MARTIN SEYMOUR-SMITH

Robert Graves:
His Life and Work

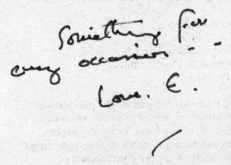

PALADIN
GRAFTON BOOKS
A Division of the Collins Publishing Group

LONDON GLASGOW
TORONTO SYDNEY AUCKLAND

Paladin
Grafton Books
A Division of the Collins Publishing Group
8 Grafton Street, London W1X 3LA

Published in Paladin Books 1987

First published in Great Britain by
Hutchinson & Co Ltd 1982

Copyright © Martin Seymour-Smith 1982, 1987

ISBN 0-586-08622-6

Printed and bound in Great Britain by
Hazell Watson & Viney Limited,
Aylesbury, Bucks

in memoriam

Norman Cameron
James and Mary Reeves
Alan Hodge

Contents

Introduction   v
Introduction to the Paladin Edition   vii
Acknowledgements   xi
Chapter One   1895–1900   1
Chapter Two   1900–1914   12
Chapter Three   1914–15   31
Chapter Four   1916   45
Chapter Five   1917–19   54
Chapter Six   1919   73
Chapter Seven   1919–25   80
Chapter Eight   1925–26   103
Chapter Nine   1926   122
Chapter Ten   1926–27   131
Chapter Eleven   1927–28   144
Chapter Twelve   1928–29   153
Chapter Thirteen 1929   170
Chapter Fourteen 1929–33(I)   186
Chapter Fifteen 1929–33(II)   201
Chapter Sixteen 1933   223
Chapter Seventeen 1933–36   241
Chapter Eighteen 1936–37   265
Chapter Nineteen 1937   282
Chapter Twenty   1937–38   299
Chapter Twenty-One   1938–39   311
Chapter Twenty-Two   1939–40   329
Chapter Twenty-Three 1940–46(I)   353
Chapter Twenty-Four 1940–46(II)   377

Chapter Twenty-Five 1946–47(I)   389
Chapter Twenty-Six 1946–47(II)   410
Chapter Twenty-Seven 1947–50   424
Chapter Twenty-Eight 1950–52   440
Chapter Twenty-Nine 1953–59   457
Chapter Thirty 1959–60   490
Chapter Thirty-One 1961–63   507
Chapter Thirty-Two 1964–69   530
Chapter Thirty-Three 1969–81   550

Notes   569
Books by Robert Graves   579
Index   585

Introduction

Robert Graves is unique in English letters: in his paradoxical versatility – as brilliantly successful popular historical novelist, eccentric but erudite mythographer, translator, pungent and outspoken critic, and as arrogant poet oblivious to public opinion – and in his lifelong refusal to conform. It is of course as a poet that he will be chiefly remembered, and by general readers as well as by the critics, who are certain to accord him major status (a phrase he hates). But he will be remembered, too, as a man, as a personality, and perhaps as a kind of prophet of 'the Return of the Goddess'.

Only by 1960, when he had reached the age of sixty-five, was Graves's reputation as a poet of genius secure. He had to wait a long time to be recognized as the foremost English-language love poet of this century – and probably of the two preceding ones, too. He added to his fame by continuing to produce a plethora of fervent and hot-blooded love poetry until he was eighty: something no other poet has done or tried to do. He 'invented' the White Goddess, his book about whom, published in 1948, continues to exercise a wide influence.

His personality is also famous, and has puzzled and fascinated both his admirers and those who regard him as the 'literary nuisance' he wants to be. 'What is this iconoclast, who can be so cuttingly rude and "personal" in controversy – and yet is known for his wild generosity – really like?' 'Is he as arrogant and contemptuous of others as he seems?' 'Does the creator of the grotesque, intelligent Emperor Claudius at all resemble his creation?' Such questions are often asked. So also are such solemn questions as these: 'Is he really father of at least half the children born on the island of Mallorca between 1929 and 1975?'; 'Did he push Laura Riding out of a window and flee the country with her?'; 'Has he been grilled by the police on a suspicion of murder?'

These and many other such questions are answered in the course of this book.

I have known Graves – and his wife Beryl – very well since March 1943. My father (who used to obtain books for him) knew him before that; both were friends of the bookseller Harold Edwards. I wrote the first full-length monograph on him, in 1956 (it has been three times revised since then, and is now overdue for another full revision). I was a frequent visitor to Galmpton during the war, and stayed with him and his wife for a long time in Mallorca in 1949. From 1951 until 1954 my wife and I worked for and with him in Deyá and in Palma (where for much of the time we lived under the same roof). I continued to see and correspond with him in the ensuing years – and I spent a considerable amount of time with him while working on this book.

I have therefore much depended on his confidences to me, on a large variety of matters both literary and personal; but I have never done this uncritically, or without cross-checking where I could. I am of course most grateful of all to him for his friendship and confidence – but I am also grateful to him for allowing me to write this book, to quote from all his writings, published and unpublished, to make reference to his 1935–39 diary, and to other more scrappily kept diaries of later years, and for directing me to the whereabouts of his correspondence and other confidential documents.

I am equally grateful to Beryl Graves for her cooperation in all the foregoing; and for her unfailing hospitality while I was working at Deyá, for her kindness and patience and sense of humour. She went over every word of the final draft of this book with me, and over the proofs, and made many invaluable corrections and suggestions – but resolutely refused to try to influence me in any of my interpretations. She only corrected errors of fact.

January 1980

Introduction
to the Paladin edition

When this book was published in 1982 Robert Graves was still alive. He died in early November 1985, three months after celebrating his ninetieth birthday. There was nothing dramatic about his death, although much had been in his earlier life. He simply did not wake up after one of his many sleeps. The people of his adopted village of Deyá were much moved, and he was buried in the churchyard on the hill within two days. Over his grave is a simple stone, reading: 'Robert Graves, Poetá'. His work-room has been beautifully preserved by his wife. It is all exactly as he would have wished.

Nothing 'happened' in his life after the publication of my biography, and so, for this new paperback edition of it, I – and the publishers – decided that it ought to stand as it was written. Furthermore, there is little to add by way of introduction.

Since 1982 the first part of a new biography of Robert Graves has appeared: it is called *The Assault Heroic* (1986) and it is written by Richard Perceval Graves, the son of Robert's younger brother, the late John Graves. It takes the reader up to 1926, to Graves's first meeting with Laura Riding. It is – as I have written elsewhere – a charming account of Graves's early career from a family point of view, rather than from that of a person who knew Graves himself at all well. This is to say, Richard Perceval Graves's father always planned to write a biography of his brother – a venture towards which Robert Graves had a somewhat sardonic attitude – and his son has started to fulfil this. Before his death, which preceded that of Robert, John Graves – an exemplary man, but not one well able or well disposed to understand Robert – was generous enough to provide me with much important material. He drew upon his own recollections and the diary kept by his (and Robert's) father, Alfred Perceval. But I was not given access to the diary, whereas of course Richard Perceval has inherited it. Thus, although he adds little to what his father so wisely, and with such excellent judgement, told me about Robert (and about Laura Riding) in his letters to me and in his telephone conversations with me, he has been able to cast more light on the family's attitude towards Robert in the early years. This gives his book a fine period air, and its consequent charm is increased by his own familial expertise.

Richard Perceval Graves has been as magnanimous to me as his father was, speaking of my book as a 'pioneer' effort; and even generously conceding, apropos of it, that 'a man is entitled to his opinions'. Almost all of his differences with me – relegated, he writes, to the 'decent obscurity' of footnotes – are of opinion rather than of fact, and, considering that most of these stem from his family feelings, I have seen no reason to change any of my views. Our styles and outlook are very different.

However, he has corrected me in a few small instances: I (following Graves himself) got the date of his confirmation wrong; and he was at Charterhouse for five, and not for seven, years. Some might carp at these corrections as petty. But, although not important in themselves, the meticulousness with which they have been applied is admirable and exemplary.

On two other matters he is, at least partially, mistaken. He attempts to minimize Graves's part in Siegfried Sassoon's deliverance from a court martial, and thinks a letter of Robert's to Bridgman (pp. 57–8 of this book) was written well after 19 July 1917. I should have given the date of this letter, which is in the Russell archives in Canada: it is 19 July 1917. Graves's part in this matter cannot be minimized, simply because it was he who was instrumental in getting the reluctant Sassoon off the court martial.

On the question of Graves's and Sir William Nicolson's unfavourable reaction to Laura Riding on the occasion of their first meeting, Richard Perceval – prompted by Laura Riding herself – suggests that my account might rely solely on T. S. Matthews's book *Jacks or Better*. I relied on Graves's own account (the matter came up more than once when 'first impressions' were being discussed), and on written evidence of William Nicolson. It is no discredit to Laura Riding: it is just how things were. In any case, Graves's remark was known to her.

On the matter of Ms Laura Jackson: she has, albeit gently, objected in a number of quarters to what she feels is this book's misrepresentation of her and her life's work. She has written that I have 'virulently defamatory intent', and that I have a 'maniacal animus' against her: 'the vindictive resentment towards myself that is the main driving force of his book'. Alas, the main driving force of the book was always to give an account of Robert Graves. I could even, at times, have wished that Ms Jackson were not an essential part of the life that was my subject. All that I have written of her is supported by good evidence or is the result of sincere irritation rather than malice. However, had she precisely detailed her objections, I should have discussed every point with her as exhaustively as she wished. She has so far refused to do this, despite my offers.

Graves did suffer greatly on account of his association with Laura Riding. But he would have suffered as much anyway, just as all other men would have become 'the devil' for her. Her influence upon him was of course profound; I do not in this book seek to deny it. All I have done – and it offended Ms Jackson – is to point out that his influence upon her was also profound. Not only should we be grateful that Robert Graves found Beryl, his second wife: we should also be grateful for Laura Riding. He always was. When I was about to go up to Oxford he suggested to me, not that I should start a back-to-Robert-Graves movement, but a back-to-Laura-Riding movement – though his own poetry was at that time neglected enough. That her ultimate view of him should be so much less generous than his ultimate view of her is certainly tragic; but it does not alter the fact of their mutual debt. We could profitably devote more time to the wonderful friendship between Wordsworth and Coleridge, and less to their falling out. Likewise Graves and Riding – whatever she may feel.

Martin Seymour-Smith
July 1986

Acknowledgements

The matter of acknowledgements is a delicate one. Certain institutions which supplied me with copies of Gravesiana (and therefore Ridingiana) did so only under the strict condition that I should not mention them by name. I respect and understand their motives, and thank them for their discreet cooperation. The same applies to two private collectors.

It is much the same with those living individuals who gave me information, especially about the period 1926–39; they generously told me all they knew, showed me and even allowed me to take copies of letters and other documents – but begged me not to mention their names. I thank them all very warmly, and (once again) fully understand their reasons for wishing to remain anonymous.

I obtained most help – in the first instance long before I was aware that I would ever write this book – from four people who, alas, are no longer alive to read it. It is dedicated to their memory, for they were all highly valued friends of mine, as of Robert and Beryl Graves. They are Norman Cameron, James and Mary Reeves, and Alan Hodge. Norman Cameron talked much to me about 'the Laura Riding years', and about Laura Riding, when I used to see him during the latter part of the war and in the years immediately after it. His reports on and views about the Graves–Riding relationship were invaluable, as were his personal memories of Riding. He was a most truthful man. James and Mary Reeves were a mine of information – and James Reeves was able to give me some specific help on this book, before his death in May 1978. Alan Hodge was helpfully answering my questions, and going over ground we had gone over before in many conversations, both on the telephone and by letter, until shortly before he died in May 1979.

Others to whom I am grateful, and can mention, are the late John Graves, Ronald Bottrall, Margaret Bottrall, Paul O'Prey (who has arranged and annotated a valuable collection, *In Broken Images*, of Graves's letters on literary subjects published in 1982), Peter Quennell, John and Gretl Aldridge, Desmond Haynes-Royer, Catherine Dalton, William Graves, Jack Lindsay, Roger Machell, Geoffrey Grigson, Anthony Powell, Eric Quayle, Eirlys Roberts, the late Jacob Bronowski, the late John Cullen, Miron Grindea, Judy Karasic — and the novelist Giles Gordon, my indefatigable, long-suffering and always encouraging literary agent. I am also grateful to David Day for getting me two rare books.

I suppose I am grateful for a large bundle of material relating to Laura Riding — it includes photocopies of letters to and from her written over a period of forty years — but I do not know whom to thank. It arrived anonymously. I have made use of whatever was relevant to Graves, but not of the rest. Clearly it had been assembled by an assiduous collector with access to many files. Certainly it did not come from anyone I know well.

Karl Gay furnished me with an invaluable list of corrections, for which I am deeply grateful.

I should also like to thank the East Sussex County Library, and the London Library, for helping me with difficult books.

I must not forget my editors: Tom Wallace of Holt, Rinehart and Winston, and Jim Cochrane of Hutchinson, who took over from Philippa Harrison (to whom I am grateful for initial help). Tom Wallace steered me off a wayward course at a crucial stage — and then came up with an exhaustive list of corrections and suggestions, of which I have taken full advantage. Jim Cochrane made sensitive and useful suggestions about the final revision — all of which I have adopted. Both editors have shown sympathetic understanding of the difficulties involved in writing the book, some of which were considerable. I thank them both for their realistic and constructive attitude; they have done much to improve a book in which, of course, any errors of fact or of judgement remain my own. I am also greatly indebted to the book's final editor, Sue Hogg.

My wife's contribution, as always, amounted to far more than the term assistance can cover.

Chapter One
1895–1900

I

Robert Graves was born at 4.26 on the morning of Wednesday, 24 July 1895, in Wimbledon, then a fashionable, pleasant area south of London. It was into a sharply different world from that to which he later had to accommodate himself: the last late flowering of a solid age.

In the week of his birth a general election had confirmed Lord Salisbury's Unionist ministry in power. There were now 340 Conservatives, 71 Liberal Unionists, 177 Liberals and 82 Irish Nationalists in the House of Commons. At the beginning of the following week Kaiser Wilhelm II came to Cowes in the Isle of Wight to discuss the partition of Turkey, which Lord Salisbury casually but confidently proposed to him. In May Oscar Wilde had been found guilty – at a sensational trial – and sentenced to imprisonment on charges of homosexuality. The third volume of *Das Kapital* was published; Marconi invented wireless telegraphy, Auguste and Louis Lumière cinematography. The first main-line railway was electrified. In Austria Freud laid the foundations of psychoanalysis with the publication of *Studien über Hysterie*. The famous conductor Gustav Mahler published his Second Symphony, of which small note was taken; the equally famous conductor Richard Strauss published *Till Eulenspiegel*, of which much note was taken. The first Henry Wood Promenade Concert was held. Not far from the baby's home Peter Latham became world lawn tennis champion; he already held the same title for rackets. Great Britain produced 190 million tons of coal. The Armenians of Constantinople were massacred on 1 October of this same year; shortly thereafter Britain sent a squadron to the Dardanelles. The total government expenditure for that year, including the costs of the Dardanelles exercise, was just £110 million – as against £58,506 million for 1976.

But Robert Graves would not be much concerned in his long life with politics, sports champions or national production and expenditure. He would instead become the most widely praised and widely read of twentieth-century love poets, and a famed historical novelist.

And so, despite these and other 'merely local', 'historical' – as Graves would later class them – events, what was the state of literature, a less transitory activity, in that year?

The novel thrived. Joseph Conrad, a Polish sea-captain who was busy making a strange but powerful form of English his own, published his first novel, *Almayer's Folly*; H. G. Wells, with *The Time Machine*, began an auspicious career. The last of Thomas Hardy's novels, *Jude the Obscure*, appeared, offending his genteel readership and giving the author the excuse to do what he really wanted to do: devote himself to poetry. Graves was to meet him, and was to admire and love him. Many of the nineteenth-century novelists were still active: Gissing published three novels in that year, Meredith one; and, at a lower level, Marie Corelli added to her fortune with *The Sorrows of Satan*. But the novelist Robert Graves was never to take a serious interest in fiction, nor even to have much knowledge of it.

No: poetry was to be, in his own words, his 'ruling passion'; and all his subsequent activity, with the exception of a long period served in war and a short one as a professor, was to be prompted by poetic motives. And he was to take a view of poetry startlingly different – more dramatic, absolute, intense – from anyone else's of his time. He was to insist – more strongly than any other poet – that poetry was an entity different from all others: not an amalgam of philosophy, religion, romance, or anything else, but a mysterious thing in its own right, demanding special and rigorous dedication from special people. The poet was never, for Graves, the expresser of ideas, the man or woman with a 'message'; he was the discoverer, albeit often self-acknowledgedly inept, misguided, unworthy, of the *poetic*. This word means something different in Graves's vocabulary from what it means in anyone else's. His life may be seen as a quest for exactly what that something is.

So, in this year of his birth the situation in English poetry is pertinent. The three Victorian giants, Tennyson, Browning and Arnold, had not long died. William Morris refused the office of Poet Laureate in 1892, on Tennyson's death, and it was vacant until 1896, when Salisbury gave it to Alfred Austin, supposedly on the strength of his politics (although he could only answer, when asked why he had done it, 'I don't think anyone else applied for the post'). There have been bad Laureates, and none since Tennyson has been a substantial poet, but there has never been a worse or more pompous one than Austin, who has been a laughing stock ever since, especially for his (pre-Laureate) lines on the illness of the Prince of Wales in 1871:

> Across the wires the electric message came,
> He is no better, he is much the same.

The state of British poetry was not as bad as the verses of Austin suggest; but it was not much better – and it was not to improve until the second decade of the new century. True, an Irishman, W. B. Yeats, born thirty years before Robert Graves – and the object of his unrelenting and lifelong dislike – issued in 1895 his first substantial collection, *Poems*; and true too that a few poets, such as John Davidson, who were working in comparative isolation, would later be seen as superior to their contemporaries. But the public taste, which did not yet take in Yeats, was satisfied with a type of verse more banal than it ever had been since a public taste for poetry existed. This is why Edward Marsh's Georgians, with whom Graves was to be associated, seemed so much better when they emerged early in the second decade of the century. Swinburne, now the prisoner, at Putney, of the wily solicitor Watts-Dunton – and a near neighbour of the new baby and his family (he used to pat baby Graves on the head) – continued to produce verse, but not even his few modern admirers have anything to say about this. A handful of poems by Gerard Manley Hopkins, who had died six years earlier, had appeared – in mutilated form – in an anthology; but no one had taken any notice of them. His poems were not to appear in book form until 1918, when his prim, learned friend Robert Bridges decided that the world might just be fit to receive them. Bridges himself was perhaps one of the best poets of the nineties – an apt index to the state of poetry at that time. He became Laureate on the death of Austin in 1913.

It was a situation that Graves would help to improve; but as a mature adult he was not interested – as were contemporaries or near-contemporaries, such as T. S. Eliot and Ezra Pound – in whether he did so or not. From *On English Poetry* (1922) onwards, his attitude has been that poets should do their own job and let the history of poetry look after itself.

II

The Graves family pedigree on his father's side goes back, according to him, to 1485, when a French knight called Graves landed with Henry VII at Milford Haven. It has been confidently asserted by other members of the family that there is no question of Norman or Breton origin. Rather, these people, Graves, Greaves or Reves (originally Gerefas), adventured in Ireland. There was a Colonel Graves who fought for the Parliamentarians in the English Civil War, had charge of Charles I during his imprisonment at Carisbrook Castle on the Isle of Wight, and eventually turned Royalist. And there is a long tradition of literature and scholarship. One of the most notable of Graves's ancestors is Richard Graves (1715–1804). This Graves has his niche in English literature as the author of *The Spiritual Quixote or The Summer Ramble of Mr Geoffry Wildgoose* (1772). A Fellow of All Souls, and eventually rector of Claveston, near Bath, he wrote poems, stories, a translation of Marcus Aurelius, and other works as well as his successful main novel, a satire on the fanaticism, illiteracy and narrowness of certain types of Methodists. Richard Graves was also one of the teachers of the economist, author of *Theory of Population*, the Rev. Thomas Malthus. But we cannot blame Malthus's doctrine – if we dislike it – on Graves, for Malthus himself said that he learned from him only 'Latin and behaviour'. He loved him enough to officiate, as priest, at his deathbed. Richard Graves was more genial than his descendant, but could be cruel in his exposure of hypocrisy. The real victim of *The Spiritual Quixote*, the missionary Calvinistic Methodist George Whitefield, does not come off lightly. Richard Graves is Robert's most distinguished literary forbear; and it may also be significant that the subtitle of one of Richard's minor novels, *Eugenius* (1785), is 'An Embellished Narrative of Real Facts'.

In 1776 John Crosbie Graves, barrister and chief police magistrate of Dublin, was born. He married Helena Perceval (which accounts for the number of times the name Perceval crops up in the Graves pedigree). Her ancestor, Sir John Perceval, was the First Earl of Egmont; he sat in the Irish and the English parliaments, and was one of those who established the American colony of Georgia. His son of the same name, Second Earl of Egmont, was a partisan of Frederick, Prince of Wales, the son and enemy of George II. Later he became First Lord of the Admiralty, but resigned because of his disagreements with the Earl of Chatham. Spencer Perceval, his son, was the only English Prime Minister (so far) to be assassinated.

John Crosbie and Helena had six children, four sons and two daughters. One of the sons, Charles, was Protestant Bishop of Limerick, a gifted mathematician who specialized in spherical conics, and an archaeologist. He was an authority on Ogham script. He was Robert's grandfather, and lived until 1899 – long enough to bless his grandson, who does not remember the occasion.

One of John Crosbie's daughters, Helena Clarissa (Clarissa is another name that crops up often in the family; Graves had an elder sister of that name, and his granddaughter, born in 1977, has it), married the German historian Leopold von Ranke, Robert's great-uncle. Graves's father, Alfred Perceval, son of the Bishop of Limerick, also married a von Ranke: his second wife, Robert's mother. In 1929, Graves said that he owed 'his historical method' to this famous historian, whose works he had not then looked at; in 1957 he modified this to 'I owe him something'. It is evident that he does, even though he has still not read Leopold's *chef d'œuvre*, the massive *History of the Popes in the Sixteenth and Seventeenth Centuries*. The genetic contribution of the sturdily empiricist, satirical and anti-puritanical Richard Graves has been unduly neglected; but the effect of von Ranke, well acknowledged, has not been exaggerated.

Leopold von Ranke has been described as 'the G.O.M. of German historians'. He founded a school of objective history, which set out to establish sound sources and to state the facts. Graves quotes him as saying 'I am a historian before I am a Christian', by which he seems to think that von Ranke meant that facts were more important than faith. Actually his view was that if you recorded the facts then Christian Providence would do the rest. And that, with a twist, is just what Graves inherited from him. He too has a passion for facts (though he denies that they constitute 'truth'), and has never cold-bloodedly invented one (though he has 'inferred' plenty of non-facts), and he too believes that Providence will do the rest – but the Providence in which he believes is that of the White Goddess, and not that of her 'rival' Jesus Christ.

Two other of Graves's many illustrious ancestors ('thin-nosed and inclined to petulance, but never depraved, cruel or hysterical', he tells us) who deserve mention are the Dublin physican Robert Graves, who discovered toxic goitre, called Graves' Disease after him; and Robert

Perceval Graves, who was curate to William and Dorothy Wordsworth, and who wrote the encomium for the latter.

But on this side of the family it was to his father Alfred Perceval that Graves owed most – though it took him a long time to recognize this. In his eighties he speaks of him with an almost rueful love.

Alfred Perceval was born in 1846, and was the son of that Anglican Bishop of Limerick who occupied himself with spherical trigonometry and Ogham script. The bishop was close about money but generous in spirit, begetting eight children. Alfred Perceval graduated from Trinity College, Dublin, with high honours, and entered government service; he was clerk and private secretary in the Home Office from 1869 until 1875. He married Jane Cooper in 1875, and by her had five children. The eldest of these was Philip Graves, a notable journalist who worked closely with T. E. Lawrence in the Middle East, attained fame when he exposed the Protocols of the Elders of Zion as a forgery, and was the father of Elizabeth (Sally) Chilver, anthropologist and historian who became Principal of Bedford College, London, and then of Lady Margaret Hall, Oxford. There were two sisters, Mary (Molly) and Susan, and two more brothers, Perceval and Richard (Dick), a diplomat who was Mayor of Jerusalem during the last days of the British mandate. Jane Cooper died of consumption in 1886.

Alfred Perceval's true interests lay in literature, folklore and the education of the people in these subjects. He was editor-in-chief of the magazine *Every Irishman's Library*, a founder of the Folk Song Society, and President of the Irish Literary Society. He had a gift for writing graceful, merry lyrical poems. The most famous is 'Father O'Flynn', because it was set to music by Sir Charles Stanford to the melody of 'The Top of the Cork Road'. For his harmonization Stanford received substantial royalties, and Boosey the publishers made, says Robert Graves, 'thousands'. Alfred Perceval got one guinea, but never complained.

In introducing his *Irish Poems* in the first decade of this century A.P. stated his hatred of 'Stage Irish Songs', and spoke of his admiration of the 'great body of Gaelic Folk Song' – in the revival of which he played an important part. If, he wrote, he had had any success in his entrance into the 'newly-opened lyrical field' of the Gaelic folk song, then this was

> because I have not only had an Irish Countryside up-bringing and the
> advantage, therefore, of constantly having in my ears that translation

into English of Irish idioms which renders the speech of the Kerry so peculiarly poignant and picturesque, but because ... I have also had before me the best published examples of the Western Gael to ponder and profit by.

He had 'danced and sang to as a boy', he went on, 'the music of the old Irish airs'; they had 'haunted him through life'. He ended by explaining that he had not supplied a glossary as he had 'endeavoured as far as possible to indicate the meaning of strange words by their place in the context'.

This was to be the practice of his son, who introduced his own *Collected Poems* of 1938 with the remark: 'No notes are given; for I think that poems should supply their own illumination – otherwise they are incomplete fancies which no glosses, however numerous, can perfect.' The inheritance of the ability to write melodiously and gracefully, an absolute requisite for a lyrical poet, is obvious; but that of the notion that poems ought to 'stand up on their own', as Graves has often put it, is less obvious.

Graves wrote (1929): 'That my father is a poet has, at least, saved me from any false reverence for poets.' This is double-edged. And, he continued: 'He never once tried to teach me how to write, or showed any understanding of my serious poetry; being always more ready to ask advice about his own' – a statement A.P. indignantly denied. Yet there was a quality in the father which the son inherited without either of them knowing it – but in A.P., who was two days past his forty-ninth birthday when Robert was born, it remained suppressed. A gift of lyrical intensity that remained merely cheerful, convivial and pleasant in the father was more spectacularly fulfilled in the son. Graves believes A.P.'s earlier, light-hearted work to be his best, and says that 'After marrying my mother and turning teetotaller, he is said to have lost something of his playfulness.' In conversation he puts it rather more bluntly: 'he was all right until he stopped "drinking".' By this he does not mean that A.P. had ever been a drunkard, which he had not, but that he became puritanical.

Although Graves's pedigree on his father's side is scattered with all kinds of clerics, religious strictness is stronger on that of his mother, although it mostly concentrated itself in the women, whose husbands gave them plenty to pray about. His grandfather Heinrich von Ranke, a doctor, was an atheist who turned into an agnostic. He died saying: 'The God of my fathers, to Him at least I hold.' His wife, a

Schleswig-Dane, daughter of the Greenwich astronomer Tiarks, was a devout Lutheran ('tiny, saintly, frightened'), who prayed much for her husband and more for her children. Hence perhaps the extreme devoutness of her daughter, Robert's mother, Amalia Elizabeth Sophie von Ranke. A.P. met Amalia through their von Ranke connection, and she immediately told him that she liked 'Father O'Flynn'. She was a courageous and high-principled woman, as her fragment of autobiography, unpublished, demonstrates. She had real devotion to duty – and the moralistic obstinacy that sometimes goes with it. She was eminently practical, eminently scrupulous – once some visitors left behind some sandwiches, and she sent them on – and it is from her, rather than from his father, that Robert gets his practicality. Suffering, for Amalia, was something sent by God, and was the easier to endure because of this (for her son it is sent by Woman, and is easier to endure because of that); but she had her feet firmly planted on the ground, and was in no way the sort of woman to invite suffering upon herself for the sake of pleasing God. She assumed that God, too, was practical. She had an admirable simplicity, could neither understand nor countenance modern ways, and was seldom stupid.

Her marriage to A.P. in 1891 was no love match. Jane Cooper had been a gay, laughing, light-hearted woman who practised no kind of piety. Graves believes that his father was always in love with her memory. But he had had five children to look after for five years (the eldest, Philip, was fifteen), and this was expensive and time-consuming. They needed a mother, anyway. Amalia liked A.P. and admired his probity, and saw that he was a good man (as he was). But she insisted that he give up alcohol – he signed the pledge – for she was a ferocious missionary by nature, and saw alcohol as an obstacle to goodness. Graves says that she regarded marriage to his father as presenting her with as good an opportunity for 'mission work in the . . . field' as she might have found in India, where she had intended to go as a medical missionary. The tragedy is that she reduced A.P. to a ghost of his former self: knocked most of the gaiety out of him.

For all her sense of righteousness, she was shrewd – often warning her excessively gullible son not to rely on those he believed to be trustworthy. Graves has suffered greatly in his life through his inability to judge the extent of his friends' (and lovers') loyalty to him, as well as from his tendency to demand too much from people; but he has almost always been able to support his family without doing anything he did not really want to do. He owes that capacity, too, to Amalia

8

(hereinafter Amy, as she was always called) Elizabeth Sophie von Ranke.

From 1875 until his retirement in 1910 A.P. was an inspector of schools. He left Ireland – his son says that he is grateful to both his parents for making the 'geographical break' with Ireland – and came to live in Wimbledon. A.P. wrote in his autobiography, defiantly entitled *To Return to All That* as an answer to his son's *Goodbye*:

> In June 1894 we moved into a new house in Lauriston Road, near Wimbledon Common. It was simply designed, without billiard-room or conservatory, but with bedrooms enough to supply the demands of a growing family. Large over-hanging eaves and green Cumberland slates were special features. . . . A fine chestnut tree overshadowed the garden. . . . We named it Red Branch House after the Knights of the Red Branch, celebrated in Irish chivalry for their poetry and hospitality. . . . In further justification of the name we soon could show red hawthorn blossom, red yew and holly berries, and other red branches in the garden.

Before Robert there were two sisters: Clarissa (1892), who never married, and who became an artist and a devout Christian Scientist – she published one volume of poetry; and Rosaleen (1894), who became a doctor, married another doctor from whom she was later divorced, and is the mother of three children. Rosaleen is still living, in south Devon; Clarissa died in 1976. After Robert came Charles (1899), a journalist infamous for his vulgarity, and John (1903), a civil servant and then headmaster, who had originally – his father said – wanted to be a tram conductor. He died in January 1980. Charles died in 1971.

As was customary in England amongst well-to-do people, the children did not see a great deal of either parent. They had a nurse – and, as Robert writes, 'each other'. That, he found, was sufficient. When his father had time, he was 'sweet' (the word is Robert's) to the children, telling them jokes and playing games.

Amy, though essentially gentle, was firm and influential; she instructed her children in good manners and morality, sometimes with a hairbrush, and they believed what she told them. She was no hypocrite. She was not shocked when her son, at the age of four, asked her, after she had heard their evening prayers, if, when she died, she would leave him any money – if it amounted to five pounds he could buy a bicycle with it. 'Surely you'd rather have me, Robby?' she complained. 'I could ride to your grave on it,' he replied.

She led an exemplary life. She inculcated strict morality, and the boy

Robert's highly moralistic analyses of his own behaviour were grimly serious; his good resolutions were kept. There was none of the young pretender in him. He was not mischievous, and was not expected to be; that was not part of his mother's philosophy, though it might have been a concealed part of his essentially ebullient father's. But although Amy saw to it that A.P. looked as though, and was treated as though, he were head of the household, it was she in fact who controlled it.

Graves simply accepted the values of his parents; it did not occur to him, as it does to children more exposed to the outside world, to question or to challenge them.

In all innocence his strict-minded mother inculcated in her imaginative son terrible fears. Such childhood fears are never forgotten. The ungainly, large boy, with the thick curly hair, was not only terrified of eternal damnation, of burning fiery furnaces and of fearful prophecies, but was also excessively superstitious. Frightful penalties would follow, without warning, if he were rude or if he ate too many sweets or if he coveted his neighbour's goods; and he would imagine, of course, that he was guilty of all these sins, even when he was not. Only the figure of Jesus Christ consoled him, for did not Christ forgive and save? That figure, though eventually painfully rejected as the Saviour of mankind and the Son of God, was to obsess him until he felt that he could rewrite his story (twice, no less).

And then, eventually, there was sex, from which there is no escape. He mentions the 'sexual embarrassment from which I have found it very difficult to free myself' – and retains that remark in the 1957 revision of his 1929 autobiography. There is one sense in which he never has freed himself from this 'embarrassment'. It explains much; and to this 'failure' to free himself, in fact, we owe the notion of the White Goddess.

So here the poet was born: in the nursery, and then in childhood. His father had danced and sung to ancient melodies, and carried their lilt in his heart. The temperance man and conscientious school inspector could still write words to a tune; it came naturally. Robert inherited that, and he too, in his childlike way, danced and sang to what was going on in his father's innermost being.

But in his early boyhood, even before he became sexually aware, Graves's mysteries and fears failed to coalesce satisfactorily with the melodies – those arrangements of words which so strangely 'sing' like music, but which convey a greater meaning. Terror challenged beauty, and the paradox disturbed him. He would, throughout the course of a long, full and difficult life, do no more – in one sense – than try to reconcile his nightmares with the beauty of songs that he was already hearing in his heart and as yet unformed mind.

Chapter Two
1900–1914

I

No one has satisfactorily answered the question as to what prompts a person to wish to 'become a poet'. More people than is generally recognized have at some time expressed themselves in verse. The majority of these do not, however, form intentions, at the time, of wanting to be 'poets'; the profession is notoriously unprofitable, and is even associated with a lack of respectability. We have in Robert Graves, though, an example of one who decided to become a poet when he was fifteen years old, in 1910. Since that time, he has written in *The White Goddess*, 'poetry has been my ruling passion'. He had started to write two years before, in 1908. Few poets have taken the decision so young. This was no question of something he thought he'd like to do; it became, then and there, a 'ruling passion'. Why? For it is irresistible emotional pressure that first causes a true poet to write.

This pressure goes back to his early fears and imaginings. They are common in all children, but the young Graves was possessed of a most powerful individuality – an individuality which found a rigid morality highly inconvenient. When at his various preparatory schools, then at his public school, he found himself having to cope with a strange environment, he was forced back on himself, and so onto the conflict in him between maternally induced morality and independence. There was, too, the challenge of his awakening sexuality. His poetry arose directly from his urgent need to reconcile the opposing forces in his nature. The alternative would have been mental breakdown.

He went to several preparatory schools. There was the junior school of King's College School, Wimbledon, where he had to play rugby football without having been told the rules, and where he felt dwarfed by what seemed to be the hugeness of the place, and by the largeness of the other boys. There he was taught Latin by rote and also learned strings of dirty words whose meanings he did not understand. It was lucky he picked these up: his father, hearing him use some one day, promptly removed him. At another Wimbledon school, Rokeby, not quite so pretentious, he stayed from eight until eleven. It was here that his powerful ego first began to manifest itself.

This was not then altogether pleasant; as he says, 'quarrelsome, boastful . . . domineering'. He was being trained to be a 'young gentleman', but could make no sense of the process. The other boys collected stamps, so he collected coins. His fellow-pupils did not like him; but he could now look after himself. He was aloof, felt isolated and lonely – though he was too proud to tell anyone else. The staff disliked him, but he showed scholastic aptitude.

There were three more preparatory schools. One in Wales where he spent a term, and where he was caned for learning the wrong collect. Then a strange one, at Rugby, where there was some competent teaching, but where the headmaster had a sinister secret. Graves tells the story of how he one day came into class beating his head with his fists and moaning, 'Would to God I hadn't done it! Would to God I hadn't done it!' He was 'given twenty-four hours to leave the country'. He was succeeded by a good man, who two weeks later fell out of a train on his head – and that, Graves writes, 'was the end of him'.

The last of the preparatory schools was what Graves calls, with the kind of irony in which he specializes, 'a typically good school': Copthorne in Sussex, where his brother John was a distinguished pupil and later a teacher. John, Robert tells us, was a 'typically good, normal person', and because of this he 'naturally went back as a master to his old, typically good preparatory school. . . . That is the sort of typically good preparatory school it was.'

But Copthorne, apart from teaching what he calls a 'high moral sense', did help to get him into Charterhouse, one of the leading English public schools. He failed to get into Winchester (which he preferred), but was first on the list for Charterhouse. He was there for seven years.

What he felt about Charterhouse is made evident by his worst recurring dream – from which he used to wake, for some fifty years afterwards, in a sweat of terror – that he was back there. He did not like it at all, and has never changed his mind. When he was looking for a school for the eldest son of his second marriage (he had no control over the schooling of the children of his first), he made sure to find one (Oundle) that he felt was as unlike Charterhouse as possible.

His objections to Charterhouse, as he expressed them in *Goodbye to All That*, are, characteristically, based on how he found it uncongenial. There are few abstractions about the evils of the educational system of the first decade of this century. The only complaint he makes is that the system produces what he calls 'pseudo-homosexuals'. That matter was to play – or so he believed – an important part in his adolescence; and his experiences in this respect explain much – both about his emotional make-up and his subsequent sexual attitudes.

II

Like many young people who have troubles, Graves took refuge in study. When he got to Charterhouse, which he took to be an institution primarily intended for learning, he was disconcerted to find that school work was despised by the pupils. Moreover, the masters gave no sign that they knew anything, or were going to do anything, about this. He has written that the 'oppression of spirit' which overtook him at that time is something that he hesitates to 'recall in its full intensity'. His recurring dream is no jocular metaphor. To feel absolutely alienated at the onset of adolescence is a terrifying experience – and all the worse if one has discovered values that make no sense to anyone else. He had discovered such values. At one of his earlier schools he first came across the old ballads. He mentions 'Chevy Chase' and 'Sir Andrew Barton', adding laconically, 'I saw how good they were.' But apart from seeing how good they were, he could hardly at that stage realize exactly why they seemed so 'good' to him – or what spirit they represented. The *Iliad*, too, excited him immensely.

At public schools in those days, much lip service was paid to 'Literature'. Such lip service is worse than straightforward condemnation. It is the very antithesis of what literature is about. So Graves felt even more isolated. He had no one to whom he could convey his feelings about his new discoveries, and so of course he doubted them – and even, at times of particular depression, equated them with those terrors which had begun to haunt him as a child.

Other things were against him. He wasn't dressed like the other boys. His clothes were regulation, but of poor material. His parents, he explains, had no regard for 'the niceties of dress', which made him feel even more awkward. He had little pocket money – much less than his fellows – and so could not treat them at the tuck shop (one of the most sacred of institutions in English public schools) as was the custom, nor could he accept their offers. In his refusal he seemed boorish and arrogant, nastily superior. He withdrew into himself, and appeared churlish and unfriendly.

Then a revelation about his name reared its ugly head. His name was registered on his birth certificate as Robert von Ranke Graves, and this was how he appeared on the school register. Someone found out. He had hitherto believed his middle name to be merely Ranke, which he could have 'passed off'. But the 'von' was too much. Anti-German feeling was rampant at the time Graves entered the school; all the popular magazines – especially those read by boys – were full of it, and it was stated in the crudest fashion. Graves himself has summed it up thus: ' "German" meant "dirty German". It meant: "cheap, shoddy goods competing with our sterling industries". It also meant military menace, Prussianism, useless philosophy, tedious scholarship, loving music and sabre-rattling.' It was even worse when someone started the rumour that he was not only a German, but a German Jew. His claim that he was Irish proved fruitless, and more so because a boy older than himself, pure Irish, started a ragging campaign against him on the grounds that no dirty German Jew was going to be allowed to make a claim to be an Irishman. He drove Graves near to breakdown; only his inner resilience, pride and natural toughness enabled him to survive. There was no one who could understand, and he himself felt bewildered. He did not, of course, 'sneak' (the then uniform school word for 'inform') on his persecutor. Few public schoolboys do. But he finally felt, after this had been going on for one and a half years, during which he kept silence, that he must tell someone. He wrote to his parents. It was his only resort. British public schools are divided into houses, so that the pupils have to contend with two 'spirits': the 'school' and the 'house'. He told his parents that his house had made it clear to him that he did not 'belong'. His Irish enemy's tales about how he was not really prudish at all, but a fierce masturbator and secret seducer of boys, had not helped. All that had been taken as a great joke, not only by the other boys but also by the house monitors who were supposed, in theory, to maintain justice. He wrote in confidence, leaving out only the sexual details. His parents came to see him, told him that he must 'endure all' – and then, without his knowledge, saw his housemaster.

That night the housemaster preached against bullying to the assembled boys. But, with more conviction, he also told them how he detested 'informers'. He did not name anyone, but since his parents had been seen, and on a non-holiday, everyone knew that von Ranke Graves was not merely a super-masturbating Jew-prude who preached virtue, but also a sneak. His locker was interfered with, his study wrecked, his clothes went missing or were urinated on – he had to remove these to an abandoned shower-bath.

Some new stratagem was called for. Graves not only knew his Bible, but also believed in it. The name of David ('beloved', 'faithful') has had great significance in his life: his close friend who was killed in the war was called David; so was his first son. He saw himself, in his desperation, as the 'cunning player on the harp', who was now persecuted and the object of murderous thoughts. He was a boy determined to avoid anything which might be regarded as sinful; he was virtuous, and was terrified of the consequences of wrong-doing. But what could be sinful in doing what King David had done: feigning madness?

Just at that time his heart had, he writes, 'gone wrong' (this was clearly psychosomatic) and he had consequently been forbidden by the school doctor to play football. His feigned madness worked wonders. He was shunned, which was just what he wanted. When he started writing poetry his fellow pupils regarded this as confirmation of his insanity. Writing of these early poems in his 1929 autobiography, Graves made a revealing remark, which he omitted from the 1957 revision:

> The poetry I wrote was not the easy showing-off witty stuff that all the Graves write and have written for the last couple of centuries. It was poetry that was dissatisfied with itself. When, later, things went better with me at Charterhouse, I became literary once more.

One of the chief features of his mature poetry is the dissatisfaction it expresses, both with itself and with its author. Graves's is essentially an existential poetry, one written as a means of attaining virtue through love of women. As for the aside about becoming 'literary' again when things got better for him, this is an indication of his state of mind when, at white heat, he wrote *Goodbye to All That*. By then 'literary', as it is normally understood, had become a dirty word, and Graves was busy purging himself of it and all its connotations. The poems he refers to are unfortunately lost – what he describes and publishes in part, for the first and only time, as his 'first' poem in the foreword to his 1938 *Collected Poems* is no more than that which he regards as his first technically competent one. What he let slip in 1929 was a barely conscious realization that, at the very beginning, he had not been 'literary' in what for him is a bad sense – a sense with which we shall become familiar soon enough.

Curiously enough, it was through the 'lunacy' of poetry that Graves found an avenue of escape from his oppressive circumstances. He sent a poem to the school magazine, *The Carthusian*. One of the more enlightened boys sent him a note suggesting that he might like to join the poetry society. The existence of this body, which boasted seven members, was an embarrassment to the school. The trouble was that the society, which could not be seen to be openly discouraged by the authorities, cut across sacred custom. This was that no boys from different houses were allowed to be friends or to associate with each other or to play a game – even if they were related. This was part of the 'house spirit', which was of course the backbone of the 'school spirit', which was the backbone of the national spirit, which was why we had a Glorious Literary Heritage and why the Square did not break at Waterloo. . . . All Englishmen born before about 1930, and some later, will recognize the impeccable logic of this argument.

But how could even the most zealous master prevent two boys from different houses talking to each other about poetry? Besides, the law was an unwritten one. So when Graves formed a close friendship with a boy of about his own age called Raymond Rodakowski, nothing could be done about it: Rodakowski was a member of the poetry society. Anyone with a surname like Rodakowski was bound to have found almost as much trouble as someone with a middle name of von Ranke. Graves confided to Raymond, who cheered him considerably by telling him that he was a good poet and a good person; he also told him how he had solved the problems caused by his own name – he had taken up boxing. Why, he asked Graves, didn't he do the same? Graves took up the advice.

He trained 'savagely'. A new year began, and he found himself matched against Rodakowski. They took care not to hurt each other badly, gave each other a good fight, and thus earned some respect.

Graves now gained in self-confidence. His school work was good; and there were now a few boys ready to defend him when he was verbally attacked. The accusations of sexual hypocrisy were forgotten: the Irish boy left the school, and even went so far as to write to Graves begging his forgiveness – adding that if he didn't get it then he'd have him 'done' by a friend still in the house. Graves did not reply.

But, although his circumstances were becoming more tolerable, there were still problems. He was still an odd man out. He could not get on with many of the senior pupils, of whom he was now one. He was in his fifth year at the school and a sixth-form boy. He had done well in the last set of examinations. But his position was anomalous because his real friends – one particularly important – were 'juniors'. The hierarchy in the British public school was rigid. You should not go around with boys younger than yourself. So although Graves was now regarded by his contemporaries with tolerance, because he could play games like any 'decent chap', he was still looked at askance.

Graves's house games captain, whom he liked, persuaded him to allow his name to be put down for the welterweight division of the inter-house boxing competitions. He pointed out that this would make things easier for the favourite, a house colleague, by 'damaging one or two of the stronger men'. Graves didn't like this, but realized that he would have to do it. But he knew that his wind was not good enough for the ordeal of three rounds of boxing, and so he got the house butler to procure a bottle of cherry whisky for him; these fights, he determined, were going to be short.

He had never drunk alcohol before. He explains how he steered his conscience around the problem. His mother had made him sign a pledge card, not at all uncommon in those days, but she had put this card amongst the family treasures. So, he speciously writes, 'I regarded myself as permanently parted from my pledge.'

When the fights got under way, Graves, 'delighted' with his cherry whisky, found himself drawn against the favourite – just what his house captain had not intended. But he refused to scratch, and the captain urged them to do the sporting thing: box but not hurt each other. The favourite began to show off, so Robert promptly knocked him out with the most unorthodox blow in boxing, the inevitably 'telegraphed' right swing, which landed on the side of the neck. He had been made angry.

When Graves went to the changing room the gym instructor suggested that he put his name down for the middleweight division, which, in the euphoria of victory and cherry whisky, he 'cheerfully' did. His blood was now up. He fortified himself with more alcohol.

His next opponent, to whom he was conceding a stone, was a more formidable proposition. When Graves knocked him down, he obstinately got up. But eventually he did not.

He went back to his house and took a cold bath – and some more drink. He noticed that some of the others were looking at him admiringly.

18

Naturally – for he must by now have been quite drunk – he does not remember the rest of the fights. But he ended up as victor at both weights. He received two silver cups, which – like the gold medal the Americans awarded him over fifty years later – turned out not to be what they seemed: when, some years afterwards, 'starving in the proverbial garret', he tried to sell them, he found out they were only silver-plated.

III

Graves's two most pressing problems were religion and his now rapidly developing sexuality – matters intimately connected.

First, religion. In the term when he made friends with Raymond, Graves was being prepared for confirmation by a 'zealous', narrow-minded and unimaginative master. Graves none the less looked forward to the coming event with naive spiritual joy. He was going to experience a revelation. But, as he wryly puts it, the Holy Spirit did not descend in the form of a dove, he did not find himself gifted with tongues – all that happened was that another boy who was being blessed (by the Bishop of Zululand, who was officiating) slipped off the footstool on which they were both kneeling. He felt wounded and devastated – and also that he must have done something very bad. He did not yet question the Christian religion. He was puzzled and afraid.

He confided in Raymond. But Raymond, instead of having something useful to tell him from 'within the faith', laughed it off and told Graves that he was an atheist. That was a double blow. He was profoundly shocked, and by one he now idealized: for Graves has in him a strong need to idealize someone. His mother had failed him. The clumsiness of her intervention at the time of his greatest unhappiness had disqualified her from fulfilling this role. He tells us that Raymond asked him, 'What's the use of having a soul if you have a mind? What's the function of the soul? It seems like a pawn in the game.' He felt that he should answer Raymond because he 'loved and respected' him. But instead, as he says, he did not answer; he broke off entirely with Raymond. There could be no compromise, because salvation came before 'human love'.

This is a revealing early example of a marked characteristic of his behaviour. He has continued to break off relationships, ruthlessly, relentlessly and suddenly, 'on principle'. He later tried to approach

Raymond with some sort of what he calls 'broad-Church' compromise. He was surprised to be bluntly repudiated. He simply hadn't seen how deeply he had hurt his friend. (In 1917 he sought him out in France and 'felt as close to him as I had ever felt'. Raymond was killed a few days later.)

Graves's feelings for Raymond, according to him, were 'comradely' rather than 'amorous'. But soon after his break with Raymond he 'fell in love with' a boy three years younger than himself. (In *Goodbye to All That* Graves calls him Dick; in his letters he refers to him as Peter, though this seems not to have been his name. He was G. H. Johnstone, 1898–1949, family name of Vanden-Bempde-Johnstone; he became Baron Derwent – and left Graves some of his books, which were refused, in his will.) Graves carefully writes that he was 'unconscious of any sexual desire for him': he loved him, he believed, because he could talk about poetry and was intelligent in a way in which his contemporaries were not. They met because both were in the choir; when Graves was warned off Dick by a master who also sang in the choir he refused to limit his friendship with him – and, as he puts it, 'lectured' the master (who let the matter drop) on the virtues of Platonic love, citing Michelangelo and other eminent figures. He was already both resourceful and absurdly naive.

This episode was bound up with what he felt and thought to be right (and wrong) – and that in turn was, of course, bound up with religion. He could feel 'parted' from his pledge not to drink liquor easily enough when put in a tight corner, but he could not so easily give up his faith (the faith he was convinced he must have if he were not to be, in some inexplicable way, damned). He repressed his anxieties, but they kept surfacing.

The composition of technically difficult poetry acted as a spell to frighten his terrors away. But that poetry did not treat of the anxieties themselves, which were too acute. Only later, during the war, could he lose his faith and keep a good conscience about it – and even this was painful, as it is to most of those brought up as Christians. He went on studying the Bible.

In the 1929 *Goodbye to All That* he wrote:

In English preparatory and public schools romance is necessarily homosexual. The opposite sex is despised and hated, treated as something obscene. Many boys never recover from this perversion. I only recovered by a shock at the age of twenty-one. For every one born homosexual there are at least ten permanent homosexuals made by the public school

20

system. And nine of these ten are as honourably chaste and sentimental as I was.

In the revision the passage reads identically except that 'ten permanent homosexuals' now reads 'ten permanent pseudo-homosexuals' – and the sentence beginning 'I only recovered . . .' is deleted.

When Graves left Charterhouse he still loved Dick, and corresponded regularly with him, mostly about poetry. When his brother John sent him news, at the front, to the effect that Dick was not what he seemed to be, he took no notice. But in early June 1917, a cutting from *John Bull* reached him. Only the other day, it said, a sixteen-year-old boy at Charterhouse School had approached a Canadian soldier with a 'certain proposal'. The soldier had put him in charge – but because the boy had aristocratic connections he had been bound over in the care of a doctor.

The boy was Dick; and 'this news nearly finished me', Graves recollected. But he rationalized: Dick must have been driven out of his mind by the war, especially since there had been 'madness in the family'. He told Edward Marsh in a letter that this 'worst possible news' was explicable only by a 'mental breakdown'. Previously he had called him 'radiant', 'wholesome and clean-living'. That was the 'shock' which Graves originally, before reconsideration, thought had contributed to his 'recovery' from what he defines as 'pseudo-homosexuality'.

He was right to cut the sentence out. He was very different from the other boys at Charterhouse both in his attitude to sex and in his observance – though this became rather more private as he went up through the school – of religion. Both homosexual practices and ideal-istic 'pure' love flourish at British public schools. However, it is not really 'homosexuality' (the precise aetiology of which remains obscure), but a phase through which the majority of boys naturally pass, a phase of finding out about sexuality.

Graves ascribes his early difficulties at Charterhouse, the 'horror' with which he reacted to 'the many refinements of sex constantly referred to in school conversation', to his mother. 'I remained as prudishly innocent as my mother had planned I should.' This is a little unfair, though Amy Graves did unwittingly have the effect, as mother, of savage moralist. Almost all mothers of those days planned to keep their sons in a state of 'purity'; but the sons had other means of getting to know the facts. But, always aloof, Graves took his virtue with an intense idealistic seriousness. Retrospectively, he comments on the distinction, supposed to have been made by G. H. Rendell – headmaster at Charterhouse when he arrived: 'My boys are amorous, but seldom erotic.' He agrees with the

> distinction between 'amorousness' (by which he meant a sentimental falling in love with other boys) and eroticism, or adolescent lust. The intimacy that frequently took place was very seldom between an elder boy and the object of his affection – that would have spoiled the romantic illusion – but almost always between boys of the same age who were not in love, and used each other as convenient sex-instruments. So the atmosphere was always heavy with romance of a conventional early Victorian type, complicated by cynicism and foulness.

Any schoolboy can vouch for this. But Graves does not allow for the immense strain his love for Dick put him under. For although innocent, even ignorant by comparison (he got used to 'bawdy talk' only in his last two years at school, and 'hardened' to it only after some time in the army), he was convinced that underlying his idealization of Dick there was desire. His notion that this desire existed hurt his immense pride. It was a terrible bogey in the ever-fearful back of his mind.

One of the keys to Graves's personality, and therefore to his poetry, lies in the fact that he is in a continual state of terror; he relieved this, challenged it, by an increasingly sophisticated romanticism – but a romanticism that is wilfully designed to punish him for his pride, which prevents his loving wholly, and which in that special sense may well be the 'ancestral sin' of the poem 'Reproach'. His terror is doubtless simply of being alive – this notion and its meaning have become familiar to us in modern times; but, being an empiricist at heart, he has made his 'fright' (the word used in one of his most famous poems, 'The Cool Web') concrete. Physical desire and the sexual act, the 'thing', is what terrifies him. It is, after all, the urge to reproduction that maintains existence. He was intuitively aware, from very early on, of the biological truism that 'the price of sex is death'. This was an instinctive realization of a biological fact that has always been relevant to poetry, and indeed to literature as a whole. The simpler organisms divide by fission and therefore seem to be 'immortal'. Truly individual organisms are strictly finite: the price, for human beings, of individuality is death. The more individuality (pride), the more death. From the start Graves's uneasiness took the form of locating his individuality

– it is an extremely powerful one – in his sexual desire. When he was young it had no object at all; it was too terrified.

While in his last years at Charterhouse, Graves formed an attachment for another 'hero-figure' – someone older and altogether more impressive than Raymond. Graves writes: 'The most important thing that happened in my last two years, apart from my attachment to Dick, was that I got to know George Mallory.' Mallory is famous as the mountaineer who, with his companion Irvine, disappeared near the top of Everest after beginning an attempt on the summit. No one knows if they succeeded, but Mallory became a hero-figure to thousands of youngsters during the late twenties and thirties.

As a master he was easy-going and enlightened, and treated such boys as Graves as equals. He took him for walks, entertained him in his rooms, and introduced him to the works of writers of whom he had never heard: 'Shaw, Samuel Butler, Rupert Brooke, Wells, Flecker . . . Masefield', and thus excited in him a sense of discovery. Butler in particular made a great impact upon him, and he struck all his friends as 'Butlerian' in his views for the next decade. *The Way of All Flesh* profoundly influenced his attitude to his parents.

Mallory introduced him to Edward Marsh, who was then Prime Minister Asquith's secretary. Marsh, inspirer of Georgian poetry, and certainly for the war decade an important arbiter of taste, liked Graves's poems but 'pointed out that they were written in the poetic diction of fifty years ago and that, though the quality of the poem was not necessarily impaired by this, many readers would be prejudiced against work written in 1913 in the fashions of 1863.'

This is interesting. Graves had been writing poetry now for five years – and one wonders what he showed Marsh, whose judgement was less poor than it was limited. For although most of such juvenilia as he did not publish in his first volume seems to be lost, he has quoted from one or two early poems. One of these quotations is the beginning of what he describes as his first poem, written in 1908 at the age of thirteen:

> I sat in my chamber yesternight,
>   I lit the lamp, I drew the blind
> And I took my pen in hand to write;
>   But boisterous winds had rent the blind
>   And you were peering from behind –
> Peeping Tom in the skies afar,
> Bold, inquisitive, impudent star!

The diction is indeed archaic; but the theme – for a thirteen-year-old – is fairly original. It is self-observant rather than profound. Graves in 1938 had this to say about it: 'The temptation to digress has always vexed me. Indeed, it was the subject of my first poem. . . . This was about the mocking interruptions of a poet's privacy by a star. . . .' It was prophetic that Graves's 'first' poem should be on the subject of digression, since the 'vexing' temptation to digress amounts to evasion of the problem that is really bothering the poet. One must suppose, however, that he showed Marsh the 'literary' poems, not those which were 'dissatisfied' with themselves. On 28 June 1914, a few weeks before he left Charterhouse, he listened to Marsh reading excerpts from Gordon Bottomley's play *King Lear's Wife*, which much impressed him – as did the work of Rupert Brooke, Masefield (in particular *The Everlasting Mercy*) and W. H. Davies (whom he continued to admire). These writers were indeed lively compared to what had been the fashion for the first ten years of the century.

Since his *Collected Poems* of 1938 Graves has been guided in his choice of what to include in his canon by the notion of what he calls (1938) his 'poetic seriousness at the time'. If he has felt that a poem 'misrepresented' this at the time it was written, then he has suppressed it. His notion of 'poetic seriousness' is a concatenation of various principles; but paramount amongst these is that of the bad effects, on truth (purity), of evasion, which in 1938 he called 'digression'. He was from the very beginning obsessed with ideas of purity and truth – even though in 1926 he dramatically, drastically, impulsively, mistakenly believed that he had repudiated his earlier poetic self.

One cannot overemphasize the element of desire – craving – for purity in his nature, even though in drawing attention to it one risks giving the false impression that the adult Graves is prudish, or in some way unsophisticated or unworldly. But the boy, though moved inexorably by the need to express himself in poetry, was seriously blocked; he was a prude and a prig, even if he was developing defences against the coarsenesses and insensitivities of his contemporaries. When a brash fourteen-year-old boy sent him some of his early poems, written at a public school, he began his reply:

> Yes, it is at 14 that one knows for sure that one is a poet, and that one will always be one. Most letters that come to me with poems in them are from the 18–22 age-group: they want to be told that they are poets, they want to be told how to publish their poems so as to make other people think that they are poets. But in their hearts they know they are

not really: they are people in love, or sorry for themselves, or [with] a social conscience or something. . . . So I was very glad to get your poems, because I know how you feel: a wild, invincible feeling. . . . [To M.S.-S., c. February 1943]

From 1908 onwards Graves gained strength from feeling wild and invincible; but he was the victim not only of the puritanical overkill of his upbringing but also of his own inner drive towards virtue, which he sought because he terribly feared the consequences of vice. However, he had no very clear notion of what vice was.

These early difficulties were hard to bear; but that Graves wrote in what Marsh called 'archaic style' may well have been one of the factors that confirmed him as a poet. For since he was not acquainted with current fashions until he met Mallory, he at least was not tempted to 'digress' in their disastrous direction. By the time Mallory showed him the poems of Brooke and others, he had formed his own technique – even though he was excited by this new Georgian poetry. Of course the boy could not now begin to write on the dark themes which obsessed him, and which he hardly consciously understood anyway. Instead, as he says, he made 'difficult technical experiments in prosody and phrasing'. He was, in his boyhood, as he writes in the foreword to *Poems 1970–1972*, 'indoctrinated by "Gwynedd" . . . in *Cynganedd* and other ancient metrical devices. . . .' In 1909 he tried his hand at translating some poems by Catullus; and at the same time was trying to adapt Welsh technical procedures to English. These are amongst the most complicated in world poetry. The group of *englyn* metres, which especially attracted Graves, requires extreme verbal economy, complex alliteration and internal rhymes; there are numerous strict rules. Eventually he found that complete adaptation of these procedures to English was not possible; but that all his energy went into trying to make it possible meant that he would be the finest and most versatile traditionalist technician in English-language poetry of his century. He gives us, in the 1938 *Collected Poems*, a couple of early examples:

> Thou, a poor woman's fairing – white heather,
> Witherest from the ending
> Of summer's bliss to the sting
> Of winter's grey beginning. . . .

and

> ... Woodland fauns with hairy haunches
> Grin in wonder through the branches,
> Woodland fauns who know not fear:
> Wondering they wander near,
> Munching mushrooms red as coral,
> Bunches, too, of rue and sorrel,
> With uncouth and bestial sounds,
> Knowing naught of war and wounds.
> But the crimson life-blood oozes
> And makes roses of the daisies. . . .

Another couple of early lines he quotes are:

> Green terror ripples through our bones
> We yearn for careless day.

This was a valuable apprenticeship – and it should be observed that Graves found his sources, which were obscure, amongst his father's extensive collection of books.

As to the subject matter of the poems, he was being truer to himself, even then, than he later gave himself credit for. Concentrating on the physical side of poetry, as he has acknowledged, he expressed his apprehensions about nature and brutish sex (those fauns are, in a very generalized and conventionalized way, horrid representatives of lust). The terror that ripples through his bones so that he yearns for careless day is *green*. He here anticipates the nature theme which runs through his work. This poem bristles with horrors already. But he does not want to be dead: the green terror *ripples* through his bones with vitality. The verse itself, even though that of a boy, is highly energetic, full of nervous vigour. There is in him, already, a spirit of challenge, a racy, fluid lustiness which rises to meet terror, which in a sense welcomes it as a quickener, something to make the blood flow. There is also an absolute ignorance about sexual 'vice', only a horror of it. At this time all sex to Graves was vice.

The last year at Charterhouse was mostly easier. He was out of reach of boy-persecutors, and in late 1913 sat successfully for a classical exhibition to St John's College, Oxford. This meant that he did not have to put so much energy into his work, and could therefore find time (partly as coeditor of the school magazine) to express his contempt for the traditions of Charterhouse. He became known as arrogant and intractable; but, because of his reputation as a boxer, no one was prepared to take him on. 'Poetry and Dick were still almost all that really mattered,' he wrote. George Mallory and those to whom he introduced him are covered by the 'almost': Mallory made him feel an equal in the adult world – which he was now so keen to reach, so as to escape once and for all from the restrictions of school.

But he had two more difficult encounters with authority. The first was when one of his fellow house monitors scratched 'up a pair of hearts conjoined, with Dick's initials and mine above them' in the bathroom. All or most of these monitors had physical affairs with younger boys, but they looked on Robert's love for Dick as being holier-than-thou, 'wet', superior. They cannot altogether be blamed. Superficially he must have seemed an arrogant prig – even if not to Mallory, whose heart was no more in Charterhouse than was Graves's.

He caught the monitor while he was scratching up the initials, and pushed him into the bath – conveniently at hand – and turned the taps on. This was too much for the other monitors, who (with the exception of one) now ganged up on him. They picked up a manuscript book which he had left in their commonroom – it contained essays – and each annotated it facetiously in blue chalk, signing his initials.

Graves's reaction was 'true British'. He demanded a signed apology, and announced that if he didn't get it he would knock down the first monitor he saw. He didn't get his apology, and soon met a monitor in a corridor – it happened to be the head monitor. He knocked him down, and blood spurted. The incident was witnessed, and news of it spread. The housemaster, known as 'Gosh' Parry because of his difficulty in controlling his saliva when worked up, was beside himself, and told him that he had committed a 'brutal act'. As Graves tells it, 'his mouth bubbled with spittle: I jumped up and clenched my fists too, saying that I would do the same thing again to anyone else who, after scribbling impertinent remarks on my private papers, refused to apologise.' Parry, he says, replied, 'Private papers? Filthy poems!'

Probably Frank Fletcher, the headmaster who succeeded Rendell, would have liked to expel Graves. But he had won an exhibition to Oxford, and his grounds for action would have involved mention of 'amorousness' – if not 'eroticism'. Parry sent him to Fletcher, who discussed the causes of the incident with him. When Graves frankly confessed his love for Dick – still perfectly rightly seeing this as 'unsullied' – he was puzzled; but he was impressed, for later Graves learned that he described it as an 'essentially moral' friendship.

There was one other incident. It exemplifies, once again, Graves's ferocity in the cause of what he holds to be virtue – and his habit of concealing 'murderous' feelings under the guise of 'moral outrage'. For although in relating this incident he writes that doubtless 'my sense of moral outrage concealed a murderous jealousy', the capacity for this insight has not always prevented him from indulging in the same sort of behaviour.

The master who sang in the choir warned Graves, who was 'infuriated', about exchanging glances with Dick. But another choirboy then told him that he had seen this same master surreptitiously kissing Dick. Graves went straight to the master in a raging temper: 'You have been seen kissing a boy. It is a criminal offence. You can go to prison for years for this. I demand your immediate resignation or I will go to the headmaster, and you will go to penal servitude!'

The unfortunate master denied it. But he was in a spot. He had kissed lots of boys, although no more than that – and the whole school (except Graves) knew it. The master prevaricated, and suggested that they send for Dick himself. For Graves, beside himself, had not yet even bothered to check up. Dick, asked directly whether he had been kissed, replied that he had. The master, already near breakdown under pressure of guilt, collapsed, promised to resign (which he did), and even thanked Robert for not reporting him.

This was the summer of 1914; he went into the army and was killed the following year. Dick told me later that he had not been kissed at all, but he saw I was in a jam – it must have been some other member of the choir!

This is all Graves has to say about the matter. In his record of the affair he tacitly reproaches himself for his callousness by mentioning that he 'went quite mad without asking for any details or confirmation'; but he has continued to do exactly this throughout his life. The baldness of the account is likewise characteristic. In fact he did have a bad conscience about it, but his style is not at all apologetic. If challenged with callousness he might say that any fool could see that he felt bad about it: 'never apologise, never explain'. Repentance has aroused his scorn since he was a young man: it is 'wet'. But this aversion to wetness conceals an extreme 'wetness' in himself – a high emotionalism which, when he recalls it, causes him to shudder with embarrassment.

His headmaster's final advice to him on leaving Charterhouse has become legendary: 'Well, goodbye, Graves, and remember that your best friend is the waste-paper basket.'

IV

Graves so disliked Wimbledon that in his autobiography he writes: 'I don't like thinking of Wimbledon.' Above all he hated the social life in which he was forcibly involved; he was expected to behave at his 'best', in the conventional sense, and this seemed unnatural and time-wasting to him. Though his father encouraged his interests in Irish and Welsh mythology, and ancient poetry, his actual home life was more German in style than English. Christmas was celebrated in the German tradition, which means heavily overjovially and overactively. He often visited Germany in the summers, and well remembers his eccentric grandfather and the supposedly haunted manor house Laufzorn ('Be-gone, anger!'), not far from Munich. He enjoyed the German fun, the practical jokes of his grandfather, and the countryside seemed more like home than Wimbledon; but he found Munich 'sinister', and was afraid of the realistic wayside crucifixes: 'Though brought up to believe in hell, we [the children] did not like to be reminded of it.' He learned to speak German, but was, from his entrance to Charterhouse onwards, consciously trying to reject the German in himself; he has only ever read in the language with the greatest reluctance – and has never read a whole book in it.

Graves was overjoyed when A.P. bought a holiday house in Harlech. He says that the first poem he wrote 'as himself' was about the Harlech hills. 'On our visits to Germany I had felt a sense of home in a natural human way, but above Harlech I felt a personal peace independent of history or geography.' He has still never discovered any country like that around Harlech – which lies south of Caernarvon, in wild country in North Wales, and has a famous castle. It 'seemed independent of formal nature'. He experienced the place as non-geographical, ghostly but peaceful; there one 'hardly noticed the passage of the seasons'. The 'rocky skeleton' of the hill gave peace to his mind and heart. There is something about the detail in nature (branches, flowers, birds, even moss) which attracts but also frightens him. He likes bare rock – you can see a good deal of this in Mallorca.

In Wales he learned to conquer his fear of heights. He would invent difficult climbs for himself, then lie down 'twitching with nervousness'. It was a secret existence; although as a child he had been very close to his sister Rosaleen, and written songs and stories with her, he now had no real confidant.

Dick was a special case: he was younger than Graves and needed to be protected from the 'facts of life' (of which he knew very many more than Graves). Mallory came nearest to the role of confidant. Not until he met T. E. Lawrence was he to find an older friend in whom he could place full confidence, and in whom he could believe fervently.

Mallory made him feel like an adult with opinions of his own, and took him climbing with eminent mountaineers on Snowdon in the school vacations. His achievements in climbing meant a great deal to him. Though a poet and writer, and therefore a man who perforce must spend time at a desk, he believes that true poetry (and all other writing, for that matter) springs from experience – he is emphatically a 'doer' rather than a 'thinker'. In all his poetry experience is primary. With Mallory he did mostly rope and ice-axe climbing; his companions included Geoffrey Keynes, surgeon and editor of Blake, the well-known climbing technician H. E. L. Porter, and the poetaster Geoffrey Winthrop Young, a courageous man who, after he lost a leg in the war, went on climbing with a wooden one. He told Robert that he had the most perfect sense of natural balance that he had ever seen in a climber – and this pleased him so much that he always refused to look at Young's banal verse.

Chapter Three
1914–15

I

Finishing with Charterhouse was a great moment. He could still see Mallory; and there was no one else there, with the exception of Dick, with whom he wished to keep in touch. He went off to Harlech and wandered about the hills, as he always did when he could. There was one thing that he was dreading above all else: Oxford. He was dreading it so much that he has told many people (rather shocked at himself) that, at the very first, he welcomed the war as an escape. He says as much, too, in *Goodbye to All That*. In common with most people he had no idea of how long the war would last, or what its nature would be.

He dreaded Oxford because he had come to despise the educational system, which seemed to him stultified and operated by hypocrites. He thought he would get more of this kind of thing at Oxford, more of being taught dry facts in which he had no interest. His spirit rebelled against it, although he had very little idea what he actually did want to do, except that he knew that he would be a poet. This sense of vocation was certain enough, but somewhat vague. Even then he did not equate being called a poet with being one, although he was still ambitious and idealistic.

Then Great Britain declared war on Germany. Public opinion, and Graves with it, thought that the war would be over before Christmas; all he hoped for was that it would last long enough to keep him from Oxford until at least the following year. He thought that any fighting would be done by regular soldiers. But he felt disgusted by Germany's behaviour – though he was realist enough not to believe all the wild atrocity stories that were being put about.

His decision to enlist immediately was prompted not only by the notion of getting out of Oxford but also by the fact that he felt compromised by his German blood. Several of his relatives were high-ranking officers in the German army; one was a general. Fortunately his uncle on his father's side, Rear-Admiral Sir Richard Poore, was commander of the Nore from 1914 until 1916; he concentrated on him whenever the matter of relatives came up.

He did not enlist through the ranks. The secretary of the Harlech golf club suggested that he should 'take a commission'. You could do that, if you were a gentleman, in those days. Graves felt pleased; things were working out well. A telephone call to the nearest regimental depot, at Wrexham, and he was in. The secretary told the adjutant that Graves had been in the Officers' Training Corps at Charterhouse (but not that he had resigned from it), and was told to send him along. The regiment was the Royal Welch Fusiliers. His family (including his mother, who lamented, 'Our race has gone mad!') rejoiced: he was already a hero. He was indifferent to this; nor had he any intention of making the army his career.

It was on 12 August that he joined up. His father recorded in his diary:

> Up at six a.m. to see Robbie off to join the Royal Welch Fusiliers at Wrexham. He started in good spirits and was waving to us as long as possible from the carriage window.

The next day he wrote to his family (he was then a dutiful and affectionate son, something that hardly comes over in *Goodbye to All That*), telling them that he was 'keen over his work' and hoped to be gazetted in 'the next few days'.

After what passed for training in the months before the war was taken seriously, Graves was transferred to Lancaster, where he was put in charge of recruits and German prisoners. He found the experienced Special Reservists difficult to outwit: they were tough Welshmen, always fighting, breaking bounds and seducing women. He kept himself aloof from their animal spirits, but dwelled upon what he thought must be their hyper-bestial experiences, and magnified them, in the secret parts of his mind.

By October he became impatient. 'Guarding prisoners seemed an unheroic part to be playing ... I wanted to be abroad fighting.' His adjutant did not like him: he was untidy, 'unsoldierlike and a nuisance'; he was unsporting – the only officer in the camp who had not wanted to attend the Grand National (at nearby Aintree) in which the adjutant had a horse running. Besides, what right had so slack-looking a soldier to put on airs?

On 20 October he had a short leave. His father noted that he was 'fatter', and did not expect him to be sent to the front 'for some time'. Graves became more and more impatient as, one by one, his fellow-officers were packed off to France. It was boxing that came to his aid once more. Johnny Basham, a Royal Welch sergeant and professional welterweight, was training for a title fight. He was making some of the young officers look silly when they offered to go three rounds with him. Graves offered, and he managed to catch him unawares, by pretending to be more of a novice than he was; he knocked him across the ring. Basham allowed him to seem 'a much better boxer than I was, by accommodating his pace to mine'. This impressed even the adjutant. Graves's reward: he would be put down for a draft to France due to leave in a week.

But this did not happen until May 1915. In the meantime he learned a great deal about army life, and about the history of his regiment – which was a 'good bloody' one. He was glad to be a member of it, and glad to become an honorary Welshman by eating raw leeks, with one foot on a chair and one on the mess table, to the roll of drums, on St David's Night (1 March).

Meanwhile a batch of his poems had been sent, either by Mallory or his father, to the Gray's Inn home of Edward Marsh. Graves wrote to Marsh: 'I think he [Rupert Brooke] is really good. . . . What a torture his sensitiveness must always be for him, poor fellow!' But Marsh still insisted that Graves's work was old-fashioned in diction and technique. He hoped his criticisms would not annoy him. 'No, I'm not annoyed, why should I be?' Graves wrote in February 1915 from his camp in Lancaster.

> I always try to look at myself objectively and dispassionately because this helps me to get the full flavour of romance out of life, so now I can see that it would be most extraordinary if my technique wasn't obsolete. . . . However, I am still in my teens and when this ridiculous war is over I will write Chapter II at the top of the new sheet and with the help of other young Georgians to whom I trust you will introduce me, will try to root out more effectively the obnoxious survivals of Victorianism.

Later he would feel that he had been untrue to himself in being ambitious, and in offering to become part of a 'school'. He also changed his mind about the worth of Brooke. But the letter shows the useful work Marsh did in trying to get young poets to write in a less archaic manner.

When Graves got out to France in May and was posted to the line – to the Welsh Regiment, to his disgust, and not to the Royal Welch Fusiliers – things soon appeared very differently to him. What struck him most forcibly, and shocked him, was the state of unpreparedness of the forty men in the platoon of which, as second lieutenant, he was given charge. One of them asked what 'this here arrangement' at the side of his rifle was. It was the safety catch. He was aged sixty-three – had given a false age on enlistment – and had last fired a rifle in Egypt thirty-three years before. This man had been rejected as too old when he tried to enlist for the Boer War. Others were mere boys, who had also given false ages.

II

The Great War finally shattered the myth of human progress by which the Victorians fortified themselves against those aspects of the technology from which they benefited materially, but which seemed to menace their spiritual lives. Another word for this myth, more used in America than England, was 'meliorism'. Even Thomas Hardy, who accurately prophesied the gloom to come in many poems written between 1870 and 1914, was wary about how he denied that he was a meliorist. It looked very bad not to be a meliorist if you were not a Christian. There had been no war between the major European powers since 1871, and no one – including Robert Graves, Siegfried Sassoon, Wilfred Owen and others – had any real idea of what a new one would be like. The old wars had been decided by heroic battles; those battles which ended in stalemates had then been settled by other battles. A war would be a quick affair; or if it were by any chance to be drawn out, then it would be simply a matter of a series of several battles. Graves had read about the battles in which his regiment had been involved, and himself formed this notion.

But the battles of the First World War were unlike any that had preceded them. The first months of the war made this plain. Twenty days after Britain declared war on the Central Powers, Sir John French's four divisions found themselves outflanked. They were forced to retreat from Mons. In the next week, in a series of bloody and costly engagements on the Marne, the Allies stopped the German advance on Paris – and probably saved the war.

By Christmas 1914, after each side had vainly tried to fight its way to the Belgian coast, the two armies found themselves locked into the trench system. A week or two before Graves found himself in France, the Germans used chlorine (they had used tear gas in October) for the first time – at Ypres ('Wipers'); he was luckier than his friend-to-be, Edmund Blunden, who suffered from bad health for the rest of his life through being gassed. The horrors of the trench system have become notorious – and they are not susceptible to exaggeration.

Graves was at first sent up to the line at Cambrin, not far from Béthune, which is in the area around Lille where so much of the war was fought. He was introduced to his company commander, Captain Dunn – a Scotsman two months younger than himself, but already a veteran. Dunn told Graves how they had at first thought of the trenches as 'temporary inconveniences', and had paddled about in them; now they lived in them for 'safety' and 'health'.

He spent his first watch learning not to move at peril of his life, and discovering how wet and uncomfortable it was. He also saw his first corpse. At the end of this watch he saw a man lying face down in a machine-gun shelter; he had no boot or sock on. Graves was going to speak to him, but a machine gunner told him, 'No good talking to him, sir.' 'He had taken off the boot and sock to pull the trigger of his rifle with one toe; the muzzle was in his mouth.' He had been sent a 'bit queer' by the 'last push' – and had then got bad news about his girl and another man. An officer ordered the incident not to be reported as suicide: 'Usual sort of letter; tell them he died a soldier's death, anything you like. . . .' Graves soon learned of these and other realities, and how to get on with his platoon.

He fills a chapter of *Goodbye to All That* with extracts from letters he wrote at the time; his father printed some more in his autobiography *To Return to All That* (1930); the latter had in fact already appeared, as letters from a soldier at the front ('Some Trench Scenes') in the *Spectator* of 11 September 1915. The style of these *Spectator* letters is more youthful than that of the ones Graves himself prints, which he edited, doubtless to cut out any 'wetness'. They are all interesting as showing how he represented himself at this time to his father – and as showing that his father was in no way whatever ashamed of his son's anti-war feelings, or a prude (though what Amy Graves thought about the woodpecker song, which has been current ever since, I cannot imagine). Here are some extracts from the ones A.P. printed, in chronological order:

On Sunday ... I was in charge of a hundred or so ... doing fatigue work down at the quay in the immense storehouse, built by certain busy Teutons. It is over half a mile long, a third of that broad, and choked up to the rafters with stuff (know that picture of 'Little Porgie' in Just-So stories? this place knocks that into a cocked hat) – well, I was down there and got a sudden order to return and report, which I did, and next morning a great column of us marched to the station and entrained. We took twenty-five hours to go as many miles, travelling, the five of us Flash Mob, in one carriage with packs and valises, which was cheery, but not good for sleeping. We had a rowdy dinner beforehand, with *homards, pain d'épice,* bully beef which isn't bad stuff – for a time – marmalade, tinned sausages, sang a lot of songs, and did the 'Tomorrow Comrades we' touch. When we arrived at the railhead, a small town (ask no names), we disembarked feeling a bit like the bottom of the proverbial parrot-cage, and were told by the guide who met us that we were to go straight to the trenches. Which we did after a five-mile march by cobbled road and a mile and a half down a muddy communication trench in the dark, lit by occasional star shells. I was posted to — Company and put in charge of no. — platoon. After a cup of tea, some cake, and an Egyptian [cigarette], I retired to — 's dug-out, where I slept like a top (broken only by the 'stand-to' for an hour before dawn). The trenches are palaces, dug by the French who had occupied 'em for six months, wonderful places. I wish home was as tidy always. Clay walls, bomb-proof ceilings, pictures on the walls, straw-filled berths, stoves, tables, chairs, complete with a piebald cat. I wasn't frightened by the guns which bang away all day and night. The noise is just like the Blaenau Festiniog [near Harlech] slate-blasters, with the rocket-like whistle of the shells going over.

I have a servant. . . . He is a good servant but a bad man. The worse the man, in fact, the better the servant. What constitutes the good servant is the faculty of coming back with more than he sets out with: mine got hold of a new Webley revolver complete with lanyard, an excellent weapon. Some poor beggar must have cursed, but I couldn't trace the ownership, so remain the possessor. . . .

I can't stick those horrid fellows who write home to say war is adorable. Let me explain what I mean. Last night – we had seventeen casualties yesterday from bombs and grenades – I went round the fire-trench, which averages fifteen yards from the Germans' and at one point is ten yards off, to see if all was correct, and turning a traverse sharply almost

36

stepped on a Horrible Thing lying in the parados [bank of earth]. We can afford to laugh at corpses, if we did not know them when alive, because then it is a case of what the men call 'nappoo fineesh': we can joke with men badly wounded who are going to recover: but when a German bullet – and a reversed one at that – strikes a man on the head and takes the scalp and a lot of his brains clean away, and still lets him live for a few hours, the joke is there no more. An R.E. sergeant met me there and told me that his sap had just come through into an old crater where a mine had been exploded, and that the time was ripe for bomb-throwers. So with this Horrid Thing still lying there the bombers filed past, and creeping down the sap lobbed the bombs over into the German trenches: they threw twenty over, and now doubtless the Prussian subaltern opposite, if he is a decent fellow, is being sickened by more than one Horrid Thing in his parados.

And from amongst the many songs the men sang he quotes the famous

> I shoved my finger in a woodpecker's hole
> And the woodpecker screamed GOD STRAFE YOUR SOUL
> Take it out!
> Take it out!
> Take it out!
> REMOVE IT!

At this time he had with him, for reading, the *Odyssey*, *Erewhon* (which he was reading for the sixth time – 'there is always some new reading to be got out of Butler's twisted accounts of Erewhonian customs'), Blake and Keats ('about the most soothing poet going'). Whether or not he had a Skelton – Henry VIII's tutor and 'laureate' whom he has loved lifelong – he claims in his autobiography that he already knew his poems from the Dyce edition (in the old spelling). The 'clean, dry' corpse of a dead parrot in a cage which he and his company used as a wicket for an afternoon cricket match reminded him (he wrote) of Skelton's

> Parrot is a fair bird for a ládye.
> God of His goodness him faméd and wrought.
> When parrot is dead he doth not putrify,
> Yea, all things mortal shall turn into nought
> Save mannés soul which Christ so dear bought,
> That never can die, nor never die shall.
> Make much of parrot, that popajay royál.

But this may be an error: from his letters one gathers he discovered Skelton two years later.

He was also writing to Edward Marsh in much the same terms as to his father at this time, except that he took the opportunity to denigrate his father. Brooke had died on his way to Gallipoli a month before:

> My Father (dear old man!) said that this was a fitting end for Rupert, killed by the arrows of jealous Musagetes in his own Greek islands; but fine words won't help. . . . I feel exactly like a man who has watched the 'movies' for a long evening and then suddenly finds himself thrown on the screen in the middle of scalp-hunting Sioux and runaway motorcars; and rather surprised that I am not at all frightened. . . . You may disbelieve the following, but I swear to you, Eddie, it's a true bill, that a violent artillery duel going on above my dug-out two nights ago simply failed to wake me at all though I was conscious of the whole place rocking but, when this had ceased, I was wakened by a very persistent lark. . . . I know it is very rude and inconsiderate of me, inflicting my verses on you, but last January you told me to bring my technique up to date and try to do a bit better than what I showed you so I send you a thing ['The Poet in the Nursery'; a draft of 'It's a Queer Time' is incorporated in the letter] I wrote . . . with your advice still ringing in my ears. . . . Tomorrow we go, they say, into some trenches where we and the Boches are sitting in each other's pockets, the whole place mined and countermined, complete with trench mortars, gas, and grenade throwing parties. So now for a little sleep. Yours in the Muses. . . .

He remained in the area near Béthune, in the Cambrin and Cuinchy trenches. Soon he 'caught the pessimism of the First Division'; casualties were very heavy, although the policy was not to provoke the Germans. He found himself getting 'trivially superstitious'. And he did not much like his second sergeant's account of his predecessor, who had told the sergeant that he was going to be killed on the day he was killed.

Some officers' and men's nerves were already torn to shreds. Robert's account of a Major Furber nearly got him into serious legal trouble (I quote here from the first version of *Goodbye to All That*; the second scarcely differs in this passage):

> There is a company commander here called Furber. His nerves are in pieces, and somebody played a dirty joke on him the other day – rolling a bomb, undetonated, of course, down the cellar steps to frighten him. This was thought a great joke. Furber is the greatest pessimist out here [second version reads 'in France']. He's laid a bet with the adjutant that the trench lines will not be more than a mile from where they are in this sector two years hence. [Footnote added to second version: 'He won the

bet.'] Every one laughs at Furber, but they like him because he sings sentimental cockney songs at the brigade gaffs when we are back at Béthune.

When Major Furber read this in 1930 he did not like it. His solicitors wrote to the publisher (Jonathan Cape) on 21 October 1930 telling him that they would be glad to hear whether he would compensate their client, who would otherwise 'commence proceedings to enforce his rights'. But they were told that their client would under no circumstances be compensated, whereupon he may have sung a sentimental cockney song; but he did not 'commence proceedings to enforce his rights', whatever these may have been.

Graves's 1929 account of the snobbery that usually prevailed in the officers' messes did not involve him in a libel suit, or even the threat of one; but it caused certain regular officers to speak of him as a cad, bounder and traitor wherever the British Army was stationed – right up to the outbreak of the Second World War – as Brigadier Desmond Young, biographer of Rommel, told him in a letter of 1952. One glaring instance of this snobbery, at a mess at Laventie, caused him to say to himself (but well under his breath): 'You damned snobs! I'll survive you all. There'll come a time when there won't be one of you left in the battalion to remember this mess at Laventie.'

It was at Laventie that the going started to get even tougher for him. He had never before been in no-man's-land. But by now he had joined his own regiment, the Royal Welch, who 'made it a point of honour to dominate No Man's Land from dusk to dawn'. No-man's-land was the strip between the two front lines, littered with unretrieved corpses. One of the most horrible of all places for those who fought in France in the First World War, it was almost always 'ridiculously' narrow, but did not seem so to the men who patrolled it in the dark. On Graves's first visit to it, on night patrol, wriggling along a few yards at a time, he surprised and horrified himself by putting his hand 'on the slimy body of an old corpse'.

Meanwhile, although he had already received the disquieting letter about Dick, he still drew great solace from correspondence with him. He had had a reassuring letter from him explaining that he had 'been ragging about in a silly way', 'but that nothing bad had happened'. Graves was uneasy, but smothered his doubts. He was still very dependent on this relationship, although aware that it had become tenuous. His morale was becoming steadily sapped by the fighting.

But the instinct for survival was strong in him. As we have seen from the letters he sent to his family, and to Marsh — especially the one complaining about people who write home saying how 'adorable' war is — he soon saw through the nature of the war. He is candid about how he felt. Having described, in *Goodbye to All That*, his first alarming patrol of no-man's-land, he goes on to say:

> After this I went on patrol fairly often, finding that the only thing respected in young officers was personal courage. Besides, I had cannily worked it out like this. My best way of lasting through to the end of the war would be to get wounded. The best time to get wounded would be at night and in the open, with rifle fire more or less unaimed and my whole body exposed. Best, also, to get wounded when there was no rush on the dressing-station services, and while the back areas were not being heavily shelled. Best to get wounded, therefore, on a night patrol in a quiet sector. One could usually manage to crawl into a shell hole until help arrived. [This is the later version.]

On 9 September 1915 he went home on leave for the first time. He found the people in London strangely unaware of the reality of the war — and hurriedly went off to Harlech, where he wandered about 'in an old shirt and a pair of shorts'. When he returned and was posted he recognized, 'with some disgust', that he was back where he had begun in the previous May. Throughout the month of September he was involved in the notorious 'dud show' (or 'bloody balls up' as one of the officers called it), the Battle of Loos. The action of Graves's brigade, if such a shambles can be described as action, was to create a diversion. He lost most of his brother officers and many of the men he had known. In eight days he snatched eight hours' sleep — all short naps which, he has said, were physically irresistible when the rare opportunity offered, but which seemed even worse than continual sleeplessness because he had to wake up too soon to responsibility and drastic action. Large quantities of whisky kept him going. One man who served under him, as a private, and was with him at Loos, remembered him as a 'capital officer' — but even forty years later was unaware that he was 'the famous writer'.

Soon after Loos Graves was gazetted a Special Reserve captain, the rank he held until he was demobilized. This was useful financially, but put him in an awkward position because he was not (officially) 'efficient', and was being promoted over the heads of older and more experienced men who knew how to look efficient. Anyhow, promotion did nothing to allay the 'black depression' into which he had sunk —

a result of the battering he had taken in the Loos fiasco, and of his misgivings about Dick. At this stage he began to have suicidal feelings; and in those circumstances a man does not have to take the decision to kill himself, he just has to allow himself to be killed. In the First World War, especially, this was an art easily and often learned.

With the late autumn of 1915 things temporarily became easier. He went back to the now reorganized First Battalion, a mile or so from Cambrin, where he found it 'more efficient and regimental'. He liked this.

At his new posting he heard the noise from yet another 'dud show', in which his brigade expected to be involved (but was not). In this, an assault on the so-called Hohenzollern Redoubt, the poet Charles Sorley was killed.

When he was ordered to join the First Battalion at Locon, north of Cambrin, he was attached to A Company mess; but he made a social call on C Company mess, and was surprised to find lying on the table *The Essays of Lionel Johnson*, a highly esoteric item to find in this part of the world. He looked surreptitiously at the flyleaf, where he found written the name Siegfried Sassoon. He had never heard of it – and reasonably enough. Sassoon, nine years his senior, had published little, though he already knew many literary men through his uncle, who knew the influential Edmund Gosse. Sassoon (whose father was of a notable Sephardic Jewish family) had grown up with his mother, a sister of Hamo Thorneycroft – a well-known sculptor – who had separated from her husband. He had been educated at Marlborough and Clare College, Cambridge – from which he was sent down for not working. He was interested in sport, hunting – and writing poetry. The only notable poem he had so far written was *The Daffodil Murderer* (1913), a strange parody of the then lively and candid Masefield which got out of hand and turned into something with an odd life of its own. But he had published this under the pseudonym of Saul Kain, to make his target obvious (Saul Kane is the name of the central character in Masefield's famous narrative poem of 1911; another narrative poem, of 1913, was called *The Daffodil Fields*).

Meeting Sassoon was the start of an exciting new friendship for Graves. It seemed to them, in those dark days, that they would always be kindred souls, that they would share the same views about poetry. It was a bitter experience for both, though mostly for Sassoon, to discover – after the shadow of that war had passed – that they violently disagreed, Graves being, in his own individualistic way, forward-looking, and Sassoon backward-looking.

Graves was just then preparing his first book, *Over the Brazier*, for the press. A.P., who had been offering the poems around, had arranged this publication with Harold Monro of the Poetry Bookshop, a house which steered an incautious but exciting way between the conventional and the unconventional. Graves had met the unknown and unpublished Robert Frost while browsing in the shop, in 1914. Siegfried was shocked by his new friend's candid approach to the war in these poems. War, he told Graves, should not be written about realistically. He showed him one of his own poems:

> Return to greet me, colours that were my joy,
> Not in the woeful crimson of men slain . . .

Graves told him that when he had been in the trenches he would soon change his style.

Graves liked 'Mad Jack', as Sassoon soon came to be called when he went into action, because he hated all the 'sergeant-major business', 'and used sometimes on [the] barrack square to be laughing so much at the pomposity of the drill as hardly to be able to control his word of command.' Graves spent a good deal of time with him in France in the next months, and both became friendly with a young Third Battalion second lieutenant called David Thomas, a Welshman: 'He, Siegfried Sassoon, and I always went about together.' In *Memoirs of an Infantry Officer* David Thomas is Dick Tiltwood.

Graves wrote to Marsh to tell him that he found it difficult to talk to Sassoon about poetry

as the other officers of the batt. are terribly curious and suspicious – If I go into his mess and he wants to show me some set of verses he says 'Afternoon, Graves, have a drink. . . ; by the way I want you to see my latest recipe for rum punch.' The trenches are worse than billets for privacy.

Early in 1916 Sassoon wrote to Marsh, whom he already knew through Gosse, that Graves was

a strange person, full of ideas and originality. I am rather disappointed with his poems. Do you think it wise for him to publish them? I am sure he will do some much better work before long when he has recovered his balance. . . .

Marsh thought better of the poems and told Sassoon – who then regarded Graves as a promising boy – that he had been very interested in them: 'fresh, pleasant things (some I don't like at all) I shouldn't be at all sorry to see him publish. . . .'

A. P. Graves had been 'trying to pin Marsh down to a discussion on the young man's literary future' (says Marsh's biographer) for months. Robert resented this bitterly, and told Marsh that both his parents took him overseriously: 'last month I had an absolute *snorter* from Father about some verses giving a point of view he regarded as immoral.' He was therefore sending this new lot 'in strict confidence'.

Sassoon left a vivid picture of Graves (David Cromlech) at this time, in *Memoirs of an Infantry Officer*. He and the 'big, impulsive' Cromlech were 'close friends'. He had a 'remarkable' face, 'sallow, crooked and whimsical', and would make 'desperately cheerful ejaculations' just before going into battle.

At his best I'd always found him an ideal companion, although his opinions were often disconcerting. But no one was worse than he at hitting it off with officers who distrusted cleverness and disliked unreserved utterances. In fact he was a positive expert at putting people's backs up unintentionally. He was with our Second Battalion for a few months before they transferred him to 'the First', and during that period the Colonel was heard to remark that young Cromlech threw his tongue a hell of a lot too much, and that it was about time he gave up reading Shakespeare and took to using soap and water. He had, however, added, 'I'm agreeably surprised to find that he isn't windy in trenches.'

David certainly was deplorably untidy, and his absent-mindedness when off duty was another propensity which made him unpopular. Also, as I have already hinted, he wasn't good at being 'seen but not heard'. 'Far too fond of butting in with his own opinion before he's been asked for it,' was often his only reward for an intelligent suggestion. Even Birdie Mansfield (who had knocked about the world too much to be intolerant) was once heard to exclaim, 'Unless you watch it, my son, you'll grow up into the most bumptious young prig God ever invented!' – this protest being a result of David's assertion that all sports except boxing, football, and rock climbing were snobbish and silly.

From the floor of the tent, Holman (a spick and span boy who had been to Sandhurst and hadn't yet discovered that it was unwise to look down on temporary officers who 'wouldn't have been wanted in the Regiment in peace time') was now saying, 'Anyhow, I was at Litherland with him last month, and he fairly got on people's nerves with his hot air about the Battle of Loos, and his brain-waves about who really wrote the Bible.' Durley then philosophically observed, 'Old Long-neck certainly isn't the sort of man you meet every day. I can't always follow his theories myself, but I don't mind betting that he'll go a long way – provided he isn't pushing up daisies when Peace breaks out.' Holman (who had only been with us a few days and soon became more demo-cratic) brushed Durley's defence aside with 'The blighter's never satisfied unless he's turning something upside down. I actually heard him say that Homer was a woman. Can you beat that? And if you'll believe me he had the darned sauce to give me a sort of pi-jaw about going out with girls in Liverpool. If you ask me, I think he's a rotten outsider, and the sooner he's pushing up daisies the better.' Whereupon Perrin (a quiet man of thirty-five who was sitting in a corner writing to his wife) stopped the discussion by saying, 'Oh, dry up, Holman! For all we know the poor devil may be dead by now.'

Chapter Four

1916

The soldiers had been aware since late 1915 that there was to be an offensive on the Somme. Graves went at New Year as a training officer at Harfleur; in March he rejoined the First Battalion on the Fricourt sector. Very soon after this, before the offensive, young David Thomas was shot through the neck. At first it was thought that he was all right: he had been seen walking to the dressing station. Graves records that he was 'delighted': his friend would miss the offensive and perhaps the whole war. But David died. The doctor (or so the story went) warned him not to raise his head, but he did so while handing a letter to an orderly to post for him; it had been written, to his girl, for delivery only if he got killed. 'I felt David's death worse than any other since I had been in France, but it did not anger me as it did Siegfried,' Graves writes. It prompted him to write an elegy, one of the better known of the poems he rejected from his *Collected Poems*. He had it privately printed, and it was issued in pamphlet form towards the end of 1916. It is a good example of his best war poetry; but it demonstrates, against almost any of the well-known Sassoon poems of later in the war, that he certainly did not feel 'anger'. Having written this, and seen it through the press, he felt – he says – some kind of strange compensation for David's death. In parentheses below the title *Goliath and David* are the words: 'For Lieut. David Thomas, 1st Batt. Royal Welch Fusiliers, killed at Fricourt, March, 1916'.

> 'If I am Jesse's son,' said he
> 'Where must that tall Goliath be?'
> For once an earlier David took
> Smooth pebbles from the brook:
> Out between the lines he went
> To that one-sided tournament,

A shepherd boy who stood out fine
And young to fight a Philistine
Clad all in brazen mail. He swears
That he's killed lions, he's killed bears,
And those that scorn the God of Zion
Shall perish so like bear or lion.
But . . . the historian of that fight
Had not the heart to tell it right.

Striding within javelin range,
Goliath marvels at this strange
Goodly-faced boy so proud of strength.
David's clear eye measures the length;
With hand thrust back, he cramps one knee,
Poises a moment thoughtfully,
And hurls with a long vengeful swing.
The pebble, humming from the sling
Like a wild bee, flies a sure line
For the forehead of the Philistine;
Then . . . but there comes a brazen clink,
And quicker than a man can think
Goliath's shield parries each cast,
Clang! clang! And clang! was David's last.

Scorn blazes in the Giant's eye,
Towering unhurt six cubits high.
Says foolish David, 'Curse your shield!
And curse my sling! but I'll not yield.'
He takes his staff of Mamre oak,
A knotted shepherd-staff that's broke
The skull of many a wolf and fox
Come filching lambs from Jesse's flocks.
Loud laughs Goliath, and that laugh
Can scatter chariots like blown chaff
To rout; but David, calm and brave,
Holds his ground, for God will save.
Steel crosses wood, a flash, and oh!
Shame for beauty's overthrow!
(God's eyes are dim, His ears are shut).
One cruel backhand sabre-cut —
'I'm hit! I'm killed!' young David cries,
Throws blindly forward, chokes . . . and dies.
Steel-helmeted and grey and grim
Goliath straddles over him.

This poem is really a personal, rather than a 'war', poem; and while Graves's attitude is disillusioned and against 'Christian comfort', his diction is still conventional.

A sentence or two after describing his feelings over David's death, Graves in *Goodbye to All That* writes that his 'breaking-point was near now . . . a general nervous collapse, with tears and twitchings and dirtied trousers'. He had seen 'cases like that'. Something had to intervene, he felt, to prevent it. But he was tougher than he thought – as were so many others caught in that conflict.

It so happened that just then he needed a nose operation, so as to be able to wear a new, safer type of gas-helmet; his boxing had displaced his septum, and he could only breathe through his mouth. His nose was to be a trouble to him again and again, but this time, although the operation was very badly bungled, it may have saved his life. He missed the beginning of the offensive, in which three-fifths of his fellow-officers were killed.

He went on leave for his operation – an inept army surgeon did it in London, at St Edward's Hospital. At home he had a row, which he did his best to avoid, with his parents about attending Good Friday service. No one has put it better than he has: 'if they believed that God stood squarely behind the British Expeditionary Force, it would be unkind to dissent.' When he took the Sacrament at the end, to please his mother, it meant nothing at all to him. This gave a certain relief.

Then he went off to Harlech again, where he bought from his mother a small simple cottage. He defied the war, thinking only of what he'd do after it. But underneath his defiance he still felt 'empty and lost', that same misery that had pervaded him since David Thomas's death. It is testimony to his powers of endurance that he actually wrote a few poems in anticipation of the good times to come; they were really exercises in defiance (he seems not to have published any of this batch), for he did not even feel defiant. He possesses this capacity to practise defiance when he feels absolutely lost; the paradox is one of the generators of his poetic impulse. One recalls his statement of 1965, made at the age of seventy: 'My main theme was always the *practical* impossibility, transcended only by a *belief in miracle*, of absolute love continuing between man and woman' [my italics].

During this leave he was introduced, while in London, to Lloyd George, whose eyes reminded him of a somnambulist's; but he found it hard to resist his rhetoric while listening to a speech he made at a dinner, though he realized that it was empty of content. Then, still in

March, he was posted to the Third Battalion at Litherland near Liverpool. He stayed there in comparative peace for two months; but on 1 July 1916 the Somme offensive began. He found himself with the Second Battalion (he would have preferred the First) by 5 July, in the trenches at Givenchy.

The instant he arrived he found a raid in progress; four days after that was over he and the rest were on their way to the Somme About 10 July he arrived just behind the line, where he found Siegfried Sassoon – and one or two others who had not been killed. Sassoon had been distinguishing himself, though in a somewhat eccentric manner; his chief feat until then had been to take, single-handed, a battalion frontage which the Royal Irish Regiment had failed to take the day before. But he had broken the rules by then sitting down in the trench and reading a book of poems – and by not reporting his achievement. Some time before this he had sent a rhymed letter to Graves. Graves now replied, using a transport man as postman; he spoke of the things they'd do after the war, ending 'And God! what poetry we'll write!' But tacked on was a 'fragment' describing how that very day (13 July), he had discovered a 'certain cure for lust of blood': a 'dead Boche', scowling, stinking, dribbling blood, propped against a tree.

For the next few days he was fighting in the area around Mametz Wood – the most serious obstacle to the advance – and the Bazentin–High Wood road. High Wood, from which the Germans could see some miles behind the old British line of 1 July (the date of the offensive), was captured in the face of savage resistance; but two days later it was evacuated, the German counterattacks on it being too frequent and heavy.

The Royal Welch, now reduced to some 400 fighting men, were informed, on the evening of 19 July, that they were to attack it. They could see it 'a thousand yards away to the right at the top of a slope'. Early on the morning of 20 July Graves and the company he commanded (B) were in the churchyard of Bazentin, due east of Mametz Wood and about half a mile south of High Wood. The company commanders were briefed: at 5 a.m. the Cameronians and the Fifth Scottish Rifles were to attack first, with another battalion in support. It was not clear if the Royal Welch would be called upon or not; but they expected to be. At 11 a.m. they were. But by then Graves was out of it.

The Germans, knowing of the supporting presence of the Royal Welch, began to shell their positions very heavily: 'we lost a third of our Battalion before the show started.' The shelling was so dense that the battalion decided to move back fifty yards, 'in a rush'. Just as Graves started to run, an eight-inch shell exploded behind him. A splinter of marble, perhaps from a headstone, lodged above his right eyebrow, and he got a couple of minor wounds on his right hand; more seriously, a piece of shell went through his left thigh – 'I must have been at the full stretch of my stride to escape emasculation'; worst of all, a fragment had entered his back, below his right shoulder-blade, passed through his lung, 'and came out through my chest two inches above the right nipple'. Altogether he had eight wounds, but only this and the one in the thigh were serious.

The wounds were dressed fairly quickly, and he was removed to an old German dressing station at the top end of Mametz Wood. He lay unconscious there, on a stretcher in the corner, for more than twenty-four hours – given up for dead. But someone whose duty it was to collect the dead for burial noticed that he was breathing – though he was barely alive. He was put in an ambulance for the nearest hospital. Its jolting made him scream for half the time; for the rest he lost consciousness.

His parents, meanwhile, were confused. The first letter they received was from him; he says that he wrote it on his birthday, 24 July, but Alfred Perceval says in his autobiography that it was received on that day. It was addressed to his mother, written in pencil, and told her that he had been wounded on 20 July but was 'all right'. A.P. could get no information from the War Office; but his wife received three more letters. The first was from her son, and reassured her that his condition was not too bad, he was recovering. The second was from the matron of No. 8 hospital in Rouen, and said that he was critical but was being well looked after. The third was from his commanding officer:

> I much regret to have to . . . tell you your son has died of wounds. He was very gallant, and was doing so well and is a great loss.
>
> He was hit by a shell and very badly wounded, and died on the way down to the base I believe. He was not in bad pain, and our doctor managed to get across and attend to him at once.
>
> We have had a very hard time, and our casualties have been large. Believe me you have all our sympathy in your loss, and we have lost a very gallant soldier. . . .

All this was true – except that Graves had not died. He had spent two fearful nights, those of the 22nd and the 23rd; on his birthday he was transferred by train to No. 8 hospital in Rouen. Meanwhile his parents had received a telegram from the Army Council 'confirming' his death. He was put on the casualty list as having died on his birthday. On 30 July his commanding officer sent him a letter telling how glad he was that a mistake had been made – and describing how many of the 'Jocks' had 'legged it' (their Roman Catholic chaplain later led many of them back) – 'that rotten crowd'. The colonel would hardly have expected to be quoted in print thirteen years later, though in the first version of *Goodbye to All That* his name is not given. This allegation of the 'Jocks' running away caused much ill feeling; but it seems to be generally true, though, as Graves himself adds in his second version of these events, 'Nor did the Scots all behave badly.' The reflection is not, of course, on the fighting ability of Scots; but most of those at High Wood that day agreed with Graves's colonel about this particular group: 'it is not fair putting brave men like that alongside that crowd.' To an inquirer Graves wrote, in 1960: ' . . . I never reached High Wood. . . . The rest of the Battalion who did get there were *terrific*: no other adjective will fit the case. They advanced across that catastrophic slope with parade-ground coolness. . . . '

Within a few days, out of danger, he was in Highgate, at the Queen Alexandra's Hospital. By now he had sufficient energy to ask *The Times* to cancel the obituary of him which they had published; they inserted the announcement in their 'Court Circular' 'without charge':

> Captain Robert Graves, Royal Welch Fusiliers, officially reported died of wounds, wishes to inform his friends that he is recovering from his wounds at Queen Alexandra's Hospital, Highgate, N.

His recovery was rapid; and, ostensibly anyway, he enjoyed the 'joke' of his supposed death. He suffered no permanent injury except that, as he wrote at the end of *Goodbye to All That* (first version), his lung was 'barometric of foul weather'.

Sassoon had written gloomily to Marsh on 21 July: 'Robert died of wounds yesterday. . . . Won't they leave anyone we are fond of?' But Marsh already knew the truth, and wired him from Whitehall. Sassoon 'felt a sort of glow spreading all over' him, in his relief, and Marsh, too, felt that he 'could not have borne those poems [one of them 'The Dead Boche'] if he'd been dead. . . .' Sassoon records in *Memoirs of an Infantry Officer* that he thought, with pleasure, 'Silly old devil . . . he always manages to do things differently from other people.'

From Rouen Graves had already written to Marsh:

> This afternoon I had a sort of waking dream about meeting and making friends with Rupert; it was absolutely vivid. . . . We talked poetry most of the time. . . . I wonder what suggested it? . . . I came of age on the 24th, think of that!

And later from Highgate:

> I *did* die on my way down to the Field Ambulance. . . . To cut a long story short old Rhadamanthus [one of three judges of Hades in Greek mythology] introduced himself as my judge but I refused. . . . The Doctor was saying 'Hopeless case' . . . and I winked at him and said 'Dear old doctor' and went off again to sleep. . . .

He then went on to describe how he had been made to laugh 'until I was nearly ill' because his brother John, still at Charterhouse, had been made to write '100 copy lines' 'to the effect that he must not be a baby' – 'I must endeavour to emerge from my present stage of infantility' and so forth.

He asked Marsh to bring the glamorous young actor and song-writer Ivor Novello with him when he came to visit him on the next Saturday; Novello set, or began to set, some of Graves's poems. Nothing came of it, and Graves's comment on Novello in *Goodbye to All That* is scathing.

Underlying Graves's relief – indeed, his ebullience at having survived – the experience was traumatic. Many of his poems dealing with the theme of death-in-life – a notion which has always obsessed him – draw on the experience of actually having been reported 'dead', though not directly so; rather they gain their power from the experience. The poem 'Escape', in which he treated the subject directly – he seems to have finished it by 6 August, for it is headed 'August 6th, 1916. – Officer previously reported died of wounds, now reported wounded. Graves, Captain R., Royal Welch Fusiliers' – is, not surprisingly, superficial, and he suppressed it. Its light, almost facetious tone disguises deep dreads and anxieties, as well as a fast-developing 'neurasthenia', as battle fatigue used to be called. In fact the word means only 'nerve' (*neuron*) 'weakness' (*asthenia*).

His nerves were indeed greatly weakened, in the sense that his range of activities was becoming rapidly limited. He found it frustrating to talk to his parents, and was disgusted by the 'newspaper language' in which the people at home spoke of the war. Fortunately for him,

Siegfried Sassoon was in England, sent back with suspected lung trouble. The two met at Paddington Station, and discovered that they need waste no time in understanding each other's mood. They went off to Harlech together and on the journey Graves could not help 'crying all the way'.

At Harlech they worked on their writing, achieving so close a rapport that they were able to suggest amendments to each other's poems without any offence being taken (rare amongst poets). They also talked of peace. Siegfried spoke of countryside pursuits, and music; Graves thought chiefly of children: 'In France, I used to spend much of my time playing with the French children of the villages in which we were billeted.' His chief dream, then, was of a happy marriage blessed by a remarkably large number of children.

Then they went on to visit Sassoon's Kentish home; but Graves left early. Sassoon's mother was trying to make spiritual contact with another son, killed in the Dardanelles. Graves was unnerved when he was awakened in the middle of the night by rapping sounds and shrieks. Mrs Sassoon had been influenced by Oliver Lodge's book *Raymond*. He told Siegfried bluntly that he was leaving because he found it 'worse than France'. He did not take his leave gracefully, and Siegfried was offended, though he did not then show it. Graves's description of this incident in *Goodbye to All That* was one of the sources of their later, bitter quarrel.

In November Graves and Sassoon found themselves sharing a hut at battalion headquarters at Litherland. Graves, at this time very much under Siegfried's influence, agreed with the older man that they should make no public protest against the war; their job, they romantically decided, was to keep up the reputation of poets as men of courage – by being back in the line. Home service was 'shameless madness'. And so in December, offered the opportunity by a medical board of spending a few more months in England, Graves declined and asked to be sent back to France.

He had already learned about methods of surviving; but the shame he saw and felt in England overcame even his desire to live. When he was posted, in January, he took with him to Harfleur – this was the 'Bull Ring', the base at which troops newly arrived in France were instructed – a Bible, a Shakespeare, and Catullus and Lucretius in Latin. The last two choices are interesting: he remained obsessed with Lucretius for many years, and eventually wrote an intriguing essay on him and the theories of the physicist James Jeans; Catullus is one of the poets who helped form his mature style.

He disliked Harfleur, and was delighted to be returned to trenches on the Somme. But the doctor, Dunn, who had saved his life on the previous 20 July – thought him unfit, and had him sent back from Bouchavesnes, on the line, to Frises, where he took command of the transport company, which could be called upon to provide riflemen if needed. It was very cold, his weak lungs could not stand the weather, and he fell ill with severe bronchitis. He had been walking every day six miles to the line, and back, with the rations. When he arrived, once again, at No. 8 hospital, Rouen, a doctor who recognized him told him that if he found him, with his lungs in that state, in France again he would have him court-martialled. His active service was finished.

Chapter Five
1917–19

I

In 1914 he had welcomed war as a means of avoiding Oxford. In 1917, asked at Rouen where he would like to be hospitalized, he told them Oxford. And so to Oxford he was sent – to Somerville College (then exclusively for women), which had been turned into a hospital for the duration. He felt bad about not being in France; but better about being through with active service, since he knew he could take no more. When he had recovered his physical health to his own satisfaction he joined the Wadham Company of the University Officer-Cadet Battalion as an instructor. He ran it toughly; but it was all too much for him, and after collapsing down a staircase and cutting his head he was sent back to Somerville. But this was not before he had been elected a member of the Wadham senior commonroom. It was characteristic that he should find himself a member of a senior commonroom (for dons and graduates only, in normal times) before he had even become a freshman undergraduate. When Professor of Poetry at Oxford in the sixties he would point out to one of Oxford's most formidable characters, C. M. Bowra, that he was senior to him in his own commonroom.

During this time at Oxford he made the acquaintance of Aldous Huxley – he did not then take to him (' . . . he had read too much and wished to make some sort of synthesis of his reading, but could not face the task . . .'); and he became a good friend of Huxley's brother Julian. He also got to know the critic Tommy (T. W.) Earp, and the famous, or infamous, pacifist friends of Siegfried's, Lady Ottoline Morrell and her husband Philip. They lived in Garsington, not far from Oxford, and he went out there on many weekends. He was hardly at home amongst this (from his down-to-earth, ex-trenches point of view) effete and arty crowd, but he learned a lot about them, and met many well-known people: Lytton Strachey, Bertrand Russell and the art critic Clive Bell. He found their pacifism impractical; but at first he respected the moral conviction which lay behind it. For their part, the Garsington people found him arrogant and awkward; he did not fit in with their version of high 'enlightened' society, or with the attitude that caused them to regard D. H. Lawrence as a hero. But because they were kind at heart, and he was so mauled by war, they accepted him – and he was then grateful for their sympathy.

It was while he was in hospital at Somerville that he first fell in love. She was a probationer nurse, a concert pianist in civilian life who tried to teach him about music. But he did not tell her he loved her. 'My heart had remained whole, if numbed, since Dick's disappearance from it, yet I felt difficulty in adjusting myself to the experience of woman love.' He rather skates over this in *Goodbye to All That*; but it seems as though he was almost relieved to be able to stop writing to her – which he did when he heard that she was engaged to a lieutenant serving in France.

Eventually he was sent off to convalesce at Osborne in the Isle of Wight, where he was bored by everything and everyone except the famous Benedictines of Solesmes (driven from their home by the anti-clerical laws of 1906), under the spell of whose plainsong he fell. While there he got up to a few frivolous pranks with a fellow officer: for example, they switched all the pictures in the local art gallery, leaving the original labels. As he later said, they needn't have bothered.

Siegfried was by this time back in France with the Second Battalion. He behaved heroically, as was his wont, and was even recommended for a Victoria Cross. He deserved it, but did not obtain it, owing to a clerical technicality, but he was shortly thereafter awarded the Military Cross. In one action, he was shot through the throat and was returned to London. He was now in a state bordering on madness. He saw corpses lying around him in the streets, and raved at the incompetence and callousness of the authorities. He told Graves that he would like to shoot Lloyd George or General Haig; and he meant it. He threw his Military Cross into a river. But he also felt an irresistible compulsion to go back and get killed.

Siegfried came to Oxford to see the Morrells (he had known them since before the war) but missed Graves. Then in July a letter arrived at the Isle of Wight which seriously alarmed Graves. It contained a newspaper cutting, and nothing else. The cutting quoted Second

Lieutenant Siegfried Sassoon's explanation to his commanding officer of the reasons for which he now refused to serve further in the war.

> I am making this statement as an act of wilful defiance of military authority, because I am convinced that the war is being deliberately prolonged by those who have the power to end it. . . . [It] has become a war of aggression and conquest. . . . . On behalf of those who are suffering now I make this protest against the deception that is being practised on them; also I believe that I may help to destroy the callous incompetence with which the majority of those at home regard the continuance of agonies which they do not share, and which they have not sufficient imagination to realise.

Graves agreed with every word of this, but was 'filled with anxiety and unhappiness'. He now felt bitter about those (the Morrells and their circle, but mainly Bertrand Russell) who had put Sassoon up to this gesture, as 'mad' in its way as those for which he was famous on the battlefield. Sasoon himself wrote, in retrospect, that he was a 'believer in the power of spiritual presences', and that as he made his protest he felt that his 'companions of the Somme and Arras battles were around me. . . . Perhaps the dead were backing me up, I thought. . . .'

In 1974 Graves wrote to Ronald Clark, the biographer of Russell, that

> Sassoon's disapproval of the war was largely taught him at Lady Otto-line's home near Oxford. There he had met the anti-militaristic Huxley brothers. I never became an anti-militarist myself. . . .

This is confused and a little misleading. Graves disapproved of the war as much as Sassoon, as he makes clear. And in *Goodbye to All That* he says that Aldous Huxley would have been at the front had it not been for his poor eyesight. But the Garsington circle, and most especially Russell, did in truth encourage Sassoon in his reckless behaviour; it was Russell's impracticality that Graves had to, and did, counter. Sassoon had become 'a military hero among pacifists', and Russell decided to exploit his traumatized condition in the interests of his pacifist programme.

It was Russell (Tyrrell in *Memoirs of an Infantry Officer*) who encouraged Sassoon to write his statement, and who influenced the form it took. It was printed by Francis Meynell as a leaflet, and circulated – until the police seized the remaining stock. The pacifists were delighted; Sassoon was back at Litherland and, although he met with nothing but kindness and understanding from the military authorities, he remained determined to continue his stand. Russell was meanwhile calculating how to turn the affair to the advantage of the Non-Conscription Movement, being of the foolish – or wilfully selfish – opinion that there was 'nothing in the faintest degree hysterical or unbalanced in [Sassoon's] attitude'.

When Graves received the cutting – sent him by Sassoon – he decided to intervene. Sassoon acknowledged in his memoirs that this intervention saved him from needless suffering.

Graves managed to get himself posted back to Litherland, whereupon he immediately tackled Sassoon, telling him bluntly that he must give up his protest. His reasons were practical. He tried to persuade him to appear in front of a medical board. He had arranged with a sympathetic officer at Litherland that if Sassoon would agree to this he would be granted leave, and the affair would be smoothed over. Sassoon refused – until Graves informed him that he had been told, on the highest authority, that if he persisted in his refusal then he would be certified insane: 'they would lock me up in a Lunatic Asylum for the rest of the war.' He would not get the court martial for which he was angling. He wanted it in order to give maximum publicity to his infuriated feelings – which were understandable and, indeed, justified. But Russell and his friends desired this publicity even more. Sassoon's misery was of the utmost value to them.

Graves swore to Sassoon, on an 'imaginary Bible', that what he had said was true. Sassoon says that he was lying, though in his memoirs (at least) he expressed wry, good-humoured gratitude for the lie. No doubt Graves was lying; if so, it was in a worthy cause. 'At last, unable to deny how ill he was, Siegfried consented to appear before the medical board.' Graves was able to rig the board, with, as Ronald Clark says, 'a good deal of skill'.

He was able to arrange to appear as witness for Sassoon, 'as a friend of the patient', and managed – with the help of the one sensible man on the board, a doctor who understood Sassoon's condition – to attain the desired result: Siegfried was to become a patient at a convalescent home for neurasthenics at Craiglockhart, in Edinburgh, and Graves was to escort him there. (Siegfried arrived at the hospital before him, as he characteristically missed the train. He has almost always missed trains unless there has been someone to put him on them.)

Graves now wrote to a Welsh acquaintance, Evan Morgan. Morgan, interested in poetry, was private secretary to the Minister of Labour, W. C. Bridgman:

> You have I expect heard about the poet Siegfried Sassoon being exploited by the pacifists Bertrand Russell and Lees Smith [a pacifist MP, like Philip Morrell] when in a state of (now certified and official) nervous breakdown after being wounded in some marvellously brave fighting in France. . . . After enormous struggles I've smoothed things down & got him certified suffering from nerves, etc. by a Medical Board & told the pacifists that they've been thwarted, & that their protégé is now in a convalescent home in Scotland. Well, you belong to the Trade Union of poets & so you must see what you can do in connexion counter-propaganda bureau to stop his 'defiance letter', copies of which he has sent to B. Russell & to Henderson's 'Bomb Shop' [a pacifist bookshop in Charing Cross Road] going any further. Everything is being hushed up now. James Hope the M.P. has been working on behalf of a quiet solution to the business. . . . Any scandal would spoil all our efforts.

It would: Sassoon could still have been prosecuted had the affair gained wide publicity. But Russell, whose unwittingly cruel obstinancy knew no bounds, wrote to Ottoline Morrell that he had thought 'better of Graves. . . . Could you not make him see that he is not acting the part of *real* friendship, tho' he thinks he is?' And he contacted Lees Smith in order to induce him to raise the matter in the Commons: '*We* have to see that there *is* scandal, & no Hushing-up.' In some way he had got hold of Graves's letter to Morgan. But when Lees Smith raised the matter he was effectively silenced by the Under-Secretary of State for War, who pointed out that Sassoon *was* suffering from shellshock, and that was that. Graves wrote to Russell:

> Sassoon has been forced to accept a medical board & is being sent to a place in the country as suffering from nerves: which is certainly the case as anyone can easily see. . . . His opinions are still unchanged but there is nothing further for you to do (with him for your cause). I blame you most strongly for your indiscretion in having allowed him to do what he has done, knowing in what state of health he was (after his damnable time at Arras). Now you can leave things alone until he's well enough to think calmly about the War & how to end it.

Graves's attitude was both anti-romantic and anti-heroic. He did not believe that Sassoon was in any state to face court martial and the inevitable imprisonment that would follow. This was surely right. His efficient intervention probably saved Sassoon's sanity. Further, he felt that the gesture, though he sympathized with its spirit, would do no good at all: no one would follow the example set.

Sassoon had thus been saved from what would certainly have been an overwhelmingly terrifying experience; but he had also been cheated of taking up the martyr's role which, in his weakened and enraged state, he then wanted. A deep-seated resentment against Graves may well have formed then, though he was perhaps unaware of it. Sassoon had strengths, passions and (then homo-) sexual agonies; but he was not sharply self-aware, self-analytical or outstandingly intelligent. In Craiglockhart he immediately set to writing the poems which appeared in the next year as *Counter-Attack*. These are the most terrifying of his poems, and it is unlikely that he would have had the opportunity to write them had Graves not ensured his residence in a hospital (where he belonged) instead of a gaol. Graves deeply admired this sequence – and was well aware that he had not yet got it in him to write as well. For the time being the friendship continued intact.

II

Having got himself declared fit when he wasn't in order to extricate Sassoon from his own quixotism and the clutches of the pacifists, Graves had to take the consequences: dull duties at the repulsive, dirty, and by now only too familiar Litherland, Third Battalion headquarters. He should have been in Craiglockhart himself; his nerves were in pieces, strange smells put him into trembling sweats, and any bang sent him flying for cover. Unable to bear the idea of France again, he decided to try for Mesopotamia, where conditions were not so severe. The first step was to get himself sent to Oswestry, the Third Garrison Battalion; from there, he reckoned, he could get out to Palestine. He got as far as Oswestry (and soon afterwards to Rhyl), where he trained young officers; but he failed to get himself a posting out of England. However, he felt better out of the fumes of Litherland. And it 'was at this point that I remembered Nancy Nicholson'.

England was horrible to him mostly because of the civilian attitude to the war. He must look for something or someone different and better, and beautiful. War had done nothing to shatter his beliefs in such things, it had whetted his appetite for them. He remembered Nancy from when she was sixteen. He had met her at Harlech in April 1916, after the operation on his nose. She came from a distinguished

family: her mother, Mabel, was a painter, her father, William Nicholson, a better known one, with many aristocratic connections. Her
brother was Ben Nicholson – kept out of the war by asthma – who
became one of England's foremost painters. Sir (as he later became)
William was then forty-five years old. With his brother-in-law James
Pryde he had done pioneering work in the field of the artistic poster;
he was also well thought of for his still lifes and his woodcuts of
Victorian scenes and people. He and Pryde were known as 'The Beggarstaff Brothers'. Ben, then twenty-three, soon attained fame. Graves
and he never became friends. There existed between Graves and Sir
William much warmer feelings. As for Nancy, her mother had brought
her up to expect little of men, since she was more embittered by Sir
William's frequent infidelities than she let on – to anyone but Nancy
and perhaps to some women friends.

Nancy – her full name was Annie Mary Pryde Nicholson, but she
was always known as Nancy – was 'ignorant, of independent mind,
good-natured, and as sensible about the war as anybody at home could
be'. Soon after the non-affair with the probationer nurse had finished
Graves had taken her to the theatre, at that time thinking of her more
as a schoolgirl than as an adult. Now he began to write to her about
some poems for children which she had agreed to illustrate.

She had by now left school and was working on the land, at a farm
at Hilton, Huntingdonshire. In October 1917 he visited her there, and
decided that he was in love with her – which he was, to the extent
that his war-torn state of mind and young age allowed. (Twelve years
later he was to pay another visit to this farm, under much more
dramatic circumstances.) It was an innocent, charming, childhood-
ridden kind of love, infused with pastoral, its whimsical romanticism
a deliberately contrived antidote to war, terror and the, to him, still
terrible fact of lust.

Just at the time he fell in love with Nancy, his plans for getting sent
to Palestine went awry: it seemed as though he was bound for Gib-
raltar. Therefore, he did one of the things he most enjoys doing: he
pulled strings, by using a friend at the War Office, to get the order
cancelled. The men of the Third Garrison were soon afterwards ordered
to York; but, because a morse message substituted a 'C' for the 'Y',
they were sent to Cork instead. Graves was given the job of looking
after that part of the battalion which remained in Britain. Life was not
so bad at Rhyl, although his nervous state was still poor, and his
wounded lung had only a third of its full expansion.

In December 1917 Graves visited London on leave; while there he proposed to Nancy, who accepted him. They were married in January 1918. It was an odd courtship. The two were not compatible; but this is not unusual, especially in war marriages. As well as being anti-war, Nancy showed every sign of being independent, and he needed this above all from a woman. His mother was too conventionally moralistic for him, yet he yearned for instruction. And he longed for children.

As for Nancy (who died in 1977), her true psychological make-up was delitescent, but she was not, perhaps, a very interesting person. The keynote of her character was obstinacy. It is hard to discover a core of conviction in her, a sense of true direction. It is almost as if she contrived her obstinacy in order to conceal a lack of robustness. She was well brought up, winsome, charming, teasing in an innocently sweet and unvulgar way – but shallow. Graves fancied that he loved her for her feminist candour, which was indeed refreshing in those days, and because she dismissed the Christian religion on the grounds that it must be rubbish if God was represented as a man. This view attracted him; he never had to learn from anyone his resistance to assumptions of male supremacy.

Nancy was feminist, or so she forcefully claimed. But she was neither suffragette nor suffragist. She maintained an attitude of constant fury at the way men behaved, both at an international and a personal level – and she warned her husband that he would have to be 'careful' in the way he spoke of women. She would have no truck with the convention of taking his name, and on at least one occasion Graves had to show his marriage lines to a suspicious hotel manager before being allowed to take a double room. Yet Nancy's indignation, unconventionality and general propensity to make herself difficult when she felt like it (Sassoon was to complain of this, and T. E. Lawrence and others noticed it) seems to have been – at least in part – cultivated in order to compensate for feelings of inadequacy. Possibly she was obsessed with doubts about her artistic abilities. Her father was a confident and successful artist, whereas her mother was an unconfident and much less well-known one. Nancy's noisy protests against men in general may have been a protest against her father – fortified by emotions of anger because he was more artistically accomplished than she (though some of her later design work has attracted admiration). Her unquiet nature and propensity to criticize was something that Graves was no doubt unconsciously seeking out.

They were married in St James's Church, Piccadilly, on 23 January

1918. William Nicholson liked social affairs, and this, the war not-withstanding, was made into one. Nancy was in a fury. She had read through the marriage service for the first time that morning; if she was going to have to promise to 'obey' her husband, she said, then she would not be there. But Graves quickly arranged for the ceremony to be 'modified and reduced to the shortest possible form', and she turned up.

'Another caricature scene to look back on,' he wrote in *Goodbye to All That*:

> myself striding up the red carpet, wearing field-boots, spurs and sword; Nancy meeting me in a blue-check silk wedding-dress, utterly furious; packed benches on either side of the church, full of relatives; aunts using handkerchiefs; the choir boys out of tune; Nancy savagely muttering the responses, myself shouting them out in a parade-ground voice.

As soon as the formalities were over Nancy seized a bottle of champagne (then scarce), drank a few glasses, and disappeared. She had exclaimed, 'Well, I'm going to get something out of this wedding, at any rate.' She soon reappeared, much to her new mother-in-law's discomfiture, dressed in her land girl's outfit of breeches and smock. She wasted no time at all in proclaiming herself a termagant – and her husband had no desire to tame her.

Choirboys are often out of tune at weddings and doubtless the organists are annoyed. Usually this is not very interesting; but in this case the possible annoyance of the organist adds a tiny footnote to the story of another man who pursued an entirely different career. In late 1969 Graves agreed to be a sponsor to the Pablo Casals benefit. The organizer of the benefit wrote on 6 January 1970 to thank him:

> Dear Robert Graves:
>
> It is kind of you to be willing to be a sponsor ... and I am glad I had the pleasure and honor of playing for your wedding in St James, Piccadilly!!
>
> Happy New Year!
> Leopold Stokowski

Many well-known people attended, including Max Beerbohm, the caricaturist George Belcher (in 1870 costume), William Heinemann, Edward Marsh, E. V. Lucas; George Mallory was Robert's best man. Also there was Wilfred Owen, who had been corresponding with Graves. His wedding gift was a set of eleven apostle spoons; 'he said the twelfth had been court-martialled for cowardice and was awaiting execution for cowardice,' Graves later wrote, to the editors of Owen's letters.

Owen wrote to his mother on 19 January that 'It is a kind of duty both to myself and Graves to go to the Wedding.' The day after it he wrote to his sister Susan:

> ... The wedding was nothing extraordinary. Not a great crowd of people, but a very mixed one. Some were dressed in the dowdiest unfashion. Possibly these were celebrities in their way? ... Graves was pretty worked up, but calm. The Bride, 18 years old, was pretty, but nowise handsome.
> Heinemann was there. He is jibbing at Sassoon's new book, because of the 'violent' poems.

And in another letter, to a friend, he gives an intriguing glimpse of Beerbohm, referring to his prowess as caricaturist:

> Max B. dressed fairly ordinarily, but when he looked at me, I felt my nose ti-tilting in an alarming manner; my legs warped; my chin became a mere pimple on my neck.

Wilfred Owen gained the poetic confidence he needed to write his last, and incomparably best, poetry from his meeting and subsequent association with Sassoon as Craiglockhart – where he, too, had been sent as neurasthenic.

Graves first met Owen when he visited Sassoon there on 13 October 1917. Owen recorded;

> He [Graves] is a big, rather plain fellow, the last man on earth apparently capable of the extraordinarily delicate fancies of his books.

Graves described him in *Goodbye to All That* as a 'quiet round-faced little man'. From his retrospective comments one might infer that he did not approve of Owen from the start. But this is not the case, even though he wrote in 1943 that

> Owen was a weakling, really; I liked him but there was that passive homosexual streak in him which is even more disgusting than the active streak in Auden. [To M.S.-S., undated]

But this was not his first impression, for they carried on a lively correspondence, and Graves was obviously excited about Owen's poetry. Owen became so interested in Graves that he asked his sister Susan, just after Christmas 1917, to get him an October issue of

Chambers's Journal which carried an article praising Graves, Sassoon and F. W. Harvey (a now forgotten poet). In the previous month Owen had ordered 'several copies' of Graves's *Fairies and Fusiliers* (published by Heinemann) at more than one Shrewsbury bookshop, 'but shall not buy all, in order to leave the book exposed on the Shrewsbury counters!' When he saw the collection, some of which Sassoon had already read to him at the convalescent home, he told Sassoon (27 November 1917):

> [Harold] Monro [and I] ... exchanged some delicious winks [Monro was bisexual, and much tormented by his penchant for young men of bad character]. R.G.'s book came in during the hour I was there [the Poetry Bookshop]. I should never stop if I started to rejoice over these poems.
>
> You read many to me: but, wisely, not the best: – or the most charming. . . . Oh! world you are making for me, Sassoon!

Owen had already told his mother that he was under the impression that Graves – at their first meeting, when Owen's poem 'Disabled' was shown to him – considered him 'a kind of *Find*!!' ('No thanks, Captain Graves! I'll find myself in due time.')

Indeed, Graves actively cooperated with Sassoon in encouraging Owen. As soon as he returned to Rhyl from Craiglockhart he wrote to him:

> Do you know, Owen, that's a damn fine poem of yours, that 'Disabled'. Really damn fine.
>
> So good the general sound and weight of the words that the occasional metrical outrages are most surprising. It's like seeing a golfer drive onto the green in one and then use a cleek instead of a putter, and hole out in twelve.
>
> <u>For instance you have a foot too much in</u>
>
>   In the old days before he gave away his knees
> & in He wasn't bothered much by Huns or crimes or guilts
> &   They cheered him home but not as they would cheer a goal
> &   Now he will spend a few sick years in institutes
>
> <u>There is an occasional jingle</u>
>
>   Voices of boys
> &   Voices of play and pleasure after day
> And an occasional cliché
>   Girls glanced lovelier
>   Scanty suit of grey

I wouldn't worry to mention all this if it wasn't for my violent pleasure at some of the lines like the one about 'the solemn man who brought him fruits' and the 'jewelled hilts of daggers in plaid socks' and the 'Bloodsmear down his leg after the matches'.

Owen you have seen things; you are a poet; but you're a very careless one at present. One can't put in too many syllables into a line and say 'Oh, it's all right. That's my way of writing poetry'. One has to follow the rules of the metre one adopts. Make new metres by all means, but one must observe the rules when they are laid down by the custom of centuries. A painter or musician has no greater task in mastering his colours or his musical modes or harmonies, than a poet.

It's the devil of a sweat for him to get to know the value of his rhymes, rhythms or sentiments. But I have no doubt at all that if you turned seriously to writing, you could obtain Parnassus in no time while I'm still struggling on the knees of that stubborn peak.

Till then, good luck in the good work.

Yours Robert Graves.
Love to Sassoon.

And in December he followed this up with,

'Scuse pencil – lazy – Saw old Sassoon yesterday and he showed me your poems – Don't make any mistake, Owen, you are a damned fine poet already and are going to be more so – I wont have the impertinence to criticise – you have found a new method and must work it yourself – those assonances instead of rhymes are fine – Did you know it was a trick of Welsh poetry or was it instinct?

Two things however you'll forgive. Best thing, I find, is never to marry two colloquialisms in the same line, put a stray one in here and there but always mate it with better quality words and make it seem meritable and so poetic. S.S. often overdoes it: he started sparingly but its a temptingly easy path to run down to bathos by –

For God's sake cheer up and write more optimistically – The war's not ended yet but a poet should have a spirit above wars – Thanks awfully for cheering S.S. up: he actually talked of *après la guerre* yesterday and looks as fit as your soulful flea [refers to an early draft of Owen's poem 'A Terre'] – I will send your poems to R.N. [Nichols] . . . Robert is a ripping fellow really but any stupid person would easily mistake him for an insufferable bounder; This sounds funny, but true – I am devoted to him. Puff out your chest a little, Owen, & be big – for you've more right than most of us. . . . I don't want to lose sight of you – you must help S.S. and R.N. and R.G. to revolutionise English Poetry – So outlive this War.

Owen acted on most, although not all, of Graves's criticisms of 'Disabled'. And he wrote to his mother, about the second letter quoted above, that he could think of 'nothing at the moment but Robert Graves' letter'. Later, in May, he wrote from Ripon:

> ... I want no limelight, and celebrity is the last infirmity I desire. ... I have already more than [his peers'] recognition: I have the silent and immortal friendship of Graves and Sassoon. ... Behold are they not already as many Keatses?

Owen was killed on 4 November 1918; on 3 November he sent Graves a field postcard, which was lost (as were some three of his letters to Graves, and about seven to Sassoon).

What Graves then thought about Owen is confirmed by his excited remarks about him to Marsh. Soon after their first meeting he wrote:

> ... I have a new poet for you, just discovered, one Wilfred Owen: this is a real find, not a sudden lo here! or lo there! which unearths an Edward Eastaway [Edward Thomas's pseudonym], but the real thing, when we've educated him a trifle more. R.N. and S.S. and myself are doing it.

And in January 1918:

> I send you the few poems of Owen I can find, not his best but they show his powers and deficiencies. Too Sassonish [sic] in places. Sassons [sic] is to him a god of the highest rank.

It is odd, in view of all this, that in the 1957 revision of *Goodbye to All That* Graves should have dismissed Owen with the remark that he was 'an idealistic homosexual with a religious background' (this was deleted by request of the late Harold Owen, Wilfred's brother, who always refused to acknowledge his brother's homosexuality). But this is not Graves's last thought on Owen. He has explained to me that he assumed everyone responded to the poetic power of Owen at his best, that it went without saying – forgetting that in the case of Graves one can assume nothing.

III

Graves passes over his wedding night tersely: 'The embarrassments of our wedding-night (Nancy and I being both virgins) were somewhat eased by a [Zeppelin] air-raid. . . .' The bombs dropped nearby set the hotel in an uproar. He added the parentheses in the later version. The essential story of his marriage is in his poetry, which is always candid where it has to be.

A week later Nancy went back to her land work, and he returned to his command at Rhyl. But Nancy soon found a gardening job, and was able to come to live with him in Wales. When she discovered that she was pregnant she gave up the gardening and spent her time drawing.

Meanwhile Graves was hearing from Siegfried, who was now complaining to him of the way in which he had handled his affairs. He criticized him for identifying himself with 'good form' – and for lacking the courage to protest against a stupidity, cruelty and folly which he fully admitted existed. Yet, paradoxically, Siegfried was now itching to be off to battle again – to kill, unpacifistically, more Germans. Graves comments that he was himself 'both more consistent and less heroic', and recalls that this is the gist of what he told Siegfried at the time. When Graves wrote in *Goodbye to All That* that Siegfried's 'unconquerable idealism changed direction with his environment: he varied between happy warrior and bitter pacifist', he put his finger on the matter, in the kindliest possible manner. For all that was consistent about Sassoon was his determination to be conspicuously heroic; 'unconquerable idealism' was an element in this, but not the only, or even the main, one.

But their friendship held. Siegfried was sent to Palestine, then back to France. Graves heard in July that he had been shot through the head patrolling no-man's-land, but had not been killed; he was in hospital in London and soon sent Graves a poem from there. This much moved Graves at the time, but caused serious trouble ten years later.

In the summer of 1918 Graves stayed with his wife's family at a large Tudor house near Harlech. It was haunted in the classical manner – raps on the panelling and, more frightening, a small yellow dog which appeared to announce deaths (Nancy saw it not long before her mother, one of the first victims of the Spanish influenza epidemic which claimed more lives than the war, died). He records this with sang-froid, but it made a deep impression on him, for his postwar poetry is pervaded with the notion of being haunted.

The Armistice came, but it was no armistice for him. He still had a war to fight, and this time it was one for which he alone – as he felt – was responsible. He went, he tells us, on a long walk, 'cursing and sobbing and thinking of the dead'. In 1929 he was even ruder, in *Goodbye to All That*, about the book of poems he was working on at this time (*Country Sentiment*, 1920) than he was in his 1957 revision. All he has to say, in the long view, is 'To forget about the war, I was writing *Country Sentiment*, a book of romantic poems and ballads.' In 1929 he speaks of having, in the poems, 'used' Nancy, rather than children (always his solace), to forget about the war. And he mentions one poem, in the group of 'pacifist war-poems' at the end of the volume, in which he lied about an old French lady's gift of a plate to him: 'I cannot think how I came to put so many lies in it. . . . This is only one of the many of my early poems that contain falsities for public delectation.' But he was right to cut out his disparagement of this collection in his 1957 revision: it is less escapist than he thought. It contains one of the best of his early love poems, and is preserved (without a word altered) in his last (1975) collection:

> *One Hard Look*
>
> Small gnats that fly
> In hot July
> And lodge in sleeping ears,
> Can rouse therein
> A trumpet's din
> With Day of Judgement fears.
>
> Small mice at night
> Can wake more fright
> Than lions at midday;
> A straw will crack
> The camel's back —
> There is no easier way.
>
> One smile relieves
> A heart that grieves
> Though deadly sad it be,
> And one hard look
> Can close the book
> That lovers love to see.

This demonstrates Graves's innate lyrical gift as perfectly as any of his poems. But, apart from the lyric quality, the content is of interest, both procedurally and psychologically. This is a poem written by a very newly married man, who is safely out of the war. There is a hint of his later paradoxical and metaphysical manner in the statement about the straw and the camel. Usually the straw that breaks the camel's back is taken to be the ultimate small blow that cracks a man's endurance after he has taken a series of much heavier blows. But this is a poem written in the context of young love, not war (the heavy blows). It is almost as if the poet is awaiting disillusion – even acknowledging it.

Biographically, it is an indication of how he experienced Nancy's general demeanour towards him, of the disenchantment he already felt with the concept of married love. The simple statement the poem makes is uttered as if by one who has had the experience of that 'one hard look': the book of love is closed; the hard look has been assimilated, as a lack of love. But it is not yet a matter of the poet's revealing a morbid oversensitivity; the lyrical tone denies that. The ears were 'sleeping' in that July of 1918. But the nature of that 'one hard look' has awakened unbearable ('Day of Judgement' – when one's sins will be revealed and punished) apprehensions.

In this volume are other acutely apprehensive, not to say melodramatic, poems which have also survived Graves's relentless scrutiny – 'Apples and Water', 'Outlaws' and 'Vain and Careless'. 'Apples and Water', in which a mother warns her daughter against her good-natured impulse to give soldiers marching to war apples and water ('Once in my youth I gave, poor fool,/A soldier apples and water./So may I die before you cool/Your father's drouth, my daughter') may easily be read as self-reproachful, especially in the light of the fact that Nancy was not taking her pregnancy any more serenely than she had taken the formalities of their union. The theme of 'Vain and Careless' is incompatibility. 'The Beacon', early suppressed, is alarmingly enigmatic, despite its innocently pastoral context:

> The silent shepherdess,
>   She of my vows,
> Here with me exchanging love
>   Under dim boughs.
>
> Shines on our mysteries
>   A sudden spark.
> 'Dout the candle, glow-worm,
>   Let all be dark.
>
> 'The birds have sung their last notes,
>   The Sun's to bed.
> Glow-worm, dout your candle.'
>   The glow-worm said:

'I also am a lover;
  The lamp I display
Is beacon for my true love
  Wandering astray.

'Through the thick bushes
  And the grass comes he
With a heart load of longing
  And love for me.

'Sir, enjoy your fancy
  But spare me harm.
A lover is a lover,
  Though but a worm.'

This is not fully worked out; but it is in no sense a happy poem. True, Graves's outward demeanour is almost invariably that of high optimism. One of the many conflicts in himself, with which he was soon to become obsessed to the point of erecting a theory – or at least a practice – on it, was between external optimism and internal gloom and terror.

IV

The rest of Graves's army career is soon told. He was ordered to report to Limerick, to the Third Battalion, in late December. He postponed his journey – thus being technically absent without leave, though he 'lied his way' out of it – until the birth of his first child, who turned out to be a daughter, Jenny. She was born on Twelfth Night, 1919, at a house in Hove which the ever-generous William Nicholson had taken for the occasion. She became the best known of Graves's eight children, eventually as a journalist. It had been agreed that the girls born to the couple would take their mother's name of Nicholson, while the boys would take that of Graves – so Jenny was Jenny Nicholson.

Robert found Limerick amusing, even though it was a Sinn Fein stronghold. But he found the charm of Ireland 'dangerous', and has said that whenever there he felt strangely oppressed by his ancestry. There were people who remembered his Limerick grandfather, and although he was superficially amused by the gossip, he still felt uneasy. He was apprehensive, too. On top of her unnerving and unpredictable behaviour – alternating between a light-hearted sweetness and a dark moodiness which entirely shut him out – Nancy had never been told what it was like to bear a child. He wrote that 'it took her years to recover from it'. She was consoled that it was a girl – but her feelings about the male sex were not softened. Graves was enraptured to be a father, and of a daughter at that; he started composing charming light verses addressed to both mother and child. But his unease persisted. He decided to get out of the army – which was not so easy – as soon as he could. He pulled strings (now customarily available to him), and eventually orders for his demobilization came through.

But another order, countermanding them, rapidly followed: no soldier on duty in Ireland was to be demobilized, on account of the Troubles. Though unwilling to be involved in the British solution of the Irish problem, he would have stayed. But illness intervened, and made it necessary to his very survival for him to get out – by hook or by crook. For on the previous evening, while staying with one of his uncles who lived nearby, he recognized the first symptoms of Spanish influenza. He had seen his mother-in-law die of it; after what he had survived, he wasn't going to follow suit. To be treated in an Irish military hospital, with his lungs in the state they were, was out of the question: it would have been suicide, he felt. By a daring and desperate trick he prevailed upon a senior officer to sign his demobilization papers in time to catch the last train to leave Limerick before all demobilization from Ireland was officially ended.

Then, back in England, he had an astonishing stroke of luck. When he arrived at Paddington he was so ill that, upon getting out of the train, he fell over. He was in a rush to get to Wimbledon – not because he had been born there, but because it happened to be the demobilization centre. As he had been unable to get his secret code numbers before leaving Limerick he was sure that the officers would refuse to release him; but at least he knew that they would have to get him into a hospital – an English one.

However, the London underground staff were on strike that day; there was no chance of getting to Wimbledon by tube. He managed to seize a taxi, but having left his luggage on the rack, he had to bring the taxi to the train. He offered the man who had been his travelling companion a lift. His lift 'happened to be' the Cork District Demobilization Officer, who had the necessary forms with him, and filled in Graves's.

And so he was released at Wimbledon without fuss. He paid a lightning call on his parents, a few hundred yards away, and then went on to Hove, determined to recover from his Spanish influenza. The doctor there was gloomy, telling him that he had septic pneumonia; but he had been through too much to worry unduly, and contented himself with taking a poem he had started (still preserved in the canon, though at one point excised from it), called 'The Troll's Nosegay', through over thirty drafts. He recovered; so did Nancy, who had a lighter attack. Jenny did not contract it. Not long afterwards he and Nancy set off for Harlech. They were to remain there for a year.

Chapter Six

1919

I

In his widely read *The Great War and Modern Memory* (1975) Paul Fussell, an American, deals with the connection between the war and sexuality – and with homosexuality in particular. In the course of this he touches on Graves. The result is provocative – but inaccurate, and very misleading. Fussell believes that Graves would like us to forget that he ever wrote a play called *But It Still Goes On* (1930), in which one of the main characters is a homosexual; and that his deletion of the sentence about his 'recovery' from homosexuality in the second version of *Goodbye to All That* is 'not unconnected' with this wish. His basis for this belief is that Graves did not choose to include 'its title' 'in the list of his works prefixed to his *Collected Poems* of 1955, although that list includes thirty-five books'. Fussell is unaware, therefore, that the book *But It Still Goes On* contains much more than a play – or that Graves reprinted the play itself in *Occupation Writer* (1951), listed in the 1955 *Collected Poems*. Graves has thus never sought to suppress it, or even thought of doing so. He deleted the sentence about his 'recovery' from homosexuality only because he knew it to be an oversimplification.

Fussell continues his general discussion of the topic of 'homoeroticism', leaving his view of Graves's involvement in this manifestation hanging in the air like a question mark; and the discussion itself peters out.

But the matter he raises is important in terms of Graves's psychological development, even though Graves's involvement in the 'homoerotic tradition' (as Fussell chooses to call it) is non-existent.

Fussell uses the term 'homoerotic' to describe what he calls 'a sublimated (i.e. "chaste") form of temporary homosexuality'. There was, he rightly if unimaginatively remarks, little active homosexuality at the

Front. Sublimation involves rechannelling. Fussell directly relates what he takes to be the 'homoeroticism' amongst British soldiers in the First World War to Victorian homoeroticism, as exemplified by Oscar Wilde, Gerard Manley Hopkins, John Addington Symonds and others; but his discussion becomes confused because he fails to separate active pederasts (such as Symonds) from non-practising homosexuals such as Hopkins. He also spoils the force of his observation – that the expression of feelings about the deaths in the First World War was in certain cases directly influenced by the Aesthetic Movement of the nineties and by the poetry of A. E. Housman – by failing to distinguish between true homosexuality, such as that of Sassoon and Owen, and 'aesthetic' expression such as that found in the verse of the heterosexual Robert Nichols, for a short while Graves's close friend and correspondent, and a popular 'war' poet. The golden-haired Rupert Brooke attracted people with strongly developed homosexual feelings – including D. H. Lawrence, Henry James and the more sentimental Edward Marsh – but he also attracted heterosexuals simply as an aesthetic 'object'; he was himself heterosexual.

So was Graves. But because of his awkward innocence, and his ignorance of sex, he found himself in the position of being unable to distinguish between love and friendship. He was a virgin until his marriage (as he tells us), but he was, perhaps unusually, never homosexual. He was, however, intensely anxious that he might be – and that he would discover himself incapable of loving women. It haunted him to the point of driving him into an ill-considered marriage (he would at that time have considered the notion of a sexual relationship outside marriage as unthinkable). Nancy Nicholson, if she would have him, was the woman with whom he could prove himself to himself. Thus he relieved himself of the stress of thinking that he might be 'doomed' as a homosexual. But he felt guilty, since, as his attempts to write love poetry in this period testify, he did not really love his wife any more than she loved him. His poetry gained power just as soon as he began to question the quality of his love. Many have been in the same case as Graves then was – but with the difference that they lacked his persistent sexual puritanism.

Graves survived his war experiences through his friendships and his feelings for children, whose company he sought out as much as possible in France. His parents proved to be no consolation to him, because, although affectionate, they understood neither him nor the nature of the war. First he had, as he writes, got by mainly on the strength of his correspondence with Dick, whose letters had been his 'greatest stand-by'. When that friendship was shattered by the news that Dick was 'homosexually immoral' (as he felt it), he almost immediately turned to Nancy Nicholson. It is noticeable that he did not feel in the least sorry for Dick, as one who had been in trouble. He was disgusted with him, and so rejected him out of hand. But, to be fair, his account of his reaction to the news he received in *Goodbye to All That* is deliberately laconic, and is contrived to reveal his own lack of sophistication at the time. (Though by now self-reliant, he was still a moralizing prig. One recalls Sassoon's story of how he lectured a fellow-officer for fornicating.) In the autobiography the incident is put back some fifteen months.

The priggishness was a result not only of ignorance but also of a stubborn and unconscious determination to discover a virtuous reality for himself. He did not know the difference between lust and love or between friendship and love. Only much later would he be able to make this careful and exquisite distinction:

> 'Love at first sight,' some say, misnaming
> Discovery of twinned helplessness
> Against the huge tug of procreation.
>
> But friendship at first sight? This also
> Catches fiercely at the surprised heart
> So that the cheek blanches and then blushes.

At the age of twenty-one he was confused by his feelings of friendship. Clearly there was a 'huge tug' between him and Nancy, even if both were embarrassed by it. Simply being married and begetting a child, as he so soon did, meant a great deal to Graves, but alienated Nancy by what seemed, to her, his clumsy sexual urgency. She became increasingly unsociable, and often complained of feeling unwell – so that she would neither have to go to bed with him nor greet his friends. Probably she often did feel unwell. But he worked hard at improving the relationship, and insisted on taking the full responsibility for its failures upon himself. Later (in 1926), exasperated by Nancy, he would bitterly refer to himself in a letter to T. E. Lawrence as a 'servant'.

The late F. W. Bateson wrote that the situation in Wordsworth's house, after he had settled down to marriage, centred around the question: 'What must Wordsworth do to be happy?' Everyone in the poet's household, Bateson implies, was dedicated to finding the correct answer to this. Nancy wasn't much concerned with Graves himself, expected nothing from him (or any other man), and did not understand him. But for Graves himself, who was – unlike Wordsworth – a solitary in his search for happiness, the central question was, and always continued to be, 'What must Robert do to be virtuous?' This was difficult to answer because Nancy – unlike Mrs Wordsworth and the other women round Wordsworth – wasn't bothered; and in any case he hardly knew what virtue was, except in the negative sense that it involved not doing wrong. He wrote poetry, then as always, to find out all about it. But most of this poetry was, so he retrospectively felt, escapist. For the present he tried, although with characteristic clumsiness, to pursue the purely conventional virtue taught him by his mother (though he blamed his father for it), even while rejecting it as silly. His 'view of life', Peter Quennell writes of him when he was an undergraduate at Oxford in the early twenties, 'was still intensely puritanical; and he even asserted that a "bad man" – bad in the accepted moral sense – could scarcely hope to be a good artist.' He has continued to insist on just this – except that he has dropped 'the accepted moral sense', and changed, deconventionalized, his view of what is 'bad'.

II

When Graves was demobilized he was officially suffering from neurasthenia or shellshock. After the First World War the term 'neurasthenia' was used vaguely, as a synonym for 'war neurosis'. But the neurosis was not caused by war experience, but relentlessly uncovered by it. Men found themselves stripped of their necessary psychological defences; they found themselves having, at a too early age, to face aspects of themselves of which they were ignorant, and which therefore terrified them. This drove the novelist Henry Williamson into active Fascism, the poet Ivor Gurney into madness, and countless others into despair and failure.

Graves was in an excessively nervous state; but he was exceptionally dogged. One of his resources, developed early on – even in his schooldays when he suffered most from being at the mercy of others – has always been to make the best of his situation. If he must always ask the question, 'What shall I do to be virtuous?' he also always states, often untruthfully, but to useful effect, 'I am happy.' During the war itself, especially at the front, this simply would not do at the very worst times; like the rest, he just had to endure. He learned that lesson thoroughly. But as soon as he got out of the army he vowed that he would never again put himself into anyone's hands, he would never 'take orders'. In 1920 this vow gave him strength – and indeed he never broke it, except when he worked for a short while for the University at Cairo.

Externally he was nerve-wracked. As he describes it, shells would burst on his bed at midnight, strangers would take on the faces of comrades killed in the war, he could not use a telephone, he considered everything – even the beloved landscape of Harlech – in terms of war (how could he hold or capture this or that piece of land, and so on), if he met more than two new people in one day he could not sleep. He commandeered everything 'of uncertain ownership', an army habit (his story 'Bins K to T' is on this theme). And he describes how he lied his way out of everything in the time-honoured army style. He was 'rough', and many considered him uncouth. But he 'got by'.

Internally, too, he was seething with anxiety. He was riddled with guilt about the people he had killed in the war, though commonsense prevented his talking of this. His extreme sexual puritanism was outraged by his bodily desires to an extent that it is hard for people of later generations to imagine. As a consequence of what he has himself described as the 'sexual embarrassment' from which he has found it 'so difficult to free' himself, he was still clumsy, and so further invited Nancy's hostility. She would tell him that his experiences in war were as nothing compared to the general sufferings of women at the hands of men – and she frequently got at him because he was male. She had a point; but in the state he then was he found himself dismayed by his feelings of dislike for her. For a state of virtue and happiness had, for him, to preclude hostile emotions, even occasional ones. So he suppressed them, a procedure at which, in terms of day-to-day living, he is adept. Little went right between the two, despite his efforts. Nancy spent a good deal of time, he tells us, illustrating 'some poems of mine'. But these illustrations never appeared. The woodcut of the little girl looking into the treasure box on the title page of the privately printed pamphlet *The Treasure Box* (Chiswick Press, 1919) was the only illustration Nancy ever published for any of her husband's books. *Country Sentiment*, published by Martin Secker in England and by Knopf in America in March 1920, in an edition of 1000 copies at five shillings each, was dedicated to her – but contained no drawings. *The Pier-Glass* of February 1921, again published by Secker and Knopf, was likewise dedicated to her – but the only picture in it was a portrait of Graves by his brother-in-law Ben Nicholson as frontispiece. In refusing to allow him to use her drawings, which he yearned to do, she hid her lack of self-confidence under a show of belligerence about the suitability of the drawings to the poems, or, more nastily, vice versa. His dogged devotedness made his friends wonder, and irritated her. But Graves, although he retrospectively regarded this period of his life as mistaken, 'wet', untruthful, still pronounced to all and sundry that he was happy, and happily married. And so he believed himself to be. Only certain of his poems gave him away; but no one, and certainly not he, saw this clearly and consistently. Later he got into the habit of talking at length to others about his problems; but this habit did not begin until a year or two later.

While at Harlech he indulged himself in living as though he had 'an income of a thousand a year' (this represented, until well after the Second World War, comfort and even luxury in Great Britain). Actually he had a little capital, an annual disability pension of £60, and some literary fees. He got a nurse for Jenny, and a general servant. He was able, for a while, to devote substantial time to work: to his poems and to reviewing – Sassoon, for the time being a militant socialist, had become literary editor of the *Daily Herald*, and sent him books for review. He could get his poems published in more or less any magazine he liked, and at this time he was as ambitious and as idealistic as any other young poet; he did not yet realize that his extreme independence, pride and individualism would inevitably lead to unpopularity. He held, for the only time in his life, a political attitude, although it was never intense – and never crept into his writing. But he does say that both he and Nancy took postwar conditions 'to heart'. They were disgusted with the complacency of the press – all but the Labour *Herald* – which concentrated on such items as the marriage of Lady Diana Manners even while the Versailles peace talks were going on. 'Nancy and I . . . called ourselves socialists.' This does not mean that he had any faith in politicians: he did not, and never has had. Nor of course had Nancy; they were practically all men, she rightly reasoned, and were therefore bent on enslaving women. Her feminism was sincere but shrill; he made it his business to support everything she said with vigour.

His political attitude was not really 'socialism', in the sense that Siegfried was just at that time embracing it. But it deeply shocked Graves's family. The real horror emanated from his mother; his father would have been more easygoing had he had the chance. It was not easy (as Graves says) for the family to reproach him, for, of all the boys, he alone had seen active service and been wounded 'in the service of his country' (a phrase he, but not they, distrusted). But they bombarded him with anxious letters, and gently remonstrated with him whenever they saw him.

A.P. was given the task of 'dealing' with him, and fulfilled this in the best Victorian manner; but Graves is unfair to him – as he generally is in *Goodbye to All That* – in blaming him, rather than his mother, who was responsible for the pressure. He was then and for some time after resentful that he owed to his father his first appearance in book form (*Over the Brazier*), and to him also some, at least, of the influence he was building up with literary editors; he did not record these debts even in his 1957 revision of *Goodbye to All That*.

The family was somewhat less ultra-conservative in politics than Graves makes out – though he could hardly exaggerate the quiet moral ferocity of his mother. What shocked them was his sympathy for the Bolsheviks, which they misinterpreted as being 'revolutionary' – whereas it was really no more than an acknowledgement of Tsarist corruption. His mother was even more appalled by his and Nancy's refusal to go to church, or to have Jenny baptized – and by their membership of the Constructive Birth Control Society, whose literature they distributed locally. She disliked the practice, which was Nancy's idea, of the children calling their parents by their Christian names. Amy Graves thought that her son exercised too little 'control' over his wayward and misguidedly feminist wife, whose refusal to use the name 'Graves' under any circumstances personally offended her – she was herself proud to have taken it. Nancy impressed those who knew her at the time of her marriage to Graves as being wilful rather than intelligent. By the time he went up to Oxford, in October 1919, she had become something of an embarrassment to him; but he would not admit it to himself, and was on the sharp lookout for anyone who dared to criticize her. He was already very good at not noticing what he did not want to notice. Meanwhile he took it out on his own parents by cultivating his wife's father, who was altogether more congenial.

Chapter Seven
1919–25

I

Graves now wanted to go to Oxford, but on his own terms – which he was able, as a wounded ex-serviceman, to negotiate. The rule was that students must live within three miles of Oxford. But rooms were expensive and scarce now that the war was over; and St John's College could not accommodate married undergraduates. So he got permission to live out on Boars Hill, on account of his bad lungs. Here John Masefield offered to rent him a cottage at the end of his garden: he 'thought well of my poems'. He owed Masefield's interest in him to Marsh and to Sassoon, who had been living in Oxford during 1919 and had pleaded his cause – which Masefield was glad to further. Blunden, whose lungs were in an even worse state than Graves's, also had permission to live out on Boars Hill, and the two men often met and talked. They remained friendly for some time, but Blunden was already unhappy about Graves's *hauteur* (his brother was once so upset by Graves's aristocratic manner that he walked out of Blunden's house) – and Graves disliked Blunden's 'meanness and ambitiousness'.

The School of English at Oxford was then fairly bad, although not as bad as it later became; but Graves none the less wanted to read English rather than Greats (the Classics course at Oxford), for which he had been given his exhibition. The head of the English School was Sir Walter Raleigh (author of the famous lines beginning 'I wish I liked the human race'), of whom he was fond. Graves's moral tutor, J. V. Powell, had been a corporal in the General Reserve, and had many times saluted his future pupil in 1916. Powell persuaded the college to let Graves have his annual classical exhibition but read in the English School.

He soon found the English teaching tedious, though he liked his tutor, Percy Simpson, who (with C. H. Herford) was responsible for the first decently edited complete works of Ben Jonson. It was Simpson – of whom he wrote, when he died at an advanced age in the sixties, that 'he was a darling' – who made him aware of the loss to the poetic sense that resulted when seventeenth-century texts were modernized and repunctuated. He found, like many others who read English at Oxford, the Anglo-Saxon language difficult; but he did not agree with his lecturer that the poetry had no merit. He found it vivid, and liked it much more than the eighteenth-century periphrastic elegance which he felt was too hard pressed upon him by the authorities, and which he regarded as artificial.

Graves's critical opinions are unabashedly based on his own poetic practice. And this practice has always been fundamentally romantic. The basic romantic element became tempered and modified by an increasingly robust metaphysical, sometimes even Restoration, sophistication and worldliness (one thinks principally of Rochester). Pope, in Graves's view, could not be 'any good' (as he so often puts it) because he 'thought out his poems before committing them to paper'. He wrote in a letter a quarter of a century later:

> Pope was a little devil who put it over everyone by fear: he was not a poet but a satirist in the primitive Irish sense. . . . His *Dunciad* is his best work because the evillest. He was not a 'good craftsman' as is supposed; and his poems consist of a series of couplets, not of an orderly procession of sense. His [non-satirical] poems are flat – 'Windsor Forest' for example. [To M.S.-S., 8 March 1945]

Graves liked his landlords, the Masefields, and respected Masefield's poetry. He had first met him in 1917. In his address at the memorial service for Masefield in Westminster Abbey (20 June 1967) he said that he had written 'from the heart'; although Kipling had influenced his first (1902) volume, he 'got inside [the] skins of his characters in a way that Kipling could not'. With *The Everlasting Mercy* he had 'set the Thames on fire':

> a fresh wind that carried English poetry clear out of the Edwardian doldrums. . . . Those pungent, urgent, violent lines . . . exhilarated us youngsters.

He remembered his

> shy morning smile and hello, when I used to trudge by his garden workshed half-hidden among gorse-trees. . . . I grew greatly attached to John Masefield, as also did our neighbour Edmund Blunden. . . . Though

members of a rebellious new generation we declined to ally ourselves poetically with the Franco-American modernists – the Sitwells, Eliot, Pound, H.D. [Hilda Dolittle, poet-wife of Richard Aldington], Flint, Read and the rest. We remained as obstinately rooted in the early English tradition as Masefield himself, who was Chaucer's man.

Graves went on to make it clear – though in the polite language required on such a solemn occasion – that he thought Masefield's poetry went off after 1911; but he concluded by saying that 'he never lost what is the supreme poetic quality: an unselfish love for his fellow men.'

Masefield for his own part thought Graves 'the most likely young man in literature over here', as he told an American woman correspondent (7 April 1919) some months before Graves became his tenant. Constance, Masefield's shrewd, shrewish wife, thought less of him – and of Nancy. 'She has not got enough adventure in her to be a poet's wife,' she recorded in her diary for 20 February 1920:

Nancy is a strange shy boyish girl, very clever with her fingers and quick in brain. Affectionate too, but spoilt in a sort of artistic way, ready to find fault with anyone else's work. I quite like her, but I wish she weren't so mulish. For some reason she insists on calling herself Miss Nancy Nicholson.

Graves she found 'tender-hearted, rather vain, very domestic. . . .' She disapproved of his confiding in her about 'his domestic life' ('tells me more than he should'); and he was 'sometimes a little garrulous'.

The Masefields found Graves's habits 'rough', and Masefield (forced to it by his wife) wrote to him (22 April 1920) to tell him that he and 'his charming family' must not visit except between '4.15 p.m. and 5.15 p.m. on weekdays, or between 4.00 p.m. and 6.00 p.m. on Sundays': 'We attach a rather old-fashioned importance to our visitors entering by the front door.'

In other words the Masefields failed to understand either their tenant's rough trench manners or his idealism (why shouldn't poets walk into one another's houses?). Masefield had served in France – but not in the trenches. And he was in any case by now helplessly in the thrall of his wife, for whom literature consisted entirely of Jan's (as she called him) works.

Eventually Graves came to feel that there were too many poets and literary men where he lived. Not long before his death F. W. Bateson, the critic, recalled 'sitting at the feet of Robert Graves' in 1920. There were others. His personality was beginning to assert itself. But his notion of starting a movement from Boars Hill was short-lived. There were now few poets, aside from Blunden, whose work he really admired. He mentions Robert Bridges, then Poet Laureate, in *Goodbye to All That*, as a man with a 'bright eye' and 'abrupt challenging manner'; he does not add that he thought his poetry effete and unexciting, although metrically accomplished. Graves had got to know the flamboyant Robert Nichols early in the war, and had introduced him to Sassoon; there is a war piece from Graves called 'To R.N.' Nichols, who had written some lurid war-style poetry (his *Ardours and Endurances*, 1917, was a popular success) started a legend, on a lecture tour of the USA, of himself, Sassoon and Graves as 'the New Three Musketeers'. This annoyed the other musketeers, as they had never all three been in the same room together – and in any case Nichols, although this is, decently, not stated in *Goodbye to All That*, had seen no active service. He had been in the Artillery, and had spent three weeks near the front line in 1917. But before seeing any action he managed to contract syphilis – and to fall off a roof. He cracked up, became hysterical, spent five months in hospital, and was treated for neurasthenia by Henry Head, a colleague of W. H. R. Rivers, who treated Sassoon.

It so happened that the ideas of both these men became increasingly important to Graves in the years after the war, as we shall see. Rivers was an eminent Cambridge professor: psychologist, neurologist – and something of a pioneer anthropologist, as well. He treated his neurasthenics through a modified Freudianism, and was therefore particularly interested in their dreams. He treated patients less for money than because he liked helping people.

David, Robert's and Nancy's second child, was born in March 1920. Amy Graves was delighted; at the birth of Jenny she commented (Nancy was not amused), 'Perhaps it's as well to have a girl first to practise on.' Just at this time Nancy began openly to regret their marriage: 'We wanted somehow to be dis-married – not by divorce, which was as bad as marriage – and able to live together without any legal or religious obligation to live together,' Graves wrote. In his 1957 revision he attributes the regret to Nancy alone. He did not want to be 'dis-married' at all, and was appalled when Nancy suddenly announced that she did. But in 1929 he was still too proud to admit it.

What really happened is revealing. Nancy told him that she regretted their marriage. As is his wont when confronted with bad news, he made the best of it. Playing on her feminist convictions, he prevailed upon her to admit that the marriage laws – slanted to favour men – were responsible. He was thus able, for the time being, to agree with her that 'dis-marriage' was the desideratum.

II

In the same month as David's birth Robert met T. E. Lawrence ('of Arabia'), who was now a Fellow of All Souls. The two men immediately developed a strong feeling for each other, although many of those who knew Graves felt that he hero-worshipped Lawrence – and that knowing him well had gone to his head. However, it would have been difficult for any young man, even a war veteran, not to have been flattered by the fact that Lawrence showed a peculiar liking for him – and for his poems.

The occasion on which they met was a guest night at All Souls. Graves was an 'accidental' guest, he says; he was in fact invited because his father had been invited, and thus it was that he met Lawrence. Graves had already heard much about Lawrence from his half-brother Philip, who worked with him in the Intelligence Department in Cairo before he became involved in the Arab Revolt. To an inquirer, a stranger, in 1974, Graves wrote of his first meeting with Lawrence thus:

> He asked if I was Robert Graves the poet – which embarrassed me, but it turned out that my brother Philip and my Uncle Robert had been directing activities from Egypt when he first appeared in Arabia – which put things right. . . . He became my best friend. . . .

Lawrence told Graves that he had read a book of his poems in Egypt in 1917, and had thought them 'pretty good'. This book could have been *Over the Brazier* or *Fairies and Fusiliers*. Doubtless Philip had passed it on to him. Lawrence, now toying with the possibility of a literary career, then and there decided to ask Graves's advice on all matters pertaining to modern poetry. Robert eagerly took this up – and was soon asking Lawrence's advice on his own poems, which was unwise but natural. Lawrence, who had strong literary yearnings but rightly lacked confidence in his literary judgement, needed the reassurance of one whom he felt to be 'in the know', and Graves gives out an aura of this.

Graves had already become exhausted by the difficulties created by his own idealism and conventional moral rectitude, by his struggle to reconcile a rigid personal morality with a growing hatred and distrust of conventional morality (the 'morality' which produced the war). He compensated by indulging in a robust opposition to the Establishment, in which Lawrence – an accepted figure – also shared. Lawrence wanted to 'wake Oxford up'. He was thus congenial to Graves; he offered him an example of the kind of sophistication, almost a sort of ataraxia, with which he sought to relieve himself from too much virtue.

Lawrence loved and admired but did not wholly understand Graves. His Irish intuition recognized a dedicated poet in him – probably he was the first man to make this recognition – and he was fascinated, even though he did enjoy teasing Graves's susceptibilities from time to time. The friendship between them was intense, and though Lawrence knew dozens of eminent men, he confided in Graves as fully as he confided in anyone (which was not very fully). Graves confided in him, too – particularly at the time when he was writing the poems in *The Pier-Glass* – about his sexual problems. Lawrence invariably hid himself behind cryptic utterances; but Graves was one of the very few of his friends to whom he gave detailed information about his irresistible compulsion to be punished.

Lawrence was impressed by the extent to which Graves was steeped in poetry. This was the time when Graves read most eagerly, particularly in folk song and ballad (his *The English Ballad*, 1928, was the result of this) and once more in Skelton. Graves refused, as he always has, to treat of poets as 'major' and 'minor', preferring to concentrate on their virtues as individuals:

> Donne (for example's sake),
> Keats, Marlowe, Spenser, Blake,
> Shelley and Milton,
> Shakespeare and Chaucer, Skelton –
> We love them as we know them,
> But who could dare outgo them
> At their several arts,
> At their particular parts
> Of wisdom, power and knowledge?
> In the Poets' College
> Are no degrees or stations,

Comparison, rivals,
Stern examinations,
Class declarations,
Senior survivals. . . .

Already in this poem, 'In Procession' (first published in 1922), he is voicing his impatience with the 'evaluations' of academic critics.

Whom did he admire in these very early days, apart from Skelton – whom he had certainly discovered for himself? He was interested in T. S. Eliot, but suspicious – not at this time of his modernism, but of his friendship with and admiration for Ezra Pound. Pound he met in Lawrence's rooms at All Souls: 'you will dislike each other', Lawrence said as he introduced them. Graves did dislike Pound, who had, he says, 'a wet handshake'. He granted him technical skill of a sort, but did not like the rhythms he achieved. He was put off by Pound's yankee manner and his jocose slang; he also felt that Pound was trying to bring 'continental' influences into English poetry – he was, then as now, largely insensitive to non-English poetries, and chose to ignore the influence they have exercised on English poetry at various times. But Eliot's pre-*Waste Land* poems he admired for their sense of fastidious satirical disgust and their 'poetic feeling'. Although he disliked *The Waste Land* as a whole, he was friendly enough with Eliot to contemplate collaborating with him on a book of critical essays in 1925 – but nothing came of it. But as hopes for a Georgian revival faded, which they quickly did, he became increasingly sparing of praise for his contemporaries, though he thoroughly admired the American John Crowe Ransom, whose work he introduced to England. He liked W. H. Davies for his simplicity (and later on felt sorry for him, because 'his wife gave him a dose'), and Walter de la Mare (particularly the poem called 'Quartette' – but he detested de la Mare's 'anthology' poems, and later castigated one of them, 'Arabia'). He also liked Davies because he was supposed – William Nicholson told him the story – to have made a long list of poets and then started crossing out the ones who blotted their copybooks. At last only his own and Graves's names were left. Nicholson warned him that his would be the next to go. He was writing reviews of contemporary poetry for the *Herald* and the *Nation* and other periodicals, and was as critical as he dared be. (He needed the money, and resented having to sell himself. As soon as he could, he vowed, he would make himself independent of having to review for a living.) As 'Fuze' he contributed twelve 'Books at Random' pieces to the *Woman's Leader*; the one he most enjoyed writing was on 'neglected and recently rescued poets': Traherne, Campion, Donne, Gavin Douglas, Henryson, Darley, Clare and Skelton. He fully supported Blunden's (and Alan Porter's) work to get the poems of John Clare ('one of the glories of English poetry') into print.

Wishing to shake up his Oxford contemporaries, he managed to persuade Sir Walter Raleigh to give him permission to invite the Illinois poet Vachel Lindsay, then in England, to read in Oxford. He describes Lindsay as 'Middle-Western clay with a golden streak', but was hardly himself prepared for the shattering effect this 'jazz Blake, St Francis of Assisi playing the saxophone at the Firemen's Ball' would create. Lindsay gave electrifying performances of his work – in the rhetorical style he had originally based on the poetry readings of Professor S. H. Clark, of the University of Chicago. He and his mother were entertained in Lawrence's rooms. Of the reading, which took place in the morning, Graves on 19 October 1920 wrote to a friend:

> Vachel Lindsay was a most staggering success. I meant to hit Oxford a pretty heavy blow by arranging for his invitation by the University, but did not expect to inflict a knockout, as occurred. . . . By two minutes, Lindsay had the respectable and intellectual and cynical audience listening. By ten, intensely excited; by twenty elated and losing self control, by half an hour completely under his influence, by forty minutes roaring like a bonfire. At the end of the hour they lifted off the roof and refused to disperse, and Raleigh in returning thanks said he had never been so moved by a recitation in his life – quite like the pictures.

Of the older living English poets he only unreservedly admired Hardy, whom he and Nancy visited in the course of a bicycle trip they took in the summer of 1920. They had already met him, briefly, when he came to Oxford in early February of that year to take an honorary degree – and to see a performance of *The Dynasts* by the University Dramatic Society. They had then thought him rather confused; but at his own home, in Dorchester, although now just eighty, they found him 'active and gay'. Graves's account of Hardy in *Goodbye to All That*, based on notes he made at the time and written up in a hurry, is poor; he wanted to show his love for Hardy, but was inaccurate, careless and managed to sound patronizing – and failed to convey the warmth he felt. Nevertheless, his meeting with the old poet deeply affected him. He was most of all impressed with Hardy's disdain for critics, his loyalty to his friends and his dislike of *vers libre*.

On leaving Hardy the couple went on to Tiverton, in Devonshire, where 'Nancy's old nurse kept a fancy-goods shop'. Nancy got so much pleasure in cleaning and rearranging this shop that it gave her a disastrous idea: to start a shop on Boars Hill, where many people lived but which had no shop nearer than three miles. Graves was privately unenthusiastic, but put his soul into it none the less, and promised to help. Now began a bad nine months in both their lives.

They had a hut – designed by Nancy – built in too much of a hurry, and rented a corner of a field for it. Graves, who has a knack of attracting attention whenever he needs to, saw to it that the opening was well advertised. The *Daily Mirror* carried the headline 'SHOP-KEEPING ON PARNASSUS', and a large number of people from Oxford came up to gawp at the eccentric poet-turned-tradesman. It might have been an auspicious beginning, but they had not thought enough about what exactly they wanted to do. Should they just run a small sweet and tobacco shop, offering no provocation to the big Oxford tradesmen who were used to the custom – or should they set up as rivals to them? They chose the bolder course, and were soon in trouble.

Nancy had taken a neighbour – a Mrs Michael Howard – into partnership; but this lady, who had offered to keep the books but had no knowledge of book-keeping, soon let them down. They quarrelled; Mrs Howard, in high dudgeon, withdrew, and Graves and Nancy began to get talked about as being odd (it did not help that they were). Nevertheless they obtained the custom of most of the residents, who could not resist the genteel thrill of 'supporting a poet' who, another popular newspaper asserted, 'made his own clothes'. But Nancy's convictions did not endear her to the local people; nor did they much care for the contempt with which she seemed to regard her husband, who was by contrast admired for putting in so much time in the shop. Still, they added stock to their original purchase, and seemed to be doing well. So well that they played Robin Hood (at Nancy's behest), over-charging the rich and undercharging the poor, and getting away with it. But things were not going well with Nancy, though Graves would not admit this until the very last moment. She was neglecting the house – and even the two children, to whom she had hitherto given exemplary care – in favour of the shop. She thought that she could become rich, and thus in some way outdo her husband – whose gifts she undoubtedly resented. When Mrs Masefield tactlessly told her that if she wanted to 'hold on' to her husband she should keep up with him intellectually, she glowered with rage. Normally she was efficient with the children;

but for the duration of this adventure she was beside herself. At first she went round herself to collect orders; later they employed a boy. Graves got no work done, and hardly put in an appearance at lectures. He struck his customers as he meant to strike them: absent-minded and tousled – and just like a poet. His manners behind the counter were never servile, and some were even made nervous by his authoritative manner.

Then prices began to fall at the rate of about 'five per cent every week'. Nancy became tired and ill, and suddenly interested herself again in the children – she even accused Graves of overoptimism, inefficiency and recklessness. She began to speak of him to the customers with an outright rudeness. She dismissed the nurse she had engaged – leaving him to deal with the rapidly running-down shop. But he got a bad attack of influenza, which made it no easier for him to decipher Mrs Howard's crazy book-keeping. The attitude of Mrs Masefield, who kept the timid future Laureate himself on a short string, was of no help. She disliked having anything as vulgar as a shop, and in a hut at that, so near her house, and she made it clear that she was sorry that she had ever let her property to this couple. The job of a poet was to write comprehensible poetry, like her husband's, not keep shops – and she considered that Graves should control Nancy more effectively. She refused them her custom except for a nominal visit, once a week, to buy Vim and Lux, with which she cleaned her conscience, and doubtless appeased Jan. Such was her horror of 'trade' that she saw to it, at the end, that they would be unable to recoup their losses. A big Oxford grocer offered to take the shop over from them; they would have made a small profit. But Mrs Masefield persuaded the people who had rented them the field not to permit this. Masefield was embarrassed, but had no power over his wife – so, in disgust, they gave notice that they would leave at midsummer, 1921. A lawyer reduced their debt to about £300, William Nicholson gave them £100 – and T. E. Lawrence, by this time sorry for Graves's predicament as a husband, gave him some fragments of the second draft of the much-rewritten *Seven Pillars of Wisdom* to sell for serial publication in America. This saved the situation. Graves sold the fragments to *The World's Work*.

But he was again near the end of his emotional tether. He had actually begun to feel better, to have better nights, in the summer of 1920. Now, as the summer of 1921 began, he felt ill and haunted again. He became physically very ill; his influenza turned into severe bronchitis, and, with his as yet not fully healed lung, he was forced to take to his bed. He was on a shortened, two-year-and-one-term course, and due to sit for his finals at the end of that year. But he was able to postpone taking these on grounds of ill-health. He never did sit them: he did not want to be 'examined'; but in 1925 he obtained his BLitt – without taking the necessary BA – owing to the good offices of Raleigh.

III

Nancy looked after him while he was ill, but managed simultaneously to give him the impression that he was a weakling. She was changeable, sometimes agreeing with his wish for independence, and sometimes not. He promised her – and himself – that he would pull himself together. She had little sympathy with his sufferings in the war, since she still believed that 'all that' was as nothing compared to the suffering endured by women throughout the ages. She was right, and he agreed with her; but, if only in the privacy of his mind, it was difficult for him. He sometimes even inclined to the view that he had not *personally* caused all the suffering of women throughout the ages. He even toyed with the idea of finding a psychiatrist. But two things worried him: would the 'cure' deprive him of poetic power, and would he become dependent on the doctor? He worried that he was being perversely, wilfully, ill in order to write poetry. But, as he wrote in 1929 (he deleted the passage in 1957):

> I decided to see as few people as possible, stop all outside work, and cure myself. I had already learned the rudiments of morbid psychology from talks with Rivers, and from his colleague, Dr Henry Head, the neurologist.

But first they had to have somewhere to live. Nancy specified the kind of cottage she wanted, and he managed to find one just like it in the village of Islip, some eight miles north of Oxford. It is possible that the World's End, which was the name of the cottage in which they were to live for the next four years, was not quite so exactly what Nancy had specified as he relates in his autobiography, where he tells us that after listening to her precise specifications he laid a ruler across a map, found the position required, and went into a house agent and said:

What I want is a cottage just outside the village of Islip, with a walled garden, six rooms, water in the house, a beamed attic, and at a rent of ten shillings a week.

Whereupon, according to Graves, the clerk said, 'Oh, you mean the World's End cottage . . .' and told him that it was for sale, not rent. Anyway, it was near enough to what they wanted. They had no money to buy the place. Amy Graves, more kindly than severe in an emergency, came to the rescue. She bought it and rented it to them at ten shillings a week. But she put a clause into the agreement (to restrain Nancy, and with Graves's tacit approval) to the effect that no trade or business could be conducted from it. So began a four-year period in Graves's life in which, once again, he tried to consolidate his position.

Nancy believed in having her children as early and as close together as possible: Catherine was born in 1922, Sam in early 1924. Both Graves and Nancy found they could fit themselves into the agricultural life of Islip much more easily than into that of Boars Hill, whose concentration of would-be poets now depressed them beyond measure, though for different reasons.

Graves had all this time been working tentatively on his first prose book, trying to discover the origin of what he has called his 'haunted state'. He published *On English Poetry*, a series of short critical essays, in July 1922, with William Heinemann – who had previously published *Fairies and Fusiliers*. The book, subtitled 'an Irregular Approach to the Psychology of This Art, from Evidence Mostly Subjective', was printed in the United States, and had already appeared there in the previous May under the imprint of his (for the time being) regular American publisher, Alfred Knopf.

These essays, taken with *The Pier-Glass* – the first book of poems in which he found his own distinctive style – contain, in embryo, the Graves with whom we are familiar. T. E. Lawrence, in his letter to Edward Marsh accompanying a copy of what he called the 'MS. story of Feisal's campaign' – the very 'fragments' which he had given Graves to sell in America – said of the volume:

> I hope you like R.G.'s little book *The Pier-Glass* – I'm immensely struck with it. A good deal of it is rather odd, but I think there can be no two opinions about the excellence of the writing, and much of it is sheer beauty.

Two of the most distinctive and revealing poems in *The Pier-Glass* are the title poem, and 'Down'. 'The Pier-Glass', the last twenty-five lines of which have been cut from all editions of the subsequent *Collected Poems*, is one of Graves's most cryptic poems. It is a key poem, but has not been well or fully understood by commentators on Graves's poetry.

The narrator is a living woman who, whenever she is sleeping, is doomed to haunt a 'lost manor', and in particular a room containing a 'bed of state' and 'a sullen pier-glass'. The implication is that she is a sleep-walker, and this in turn suggests that her whole life is a nightmare because, although she tells us nothing of her waking self, she gets no rest. The pier-glass is cracked and old, and 'scorns to present the face (as do new mirrors)/With a lying flush, but shows it melancholy/ And pale, as faces grow that look in mirrors.' In its later versions the poem ends:

> Ah, mirror, for Christ's love
> Give me one token that there still abides
> Remote — beyond this island mystery,
> So be it only this side Hope, somewhere,
> In streams, on sun-warm mountain pasturage —
> True life, natural breath; not this phantasma.

This reflects above all Graves's own neurasthenic state, his proneness to return involuntarily to war experience (which did not leave him until 1928). He can put himself into the situation of his woman narrator because he, too, is haunted by guilt and he, too, lives in a 'phantasma'. But neurasthenia is not, as he knows, explained simply by war experience. War experience uncovers it, exposes what might well otherwise remain hidden. Thus, the explanation of the poem as a representation of his war neurosis, the usual approach taken by critics, is correct — but does not go half far enough. No one seems to have been able to explain why Graves chooses here, as he very seldom does, to speak as a woman. But there was good reason for it. Even when he cut the poem by a third of its length he left it as spoken by a woman.

The twenty-five line final stanza of the original poem, last published in the *1914–1927* collection of his poems, offers an explanation for the woman narrator's traumatized state. It is less good than the rest of the poem, and Graves was right to reject it. As an attempt to round off the poem it is a failure, but it is none the less interesting. The woman begins, in this final section, by stating that she knows that 'death prevails not yet'. And her contrived speech — in marked contrast to the haunted first part of the poem – attempts to conventionalize the poem. It turns out that she is a maidservant haunted by the guilty fact of having killed, rather than forgiven, her master who has enslaved her as his whore. This revelation makes more explicit the following lines from the first part of the poem:

> At my right hand
> A ravelled bell-pull hangs in readiness
> To summon me from attic glooms above
> Service of elder ghosts. . . .

She now knows that 'death prevails not yet' because a hive of bees is 'pent up' between the pier-glass and the outer wall, and

> This new mood
> Of judgement orders again my present duty,
> To face again a problem strongly solved
> In life gone by, but now again proposed
> Out of due time for fresh deliberation.
> Did not my answer please the Master's ear?

And, faced again with the 'paltry question' of whether to kill or to forgive, 'the wronged lover' comes to the conclusion: 'Kill, strike the blow again, spite what shall come.' The poem concludes messily, failing to resolve the situation of the speaker. But it does invent a destructive female figure.

'The Pier-Glass' in its original form is dedicated to T. E. Lawrence, 'who helped me with it'. Lawrence helped him with all the poems in *The Pier-Glass*, and was very proud of the fact. But, as Graves explains in the revised *Goodbye to All That*, Lawrence (as he came to see only later) thought of poetry as simply some 'technical secret', rather than as a way of life. His suggestions were not pertinent. He could scent the 'differentness' of a dedicated poet; poetry itself defeated him.

In this instance, Graves wrote the first part of the poem more or less as we know it – and then showed it to Lawrence for his approval. Lawrence could not understand it, but was fascinated by it; he suggested to Graves that he keep it cryptic, but add a few tantalizing clues. So Graves 'manufactured' an ending giving such clues, became interested in the section on its own account, and therefore did no more than confusedly adumbrate the White Goddess.

There was a certain moral capriciousness, a lack of firmness, about Nancy which made her unsuitable as a Muse; he was painfully and reluctantly realizing that he could never learn to love her. The young and war-stricken Graves of 1917 and 1918 had yearned for a loving, devoted wife and a long life of pastoralized bliss blessed by scores of children. But not even Nancy's feminism was convincing. His fate, as he now secretly admitted to himself and to Lawrence, was to be misunderstood – to be subjected to the whims of a scatterbrain.

He began to accept his fate; but he projected the old maternal strictness onto his conception of it – transforming that strictness, however, into something sophisticated, enlightened, and understanding. He would still *feel* misunderstood; but at the hands of this (so far) phantom woman of his imagination he would learn that such feelings were misguided – and so be purged of his 'ancestral sin', his guilt. Thus, in one sense, was Laura Riding born. The only eventuality upon which he did not then reckon was that his exploration of the meaning of lust would have, for a considerable period, to be conducted in the absence of the exercise of it. In all other respects he had, in the context of his own life, already invented Riding. *The White Goddess* is not, as it has too often been called, simply a 'rationalization of Riding'.

'Down', this time written in the voice of a man, is a more straight-forward account of his neurasthenic condition, in which the nerve-shot speaker investigates the guilt associated with the creation of poetry itself:

> How had he magicked space
> With inadvertent motion or word uttered
> Of too-close-packed intelligence (such there are),
> That he should penetrate with sliding ease
> Dense earth, compound of ages, granite ribs
> And groins? Consider: there was some word uttered,
> Some abracadabra – then, like a stage ghost,
> Funereally with weeping, down, drowned, lost!
> Oh, to be child once more. . . .

There is no doubt of the nightmare state in which Graves now found himself. Confusion was compounded by confusion: on the one hand he was seriously worried as to whether a cure – specifically one by psychoanalysis – would destroy his capacity to write poetry; but on the other he was treating his poetry, or trying to treat it, as psychotherapy. Since poetry was for him essentially a quest for purity, however – even though, as he tells us, he had not then 'learned' enough to know that it was a 'way of life' – this attempted use of it, for psychotherapy, increased his guilt feelings. He was in a vicious circle.

One component of his guilt, however, is so obvious that we may even be in danger of ignoring it: he was ashamed of having killed people, of having been turned into a murderer by his participation in war. This is the context of his poem 'Reproach', included in *The Pier-Glass*. One night while in France, in 1917, he looked up into the sky and fancied he saw a face staring down at him; it was the moon, but the moon transformed into a face, which he took to be that of Christ, reproaching him. He had by then lost his orthodox faith, but not his belief in a redeeming Christ. I give the poem in its original version.

> Your grieving moonlight face looks down
>   Through the forest of my fears,
> Crowned with a spiny bramble crown,
>   Dew-dropped with evening tears.
>
> Why do you spell 'untrue, unkind,'
>   Reproachful eyes plaguing my sleep?
> I am not guilty in my mind
>   Of aught would make you weep.
>
> Untrue? but how, what broken oath?
>   Unkind? I know not even your name.
> Untrue, unkind, you charge me both,
>   Scalding my heart with shame.
>
> The black trees shudder, dropping snow,
>   The stars tumble and spin.
> Speak, speak, or how may a child know
>   His ancestral sin?

It is impossible to take this poem as having, for its 'target', 'Original Sin', as one critic would have us do. Christ is here being asked, by a soldier who is supposed to be doing his duty by killing, to tell him what he should do and feel. But the original Flanders context is removed, justifiably, because the question can legitimately be generalized. Christ did not speak to him, and Graves eventually rejected even him. He told me in 1945, 'I thought then that it was Christ, but it must have been Hercules.' The Gravesian Hercules did – if only metaphorically – supply him with an answer: learn to love woman. And the moon turned back into the moon. But it was a terrifying process. 'Reproach' shows that although Graves had long made his farewell to conventional Christianity, he was still considering some private form of it based on the person of Jesus.

IV

Graves came to see that he could not go on in 'The Pier-Glass' vein any longer. So he turned to theory. The sort of theory is demonstrated in his first two critical works: *On English Poetry* (1922) and *Poetic Unreason* (1925). Now although in these – and in *The Meaning of Dreams* (1924) – Graves felt that he had been erecting theories, and that this had been reprehensible, he was making a necessary investigation and exploration of his own practice. It is extraordinary to what an extent, in these works, he anticipated himself. He was doing better than he was shortly afterwards led to think, and especially so if we allow for his comparative youth – he was not, after all, thirty until July 1925. When in the mid-1940s he began to revise his literary essays for collection in *The Common Asphodel* he wrote:

> They are very badly written and inaccurate, but I find that I had already in 1920 planned a line that I have been following ever since. I daresay they'll make a book if I'm ruthless enough. [To M.S.-S., 25 July 1946]

This discovery, twenty-six years after, that he had 'planned a line' to which he had adhered, is remarkable; until then he had been conditioned by Riding to assume that few of his critical notions had been his own, but had been learned from her. He never suspected the enormous extent of her debt to him. He simply had not reread his earlier work.

He ended the prefatory note to *On English Poetry* cannily: '. . . when putting a cat among pigeons it is always advisable to make it as large a cat as possible.' Thus Graves on page viii of his first prose book – a Graves surely familiar to us all. But this work neither sold nor was much reviewed – though it was read, and some of its ideas were lifted by other critics.

On English Poetry seems a logical enough predecessor to *A Survey of Modernist Poetry*, which was written (in word for word collaboration), in 1926 and 1927, with Laura Riding. As he wrote in a formal letter of 1966, correcting some inaccuracies perpetrated in an ill-informed article in *Modern Language Quarterly* (27).

> My more recent writings on poetry . . . proceed from views I first clumsily expressed in *On English Poetry* (1922) and then developed in collaboration with Laura Riding. . . . We both agreed with our friend Gertrude Stein's simple view of literary criticism: 'the way to say it, is to say it'. I at least still stand by that.

On English Poetry for all its immaturity is in many ways even now a salutary and lucid book, and although Graves has preserved parts of it, in revised form, in *The Common Asphodel*, it could usefully be reprinted. It contains Graves's view of poetry in embryo, and is invaluable as a young poet's immediate record of his practice – and as a record of the principles which guided him. It is the first book of its time to take a truly psychological approach to poetry, and to make use of modern psychological methods.

This is at first surprising. We tend to think of the advent of 'modernism' as having been characterized by the 'depth psychology' approach to poetry – as well as by the development of *vers libre*. But neither Eliot nor Pound, the acknowledged proto-modernists, ever showed any interest in Freud – or in the subject matter he introduced. Eliot had too much to hide to interest himself in anything so potentially menacing. And Herbert Read, who was a pioneer of depth-psychology criticism, did not publish his first prose book until 1924 – and did not in any case venture into this field until some time after that. But when literary historians come to record the development of modernism, not only do they forget *On English Poetry* – they ignore Graves. This is mainly because his criticism has too studiously ignored non-English poetry – although a subsidiary reason may well be that he himself took every possible opportunity of condemning the work (and *Poetic Unreason*) in the period when it might still have been influential, namely, the later twenties and the thirties. The style, too, is markedly informal, whereas Eliot's (say) is pontifical, and therefore appealed more to academics.

The book is dedicated to T. E. Lawrence and to Rivers. Graves was never a patient of Rivers, but determined to get what knowledge he could from him – and from Head. As he put it, in the same letter to *Modern Language Quarterly* (27) from which I have already quoted:

> I was never a patient of Dr W. H. R. Rivers, as were Siegfried Sassoon and Wilfred Owen. But he and his colleague Henry Head (Robert Nichols' psychiatrist) were my friends and for a while I accepted their general theory of a 'subconscious self' . . . but not Freud's deformation of it. No Freudian I, nor were they. . . .

Graves knew Freud only through Rivers and Head – and a hasty reading of *The Interpretation of Dreams* (the first, imperfect, English translation of this, by A. A. Brill, appeared in 1913); he therefore tends to attribute to Freud himself the excesses of some of his disciples.

However, he desperately needed, at this stage, an explanation for his guilt feelings; neither simple escapism, nor an Eliotian concentration on tradition, nor a Poundian one on 'making it new', was acceptable to him. It was a relief to him to find that his 'ancestral sin' might reside in his 'unconscious'.

The theory of poetry presented in *On English Poetry* is a concatenation of nineteenth-century romantic poetic theory (as found notably in Coleridge, and in Edward Young and others before him), with ingredients from the early twentieth-century protoanthropology of Tylor, Marett, Frazer and others – knowledge of which Graves acquired from Rivers and, to a lesser extent, from Head, and from his reading. But his specific formulation of all this material was then new – and unfashionable. In the highly influential *The Sacred Wood*, of 1920, T. S. Eliot pleaded for 'detachment' in poetry, and for the 'development of sensibility'. Graves found this intelligent as far as it went, but strained and evasive. Eliot was at this time experiencing great difficulties with his first wife, who was mad; his way of dealing with this was to withdraw into 'objectivity', the consideration of the larger social and religious issues. By contrast, Graves's way of dealing with his problems was to make, as nearly as he could, the fullest possible acknowledgement of them. Eliot's ideal poet (himself) is a man of such exquisite sensibility that he can modify the 'ideal order' of the 'existing monuments' by being 'really new'; he

> must develop or procure the consciousness of the past. . . . The progress of an artist is a continual self-sacrifice, a continual extinction of personality.

For Eliot '*significant*' (his italics) emotion 'has its life in the poem and not in the history of the poet'.

Graves's ideal poet (himself) is a less ambitiously rarefied creature: more empirical, more pragmatic, classical only in his craftsmanship – but otherwise a member of the romantic, individualistic tradition to which Eliot was opposed. Eliot has little serious to say about the origins of poetry, preferring – ultimately – to put it at the service of a political and religious conservatism. Graves, to his own guilty embarrassment, insists on its origin in painful personal conflict. Yet he would agree with Eliot that the *significant* life of emotion lies in the poem (although he would always avoid the use of the particular word 'significant' on account of its academic connotations). But he needs to explain how it is that a poet manages to transcend his 'local' passion, to make it mean something to his readers. His attitude is more subjective than Eliot's, more disturbing to himself and others – and more informal. He explains poetic power, about the retention of which he is perpetually superstitious, in quasi-anthropological terms. And as early as 1922 he acknowledged the necessity of arrogance:

> ... with the poet there is always the tinge of arrogance in the thought that his own poetry has a lasting quality which most of his contemporaries cannot claim. . . . They have most arrogance before writing their poem of the moment, most humility when they know that they have once more failed.

These are uncomfortable truths, which cannot be wrapped up in 'larger issues' – for his apparent avoidance of which Graves, understandably if not rightly, was until recently written off as inexorably 'minor' as compared to Pound, Eliot, Auden or even Lowell.

The poetic impulse, Graves postulates, originates in conflict:

> When conflicting issues disturb [the poet's] mind, which in its conscious state is unable to reconcile them logically, the poet acquires the habit of self-hypnotism, as practised by the witch doctors, his ancestors in poetry.

Why, he asks, do some poets 'suddenly come to a dead end' – fail to 'go into trance'? Graves explains that this is the result of either a transmutation of the 'clash of emotions' into a 'calmer state of meditation' or of the final settlement of the conflict 'by some satisfaction of desire or removal of a cause of fear'. He has made sure, always, that *his* desire has never been satisfied, the causes of *his* fear never removed. For, as he points out, the 'temporary writing of poetry by normal single-track minds is most common in youth . . .' for the obvious reasons (love, rebelliousness, and so forth). He was always terrified of drying up, since he could not write poetry unless he felt that it originated in 'trance'. 'Trance' is important to him because it implies a state – one which approximates to that of 'waking dream' – in which all inhibitions and defences are removed. In such states words, magical entities for Graves, are allowed to exercise their full power, untrammelled by considerations of what the poet dislikes acknowledging in himself. Thus secrets are revealed. It is worth adding that hypnogogic trance, in which the brain emits the 'theta rhythms' associated with meditation and ecstasy, is now a well-recognized physiological state – a veritable 'waking dream'.

One might think, from this description of *On English Poetry*, that

Graves was the advocate of a rhythmical surrealist poetry, such as certain mostly French surrealists who eschewed *vers libre* did write. But that is not the case. For he shows an extremely scrupulous concern for the reader, and does not believe that surrealism can satisfy. He tolerates *vers libre*, but argues against it that 'there is no natural indication as to how the lines are to be stressed'. His insistence on 'regulated' verse reflects his urgent need for his poetry to do its job: resolve his conflicts in a disciplined way. 'Regulated' verse is right – for him; but his objection to others' use of a freer verse, or of metrical irregularities, sometimes amounts to a prejudice. Did it really matter if Owen put 'a foot too much' in some of his lines, or was Graves overindulging his passion for tidiness? He makes it clear that he believes a regular metre (upon which one can, indeed must, make variations) is always 'available' for a set of emotions, even if one has to invent it; he is absolutely against imposing a metre on emotions – as he thinks Swinburne, for example, did in 'Hertha'.

However, his insistence on spontaneity does need explanation in the face of his famous – indeed, to some notorious – habit of revision. No twentieth-century poet has put his poems through so many drafts, or revised so consistently. Graves's revising habit, however, is not primarily a cerebral process. Its main purpose is to sort out, into coherent order, the material 'given' in the original trancelike state, which, it is acknowledged, has no organizing power. Sometimes two or even three poems are 'given' at one time: these need to be separated. Also the trance state is recognized as being an essentially transitory one. The full poetic sense needs to be restored, recovered. The right technique may need to be found for the set of emotions 'given'. The poet is seen as one who perpetually struggles against not only his own stupidity but also against his defensive disingenuousness. He doesn't – and this comes straight out of Freud, though Freud wasn't the first to think of it – want to know the truth about himself. Hence the pain of writing poetry.

Graves's concern for the reader extends beyond technical matters, however. Even at this stage he had worked out an elaborate explanation of how poetry works for the reader. There is, or seems to be, an element of trickery involved – and he criticized himself for this later on. The reader is, he says,

> thrown off his balance temporarily by the novelty. . . . He has no critical
> weapons at his command, so he must follow the course which the poet

has mapped out for him. . . . Even where a conclusion is definitely expressed in a poem the reader often deceives himself into saying, 'I have often thought that before, but never so clearly,' when as a matter of fact he has just been unconsciously translating the poet's experience into terms of his own, and finding the formulated conclusion sound, imagines that the thought is originally his.

This is deliberately mischievous as well as arrogant, and is just the kind of thing to lead earnest critics to the conclusion that Graves is 'cynical'. However, though Graves had to struggle against sexual ignorance (or at least lack of sexual sophistication), and to combat his tendency to a holier-than-thou profession of purity (lecturing people about their womanizing and other 'vices' in surprisingly Victorian terms), earnestness, solemnity were never hindrances to him. Furthermore, he saw 'a sly sense of humour' as a necessary quality in poets; humour, like poetry – he says in *On English Poetry* – reconciles incongruities. There is little or nothing in the Graves canon that suggests itself for inclusion in *The Stuffed Owl*, that famous anthology of unintentionally funny verse. But although the genuine poem originates in a 'dream state' which has arisen from inner conflict, it must, according to Graves, be 'controlled': '. . . both the controlled and uncontrollable parts of the art . . . [are] helpless without the other'. The poet's 'conscious scrutiny' of his poem must satisfy him; the poem must not only be a sucessful and honest resolution of a problem, but also must play fair with the reader. The worst offence is to be a 'fake' poet. A 'bad' poet is someone who 'solves his emotional problems to his own satisfaction but not to anybody else's'; but fake poetry is 'the decay of poetry'. The fake poet is one who, unable to go into trance like the priest of old, 'imitates a state of trance', if necessary with the aid of drugs, and

> recalls someone else's dream which he alters slightly, and wraps his oracular answer in words recollected from the lips of genuine witch doctors.

His paradigm of the fake poet was later to be W. H. Auden, 'a synthetic poet who probably never wrote an original line in his life'. He never changed this view.

For the rest, *On English Poetry* is characterized by its concentration on the practical and by its irreverent humour (though the irreverence is only beginning to break through). His (then laboured) conception of the poet is as follows:

A poet in the fullest sense is one whom some unusual complications of early environment or mixed parentage develop as an intermediary between the small-group consciousnesses of particular sects, clans, castes, types and professions among whom he moves. To so many of these has he been formally enrolled as a member, and to so many more has he virtually added himself as a supernumerary member by showing a disinterested sympathy and by practising his exceptionally developed powers of intuition, that in any small-group sense the wide diffusion of his loyalties makes him everywhere a hypocrite and traitor.

But the rival sub-personalities formed in him by his relation to these various groups constantly struggle to reconciliation in his poetry, and in proportion as these sub-personalities are more numerous more varied and more inharmonious, and his controlling personality stronger and quicker at compromise, so he becomes a more or less capable spokesman of that larger group-mind of his culture which we somehow consider greater than the sum of its parts: so that men of smaller scope and more concentrated loyalties swallow personal prejudices and hear at times in his utterances what seems to them the direct voice of God.

In this confusion we see social conscience struggling with independence – but above all plenty of 'necessary arrogance'. However, Graves cannot be accused of trying to make it easy for himself. He argues for the (initial) spontaneity of true poetry, and acknowledges that what he calls 'the real stuff' is often slow to arrive.

He had the technical equipment to turn himself into an Augustan, or a didactic poet, or a really great translator. But he attacks this type of intellectual poetry; he chooses the most difficult way, and begins to heed internal rather than external pressures. To all intents and purposes, poetry is his religion, and magic (the magic, the mysterious qualities, of words) is his means.

Chapter Eight
1925–26

I

Living at Islip allowed Graves to settle down to some degree. He was able to effect a partial cure for his malaise, if only by having the opportunity to pull himself together in comparative isolation. Peter Quennell has given an impression of him at this time. Quennell was still a schoolboy, in Oxford to take an examination. He went with his father to visit Graves at his home at Islip. His father, who, according to Quennell, had a 'pure' mind, found Graves 'rough' but a 'decent sort of fellow'. Nancy they found 'fresh-cheeked and unaffected'. Robert's corduroy suit was, says Quennell, even rougher than he was. A number of 'wholesome noisy children' ran 'wild around their small house'. The food was 'plain and sensible', and Quennell senior was pleased to note that neither 'drank'. Quennell studied the poet's appearance: 'a nose broken like that of Michelangelo, and thick dark hair that curled on his forehead like the locks of Michelangelo's *David*, together with a sallow [the sallowness vanished when he got over his war neurosis] skin and mobile, slightly twisted mouth.' To his children, Quennell noticed, he was 'remarkably affectionate'; he told him that a poet ought to work in the midst of his family 'while he minded a fractious child or kept his eye on a bubbling saucepan'. But he 'wore the strained and troubled expression of a young man who had lately emerged from an inferno'. The inferno was doubtless the shop as well as the war.

Although Graves was, marginally, happier at Islip than he had been at Boars Hill, he was still extremely short of money – and at the mercy of a scatty wife who might one day ignore him and be rude to his friends, and on the next suggest a sudden trip (children and all) to get away from routine. On one occasion, in 1922, they spent a month touring the south coast in a 'derelict baker's van' drawn by a horse

103

that had been pensioned off in 1917. Catherine was then only four months old, and it rained for the whole time they were away. Later they 'adopted' the daughter of a tramp; fortunately she left after one winter.

Graves fitted in better with the village than he had at Boars Hill. There were no literary people, and he liked the rural ways. The villagers called him Captain, and his appearances for the football team aroused extreme controversy – his method of play was highly aggressive, for he considered the village standards 'ladylike'; his football was nothing like as elegant as his poetic technique, and he was not regarded as 'playing fair'. He and Nancy still called themselves socialists, and he was elected as Labour member of the parish council, on which he served for a year. He made himself unpopular with the gentry – but hardly toed a party line. He became disillusioned with parliamentary socialism before Labour formed a government, and was for a short time more sympathetic to communism – though he dropped all political opinion for good after 1926.

Marsh's *Georgian Poetry* volumes (1912–22) had made Graves's name well known. His first books had attracted some attention; but the postwar ones were mostly ignored. He might have done better to stick to Heinemann, but left him (temporarily) for Martin Secker when William Heinemann 'tried to teach me to write poetry', which he resented. He had an income of about £130 a year; this included presents from relatives as well as £16 rent from his cottage in Harlech, income from reviewing and poetry, and his war pension. There were also substantial gifts from Lawrence, and Sassoon generously helped more than once with what he called his 'Jew money'. His college exhibition dried up at the end of his course, though he had obtained permission from Sir Walter Raleigh to skip his finals and proceed to the degree of BLitt (the remarkably understanding Raleigh agreed to be his tutor on the understanding that he need not actually tutor him). Eventually *Poetic Unreason* (1925), already printed, was accepted as a thesis, and he obtained the BLitt, having been 'deemed' to have received his BA. The regular money was not enough – and, worse, his reputation had slipped badly. But he was, as he explains, idealistic in those days.

> I used to take the reviews of my poetry-books seriously. . . . I still believed it was possible to write poetry that was true poetry and yet could reach, say, a three or four thousand-copy sale. I expected some such success.

However, it was at Islip that he began to change his attitude. There were a number of reasons for this. He had become disenchanted with the notion of 'Georgian poetry'. When his volumes stopped selling he began to understand that he did not even really want them to sell; he did not want to be a 'popular' poet. He was becoming increasingly identified with his more pessimistic view of himself: as a man who was destined to have to write poetry to keep sane – to resolve his conflicts – and who would yet fail to be, as he put it, 'of public utility' (that is, his poetry would not help to resolve the conflicts of others – with whom he was getting out of sympathy – although his theory had stated that true poetry did just this). In short, he was in a state of depression. It is fortunate that he was, that he did not get taken up as a popular Georgian, and subsequently fade out at the end of the twenties – which is what happened to Sassoon and others less well known.

He had already shown, however, signs of disillusion at Boars Hill, and as early as 1919 had exhibited an unfashionable eclecticism in his literary editorship of *The Owl*, which ran for two numbers (it was revived as *Winter Owl* for one issue, November 1923). He had editorial help from W. J. Turner and from J. C. Squire, a good-hearted boozer who was far more conservative than Marsh – and by then in a position of greater literary power. Squire championed *Georgian Poetry* because it printed the feeble verse of his friends Edward Shanks and John Freeman, and of the rather more interesting Turner. The money for *The Owl* came from William Nicholson. The first number contained work by Masefield, Hardy, Sassoon, W. H. Davies, Max Beerbohm, Squire and Graves himself; the second took in poetry by Vachel Lindsay, Blunden and de la Mare. William Nicholson drew the picture of the owl that adorned the back cover, and Graves wrote the quatrain

> Athenian owl with feathered legs
> Stand emblem of our will
> To hunt the rat that sucks the eggs
> Of virtue, joy and skill

beneath it. The tone of the editorial foreword is unmistakable:

> It must be understood that 'The Owl' has no politics, leads to no new movement and is not even the organ of any particular generation – for that matter sixty-seven years separate the oldest and youngest contributors.
>
> But we find in common a love of honest work well done, and a distaste for shortcuts to popular success.
>
> 'The Owl' will come out quarterly or whenever enough suitable material is in the hands of the editors.

This is the familiar Graves speaking. And so he does himself something of an injustice in *Goodbye to All That* when he accuses himself, by implication, of perpetually seeking popular success for poetry in his early days; he had, in all the flush of confident youth, already denounced short cuts to it in his early twenties. But the public did not want this sort of candour. The magazine died. He had had high hopes for it, and must therefore just then have felt consoled by the publicity he was getting from *Georgian Poetry*.

Gordon Bottomley, then widely read and one of the main props of Marsh's venture, had written of 'his nimbleness and variety and the promise implicit in the vivid contrasts of his reactions' – this was passed on to him.

When Marsh's *Memoir* of Rupert Brooke appeared, as an introduction to *Collected Poems* (1918), Graves had been grateful enough to give his moral support to Marsh, who had had a dreadful time with Brooke's jealous and stupid mother – and who was depressed by the inevitable reaction against the notion of Brooke as the perfect twentieth-century man and great poet:

> How wrong about Rupert [Graves wrote to Marsh]. We all look up to him as to our elder brother and have immense admiration for his work from any standpoint, especially his technique, on which we all build. I know it is fashionable to dislike him: but no one does really, least of all R.N. [Nichols], S.S., or R.G.

He did not quite mean this, and thought Charles Sorley, Owen, Isaac Rosenberg and Sassoon far superior as war poets; but he wished to act in the role of comforter. He could be honest, too, in saying that, although himself more optimistic than 'all' his friends, 'my capacity for such prehistoric happiness as Rupert had is nothing'. Whether Rupert was really so happy is beside the point; what they all embodied in their memories or ideas of him was their feeling for the prewar days, now for ever lost. In 1945 he wrote a more considered judgement:

> Rupert Brooke . . . seemed very original to me in 1914. He would have become a man of affairs (had he lived), a liberal M.P., and written very little more worth reading. He was intoxicated with the high society to which Eddie Marsh introduced him, being a simple Rugby and Cambridge chap. [To M.S.-S., 8 March 1945]

This shows that Graves finds nothing to forgive himself for in having once admired Brooke.

Graves could not, however, conceal his feelings about the fourth volume of *Georgian Poetry* (1919). He told Marsh that he felt that the similarity between the verses of some of the contributors was 'a signal for someone with a personal style to take over the torch'. He recommended Blunden to Marsh's attention, but referred to himself as a 'Georgian infant'. On the subject of the fifth and last anthology (1922), put out when Georgianism was losing its hold on the public, he made himself plain: he told Marsh that he ought to divide it into two parts, one representing the 'senior' contributors and one the poets 'whose characters are entirely moulded by war experience'. Marsh ignored this, though he did include Peter Quennell and Frank Prewett (an Oxford friend, whose posthumous selected poems Graves introduced long after the end of the Second World War) at Graves's suggestion. Marsh was probably hurt by Graves's declaration that, while 'wild horses' would not drag names from him, the chief characteristic of the 'old' Georgians was their 'damnable dulness'. Still, though disenchanted, he did not have the heart to secede – which even the gentle de la Mare tried to do.

Graves's first publisher, Harold Monro of the Poetry Bookshop, put out a hurried book of criticism, *Some Contemporary Poets*, in November 1920. In it Monro dealt with almost every living poet. He waspishly wrote of Graves:

> He barks at the critics in truly dogmatic style . . . but we are not much daunted, not proposing to examine him too closely. The kindly, and ballad-like, and sometimes jocular intention that informs most of his verse is more suited to comment than criticism. One cannot say of him, at present that his poetry is either good or bad. . . . Too much importance has been attached to a pleasant and congenial instinct for making Rhymes. . . . He has shown insufficient profundity to justify a definite faith in his future. His art, as it may be at present understood, is one rather of intelligent adaptation than of personal invention.

This was written before publication of *The Pier-Glass*; but that volume failed to attract notice, although it deserved to do so. The passage depressed Graves, as he felt it partly true; but he never held a grudge against Monro, some of whose poetry he liked, though he insisted that he experimented 'with too long lines'.

He still felt defeated and worried about what was to become of himself, though he concealed it. To Nancy he decided that he must appear cheerful at all times, even when she scolded him. He vainly tried to work out the poison of his war memories in the form of a novel – but it would not come right. Although he had plenty of friends and acquaintances among the poets, Nancy made it difficult for him to entertain them at Islip. He felt uneasy in the company of Osbert and Sacheverell Sitwell, though he saw more of Edith Sitwell, to whom Nancy did not object:

> It was a surprise, after reading her wild *avant garde* poems, to find her gentle, domesticated, and even devout. When she came to stay with us she spent her time sitting on the sofa and hemming handkerchiefs. She used to write to me and Nancy frequently, but our friendship ended in 1926.

He dedicated a book, *Contemporary Techniques of Poetry*, to her 'in friendship'. But she quarrelled with him in 1926 on the grounds of his 'defiance of conventions'.

He published two books of poetry in 1923, *Whipperginny*, for which he went back to Heinemann, and *The Feather Bed*, the first of five small books and pamphlets he published with Leonard and Virginia Woolf at their Hogarth Press. Later he wrote that the reader he envisaged for these works 'was no more real a person than the conventional figure put in the foreground of an architectural design to indicate the size of a building.'

II

A letter Graves wrote to T. E. Lawrence in early 1922 records his state of mind. Parts of it are cryptic: the two men enjoyed teasing each other with learned riddles, some of which can never now be unravelled. Lawrence had certainly confided some of his problems to Graves; Graves, much more fully, had reciprocated.

Indeed, Lawrence was the only person to whom he could confide just at this time. The friendship with Blunden had cooled, and he had had more than enough at Boars Hill of the hysterical Nichols.

When T. E. Lawrence left Arabia in December 1921, he became depressed, sleepless and temporarily poverty-stricken. Whenever they met, and in correspondence, the two men discussed the problems of sexual desire. Lawrence told Graves as much as he told anybody about the famous Der'a incident: that he had been flogged, beaten up and sodomized – and that he had sexually enjoyed it. But he pretended that the affair had left him impotent, which it had not – for one of the conditions of the floggings which he began in 1923 to pay Bruce to inflict upon him was that they should be severe enough to produce 'sexual emission'. (He may, however, have meant 'impotent with women'; though he never went to bed with a woman.)

Prince,
Out of it seems a salty & desolate kingdom, Prince, you terrify me that such things can silently happen to princes & the world go wobbling contentedly on, & other princes continue to drink each other's healths, as if all was well & Nemesis had ended the reign of Croesus –

I must say, I had doubted you the monster you pretended to be, because *Belle Dame Sans Merci* & *Song of Contrariety* would have been as meaningless to you as my domesticities if that have [*sic*] been the truth. . . .

The poem [Lawrence's] is neither prose nor verse, but poetic quartz in which the veins of metre run. To be prose, the ear must not be drawn at all where into [*sic*] blind-alleys of iambic rhythm; you tempt and disappoint with blank-verse promises.

To be verse, the ear must be kept under control, & the delight the ear gets is in the variations from a norm or a sequence of norms; where there is no norm the hypnotic spell has no chance of taking effect. [There follow a few lines of specific criticism of Lawrence's text.]

I was so upset by your letter & the poem that I found myself looking at it as if it had been dictated to me (so you may have seen in some rough draft of mine a poem very often exactly in this form and I stare at it and there is a sort of Dry Bones miracle & the poem takes form and breath) and I don't know if you'll forgive my childishness in sending you what occurred but I did it to banish my own terrors:

(The Crusader on his dead Mistress)

Death, eager always to pretend
  Himself my servant in the land of spears,
Humble allegiance at the end
  Broke, where the homeward track your castle nears,
Let his white steed before my red steed press
And rapt you from me into quietness.

If anything happened to Nancy (whatever nonsense I talk now for fear of Nemesis) I naturally *would* react to self-imposed hunger, sleeplessness & avoidance of women: even the children about would hardly make me marry them a stepmother: the spirit cannot it seems be conjured into the grave. It may satisfy you to know that but for your £200 and £50 we could not have avoided a complete smash; and you are therefore already a more-than-godfather to the baby due today or tomorrow.

(The cheque restores an overdraft and enables me to face baker and milkman – bless your wit). . . .

Graves goes on to invite Lawrence to read Isaiah xxix 'with intelligence', dwelling on certain points, and to 'answer, mentally, to what does all this tend?'

He ends by quoting an early version of the famous 'Children of Darkness' ('We spurred our parents to the kiss . . . '):

> When biking to All Souls last week, I had started a poem which your last words in the college about the futility of Being, finished; and also your remarks about parental difficulties, I suppose. . . .

He writes out the poem and ends 'signature to record that I think it's one of my better efforts', and adds a postscript: 'That's all, but come & stay with us in March if you can. Neither Nancy no[r] I nor the children will molest you.'

The first two paragraphs of the letter refer to Lawrence's sexual difficulties in general. 'The poem' of the third paragraph accompanies the dedication of *Seven Pillars of Wisdom* to 'S.A.', which Lawrence had submitted to Graves for revision. Graves, shocked, at first guessed that 'S.A.' was Dahoum, the Arab waterboy whom Lawrence had loved and desired but not possessed; but Lawrence deliberately misled him, thus causing Graves later to erect an ingenious but false theory that S.A. was a woman. In the end he came to believe in this, and even devoted a lecture to it – until reminded of the truth.

'Song of Contrariety' is clearly a poem of sexual disillusion, though it retains faith in romantic values (I quote the original version):

> Far away is close at hand,
> Closed joined is far away,
> Love might come at your command
> Yet will not stay.
>
> At summons of your dream-despair
> She could not disobey,
> But slid close down beside you there
> And complaisant lay.
>
> Yet now her flesh and blood consent
> In waking hours of day,
> Joy and passion both are spent,
> Fading clean away.

Is the presence empty air,
　Is the spectre clay,
That Love, lent substance by despair,
Wanes, and leaves you lonely there
　On the bridal day?

'[La] Belle Dame Sans Merci' is an essay on Keats which Graves had shown Lawrence; it appeared in *On English Poetry*. The theory put forward in it is that Keats saw in his dead young brother Tom's face 'Fanny's mocking smile and sidelong glance'. This refers to Graves's version of Lawrence's reaction to the memory of the dead Dahoum.

It was to be a bitter disappointment to Graves when Lawrence vanished into the RAF later that year.

III

The poems of *Whipperginny* have been discussed by critics on the assumption that they are 'cynical', apparently an offensive state of mind. They are, however, the exact opposite: the main theme of the volume, when viewed overall, is the possibility of being honest with oneself and with other people without being cynical. The tone is clearly anti-cynical:

Is whiteness white?
　O then, call it black:
Farthest from the truth
　Is yet half-way back.

This stanza, from 'The Dialecticians', is indeed sarcastic – yet it acknowledges, under this guise, that absolute denial of the truth, embracement of the false, is indeed one way of learning the sweeter although more unkind taste of truth. It seems as though at least some critics have denied the tone of the poem and taken its last (not very effective) stanza as a literal injunction, instead of as ironic:

Contentions weary,
　It giddies all to think;
Then kiss, girl, kiss!
　Or drink, fellow, drink!

Graves was doing little kissing and no drinking. He was desperately unhappy with a marriage that had broken down but was none the less proceeding; and he now felt isolated from almost all his fellow poets. He did not publish this exquisitely unpleasant brief poem (I quote the original version, written in 1922) until many years later, but it records how he often felt:

> I'd die for you, or you for me,
> So furious is our jealousy –
> And if you doubt this
> Kill me outright, lest I kill you.

Of course he and Nancy did not by any means hate each other all the time. Only for most of it. She felt angry that she had married him; and he (although he tried to hide his immediate feelings because he felt that they were not virtuous) was in despair because he had seriously sought true and perpetual love in marriage. There was often an atmosphere of hate in the house. What he found particularly painful to accept in himself was that he had fallen out of love. This presented him with an intolerable puzzle. Many of the poems in *Whipperginny* are downright nasty about it, in a Swiftian manner. Graves, like many other poets at such times, enjoyed jerking the sentimental complacency of his reader; it relieved his sense of unease. But true cynicism in a poet would amount to the abandonment of true for false poetry (in the sense he had shortly before set out). The tone of *Whipperginny*, with the exception of a few poems like 'An English Wood', is self-castigatory; but it is also hostile to a public that would not accept either his poetry or its reasons. In the Author's Note prefacing the volume he spoke of the 'increasing emotional stress' within him, relating it to 'war neurosis'; and he stated that in the following poems there were 'evidences of a greater detachment', of 'less emotional intensity' – 'and the appearance of a new series of problems in religion, psychology and philosophy'. What he could not forgive himself for – later – was what he diagnosed as his surrender in these years to critical precepts, to the composition of poetry along preconceived, 'philosophical' lines.

He was unfair to himself. *Whipperginny* is an interesting volume of poems by a man of only twenty-eight – and often more than interesting; a fair number of the poems in it were destined to end up in his *Collected Poems*.

Though he now lacked public attention there were several writers interested in his poetry, as there always have been. Eliot was one of them – but he never managed to write about it, because he could never make up his mind what to say; the effects Graves achieved mystified him, as he was to tell him twenty-odd years later when Faber and Faber published *The White Goddess*. The critical reception of *Whipperginny* was bad. He laid himself open, he wrote, to 'accusations of trying to get publicity and increase . . . sales by a wilful clowning modernism'. The fact is that he started, in this volume, to go in a direction that few could follow; and when they could understand, they did not like what they understood. Graves seemed morbid and sexually unpleasant – although one wonders why the now famous and witty 'Richard Roe and John Doe' did not give immediate delight. Yet even this has been called an 'exercise in cynicism' – in which case all anecdotal and epigrammatic poetry with a down-to-earth psychological point to make is also 'cynical'.

In this book, which includes the disturbing and deliberately anti-romantic 'Children of Darkness', Grave's diction becomes markedly more individual. It is obvious that he had been rereading the metaphysical poets – and Rochester, too – more carefully. The volume was certainly 'modernist', but not fashionably so. It firmly rejected Georgianism, but, in contrast to the kind of poetry being written by Eliot, Pound and their imitators, which concerned itself almost exclusively with public themes, it concentrated on private ones. Eliot influentially commended the metaphysicals; but Graves resembled them more closely. Yet the book was dedicated to Edward Marsh, doubtless in order to console this overflowingly good-natured man for its author's desertion from the Georgian fold. Asking him to accept the dedication, Graves wrote in a letter:

> The psychology of the human race is the same as it ever was, but the proved research by capable scientists is getting on paper now, and the Poet may take advantage of it surely. Freud is unattractive but his self-analyses are the more likely to be fairly true to Truth if they show him in an unattractive light. Dr Rivers is my mentor in these matters and I am inclined to believe in his theories because they are all tested by the treatment of war-neurosis cases – including Sassoon, Owen, and Frank Prewett [Owen was not in fact treated by Rivers].

All this was beyond Marsh, and Sassoon – even though he personally worshipped Rivers – shared his feelings. He had always envied Graves as possessing superior knowledge to himself ('he knew so much more than I did about almost everything except foxhunting'), and he now took up the pose of an 'ordinary man' (as befitted one who would remain a Georgian): 'surely poetry should be comprehensible to ordinary intellects without any scientific jargonry about dreams, etc., being dragged in by the lunar complex?' Sassoon was in a way quite right; but was deliberately missing the point. Graves was prepared to face up to the unpleasantness of human nature, even though he loathed the process; for his pains he was dismissed by the Georgians, who yearned for a past which no longer existed, and yet was ignored by the 'modernists', whose procedures concentrated on the break-up of traditional technique and on the 'objective' expression of cultural despair. If Eliot had taken the path Graves took he would have written about his unhappy (first) marriage; Pound would have examined his own tendency to drift into schizoaffective illness. While these poets projected themselves and their intelligences, so to say, into the mainstream of culture (largely an abstraction, except in strictly anthropological terms), Graves subjected himself to critical self-examination, and used very modified Freudian concepts to do it. He was the only English poet to take this line, and it is no wonder that readers found *Whipperginny* bewilderingly difficult. The choice of the title 'Whipperginny' is indicative: this is not only a name for purgatory and for an old card game, as the title poem states – but also, as he knew perfectly well, a term of abuse applicable to women.

During the time he was writing the *Whipperginny* poems Graves came under the direct influence of philosophy, in the person of a Bengali lawyer called Basanta Mallik. Mallik, after graduating from Calcutta University some years before the war, became assistant tutor to the children of the Maharajah of Nepal, and in due course his trusted servant. Mallik had been in Oxford for more than ten years studying 'British political psychology'; this experience turned him, perhaps not unsurprisingly, into a philosopher. His philosophy, as Graves describes it, seems to have closely resembled the views of the sceptic Graves himself; only he had thoroughly formulated his ideas, and thus oversimplified them. And his 'characteristically Indian insistence on ethics . . . [and on] the necessity of strict self-discipline' appealed to the virtuist in Graves. (It inevitably happens that those who influence Graves do so because they reflect, or seem to reflect, his own inner thoughts. This was the case with Laura Riding, and, later, with the Shahs.) Mallik's was essentially a subjective philosophy: he 'believed in no hierarchy of ultimate values or the possibility of any unifying religion or ideology', and he rejected those conventional social values which Graves also could not stomach. But he 'recommended constant self-watchfulness against either dominating or being dominated by any other individual'. Graves should have been warned.

The volume in which Mallik's hand is most clearly seen is *Mock Beggar Hall* (1924), another Hogarth Press publication. 'Interchange of Selves' purports to be a 're-Englishing' of an 'actionless' drama, in prose, by Mallik himself. Actually Graves, in his temporary enthusiasm for Mallik, got him to write a play on lines he suggested, and then completely rewrote it. Its message is that conflict is all evil, that stoical endurance is the only solution. However, being didactic, stoicism did not satisfy Graves even then, and Mallik's ideas only served to get him through a difficult time. Didacticism and a philosophy which owed much to the Indian tradition of indifference to life could act as only a temporary refuge for a man whose appetite for life was so voracious.

The poems of this period challenge the conventional notion of history, anticipating, though in a more playful way, his acceptance of Laura Riding's insistence that 'history' had 'finished'. 'Knowledge of God' is a comparatively subtle poem, suffering but little from Graves's short-lived attempt 'to be more philosophical'. It begins 'So far from praising he blasphemes/Who says that God has been or is', and ends by telling the reader to do what he likes ('Rule, or be ruled by certain fate') but on no account to 'cast [a] net for God'. At the core of these supposedly philosophical poems there is a mockery of philosophy. The true message, not only of this but of many of the other poems written in the Mallik period, is that it is foolish to seek for first causes. What is taken for 'God' in all the orthodox religions is now seen as evil (as Graves wrote later: 'The true fiend rules in God's name'). He was beginning to take the line of thought expressed in the essay *Mrs Fisher* (1928): that life was 'goddawful' in what he called an 'anti-poetic sense'. It was in this anti-Establishment spirit that he recommended Lawrence to read Isaiah xxix – about the 'hosts of iniquity besieging Ariel [Jerusalem]' and their dire fate (though there was a meaning pertinent to Lawrence alone in this, too: a reference to those officials who had frustrated what he had tried to do for the Arabs).

> We do not laugh only because to laugh would mean seeing goddawful things as they are; and if we did this, we should do something about them before we laughed. Perhaps even then we should not laugh, and perhaps even posterity will not laugh – either because it will see how goddawful things really were or, more likely, because they will still be equally goddawful and posterity will have inherited our capacity for looking absent-mindedly away from them.

From almost the beginning of the time (a year or so) during which Mallik seemed to influence him, he was, at the heart of himself, already rejecting all 'systems' as useless. It was inevitable that, for a time, he would tend to try to turn poetry itself into a system, if only in order to oppose all the others. He needed meanwhile to put systems-in-general to practical test, in order to complete this rejection.

The Mallik episode saw a distinct increase in poetic power and concentration, and the beginning of an ability to come to terms with the 'goddawful' external world. Graves was learning that he could express his disdain for head-in-the-clouds, nominally logical public behaviour, in satire and grotesquerie. One of the most sustained of his early poems, 'Alice', combines the two.

Later Graves's imagination, the 'unconscious' as revealed in dreams, would be projected upon the outside world – which will be emptied, so to speak, of all its nonsense (goddawfulness) about politics and (to quote again from *Mrs Fisher*)

ABBEY ENLARGEMENTS. . . . WHAT CONSTABLE FOUND. . . . PITH BATH DEATH MYTH: No further development reported today. . . . MAN WITH 14 SONS. . . . FASHION NOTE. . . . Does any reader know a poem which describes life as a lump of clay which, with a bag of tools, man can fashion into a stumbling block or stepping-stone?

And so on and so forth: read any newspaper or American thesis on the meaning of meaning of meaning, or examine 'the book-reviewing system'. It is not a question of misanthropy, of which Graves's more obtuse critics have accused him, but of seeing public life as loveless. No wonder the concept of *báraka* appealed to him when he encountered it some forty years later.

The poem itself, if it can be dragged out into the light, is for Graves the residue of good in whatever situation produced it. We must always be at it: delving into the imagination, producing mysteries, invoking the power (magic) of words; what is involved is a perpetual process of self-revelation, which will hopefully end when the act of loving has been learned. But it never is. . . . At its most serious, then, this existential poetry must of necessity be self-critical, at least when it is not jeering at the pretensions of the world.

Like every poet in the romantic tradition Graves felt guilty because he wrote poetry. It seemed to him 'less important to be well than to be a good poet'. As early as 1920, when he wrote the still-famous 'Lost Love', he had become consciously aware that his compulsion towards poetry was irresistible. The man who has lost his love (we can take it either way: she has gone to another man, or he has fallen out of love) is turned into a seer, given magical powers. He 'wanders god-like' and, like the mythical heroes of Irish legend, he can see through walls and watch the spirit of a dead man flying up from his mouth. 'Lost Love' is in this sense the first fully realized White Goddess poem. Another early example is 'Full Moon', written in 1923, and included in *Mock Beggar Hall*. Here the moon, which figures throughout Graves's – as throughout others' – poetry as a symbol for woman, is already 'the tyrannous queen above', 'sole mover of . . . fate'. But at this time the nature of love is unknown to him; he is busy transforming it from an abstraction, and to do that he must write a poetry that dwells upon erotic detail, upon lust, upon what distracts from love and yet, paradoxically, leads to it. In Graves's work of the Islip period we have what is often no more than a flash of guilty understanding presented to us in a vivid, dramatic and concentrated form.

The Shout, a story he wrote in 1924, was probably, in its original (8000 word) form, the fullest representation of his haunted state that he achieved in those years. The film of it (1978) rather alters the plot, but realizes the atmosphere well. Unfortunately Graves could not find a publisher for it in 1924, and had to wait five years. When one came up he insisted that Graves should cut it to 5000 words, to fit into a series of uniform format, 'which was too drastic a condensation, and I have since lost the original version'. He has said that the victim-figure of the tale, Richard, was a 'surrogate for myself'. But in fact all the five main male characters – a learned madman called Crossley, a psychiatrist, Richard (whose happy marriage is wrecked) and the magician Charles, as well as the narrator – are 'sub-personalities' of the author. But at another level the story functions as prophecy, as he recognized soon after he wrote it.

The fundamental thesis of the story, though it does not mention poetry, is that the practice of poetry (magic) turns a man into a monster, and his hitherto 'ordinary' beloved into a tyrannous, capricious, cruel and sinister being. Rachel, Richard's wife in the story, falls in love with the murderous magician Charles, whereupon she immediately hates Richard 'for being ill . . . lazy . . . and a sham'. When he groans in agony she pushes him down into 'nettles and old iron' and laughs 'loudly'. Later the brutal Charles tells Rachel, 'At ten o'clock . . . you and I sleep together.' Richard thinks that Charles has 'gone mad'; but Rachel answers Charles, 'Why, of course, my dear.'

Richard decides that he himself is mad, and that he has lost his 'luck', and so goes out to smash up his own soul, with a hammer. However, 'one may recognise the soul of another man or woman but one can never recognise one's own. . . .' Then he comes across Rachel's 'and recognised it (a slim green stone with glints of quartz in it) because she was estranged from him at the time. . . .'

The 'glints of quartz' here recall what he had told Lawrence in his letter about his botched poem; but now they run not through Lawrence's prose but through the soul of Richard's wife. He was already more than merely fumbling, here, for the sovereign Muse he needed. As he wrote, to Riding, in his 'Dedicatory Epilogue' to *Goodbye to All That* in 1929: 'Let me . . . recall . . . *The Shout*, which, although written two [*sic*] years ago, belongs here; blind and slow like all prophecies – it has left you out entirely. . . .' It seemed to leave her out because she to him, then at least, was pure quartz.

But why mention *The Shout*, and near the end of a passage of supreme importance to him at the time? Why did it 'belong' there? Because of course it omitted 'her' so absolutely that its deepest meaning (expressed in the title) lay in that omission. The magician Charles certainly stood for Graves-the-poet in the story-as-autobiography: it was a recognition of the destructiveness inherent in the practice of poetry, and of overtones even more sinister. But Charles's terrible, magical and killing shout obtrudes; it makes the sleeping Rachel's 'nerves [cry] out in pain at once' and pierces her 'through and through with a beam of some intense evil light' and twists her 'inside out.' It is superb as a component of a regular supernatural yarn, but its function is not explained. And it is not delivered by one of the right sex. He was one day, no surrogate for himself, to hear that dreadful magic shout – but not from Charles. The prophecy was blinder and slower, and yet more exact, than he dreamed in that time when

> Snows melted,
> Hedges sprouted, the moon tenderly shone,
> The owls trilled with tongues of nightingale

and when he did not know that 'These were all lies, though they matched the time' – or that they would bring him 'less than luck'.

IV

Graves wrote few other books during the Islip period. The most substantial was *Poetic Unreason*. *The Meaning of Dreams* (1924) was a hurried hash-up of Freudian dream-theory which 'fell flat; as indeed it deserved to do'. *John Kemp's Wager* (1925), a ballad opera, failed to get off the ground because it made the error of treating its folk sources too self-consciously.

The Marmosite's Miscellany (1925), a 421-line satire, with notes, demonstrates Graves's growing independence of 'schools' of poetry, but is not venomous enough to draw blood; he published it, first in a magazine and then with the Hogarth Press, under the pseudonym of 'John Doyle' – but made no serious attempt to hide his identity. The seven-line stanzas are skilfully handled, and the punch is there – but concealed behind too much facetiousness and effortful good temper.

The underrated *My Head! My Head!* (1925) is more interesting as being the first of his unorthodox biblical exegeses; 'it was', he writes, 'an ingenious attempt to repair the important omissions in the biblical story' of Elisha and the Shunamite woman (II Kings). This little work exemplifies his lifelong fascination with the Bible – his passion for 'restoring' ancient and sacred texts, the more eminent the better, along matriarchal rather than patriarchal lines; and his conviction that the key to truth lies in Woman and her mysteries. He had been reading deeply in the works of James Frazer, which he then accepted more or less uncritically; and had been studying the early history of the Jews, chiefly in Frazer's *Folklore in the Old Testament* (1918).

Contemporary Techniques of Poetry (1925) is a witty essay gently dissociating himself from all his contemporaries except Hardy and Frost. This was his third Hogarth Press publication. It is presented as a political analogy: the conservative traditionalists like Herbert Trench (by then a figure of fun) who abjure all 'filth'; the left-wingers who are 'hooligans' and towards whom his hostility is modified if only because a few of them (including Sassoon and Edith Sitwell) were his friends; and the 'Liberals' such as Blunden and Masefield. He has some acute things to say about technique, and although the whole piece is presented as a good-natured joke not to be taken seriously, it can easily be seen, by reading between the lines, that Graves was growing exasperated by the necessity of being 'nice' in order not to be put on the breadline. He has recorded that he was becoming increasingly weary of sounding tolerant about the 'dud books of poetry', which he had been reviewing, fairly politely by his standards, for some five years in various magazines.

Another Future of Poetry (1926) is a short essay, again published by the Hogarth Press, which attacks rhetorical poetry and the notion that science must be the 'way of the future'.

Poetic Unreason (1925) is a longer book. It is not such a bad one as Graves thought, for much of its description of the psychological processes attending the creation of poetry remains true. He himself has put his finger on its main weakness: it failed to distinguish between the 'supra-logical' thought processes of the poet and the 'sub-logical' ones of 'the common psychopath'. There is a difference, certainly; but no one has yet successfully made the distinction – and Graves of all people has reason, if not from his own practice, to know that the relationship between the two processes is not necessarily a tenuous one. He has met poets who were 'psychopaths' (in the loose sense in which he here uses it), though hardly 'common' ones.

Poetic Unreason is his most overtly 'Freudian' book – especially in its dissection and revision of his own poem 'The Bedpost'. It was useful to him as an exercise, too, even though he wrote it some ten times over. It confirmed his view that words, when combined in a certain way, possess a latent as well as a manifest meaning. He blamed himself bitterly, soon afterwards, for having given the impression that the sole use of poetry was to 'cure' people (poets and readers) of their neuroses; and for implying that the poet could 'manufacture' it. (In the criticism of his old age he rather lazily reverts to this view.)

It is certainly a confused book, and he says as much in *The Common Asphodel*. But underlying its uncertainties is the clear belief that poetry is 'given', and that, once given, it must be respected by its receiver, put into decent order. The crypto-Freudian theories put forward here, and the rest, are substitutes for what he truly needed: something exterior to himself, to which he could devote himself. His unhappy mind was busily conjuring up some phantom woman.

But it was not to be Nancy. She was becoming ill and she fitted in less and less well with his vision of a Muse. He felt desolate. In those bad years spent at the World's End Mallory died on Everest, Sir Walter Raleigh of typhus while out East, Lawrence went to the Tank Corps, Mallik returned to India – and other close friends died unexpectedly or vanished from the scene. He felt increasingly bitter. Was this a punishment? What for?

But there were lighter moments. Nancy acquired a car which was not only mechanically unreliable and unsafe, but was also driven by her with a recklessness that became the talk of Islip. He could laugh at that, and hotly defend her mistakes to indignant neighbours. Like an economist defending a money policy he had a great strength here: he knew nothing about the subject. But such diversions were few, and even these held physical dangers.

Then the doctor told us that if Nancy wished to regain her health she must spend the winter [1925–26] in Egypt.

And so he acquired a 'job in Egypt, at a very high salary, and with little work to do'. It was 'Professor of English Literature' at the new 'Royal Egyptian University' in Cairo. He drops, in his autobiography, the names of several of the people who, he claims, helped him obtain it: Lawrence, Arnold Bennett, John Buchan, 'Mr Asquith, now the Earl of Oxford, who had taken a fatherly interest in me, and often visited our cottage. . . .'

It was the end of an epoch in his life. And it is unlikely that even this gifted seer through flint walls, this poet enamoured of the moon in its phases, recollected – as he packed up to leave England at the end of 1925 and contemplated the future – these lines from his own poem 'Witches', which he had included in *Mock Beggar Hall*:

> Be wary, lest on unbelief
> The cloak of dark one day be spread,
> Time shall be grief and Space be grief
> And Love in accidie lie dead,
> And broomstick rites alone remain
> To lend your cramping pain relief.

Chapter Nine
1926

Robert Graves first met Laura Riding in person on 2 January 1926. She was within a fortnight of her twenty-fifth birthday. He went, accompanied by William Nicholson, to meet her at Waterloo Station. He caught sight of her, a small, tired, over-made-up figure in the crowd of passengers disembarking from the boat train from France.

'My God!' he said to Nicholson, 'what am I going to do?'

Nicholson did not stay to give an answer; he left in robust horror. But Graves soon changed his mind. He tersely commemorated the event in the 2 January entry of his diary for 1936: '10th anniversary of first meeting Laura.'

Who was Laura Riding, remembered by Peter Quennell as a 'pale mop-headed young woman' and by Tom Matthews as 'small, severe', 'primly neat', 'very nearly ugly, or at least repellent – when her deep-sunk eyes went dead as stone (or a lidded snake's) and her normal pallor faded to the tone of chalk . . . old enough to be my mother' (Tom and she were born on the same day)?

She was born in New York City on 16 January 1901. Her mother (her father's second wife) came from what she describes as 'downtown Manhattan'. Her father, Nathaniel Reichenthal, Austrian born, had emigrated to America when he was about fourteen. Both parents were Jewish, 'but' – Riding has added – 'not religiously so'. Reichenthal was a tailor; but he soon took to 'consistently unsuccessful' business enterprises and, more enthusiastically, to socialism.

He was active in the American Labour movement, and Riding inherited from him her notoriously unrelenting persistence in exercising her principles in face of opposition and misunderstanding (both real and imagined). Her own principles, however, have never been socialistic although (she has written) her father brought her up 'sternly in his political faith', and hoped that she would become 'an American Rosa Luxemburg'. His idealism and proneness to 'unsuccessful enterprises', however, she did inherit; she transformed and intensified those tendencies.

Nathaniel's unhappy business affairs necessitated many hopeful changes of address, so that Riding attended some dozen primary schools. However,

> ... I was lucky enough to be able to spend all four high-school years at Girls' High School, Brooklyn, where I received a remarkably thorough education in a number of subjects. ... With the help of three scholarships I went to Cornell University, where I took a general arts course.

In 1920, while at Cornell, Riding married a teaching assistant in history there called Louis Gottschalk. The marriage did not work out, and (Louis Gottschalk wrote in the early fifties) 'ended [1925] in sheer incompatibility and divorce'. Gottschalk regarded her as 'undereducated'.

Having married, Riding abandoned Cornell and enrolled in some courses at Illinois, where her husband had obtained a post. In 1923 Gottschalk went on to the University of Louisville, as an assistant professor; here Laura Riding got her first taste of the South – and became aware of the powerful and influential Fugitives, a group of poets of whom the most enduring, in the public eye, have proved to be John Crowe Ransom, Allen Tate (both now dead) and the later entrant, Robert Penn Warren. It was through their respective links with the Fugitives that Graves and Riding were brought together.

The Fugitive group, whose official inception dates from the publication of their poetry periodical *The Fugitive* in April 1922, emanated from Vanderbilt University, Nashville, Tennessee. It could never have come into being had it not been for Sidney Mttron Hirsch, who (presumably) conferred upon himself his middle name (pronounced 'Met-tát-ron', so that the first syllable is scarcely heard). Hirsch was the only fully fledged Fugitive not a student or teacher at Vanderbilt; but he lived only a block from the campus. From a wealthy Jewish Nashville family, Hirsch (1885–1961) had been sailor, boxer, socialite, mystic, numerologist, Cabalist (in the Cabala – and elsewhere in Jewish mysticism – Metatron is an angel who is none other than the 'lesser YHVH [Jehovah]', the supreme angel into whom Enoch was transformed after his ascent to heaven), occultist, poetaster, pageant-playwright – and, chiefly, charming, vaguely sinister and persuasive catalyst to a group of eager, intelligent and mostly gifted young men. In retrospect they were to regard him with affection, but also as an eccentric crackpot. The other leading spirit was Ransom, who had more coherent notions about the function and future of poetry. Inasmuch as *The Fugitive* had any one coordinating editor it was he (though Donald Davidson and Allen Tate took their turns in editing it); but the title of the magazine was certainly Hirsch's. His notion of the poet was that of a gnostic wanderer ('fugitive') possessed of mysterious knowledge.

The view of poetry held by Ransom, who was the chief theorist of the group, is pertinent. When Graves published his *On English Poetry* with Alfred Knopf in New York, Ransom reviewed it in the third issue of *The Fugitive* (October 1922), making it the subject of his editorial. The book hardly touched on prosody, and Ransom used this fact as a point of departure to express his own ideas about what he considered to be the most important issue in American poetry at that time. But Ransom's attitude to Graves himself was sympathetic:

> The charming personality of Graves expresses itself without embarrassment in prosodical verse. But some of the most brilliant of contemporary minds [he meant Eliot and Pound] have apparently been unable to do this.

This review led Graves to write a grateful letter to Ransom, whose *Poems about God* (1919) he had greatly admired – with two immediate results. Two poems by Graves appeared in the fourth *Fugitive*; and, on 30 October 1924, at Graves's (and, oddly, Eliot's) instigation, Leonard and Virginia Woolf published at their Hogarth Press a selection of Ransom's poems, *Grace After Meat*, with an introduction by Graves (and a dedication to him from Ransom). The twenty poems were selected by Graves. Thus Graves first introduced an important American poet to the English public. *The Feather Bed*, his own most thoroughgoing 'Freudian' poem, has an 'introductory letter' to 'Ransome' [*sic*].

What is interesting in Ransom's view of poetry is what has been called his 'fury against abstractions'. He rightly discerned a similar tendency in Graves.

Ransom at this time was most concerned to attack the smug claims of the scientific attitude (as Graves did in *Another Future*); he was then less interested in the (themselves abstract?) concepts of 'structure' and 'texture', or in 'close analysis' of texts. These concepts, and variants of them, became the chief features of the 'new criticism' which Ransom helped to create – but later found wanting. In his early days the American was concerned to demonstrate that whereas complacent scientism was 'monistic', poetry was 'pluralistic', and 'satisfied the whole man': 'the excellence of art is in its superfluities, since it accompanies these abstracts [the scientific processes which "crucify our organic sensibility while they drive furiously towards their abstracts"] with much of that tissue of the concrete in which they were discovered.' This is certainly a language and an attitude with which Graves sympathized. It influenced him deeply.

Ransom immediately saw that the best of Riding's poetry, of which he first became aware in 1923, when she sent him 'sheaves' of it for consideration, was *not* abstract, even though this charge was persistently made against it, and over a very long period. Furthermore, though Ransom was convinced of the necessity of a classical kind of prosody, he was not so dogmatic that he rejected Riding for her non-metrical technique. Her 'The Quids' (of which I give the first stanza), which appeared in the eleventh issue (February 1924), can hardly be called 'metrical':

> The little quids, the monstrous quids,
> The everywhere, everything, always quids,
> The atoms of the Monoton,
> Each turned an essence where it stood,
> Ground a gisty dust from its neighbours' edges,
> Until a powdery thoughtfall stormed in and out –
> The celebration of a slippery quid enterprise.

Tate, too, was impressed with the poetry Laura Riding sent; he asked for more. As any other young poet would be (she was just twenty-two) she was excited. But her reaction was hardly what the members of the group expected.

Before her recognition by Ransom and Tate – whom she would have seen as the leading runners in a group now capturing wide attention – she had published a few poems in *Poetry Chicago* and other magazines, had written a novel (unpublished) and part of another, and was, by every available account, an 'intense, unhappy woman'. The interest with which the Fugitives viewed her poetry impelled her – intense and unhappy or not – into an outburst of oversanguine activity.

The group was running short of money, and decided to launch a campaign to obtain some, partly through raising more subscriptions, and partly through pledges from patrons. Their most fervent supporter was Riding, who 'adopted *The Fugitive* cause as her own', and even offered herself as 'secretary to the board of editors', which the board of editors neither wanted nor could afford.

She worked unceasingly and untiringly to gain support for them, even asking, for example, permission to speak of them to women's clubs. She sent them lists of her acquaintances, with details of their finances, personal habits and likes and dislikes; and she told them that when she returned from New York – to which she had gone to find a job – she would continue to work for *The Fugitive*. John L. Stewart, basing his judgement on what he learned from other members, calls her collection campaign

> pathetic, funny, and unsuccessful in its attempt to flatter and cajole support from prominent people who had never heard of the group.

She approached the bemused philistines (among them 'wealthy Louisville dowagers') from whom she hoped to raise funds or subscriptions by informing them, in proselytizing and self-righteous terms, of what they ought to do. Her main motive seems to have been the advancement of her own work, since although she was, verbally, lavishly grateful to the Fugitives ('Dear Present Editor of the Fugitive', she wrote to Davidson in July 1924), she did not, apparently, take any interest in their poetry, even though she supported their programme by implication. (When in August 1924 Tate felt that Davidson should reject some of her poems, he warned him to use tact; she had, he told Davidson, an 'extreme sensitiveness to rejection'.) Yet Riding has insisted upon a quality of rectitude especial to herself ('my word-style had a peculiar rectitude of accent', she was to write in the mid-fifties), and has resolutely denied that criticism of or even simply writing about her is anything other than offensive, untrue, 'malignant drivel' and so on.

She wrote (1975)

> I have no influences on myself to record, or membership of any school. (In the early twenties I was made an honorary member of a group of Southern poets that called itself 'The Fugitives'. But I had no programmatic association with them. . . .)

When Laura Riding turned up in Nashville she was found to be 'frighteningly intense', wanting 'life on terms of immediate, instinctive action, however grotesque or absurd it might seem to others'; 'she expected a more emotional involvement with her fellow poets than any of them cared for'. She 'claimed that her consciousness of a situation *was* the poetry of that situation'.

The visit went badly: 'to these serious, rather courtly gentlemen, it must have seemed odd to admit a pert young woman on an equal basis. . . . Mrs Gottschalk and Hirsch quarreled, and the whole event ended in confusion.' Despite this, she was elected – mainly at Ransom's behest – an honorary member of the group (in early 1925); and she paid another visit to Nashville, where she is said to have 'overstayed her welcome at the hospitable Frank home [Sidney Hirsch, now a semi-invalid, was living with his sister, Rose Hirsch Frank, and her family] . . . and left at last in a temper'.

The general conclusion of the historians of the Fugitive movement is summed up by Louise Cowan: 'Miss Riding had tried to assume leadership in the project and ended by causing some little dissension. . . .'

Of the Fugitives, only Tate had met her before she visited Nashville – when passing through Louisville in early 1924. How intimate the two became has not been recorded. He told Davidson in a letter of 21 February 1924:

> Her intelligence is pervasive. It is in every inflexion of her voice, every gesture. . . . But always you get the conviction that the Devil and all Pandemonium couldn't dissuade her of her tendency.

Nearly fifty years later, asked at a London party 'what she was like', he replied with unforgivable terseness, 'All right from the neck down.'

In the summer of 1924 Allen Tate married the novelist Caroline Gordon, in New York. In the early autumn of 1925 Laura Riding moved to New York, where she lived near the Tates and met many of their friends – in particular Hart Crane, whom she and Graves were to encounter, briefly, in London a few years later. Despite her unfortunate experiences at Nashville, she retained all her idealism and enthusiasm, and, writes Stewart, impressed Tate's circle in New York – who were not Fugitives – with her 'brilliance and energy': 'it was not long before she was involved in a number of projects.' Tate, in a letter to Davidson written in the autumn of 1925, commented: 'Laura's successes drive on apace. That young lady has more energy than a phalanx of dynamos, with seven billy-goats thrown in.' Crane wrote to Slater Brown, for some time an associate of certain of the Fugitives, 'The engrossing female at most of these ["numerous 'celebrations' "] has been "Rideschalk-Godding" [later he changed this to "Laura Riding Roughshod"], as I have come to call her, and thus far the earnest ghost of acidosis has been kept well hence.' The 'earnest ghost of acidosis' is a reference to Riding's venomously exact and yet often simultaneously wrong-headed appraisals of others which were to be discussed more frequently than her poetry. This period Riding was later to describe to a correspondent as that of her 'drinking and dancing days'; but they did not last long.

The repercussions of her brief affair with Tate led her to form a special attachment for a Deyán child, Francisca, six years later, and she began her poem *Laura and Francisca* (1931):

> My name, as the title shows,
> Is Laura, and hers Francisca.
> And my age must be thirty,
> And hers must be I should say six,
> Judging by and judging by.

By the end of 1925 she had got through some of her difficulties, and recovered some of her composure, though not without making herself the subject of gossip. For example – and it is only one of many – the poet Louise Bogan, who was jealous of Riding's poetic accomplishments and anxious to suppress her work, described her in a (now published) letter to Morton Zaubel (19 February 1940 – when Riding had provided new material for talk on her return to the States) as 'Blue Butter Balls', a phrase whose meaning may be inferred from, say, Wentworth and Flexner's *Dictionary of American Slang*.

Riding now rejected America as a land of hope for herself or for humanity, and left hurriedly for Europe. Her most recent statement about the reasons for her decision to emigrate appears in *Contemporary Poets* (1975).

At the close of 1925, after a period of uncertainty, I went abroad to live. I had found my American fellow-poets more concerned with making individualistic play upon the composition-habitudes of poetic tradition than with what concerned me: how to strike a personal accent in poetry that would be at once an authentic truth-compulsion, of universal force; I saw them as combining something less than complete poetic seriousness with something less than complete personal seriousness. In the English and cross-Atlantic atmosphere, there was, instead of crowding individualism, a loose assemblage of unsure position, occupied with a varying show of modernistic daring: I had there solitariness in which to probe the reality of poetry as a spiritual, not merely literary, inheritance.

Just before she first visited Nashville, in November 1924, Ransom suggested to Riding that she might like him to send some of her poems to Graves, who could use his influence to get them published in England; she was pleased, and asked for Ransom's advice in their preparation. Ransom wrote to Graves of her, then, in prophetically worried but commendatory terms. 'The Quids' had appeared in the February 1924 issue of *The Fugitive*; whereas she had no less than twenty-seven poems printed in the magazine, Graves had had only three. Graves noted 'The Quids' towards the end of 1924, and began a correspondence with her; at some time it was mooted that she would come to England to collaborate with him on a book on modern poetry. But she took the decision to come very suddenly. In the time of her difficulties the correspondence had lapsed. When she wired, Graves had begun packing for Egypt. In the 'Dedicatory Epilogue to Laura Riding' which ends the first version of *Goodbye to All That* he writes:

> For how could the story of your coming be told between an Islip Parish Council Meeting and a conference of the professors of the Faculty of Letters at Cairo University? How she [Nancy] and I happening by seeming accident upon your teasing *Quids*, were drawn to write to you, who were in America, asking you to come to us. How, though you knew no more of us than we of you, and indeed less (for you knew me at a disadvantage, by my poems of the war), you forthwith came. And how there was thereupon a unity to which you and I pledged our faith and she her pleasure. How we went together to the land [Egypt] where the dead parade the streets and there met with demons and returned with the demons still treading behind. And how they drove us up and down the land.

Laura Riding arrived in England on 2 January 1926, and left there – with Nancy, Graves and their children – for Egypt on 9 January.

Graves's family saw 'nothing to explain' in Laura's presence at this time; and Nancy, for the moment mollified, shared her husband's admiration for her poetry and, more, for her personality. She also, according to John Graves, saw 'her as an extra nursemaid for her four small children'. Alfred Perceval recorded in his diary for 5 January 1926 that he 'supped with R., N. and Miss [she now called herself Miss] Gottschalk (German [*sic*] Jewish poet etc. etc.).' 'She took pains to get on well with Nancy,' John Graves has added retrospectively. But the two women really did get on well. Certainly Graves has always emphasized this: 'At first everything was wonderful,' he said ruefully in 1943, and again several times after that.

Graves was in good heart as he set off for Egypt on 9 January 1926, 'second-class, by P. & O. . . . with a nurse for the children, new clothes in the new cabin trunks, and a Morris-Oxford in the hold' (Nancy would not give up her passion for driving, but had consented to change cars with the help of the handsome advance her husband had received on his salary). Sassoon, full of good will, good spirits and good wishes, came to see them off.

Chapter Ten
1926–27

I

Graves did not enjoy this new phase of his life for long, though the reasons for his disenchantment did not lie wholly in his dislike of Egypt. Egypt became a lurid symbol of the goddawful world in general. Despite the light-hearted tone of his own account, the few months spent in Egypt saw the beginning of the 'story' which, in *Goodbye to All That*, he refuses to tell. The autobiography records his 'history', and Riding he sees as outside such history; therefore he does not mention her in the main text – only in the epilogue. In the revision he calls that part of the story he omits 'dramatic but unpublishable'.

> But to end [the story] with the return from Egypt would be to round it off too bookishly. . . . From a historical point of view [it] must be read . . . as one of gradual disintegration. By the summer of 1926 the disintegration was already well advanced,

he wrote in the 1929 text. Certainty about this 'disintegration' – by which he means 'disintegration of my post-war personality' – began to crystallize rapidly in his mind as soon as he had got to know Laura Riding, whose personality – however anyone may wish to assess it – was, although unhymned except by him, both explosively freakish and characterized by acute though not learned intelligence. She was soon able to dissolve any doubts he may have had about her. Her husband had already noted her capacity to influence others – and to use them as repositories of the information she lacked.

Graves's sketch of the Egyptian episode makes it sound, in the main, farcical. And that country did have, at least until 1952, its unavoidably farcical side. But, as he remarks in the 'Dedicatory Epilogue', he and Riding also found it a 'land where the dead parade the streets'. He was referring not only to Egypt itself, but also – metaphorically – to what he and Riding went through there together (and, as well, to her unhappy love affair with Tate), to the experiences which led them to a rejection of the 'world'. He had already been beset, in the Islip years, by a sense of 'bad luck', and had reached a crisis in his own life. In the Egypt of that period, as Lawrence had told him, the 'beings are curious and disgusting'. ('My God,' Keith Douglas ended a memorable 1942 poem, 'the King of this country must be proud.')

Graves soon came to feel disgusted by the conditions there, which reinforced his general discontent and his growing sense that the opportunity to make a drastic change was at hand. His youngest son, the baby Sam, was neglected at an isolation hospital to which he and the other children were sent when they contracted measles; he came back with eardrums so badly scarred that he was left with a permanent deficiency of hearing.

Graves began to feel that he could bear it no longer. In May he decided to resign. His half-brother Richard, who had been in the diplomatic service in Egypt for some time, and his wife had made things as easy as they could for the Graveses, even though they had heard, and were acutely nervous of, Robert's alleged 'socialism'. His eccentric half-sister Molly (she was among other things a dowser), who also lived in Cairo, did her best too. But he felt he had to break his contract. He could no longer put up with the absurdities of his job: the strikes, the foolish student essays which no longer seemed funny, the surreal political situation. His children's health was not prospering, and Nancy was not better. He hated the architecture of Heliopolis, which had been constructed by a Belgian company. (For ever afterwards he has contemptuously referred to bleak, 'contemporary' suburban districts as 'Belgian'.) Nancy concurred in his decision; the situation between Graves, Riding and Nancy was, for the time being, stable. Graves and Riding pledged themselves to a 'unity', and Nancy pledged her 'pleasure' in it. It was, he told Lawrence, 'pure'.

It was while he was in Egypt that Graves arranged his first retrospective collection of poems. It bears the title *Poems 1914–1926* (it was published by Heinemann on 2 June 1927), but the running head is 'Collected Poems of Robert Graves'. (The *Poems 1914–1927*, issued at the same time, is almost the same book, except that it is printed on better paper, is limited to 115 copies, 100 of which are signed by the author – and it adds nine poems completed in England in 1926–27). It is dedicated to 'N[ancy] and L[aura]'.

He has called his arrangement of this first 'collected book of my poems' 'a process of tidying-up'. The tidying-up process in no way matches the severity of that seen in the *Collected Poems* of 1938; but, he later wrote,

> it was selective rather than collective, intended as a disavowal of over half the poetry I had so far printed. As Skelton told Fame, speaking of his regretted poem 'Apollo Whirléd Up his Chair', I had done what I could to scrape out the scrolls,/To erase it for ever out of her ragman's rolls. . . . I stopped contributing new poems to English and American periodicals.

In November 1927 he published a poem in the *London Mercury*; his next periodical publication of poetry was to be in the *Scholastic* of October 1940. Periodicals, with a few exceptions, would not accept Riding's work.

He wrote little else in Cairo except the final draft of his essay *Lars Porsena, or the Future of Swearing*, first published in April 1927. This witty, entertaining little work has been several times reprinted, and revised twice.

II

Graves's parents' anxieties when they eventually learned about his resignation were profound. They wanted him to have financial security, status – and a reputation for moral probity. His brother John told me as late as 1977 that his throwing up of a 'safe post' was 'reprehensible'. While they believed that he could have a steady job *and* be a poet, he saw that their conventional morality could never do for him, even though they were far from hypocrites.

The twenties was the decade when the moral style of the nineteenth century first came under wide (and not always understanding) scrutiny; many found D. H. Lawrence and Bertrand Russell (in particular) liberating influences. Graves was influenced by neither; his mentor, in so far as he had one, had been Samuel Butler. He found D. H. Lawrence's ideas muddled and irrelevant – and he had already run up against Russell over the Sassoon affair. He 'looked', he 'loved', and 'therewith instantly' (to quote from a poem he wrote at this time) discovered a dazzling route out of the besieged Ariel (Jerusalem) of which he had spoken to T. E. Lawrence in early 1922. In that remarkably prophetic letter (most of which is quoted on pp. 109–10) he had asked Lawrence, in reading Isaiah xxix, to comment 'mentally' on:

a) the bit about the closed book
b) the hosts of iniquity . . . and 'it shall be unto Ariel as unto me'
c) the familiar spirit
d) the bit about the drunken men
e) the date of the Authorized Version

and, when he had done this, answer 'to what does all this tend?' So far as he himself was concerned, it tended to Laura Riding.

He took to heart verses 5–8 of Isaiah xxix, which refer to a miraculous deliverance. The 'closed book' reference is simple:

> And the vision of all is become unto you as the words of a book that is sealed, which men deliver to one which is learned, saying, Read this, I pray thee: and he saith, I cannot; for it is sealed. [v. 11]

He was obsessed, then as ever, with the themes of 'miraculous deliverance', and of 'that day' when 'the deaf shall hear the words of the book, and the blind see out of obscurity, and out of darkness' (v. 18), when a book of secret knowledge should be opened – to him.

Now not only the 'closed book' but also, he believed, its authoress had arrived, and had been discovered in 'a land where the dead parade the streets'. He was dazzled. Those who believe in miracles, as Graves always has, give up hope of them the more absolutely (the wilder the hope, the wilder the despair) – and are thus the more bedazzled when they seem to occur. But in spite of the sudden appearance of this 'Queen of Night on her moon throne', who could reveal all to him, who would 'mercilessly', 'lovingly' pluck 'out the lie', and to whom he 'thankfully' consented to his 'estrangement' from himself 'in' her – despite this, he was not ready for a complete breaking away, either from Nancy or from his family. Nor did Riding for the time being encourage this. It is natural to Graves not only to 'want to be nice' but also to arrange things in such a way that 'truth' is suited without anyone's being made unhappy – and as natural to him, in his behaviour, to fail to discern that 'truth' sometimes makes people as unhappy as other lesser matters.

So it was natural that, not wishing to offend their susceptibilities, he failed to keep his family fully informed of his circumstances. He led his father and mother to believe that he was getting on with his work at Islip, whither he had returned in June, in what was no more than his first vacation. They understood that he and Nancy (with Laura a kind of intelligent servant) had come to Islip because a plan to spend the vacation in Cyprus had been frustrated by news that the food there was unsafe, especially for children.

Then Robert's doctor sister, Rosaleen, 'reported' that he had given up the Cairo post. There was intense consternation, based for the most part on extreme anxiety over the prospects for Robert and his large family: what would they do? Graves had at this point shown a capacity to earn money – and good money at that – by what his family no doubt believed was teaching; but none whatsoever by writing prose. And A.P. was not such a fool as to imagine that serious poetry alone could keep a family.

The first action they took was to urge him to withdraw his resignation. It was too late for him to do so, but they did not know this. To A.P.'s letter asking him to 'reconsider' Robert sent, according to John Graves, 'a haughty and self-contradictory reply'. He was in a spot, since he had been misleading them from the start. Naturally, he played the danger to the children's health – if made to live in Egypt – as his trump card. It was a valid one, as Sam Graves can still testify. But he also gave A.P. to understand that he was seeking a job in an American university to 'avoid bankruptcy'; this was true, although it came to nothing.

So he was once again broke. And Laura Riding had no means of raising cash. Graves, then, had not only his wife and children to support, but Laura's genius to protect from Mammondom. Eventually, though he didn't enjoy it, he had to learn to keep the efficient Mammonite in himself separate from the anti-Mammonite poet. But in the summer of 1926 there was no such prospect. He didn't even know if he could earn money from prose, and certainly had no proof of or confidence in the possibility. He could depend on no royalties from previous publications.

It was T. E. Lawrence (by now T. E. Shaw of the Royal Tank Corps) who came to the rescue – yet again. He sent Graves a copy of *Revolt in the Desert*, an abridgement of *Seven Pillars*, with an inscription: 'please sell when read'. This was a valuable property, for a regular trade edition of *Seven Pillars* in full did not appear until 1935. Graves got over £300 for it – and so, together with the sale of some autographed first editions, he made himself temporarily solvent to the extent of some £400.

One of the autographed copies he sold was of Edith Sitwell's *The*

Sleeping Beauty (1924), which she had inscribed 'For Robert Graves and Nancy Nicholson in admiration from Edith Sitwell'. Edith Sitwell later bought it back, then sold it again, with the following postscript:

> I wrote this dedication at a time when Robert Graves was still a tentative English nightingale [*sic*] and not an American loon or screech-owl. Though poor, I am happy to buy this book (from the shop to which he sold it) for the sum of 15s so that no one can accuse me of being a hoot-fan
>
> *Edith Sitwell*

III

Graves and Riding did not stay long at Islip. They had begun writing in collaboration, and the fuss the children made was too much for them. Nancy concurred. She approved of the influence Laura was exercising upon Graves, and was convinced of the importance of the work they were doing. She had fallen under Laura's spell no less than had her husband. Laura made a point of telling Nancy how impossible and awful men were. Laura liked children when they behaved themselves, but that she had certain reservations about them may be inferred from the horrible but powerful fragment she had written, doubtless with good cause, while still in America:

> Mothering innocents to monsters is
> Not of fertility but fascination
> In women.

Nancy liked these lines, and was full of admiration for a woman whose fertility was so determinedly mental. She was led to believe that Graves could better be reformed by Laura than by herself.

She willingly acquiesced in a new arrangement: Graves and Laura would share a flat at 9 Ladbroke Square (not far from Notting Hill underground station). In any case, as she told a friend, she 'was glad to run her own house'.

But Graves and Riding were not alone in Ladbroke Square. Rosaleen was living in with them, as, it was understood by the family, 'chaperone'. So by the standards of Graves's parents things were just about respectable, though 'dangerous'. But such was the force of Riding's persuasive powers, and of Graves's assurances of her virtue, that A.P. and Amy were able to accept that work of epoch-making importance was being carried out in Ladbroke Square – and nothing else. They believed that the two were not lovers. Nancy helped smooth over any doubts that they may have had. Yes, she told them, it *was* important work, and of a deeply spiritual nature at that.

Nancy seemed in no wise shocked by the moral considerations which concerned A.P. and Amy, who were kept in the dark until the last moment. At this stage she felt glad that some other woman was willing to take her place. Her husband, for all his servitude and helpfulness and unimpeachable guilts, somehow possessed a demanding air, ghostly though this was. He had often made her feel that she was doing or being something wrong. Laura could handle him better. It would all work out very well. They were 'dis-married' at last. She was, after all, a modern woman – and no one could have been more solicitous of her rights, or understanding about her feminist feelings, than Laura. She had never met anyone like her. At least Robert was right in that. And hadn't she agreed with him from the start?

In 1926 Riding published her first collection of poems, *The Close Chaplet* (as well as a translation of Marcel LeGoff's *Anatole France at Home*). Graves was responsible for the publication of the poems, by Hogarth; Adelphi Press of New York took a few copies, but sold virtually none. *The Close Chaplet* (the title is from one of Graves's poems), the translation and the long poem *The Vain Life of Voltaire: A Biographical Fantasy* (Hogarth Press, 1927; 1969) were all issued as by Laura Riding Gottschalk; but in the last-named book the 'Gottschalk' is overprinted, though still legible. They were remarkable poems, quite distinct from anything else that has ever appeared in the English language. Little notice was taken of them by reviewers.

In these years, Graves once said to me, she 'glowed with a sort of light'. He has never gone back on this, or changed his view of her as she was then. By his choice and need, and her own inclination, hers was the purer – indeed, the paradigmatic – genius. As time passed, his subservience to her increased. But he continued to write his poems in his own voice, and they rarely take on the tone of hers. Their technical approaches were entirely different.

The books Graves and Riding wrote in collaboration before their departure from England for Mallorca were *A Survey of Modernist Poetry* (published in early November 1927) and the ferocious *Pamphlet Against Anthologies* (July 1928). On her own she published two books of essays, *Contemporaries and Snobs* (1928) and *Anarchism Is Not*

Enough (1928). Her essay on Gertrude Stein, 'The New Barbarism, and Gertrude Stein', included in an expanded form in the former collection, appeared in Eugene Jolas' Paris-based *transition 3* in 1927 – and she contributed a number of poems to the 1927–28 (first) series of this magazine, as well as a review of Hart Crane's first collection of poems, *White Buildings*. Graves himself contributed one poem. Through the *transition* contributions Riding established a relationship – to become important to both partners – with Gertrude Stein. It was Graves who persuaded Jonathan Cape to publish Riding's own two books of essays, which attracted little attention. Many of them (particularly 'The Damned Thing', about sex) are fifty years ahead of their time; but their language is often unnecessarily obscure, and could have been improved by extensive rewriting. The two collaborations with Graves are better written, and attracted much more general attention. Certainly Graves helped teach her to write more lucidly. He also served her as a source of information. Gottschalk met Graves on a visit to England in 1926 and got the impression that he wrote most of the 'collaborations'; the evidence, documentary, stylistic and otherwise, confirms this.

At Ladbroke Square they were working on *A Survey of Modernist Poetry*, and Graves was listening with increasing excitement to what was in effect a clarified version of his own convictions, that

> There is a sense of life so real that it becomes the sense of something more real than life. . . . It is the meaning at work in what has no meaning; it is, at its clearest, poetry.

Those are the opening words of *Contemporaries and Snobs*. In a 'Letter to M[allik] in India' prefacing the satire *The Marmosite's Miscellany*, he had written of having 'no ambition'. 'Except this only, to have no ambition'; of having 'no sure knowledge but that knowledge changes/ Beyond all local proof or local disproof'; of 'friendship' that is independent of geographical location, and that 'thrives on absence', drawing strength, even from 'soured earth'. This passage, and many others from his Islip period criticism, are expressions of essentially the same point of view. But Riding was less tentative; and from a very early age the poetry she had been writing had assumed such a viewpoint without struggle or effort. Yet, and with tragic hubris, she still retained enough confidence in her own rectitude to feel that she herself, as well as poetry, could work effectively as 'meaning' in 'what has no meaning'. She *was* her poetry, she believed. This gave her work power, but led to its collapse into the turgid, contorted and messianic prose of the postwar years.

Graves often visited Nancy at Islip, and sometimes Laura came with him. The situation in August and September was fairly stable from the family's point of view, since John Graves felt able on 9 August to travel back from Oxford (where he had been taking his BA degree) with the couple, who had been visiting Nancy.

But on 21 September 1926 A. P. Graves's diary entry showed alarm:

> A consternating letter from Robert, who is going with Nancy's consent with Laura to Vienna till over Xmas.

The business of 'Nancy's consent' was no more than a sop to the Graves parents' morality. A.P., Amy and sister Clarissa wired Nancy to 'withdraw consent'. She told them not to worry. But as they had never trusted her soundness in any case, her attempts to reassure them failed. They were in a state of panic: Robbie had at all costs to be saved.

But Graves and Riding went off to Vienna notwithstanding – and chaperoneless. A.P. and Amy were at a loss to know what to do. They were still prepared to believe that their son's relationship with the 'German poet etc. etc.' was no more than what they had been assured it seemed; but what would everyone else think?

Amy told A.P. that it was no less than their duty to winter that year in Austria; so he laid that down, and she obeyed. So as not to seem to be too near Graves, they went, on 4 October 1926, to the spa of Bad Hofgastein.

Graves, anxious to placate his parents, promptly wrote to his father, who reported in his diary for 10 October:

> A really wonderful letter from Robert about the strange Trinity of friendship and love between him, Nancy and Laura.

The letter was truthful, though overenraptured; to cause A.P. to react so favourably it skilfully concentrated on the Platonic aspects of the matter. The 'strange Trinity', as a concept, derived from Riding.

Alfred Perceval was so impressed by this letter that he determined to confirm his newly found confidence by inviting Graves and Riding to visit himself and his wife at Bad Hofgastein. They arrived there on 13 October and returned to Vienna on the 17th. A.P.'s diary mentions long talks about poetry, but no discussion of the nature of the relationship between his son and Laura. He was, for the time being, sold. We may doubt if the shrewder Amy was.

However, the collaborative work on which the couple were engaged was not enough to earn them a living. On their return to England in 1927 they were again finding it difficult to make ends meet. For a time they managed on the *Revolt in the Desert* money, working hard on *A Survey of Modernist Poetry* – and on initiating and then abandoning various projects because they could not finance them. Nancy went off for a time to Cumberland to work on a farm, taking all four children with her. Thus Graves was relieved of part of the burden of supporting her. Graves and Riding visited her there.

When she returned, the couple had moved to a two-part, fourth-storey flat, No. 35A St Peter's Square. The flat was taken in Riding's name, but Graves paid the rent. For Nancy and the children he rented a barge, the *Ringrose*. The Trinity was still flourishing.

St Peter's Square, Hammersmith, London, W6, is an attractive small square immediately north of the Great West Road (now the A4), at that point running alongside the Thames, which makes a sharp north-wards bend from Fulham in the east to Sheen in the west. Just across the river from St Peter's Square lies St Paul's School, on the south bank. Along the Chiswick Mall, a stone's throw from St Peter's Square, a number of barges, houseboats, were moored. The *Ringrose* was one of them. The people living on the barges and in St Peter's Square and the other small streets thereabout were generally of an 'artistic' or 'bo-hemian' kind, and formed a little community of their own. Graves and Riding, being busy, kept their distance; but they were not unfriendly, and were known and tolerated – though their domestic arrangements were commented upon.

Laura Riding, now absolutely minus the Gottschalk, had accom-plished a good deal for herself in the six short months since she left America. When she left she had done so in a state of physical and mental demoralization. She had been through a bad personal experi-ence; all her takeover bids had been turned down.

She had now taken over the Graves–Nicholson enterprise, which was functioning better than it had ever done before, as a wonderful Trinity, and a decently Nicaean one at that. No doubts were entertained as to which of the three persons was ungenerated. Graves had found what he needed. In place of Nancy's milk-and-water feminism, man-nered rather than powerful, he had someone who was asking:

when will man grow up ... become woman, when will she [woman] have companions instead of children?

This question she asked in 'The Damned Thing', included in *Anarchism Is Not Enough*. Neither Graves nor she desired to undergo a sex change; that was not what she meant at the time. What she meant was that she would initiate a programme of the education of men – starting with Graves. Ironically, he was educating her; but he said nothing of it. But many besides Louis Gottschalk noticed it.

On the financial front no luck had yet come their way. Laura not only supported Graves in his feelings of obligation towards his immediate family (she was always meticulous in this), but made them, not herself, a priority. By midsummer 1927 they were finding it increasingly difficult to make ends meet. But she was cheerful, helpful and encouraging. Nancy teetered between compliance and hysteria; Graves grumbled a lot about it in letters to Lawrence.

Once again the situation was saved, and once again it was Lawrence (although this time more indirectly) who saved it. It marked for Graves the beginning of solvency. From then on he was a writer who could command good fees, and be certain of getting commissions.

The astute publisher Jonathan Cape of London, in association with George Doran of Doubleday Doran in New York, realized in 1927 that Lawrence was soon going to withdraw *Revolt in the Desert*, which had now been published: he wanted to prevent inferior authors from exploiting the material. He had loathed the American publicist Lowell Thomas's book about him, published in 1924, but could not prevent him from writing more. It was (and still to some extent is) Thomas who was responsible for the 'Lawrence legend' – though he had no bad intentions, within his journalistic limits. So Cape, with Lawrence's at first secret connivance, commissioned Graves to provide the inevitable popular book: T.E. assured Cape he would give all the help he could. At first it was to be a brief book for boys. To a friend Lawrence wrote:

Robert Graves, a decent poet [is doing the book] by a conspiracy of my friends, to keep the job out of bad hands.

He could not help suggesting to another friend that Graves would no doubt devise some 'psychologically plausible explanation' of his 'spiritual divagations'. But he distrusted Graves least.

Graves had only six weeks (by the terms of his contract) to collect, organize and write his material, and so had to work at the job for eighteen hours a day. He dropped everything else. He was greatly aided by Lawrence, who sent him a series of long letters throughout June and July. Lawrence was then in India, which did not make matters any easier. (In the *Goodbye to All That* of 1929 Graves wrote that he had to get 'Lawrence's permission'. He did not know of the 'conspiracy' when he received Cape's initial letter.)

As Lawrence sent him material, so Graves sent him his work-in-progress. Lawrence went over it in detail, making many additions and alterations. The book may thus be regarded as a collaborative effort, though the two men were not able to meet personally to discuss it. Lawrence deliberately mystified Graves on certain crucial points – as he was prone to do to everyone. The responsibility for the final text lay with Graves because of the shortage of time. The book was out by early November.

Speed became an even more urgent matter at a very early stage. Lowell Thomas stymied the original project of a short book for boys by issuing his 1924 work in Great Britain. To get the market, Graves, with Cape's agreement, had suddenly to produce an adult book, of three times the originally stipulated length. But he succeeded in producing a readable book, and one reasonably accurate in view of the circumstances under which it was written. It had gone into a fourth impression by the end of November, and was selling at the rate of 10,000 copies a week throughout December. Doubleday issued an edition of 20,000 copies on 30 March in the following year – and Graves benefited further when a concise edition appeared in 1934, and again in 1940 when a 'school edition' was issued.

We are informed in a book on Graves's poetry (by Douglas Day) that '*Lawrence and the Arabs* is, incidentally, a very hero-worshipping sort of biography, and it seems to have caused Lawrence no little embarrassment. . . .' This remark – demonstrating that its author knows nothing of the circumstances under which the book was written – should be severely modified. The book is a potboiler, was meant to be – and Graves has never claimed otherwise. Lawrence did write (to Mrs Bernard Shaw) that it was 'too laudatory', but that was false modesty, and he was in a bad state at the time. He knew very well that his old friend, who needed money, and had no time for niceties, had been obliged to take up a laudatory tone. What depressed him was reading over the accounts of his past: 'So soon as I insulate myself,' he wrote to Shaw's wife, 'the needle swings back to self-condemnation.' As John Mack, Lawrence's most able biographer, has put it: 'His close participation in the creation of Robert Graves's book about him revived again for Lawrence ... painful memories and feelings. ...' The bad feeling between Graves and Lawrence was yet to come – and it was painful for both of them.

Graves got £500 advance from Cape for the Lawrence job. Thus money was available again and thus the Seizin Press was brought to birth: this would actualize the new thinking, bring some of the right people together, and provide practical examples of how writing should be done. The implied precepts of *A Survey of Modernist Poetry* (published in July 1927) required illustration.

Chapter Eleven
1927–28

I

Riding's presence clarified Graves's thinking. On the physical and mental planes he loved her; for a short time he was able to feel that, in her, body and intellect were one. He enjoyed being 'lessoned' (a word she later grandiosely used of her role); it increased his love for her. She sympathized with his sexual difficulties, his guilts, in a manner in which Nancy had not; and she reciprocated in such a way as to make him feel happy. She was perhaps herself happy for a brief time.

Provided that it is understood that she despumated him, reorganized him, relieved his mind of its obsession with psychological theories of poetry – and that he had been asking for exactly this – then their respective contributions to *A Survey of Modernist Poetry* are about equal, although the book is ultimately more his than hers, because he possessed a literary background whereas she did not. They agreed to call it a 'word-by-word' collaboration; and so it was.

The organization of the book's argument, and the lucidity of its style, are his. Her own solitary prose efforts make this abundantly evident. The basis of the work, that poetry must be independent of fashions, fads, 'dead movements' (public psychological moods that pass 'leaving no trace but waste material'), is joint. The 'modern' poet is not a poet; he is playing for fame. He had already said this in so many words; she had not. The 'modernist' poet, the authors say, may be better; he rejects 'history' (in the sense of fashion, the *Zeitgeist*) in favour of general truths and true clarity of communication. The latter understands that poetry is a special, a unique means of making 'timeless' statements. He will avoid fashionable tricks (exemplified by Pound and the Imagists, who are here branded as 'modern'), but if what he has to say involves *seeming* obscure to the reader then he will go ahead regardless of reader reaction. The modernist does not write to anyone's 'taste'. Thus Hopkins's difficult 'Betweenpie mountains' (from 'My own heart let me more have pity on') is ingeniously and convincingly defended and explicated on the grounds that this was the only way Hopkins could say what he needed to say. Hopkins is a 'modernist', not a 'modern'. Cummings, too, is shown to be perfectly intelligible; his quirks are necessary to express his meaning.

The book is a defence of the true poet's right and duty to *seem* 'obscure' if he cannot find a means of saying what he has to say in a conventional manner. D. H. Lawrence (surprisingly) could be a poet if he gave up his obsession with sex. Graves's hand is seen in the praise of Frost as a successful poet of nature – and more so in the over-generous approval of Sassoon, who was not then writing at all interestingly.

The most influential section of the book proved to be an analysis of Shakespeare's Sonnet 129 ('Th' expence of spirit in a waste of shame'). The analytical method employed there enabled William Empson to evolve his own method. Neither Riding nor Graves liked *Seven Types of Ambiguity* ('Empson is as clever as a monkey & I do not like monkeys,' Graves wrote in 1944), as they considered it a corruption and not a development of their own methods. However, like it or not, the method employed here led not only to 'Empsonianism' but to one of the main features of the New Criticism: its concentration on the text. More important, however, is the insistence Graves–Riding make on sticking to the original spelling and punctuation, their demonstration that modernization leads to distortion. This contribution to Shakespeare criticism has been extremely influential; even if some of the subsequent work has been more scholarly, this is its source. The basic concept is Graves's, though influenced by Simpson.

The shorter *A Pamphlet Against Anthologies* is a development and elaboration of a letter Graves wrote to the *Times Literary Supplement*, (1 December 1921, four years before he met Riding) supporting T. S. Eliot, who had attacked certain anthological practices in a previous issue. The mockery of the stock anthology piece (de la Mare's 'Arabia' and Yeats's 'Lake Isle of Innisfree' come in for fearsome thrashings) is very Gravesian in tone; the sharpness and intelligence are a combination of two critical minds functioning at their best.

The argument is simple. The stock-in-trade anthology, which gives readers the 'beauties' they desire, often bowdlerized, and aimed at a wide, 'stupid' market, is a mere joke. It further debases public taste. Anthologies of ballads, folk songs, Elizabethan lyrics and such are valuable because they collect material otherwise difficult of access. And editions of unpublished private, personal anthologies are interesting in their own right. It is a light, brilliant piece – and was not calculated to gain its authors popularity.

II

Cape's £500 advance on the Lawrence book gave Graves and Riding the opportunity to proceed with their plans to found the Seizin Press. Riding had the title of 'chief manager'. Graves was her self-styled 'partner'.

The name chosen by Graves for the new Press has been a source of puzzlement to many. 'Seizin', usually spelt 'Seisin', derives from 'seize'. It is now used only as a legal term, denoting 'possession as of freehold'; 'the possession which a freeholder has'. The *Oxford English Dictionary* also lists its meaning in Scottish law ('The act of giving possession of feudal property by the delivery of symbols . . . the instrument by which the possession . . . is proved'), and its meaning in the old phrases 'to give' or 'take' 'seisin' – 'in popular language *seisin* has been occas[ionally] applied loosely to the object (e.g. a tuf, a key, a staff) handed over in "livery of seisin" as a token of possession'.

One commentator, Hugh Ford, writing solely on Riding's authority, ponderously says that 'all the later ideas could not have been specifically in her mind at the time the name was fixed on. . . .'

> The notion of possession was central in her mind as the problem of finding a name for the Press presented itself, but not merely in connection with the fact of ownership of the instrument of a new activity – that of actually printing books – and identification with that activity; attitudes and ideas on a befitting spirit of possession were involved, though not in explicit form.

Ford, whose account is written in a contorted style oddly reminiscent of Riding's own, then quotes remarks she made on 'possession' in *The World and Ourselves* (1938), 'enunciating' what he describes as 'a morality of possession':

> It is a general good effect of life to be able to possess things which are one's very own by their difference from what others would want to possess; and to have the power to care for them so well that one can feel a free agent of control over the domain of one's possessions. . . .

'She associated possession,' he continues,

> and the consequence of proprietory devotion with the principle of hos-
> pitality as a new (potential) dynamics of general human behaviour,
> extending from the field of personal possession. One may, hence, read
> back into the launching of the Press with 'Seizin' for its name a spirit of
> moral resolve to use it well.

All this is more tersely summed up in the *Webster's* definition: 'possession with quiet enjoyment', which is what Graves himself had in
mind when he put the name forward for her approval.

Seizin One, of great length in terms of the Press, its resources, and
the extent of its managers' knowledge of printing and book-making,
was *Love as Love, Death as Death*, Laura Riding's first collection of
poems since *The Close Chaplet* and *The Vain Life of Voltaire*.

Graves had now to find a suitable machine – and he and Riding to
learn how to print on it. It is remarkable, in the light of their initial
ignorance of theory and practice, that they were able to publish four
books in the two years before they left England – and to carry on in
Mallorca. It was Graves's friend Vyvyan Richards who gave them the
help they needed; indeed, without Richards there might very well have
been no hand-printed books from the Seizin Press.

Richards had been up at Oxford, before the war, with T. E. Lawrence. The two had planned a private press venture, but it never came
to anything because of Lawrence's other activities. Richards himself
now owned a private press, from which he had just issued an edition
of William Caxton's *Prologues and Epilogues*.

The Seizin machine, a large Crown Albion of 1872 (patent 2937),
weighing some seventeen hundredweight, was procured for them by
Richards. It was installed at the St Peter's Square flat, where he gave
them their first lessons. They learned the difficult business quickly. On
Richards's advice they bought a large supply of Batchelor hand-made
paper. They did not at first do their own setting, but employed a
Monotype firm for this purpose; they made their alterations and corrections from their own stock of type – this, used by the Press in all its
own productions, was Caslon Old Face.

With *Seizin One* the partners had the usual difficulties of beginners.
Correcting the type was easy; so was pulling rough proofs. What came
hard was producing the finished book. They shared the work equally.
They found that the dampening of the sheets presented the greatest
problem: the paper had to be saturated, to a very critical degree, to

ensure a uniform impression. There were many failures, but at last an edition of 175 acceptable copies was produced. The pages were bound in linen buckram. The author signed all the copies, which were numbered; the price was 11s. 6d. One of the subscribers was W. H. Auden, who had already read *The Close Chaplet* of 1926, as his earliest poems – with their profuse borrowings from Riding (as from Graves) – demonstrate. A London bookseller, A. W. Bain, handled and distributed the rest of the stock.

The Seizin prospectus was carefully worked out. Its policy was 'to print necessary books by various particular people'. Most private presses, then as now, printed primarily for collectors; the content of their books was secondary. Graves and Riding, though concerned to give each work the presentation most graphically suitable to it, took pains from the start to divorce Seizin from any notion that its products were for collectors. The editions were

> decidedly not addressed to collectors but to those interested in work rather than printing – of a certain quality. That is as far in prophecy as we care at the moment to go. You must take our word for it that our reticence is due to something more than an uncertainty of standards. Quite the contrary.

This is from an early prospectus. There are a number of other such items, produced as printing practice for the partners as well as advertising material; some are now very rare.

The Seizin Press was the first public expression of Riding's hopefully 'supra-individual', anti-temporal project that was not entirely unsuccessful. At first, and consistently until 1939–40, she saw poetry as the only true reality: a form of words independent of time. An ancient idea, but in the new clothes of a bizarre personality of limited but powerful genius. That 'sense of life so real that it becomes the sense of something more real than life' of which she had spoken in her *Contemporaries and Snobs* could not, she asserted, be fully expressed in 'spatial' or 'temporal sequences'. 'It is the meaning at work in what had no meaning; it is, at its clearest, poetry.' This is at bottom pure Gnosticism – and there is evidence that Riding had certain hazy notions about the Cabala, though she was no scholar of it. Once you reached the point at which 'there is no temporal interruption between one poetic incident (poem) and another, then we have not merely poems', she wrote in 1938, 'we have poetry: we have not merely the immediacies – we have finality. Literally.'

Many wondered what she meant by this. Graves, himself a student of Gnosticism from his schooldays, accepted it; it fitted in with his interests and above all with his devotion to poetry. But his acceptance was in the framework of a love relationship. Riding herself did not understand at this time the road along which she was travelling; she knew only that she intended to change the world. But she harboured the suspicion that she might have one thing, at least, in common with others: she would die. This was the idealistic dream of one who carried along with her completely only one person: Robert Graves. Without his devotion it is impossible to say what might have happened to her.

But she made Graves feel a changed man – and in doing so saved herself from total withdrawal. It was a reciprocal relationship, and each owes the other much for what they did for each other, in love, in those years (1926 to early 1929). She has now forgotten this.

Since the end of the war, with only brief remissions, Graves was still plagued by the alarming 'day-dreams' of the war. They 'persisted like an alternate life'. Laura's presence gradually relieved him of these too vivid, nerve-shaking recollections. He became calmer, gained a steadier sense of purpose and direction. He had for long regarded poetry as a vocation essential to him, but had not fully understood why. For a very short while he remained independent of her only at the profoundest poetic level, as his panic-stricken poem 'Sick Love' demonstrates.

Only two more Seizin items were published in England: Gertrude Stein's short *An Acquaintance with Description* (1929), and Graves's own slim *Poems*, published in London in December 1929, two months after the partners had left England. Both Graves and Riding admired Stein's persistence in trying to preserve linguistic integrity in the face of the nothingness of commonplace 'reality'. Both fully appreciated that, however exhibitionistic Stein was, she paid a persistent and intelligent attention to *words* themselves; this was what interested them. They were sympathetically aware that the most meaningful things she had to say were about her homosexuality – and that (in those days) she was debarred from expressing herself as she wished on this matter.

For Seizin she gave them a short piece she had written in 1926. Slips, inserted later, were taken to Paris for her signature, and the volume appeared in an edition of 225 copies, again at 11s. 6d. Stein became very fond of both, most especially of Graves, and was soon to prove a good friend.

III

In 1928 another friend came to live near Graves and Riding: Norman Cameron. They had met him in Oxford in 1927, when he was at Oriel College reading English. He was then president of the English Club – an undergraduate society which exists mainly to invite literary speakers. Christened John Norman Cameron, he was a Scot. He was born in 1905, and educated at Fettes College, Edinburgh. At Oxford his poetry gained the enthusiastic attention of Auden, Day Lewis and other of his undergraduate contemporaries. He was not ambitious, but was well represented in the *Oxford Poetry* of 1927, edited by Auden and Day Lewis. His undergraduate poems were unusually accomplished, and owed nothing whatever to Graves or to Riding. He maintained the same neat, sardonic, meticulous style until his early death in 1953.

He was tall, pale, almost always at bottom drivingly unhappy; the unhappiness was about something which eluded both him and most of those who loved him. He was a humorous and tolerant companion. His character changed little during his short life – until uncertainty, a sexual guilt he could not acknowledge and, chiefly, physical weakness (he suffered from high blood pressure, and drank more than was good for him throughout his life) drove him, first, into a course of psychoanalysis and then into the Roman Catholic Church – which he embraced with a predictably Calvinist conscientiousness. His delight in the unusual and the bizarre, his sense of the comic, his bawdiness, these are unforgettable, as are the best of his poems. His many relationships with women were disastrous – until he met his Austrian third wife, Gretl, at the end of the Second World War, and settled down very happily.

In 1928 he was, as he remained until the end, uneasily torn between poetry (which disturbed him) and a career (which he was too humorous to take seriously). He was, as Graves has recorded in the introduction to his posthumously collected poems, punctilious and yet negligent. His perfectionism is most evident in his few poems (there are only about sixty of them); but he was afraid of his poetic impulses, and of where they might lead him. He could never commit himself to a literary life. He went from job to job, mostly as an advertising copywriter, filling the gaps between jobs with translations from the French and German. Later he came to live near Graves and Riding for a while in Mallorca – an experiment which, owing to Riding's effect on him, almost destroyed him.

While Graves's and Riding's neighbour in London, he lent a hand with the Press activities, but never did any actual printing. He also helped Graves to subsidize Len Lye, an expatriate New Zealander living in London, and his wife Jane. The zany Len, who was soon to write a Seizin book, had new and original ideas about film-making, design and ways of writing prose. He was doing what Walt Disney did before Disney; and he did it better. He, too, became a valued friend.

Graves and Riding lived – and slept – together in the St Peter's Square flat, even though Riding later (for example, in a letter of 21 September 1933 to a person interested in her work) denied it, and even denied that 'their friends' believed it. Then, in fact, she was at pains to demonstrate that she was devoted to Graves. On one occasion John Graves, having time to kill in London, called at the flat and found that Robert had gone out. Could he, he asked Laura, sit and wait for Robert in 'his room'. She exploded – with good reason. 'It's not *his* room,' she pointed out. 'Can't you see it's our *common workroom!*' John apologized. On the next day he was surprised to receive a letter from her explaining to him that he was not to imagine from her behaviour that she limited her relationship to Robert 'in any way'.

The Australian critic, translator, novelist and historian Jack Lindsay encountered Graves and Riding in these years, and has left a brief account of them in his *Fanfrolico and After* (1962). In the latter part of the twenties he and friends ran a small publishing house called the Fanfrolico Press, which had issued, among other works, a translation of Petronius. Towards the end of 1927 he wanted to do a volume devoted to the ballad 'Tom o' Bedlam' and its history, and he decided to ask Graves to write an essay for it (which he did). He called on Graves at 'the flat at Hammersmith he shared with Laura Riding', whom

> I felt to be a disagreeably self-centred person with a hard discontented face. In reply to her lifted eyebrows, he elucidated his remark that the Press had done Petronius. 'A Roman high-flyer.' She replied, 'Aw.'

Lindsay goes on to describe how she cooked them some corn on the cob, which 'proved to be as hard as the dried corn given to parrots' – and adds that her remark 'I thought I'd boiled it enough' he would have 'found amusing and charming in most women'. He reports that she 'slept always on her back in a definite line of orientation, east–west I think', and that she 'had a number of similarly stern ideas'.

Graves, however, he liked a lot, as rumbustious, refreshing and

generous: 'a tall rawboned slightly gaunt fellow, with a touch of the
wilderness about him, like a mountain-dog trying to keep his tail up
among the city-tykes. I liked him at once.' He says that Graves was at
this time engaged in 'evolving elaborate plots to trip [publishers] up
and get them technically in the wrong on some point or other'; it was
'like a furiously-spun web' (this was in fact just talk).

It would not be long before Graves himself had few friends left, for,
as Lindsay says, he treated Laura 'with the utmost respect and tenderness', and turned his own crusade 'for truth and independence' into
'a crusade for Laura' (a shrewd judgement). Unfortunately few other
people liked her for long – and that, in his eyes, was the end of them.

Chapter Twelve
1928–29

I

Graves's poems of the 1926–29 period are not love poems in the ordinarily understood sense. His real, and finest, love poems belong to the forties, and were addressed to his second wife, Beryl. The poems to or about Riding are best described as 'Muse poems', in the sense which he has made famous. Muse poems are often not 'love poems', though they are *about* love. He was never 'in love' with Nancy, in the sense that love naturally and beautifully defines itself in those poems of the forties. He might have achieved this state earlier than 1940, but his circumstances did not allow him to develop his feelings to that point.

With Riding he undoubtedly fell *in love*. He spread the good news of her with all the fervour of a previously helpless and ignorant St John the Baptist. But what he gained from the relationship, even while it lasted on its initial basis, was never peaceful enjoyment.

On the physical plane she managed (at first) to keep him happy without cutting him off from his needed unhappiness (that is, from his natural puritanism and delicacy about sex). He felt that he fully merited the scorn she increasingly – as she grew more confident – bestowed upon him. But the fully functioning poet in him knew that he was apprehending 'the terrible' – the terrible in the sense Rilke means it in the first lines of his *Duino Elegies*: 'for the beautiful is nothing but the first apprehension of the terrible'. He was at the height of his powers when he wrote 'Sick Love' (first entitled 'Between Dark and Dark', then 'O Love in Me').

'I knew something absolutely frightful was going to happen,' he said about this poem, long after he had written it, 'even though everything was fine at the time. I just knew.'

153

O Love, be fed with apples while you may,
And feel the sun and go in royal array,
A smiling innocent on the heavenly causeway,

Though in what listening horror for the cry
That soars in outer blackness dismally,
The dumb blind beast, the paranoiac fury:

Be warm, enjoy the season, lift your head,
Exquisite in the pulse of tainted blood,
That shivering glory not to be despised.

Take your delight in momentariness,
Walk between dark and dark – a shining space
With the grave's narrowness, though not its peace.

Graves's foreboding was shortly to be justified: something 'absolutely awful' did happen.

II

'The place where I was living in 1929,' Graves told an acquaintance in a skittish letter of the late fifties, 'was known as Free Love Corner.' But there wasn't much *love* (in any of that word's normally accepted senses) in evidence in the situation that began to develop in the vicinity of 35A St Peter's Square in spring 1929; and no freedom at all.

The affair, once notorious, is not completely explicable. It is unlikely that it could be, for it involves such enigmatic, trivial and diverse factors as a relationship thought of by the participants as 'The Four' (the successor to the 'wonderful Trinity'), an almost fatal descent from a fourth-storey window, another dangerous one from a third, the question of whose underpants and whose books really belonged to whom, the break-up of a marriage, the issue of a writ, the rejection of England as a dwelling-place – and a unique mixture of anguish and farce.

In any case, the emotions attending the matter were so burningly intense, and the sickness of one party so extreme, that it never did make complete sense. Nancy was at heart less affected than the others by the philosophical theories of the complex relationships which developed, or were said to have developed. Riding, the meticulous definer of every situation (whether definable or not), supplied the system, which rapidly ran away from reality.

154

Not much is now remembered about Geoffrey Phibbs, the fourth participant. He changed his name to Geoffrey Taylor when his father refused to allow his mistress into his house in 1930. His least obscure book, an anthology called *Irish Poets of the Nineteenth Century*, was published in 1951 under this name. He died just after. He also published a book on Irish gardens in the same year. In the only reference book to list him (he was cut out of a subsequent edition of it), he is described as an 'entomologist'. A relation of his by marriage (a lecturer in ethics) describes him in later life as being pleasantly eccentric and possessed of 'zoological quirks'.

Phibbs was born in 1900 in Norfolk. Soon after his birth his parents (his father was an Anglo-Irish landowner) moved to Ireland. In the twenties they were living in Lisheen, Sligo. A collection of verse composed before he met Graves and Riding has the astonishing title of *The Withering of the Figleaf*; it was published in 1928. He had married, in the mid-twenties, a woman called Norah, an artist; in 1929 he was still married to her, though in what can best be described as a state of interrupted separation – she was living intermittently with David Garnett. This finally ended in divorce, and in 1933 he married one who was allegedly – the words are those of a shrewish woman, of the Graves family, who knew him – 'some courageous young woman who seems to like men of low moral character'. His friend Frank O'Connor was fascinated by him, but thought him 'demonic'. He was unstable, revengeful and had only an iota of talent and application.

At New Year 1929 Graves, Riding and Nancy and the four children were living at the St Peter's Square premises – the two-part flat which housed the Press – and on the *Ringrose*, which was moored at Atlanta Wharf. In fact Graves and Riding were in the flat and Nancy on the barge, but who lived where was a matter of puzzlement and interest to some of the neighbours. Graves, in a 'Précis' which he hurriedly drew up in the autumn of 1929, under threat of a lawsuit from Phibbs, stated that the three were 'living together'.

As 1929 came in apparent harmony reigned. Riding, by transforming what everyone else would have described as a *ménage à trois* into a precisely formulated and 'wonderful Trinity', endowed the three-in-one with a theological glow of virtue. Only Nancy occasionally murmured.

The three had heard of Geoffrey Phibbs before New Year 1929. Like Graves, he had written to Riding about her work. He visited them in October 1928. A letter from Phibbs, to Graves, written from 'The Bungalow, Wicklow, Ireland', and dated 'Oct: 1928', reads (I have taken no liberties with Phibbs's orthography in anything I quote from him):

> Dear Robert,
> What you said yesterday about Jocasta ought to have been and was valuable, but it made me so bluddy nervous that wherever I spoke afterwards I think I put things wrong. Which in the circumstances was a pitty. God knows meaning is hard enough anyway, being the most unblessed Trinity. And one has only an idea that the idea at the other side ['end' is deleted, 'side' substituted] of the words is the same. Laura Ridings work has been getting more important for me thru the last 6 months. At present it is more important than anything else is. Naturally the important thing for me is that it is important. But it is also important for me in a different way, and perhaps less, that anyone I like, not counting work, should not think me wrong-headed & be annoyed. Because it is annoying to the edge of suicide to be admired by wrong-headed people. It would be fair of her to make allowances for the amount one has to shed, as you said, before one reaches her entire position. She may be a dragons tooth but I'm not. If you hear of a job in England will you let me know. Don't trouble about it but let me know. I'm tired of dissembling in Ireland. Don't bother answering this note.
> Geoffrey Phibbs.

Whenever Phibbs spoke, or wrote, in the ensuing months he 'put things wrong' – almost as if under some spell. But he did put an anticipatory finger on a future event when he wrote that to be 'admired by wrong-headed people' would be 'annoying to the edge of suicide'. The letter is not that of an especially articulate man – even allowing for bluddy nervousness – whereas Riding was making the matter of being articulate, to the point of absolute precision, her life's business.

None the less, her hopes were fired. So Graves was sent off in late 1928 to find out about, and possibly to recruit this admirer. Briefed by Riding, Graves told him that in order to understand and 'reach' Laura he would need to 'shed' a great deal, to change. Graves carried out his task conscientiously, but felt unhappy about forcing himself to conceal the contempt he could not help feeling for Phibbs as soon as he met him. But he indulged in his best hopes and wishes, as unfortunately he always does, and did his best.

Phibbs was tall and thin, with a lock of hair which he kept jerking back. 'Very black-looking', his face seemed 'dark and hot'. His eyes were blue, but seemed dark. He was always 'looking down as if intensely preoccupied with something that [had] just happened to him'.

156

When he came out of his brown study, it was 'always suddenly and questioningly – placing the burden of conversation on the other person'. In a number of Riding's post-1929 works he became – to the point of monotony – a synonym of the 'devil'. His appearance reminded Frank O'Connor of Proust's Baron de Charlus. O'Connor describes him in his autobiography *My Father's Son* as 'satanic and cruel', but with an 'animal beauty'.

Phibbs had already read Riding's poems; but her two prose books of 1928, *Contemporaries and Snobs* and *Anarchism is Not Enough*, were what set him off. He had difficulties with his family, was unhappy about the flippancy of his verse, disliked his journalistic work, and felt that he ought to be doing something better. He had spiritual yearnings, but of a singularly ill-defined sort. He was tired of 'being treated as an irresponsible young wit' in Ireland. The essence of his considerable charm lay in his wistfulness for the better life he knew he could not attain. When, later, he sank to his proper level, he seemed no more than odd. But in 1929 someone or something put madness into him. He was in a state of emotional lability bordering at times on madness.

So Phibbs gave up his journalist's job in Ireland, settled some of his debts there, and decided to throw in his lot with Laura Riding – and with the Seizin Press and its objectives, which he soon found he did not understand. This lack of understanding made him angry and dangerous.

He turned up with a knapsack and in rags – or, at least, in clothes of which Laura Riding disapproved and consequently 'eliminated'. He had £6, given him by his parents. Graves was prevailed upon to 'lend' him

> 7 shirts, 2 jerseys, a brown coat, a silk dressing gown, underclothes, socks and four or five neckerchiefs – value £7. Miss Riding also lent him an 18th century blue tie pin value £1, a batik silk scarf, value £2 and two other silk scarves value £1.

There is no record of his trousers, and we must assume that these were not found wanting. The 'Irish Adonis' – having been lent a further £17 by Riding for clothes (of her choice: she wished to see his spiritual virtues as well represented as possible) – was now presentable, and it was not long before he and Laura Riding, or rather Laura Riding and he, were contemplating the composition of a modest 'philosophical work'. This was to deal with 'knowledge of good and evil', but nothing more extensive.

Other women fall in love and hardly know that they are doing. But Riding fell in love, thought she knew what she was doing, and entered into a collaboration on things which most people would think irrelevant to love's vernal stirrings. As is her wont, she wanted to 'tidy up' Phibbs – which is only another way of saying that, if he wanted to reach her 'entire position', he would have to 'shed' a great deal of himself, as well as most of his clothes. Serious work on so basic a project as the knowledge of good and evil would doubtless have tidied anyone up – and everyone else as well, had it been successful. But it never got written. Composition was interrupted by events possibly definable (though we shall never now know) as at least silly.

However, Riding, having dressed Phibbs for his part, became even more intensely interested in him; and so for Graves the situation became only moderately 'wonderful' – though he made the best of it. Riding's goal has always been 'finality': end of history, end of the tyranny of time, annihilation of matter. Graves persuaded himself that in some way the Irish Adonis, and Laura's fascination with him, must be landmarks on the route: eyes front, quick march, he dedicated himself to finality and Phibbs.

Phibbs had closed his Irish bank account but had not opened one in England. He had nothing to put into any account. He was for ever dithering about his wife, and was unable to commit himself wholly to the knowledge of good and evil, though he did make some (mostly unpreserved) notes on the subject. His vacillations caused irritation; but he was more often than not able to smooth things over by his gift for making moving declarations of intent – and by his effective expression of fine repentance, which came from him as from a loop-tape.

Graves's family, and many of his friends, felt, more straightforwardly, that (as John Graves put it to me) 'Laura wanted Phibbs'. While this does not do justice to the tragic intensity with which she yearned for others to fit into her scheme, or to the absoluteness of her conviction that what she saw as the road to truth was the same for all, it does have a crude aptness. Riding earnestly 'wanted' everyone, including Robert and Nancy; but just as some people are born more equal than others, so in the late February of 1929 she found herself wanting Geoffrey Phibbs more urgently than she wanted Robert and Nancy, who were in any case already 'hers'. *How* she wanted him is obscure, because it was obscure (or just physically disturbing?) to her. Her customary precision failed her, which is why she raised a furore. Some kind of constitutional *Verrücktheit*, perhaps, supervened. Having spent two years during which Truth had not been opposed except by the correctible errors of two others, she found herself confronted by awkward and wicked bits of Untruth, by irrelevant, 'time-bound' bits of history, such as Phibbs's irritating preoccupation with his wife Norah, and his intellectual doubts. These stood in the way of Truth; and suddenly no one, least of all she, could understand in what direction she wanted to go. Phibbs in exactly her own likeness would have been night (if not daylight) robbery: she decided to make Phibbs 'happy' by doing to him what she had initially done to his clothes: throw him away and make him into a new man. But he was no Graves.

The partners began to teach Phibbs printing, and one of the many early Seizin prospectuses lists a projected short work by him. But the main emphasis was on the 'philosophical work', in which he would collaborate with Riding. In other words, Graves found himself, not for the last time, supplanted as Laura's collaborator – and in other respects – by a man whose intellect he despised.

But he swallowed his feelings whole and

bought a house-boat [*Avoca*] moored alongside the other [*Ringrose*] as a residence for Mr Phibbs and also repaired it at his expense.

All this plunged Phibbs into a state of extreme confusion. He thought he loved Laura, and was dutifully told how to do so by Graves; but he still did not feel that Riding was being 'fair' 'about the amount one has to shed to reach her entire position'. He felt, desperately, that it was a 'pitty'; good and evil, subjects he was supposed to be researching, made him 'bluddy nervous'. So did Laura. He found himself under pressure to behave properly from Graves, always officious and ferociously military when undertaking Riding's commissions. He was confused the more when Graves, seeming to change tack, would weep on his shoulder about the difficulties of his own position. Graves had needed such shoulders since he lived on Boars Hill; he must talk incessantly about his love problems. The purpose of such talk is talk; it is to no purpose, and he never takes note of any advice proffered.

Phibbs's wife Norah had just left 'little David Garnett' (as Graves had called him in *The Marmosite's Miscellany*); she wanted her husband back, and Frank O'Connor was putting pressure on him to return to her. But as O'Connor says, Phibbs was very angry with her.

So the 'Four' developed, in place of the Trinity. But Phibbs was as uneasy a fourth person as a theologian would be if obliged to accommodate a hitherto unknown divine brother of Christ into the old arrangement. The theory underlying the 'Four' is a work by Riding, the sketch for which has been lost in the fogs of time. But it lasted only some six weeks – if we allow two for the articulation of its revelation in her mind.

One afternoon – a puzzled man, bedazzled by Riding's theories, guilty about his failure to satisfy – Phibbs sat down with a pencil to try to work out his own (unentire) position. The result could hardly have been enlightening, even to him; but it is instructive as to the sort of thinking induced in people by Riding. (The initials speak for themselves; > is the mathematical sign for 'is larger than'.)

Numbers involve an undefined disintegration.
$R = L > N > R$
$L = G > R > N > L$
$L = N > G$
$N = G > L > R$
Disorder is necessary primary to order (1 to 17)
Theoretical is point of transmutation of actual from temporal
Actual = formal = potential = geometrical
Temporal *may* = historical, ('actual historical' or 'potential')
? a projection from Laura
? necessitated *by* Laura
? defined (limited by Laura (conditioned – what term?) (Not yet known)
? of myself (not yet known)

It is easy to laugh at Phibbs, but impossible not to feel sorry for him as, dressed up in one of Robert's green shirts, prettily enscarfed (even if still in his own trousers), his lock hanging over his forehead, he laboured under the rays of Riding's severe efforts to transmute him. It has always been difficult to find yourself in 17 + 1, or 18, or at the exact point at which to transmute from temporal, or whatever. Disorder certainly always = 1. He tried to persuade Laura to run off with him: immediately. But since there was no money to run off on, and doubtless for other reasons, she refused.

III

And so, on All Fools' Day, he vanished; he 'suddenly disappeared', having told 'his friends at the houseboats at Atlanta Wharf that he was dining with an aunt. No news of him could be got.' Poor Phibbs, distracted, was trying to throw up 1 to 17 and find his wife. But fate had other things in store for him: '? of myself (not yet known)'.

He had by this time received two letters from O'Connor on the subject of Norah. From one of them it seems that his actions had not been wholly unplanned, since O'Connor (who then 'loved' him and Norah 'most in the world') mentions that he hopes to see him in France at Easter (which fell, in 1929, on 31 March). O'Connor told him that for a week it had been 'touch and go' with 'Norah's reason', that Phibbs had sacrificed 'the finest woman in Ireland' (Laura made much comic play with this phrase in her feeble *roman à clef 14A*), but that he admired Geoffrey for his state of 'temporary insanity'. However, 'if I take off my hat to you I take off my head to her [Norah]' – another phrase lifted by Laura for use in *14A*. Geoffrey got off lightly, though, because he would always roast himself, 'and like Goethe I [O'Connor] have always loved that which seeks a death of flame'.

Phibbs did not lie when he told his friends that he was dining with an aunt. Having no cash, and in no position to borrow any from the three friends from whom he proposed to flee (though Graves, left to himself, would have paid him all he had to disappear for ever), he did go to the aunt – who lived in London – to get some. But he probably did not have time for dinner; he had another destination.

Very well, Riding thought to herself, Geoffrey had bolted. This was a serious mistake – but correctible. It might serve to persuade him, once and for all, which of the many causeways open to him was the heavenly one. He must be found. She had obedient assistants.

Things happened very fast from the moment of Phibbs's flight. Both Graves and Nancy Nicholson were set to work by Laura to find him. As soon as Phibbs first arrived and the 'Four' had been created, Graves had found himself being pushed, by Riding, back into Nancy's arms – this is after all one convenient way to transmute a Trinity into a Quadrilateral. But Nancy did not want Robert back in her arms. And Graves certainly wanted to be back in Riding's. He had written, some eight years earlier, of Richard Roe who, cuckolded by 'one John Doe', wished himself 'Job, Solomon, Alexander'

> For cunning, patience, power to overthrow
> His tyrant, but with heart gone so far rotten
> That most of all he wished himself John Doe.

There was one rotten-hearted sense in which he did wish himself Phibbs – but not Phibbs-in-flight. But he kept his own counsel, and, as he put it a few months later in the deliberately cryptic 'Dedicatory

Epilogue to Laura Riding', with which he concluded *Goodbye to All That*, found that 'he must suddenly hurry off to Ireland'. Riding sent him off to Sligo to seek out his own intempestive, demented rival. And he was of course grateful to her for her refusal to leave him and Nancy.

These were strange circumstances, and stranger still to a poet whose mind had not long recovered from the horrors of war. He found himself 'on the very boat, from Fishguard, that had been my hospital-boat twelve years before', and at Limerick, he saw a woman who seemed to him

> Old Ireland herself sitting black-shawled and mourning on the station-bench and telling of the Fall.

But Robert did not find Phibbs in Sligo, only two distracted parents, who had no more idea than he of their son's whereabouts. He returned to Hammersmith as soon as he could. Norman Cameron, offering a 'chance clue', suggested that Phibbs had gone off to Rouen, after his wife Norah. The three immediately set off there, via Dieppe.

They 'found him there with his wife from whom he had previously separated. He did not appear to recognise the friends. His whole behaviour was very strange.' But perhaps he did not *want* to recognize the friends. They were unable to talk to him; he avoided them. On a hilltop in Rouen Laura 'seemed to die,' Graves wrote, 'as I had seemed to die thirteen years before.'

At Rouen station Laura wrote Phibbs a letter. They then returned. For Riding the loss of him was high tragedy. She was not going to give him up without a battle – his flight had suddenly clarified his immense value to her.

IV

When the Trinity, or Rump of the Four, or whatever, returned from France they found a letter from Phibbs to Laura awaiting them. It was undated and had no return address – but it had been written and posted in Rouen. This letter, which crossed hers to Phibbs, threw light on the reasons for his departure – and got Graves into hot water with Riding, whose state of mind seems to have been fast approaching that of the Jehovah of old when his chosen people persistently failed to carry out his will and set up false idols. Phibbs, hoping to achieve his, if not her, sort of 'finality', wrote this letter:

Laura

This is to be said. I have gone away for two reasons. Last Monday whilst you were talking to Nancy in the Ringrose I talked to Robert at the Barge [the *Avoca*]. He told me, what I knew, that the only life he could have with you was when I was away. He would never have agreed to my going away even for some time. But it seemed to me then that I must go some time. Then as you know I went to dinner with my aunt. She gave me very bad news of Norah. That she was very ill and was making herself worse because of me. So when I had left my aunts I decided to go to Norah then. You must I suppose wonder that I could think of any one before you. It seemed to me that you are very strong and that you have Robert. I was between you and Robert in some way that he nor I understood. Norah simply had no one. So I did what I did and am terribly terribly unhappy. Unless you and i meet accidentally we shan't meet at present and that is not likely. You know that I know you for the most important thinker and all. . . .

Riding severely blamed Robert for not holding on to him more firmly, for telling him of his own needs, for not preserving the Four, the developed Truth, the then Final System.

In the days preceding Phibbs's departure things had been boiling up to crisis point. While Graves was betraying the Four in the *Avoca*, by admitting to what *he* would like, Riding (possibly planning to accede to Phibbs's request by reconciling the other two) was lecturing Nancy on the subject of her attitude to Robert: she was breaking the spirit of the Four by not being more loving towards him. Soon Graves, too, would have to be shown that he had been mistaken in his inclinations. For the sake of truth, or Truth, Riding must 'have' Phibbs.

From Lisheen, Sligo, Phibbs, now reunited with his wife, wrote to Graves on 10 April:

Robert,

Will you send me

1. Laura's letters to me.
2. The copy of Love as Love [*Love as Love, Death as Death*: her poems published in 1928 by Seizin] which she wrote my name in.
3. My own manuscripts & papers.

The Love as Love was in the book-case. My MSS. were some in the drawer and some were on the end of the table in the work room in a folder and on the small block. I'd like, too, the scarf Laura gave me. If you feel it would make things in a way cleaner to burn all my papers and poems please do. I don't much mind about them. Laura's letters I do want very much, but I think she may not wish me to have them, but more probably she won't mind if I have them or not.

Tell her, if you think it worth while, that I accept her letter to me absolutely (the one from Rouen station) and that I will try to do as she asked me about being silent. If it is any satisfaction to her you can tell her that I have not been happy for one minute since I left her on the Ringrose. I carry her Rouen letter with me as my most complete humiliation and I have come back to Ireland out of humiliation. God I feel bitter. Sorry. This letter is bloody. It just shews that I'm all Laura said I was.

God bless you. Tell Nancy I love her. But not furiously as I love Laura. I know all about Judas. I'll write his Gospel. Hell. I don't really care about those things, but send them if you can.

I'll never see the end of my own futility.

Nor of why.

Geoffrey.

He wrote this on a Wednesday. By Sunday, 14 April – indeed, on the day before that – he had changed his mind, for he wrote again, in a different tone, this time to Nancy. Obviously these two had been forming an understanding, on the lines of 'let's leave the two mystics to change the world while I write books and you paint'. He felt besieged by a bewildering array of women: Laura, Norah and Nancy herself.

Nancy,

Yesterday I had ready to send you 5 pages of writing & a page cut out of the Encyclopaedia Britannica [this was from the 1911 edition, 13: pages 607–8 – on one leaf – which contains the 'General Paralysis of the Insane' section of the entry on 'Insanity']. Then just when I was going to send the letter to you, came without expectation, Laura's letter to me. I had written to you a lot about Laura, her work, her brain, her health, but all supposing the letter to me from Rouen station as her finality to me. Now her letter makes everything not final. I have torn up the letter I wrote you yesterday and stuck back the page in the Encyclopaedia. Now I am bewildered – what was final is not final. I could go to Laura & you and live such a life as I want to live because it is a good life. I could do that but how can I? Norah has come here – she would not stay away from me. I have no love for her like my love for Laura ['you' is very heavily, but not heavily enough, deleted, and 'Laura' substituted]. When I left Laura & you I ought never to have gone back to her. But I did go back. And now I cannot see Norah as bad just because she is devoted to me & wants to be with me: it is a great trouble. Also she is ill: the Doctor says her lungs are all right, but that she must have absolute rest and peace. I do not see that it would be right for me to leave her again now. I do not see it as right that I should stay away from Laura. I *want* to go to Laura, but because of that I mistrust the arguments I could give for going. Will you say something? When does Laura go to Paris, if?

I love you

Geoffrey.

Graves was not the only one during this April to see Sligo. Nancy was by no means unwilling to be sent to Ireland, as Laura's envoy, to retrieve Phibbs. She was tactful and (possibly) ingratiating towards him. She persuaded Phibbs to promise to return to Hammersmith; she also succeeded in getting Norah to return to France.

But Phibbs broke his promise. He sent a wire on 22 April: 'Can't get away before Thursday.' When the time came he did not turn up. Riding became frantic. On Friday, 26 April, a wire came from Hilton, Huntingdonshire, the very place where Graves had met Nancy. It was by then the residence of David Garnett, gentleman, botanist, bookseller, farmer, journalist, hunter, novelist and, later, flier. Phibbs had presumably gone to see him, to discuss Norah. Garnett (who himself kept a wife, Rae) received him with studied distaste. But Phibbs was still reluctant, and wired:

> Difficulties innumerable insuperable too great no faith this is is is end not coming

Laura instructed Graves to go to Hilton on the instant. But that was not so easy; it was too late to get there and bring him back that night, but she wanted him back that night.

Graves hired a special train – a practice not then as uncommon or expensive as it is now. In the epilogue to *Goodbye to All That* he simply records

> my sudden journey to Hilton in Huntingdon, to a farm with memories of her [Nancy] as I first knew her, to burst in upon – as it happened – David Garnett (whom I had never met before), gulping his vintage port and scandalising him with my soldier's oaths as I denied him a speaking part in your parable. . . .

Garnett, whose own autobiography perhaps understandably does not mention this episode, was unhelpful. Graves swore roughly at him. Then he rousted out the exhausted Phibbs and took him back to London on the waiting special train. Phibbs pleaded that he had 'lost faith' in the 'philosophical work'; but he was frightened for his physical safety, for Graves looked and now was on the verge of extreme rage.

V

They arrived back at 35A very late.

> The four talked nearly all night trying to help him [Phibbs] to come to a clear decision, his reasons for staying away being uncertain and contradictory.

Riding tried to get him to stay. But Phibbs was adamant: he did not want any part of Laura Riding; he could not be happy with her or make her happy. Everyone went to bed for an hour or two. But by eight o'clock on the morning of Saturday, 27 April, they were at it again, hammer and tongs.

At about 9 a.m. Phibbs repeated that he wanted no more of Riding, that he preferred Nancy and would go with her. Riding drank Lysol, but it had no effect. While Graves, Nancy and Phibbs watched, she said, 'Goodbye, chaps!' and jumped from the window. Graves and Nancy were horrified. Phibbs took to his heels without waiting to find out whether she was dead or alive.

Riding kept returning to this topic in her writings – in the preface to *Poems: A Joking Word*, in *Everybody's Letters* and in *14A* – always describing Phibbs as 'the devil', and representing herself as poetically motivated rather than emotionally frustrated.

T. E. Lawrence, who visited Laura in hospital as soon as he could, and who stuck by Graves as he always did when the latter was in trouble, wrote about the affair to his confidante Charlotte Shaw (Mrs Bernard Shaw) on 22 May 1929. It is an almost wholly accurate report of what happened.

> . . . thence to London, where I saw Laura Riding. She has broken her pelvis, and three bones in her spine, but will recover, they say, in six months. For love of an Irishman, Geoffrey Phibbs (who did not love her any more) she had thrown herself down four stories into Graves's area at Chiswick.

Graves, he continued, jumped after her (as he did, but from the third storey). He told Mrs Shaw of how Nancy had now gone to live with Phibbs, and of how Phibbs's wife lived 'every six months or so' with

Garnett. 'They are madhouse minds: no, not so much minds as appe-
tites.' The mess, he thought, might have solved Robert's difficulties.
'He is a most excellent and truthful person, drowning in a quagmire.'

Riding landed on her coccyx, and suffered a compound fracture of
the spine. (When the surgeon came to operate on her, her spine was
'at right angles to itself', a rare phenomenon; and her pelvis was
fractured in five places.) Nancy called for an ambulance; Graves,
though very shaken by his own wild jump, carried her into it.

The double jump was reported by eager neighbours to the police,
who thought that they had an attempted murder – or, with luck, a
murder – on their hands. The now terrified Phibbs soon returned to
the district, and made an incoherent statement, which put Graves into
an even more difficult position. It led them to suspect Graves of
attempted murder, and so they grilled him more intensively. He stood
up to it – but never forgot their attitude. It was one of the experiences
that made him want to leave England.

Until well after the Second World War attempted suicide was a
crime under English law. In legal terms, Riding could be prosecuted.
But had she been charged, she would not have been sent to prison (as
some people were); as an American citizen, she would have been
deported.

She was thus not only very ill indeed – thought of at first, by all, as
a future cripple at best – but also under threat of a humiliating legal
process. So when he was grilled by the police Graves had to be very
careful what he said: he must not incriminate Laura, but was simultaneously obliged to clear himself of attempted murder, with which the
police were eager to charge him. He played his cards very close to his
chest.

Graves stated that there had been an accident, but little else. He had
to pretend that he had gone to fetch an emetic for the Lysol and that
Laura had jumped when Nancy was alone in the room, with her back
turned: Phibbs, for all he knew, had accused him of murder. Certainly
he thought Laura was dead, and accused her of having delusions of
grandeur. The police thought of her as a 'vampire'. In answer to
persistent questioning he was as cryptic as he dared to be. Later Phibbs
excused himself, in a letter to Graves, by accusing him of having told
the police what he himself in fact had told them: that 'immorality' had
been going on. 'Surely neither you nor I are *ashamed* of the way life
was led at the flat?' Graves maintained an insolently aristocratic man-

ner in face of the policemen's persistent questions, and in the end they had to give up.

As for Phibbs, he remained unrepentant. He thought (he wrote) that Riding was suffering from an intellectual disorder. But he continued to be fascinated by her.

The closest Riding ever came to describing her jump, in writing, is in the preface to *Poems: A Joking Word* (1930). This is one of her least lucid pieces (she wrote it without Graves's assistance), but some meaning may be extracted from it by those who know the background. She states here that Phibbs (who is not named) was 'the Devil and also Judas and so on'. 'Once upon a time' she was 'standing in a room with' him and with 'the Virgin Mary who was also Medea and so on' (Nancy); also there was 'a third who was about to finish with that kind of thing' (Graves). 'Myself I had already finished.' In a contorted passage, Phibbs is said to have been pretending to 'be with doom rather than with nature', but really 'with nature ... on the point of just ending'. 'Nature', to this latterday Borborite, is matter; 'doom' is 'good' because it ends time. 'My life,' she wrote in this preface – meaning by 'life' involvement in 'history' and 'nature' – 'reads all wrong to me because it is what would be me if I didn't feel doom.' 'My life is feeling myself as me, my poems are feeling myself as doom.' 'My life is me instead of doom, me postponing doom.' In her poems, she felt, she escaped 'from escaping' her life.

She wrote that Phibbs was interested only in suicide ('It was all very underhand'), and continued: 'Well, I gave him suicide.'

> And working on the Virgin Mary and so on's [Nancy's] natural (I mean not personal) feelings against doom as possible opposition, he got her to about turn against herself and go out with him. . . . Standing in that room was a quick result – I left that room, by the window of course, and poems came with me.

All this is exceedingly complex, and some passages which I have not quoted are impenetrable and tiresomely repetitious in a Steinesque manner. But there was in Riding an element of, to put it at its simplest, struggle against the flesh and what the flesh represents. The attempt at suicide was, as Gertrude Stein soon afterwards implied, poignant – rather than 'hysterical', as has been suggested. The flaw in the whole self-justificatory argument, such as it is, is that she fails to acknowledge her own jealousy, which had a physical as well as mental basis.

When she was too young to understand that personal hope is not identical with universal hope, Riding seemed beautiful to Graves. Some of her early poems are redolent with this beauty:

> As well as any other, Erato,
> I can dwell separately on what men know
> In common secrecy,
> And celebrate the old, adoréd rose,
> Retell – oh why – how similarly grows
> The last leaf of the tree. . . .

It is breathtaking, as is so much else she wrote. It exudes the spirit with which Graves fell in love; but there was not much more of it to come from the woman herself, though miraculously she went on writing beautiful poems until stopped by the man she finally fell in with. The end of 'The Mask' (written in her youth in America) answered a question that had always troubled Graves:

> Is there no pure then?
> The eternal taint wears beauty like a mask.
> But a mask eternal.

Such an altruistic beauty, even if not permanently displayed, such uncompromising intelligence compounded with innocence and ignorance, 'poignant uprightness' – such qualities, born out of untroubled and rapturous nature by whatever developed the human cortex to the point of word-making, are deadly attributes in a world disobedient to the will of any single person. There is a terrible courage in Riding's confusions.

'Mr Graves' is 'persistent', Riding wrote in 1974, when she had long hated him. She should know. She wrote of him in 1930, in that preface to her Poems: A Joking Word: 'He concentrated on living enough so that I could dilate on feeling doom.' This statement bears thinking about. It was what he craved; but could he stand it?

Chapter Thirteen

1929

I

When Riding found herself to be not dead, but a shattered and perhaps permanently crippled being whose severe pain had to be relieved by constant shots of morphia, she immediately remembered Phibbs. She still 'wanted' him. When she had recovered her health, and knew that she could not change the situation between Phibbs and Nancy, she was for some time pleasant – and generally grateful – to Graves. Immediately after the fall, however – and despite her pain and the threat of criminal proceedings – she still tried to settle affairs in the way in which she deemed they ought to be settled. The police soon satisfied themselves that Riding had not been pushed out of the window. When Graves and Nancy visited the hospital, she told them, on recovering, that she wished to take 'full responsibility for what had occurred'. This was helpful and scrupulous: it cleared everyone of suspicion.

The police were left with only one opportunity: to charge Riding with attempted suicide. But she was still seriously ill.

On Monday, 29 April, two days after Riding's jump, Graves himself was taken ill, and had to enter hospital. He often used to complain, part jokingly, of how no one sympathized with *his* fall (Riding made a point of not doing so). But before this he had written to his old friend, Eddie Marsh (who was then secretary to Winston Churchill at the Exchequer and who therefore had only indirect influence at the Home Office), asking if he could do anything to prevent the deportation of Riding as an 'undesirable alien'. Marsh replied loyally and promptly. His letter made it clear that he could offer some hope.

He told Graves that he had 'had a long talk' with a private secretary at the Home Office, 'whose sympathy I managed to enlist'. This PPS had promised to talk to the Director of Public Prosecutions. He thought that there would be a good chance of avoiding action, but that if the

DPP wanted to take it 'it would be . . . impossible for the Home Secretary to override him'.

The result of this was that 'after investigation the Home Office did not pursue the matter'. Riding later sneered at Graves's use of 'influence' in this affair, in *14A*. Perhaps he did make a little too much of it: he is fond of having influence.

On the day after Riding's jump, a Sunday, Geoffrey Phibbs had delivered to the hospital, by Nancy, this pencilled note, scribbled on a small memo leaf, to

Laura Laura Laura

I didn't understand. I was so full of my own shame. Shame at all I had made you suffer that I didn't believe you could ever want me again. You didn't tell me yesterday (Saturday). I ought to have known but I did (do) feel so unworthy. Nancy just did break down after all the strain and had this night-mare and couldn't let me out of her sight. She didn't believe that I'd go away. She thought she might wake up & find she'd dreamt it all. Oh Laura

But by the evening of the day on which he wrote this he had already joined Nancy on the *Ringrose*.

Nancy came to visit Robert on the following day, in his hospital, and told him that on the previous day she had met Phibbs, 'accidentally', in the lobby of the Plaza Cinema, 'and that she was living with him on the house-boat Ringrose'. Graves was 'very ill at the time' and told Nancy unequivocally that 'he no longer had any faith in Mr Phibbs as a friend and could not welcome him back'.

Nancy then went straight off to visit Laura, who was still 'critical'. From her she received an answer contradicting Graves's. Nancy read out Phibbs's message ('Laura Laura Laura . . . '), and then passed on the further information that he was

full of remorse for the confusion of his conduct and its consequences, and that he would obey whatever feelings she [Laura] might have in the matter.

Nancy had Phibbs in the wings, ready to be brought out to see Laura – if she would permit it. She did: she told him that 'if Miss Nicholson and Mr Graves were satisfied that Mr Phibbs should return she was too'.

But, as the 'Précis' (written later) puts it:

Miss Riding was under morphia a great deal of this time . . . nevertheless she was gradually able to work out when Mr Graves was able to leave hospital and visit her and from conversation with other friends that the friendship of the four had come to an end because Miss Nicholson, who had ceased visiting her, and Mr Phibbs had now entered into a relationship the spirit of which overshadowed the friendship of the four.

This was regarded by Graves and Riding as Phibbs's most culpable deceit of all, '*after* the fall', as Graves put it in a letter to Marsh.

Graves had forced himself to enter into the spirit of the Four as prescribed by Riding; but when he heard that Phibbs had now taken over Nancy and his children, he could no longer bear it. The sense of release from the effort of having to love Geoffrey was also triggered by his feeling that his rival was responsible for Laura's injuries. For quite some time the Trinity, however odd it may now seem to us, had actually worked. Nancy had not objected to Graves's relationship with Riding; indeed, before she ever turned up, she had found herself unhappy in her married state, as he had. But the Four put too much strain on everyone, not least Phibbs. What preoccupied Graves's mind as he lay ill in his hospital bed was the fact that this 'awful bastard' had come along and spoiled everything.

Riding, however, had physical as well as spiritual motives. Graves had blinded himself to this. Paradoxically, she craved for greater firmness than she found in Graves. The cruelty in Phibbs perversely appealed to her. And so Graves's erotic performance towards her had been undermined by his insistence on her superiority to him. Her spirit, which had sought to transform Phibbs into a fit collaborator in a fundamental work 'of a philosophical nature', was also undermined, from the start, by a vulgarity in herself so insidious that she herself could not admit of its existence. This contradiction in her unnerved even Phibbs, who saw it clearly in his closest encounters with her. But Graves wrote to Marsh that the 'sex thing' (with Phibbs) was not important to him or Laura. This was simply self-deception. The flesh is willing, and the spirit is weak – and he and she ought to have known it.

II

Some time before Sunday, 12 May, when Riding felt better and understood that Nancy had lied to her in the hospital, she told Phibbs that she never wanted to see him again. She was then certain about this, even though awaiting a critical operation (this took place on the following Thursday, 16 May, and was successful).

Phibbs suddenly felt insulted, vicious and revengeful. This new mood, induced by her total rejection of him and by Graves's sarcastic hostility, was interrupted by intermittent bursts of impudence, mawkish self-pity, envy – and genuine good will. But he was basically concerned to defend himself – to assuage what must have been a considerable sense of guilt and shame – by going onto the attack.

Graves was discharged from hospital in a day or two. His chief concern was for Laura's health and her impending operation. But the fact of his children meant that he had to get matters settled between himself and Nancy. Once again, Phibbs was in the way.

In both versions of *Goodbye to All That* Graves gives 6 May 1929 (Tuesday) as the date of his 'final' parting with Nancy. This is presumably the date on which she told him that Phibbs would definitely be standing in as father to his children, and the date on which he therefore felt that he could not have anything more to do with her – other than financially support the four children and, for the sake of them, her. To have also to support the indigent Phibbs must have been a bitter pill indeed. All the money coming in from *Lawrence and the Arabs* was vanishing fast. To make more he was now planning a candid autobiography: a book in which he would tell everything about his past, written in a mood in which he no longer cared what anyone thought about him. In any case, none of his money was destined, if he could possibly help it, to go Phibbs's way.

But while 6 May is probably the date on which he made his decision to break his marriage, he did not make this clear to Nancy until Sunday, 12 May. For on that day he had an important interview with her and Phibbs together.

She [Riding] told Mr Phibbs that she did not wish to see him again. Mr Phibbs told Mr Graves on May 12 that he was glad of this and anxious to live separately with Miss Nicholson, adding that her [Riding's] mind was maggoty and that if he thought that anything Miss Riding said could prevent this he would throw her out of another window and break her neck.

But there was more to it than this. In the first place, Riding, ill as she was, still wanted to 'tidy things up'. She had gone back on 'never wanting to see Phibbs again'. So the unhappy Graves, on the evening of 12 May, as he received Nancy and Phibbs at 35A – they had only to walk across from the *Ringrose* – felt obliged to give a full report to Riding on what occurred. (This report is extant.)

When the couple arrived Phibbs was in subdued, self-justifying mood. Nancy said little; most of the time she seemed not to be listening. She had become rigidly obstinate: *she* now wanted Phibbs, *she* could keep him even if Laura couldn't – and *she* was going to keep the children. It didn't matter what any one of them said. She later told one of her children, Catherine, that she felt Riding 'wanted to do for both men'. Towards the end of her life she said, in conversation, that she had 'quite liked Laura', who 'had a fine forehead, but whose face deteriorated in the lower half'.

On that evening Graves was in aggressive mood towards Phibbs. But Riding had a further message for the morally tattered Adonis, to be passed on by a reluctantly dutiful Robert. He was, first, to declare his 'position' (yet again), and Graves, instructed by Riding, must define for him by what means he could thus make this definition. This definition included a definition of 'definition' and of 'position'. . . . That, by Riding's standards, was elementary stuff. And Robert did his duty; but he spiced his discourse with sarcastic hostility. He wanted to see the back of Phibbs for ever. He punctuated the message with cruel taunts, especially about running away.

Phibbs, under this fierce pressure from Graves, at first did try to explain his 'position'.

'I'm hurt by Laura,' he complained. 'She's changed: that's why. It's upset and hurt me. I'm *very* upset.'

'Why?' asked Graves, mincingly. 'Why're *you* upset? Your legs are strong. You can move like a bolt from a bow.'

'She's in a complete muddle. She wants me to be like I was to her before she jumped: intense, devoted, just as I really was and felt. How can I, now? I can't be intense like that any more. She jumped – just because I said I preferred Nancy because I couldn't understand Laura. *That's* not spiritual. She's not spiritual. I can understand Nancy. She's practical. *She's* not crazy.'

Graves: 'You're a liar and a sponger. You're a liar, you know.' The verdict sounded like a court-martial finding not subject to higher review.

'First she says she doesn't want to see me again because I'm living with Nancy on the *Ringrose*. She says that this means I can't possibly *respect* 35A as a workplace. I just don't understand. You've said as

174

much to me yourself. Remember? She's just bloody well what she's always calling everyone else: *vulgar*. She's jealous of Nancy. She wants me, she wants to possess me, have me, fuck me. Isn't that just *vulgar*? Besides: she thinks she's God. She's sick.'

'You know you're lying. You've broken the Four by going off with Nancy in a squalid way, and on *my* houseboat. You owe me money, you know. You've refused to carry on with the work you and Laura were doing. *You're* vulgar. You don't give a damn for Nancy, and you can't support her. You want my support for yourself. Laura's definition of vulgarity is what we've tried to rid ourselves and the world of, both of us. Of course it's hard to understand what's holy. But you haven't even tried.'

'*She* damn well broke the Four!' Phibbs shouted back from his chair, 'by jumping out of the window. It wasn't Nancy and me. What the hell can she possibly mean by it all? She's crazy. And,' he added darkly, '*I know why*. Now, you who pretend to know everything about her, just what *does* she mean? You tell me. You didn't pretend to know so much when I first arrived!'

'You know that I can't make any statement for Laura in answer to what you say. Even you ought to understand at least that. All I can tell you is what she told me. I can't go further than that. She said that she has no desires – no ideas of being possessive – and that she wants you and Nancy to act in the way that will make you most happy. But to remember that what you want now isn't necessarily what will make you happiest in the end. Any movement, she says, must now come from you. But don't make the mistake of imagining – as with your vulgar mind you certainly do – that Laura wants you to feel that she's trying to detach you from Nancy. That's not the point.'

Phibbs now stood up and sneered petulantly, commenting that what you want now not being what will make you happiest in the end was what the choirboy told the bishop.

'Don't you have any sense at all of Laura's *holiness*?' Graves burst out.

'*Holiness*! Ha! Holiness. Oh yes. *Holiness* in sense of holes into which she wants me to fall. Holes I fall through. Maggots eat holes!'

Then, abruptly switching from abuse to mawkishness, he sat down again and started a self-pitying monologue, tears rolling down his cheeks.

'Oh God! I know I shouldn't talk like that about her. But first she wants me to think of her as *not* lying there' – he rose, went to the window and dramatically pointed down at the courtyard below – 'and then she wants me to think of her *as* lying there.'

When she had told him she didn't want to see him again, she had given as her reason that she'd left the room, 'by the window of course', in order to leave both him and what he stood for. But now she was saying – or so it seemed to him – that if he would change ('unbecome' the misguided, Nancy-preferring creature she'd left in so dramatic a manner), then he could be reconsidered: he could think of her as she had been before her jump. But he did not trust her. He meant, when he said that she *did* want him to think of her lying here, that she wanted his pity: so she was being, in his view, vulgar and possessive. He felt that although she had 'taught' him 'not to be vulgar', now she herself was being vulgar.

What, besides the material security of money that we all have to try to have, did she want? Certainly nothing he – or Graves – could provide. But no one yet realized this.

'Christ!' asked Phibbs helplessly, 'do you honestly think the Four is possible now, Robert, or not? Surely not!'

Graves had the answer. If Laura ever seemed open to a charge of jealousy or of ordinary, down-to-earth sexual desire – as she certainly did now – then her special 'holiness' was brought up as defence. It all depended on her being – and this must be emphasized – *holy*. The word was often used. Otherwise it would all have been quotidian, mundane, time-bound, goddawful.

So Graves now became almost as obscure and yet precise-sounding as Laura herself usually was – imitating her own niminy-piminy manner of expressing herself on matters to do with relationships:

'Your relationship with Nancy has defined itself in such a way that it makes the Four impossible. However, if it changes – and Laura certainly doesn't mean by that that it should grow less strong – then anything is possible. The point is that your relationship with Nancy must change in its *reference to Laura and me*.' He might have been reading from notes.

Phibbs was further bewildered – and no wonder. What Graves said in Riding's behalf does not really mean anything – unless that Phibbs and Nancy must do what Robert was doing: follow Laura's instructions to the letter.

At last Nancy intervened, although to little point: 'For heaven's sake, why can't you make it clear to Laura that always – right from the beginning — *I* put Geoffrey's relationship with her before anything else?'

Clearly the interview had gone badly, although Graves may not have been totally displeased with Phibbs's failure to toe the line. It ended with this explosion from Phibbs:

'If I thought that in any way Laura could alter my relationship with Nancy I'd throw her out of the window myself and this time I'd break her bloody neck.'

Then Phibbs and Nancy left. In the face of Graves's relentless attack on him Phibbs's thoughts turned to revenge. His vanity was wounded: Laura still 'had the greatest mind and all that. . . .'

Forty-five years later Graves, refusing to answer an inquiry about Phibbs, wrote:

> No, it's a bit close to the knuckle. He fell in love with Laura Riding with whom I had been on intimate terms ['living and sleeping' is heavily deleted], then decided to go back to his wife, then Laura tried to commit suicide ['went mad and' is deleted before 'tried' . . .] — he decamped at once and I was accused of murder by detectives — so I nursed her back to health and then he went off with my wife.

Graves never thought much about Phibbs after he disappeared from his life, though for part of the thirties he believed that Phibbs had been responsible for the destruction of Laura's 'holiness'. He abandoned this belief just before his own association with her had ended.

III

When Graves reported the details of his interview with Nancy and Phibbs to Riding she instructed him that, in the circumstances, he was not to give Phibbs any access to her papers without her consent. (There were in fact some of Phibbs's own papers among hers.) Furthermore, during the course of that unhappy interview Robert had contemptuously assured him that any papers or books that were his by right would in due course be returned to him. Phibbs was desperate to get at his property; it contained evidence of his overexcited 'lifelong dedication' to Laura, her cause, and so forth. She was as desperate to get at whatever she had written to him. She has always ferociously insisted on the return of her own letters, apparently confusing the ownership

of the copyright in letters with that of the letters themselves (which are
the property of the recipient).

But had Phibbs been given permission, in his present mood, to sort
them out himself from amongst Laura's papers, she thought he might
take some of the latter for future use – that possibly he had some kind
of insurance in mind. He knew that he had run away when she had
jumped, which was by any standards a discreditable act. He needed to
be able to make Laura look mad, the kind of person who might well
produce an action of this sort, in the eyes of ordinary people. We know
that he had, for some time, been entertaining perfectly sincere doubts
about the state of her intellect.

Graves was thus, *faute de mieux*, granted custody of all the papers
at 35A. It was a role he played with zeal, since it was in the fierceness
of his protection of Riding that he sublimated his own doubts and
miseries about her true nature – and about the future of his relationship
with her.

Phibbs made one more attempt to be conciliatory, preferring the
getting of his papers to being hostile. On 14 May he wrote Graves a
letter, heading it 'Avoca' ('his' barge, rather than *Ringrose*, where he
was living with Nancy).

> When you send my MSS will you also send the parcel of my 'Withering
> of the Figleaf' which is somewhere at the flat; also Nancy's cutting-out
> scissors.
>
> Also there are a number of my old books which were set aside to be
> sold later. We feel that we ought to have these to sell. You see we don't
> mean to bother you about money (except for the children) but at the
> same time we must get some! Would you also give me a letter of
> introduction to Bruce Richmond [then editor of the *Times Literary
> Supplement*]?
>
> Sorry to bother you & so on.
>
> Geoffrey.

There was no response; and Phibbs soon strode over from the *Ringrose*
to 35A, where he began to try to force the door. As soon as Graves
opened it, he pushed past him, rushed to where his papers were, and
began frenziedly to rummage through them. Graves says that he had
been drinking heavily. There was a scuffle, and Graves knocked him
down. Phibbs fell down a flight of steps to the floor below. Picking
himself up, he made off. But as he did so he flung back over his
shoulder fearful threats: 'I'll get you at law for this! I'll take out an

injunction for assault, theft. . . .' And so it went on until he vanished from sight.

Graves sat down at once and wrote him a letter. He here fell into an error into which he frequently falls: he brought up the question of what Phibbs owed him, in financial and other material terms. Like most generous men, Graves can – if subsequently provoked by the recipients of his generosity – seem abominably petty. This obsession with cash and property, although only ever aroused when he is put into quarrelsome mood, has often led to unfortunate results.

In his letter, besides bringing up the matter of Phibbs's indebtedness, he more reasonably accused Phibbs's letter of 14 May of being 'ironic'. Phibbs replied immediately, hurriedly, in pencil, injured and innocent.

Graves felt guilty about what his true attitude towards the Phibbs–Nancy attachment had been. The manner in which it finally resolved itself disgusted him; but then he felt guilty about that, too. Had he not been responsible? Under the powerful sway of Laura, trusting in her absolutely, he had acquiesced in the Four – but only as honestly as he could. For, quite apart from the unconscious apprehensions voiced in 'Sick Love', he could not help wanting Phibbs and Nancy to disappear together. And so he had for some time – despite himself – been actually encouraging him to go off with Nancy. Not in so many words. But by suggestion, and by the voicing of 'intuitions'. Phibbs now used this against him. His final judgement (1952) was: 'I treated Nancy badly and my punishment was Laura.'

On 16 May another letter from Phibbs arrived, apologizing for being 'bad-tempered': 'You know I didn't mean what I said. . . . Keep the damn mss., if Laura wants them.' Nancy had been getting at him. She was not now interested in anyone's manuscripts, or what prompted them – and she could not really enter into Phibbs's feelings of 'shame'.

Graves discovered from Laura what papers she thought Phibbs was 'entitled to', sorted them out, and gave them to him. But

Mr Graves was so outraged by Mr Phibbs' behaviour in view of Miss Riding's still critical condition and the fact that Miss Nicholson apparently condoned his attitude, that on behalf of Miss Riding and himself he now made a practical separation of interests with Miss Nicholson, Mr Graves and Miss Riding resigning any interest in the two houseboats and making a division of funds with her on behalf of her and the children. Mr Phibbs continued to live at the Barge Ringrose with Miss Nicholson and the four children the custody of whom Miss Nicholson insisted on having.

179

What most 'outraged' Graves was that it seemed as if he would now have to pay for Phibbs's personal needs. For Phibbs, supported by Nancy, took up a complacent attitude: he was now the children's 'father', Nancy was his 'wife', and 'they' 'had to have some [money], you see?' He was now taking advantage of Riding's denial of conventional morality in order to abandon all pretence at decency.

IV

Quite soon after Riding's successful operation, Phibbs and Nancy and the children went to the World's End at Islip, the cottage which Robert rented from his mother. They switched between there and the *Ringrose*, since Phibbs was searching for employment. Graves's mother wanted to sell the World's End, but he begged her to keep it for Nancy's use – promising to pay her the rent himself. Graves, and Riding through him, now bombarded Phibbs with an increasing number of messages. They were unpleasant messages, some doubtless metaphysical, to do with his character, with what he owed to them, and doubtless (from Graves) with his literary abilities. At first he took it all quite cheerfully: he had Nancy and he was free of the spell of Laura. On 20 May, from the *Ringrose*, he wrote Graves a jocular letter in which he made fun of the latter's unfortunate propensity to claim all his material dues. It contained the sentences:

> The frequently referred to pants. I don't know. Here are two pair; were there any more? If so please sell some of my books and replace pants.

And it concluded:

> I do hope this is the last letter I shall have to write to you for some time. Your letters and Laura's messages make me alternately cross and sorrowful.

But Graves was unable to let matters rest. His children were now in Phibbs's charge; Nancy had become obstinate, and was being obstructive about legal arrangements; and the World's End was his responsibility. Furthermore, Phibbs was now spreading an unpleasant story about. Graves felt that he had to write to him about this at once. The mistake he made was his usual one: he still could not leave the matter of Phibbs's petty indebtednesses alone.

Phibbs chose attack as his main form of defence. He seized on the notion that Graves and Riding held certain books which he had contributed to the 'joint library'. They did. As Riding put it a little later in *Poems: A Joking Word*:

> But standing in that room [from which she jumped] the quick result was that he was only the Devil and so on. And when he opened his mouth again to argue he found himself arguing of course about books. And naturally he went to law instead of to doom to argue about books. He said they were his. They were.

'They were' because, however much he had taken in goods and cash, no agreement had been entered into. But he could hardly have won a court case: he had written several letters either disclaiming interest in the books or telling Graves to sell them in order to recompense him for the pants. Taunted by Graves's cruel sarcasms, Phibbs became angrier and angrier, and sillier and sillier, and shriller and shriller.

As to the slander Phibbs was spreading, Graves told Norman Cameron (an unwilling witness to this affair) that he and Riding were planning to take legal action. Phibbs heard of this (as Graves had intended him to), and replied (from the *Ringrose*):

> Dear Robert
>
> I have heard that you (and may be Laura?) believe that I have said that Laura has or has had some form of Venerial Disease; alternatively that she is suffering from a complaint known as G.P.I. How many such stories you, knowing me as you do, are prepared to believe, I've no idea. But I'm not so uninteligent or so unscientific or so unscrupulous as to make such a statement. I don't trouble to deny such things but this is too silly.

But it wasn't silly. There are a series of worried, cryptic letters to Graves from Nancy, written at exactly this time. Nancy, influenced by Phibbs, made new inferences from some medical notes on Riding (copies of these are extent) she had seen in 1926. Her letters don't say in so many words that Riding had venereal disease; but anyone who listened to the chatter going on would certainly have believed (wrongly) that Riding was suffering or had suffered from it. The chatter spread widely, too: Louise Bogan was delightedly repeating it as late as 1940 ('Blue Butter Balls'), as we have seen.

In the course of a letter of 5 June Phibbs wrote:

> I said to you that I believed Laura to be suffering from [the disorder referred to above]. . . . As for slander actions and so on, I should be very

sorry if you thought it necessary to bring one against me. Also, quite disinterestedly, I should not advise you to do it. A successful slander action is very rare, and even if you succeeded, I could not pay the costs and damages. Libel, on the other hand, is a good deal easier, and if you feel that a civil action would clear things up, then I am prepared, against my principles, to provide you with a libel that will satisfy my conscience and your requirements. It would certainly clear things up for me, but as I said, I don't mind really.

Shortly afterwards Riding was released from hospital. Phibbs, evidently bombarded with further 'letters and messages' from both her and Robert, took the foolish step of officially demanding the return of 'his' books. On 15 July he wrote to both, from the *Ringrose*, asking them to 'agree' that it was 'fair' that he should have various titles; he suggested that he should collect them from 35A at a suitable time and date. A few days later Riding wired him; 'will send books in due course further communication impossible.' Curiously enough, Phibbs still wanted both of them – particularly Riding – to think well of him.

Graves sent Nancy more than £150 in June, for her and the children's expenses. Then, when Riding came out of hospital, and when Graves was spending all his time both in writing *Goodbye to All That* (it took 'eleven weeks from start to finish', he told Marsh) and in nursing her back to health – helping her to regain the use of her legs, and seeing that she took the ample rest she needed – Phibbs began his frenzied campaign for the books. In August Nancy ran out of money, and wrote righteously to Robert for more. Her general line was that Graves had started all this by his affair with Laura, of whose intellect she now took the same view as Phibbs.

Robert sent her £5,

and said he would send more on hearing that the children were not permitted to associate with Mr Phibbs while he was acting in this antagonistic way to the prejudice of Miss Riding's health.

She replied telling him that she had left Phibbs, and that this should 'make it easier' between Robert and her. He sent her £100. He really – and characteristically – believed that she had left Phibbs, and so did feel much 'easier'. He now felt quite safe from the threat of a renewal of the Riding–Phibbs relationship.

But Nancy had not left Phibbs (except, possibly, for a day or two to ease her conscience about writing to Graves for money). At the beginning of September Graves saw Nancy and Phibbs passing through St Peter's Square in the car. He realized that he had been duped.

Throughout August 1929 many pettinesses were practised. Two examples will suffice. Phibbs returned a Swinburne which Graves had sent him, pointing out that it was Graves's, not his. Riding sent him back a Fenimore Cooper volume which he had bought as a present for her in April; he returned it to her; she sent it back with a 7s. 6d. postal order pasted on the flyleaf; he returned it; she returned it to him – and this time he gave up.

On 7 September she wrote to Phibbs telling him that there were seventeen books awaiting him at 35A, but that he must send a 'proper messenger' to collect them. A 'proper messenger', she explained, would be a person 'unknown to her'.

She sent this message to the *Ringrose*, where he then was with Nancy. He sent Graves a long, diffuse letter (it was destroyed on receipt) in which he complained of being misaddressed; he was pretending (in order to make it easier for Nancy to get cash from Graves) to be living at a house in Shaftsbury Road (in fact an accommodation address – a newsagent). With this letter he enclosed Riding's one about the 'proper messenger'. He told Graves that he had not opened it; but it had obviously been steamed open and then resealed. Riding wrote a sarcastic postcard on 9 September, telling him that she 'noted' his '*minutiae* and *facetiae*' and that he could have 'certain books' *if* he sent a 'proper messenger, that is, one unknown to me'.

On 11 September Phibbs, in ugly mood, once more knocked on the door of 35A. Graves, being very busy with his book, his printing, and his nursing of Laura, had engaged a maid. The maid answered the door. Phibbs shouted: 'I make formal application to Mr Graves for the return of my books!'

Robert told the maid to shut the door in his face. Phibbs rushed off and immediately took out a summons against Riding alleging unlawful detention of 'about 80 books of value £10' returnable at West London Magistrates' Court on 26 September. Riding promptly obtained an adjournment, on medical grounds.

. A PC Bridger, of T Division, was delegated to serve the summons. Riding's response was to ask this constable to go over to the *Ringrose* to request Mr Phibbs to cease molesting her. When the constable saw her condition, and was told that Phibbs was living with Graves's wife, he immediately did so. Phibbs told him that he would stop bothering Miss Riding if she would return his books – and he complained to the constable that she had sent him a postcard 'half in Latin and half in English'. The constable had never heard of 'Latin' and thought Phibbs mad, though his superiors had thought very well of him.

While Riding was in hospital her sister, Isobel, had come over from America. She and a friend of Riding's, a Mrs Westgate, went across to the *Ringrose* on 11 September, the day he took out the summons, to protest to Phibbs about the trouble he was causing, and to reinforce PC Bridger's warning to him to maintain the peace. Mrs Westgate noticed that Nancy was present, and also that Phibbs had a large number of books neatly arranged in a bookcase. Nancy drew the attention of Mrs Westgate and Riding's sister to the fact that he had a worktable there. Presumably this was to imply that he was working and earning money, since Graves was casting grim aspersions on his capacity to do either. This was carefully noted in the 'Précis' the partners drew up, in case Riding should later have to defend herself at West London Magistrates' Court. It would have given the magistrate the impression that Phibbs was deceitful – living off the money of the man whose wife he had stolen. For no one, seeing Riding's condition, could imagine that she and Graves were, at least at this time, enjoying an 'illicit relationship'. Phibbs was persuaded – probably by Nancy and the police between them – to withdraw his summons. He now faded out of Robert's life. He and Nancy soon afterwards went to Wiltshire. After a few years he left her to get married, as 'he wanted children of his own'.

When Graves discovered that his £100 to Nancy had been extracted from him by a trick, he wrote her the following letter:

My dear Miss Nicholson,

I am glad to have your receipt for £100 and to hear, though not in proper form from you, that you have rented the *Avoca* for 25/- a week [this referred to a new ploy of Nancy's by which she was obstinately continuing to pretend that she was not living with Phibbs]; I am waiting for a proper statement about World's End, Islip. I wish further to say that I am delighted with the good health and spirits of our children and the fact that they seem to be getting all the good in you (and equally delighted that your other qualities are otherwise disposed of).

Yours cordially

Robert Graves

I hear that you have expressed public admiration for my loyalty to Miss Riding though a cripple. I am sure that it would please Miss Riding &

perhaps contribute to her recovery if you expressed similar admiration for her loyalty to me also (though no cripple) for (to be frank) she has allowed herself to be submitted to considerable annoyance when in a precarious state of health because of her unselfish desire to accept full responsibility for an equitable but perhaps over-ingenuous action on my part committed indeed without her cognizance. . . .

Graves continued to supply Nancy with money from 1929. He bore her no grudge.

But the scandal was one of the biggest in literary circles of its time. When Wyndham Lewis – with whom Riding became acquainted for a short while in 1927–28 – visited America in 1931–32, he amused everyone with his fund of scurrilous stories. One of them, as reported by Louise Bogan, concerned the 'Free Love Corner' affair. She wrote: 'His account of Robert Graves, Laura Riding, and the Irish Adonis ("She-devil! she-devil" remarked the Irish Adonis' grandfather from behind *The Times* in the chimney-corner) was a masterpiece.' The 'grandfather' was perhaps a concoction of Lewis's – though he may have come over on behalf of Norah.

Meanwhile, Graves was working feverishly at *Goodbye to All That*. This – he was determined – would sell well enough to finance the next phase of his life, an expensive, totally unexpected and scarifying one.

Chapter Fourteen
1929–33 (I)

I

Graves's family were outraged at his behaviour throughout the summer of 1929. He arrogantly defied them by ignoring their remonstrations and by writing them bland letters about how marvellously Riding was progressing. They now regarded Riding as a 'she-devil', Phibbs as a scoundrel, and Nancy as misguided. Amy Graves was horrified by her son's 'immorality' – but at heart she was more concerned for his welfare and for the plight of her grandchildren, which is why she went on allowing her son to rent World's End. That was hard for her: she did not like to own property in which people were living in sin.

Thus estranged from his family, Graves needed all the support he could get. But many of his friends were unavailable. T. E. Lawrence did all he could, but had his own troubles; questions had been asked about him in Parliament, and to avoid publicity he had been posted to Cattewater, a remote peninsula near Plymouth. For most of the time he was in isolation, learning to be a mechanic and working on speedboats.

Sassoon, with whom relations had become uneasy anyway, was abroad. Norman Cameron was on the verge of leaving England to become an education officer in Southern Nigeria. Other friends were either scandalized or too conventional to support him in the position he had taken up.

He was lucky to have in Jane, Len Lye's wife, a loyal and practical helpmeet. It was to her that he dictated, at top speed, much of *Goodbye to All That*. He could never have done this job so fast had it not been for her aid. Hospital expenses were mounting. Money was getting shorter, the need for it greater. He was in the appropriate mood to say just how he felt about everyone and everything, and to reject his past, which he regarded as one of Mammonolatry, wholesale. That is why he cut Riding out of the story he had to tell. But the new life of asceticism which she preached, and to which he was now preparing to devote himself (he did not yet know its extent), needed financing.

At the end of 1963 he aptly stated one resolution of the paradox he had then faced, in a lecture ('Mammon') to the London School of Economics, thus:

> What we now call 'finance' is, I hold, an intellectual perversion of what began as warm human love. . . . money can be redeemed from the Biblical curse put on 'filthy lucre' only by reviving it in the lost sense of a love-gift. . . . [*Mammon and the Black Goddess*, 1965]

As Graves worked away at *Goodbye to All That*, gripped by the notion that he had been transformed by Laura into at least a pilgrim, he was (as its sales would prove) 'making' her – giving her the opportunity to set herself up in the stable circumstances required for her enterprise, which was to put an end to history (and, oddly enough, money). He had been profoundly impressed by a fragment she had written back in America – both as a premonition of his fate at her hands, and as an illustration of the ways of the Goddess:

> Forgive me, giver, if I destroy the gift.
> It is so nearly what would please me
> I cannot but perfect it.

Laura made it clear that she had to have a new base of operations; too much was being said about her in London, for one thing. He wanted to get away, too. He was himself sick of England and of the 'goddawful' habits of English society. Besides, England belonged to a past he was busy working out of his system.

Was there some place in the world which (as Riding later put it), 'by various deductions, geographical and otherwise', could fulfil the function of being 'the home of the acceptance of the ending of the story [History, Time, and All That]' in a satisfactory way?

Such a place was to be found – in Riding's, and therefore in Graves's, terms. But as the quarrel with Phibbs, the slow painful healing of the injuries, the growth of the threat of poverty, the worry over the children, the printing, the work on the demolition of history – as all this and more went on, the partners did not know of it. Until someone, by a casual remark, changed the lives of both of them as drastically as, in his different way, Phibbs had done.

II

At that time Gertrude Stein was busy as social lioness and encourager of young writers and artists. Her love affair with her companion Alice B. Toklas was going well. Toklas acted out the incongruous role of bull-dyke – a midget butch, whose cruel erotic demands were much to Stein's taste – in their odd relationship. In exchange she acted as Stein's willing secretarial and social slave, and *alter ego*.

Despite her position, Stein was not happy. She wanted more recognition. She was greedy for it. 'It would be quite wise to have followers,' she wrote ironically.

She had a good reason to feel pleased with Riding: the latter's two prose books of 1928 showed clear signs of having been influenced by the highly experimental works she had collected in her *Geography and Plays* (1922). True, she had influenced writers more important in the eyes of the public – but Riding was another woman, and in her article on her in *transition* Riding had made large claims for her.

She became well disposed towards both partners, took an interest in their complicated personal lives, and was always ready with advice. They (and Nancy) met on at least one occasion in Paris; and she knew about and had met Phibbs – also in Paris.

None of the extant letters she wrote to Graves, or Riding, or both, is dated, but the sequence is fairly clear. The first of these letters, to Graves, was written just after Riding's jump from the window.

My dear Robert

It was about that that I feared, Laura is so poignant and so upright and she gets into your tenderness as well as your interest and I am altogether heart-broken about her, I cannot come now because of family complications but tell her and keep telling her that we want her with us, we are to be at Belley right near Aix les Bains and as soon as she can be about & strangely one thinks of her as coming together alright, you and Nancy are wonderfully good. I had an unhappy feeling that Laura would have sooner or later a great disillusionment & it would of course have to come through a certain vulgarity in another ('vulgarity' is her word. I told her that there was a dualism in Geoffrey, that he could not make it. That he was incredibly good, or just ordinary) and it will make Laura a very wonderful person in a strange way a destruction and a recreation of her purification, but all this does not help pain & I am very closely fond of you all. Tell her all & everything from me & tell her above all that she will come to us, & reasonably soon and all my love

Gertrude

Graves had not told Stein the whole story, which he did not yet know himself. Her next letter, from Bilignin (she and Alice Toklas spent their summers there, and the rest of the year in their Rue de Fleurus house in Paris), indicates that she had been told of Graves's break with Nancy:

My very dear Laura and Robert,

I am rather selfishly glad that the result of it all means you both more completely together, you do mean that to me the two of you with Len [Lye] firmly in the background because after all it is hysteria that is vulgar and the complete absence of hysteria is very rare, there is very little absence of hysteria and you two are it and therefore if not for other reasons very dear to me. We are here and wanting to see the both of you with us a quiet and yet sufficiently enlivening spot and all of it. As soon as the pain is over Laura has such real vitality that she will go on and nowadays so fortunately they can get the better of pain and it must be soon done. Do please let me hear from you as I have been doing, and all my love to you both always

Gtde

Then there were at least two letters to Riding herself, as soon as she heard she was mending. Both were from Bilignin:

My very dear Laura,

I have been thinking of you a lot lately back home, and I hope going on, and not too bad and not too anything but alright. I do hope to hear that everything is coming back, and that it would be good for you to take treatment at Aix or somewhere near us, a something that would be a pleasure to us all. Do let me hear how everything is going, yes I imagine I will be staying in France I can see how you wouldn't like it, it is not xactly a pleasant taste but it is on the whole a case of the shortest and permanentest cut to liberty and liberty that does not concern anybody not even oneself it is so permanent, but if one does not want that most and one easily may not then there is everything that jars I can see that though I do not as a matter of fact feel it it's so natural and it is very nice to feel them feeling more natural. Last years sentences were good but these years paragraphs are better. Anyway tell me you and Robert about yourselves and lots of love and are we seeing you and how and when and always

Gtde

Stein had suggested to Riding that she make France her home – and perhaps a part of France near Belley. But Riding had ruled 'geogra-

189

phically' and otherwise against this. She wrote grandly, a little later, that she 'did not really mind the French' – but 'not minding' would not be enough. So Stein explained why she herself chose to live in France (Graves and Riding would have picked up the point that France was by far the easiest place to live as a more or less open lesbian).

And a few days later or earlier:

My very dear Laura,

Just had a letter from Robert saying that you are really getting better and being more comfortable and I am as pleased as can be. I always liked Robert a lot but I've come very close to him lately and am immensely interested in his autobiography [i.e. in the project]. I guess he is going to be better and better as well as you and that means a lot to me. . . .

She was to retain her affection for Graves, and her interest in his work – but to pronounce a distinctly different, severe and partially unfair verdict on Riding.

In October 1929 – *Goodbye to All That* finished and at the printer – the couple left England for Aix-les-Bains in Haute Savoie. They did not stay long – Laura disliked competition – but it was Stein who was responsible for their eventual destination.

Stein had visited Mallorca just before the First World War, and quite liked it. She and Toklas went to Palma, the capital, where they had a good friend in the American painter, William Cook. They soon found a comfortable flat in Terreno, a fashionable district of Palma, and lived quite contentedly there until the summer of the following year. Though Stein thought the Mallorcans themselves 'a very foolish host of decayed pirates with an awful language', the episode on the island was important to her because it was there that she secured the foundations of her 'marriage' to Toklas – a marriage that was to work excellently. Curiously, she had also written much of her most experimental prose work in this period – the very work which gave Riding the basis for her own prose beginnings. She and Toklas returned from Mallorca to France mainly because of their nervousness about the outcome of the war and the fate of their property in Paris.

Graves asked Stein, 'What about Mallorca?'

'It's paradise if you can stand it,' she answered, half-jokingly, and with a sidelong look at Laura.

They went into the matter – and the more they found out the more they liked it. They made a very sudden decision, and left for the island.

There was somewhere on Mallorca, Riding immediately felt, where time could – with the aid of a sound banker – be suitably stopped.

Stein and Riding could never have got on for long. They understood each other too well. Stein's eventual public success might well have disturbed Riding close at hand even more than did Graves's – the financial fruits of which she had at least the consolation of sharing. Even at a distance Riding came to feel that Stein was 'shrewd' but 'stupid', and that her 'shrewdness [was] made up out of energetic prejudices. . . . Her stupidity [was] a shrewd avoidance of thinking about anything.' This judgement was made in *14A*, written just after the publication of the very successful *The Autobiography of Alice B. Toklas* – when Riding's feelings were also inflamed by the success of *Claudius* (closer to home), and when she was feeling generally unhappy. She has written in recent years, more generously, that Stein 'wanted to be successfully human, and yet, oh, so much, successfully, pragmatically, a creature of her time'. She adds that her purpose was 'destructive'; she wanted to have language and yet nothingness. That judgement, generous in Riding's terms, was written in ignorance of the dying Stein's own final verdict on her in a letter to Graves of early 1946.

III

Goodbye to All That made, and has continued to make, Graves money. But before it became a 'war classic' and was set for examinations in schools, it further estranged him from old friends – and it further offended his family.

We now know the state of mind which enabled him to produce what has become familiar as one of the most candid of modern autobiographies. He was writing about a past self that he hated (too much), and he didn't care what he said. He needed cash and was in a tearing hurry. He planned a best seller – but had no conscious intention of cashing in on the late-twenties boom in war books. That this boom came when he was ready to write a war book was a piece of good fortune for him. It was his publisher, Cape, who first saw the full possibilities. And Cape thought it best to let him have his head – he knew that the war would have to come into it. And so it did; more than half the book deals with his war experiences.

Graves's book, with those of Blunden and Sassoon, is generally considered to have 'most effectively memorialised the Great War as a historical experience' in the English language. He, Blunden and Sassoon the American critic Paul Fussell correctly takes to be 'the classic memoirists'. Blunden's *Undertones of War* (1928) and the two sections of Sassoon's *Sherston's Progress* which deal with the war, have literary qualities that *Goodbye to All That* deliberately lacks. They are 'composed' works of art, whereas Graves's book was written at top speed, and shows this by both its carelessness – sometimes excessive – and its urgency. Neither the book nor the intention behind it has anything to do with art. But it has something the others don't have.

Blunden's *Undertones of War*, which he began in 1924, is an exercise in ironic pastoral, exquisite within its limits but occasionally laboured. G. S. Fraser called it the best *poem* to come out of the First World War, and he makes a good point. This book's tough-mindedness consists in transforming the war-present into an ironic reflection of a desentimentalized idyllic past. It is a work that is literary in the best old-fashioned sense.

Sassoon's is a more complicated case. His *Memoirs of an Infantry Officer*, the successor to *Memoirs of a Fox-Hunting Man* (1928), was published in 1930. It is a mannered, memorable book, but, once again, literary in the old-fashioned sense. Sassoon calls himself Sherston, and chooses to see himself through a veil of artifice – albeit exquisite artifice. He was not able to put down all he felt; he was then homosexual, and to admit or even hint at it was impossible. This would have killed his reputation and his book.

Goodbye to All That sums up the fears and hopes of the generation who experienced the war with a pertinence that could hardly admit of a strictly literary treatment. The point of Blunden's and Sassoon's non-journalistic memoirs was that they had *not* rejected the past, even though they had lost it. Their accounts are poignant because they are set against, because they contrast with, the decencies and the beauties and the quietness of the traditional past. Now Graves, though a respecter of tradition, was not at that time concerned with it; he was a rebel, and he was in revolt. This revolt was not against the kind of tradition which Blunden and Sassoon loved, and for which their nostalgia is so compelling; it was against the present. Sassoon and Blunden, reclusive men, were too removed from the real present to be able to bear it. What moved them was the loss of the 'old things'; war above all symbolized this. Because they shied away from the pain of the present, the poetry of both eventually failed in power.

'All that' for Graves was the 'goddawful', which he had most carefully and extensively defined in 1928, in *Mrs Fisher*:

> politics, religion, conversation, literature, arguments, dances, drunks, time, crowds, fun, unhappiness. . . .

as he put it in his *Goodbye to All That* epilogue to Riding. The general public, however, did not take to the book because of the expression of these enigmatic sentiments. What did a literary man, a poet, mean by saying goodbye to 'literature'? The majority was unaware that Graves was speaking contemptuously of literature and religion, and so on, *as they were practised*. He wasn't against the reality of either.

But the state of mind that produced this esoteric contempt for the present also produced an account of the war itself that caught the popular imagination in a way that other English accounts did not. 'All that' for which Graves has contempt produces, as an end result, war – a profound disagreement amongst people, of which physical war is the grotesque paradigm. So that his account, in part fortuitously, has just that matter-of-factness which we find in Renn's more polished *Krieg* – and, indeed, in Hašek's *Švejk*. Among English accounts of the war only Graves comes near to achieving the sick, black humour of Hašek. It looks like 'bad taste'; but it is the nearest to the truth. It is much nearer to *Catch-22* than Blunden or Sassoon.

Because Graves didn't care what anyone thought of him he omitted heroics, respect, 'rights', honour and nobility. Sassoon and Blunden in their prose works don't. Their narratives do not aim for flatness. Graves's flat account conveys a quite different effect. And the readers, especially those who had been there (and who passed on their opinion to others), recognized the reality. Graves got hold of a large section of the non-literary public, and profited thereby.

His general contempt for all conventional values conferred upon his account yet another strength. Other writers strove conscientiously for strict factual accuracy. Graves did not even have the time to try for it – but, despite some exaggeration (especially of casualty figures), he achieved a greater realism than they.

He didn't try for exactitude because, as he wrote a year or two after, in *But It Still Goes On*:

> The memoirs of a man who went through some of the worst experiences of trench-warfare are not truthful if they do not contain a high proportion of falsities. High-explosive barrages will make a temporary liar or visionary of anyone; the old trench-mind is at work in all over-estimation

of casualties, 'unnecessary' dwelling on horrors, mixing of dates and confusion between trench rumours and scenes actually witnessed.

There are two kinds of reality. One is what actually happened – which belongs to the historian, who does what little he can with it; the other is what it was like, what happened to the person who was there – which belongs to the individual. Blunden and Sassoon might even be said to have lessened the immediacy of their accounts by laboriously mixing the one reality with the other. As Fussell writes,

> No one has ever denied the brilliance of *Goodbye to All That* and no one has ever been bored by it. . . . If it really were a documentary transcription of the actual, it would be worth very little, and would surely not be, as it is, infinitely re-readable.

The reality conveyed by *Goodbye to All That* to its readers, together with its candour, made it into a best seller. When Cape saw the typescript he knew he had a winner on his hands. Its anti- (not non-) literary quality, its 'untidiness', 'intelligence' and 'originality' (the last three were characteristics given by Sassoon to Graves as David Cromlech), all these impressed Cape's commercial as well as his critical sense. He knew that it would be worth pushing the book hard. He advertised it widely.

It was published on Monday, 18 November 1929. Ten days later Cape wrote to Graves, by now in Mallorca, that it had 'got off the mark very quickly'. Under the circumstances he offered to increase the royalties after the first 5000 copies. The original agreement had stipulated a 12½ per cent royalty on all copies sold. Now Cape offered 15 per cent over 5000, and 20 per cent over 20,000 – making the 20 per cent retrospective on the 10,000 copies already sold. He ended this generous letter:

> Of course we cannot forecast what the sale will be but we have high hopes of selling as many as 50,000, maybe even more than that [within a month sales had reached 30,000]. I don't know what the sale of *All Quiet on the Western Front* is. All kinds of extravagant figures are blowing about but the figures of sales which are quoted in the Press are like actors' salaries invented for Press purposes. We think *Goodbye to All That* might be as successful. . . . The note we want to strike is that we have the German War book which is a huge success, but here is THE English War book which is the best war book of all and one which every Britisher must possess.

Probably *Goodbye to All That* would have achieved the international success of Remarque's novel had it taken better in the USA, where it appeared under the joint imprint of Cape and Harrison Smith. But although it did fairly well there, it was too English to capture the attention of as wide a readership as Remarque's skilful, sincere but *ersatz* piece of journalism. Whereas *Goodbye to All That* was translated only into German and Swedish, Remarque's novel was translated into more than thirty languages, and made into a successful film. But Graves was able to establish himself, and Riding, on Mallorca with the proceeds – and was now a celebrity. He could not have been anything but pleased about the success of the book. But it was quickly to bring him personal difficulties, and even to prompt an ugly gesture of hatred and envy from two former friends.

IV

Siegfried Sassoon was back in England before the publication of *Goodbye to All That*. Edmund Blunden hurried an advance copy to him. His first reaction was one of hysterical rage, and he acted on it. Here is the relevant part of Cape's letter to Graves, written six days before the publication of *Goodbye to All That*:

> Siegfried Sassoon has been in to see me to-day. He had seen an advance copy of *Goodbye to All That* and was very disturbed at the story . . . which relates your visit to the house of a fellow officer in Kent whose mother having read Lodge's *Raymond*, was endeavouring to communicate with her other son who had been killed. Sassoon was very upset about this and fears that it would have a deep effect on his mother if she read it. In addition also, he takes very great exception to your having printed any of his War poem which appears on pages 321, 322 and 323 of the book. He feels so strongly about the whole book that in order to quieten him down and prevent him from taking some drastic legal action I felt that there was nothing else to do but to agree to print cancel pages and have them inserted in the book so that lines 11 to 19 are deleted on page 290, and the poem at the foot of page 321, and on pages 322 and 323 is deleted. In the blank spaces we propose to put asterisks.
>
> Because the book is to be published on Monday and we don't want to postpone publication nor do we want the book held up by an injunction, this seems the only thing to be done. It is a beastly nuisance from our point of view as the business of cutting out and pasting into bound books will take a lot of time and it will all have to be done at very high pressure. I have only consented to do this because of the

conviction that as Sassoon was so wrought up about the whole thing I felt that he would not hesitate to take drastic steps and it was quite necessary to pacify him. I must look to you to endorse what I have done as being the only and best course.

Sassoon had reason to be angry. Graves had included an unpublished poem, which he had himself rejected, without his permission. This was clear breach of copyright. Nor had Graves sent him an advance copy of a book which contained long discussions of him.

Graves readily endorsed Cape's changes – though he couldn't then understand why Sassoon should want one of his best poems cut out of it. But he knew that more lay behind Sassoon's gesture than met the eye. However, he had much in Mallorca with which to concern himself – and forgot about the matter until it was revived by an acrimonious correspondence a month or so later.

What he did not then know was that Sassoon, together with his friend Blunden, had been brooding over the advance copy for three weeks before publication. So furious were they that they set to work on a plan so preposterous that they could not have carried it out even had they tried (which eventually they did not). It is plain that Blunden had been responsible for working Sassoon up to the point of going to Cape's offices.

The two got together in October to do a demolition job on *Goodbye to All That*. They finished on 7 November, for the endpaper of the copy they used is signed 'E. Blunden, Nov. 7 1929'. It was offered for sale by El Dieff, New York, in 1976 as 'surely the outstanding memorabilia of World War I'.

A letter from Blunden to Sassoon suggests that they present their annotated version to the British Museum 'to preserve the correct version of what happened' (though Blunden could not have known much about this, having been elsewhere in France). It was of course never presented to the British Museum (who could hardly have accepted it), and it remained in Sassoon's library until his death.

There are in all 5631 words of annotation, in ink, on 250 of the book's 448 pages. The greater proportion of these are by Blunden. On the title page Blunden added a subtitle: 'Clarice, or, the Welsh-Irish Bull in a China Shop'.

The nature and quality of Blunden's and Sassoon's objections will be apparent from two examples. The annotations begin on page 1. The first words, 'The objects of this autobiography', attract this comment (E.B.):

> They are all selfish. He does not seem to guess what is the best reason for autobiography – to add one's utmost to that fund of human record which will make a friendlier and better understanding world.

The passage on page 289 about Siegfried's mother and her attempts to contact her dead son drew the comment from Sassoon that his mother was only impressed by Graves because he stayed more than a week and did not have a bath; the incidents he described were 'almost entirely apocryphal' and the passage was 'unforgivable'.

This type of comment predominates; the more specific corrections or questionings of fact are seldom substantial.

It is evident that whereas Sassoon was moved by anger towards a man for whom he still had fondness and admiration, and whose friendship he deeply regretted losing, Blunden was simply envious. As we shall see, he eventually apologized. That Sassoon regretted quarrelling with Graves can be seen from their angry exchange of letters in 1930. It is clear from this that Graves was the less wounded – and the more wounding – of the two. In his first letter, of 7 February 1930, Sassoon attacks Graves's inaccuracies ('As I am sticking pins into you I may as well . . .') in *Goodbye to All That* and says that his book ought to 'be valid against the criticisms of your "former comrades" '. Dunn, the doctor who had saved Graves's life when he promptly dressed his wounds, had written to Sassoon that he 'was very sorry that Graves wrote such a book and found a publisher for it'. This might not matter to Graves, he goes on – just the 'still small voice' of a conventional middle-aged man 'among the noise of enthusiastic reviewers'. He blames Graves for having been in too much of a hurry to check his facts.

He ends by telling Graves that he is glad he is making 'a lot of money,' and informs him that he has made a new will in which he leaves Graves '£300 a year tax paid'. That will come in handy 'unless you become a highly-paid journalist, which is, I trust, improbable' (a sarcastic allusion to the journalistic style of the autobiography). He has written to relieve his feelings, and no reply is required.

But Graves replied promptly, vigorously and unpleasantly. Sassoon's charges also prompted at least two points which he raised in *But It Still Goes On*. The first is the valid distinction between 'trench' and 'historical' reality. The second commented on Sassoon's criticism of his behaviour over the court-martial affair:

> S.S. believes that I lied when I sidetracked his defiance of the military authorities – his protest, with which I agreed sincerely, against the continuance of the War – by swearing that if he persisted he could be put not into the witness-box at a court-martial, but into a padded cell. I did not lie, unless to present an unofficial but authoritative warning as an official decision. I had learned, after discreet enquiry, that the authorities could not afford to court-martial him, for fear of the anti-war publicity, particularly in view of his magnificent fighting record. His neurasthenia, which was, as it happened, accompanied by hallucinations, would make things easy for them, I was told.

This cannot be checked; but in any case Sassoon made it clear that he forgave Graves for his oath – justified or not – in *Memoirs of an Infantry Officer*.

Sassoon's counterblast to Graves's letter came back quickly. He was still half angry, half affectionate. There are further references to Graves's inaccuracies in his reportage of the war, and Sassoon is particularly annoyed with him for having (in his letter) justified his accounts of the brothel visits of the soldiers in *Goodbye to All That* by saying, '*It doesn't take long to* ✻ .' 'Not a pretty remark, Robert. Yes, I know a little about the chronology of the act.' He is particularly pleased that Dr Dunn deprecates *Goodbye to All That* – Graves had replied that he could not reconcile Sassoon's report of Dunn's reactions with his own letter from Dunn 'correcting a few errors'. Sassoon reminds him that Dunn is a 'shrewd and forbearing Scotchman'.

After some further minor complaints, and an admission that the inclusion of his hitherto unpublished poem was 'excusable' on the grounds that Graves was not to know how it now embarrassed him, the letter concludes with a reference to a specious complaint Graves had made: that Sassoon had not sent him his collection of poems *The Heart's Journey* (which appeared in England in 1928; and in America, with some additional poems, in 1929). He wrote that he had not done so because he thought he was 'a back-number (poetically)' in Graves's estimation. He reminded Graves that he had already told him that there were only five good writers in England and America – he had not been optimistic about being among them. He adds that his companion, Stephen Tennant, has been telling him that he is too hard on Graves, and is sick of Sassoon's harping on *Goodbye to All That*.

The correspondence dragged on throughout 1930, but became more intermittent; it had petered out by the end of the year. But it flared up again in 1933. The occasions this time were Graves's *Poems 1930–1933*, published by Arthur Barker in May – and, to a lesser extent, the Graves rewrite of *David Copperfield* published two months earlier, the impertinence of which enraged Sassoon.

There exists a copy of the *Poems 1930–1933* with a 167-word denunciation of Graves's poetry by Sassoon, and with numerous underlinings by him of the text itself. (El Dieff wanted $750 for it in 1976.) The volume is not inscribed, and clearly Graves did not send it to him: Sassoon bought it in order to delight himself by attacking Graves, for whose friendship he grieved – and yet who somehow really did make him feel a 'back number'. He recognized that the poems were the record of true experience, and was distressed that he couldn't understand the nature of this.

He wrote in pencil on the front endpaper that Graves refused to be 'on speaking terms with the rest of the world', except for Riding, and continued:

> He busies himself with technical ingenuities – neat verse carpentry – makes his meaning difficult by oddity, and forbids himself to allow emotion a hearing & an outlet. . . .

This comment aptly reflects what puzzled not only Graves's old friends but also those readers who had enjoyed his earlier poems, and who were now disappointed with the work he was doing. While Auden and other younger men such as MacNeice and Spender – and, soon, Dylan Thomas – were to be widely read, Graves was now more or less ignored as a poet, regarded as an eccentric who had wandered off the right track. But among the twenty-eight poems in this volume are 'The Bards', 'Ulysses', 'Down, Wanton, Down!' and 'On Dwelling', all now much anthologized and firmly entrenched in the Graves canon as standard examples of his best work. And all the poets named above as fashionable, and many others, were amongst Graves's readers. It was the poetry-reading public and, above all, the reviewers who had lost interest in him.

This, apart from one more short acrimonious exchange, marks the end of an unhappy quarrel – except for Sassoon's brief, polite reply to Graves's congratulations on his engagement to Hester Gatty, whom Sassoon married on 18 December at a quiet ceremony (T. E. Lawrence was a guest).

Graves wrote in a note answering the question (put to him by a schoolgirl) as to whether he regretted losing Sassoon's friendship:

He lost the most; but I eventually met him by accident [in Cambridge in 1954, in King's College Chapel]. He greeted me and I responded and all was well. He had quarrelled with me, not I with him.

Chapter Fifteen
1929–33(II)

I

A Spanish guidebook of 1898 begins its short entry on the mountain village of Deyá, Mallorca, by announcing that one of its chief characteristics is 'its collection of strange and eccentric foreigners'. It has always been like that. Deyá has its remittance men, would-be magicians, refugees from scandals, suicides, murderers, confidence men, pseudo-astrologers, idlers, frauds, alcoholics, lunatics, forgers, freaks and retired military British gentlemen. Anything bizarre can happen.

Mallorca itself is the ancient Balearis Major, largest of the Balearics. At its broadest it is forty-eight miles, at its longest sixty-four. It is not much more than a hundred miles off the mainland.

A range of mountains on the north-west protects the island from the cold north winds which sweep down from the mainland of Europe. There is another, lower range of hills in the south-east. The Puig Mayor (not far from Deyá), is, at almost 5000 feet, the highest peak. The central plain, radiating out from the capital, Palma, consists of a mixture of fertile, red soil and rocky areas stripped of all topsoil. There are mountain streams in abundance – though nearly all of them dry up in summer – but no river. However, there has always been an efficient irrigation system – once using windmills, many groups of which still stand. Because of the mountains the climate is mild. Rainfall is adequate, but is normally concentrated into the last three months of the year. It seldom rains for days on end, as it does in England.

There is much lush and exotic vegetation: *algarrobos* (carob trees), olives growing on the terraced mountain slopes, orange and lemon groves, figs, almonds – and a variety of plants and herbs, in particular asphodels. It is mainly an agricultural island – many sheep, a few cattle, an abundance of chickens. Crafts provide some work: shoe-making, artificial pearls (a trap for tourists), wrought iron, some food items. The hotels and the cafés now provide an increasing source of employment.

The island is extremely ancient, redolent of many fascinating pasts. Finds of human bones besides those of the mountain antelope, *Myotragus balearicus*, show that there were human beings there by 5000 BC.

The Talayot period – *c.* 1400 BC to *c.* 200 BC – lasted until well beyond the time when the Greeks, Phoenicians and others began their invasions. A *talayot* (a word of Arabic derivation) is a towerlike monument, of which there are many examples on the island. It was then that the Mallorquíns got their name of 'slingers': they repelled invaders by hurling stones at them, with extraordinary precision. The deadly accurate, naked stone-thrower of Mallorca became a voyagers' familiar tale, and slinging continued in Mallorca until recently, when, a competitor's eye having been put out, it was temporarily stopped. It is now cautiously resuming.

But in 123 BC the Romans established themselves – and took the slingers back with them for use in war. In the fifth century AD the Vandals took over; they sharply disciplined the many Christians, who were flourishing by the end of the Roman rule. After a confused period under nominal Byzantine rule, the island was conquered in 902 by the Moors – who have left their permanent mark.

In 1229 King Jaime I of Aragon and Catalonia set out to restore Christianity to Mallorca. Three years later, after several fierce sea battles, he succeeded. Then, in 1276, his son Jaime II was crowned King of Mallorca. After a long series of struggles with his brother and with his nephew, he confirmed his position in 1298 – and until 1375 the island was an independent kingdom. Then it passed to the united Catalonia and Aragon, and finally became a part of Spain (1479).

The modern islanders differ somewhat from their Catalan neighbours. They are not as militantly nationalist, and are more cheerful and easy-going. They are religious, but markedly anti-clerical. They do not at all like politics. They are proud, but lack the Spanish vices of haughtiness and ostentation.

Now the capital, Palma, has become a tourist 'paradise', a combination of Blackpool, Clacton and a run-down Las Vegas – there is even a casino, and much bingo. This began to happen in the fifties; the process was completed by the mid-sixties. But much of the island remains unviolated, for the tourists tend to stick to the parts that have been constructed like the glittering, *ersatz* resorts of their own countries.

The tourist Mallorca is a caricature of hell, and has grown with astonishing speed; in 1891 Palma had only six lodging houses.

But the real Mallorca, out in the country, has not changed much. It is still quiet at dusk, when the sheepbells tinkle – and the strange lives of the strange foreigners are more often than not lived without noise.

You reach Deyá by taking the road that cuts up to the coast, north from Palma to Valldemosa, where Chopin and George Sand spent their famous unhappy winter of 1838–39. This winds through a flat plain, beautiful with almond blossom in the early part of the year. Towards Valldemosa you climb up, and after passing through the village (a tourist attraction because of Chopin, Sand and the local dances – but not one of the nicest of the island's villages), you go along a winding coastal road, on one side rock and on the other woods through which from time to time a glimpse of the sea may be seen. Nearing Deyá you notice, on your left, the entrance to the path leading downwards to the great projecting rock of La Foradada. At this point stands the house of the eccentric nineteenth-century Austrian recluse, the Hapsburg Archduke Ludwig Salvador. Salvador wrote a nine-volumed work on the Balearics, and was the man who said, when presented to the king by two politicians who flanked him on each side: 'I feel like a certain man between two thieves.' He did much for the inhabitants of the village.

Deyá itself, a small fishing village of some 450 inhabitants, lies on the slopes of one of the most beautiful valleys of this rugged, rocky part of the island. It is overshadowed by the Teix mountain, which is about 4000 feet. Its main street is short, and curves sharply away to the right. Most of the stone houses are built around a small, steep hill topped by the squat, low-towered village church. Some two hundred yards past the village, on the right-hand side, stands Canelluñ, Graves's house since 1932. The main street now has two general stores, three cafés and a small restaurant, a pharmacy, a baker and a butcher. The village extends down the valley slope to the left, a district of small lanes called the *Clot*. To reach the church you climb steps just before the turn out of the village and towards Canelluñ, pass another general store (the *Estanco*), and walk uphill. Before you reach this small but imposing church you pass a handsome, shuttered house called the Posada, now belonging to Graves's son William.

The slopes surrounding the village were all terraced down to the sea, centuries back, by the Moors, for olive cultivation – and this continues.

Away to the left of the road (which follows the coast on to the port of Soller), opposite Canelluñ, is a steep climb down to one of the island's most charming *calas* (beaches). Graves was a regular swimmer there until after he reached the age of eighty.

II

When they arrived Graves and Riding, who stayed at the Grand Hotel in Palma, started looking about the island, which they immediately liked. They met a painter, a cripple, in Palma, who wanted to do Graves's portrait. Graves at first refused, but then relented, and paid twenty-five pesetas for it. The painter in gratitude, told them that Deyá was the place they were looking for. (Graves threw the portrait away.)

It was, for Riding, indeed the place. If it had not been precisely defined before, it was now: a 'concentration of the limited virtue and pleasantness to be found in the earth itself'.

They rented a primitive, sunless cottage, Casa Salerosa, which stands high up just outside the village on the Valldemosa side. They stayed there for two years. The cottage, according to Tom Matthews – who lived in it for a short time in the winter of 1932 – was cold and uncomfortable. But Graves and Riding liked it, and did not complain. They transported their Albion press, and found they could accommo-date and use it. Riding's back did not permit too much press work, and both needed to spend as much of their time as possible in writing. But the press remained important, and they produced four small books on it while still at Salerosa. Three were by themselves: Riding's prose poems *Though Gently* (1930) and her long poem *Laura and Francisca* (1931), and Graves's collection of fifteen poems *To Whom Else?* (1931). The fourth was a collection of letters by their New Zealand friend Len Lye. He wrote such lively, interesting, original and intelligent letters, full of new ways of seeing familiar objects (he was mostly preoccupied with the visual arts, particularly film), that Riding suggested to him that she help him edit and revise a series of letters to the partners. Gertrude Stein had admired the 'freshness' of Lye's prose since she had been shown it in 1928. Indeed, *No Trouble* is a neglected collection of modernist prose of its period. This small but in no sense ephemeral booklet is an example of Laura Riding at her most produc-tive in the role of helper to others. Without much inhibiting, or altering, or influencing Lye's own way of seeing, she made it possible for him to articulate it effectively.

Soon she heard from Stein:

The year does roll ... and here we are and liking it we do like it there is no mistake about it and you like the islands and they are doing you a lot of good and we will see you this summer [1930] and that will do us a lot of good too and anyway here we are. ...

But nothing came of their plans to meet.

It was in these comparatively isolated years at Casa Salerosa that the distinctive 'Deyá way of life' – the confirmation of Riding as leader, the exclusion of some from their circle, the inclusion of others – was established. It was also in those years that, for Graves, Riding's 'image', to use his own phrase from 'A Love Story', 'warped in the weather, turned beldamish'. Though poetically he is able to write, again in 'A Love Story' – one of the most complete retrospective resumés of his experience of her – of the 'holiness' that went before:

> These were all lies, though they matched the time,
> And brought me less than luck. ...

The self-criticism is what is important here. The poem was written before he formulated the 'system' of the White Goddess. The 'lies' are not only what she 'told' him, but what he told himself. They matched *his* time.

It was during these years, too, that Graves and Riding ceased being lovers (if, indeed, the intervention of Phibbs had not virtually ended their sexual relationship). Her back was mending only very slowly, and by the time it was as good as it would ever be she had come to a definite conclusion, which she announced to the world, through the medium of H. W. Wilson's widely consulted reference book *Authors Today and Yesterday*, 'bodies have had their day'.

Riding's experience of men, or her knowledge of cosmic law (as one wishes to look at it), had taught her this, and, while she would from time to time admit to various friends that she as well as they were 'human' (that is, moved by physical desire), she could, she made clear, do without any sexual relationships of her own. She was frightened of thunder at night, and Graves was then summoned to her room; but no conclusions were to be drawn from this by any visitors. Later (as we shall see) the entire past situation between the two was 'revised' by Riding; but for the time being Graves got some clandestine sympathy from friends for being human and for finding it hard not to exercise the whole of his humanity.

His feelings at the beginning of 1930 are admirably and simply summarized in the retrospective sonnet 'Callow Captain' (written in Switzerland in 1937, and not published until 1938 in the *Collected Poems* of that year).

> The sun beams jovial from an ancient sky,
>   Flooding the round hills with heroic spate.
> A callow captain, glaring, sword at thigh,
>   Trots out his charger at the camp gate.
> Soon comes the hour, his marriage hour, and soon
>   He fathers children, reigns with ancestors
> Who, likewise serving in the wars, won
>   For a much-tattered flag renewed honours.
>
> A wind ruffles the book, and he whose name
>   Was mine vanishes; all is at an end.
> Fortunate soldier: to be spared shame
>   Of chapter-years unprofitable to spend,
> To ride off into reticence, nor throw
>   Before the story-sun a long shadow.

But although he then certainly felt that way, he was in somewhat of a quandary. This quandary was, ironically enough, one of the contributions to the serious deterioration in the relationship between the partners that had set in by the time they moved into Canelluñ (which in Mallorquin means 'the far house'; the proper spelling is Ca n'Alluny) in 1932.

Riding's philosophy and its development are not the subject of this book. It is Graves's understanding of them that matters here. She herself ceased to be of any importance to him when she was forced to cease to believe that the purest expression of truth could only be through poetry. When they met both believed this to be the case – though Graves's road to this position had been a more winding and tortured one. He had had more responsibilities than she, and self-doubts which she never had. His problem is his fallibility; hers is her infallibility – how to convince the world that grandeur is not always delusive.

Graves now accepted Riding's strictures on 'physicality' as 'postponing judgement'; and her certainly agreed with her that the

fundamental relation which has to be made is between the male mind and the female mind, and in this judgement the female mind is the judge, and the male mind the subject of judgement. . . . But the male mind has now had all the time there is for working up case. [Riding on herself in *Authors Today and Yesterday*]

He had believed this before he ever heard of Riding. But let us ourselves postpone physicality and judgement and sexual matters for the end-of-the-time-being, and concentrate on three things: Riding–Seizin's intentions, Graves's intentions, and money. For this last is what put Graves into his quandary.

The Seizin project did not now exist only to produce small books 'by particular people'. Riding had larger plans. For *Goodbye to All That* had turned Graves into a potential golden-egg-laying goose. Those eggs, if properly coaxed forth, could be used to expand Seizin's activities, and thus change the world.

Coleridge began the first essay of his periodical *The Friend* with this memorable paragraph:

> Antecedent to all history, and long glimmering through it as a holy tradition, there presents itself to our imagination an indefinite period, dateless as Eternity, a state rather than a time. For even the sense of succession is lost in the uniformity of the stream.

The Friend lost Coleridge money just as Seizin's miscellany *Epilogue* and its successor *The World and Ourselves* lost Graves money. And there is little difference between what Coleridge wrote in 1809 in *The Friend* and what Riding wrote in her 'Preliminaries' to *Epilogue I*, which represented the general as distinct from the particular activities of the Seizin Press. (The actual appearance of the first *Epilogue* was delayed until 1935; but the intention did not much change between 1930 and then.)

Riding distinguishes, here, between *ideas*, which obscure truth because they express only that part of it 'which it is at the moment convenient to know', and *wisdom*, which is a 'recognition of truth'. The intention of *Epilogue*, early on referred to – in conversation and correspondence – as the Vulgate, is to

> clarify a standard of reality – by making thought seek its level in the range from historical to absolute reality.

We are back with Coleridge's 'holy tradition' – and, of course, with Plato and the development of the Platonic line of thought.

Graves went along with all of this, although he saw it not as Platonic, but, pragmatically, as his only possible way of life: a means of dedicating himself to the woman whom, whatever she might do, he would continue to love. His attitude towards what he described to Cape, to Lawrence, and to several others, as the 'real work' that was going on in Deyá (to be distinguished from his money-making activities), was romantic but empirical. Riding's attitude was messianic, and on many occasions she made this clear; but she could be so genuinely charming, helpful, generous, kind and 'human' that people found it impossible to reconcile the two sides of her, which they tend to describe as the 'severe' and the 'wonderful'.

Sudden access to money made Riding ambitious; nor was she, like some hierophants, ascetic, except in the matter of sex. When the royalties from Graves's two previous successes began to dwindle, it soon became apparent that more would be needed. Both partners wanted to build a house. They soon got to know the right local people to help them in such a project – and both could soon speak Spanish. Riding's mind was already full of grandiose notions, all of which centred around one great project: the establishment of a community, presided over by herself, which would (the words are from the 'Preliminaries' to the first *Epilogue*) have the purpose of achieving 'a vivid reality of thought', the affirmation of 'a necessary final law of relation'. A community dedicated to truth, uninfected by this or that 'historical' or 'topical' fact, with the recognition of poetry as the most 'final' type of statement that can be made. A 'poem', she later wrote, 'is an uncovering of truth of so fundamental and general a kind that no other name besides poetry is adequate except truth.'

Graves, much in the public eye as an articulate war veteran, was asked if he would like to write a play – by the actor-producer Maurice Browne. Browne had in 1929 produced R. C. Sherriff's enormously successful trenches play *Journey's End*. He was after similar material, and Graves was one of the obvious people to ask.

Graves knew nothing about the theatre, having never been a theatre-goer. He also felt that all modern playwrights were in one way or another impostors, that a successful play was a sort of confidence trick. He was not interested in *Journey's End*. He had total contempt, moreover, for all the ingredients that went into West End successes. So total was this contempt that he could not resist the lure of trying for it.

But he refused to write a play set in the war. He decided to write something that would look like a study of its effects. Since he had no detailed knowledge of modern theatre or of its techniques, he chose George Bernard Shaw as his model. Although Shaw had once mistaken him for his journalist brother Charles, and had sent him a rude postcard in response to a request for information about T. E. Lawrence, he had nothing against him. In fact, if one discounted his plays (which were simply 'successes'), then Shaw (he thought) had two points in his favour: 'the world would be a duller place without him', and he regarded the use of soap as injurious to the skin, which was also Graves's view, and one which he put into constant practice.

He decided, then, to write a *drame-à-clef*, in which, as he put it later, he would tactfully reshuffle 'actual events and situations in which I had been more or less closely concerned'. This he did: the reshuffle is very thorough, and manages to combine the anecdotal with the serious. For example, he works in the tale – which he had from William Nicholson – of how W. H. Davies, suddenly jealous of Walter de la Mare, pinned up a photograph of him on a wall and took pot shots at it with a revolver. He also, in the character David Casselis, draws on certain features of Sassoon – in particular his homosexuality. The main plot hinges on the fact that two of its leading characters, Casselis and a woman called Charlotte, are respectively homosexual and lesbian. The spokesman for himself is ironically called Dick, who succinctly expresses a good many Gravesian notions such as that 'the bottom of things, after working looser and looser for centuries, has at last dropped out' and 'the War was a diversion, to distract public attention from the all-important loss'. He called the play *But It Still Goes On*.

Though no more than a period piece, it is not as bad as almost every critic has made out. Browne himself could not even consider it: its subject made it impossible, a 'curt note' accompanying the returned script informed Graves.

So no West End success. What about, then, a miscellany – mixing the serious and the trivial – to follow *Goodbye to All That*? Cape, although he had just lost money on Laura Riding's *Poems: A Joking Word* and the Steinesque prose collection *Experts Are Puzzled* (both undertaken to keep Graves on his list), was not unenthusiastic – and thought that the play's title and its subject, not taboo in printed form, might serve the book well. Described on the title page as an 'accumulation', *But It Still Goes On* appeared in November 1930. It contained, as well as the play, a 'postscript to "Goodbye to All That" ', reprinted from the *Daily Mail* (which had invited him to make a 'general reply to [his] critics'), three short stories, including a reprint of *The Shout*, and a more serious section consisting of a diary, calculated in large part to annoy his readers, called 'A Journal of Curiosities' –

and the first and last chapters of a book which he could never finish: 'The Autobiography of Baal', a longer, non-satirical version of *Mrs Fisher*.

The book was too scrappy, and the rude remarks Graves made about *Goodbye to All That* puzzled and put some of his faithful readers off. He said things like:

> When *Goodbye to All That* first appeared . . . I wrote a number of letters to the Press in answer to my critics, not unaware of the helpful effects that letters of this sort have on sales. . . . it is of no use being squeamish. . . . That [it] is selling well does not surprise me because I have been able to put into the book all the frank answers to all the inquisitive questions people like to ask about other people's lives. And not only that, but I have more or less deliberately mixed in all the ingredients that I know are mixed into other popular books . . . food and drink . . . murders . . . Ghosts, of course . . . kings . . . T. E. Lawrence . . . the Prince of Wales . . . Prime Ministers. I found three of these . . . Sport . . . school episodes, love affairs (regular and irregular), wounds, weddings, religious doubts . . . severe illnesses, suicides. But the best of all is battles. . . . So it was easy. . . .

After this gratuitous insult to the less intelligent of his readers, Graves went on to answer some more important points, including the ones raised by Sassoon.

He ran into libel trouble on two counts with *But It Still Goes On*, obliging Cape to print up two sets of cancel pages. The first one is an amusing case of characteristically hurried Gravesian inaccuracy, and is best told in the words of Cape's letter to him of 4 November 1930:

> I have been advised that there is a libel . . . in the paragraph which reads: 'I recently read a book called *The Child She Bare* by a woman who had had an illegitimate child and been befriended by the Army and was not grateful'. My information is, and it comes from a journalist . . . that the woman in question who wrote *The Child She Bare* did not have an illegitimate child. She is married and has a daughter who is believed to be legitimate. . . . She herself was a foundling. . . .

Graves had got this piece of false information from his brother Charles, who throughout his life was full of such. But the other threat to the book came from none other than Charles himself. Cape began his 4 November letter:

> Brother Charles telephoned to me this morning. He tells me that you have copied letters that he wrote to the parent of his one-time fiancée.

It is true that you used the thin disguise of altering the names, but Charles does not think this is sufficient. He says they must come out or he will take proceedings. I guess he is right when he says that you are using copyright material. . . . One would scarcely think that he would be foolish enough to take . . . action as by so doing he would only advertise very broadly something which otherwise would not be noticed or pinned on him, except by one or two intimates, but Brother Charles being righteously indignant might feel that something had to be done. He might further think, being a popular journalist, that publicity is desirable. . . .

This is one of a number of trivial but comic incidents between Robert and the famously awful Charles. Both the libel on the author of *The Child She Bare*, and that on Charles, were removed. There are therefore, in bibliographical terms, two states of the book. Perhaps Charles was justified in being annoyed. The letters (which A.P. helped him write) exposed him as a classic 'cad', as Cape recognized. Graves had lifted the drafts of the letters from Harlech and copied them without permission; it was just the sort of thing Charles himself might have done.

But It Still Goes On was a disappointment in financial terms. It went into a small second impression in England, but did badly in America. So the money problem became more acute. *Poems 1926–1930* (1931), Graves's last book for Heinemann for more than thirty years, was issued in an edition of 1000 copies, and brought in a negligible sum. *Ten Poems More*, published in 1930 in Paris by Nancy Cunard at her Hours Press (she also issued Riding's *Twenty Poems Less* at the same time), of course brought in nothing. It was in a signed limited edition of 200, in hand-set type – poets do not normally charge for this kind of publication.

Cape wanted to publish the *Poems 1926–1930*, and even asked Graves (12 December 1929) if he would care for him to take over the *Collected Poems* (i.e. the *Poems 1914–1927*). But nothing came of this, as Heinemann held Graves to his agreement that they should have first option on his next (not privately issued) volume of poetry. Like most London publishers, they now saw money in his name.

But Cape was to lose Graves (and *Claudius*) – and Graves to lose Cape – mainly as a result of an unfortunate experiment made by Riding and himself. This was a pity. Cape had not only shown enormous faith in and generosity to Graves as a writer (for example, in publishing Riding for him at a loss); he had even, at the end of 1929

211

and beginning of 1930, been considering letting him in on what he regarded as a valuable investment that the firm itself was making: 'I am of course sensible of my responsibility towards you . . . in this project, but it seems safe to us. . . .'

For a few months in 1932, and then again in 1933, things began to look distinctly bad. Graves was being written off as 'finished', and it was reckoned by most of the literary world that the person who had finished him was the unreadable Miss Riding. This was unfair, for by then she had tried as hard as he to compose a book for popular consumption. Perhaps this is why she is now so sensitive about this matter.

The beginning of serious trouble was a novel ultimately entitled *No Decency Left*. It is not a title that most regular readers of Graves will have heard of. It was published by Cape in February 1932, as by 'Barbara Rich', and although it went into three small impressions it flopped – to the extent that the last impression (of March 1935) was offered at a third of the original price of 7s. 6d (the average price of a novel in Great Britain until the Second World War; then equivalent to about $1.50). No American publisher would look at it. But it had been destined for greater heights than mere publication.

The partners had deliberately decided to 'stoop'. They would, they decided, produce a best seller – *and* it would be made into a very successful Hollywood film. Then Seizin, the increasingly-difficult-to-publish works of Riding, and the community-tuning-itself-to-a-vivid-reality-of-thought could flourish without further historical thought of the dying (or dead) world. Graves of course took the job on. He wrote it twice. In that (lost) form it might have done reasonably well.

While writing the novel Graves had asked T. E. Lawrence to supply him with a description of 'an autogyro of the future', designed by a Spanish dressmaker 'to provide the ultimate degree of private comfort consistent with safety and speed'. Lawrence did as asked, providing the machine with 'beam-antennae' which would signal the presence of anybody within 300 metres (itself an anticipation of radar).

This is what Graves wrote to Lawrence about the novel in late 1931 or early 1932, in a letter which was printed in 1938:

> That novel. It was sent off to Cape last week. It is strictly anonymous & it was not written by me. That is, I wrote it and rewrote it & had it typed & then Laura saw it & it wasn't good enough and she rewrote it with/for me and made quite a different thing of it. Made it what it

should originally have been. I shall send you a proof. Please mark anything that I have got wrong in putting your autogiro in. Please also say if any objection to joking mention of your name as a celebrated British spy (by the Lyonesse Communist leader). And if you notice any grave error in procedure anywhere.

By the time Laura had made the novel what it 'should ... have been', a best seller destined for Hollywood, it had become a romance-fantasy: a pretty office girl decides to lead a revolution, marry a prince, and make a million all in one day – and she does so. The result is disastrous. It bears all the signs of what it is: an intellectual's attempt to subsidize him/herself by writing a best seller. It is not funny, not exciting – and is far too well written. All that is worth preserving of it is the short Lawrence section – and the title.

Graves remained loyal. He was aware that his own second draft of *No Decency Left* was more commercially viable than the Riding re-write. But he hid this from himself – and of course from everyone else. What he tells Lawrence is absolutely typical. It was not subservience, although it often looked like it; it was protectiveness. Laura always knew better, and was always right. No friend, however close, could argue with Laura and expect support from Graves – ever.

Riding knew all this, too. Her pathetic efforts over *No Decency Left* finally brought home to her that she could not make money by writing.

She now knew that Graves must be the person to bring in the money to finance her projects. And it hurt her. She could not forgive him for it, although she would never admit it – even to herself. It was wrong that potboiling trash such as *Goodbye to All That* should succeed, whereas her truth-telling fell on deaf ears. Graves honestly concurred. And both were right in the sense that, for such poets as they were, believing what they did about the nature of poetry, almost any 'best-selling' prose of the present is, indeed, inferior. He worked desperately to obtain her approval; he needed that more than anything else. He believed in her with religious fervour.

It was largely the stress between his worship of her and his own powerful instincts, his empiricism, his sceptical tendencies (she was neither empirical nor sceptical: she 'uncovered the truth') that produced his tense poetry of those years.

213

III

The American Tom Matthews, a slight acquaintance of Graves from Oxford days, had returned from Oxford to America and taken up a position on the magazine *Time*. He had married a girl called Julie Cuyler, by whom he now had two children. Given the chance of a six-month leave of absence in January 1932, he decided to take it in Mallorca, to call on Robert Graves in Deyá.

When he turned up in Deyá Graves – who hardly knew him – did not at first recognize him. Then he remembered. The partners and the Matthews – who had their two children with them – quickly became friends. Tom and Julie Matthews and the children were given Casa Salerosa to live in, while Graves and Riding moved to a house in the village, Ca'n Pa Bo (House of Good Bread), for a few weeks, until their new house Canelluñ was ready for them.

Laura saw Matthews as the rising employee (as he was) of a very widely read periodical. But to the Matthews Graves, alone, was 'the well-known writer'. Laura they regarded as his mistress (Matthews describes his then unsophisticated awe at such a concept in his book *Jacks or Better*) who wrote eccentric prose and verse. They had even heard that Graves and Riding lured visitors into a courtyard, shut the door on them, and had them torn to pieces by savage hounds.

Matthews tells of his puzzlement (privately shared by almost all who knew them) at Riding's complete domination of Graves – or, to be more accurate, his complete subservience to her:

> We had read about [mistresses] and in those books the man, although he might have the wool pulled over his eyes, was always the master. It was certainly not so in this case.

The partners were also reputed to have an 'exaggerated mistrust of strangers', but this stemmed from Laura's choosiness rather than any real suspiciousness.

Matthews admired *Goodbye to All That* and told Graves so. He also admired Graves's poetry. He was surprised to be taken aside alone, by Graves, and told that his books 'were not to be brought up in conversation'. If this rule were broken, he told Matthews, he would leave the room – or even 'stop such talk by force'.

> He was more than protective of her; he seemed in a constant swivet of anxiety to please her, to forestall her every wish, like a small boy dancing attendance on a rich aunt of uncertain temper. And she treated him –

like a dog. There was no prettier way to put it. Since I admired him and looked up to him as a dedicated poet and a professional writer, his subservience to her and her contemptuous bearing towards him troubled and embarrassed me . . . she was not so much his mistress [by this time, certainly, she was not] as his master; he was *in statu pupillari* to her. . . .

Matthews saw that

the price of admission to Laura's circle was fealty to her as the acknowledged and absolute monarch of her little kingdom.

There is no reason, given a world in which men usually dominate women, why women should not dominate men without their seeming farcical. What was peculiar was that so powerful a personality as that of Graves should be, and so dramatically, in that situation. Strangers did not see that this exaggerated subservience, this 'constant swivet of anxiety to please', was, literally, worship.

Almost always he would be in that subservient position, that swivet, towards poetry – and towards what (or who) he considered to be the essence of poetry. But the attitude he then took towards Riding is a caricature of the attitude towards the power of poetry as he understands poetry. Those who seek to understand his view of the function of poetry need only take note of his treatment of her. He loved her, even when she seemed to him to be cruel, mocking, vicious and capricious, as the embodiment of poetry. Hence his later equation of her (among others) with the cruel aspect of the White Goddess. And it must not be forgotten that, since he had invented her before she came on the scene, he positively encouraged her to behave as she did.

But his influence upon her was profound. He took her seriously for much longer than anyone else was prepared to – and saw to it that others did, too. He helped her with her prose. Her fine and neglected *Progress of Stories* (1935) could not have been written without his tactful help. He remedied some serious deficiencies in her education. And he never slapped her face, 'put his foot down', or even told her to shut up. But as she admitted to him afterwards, she *wanted* to feel able to say to him 'Be happy' – but could never do so 'unreservedly'.

It was an ironic situation: the person in the subservient role the naturally dominant one – and the person in the dominant role the one who craved to be dominated.

Matthews and his wife Julie were fully accepted as members of the circle, and were much helped, although the price for this was that they were not allowed to speak with any of those who were banned from the circle: the majority of the other passing visitors, and certain ones particularly tabooed. Graves had a particular dislike for anyone who had attended the University of Cambridge – all the faults of those he did accept (for there were some, such as James Reeves) were attributed to that unfortunate experience.

At that time the 'inner circle' consisted of the painter John Aldridge (born in 1905, and a graduate of Corpus Christi, Oxford), Lucie Brown, with whom he was then living (they later married), and Norman Cameron – who had given up his Nigerian post, though not without doubts, in order to devote himself to Laura Riding's projects. He was himself building a house, Ca'n Torrent, next to Canelluñ. Cameron's relationship with Graves and Riding was always very much closer than that of Matthews, who really hardly knew Graves, as his attempts to describe his personality make evident. John and Lucie Aldridge, too (Lucie died in the seventies, and Aldridge is now married to Norman Cameron's widow, Gretl), kept in much closer touch, and (particularly John) were regarded as being at the very heart of the circle. Matthews was never in such a position – indeed, had he not worked for *Time* Laura might well have rejected him on sight. Aldridge, 'hoof-aloof' as Laura nicknamed him, was a reticent but humorous man, who with Lucie evolved a highly amusing and useful series of names for certain categories of people, such as 'day-slimers' (some estate agents, for example) and 'night-slimers' ('the sort of people who hang around garages at night').

His style of painting was already highly original, but he owed Riding a debt for her devotion to his genius, and for helping him to bring it out fully. His best-known paintings are of the countryside around Great Bardfield, in Essex, where he has lived for the whole of his adult life. He painted a fine portrait of Riding, and another (the best of all) of Graves – to be seen on the most recent edition of the Penguin selection of his poems, and in the National Portrait Gallery. He illustrated Riding's poem *The Life of the Dead*, written in French and in English in parallel text. The poem is based, as Riding says in introducing it, on the illustrations: she conceived an illustration, they then discussed it, and he drew it. She had much confidence in Aldridge, they worked well together, and he retains gratitude for the devoted help she gave him. She described him (in print) at that time, from her exceedingly limited knowledge of art, as the 'only one eloquent painter' in existence; this was nonsense. But there has been no better English painter of his generation, as the somewhat too few who really know his work readily agree.

Despite the fact that Matthews, in common with many others, believed that 'there was something occult about Laura and her gradually revealed, gradually acknowledged domination', he stayed on. He had published a short novel, and she dissected this for him, taking her usual intense trouble over the job, putting it all in writing, and trying to teach him to write. She also drew an abstract portrait of him, in which she incorporated two words: LUST and FURY. She had a reason for this.

Matthews was now working on a new novel, and she undertook to help him with it. Each morning he had to walk a mile to the Graves–Riding temporary residence, Ca'n Pa Bo. One morning when he arrived as usual, he was stopped by Riding at the door. She told him that there was a letter for him on the table in the room where they worked, and that he was to read it; she would return in fifteen minutes.

He read it. It was couched 'in complex language'. The main gist was that Riding had now become aware that he lusted violently after her, but that *if* he felt he could master his feelings, then he could stay – and when she returned they could go on as if nothing had happened. If not, he was to leave; she wouldn't hold that against him.

Instead of telling her that she had made a mistake, Matthews simply stayed where he was. So Riding 'gave a quick, satisfied nod', and returned to their joint task. Matthews (who was always being teased because he was the son of a peculiarly ferocious bishop) says that the experience so affected him that he was impotent for a month.

The Matthews did not leave before he and Riding had completed his novel (published by Seizin, in association with Constable, in 1936), *The Moon's No Fool*. The work on this was done at Canelluñ, into which Graves and Riding had by now moved. After he had left Riding spent some time in further revising it, and it reached him in its final form when he was back in America.

When Matthews arrived back at New York, ill with an ulcer, and weighing twenty-five pounds less than when he had set out, he was met by his old friend Schuyler Jackson, who was (like him) married and had children. He talked him into corresponding with Riding (though Jackson was initially sceptical). He praised Riding to Jackson, whom he had already praised to Riding – who was at first uninterested. Jackson told Matthews that her poetry wasn't poetry, but 'philosophy'. There is no record of what she then thought of him, or of his work, which was in any case very sparse, and available only in one or two back numbers of the *London Mercury*. He published no more than a few lines of verse in his life. Only Matthews then thought it important that these two should get to know each other. 'I was the pimp,' he rather foolishly wrote some forty years later.

IV

The extent of Norman Cameron's involvement in what he afterwards ironically called 'the family' was considerable. Robert Graves was always most attached to Cameron and to Aldridge, of the original 'circle' – though he later became fond of James Reeves, too, who was a late (and never in any case fully fledged) 'member'. Norman Cameron's experiences and their cost to him, during his unhappy year in Mallorca (1932), reveal the vastness – and the early genesis – of Riding's ambitions. At one point he was so bemused that when someone complained that Laura behaved as though she was God, he replied with gloomy earnestness, 'Maybe she is God.'

But first something must be said about the partners' chief Mallorquín ally. His name was Juan Marroig (pronounced Marrotch) Mas, always known as Gelat, and he had a hand in most things that went on in the village. He ran the bus service to Palma. He was married, and had a son, Juan, who helped him in his work. It was well known that he kept a mistress in the village. No one objected to this, such was his respected position. His two chief enemies were the priest (Gelat was representative of the anti-clerical element in Deyán life, and he was liked better than the priest, who was in any case a bad priest and a Fascist), and the doctor. If you wanted anything built it was best to put Gelat in charge of the proceedings. He would rob you of a bit – but not too much. Chief amongst his preoccupations during the time Graves and Riding were at Deyá was his interest in exploiting the concession to supply water to the village, the rights to which he had managed to obtain – and the desire to become mayor. He was by nature, in the context of the Mallorca of that time, a socialist; but his main reason for wanting to be mayor was that the position would help him in his business. He enjoyed this business, was friendly and helpful, and liked making money. He was the best kind of rogue that one could wish to meet: intelligent, sympathetic, an enjoyer of life. Franco's rule was custom-built to break this kind of Spaniard.

Gelat, much loved by Riding and Graves – this at least they kept in common – never allowed an opportunity to pass him by. Not even friendship. Graves liked him for this, and enjoyed his company more than that of any passing tourist, even the ones approved of by Laura.

Riding took a different, radiantly idealistic view of Gelat. She wrote of him:

> I admire no single person except a native of Deyá called Juan Marroig. He is fifty-three years old and makes the electric light there. He is rarely wrong in his judgements, and when he makes a mistake it does not stay long uncorrected. I do not believe in admiration, but when I am asked whom I admire, this is what I say. [*Authors Today and Yesterday*]

As it happens, Gelat was able to make the electric light for the village because of Laura's idolization of him. She prevailed upon Graves to advance him the money (which he never got back) to buy a hydro-electric generator. It put Gelat in a strong position in the village.

Riding believed in Gelat more than Graves – who is gullible enough – did. She took his friendship, which was merry and honest, over-intensely, though she did not show this in front of the others. He knew it, and wasn't above humouring her. He would tell her when they were alone of how badly 'they' all treated her, how she did not deserve such treatment when she was so 'good', and so forth. With the shrewd instinct of a peasant, he knew exactly what she wanted to hear. The fact of the matter was that Gelat used Laura to get Graves to do what would be most profitable for him – starting with the electricity. Not that he disliked or despised him for it, of course. On the contrary, he liked Graves more than Laura, and told some Deyáns so. But buttering up Laura was profitable.

So Gelat was put in charge of the Canellun project.

Riding had already advanced many plans for her Utopian community, though she never described it in such terms. That she would be in charge of everything was not a question that arose in her mind. In addition to this community there was to be a 'university' – and, surprisingly, a hotel. Since she disapproved of more than nine-tenths of visitors to Deyá, one assumes that this hotel would accommodate students of the university, although possibly one or two tourists could get in if they passed the test, or rejected time or 'sensuous elation' (or, from Graves's point of view, Cambridge) or whatever. For this project she needed the help of Gelat. Hence their dual exploitation of Graves.

For, in addition to the 'university' and hotel, she had a road built

– down to the sea – and planned to sell off 'lots' for villas on the property across the road from Canelluñ. She even planned at one point to sell the road 'to the Government' at 100 per cent profit. But this road was washed away in a storm, not a single lot was ever sold, and she even had at one stage to mortgage off half Canelluñ.

Graves went along with all this just as he went along with everything else Laura wanted and planned. But the relationship between the village factotum and the exotically dressed lady became so close that it even generated the rumour that the lady was 'after' Gelat. This has no known basis in fact; but it was – and still is – said.

Norman Cameron arrived in Deyá in early 1932, and left, finally, late in the same year. While he was there, he was for most of the time Riding's avid devotee; only Graves's ardour could match his. But he was not as consistent as Graves, and from time to time found himself obliged to go away, in order to 'get over' his 'bad feelings' (which he would first confess) about Riding.

In April or May 1932, while his house was still being built, Cameron suddenly developed a 'horror' of Riding. With Calvinistic zeal, he told her so, and she 'sadly' told everyone else. He went off for a time (with a German girl called Elfriede) to get over it. He did return, though, and felt for a short time that he had 'cured' himself. In fact he became so reinvolved that he made Laura a solemn promise that he would invest money in the 'hotel speculation'. This promise was to cost him a great deal. The copy I have of her letter demanding money from him, after he had left Mallorca, certainly has hair-raisingly vitriolic qualities.

Although Riding had decided that physicality postponed judgement, she was by no means uninterested in the effects her physicality had on other men – as we have seen in the case of Matthews. She did, however, exercise a real fascination over Cameron. It was, he said to me some years afterwards, a mixture of horror and awe, a feeling that at any time he might be overwhelmed into attempting to do something which would cost him his sanity and even his life, something he didn't want to do at all, something he could very seldom even bring himself to talk about unless he had had enough drinks. But his Calvinistic mentality made him into an absolute devotee while he was under the spell, and he felt himself guilty of mortal sin whenever he entertained bad thoughts about Laura. He was too sophisticated to speak in terms of 'sin'; but that is nevertheless exactly what he felt. He never rid himself of his morbid conscience. And so when Riding asked him for cash, he paid up with the feeling that he might – he told me – be free of her spell at last.

Knowing that both Graves and he were devoted to her, in their different ways, Riding put them to a test. They knew it, and Graves has described it as 'a kind of triangular situation which developed between Norman and me and Laura'. Norman wrote, retrospectively, of that situation in his poem 'The Wanton's Death', in which a wanton woman, who had two suitors, a merman and a landman, challenged them thus:

> 'To prove his love the sturdier, each abandon
> The element in which his suit was fostered
> And undergo this test of transmutation,
> Merman ashore, landman beyond the breakers.'

The suitors obey, and each suffers in the element unnatural to him:

> She, to both quarters native, found them sporting.
> At length each suitor found a spacious refuge,
> Merman a pool, landman a reefy foothold. . . .

She mocks their 'lie', but

> Her relics rot on the sea-wasted foreshore,
> Half-wooed, half-spurned by the land-tainted spindrift.

But when the time came for Norman Cameron to leave, to rid himself of what he realized he could not endure, Graves supported Riding, as he always did. He was intensely officious about this, and doubtless appealed to Cameron's feelings of Laura's 'holiness'. The general atmosphere he generated, in his role of protector, was that she was the centre of everything, and he was her colonel-in-chief. Cameron commented:

> Forgive me, Sire, for cheating your intent,
> That I, who could command a regiment,
> Do amble amiably here, O God,
> One of the neat ones in your awkward squad.

But when he left he was poorer than when he came.

In February 1948, when he was newly married and broke, he wrote thanking Graves for £100. Graves had sent a cheque on receipt of a letter from Cameron saying he had hit hard times.

Bless you, those £100 have made my life a lot brighter.
About Can Torrent, the factors in the equation were so complicated

that I preferred, when I had enough money, to regard them as cancelling out. You see, I made L.R. a present of the house (together with 10,000 pesetas to pay for getting it into a finished condition, but this apparently proved insufficient) and she gave me to understand that this was a poor compensation for my having changed my mind about investing in the hotel speculation. Moreover, although the year I spent in Majorca was expensive to me, it was much more expensive to you – and I, too, was a member of the family, so to speak. In these less well-off days, however, I gratefully accept your statement that you would like to pay me something (if 'pay' is the right word) for the place. As any payment would be entirely ex gratia, I leave the sum to you.

As for the specific £100 I mentioned (which I thought was what you were talking about at Brown's Hotel [where Graves was staying immediately prior to his return to Mallorca after the Second World War] in 1946) I gave you a cheque for that amount at a time when I had just had a legacy and L.R. was in hospital after the window event. (The reason why you never thought to 'pay back' was presumably that I shortly afterwards went to Africa, where I had more money than I needed. In those days we were both subsidising Len and Jane [Lye], and it would have been pointless for you to send money out to me, which I would probably have passed on to them, instead of giving it to them directly.) But you were under no obligation in respect of this sum either, since I had regarded it not as a loan or gift to you, but rather as a contribution to L.R. from a member of the family – or, perhaps, as a tuition fee from a student at a very advanced and therefore with-good-reason-somewhat-expensive academy! . . .

In other words, Riding extracted from him, as price of his treason, the sum of 10,000 pesetas as well as Ca'n Torrent. Furthermore, he was regarded as the villain of the piece when Graves and Riding became broke. Cameron never complained about it, though he did once grinningly remark, when someone commented that Riding never made much out of her writing: 'Not out of writing.'

But he was glad to be able to pay in money. The whole experience, he later wrote, drove him to 'madness and misery' – and more than one drastic drinking episode.

Chapter Sixteen

1933

I

Graves did not worry about the failure of *No Decency Left*. But money was getting short again. Riding's property projects were as expensive as they were unrealistic. Substantial German royalties on *Goodbye to All That* still showed no sign of turning up. There was nothing to be had from periodicals: in 1933 Graves published only one item in a periodical, and this was a letter to the *Times Literary Supplement* in reply to a review of a book he had rewritten for an old Welch Fusilier, his friend Frank Richards: *Old Soldiers Never Die* (1933). Faber and Faber published this account of a soldier's life, which Graves enlivened and 'Englished' without robbing it of its 'nap'. It did well. By 1936 it had sold nearly 10,000 copies in England, and the Angus and Robertson Australian edition sold another 2000. It was reprinted twice: in 1942 and 1964. But Graves did not, of course, receive a full 10 per cent royalty – Richards got his fair share – and the money did not go far towards paying for the improvements that were always being made to Canelluñ, Ca'n Torrent and their surroundings.

All the property, including what was acquired by 1933 and what was acquired later, though in theory 'jointly owned', was legally the property of Riding. Graves insisted on this, and perhaps Gelat 'advised' it. Later, in 1936 'she signed a deed registered at Palma . . . conveying a power of attorney for all *her* properties upon Don Juan Marroig Mas of Deyá . . .' (my italics). The properties in question were all the partners had.

During 1932 Graves rewrote Dickens's *David Copperfield* in order to produce what he called the 'real book'. He saw it as an author's deliberate falsification of autobiographical facts. Here he indulged himself in one of his favourite pursuits: 'putting it right'. He tries to do it, relentlessly, in his own poetry; and he enjoys doing it, more light-heartedly, to the works of other people.

He did not expect a big sale, although he thought that the 'cheek' – criticizing one of the most revered authors of all time as a bore, and 'correcting' his work for him – might give the work an appeal. It sold only about 2000 copies in its original form, and has never been reprinted. But in 1934 Harcourt Brace took it up in a disguised form: they called it a 'condensation', and a Dickensian pedagogue called Merrill P. Paine was given the title of 'editor'. Paine changed Graves's insolent rewrite into an 'abridged version for schools', and as such the book did well for some years – it was being reprinted in this form until after the beginning of the Second World War.

As Norman Cameron was in Mallorca at the time, Riding and Graves gave him the job of redoing the *Pickwick Papers*. Graves gave him a start, and Norman went on with some of it; but, although no Dickens lover, he decided that he could not do it better. The enterprise was not one likely to attract large sums into Deyá.

To the outraged magazine *The Dickensian* Graves wrote (5 April 1934) that his work was

> unlike the original . . . consistently readable . . . it removes the adulterations and dilutions with which Dickens has spoiled his best story . . . and may be regarded as a sincerer tribute to Dickens than the most extravagant praises of his countless non-readers. . . .

This letter was not published.

The Real David Copperfield was not published by Cape. There were two reasons for this. First, Cape was not eager for this book, which he thought a silly idea. Secondly, and more important, he was not prepared to finance the Seizin activities, or to consider, for the time being, further work by Riding. He was therefore written off.

The new publisher was Arthur Barker, who had not long before set up business under his own name in Garrick Street, near Covent Garden. Barker was interested in Graves and in Riding (he published four of her own books) and, although somewhat of a muddlehead, was a literate publisher who aimed to produce a literate list. None the less, he was early told off, in round terms, by Riding, who wrote him a letter in which she expressed her surprise that he could associate with 'shits like Agate' (James Agate then being at the height of his fame as a theatre critic). Still, he was regarded as a white hope; and he stuck by the partners – until he crossed Riding's wishes. He had made a short visit to the island and his potentialities were overrated by Riding. He published Graves's *Real David Copperfield*. He took on Laura's long poem *The Life of the Dead*. And he also published (1933) what is possibly the feeblest book that ever came out of Deyá: *Everybody's Letters*, a collection of letters edited by Riding purporting to illustrate 'The British Spirit', 'The Universal Spirit' and 'The American Spirit'. The letters are presented as having been printed 'exactly as found'.

These letters, except for a few passages, are boring and unfunny. There is an editorial postscript with some acute observations about letters (and a paragraph or two about that young man 'who turned out to be the devil'). The book might have worked had it been presented as an extended essay with selected quotations from 'ordinary' letters; as it stands, it is as boring and feeble as is the intended satire *Americans*, in badly executed rhymed couplets, which Riding published the next year with a small press called Primavera.

But no money was coming in, and by now it was badly wanted. *Epilogue* was being actively planned; by autumn 1933 it was already described by Riding as 'delayed'. The hotel project had by no means been abandoned. Nor had the 'university', though this was not yet a topic of general discussion.

Living in the village during part of 1933 were the young mathematician-cum-literary critic Jacob Bronowski and his then companion Eirlys Roberts, who after the Second World War became a household name as the founder and editor of the magazine *Which*.

Someone who knew both Riding and Bronowski well has said: 'I've known two Gods, and each was Mono.' The situation between these two did not work out. At first Bronowski seemed just what was wanted: a young literary-oriented scientist who essayed verse and who was interested in Blake and in the necessity of poetry. In particular, he and Riding worked at the problems of the relationship between poets and society – and she even acknowledged the usefulness of some of his suggestions in *Epilogue I* (1935).

Eirlys Roberts gave some help, in the form of research, to Graves in his current project, a novel about ancient Rome – while Riding and Bronowski worked together. But Bronowski could not accept being told what to do by Riding. He demanded at least equality, and found that he could not get it. He complained that Riding interfered with his independence of thought – and that she made pronouncements on subjects (particularly scientific ones) in which she was neither qualified nor informed. Eventually the affair blew up into a vulgar row, with

Riding denouncing Bronowski's character, and he telling her that she 'was no lily-white angel' (this became a legendary remark). Bronowski was no Matthews. He went off without suffering from half a day's impotence, became a don at Hull University, invented 'Bronowski's Bricks' (a form of smokeless fuel) at the Coal Board, and finally transformed himself into an academic, a television personality and a popular culture-science expert. He even wrote a prize-winning radio drama.

Graves had loathed him (but not Eirlys Roberts) all the time he was working with Riding; but he kept quiet. When Bronowski offended her a satirical poem began to form in his mind. He first published it as 'Dream of a Climber' in *Work In Hand* (1942). But its original title was 'Jacob's Ladder', and this was changed only because James Reeves, originally intended as a contributor to *Work In Hand*, objected on the grounds that he was still a friend of Bronowski's and therefore could not stand for it (though, as he told me, he always thought the poem wholly appropriate). However, Bronowski was a climber, and even gave 'rock-climbing' as his recreation in *Who's Who*. The poem, a good example of Graves in his satirical vein, speaks of 'the perfect phallo-spiritual tilt', and has his victim posing for the cameraman as 'Well-known Climber About to Ascend' –

> But in the published print, we may be sure,
> He will appear, not on the lowest rung
> But nearly out of view, almost in the cloud,
> Leaning aside for an angel to pass,
> His muscular broad hands a-glint in the sun,
> And crampons on his feet.

Luckily Graves had more profitable things to do while Bronowski was *persona grata* with Riding. Later Bronowski wrote *The Ascent of Man*.

II

In the diary (written in England) 'A Journal of Curiosities' included in *But It Still Goes On*, which covers the period 23 August–30 September 1929, the entry for 5 September reads:

> I had a dream that I had written a popular song hit called 'You surely won't charge me for that.' This is only one of dozens of winning ideas that attack me in my weaker moments of sleep or day-dream, and are

only with difficulty repulsed. It is not long since a complete historical romance or interpretative biography occurred to me – 'The Emperor Pumpkin.' I had been reading Suetonius and Tacitus. It was about Claudius, the emperor who came between Caligula and Nero. The *dramatis personae* were all ready. The only character who needed any serious enlargement was his physician and adviser Xerxes of Cos, in gratitude for whose services, it may be remembered, he gave the island its freedom from all Imperial imposts. Claudius has always been a puzzle to the historians, as indeed he was to his contemporaries. The Emperor Augustus was much surprised one day to hear his supposedly idiot grandson making a sensible speech. Claudius was to be presented in this story as an idealistic enemy of Caesardom; his father Drusus had made no secret of his own republican views and it was probably these that cost him his life. Claudius escaped both succession and assassination at the hands of claimants to the succession by a parade of his physical infirmities, an affected lowness of taste and a cultivated weak-mindedness. But in spite of every precaution the soldiers forcibly acclaimed him Caesar after their murder of Caligula. He demurred, but they insisted. So he decided, the story would show, to do his best to bring Caesardom into disrepute by playing the fool. Certainly he did issue numerous ridiculous edicts – such as that mentioned by Suetonius that no man should hesitate to break wind in his presence, if he felt so inclined, because to hold it might be injurious to health. And wrote ridiculous official letters like the one to the Alexandrians which has survived. And allowed his wife Messalina, whom he disliked, to cuckold him openly and make a laughing stock of him – until he decided (in my reading) to carry the farce further and to appear in the further ridiculous guise of the deceived jealous husband. He played the fool in the lawcourts and in the circus. He allowed himself to be ruled (as it seemed) by millionaire eunuchs. But when the city stood for all this, and more, and he saw that his fun was wasted, he became bitter. He married as a second wife Agrippina, the worst woman he could find, gave her a free hand in affairs and chose, for his successor, Nero his step-son, whom he knew to be mad, egotistical and degenerate. He was persuaded that the sequence of Tiberius in his wicked old age, Caligula the monster, himself the idiot and then Nero would be enough to bring back the republic. It nearly was.

As for Britannicus, his son, whom he loved and therefore passed over for the succession and to whom he is reported to have said, 'He that wounded thee will also heal thee,' according to the story I intended he was handed over to the care of Xerxes, who smuggled him out to Cos and found a changeling to take his place and be murdered, in due course, by Nero. I would have presented the death of Claudius not as murder by his wife with Xerxes as accomplice, but as suicide with Xerxes as accomplice. The satire of Seneca, *The Pumpkinification of Claudius*, circulated after his death, would be attributed to Claudius himself. I would have made it clear that Claudius did not play his hand as well as he might have done. He was too sincere a lover of his country to let his buffooneries prevent him from undertaking many valuable public works, and too moral a character to discredit the Imperial power by adding debauch to buffoonery.

I reckon all this here to lay the ghost of an idea which otherwise might continue to plead for execution.

As he says, Graves specifically recorded this sketch for a possible novel in order to avoid writing it. He had always expressed a dislike of ancient Rome and continued to do so after writing the *Claudius* books. But beneath his disdain for the period and the outline plot the idea had been working like yeast: it *was* 'pleading for execution'.

It was an unusual project. Most writers, especially those with Graves's gift for the grotesque, aiming to produce a popular book set in Rome, would have plumped for Nero, Caligula or at least Caesar as a central subject. The general public had heard of Claudius, if at all, as the Roman emperor who took a personal part in the invasion of Britain. Scholars tended to ignore him. At best he was a 'problem': an American classicist, T. de C. Ruth, had entitled his 1924 book on him *The Problem of Claudius*. He was an odd fish: proclaimed as emperor in AD 41 largely by accident, unpopular with the senate because he pressed them to act responsibly, a victim of ill health – and yet, as is now generally conceded, a man 'of profound common sense', with a greater grasp of Roman history than that of any other emperor, a learned writer – and the author of a lost autobiography (which, of course, Graves now supplied).

Now what had merely been 'pleading for execution', and gently at that, became harsh necessity. When some years later Graves was asked whether he knew, when he set out on *Claudius*, that it would bring in large amounts of money, he replied: 'I knew it had bloody well got to.' He felt he had been let down over money he had borrowed for Laura's land-buying and building plans; now he could not pay it back. He said in 1955 that the proceeds from *Claudius* allowed him to 'hold his head up'.

He did much preparatory work for it. The books he used are still in Canelluñ, and they comprise most of the general scholarly works on ancient Rome then available. He steeped himself in the atmosphere of the Rome of Claudius's time: its sociology, its customs at all levels, its politics, its geography, its legal system, its trade and agriculture, its military practices, and, of course, its brutal, murderous and coarse-grained history. He knew as much as anyone, academic or otherwise, about conditions in ancient Rome. Having a 'nose' (not the same as a taste) for what Sassoon had called the 'nasty', he was well equipped to deal with the excessive nastiness of Rome with just as excessive a gusto.

But the result – *I, Claudius* and *Claudius the God*, which are really one book – is anything but academic or 'historical' in the accepted sense. Graves applied his own highly idiosyncratic view to the facts he gleaned. Yet most classical students, even orthodox ones, have gained from this work a general picture of ancient Rome which they would not otherwise have had. The moral, or rather amoral, atmosphere is authentic. In certain ways Graves wanted, in fact needed, to escape from his predicament. His soaking of himself in the atmosphere of Rome served his purpose. Although this work was to be referred to – by Riding, himself and everyone else under their instructions – as a potboiler, rubbish, and so forth, it is really nothing of the sort; and he sublimated his problems in the very hard work he put into it: not the least was the assumption of a bizarre role in life.

Randall Jarrell's view that *Claudius* is 'a good book singular enough to be immortal' is shared by most critical readers – even by those who do not as a rule enjoy historical fiction, as Graves himself certainly does not. Recently the *Times Literary Supplement* referred to the work, quite casually, and in the context of a review of several historical novels none of which dealt with Rome, as the only successful historical novel of the century. Millions of TV viewers, when at last *Claudius* reached the screen, were so fascinated by it that they could not tear themselves away. Avidly discussed everywhere, it was the most successful major series ever put out by the BBC (although Graves's own financial reward for the series itself, if not for the new sales of the book thus generated, was shockingly meagre, partly owing to earlier contractual arrangements). But in 1934 *Claudius* was going to have a long wait before it reached a form other than its original one, between covers. And this despite the fact that it cries out for popular dramatic treatment.

What fascinated the mass television audience in Great Britain was by no means only the excellent acting and production, it was also, and in very large measure, the successful transference to a new medium of a certain ingredient of the original. That ingredient was the sense of immediacy, of actuality. Not all viewers believed that the events they were witnessing week by week really took place in history. But they were convinced of their essential truth. *Claudius* satisfies Aristotle's dictum that fiction (in the sense of something that is not historically true) may be more satisfying than the real: he stated, and *Claudius* is a case in point, that fiction could present the *general* truth about something more effectively – indeed, more truthfully – than could some *particular* (or even unique) historical record.

Graves once puzzled Tom Matthews by telling him that he had no imagination. Matthews thought this a strange admission for a poet to make. And so it would have been, if the poet had made it in the context of poetry. But Graves was talking specifically about his capacity for the conventional novel: the novel set in the writer's own time. What Graves meant was that he lacked the kind of inventiveness shown by an Anthony Powell, a Graham Greene, a Simenon. At one time, when they still hoped to make money through conventional fiction, Riding and he entertained the notion that to write a successful novel all you had to do was to invent a lively or odd situation. Then, in the course of the writing, 'things would happen of themselves'. This may be the way in which certain competent novelists happen to work; but such novelists are interested in the outcome, whereas Graves and Riding weren't; the contemporary world was already rejected, goddawful, historical, and 'all that'.

Graves has tried his hand at one or two novels of the conventional variety; but they proved damp squibs, and he could not finish them. The nearest he came, in published work, was in *Antigua, Penny, Puce* – but in this he was satirizing family history, family nastiness (both of a specifically English type), and certain other things he found both comic and unlikeable, such as some traits in the character of his brother John. *Seven Days in New Crete*, the most neglected of his major novels, is set in the future, and is by no means conventional.

But give Graves a set of historical facts to make sense out of, and, if he is interested in them – if they set a puzzle – then you are likely to get at least a competent novel. *Claudius* is much more than competent. Under these circumstances he has plenty of 'imagination', although he calls it 'reconstruction'.

But in 1933, settled at last in Canellun, he was telling himself that he was sitting down to turn out a potboiler. He was even more insistent on this than Riding: he needed to be. It was fortunate that the ingredients of the novel happened to be responses to the pressures he was under – though he was literally too busy to recognize this at the time

230

(he does now). *I, Claudius* is an objective correlative for his situation, and all the more powerful a one because the pressure to write it appeared to him to be solely financial.

His poem of the mid-thirties, 'The Devil's Advice to Storytellers', provides a description of his novelistic method. Part of it reads:

> . . . my advice to storytellers is
> Weigh out no gross of probabilities,
> Nor yet make diligent transcriptions of
> Known instances of virtue, crime or love.
> To forge a picture that will pass for true,
> Do conscientiously what liars do –
> Born liars, not the lesser sort that raid
> The mouths of others for their stock-in-trade:
> Assemble, first, all casual bits and scraps
> That may shake down into a world perhaps. . . .
> Sigh then, or frown, but leave (as in despair)
> Motive and end and moral in the air;
> Nice contradiction between fact and fact
> Will make the whole read human and exact.

The background against which Graves set his story of the supposed bumbling nonentity Claudius might have been tailored to match his especial, robust skills: it was one of brutality, deceit, treachery, sensuality, superstition. It was a caricature of the goddawful, and he could let himself go in his description of it without upsetting any of his readers' preconceptions. His misunderstood central character was an oblique caricature (but by no means a portrait) of himself – more particularly of his situation.

'My stutter, my cough, my unfinished sentences . . .' he began his fifties poem 'The Second-Fated'; and he has recorded in many other places his sense, physical as well as mental, of being awkward, of not 'fitting in' – even of being grotesque. Sassoon's picture of him as a soldier, not an unkind one, suggests that others felt this 'differentness'.

He does not like attention drawn, in conversation, either to this aspect of his character or to his absent-mindedness; and when his daughter Jenny Nicholson wrote a piece on him in *Picture Post* (in the early fifties), in which she said that he might well be found 'with marmalade in his hair', he was distinctly annoyed – the day it arrived in the post he said, 'I could be very annoyed', which meant he was.

The character of the historical Claudius is irretrievable, as the few scholarly non-fiction books about him make abundantly clear. So

Graves's subtle and gripping psychological portrait has, so to say, taken over: this *is*, for millions of people, Claudius.

One feature of the real Claudius's personality is known, and it attracted Graves. He was, as a classical authority puts it, 'incurably uxorious'. The concentration of evil to be found in certain of the female characters of the book, particularly in Livia Drusilla, added yet another fascinating dimension to the novel.

Arthur Barker published *I, Claudius* in May 1934, in a jacket designed by John Aldridge; Harrison Smith (who had now gone into partnership with Robert Haas) followed suit in America in June. In England the book had reached a third impression before the end of its month of publication, and a ninth (large one) by October 1935. *Claudius the God* appeared in November 1934, again published by Barker. (When Barker wound up his affairs in 1939 the rights were taken over by Methuen.) The two volumes have since appeared in numerous editions, and have never been out of print – and when Penguin released their second edition to coincide with the television series in 1976, it was on the best-seller lists for over a year. *Claudius* has been translated into seventeen languages.

But in both his and Riding's terms the work was a potboiler, and its merits were not allowed to be discussed. One afternoon Graves was forcibly reminded of this.

Both partners subscribed to a press-cutting agency. Riding took up any mention of herself (or got Graves to), and was particularly sensitive to any attribution of their joint work to Graves alone (as she had every right to be). His vitriolic letters complaining of this, a frequent habit of literary columnists, became something of a feature of thirties literary life.

When *Claudius* appeared it was hailed as a masterpiece by reviewers, and eventually (1935) received both the James Tait Black and the Hawthornden prizes. Press-cuttings poured in, and were duly filed. Perhaps he had been indulging in the universal authorial habit of secretly dwelling on the more laudatory of them – for returning one afternoon from his customary swim he discovered that they had been torn up and scattered about the floor.

It was not long after the success of *Claudius* that Graves suggested to Riding that she might write a historical novel of her own, about the fall of Troy. Appeased, she took up this idea.

Apart from rewriting another book by Frank Richards – *Old Soldier Sahib* (1936), published by Faber – and doing a translation (with

Riding) of a book by Georg Schwarz, a German neighbour, called *Almost Forgotten Germany*, Graves's next venture would be the comedy of English manners and absurdities *Antigua, Penny, Puce* (1936).

III

It is not surprising that Graves firmly believes in the anthropologically untenable theory that before the state of patriarchy there existed a state of matriarchy. This is by no means owing to his study of Bachofen, or Engels, who also believed it – but whose writings remain unread by Graves.

While he was working on *Claudius* there was established the absolute, the carefully elaborated, 'literal' rule of Laura Riding. Certainly, as everyone without exception who went there noted, she was effectively in charge by early 1932. But by the next year and the occupation of Canelluñ the laws had been drawn up. The constitution was partly written. Graves did what Laura told him to do, and he believed in what she believed. He also enforced her wishes. She did not initiate this state of matriarchy. They initiated it together. It is instructive to know something of what it actually entailed.

First, as Riding explained to a correspondent, 'quite frankly, it's not so equal' in Canelluñ as all that: 'we don't believe in equality':

> the apparatus is rather that there are certain laws of being and procedure centralised in me on which Robert relies and which I am happy to realise cooperatively with him – and others who want the same security of mind.

Of Graves's condition she wrote:

> I don't think he regards his mind as poisoned [by celibacy]: it was much more poisoned when he was leading a non-celibate life, at any rate. No doubt his mind has its brutal lapses; they are not important, only psychologically interesting.

She thought that a woman might appear with whom Graves might have 'brutal lapses'; but these lapses would be only psychologically interesting anyway – and 'it doesn't occur to him to want anyone to appear' (it did, of course).

People 'here', she wrote, 'take the clue from me and Robert that we are two very close friends, and not an establishment with a sexual definition.'

She saw herself as a dispeller of darkness, though not quite as a magician, because magicians work in the dark. 'The many . . . behind me [are] probably beings I was helping to clarify and therefore beings who were helping me to dispel dark.'

> As for Robert's knowing, or not knowing, whether I am a magician: Robert is very self-protective and on the whole doesn't let himself know more than he can absolutely help. And so it is satisfactory between us: I tell him what I am. He is perhaps the only one to whom I tell explicitly what I am. And I do not tell him that I am a magician.

And Graves, who did not allow himself to know more than he could absolutely help, was gaining the energy from somewhere to write *Claudius*.

The stress which produced Graves's thirties poetry was that between his worship of Riding and his own inclinations, instincts, beliefs, scepticisms – to which must be added his resentment, however unconscious, of her treatment of him. She was, it is true, very nice indeed to him – and often. But she continually cancelled out such gestures by making him feel acutely unhappy. She handled him with great skill when she was in control of herself; but when she lost control it simply made him unhappy anyway. He could and did hand her his powerful poem 'Certain Mercies', as he handed all his poems to her, as testimony to his willingness to be 'lessoned'; but it may be read in another way:

> Now must all satisfaction
> Appear mere mitigation
> Of an accepted curse?
>
> Must we henceforth be grateful
> That the guards, though spiteful,
> Are slow of foot and wit?
>
> That by night we may spread
> Over the plank bed
> A thin coverlet?
>
> That the rusty water
> In the unclean pitcher
> Our thirst quenches?
>
> That the rotten, detestable
> Food is yet eatable
> By us ravenous?

That the prison censor
Permits a weekly letter?
(We may write: 'We are well.')

That, with patience and deference,
We do not experience
The punishment cell?

That each new indignity
Defeats only the body,
Pampering the spirit
With obscure, proud merit?

This was shown to Riding as a poem about the spirit as the prisoner of the body, and so it should — at the initial level — be read. But its occasion is suffering; suffering inflicted by Riding as well as by the goddawful world. The poem represents Graves's willingness to suffer. But those who interpret it as a straight body–spirit metaphor woodenly miss its robust, dismayed physicality. Clearly, as a certain kind of God(ess?) might say, physicality does postpone judgement. But judgement by whom? The worms? The angels? Riding?

'Certain Mercies' offers a perfect example of a poem whose true (though then unacknowledged) personal occasion is in direct opposition to its first-level meaning. Ultimately the poem is not dualistic: it is about the body–spirit's lack of freedom to find its true self, and we may infer that this lack stems from its inability to remain 'unsplit', intact. Riding is a straightforward dualist: her post-1940 pseudo-religious system is an excellent example of poetry distorted into philosophy, and it lacks true coherence. Graves is subtler. The body ends, in 'Certain Mercies', by being defeated by its indignities. But the spirit is nevertheless *pampered*; 'obscure' and 'proud' are contradictory, though 'proud' is empirically justified. If Riding's best poetry has the quality of purity of utterance, his has that of stubborn, persistent acknowledgement of difficulties, of the sort of psychological truths unpalatable to philosophers because they spoil their theorizing.

But to hierophants difficulties become devils. If Graves had not been 'patient and deferent' he might well have found himself a Severus being burned outside the boundaries of Deyá; but 'playing safe', as he has very often said in conversation, is a strong instinct in him — even when he isn't absolutely sure what he is playing safe about. He played safe in this instance by quickly proving himself a golden goose: golden geese don't get roasted. He was never until old age absolutely lacking in shrewdness, and even then would tend to deviate into it.

But in spite of the atmosphere of unhappiness that underlay every-thing serious – Laura's dissatisfaction, and Graves's frustration at not being able to fulfil her wishes – there was plenty of fun and enjoyment, as well as much hard work, in the pursuit of which both partners temporarily forgot their miseries.

The sense of happiness then to be found in Deyá, though, was felt most strongly by those visitors who were not writers: those whom Laura did not consider as suitable for her ideal community. Towards these she (usually) behaved with an especially relaxed courtesy and light-heartedness – almost as though they provided her with a much needed excuse to drop, for the time being, the cares of the universe. There were parties – and dancing on the patio outside Canelluñ, visits to cafés, card-playing, joking conversations (many based on Aldridge's comic system of classification of human beings: his day- and night-slimers, and so on). On many of these occasions Gelat would be present.

Why Laura chose some people as 'acceptable', and others as not, was puzzling to many. One retired couple, of distinctly right-wing disposition (they were Franco supporters when the Civil War began), and without any interesting conversation or knowledge of literature, or intelligence, were singled out as good friends – yet others, more interesting, were rejected with unnecessary rudeness. People who were not members of the intelligentsia afforded Laura a sense of relief. In their presence she lacked the strain and irascibility she showed in her dealings with writers, with the work of the Press, and with the rela-tionships between her intellectual friends (with which she interfered as though she were God).

Yet the sense of lightness, of fun, of good humour, which she could induce in those around her was remarkable – and none of those who knew her has been able to forget it. It was a genuine gift. So the life in Deyá was one of strong contrasts. But she undoubtedly held sway, the others were a part of her court – and no one (witness Bronowski) who challenged her authority was allowed to stay long.

IV

Graves's official role as poet during the years in Mallorca with Riding, during which time he 'submitted' every one of his poems to her for approval, was that of a man putting himself into a state of purification so that he would be ready to be 'judged'. Thus he was 'allowed' to confess his lusts, his feelings, and to retain his individual voice – diction, tone and so forth – because this was all in the interests of his redemption. ('Redemption' is not too strong a word; later Riding would claim, through Schuyler Jackson, that she had tried to 'save his soul'.) In the *Collected Poems* of 1938 Graves ended his foreword by saying that he had to thank her for her 'constructive and detailed criticism' of his poems 'in various stages of composition'. Her detailed criticism was constructive, as other poets have testified; it had genius. She could often see, in a poem that was still in its draft stage, what was extraneous to its main theme. She could often tell a poet what he was really trying to say, when this eluded him. She helped to see many of Graves's poems of this time into more lively and exact expression. Fundamentally she did object, as she was later to tell him, to his poems 'about himself'; but in Mallorca she hoped that he would come to be able to write poems directly about the uncovering of the truth, even if not poems which, as she claimed hers did, actually uncovered it. That she was not superior never occurred to her.

But his main achievement, though largely based on his experience of her, was entirely his own. She criticized him for manifesting his 'poetic faith' in 'a close and energetic study of the disgusting, the contemptible and the evil' (he uses these words deprecatingly of himself in the foreword to the 1938 collection), but did not expect more from him. It was a fortunate coincidence that his poetic development required him to make a close study of what he found most 'evil' and 'disgusting' in what he accurately called the 'perfect confusion' of his times. There was, of course, confusion in Riding too.

'On Portents' (first published in *To Whom Else?*) was written about Riding as Muse, not about Riding as woman:

> If strange things happen where she is,
> So that men say that graves open
> And the dead walk, or that futurity
> Becomes a womb and the unborn are shed,
> Such portents are not to be wondered at,
> Being tourbillions in Time made
> By the strong pulling of her bladed mind
> Through that ever-reluctant element

This attributes qualities that are, in the Gravesian sense, 'magical' to the poet's Muse, and is one of the earliest of the pure so-called 'White

Goddess' poems. The other side of the picture is given in 'The Succubus' (*Poems 1930–1933*), another less immediately flattering – retrospective – 'White Goddess' poem:

Thus will despair
In ecstasy of nightmare
Fetch you a devil-woman through the air,
     To slide below the sweated sheet
And kiss your lips in answer to your prayer
     And lock her hands with yours and your feet with her feet.

Yet why does she
Come never as longed-for beauty
Slender and cool, with limbs lovely to see,
     (The bedside candle guttering high)
And toss her head so the thick curls fall free
     Of halo'd breast, firm belly and long, slender thigh?

Why with hot face,
With paunched and uddered carcass,
Suddenly and greedily does she embrace,
     Gulping away your soul, she lies so close,
Fathering brats on you of her own race?
     Yet is the fancy grosser than your lusts were gross?

This deals specifically with the failure of erotic fantasy (or dream) to bring a 'perfect lover' to the lust-heated imagination, but clearly refers to the reality of the human situation (which renders itself, distressingly, into the equivalent of fantasy in the very act) in which 'unity' with the beloved is thwarted by lust. It ends by blaming the 'fancy' on the unpurgeable grossness of lust. But, if only incidentally, it also shows another face of the White Goddess.

In 'Ulysses' 'flesh' had made the hero 'blind': 'Flesh had one purpose only in the act' and 'set one purpose only in the mind'; 'love-tossed/He loathed the fraud, yet would not bed alone.'

Other poems record moods of pure despair, such as 'Trudge, Body!', in which the body has no hope, nor regret: 'Before each sun may rise, you salute it for set.' Graves was aware that the course he was treading was an eccentric one, unlikely to put him in favour with readers of the poetry then currently fashionable. In 'Flying Crooked' he bitterly – yet light-heartedly – criticized his own clumsy empiricism, which involved him in a continuously experimental, backwards-and-then-forwards-and-then-backwards-again way of living, rather than one impelled by some certainty of direction (Riding's life, on the contrary, seemed to be just that). At the same time he cleverly combined this with a satire on what he called (in a letter of the sixties which he neglected to post) 'the ingenious routineness of poetry [of the fashionable kind]': scientists, he told his correspondent, 'fail to understand that the cabbage-white's seemingly erratic flight provides a metaphor for all original and constructive thinking.' He excepts Eratosthenes, Kekulé (the dreamer), Newton, Nils Bohr and Norbert Wiener from such scientists.

> The butterfly, a cabbage-white,
> (His honest idiocy of flight)
> Will never now, it is too late,
> Master the art of flying straight,
> Yet has – who knows as well as I? –
> A just sense of how not to fly:
> He lurches here and here by guess
> And God and hope and hopelessness.
> Even the aerobatic swift
> Has not his flying-crooked gift.

'Down, Wanton, Down!' is a humorous, Restoration-style treatment of the sexual problem: a poem in which a pure wit replaces the more familiar pained tension, and which demonstrates Graves's debt to Rochester very clearly:

> Down, wanton, down! Have you no shame
> That at the whisper of Love's name,
> Or Beauty's, presto! up you raise
> Your angry head and stand at gaze?
>
> Poor bombard-captain, sworn to reach
> The ravelin and effect a breach –
> Indifferent what you storm or why,
> So be that in the breach you die!
>
> Love may be blind, but Love at least
> Knows what is man and what mere beast;
> Or Beauty wayward, but requires
> More delicacy from her squires.
>
> Tell me, my witless, whose one boast
> Could be your staunchness at the post,
> When were you made a man of parts
> To think fine and profess the arts?

ROBERT GRAVES

Will many-gifted Beauty come
Bowing to your bald rule of thumb,
Or Love swear loyalty to your crown?
Be gone, have done! Down, wanton, down!

But despite all his troubles and his bad dreams and his headaches and his sexual frustration and his other ailments, Graves cheerfully told himself that he enjoyed his life; and very often he did. He worked prodigiously, and, as Riding herself noted of him in her poem *Laura and Francisca*,

Better a wrong day than none
Would Robert to himself say
Before thinking wrong to be wrong.

Chapter Seventeen

1933–36

I

Graves had tried to keep on as good terms as possible with his parents and with his children. He was glad in 1935 to hear that Phibbs had taken himself off. This meant that he could now communicate directly with Nancy – if she would with him. Hitherto he had got information about his children through his mother. But with her, and with his father, relations had not been easy. They had the whole-hearted support of all their other children – with the exception of Philip – against his 'immoral' behaviour. He had deeply hurt them by speaking of 'Grandmother Ranke' as 'intimidated', even though she had been. But what could Graves do about the kind of letter he received from his father on 21 July 1930?

This explained that his own autobiography, *To Return to All That* (the title was suggested by John Graves – supported by none other than the Society for Promoting Christian Knowledge – against the advice of Philip), contained a chapter, 'affectionately devoted' to Robert, and which put his criticisms of others 'who never wished him harm' down to 'war and recent experiences'. The chapter in question is the mildest and most affectionate of rebukes, and caused no offence to anyone.

But A.P. went on, in the private letter, to complain bitterly about the overcandid references to Dick (Johnstone) in *Goodbye to All That*; and to emphasize Robert's bad behaviour in throwing up the Egyptian job without giving 'proper notice'. He says that he is hurt by the last section of *Goodbye to All That* (the 'Dedicatory Epilogue'), 'which is Greek to all but those likely to be pained by it'. He is hurt (understandably) by the claim that he never helped with Robert's poetry. He thinks that Robert should not have forgotten that

241

it was through my asking Professor Edgeworth to let me bring you along with me to 'All Souls' that you first met Lawrence, whose first question to me after our introduction was 'Any relation to Philip Graves?'. When I said 'Only his father' he broke into high praise of him and his opinion of Philip doubtless helped you with him at the start, though no doubt his high estimate of your poems afterwards led to his friendship with you and his agreeing to let you write his life.

What followed was more difficult. The eighty-four-year-old A.P. had by now lost all his sparkle, had entered into the strictly 'pure' world of his wife. He tells Robert that he is glad that he spoke 'highly' of his mother in his autobiography, 'though not to my mind realising that she kept you pure and right minded as a child'. He can only 'hope and pray as I do daily that your future life may be directed from above and that you may lead an unselfish, honourable and useful life'. There was not much Graves could say in answer to this.

A.P. died in 1931, and the Christian moral force of the family was carried on by his widow; so far as the males of the line went, it slipped naturally onto the shoulders of John, who was well able to bear the burden.

Graves felt all this, though. Apart from youthful resentments fanned by the flames of Samuel Butler, he had been very fond of his father, and felt guilty about his treatment of him; and he worried about his mother. In 1934 he wrote inviting her to Canelluñ, adding that he and Laura 'no longer shared the same bed'. She therefore accepted, and John accompanied her, to look after her. Riding, John wrote,

> was superficially polite. . . . She regarded herself as the head of a private university, and had discussions with the group they had gathered around them. My impression was that the Group were much more interested in Robert and much more friendly and relaxed when Laura was not present. She was writing various books in co-authorship with individuals. . . . Robert's book about T. E. Lawrence, *Goodbye to All That* and his Claudius books furnished their income, and I got the impression that the Seizin Press from the first was the only way Laura could be sure of getting her poems into print. She accepted, as a matter of course, Robert's statements that his prose books were merely 'potboilers' and that her poetry was infinitely superior to his.

By now his children were well into their teens, and Graves began to take a more active interest in them. He had some discussion with his mother about them while she was visiting Deyá. He wrote to her in February 1935 about Jenny, whose earliest ambitions were theatrical.

Money was flowing in, and plans were afoot to film *Claudius*: Alexander Korda had decided to do it, with Charles Laughton as Claudius, and a cast including Emlyn Williams and Korda's wife, Merle Oberon. Now that Jenny was sixteen, Graves told his mother, she should 'start her relationship with me afresh: if she respected my feelings, I'd respect hers'. And yes, she could write to him for an introduction to Korda. But Graves and his children would meet again sooner than anyone thought.

II

On Friday, 22 February 1935, Graves began to keep a diary. It runs to 6 May 1939. This diary, which is now at the University of Victoria, was called 'really very private' by Graves in correspondence with an obsessed, garrulous ex-collector of Gravesiana (Graves has written an unpublishably savage satire on him), and thus it has acquired the reputation of being full of detailed, explicit, and highly intimate information about the last years of his association with Riding. This it is not. But it is useful to those who know Graves and can read between his lines, and is invaluable to a biographer. It is not 'private' in the generally understood sense – and contains nothing sensational. It was open to the scrutiny of Riding, and there are few overt descriptions of Graves's feelings about her. There is nothing 'intimate' about it. If Graves has refused research students (including the obsessed ex-collector) access to it then this is simply because it is something he does not want opened up to the scrutiny of strangers.

Perhaps he started it on that day because it was the one on which Laura and he – with the help of Gelat – bought the Posada, the house next to the church on the hill, then still occupied by the priest. He was at that time in the middle of writing *Antigua, Penny, Puce*, and records: 'gave Karl 3 ch of A.P.P. to type: and poem "Remembering War".' ('Remembering War' became 'Recalling War'.)

Karl was Karl Goldschmidt, a German Jew in his early twenties who landed up in Deyá in 1934. His girlfriend having left him, he was going to spend the rest of his money – and then do something drastic; fortunately Graves and Laura heard him telling Gelat off, with great efficiency, for not being on time with his bus, and took him under their wing. He was to remain a close associate of Graves for the next thirty years; he retired (1978) from his job at the University of Buffalo to live in Palma. At the beginning of the war he changed his name to Kenneth Gay, because he joined the British forces; but no one who knew him well has ever called him Kenneth.

Karl was conscientious and highly intelligent; he had left Germany because he saw what was coming there. He was a gifted draughtsman, designer and printer – he designed some of the Seizin dust jackets, and the later title-page design of the Seizin Press, which incorporated the antique insignia of Deyá. Typing he made into an art. He soon became creative secretary to Riding and Graves, and they as soon found him indispensable. During the last two years of the Mallorcan period only three-quarters, if that, of the prodigious amount of work that was done could have been accomplished without him. Karl's efficiency was unobtrusive, but he often oiled works that would otherwise have rusted up; he was never aware of the extent of his own usefulness, and hated to be praised. And, unlike almost all the others who were there from time to time, he had (refreshingly) no literary aspirations.

But first they had to teach him English. They achieved this by going through English books with him, and explaining the difficulties as they came up. He learned very fast.

Not much more Seizin work was produced on the Crown Albion press after *Laura and Francisca*. They printed two poems by Riding: *The First Leaf* (1933), and with Karl's help they were just then working at *The Second Leaf* (1935). Both these items were unbound. From 1935 the texts of all Seizin books were set by commercial printers. James Reeves's collection of poems *The Natural Need* (1935) was badly printed by a Palma printer, A. Sabater Mut. It was issued, as was Riding's story collection *A Progress of Stories*, as published by 'The Seizin Press ✳ Deya Majorca/and/Constable & Co. Ltd./London'. The rest of the books published by Seizin–Constable were printed in England. In America most were issued by Random House, who took sheets. Apart from *Antigua, Penny, Puce* (the only one that sold substantially), there was the anonymous *A Mistake Somewhere* (1935), an account of a marital mix-up master- (or mistress-) minded by Riding; *Convalescent Conversations* (1936), a feeble novel suggested by Riding to the three participants who then wrote it under the name Madeleine Vara (this was used, mostly but not entirely by her, as a signature for notes and other items in *Epilogue*), Matthews's *The Moon's No Fool* (1936), and Honor Wyatt's *The Heathen* (1937). All three *Epilogues* were issued under this imprint, and so was Riding's dull flop, her attempt to attain the success of the *Claudius* books, *A Trojan Ending* (1937).

Graves had a hand in one other Seizin–Constable book, their neighbour Schwarz's *Almost Forgotten Germany*. This was published in April 1936, as translated by Riding and Graves. Actually they freely adapted a literal crib of the original, most of it by Karl, who for some undisclosed reason refused, at a late stage, to continue the work. Riding and Graves had the last few chapters done by a Frau Thelin in Palma. *Almost Forgotten Germany* was well adapted – never against Schwarz's intentions. It is a charming, individual and informative book which never received its due. It would stand revival.

Graves was to use the Seizin imprint, which became his property, twice more: on two postwar collections of poems by young poets he wanted to encourage.

As the money supply from *Claudius* grew, so the scope of Riding's ambitions became more evident. Arthur Barker was first approached about taking on the larger Seizin books and the periodical *Epilogue*, now to be 'A Critical Summary', a series of analyses of the new world situation in which time had stopped – but had left a vacuum without values, which Riding would fill. Barker wanted no part of it; he was in any case soon dismissed because he made an offensive proposal to Graves.

On 4 March 1935 Graves received a letter from him suggesting that, in the words of his diary, 'I should write a really great book about Christ and John Bapt.' Later, as it happened, he would write not one but two important books about Christ. But at the time he was in no position to do so. For Riding had already written that any novel about Christ could only be a 'fitting subject for sympathetic disgust'. She did not so much dislike Jesus Christ himself as she disliked the worship of or interest in him by other people. In her interesting poem 'The Need to Confide' she compares herself to Christ, to the latter's disadvantage.

Robert discussed Barker's proposal with Laura on that evening. Laura was 'severe', a word frequently used of her.

The next day he wrote a long letter to Barker telling him that the suggestion was 'inappropriate and offensive', and (he wrote in his diary), he made 'it plain that he could not expect any more work from me'. Nor did Barker ever receive any more work from Graves, even though they had signed an 'all-in' contract. All the original Barker records have been destroyed; but it seems that Riding decreed that the 'all-in' contract implied that Barker was obliged to distribute for Seizin.

Riding had another grudge against Barker. In 1934 he had published her and Ellidge's novel *14A*, but had quickly withdrawn it, under threat of a libel suit. She felt that he should have resisted. She wrote *14A* in 1933, with the nominal help of George Ellidge (who eventually married Honor Wyatt) whom Graves then disliked. Graves said, later, to me (1944), that Riding had chosen Ellidge as collaborator 'because she knew that of all the people on the island I liked him least'. He was not at all bitter on the subject. Certainly there are a number of malicious jokes – some profoundly ungrateful – about Graves scattered throughout *14A*. Equally certainly it made no difference whether Barker withdrew it or not; it showed no signs of selling.

Anyway, Graves did not at this time contemplate arousing his own or anyone else's sympathetic disgust. He not only had *Antigua, Penny, Puce* to get on with, but a good deal of work connected with the 'university', set him by Laura. And he was working on a number of poems ('To Bring the Dead to Life', the retrospective analysis of how he brought off the *Claudius* success; 'The Devil's Advice to Storytellers'; and some others which he destroyed).

Since Barker would not agree to distribute Seizin books, a number of other publishers were approached. At last one showed some interest: Constable. But they wanted 'Laura Riding's' financial guarantee against loss – so eventually Graves lost £1000 on *Epilogue* alone. A cordial relationship developed between Michael Sadleir, the romantic novelist in charge of Constable, and Riding and Graves; this was continued when the partners came to London. For the time being Riding's plans remained secure; all that was needed was success. This was not forthcoming.

The first *Epilogue* appeared, at last, in the autumn of 1935. The editor was Riding; Graves was 'assistant-editor'. Contributors, besides 'Madeleine Vara', were: Matthews, James Reeves, John Aldridge (reproductions of some of his pictures), Honor Wyatt, John Cullen (a friend of Eirlys Roberts, who eventually became chairman of Eyre Methuen), Ward Hutchinson, Len Lye – and Riding and Graves themselves. Everything in the volume, with the obvious exception of the pictures by Aldridge and a photograph by Hutchinson (an American who did not penetrate beyond the fringe of the circle), was rewritten by Riding.

Matthews was the son of a bishop, and was therefore supposed to be able to ask Riding meaningful questions about God. According to him, she recast all his questions, and rewrote his contribution. *Epilogue* started (after the 'Preliminaries' already alluded to) with a series of answers by Riding to eight questions by 'Matthews', the first of which is 'Does God exist? In what sense?' This article disposes of God, setting up some shadowy woman figure in his place. The more scholarly notes on biblical matters, though mostly signed 'M.V.', are by Graves. (Graves knew Greek and was well versed in ancient history; Riding had no Greek and only a hazy, selective notion of history.)

Graves contributed five poems as a 'poem-sequence', dedicated 'to the Sovereign Muse', and two essays – one on Coleridge and Wordsworth, Keats and Shelley, and the other on the pastoral – which he later collected, in revised form, into *The Common Asphodel*.

The critical quality of *Epilogue* is high. The whole is pervaded by Riding's intelligence and acuteness. The deficiencies include over-severity, an occasional lack of scholarship (partly through being out of touch with a good library) and an unsympathetic, unfriendly air. Riding ruthlessly excised any instances she found, in her contributors' writings, of empathy. The intelligence of what is being said is therefore often vitiated by the sense that it is being delivered as an absolute judgement, sharp enough to make people feel uncomfortable about their cherished opinions. The periodical (issued in three substantial bound volumes, 1935–37) failed because its harsh tone made those readers feel safe in ignoring it. In August 1935 Constable themselves wrote to Riding requesting her to make the blurbs 'less alarming' (Sadleir and his associates found them, they said, 'distastefully apocalyptic', though they did not put it like this to her); she would not give way a jot or tittle.

III

Canelluñ, built to Riding's and Graves's instructions, is a two-storeyed house standing some thirty yards back from the coast road. It has been slightly extended since 1932, but not altered in essential structure. The garden, a wilderness when the house was built, has now become beautiful: oranges, tangerines are mixed with large trees and smaller shrubs. At the back of the house, where there is a terrace, is a low-lying piece of land which incorporates a grotto. Everywhere is planted with flowers and vegetables: all now administered by Beryl Graves and better than it has ever been.

You enter the house through a large kitchen. To the left is a dining room (now extended), to the right a hall. On this level are Graves's study and a library, which was used as the press room. Upstairs, as well as three small rooms, one of which was Riding's study, there are two large bedrooms. The house is furnished in simple semi-Mallorquín style, with matting on the floor. There are a number of pictures by John Aldridge on the walls, beautiful hangings by Len Lye and some other unusual prints.

Opposite the house, across the road, Riding very early on built a road to the sea, to the *cala*. It was badly planned – too close to the torrent at the bottom of the valley. (Further along there is another path, the usual route taken by swimmers – and campers and trippers – to the sea). On the night of 29 September 1933 part of this road was washed away. On 26 February 1935 Riding decided to begin to mend it (on *Claudius* cash). She had already, as we know, bought a wide strip of the land running down to the sea, and now had plans for this: new terraces, almonds – and the hotel or 'university', or both. Gelat was delighted. The partners had set him up financially. His account for the end of March 1935 was for 4882 pesetas (about £140): this covered four months – and the purchase of a cross between a British and a Mallorquín bulldog (so Gelat claimed), which they called Solomon, and liked.

But the plan to repair the road made the authorities suspicious: could not such a road be used for an invasion, and was it not being built at the instruction of foreigners? They were fortunate not to get into trouble, although a spy was sent (Gelat spotted him: a colonel ridiculously disguised as a peasant). In the August of 1935 someone denounced the Press as not properly licensed, and Riding was questioned by three inspectors. 'Laura much vexed.' (She was made to pay 30 pesetas annually.) They did not discover the culprit, but it was likely to have been the priest who had, with Gelat's help, been forced to vacate the Posada – or possibly the doctor, another of Gelat's enemies.

Much of Riding's severity creeps into Graves's diary. On 27 July 1935 he solemnly records that Laura 'had a talk with Karl about deportment'.

In general, with a few sly exceptions, the Mallorcan part of the diary is designed to catch Riding's approving eye; it suggests that he found her tempers and frustrations increasingly unpleasant. He speaks of her 'passing' each of his poems, and of his adoption of her suggestions.

Yet she never wrote the poems for him. Here she felt herself up against an insurmountable barrier. For one thing, he had by far the superior technical skill. He had more know-how, about poems, than she, and she knew it. That her suggestions were generally constructive and helpful, however, is beyond doubt. He also records a number of occasions on which he 'checked' her poems. Most of the aid he gave her was technical, as she was unable to write effectively in regular, conventional metres – and if she got into rhythmical trouble he helped her out of it. Her debt to him is considerable. But he had to be very tactful, since no debt could be acknowledged.

In their last year in Mallorca neither Graves nor Riding was ever entirely well. In fact, from reading his diary for this period one could easily get the impression that both were very seriously ill, which is not the case. He frequently complained of headaches, 'liverishness' and tired eyes. Riding, then a very heavy smoker, suffered from what she thought was a bad heart, but was actually nicotine poisoning. Both worked very late, but often spent the mornings in bed, reading or working on papers. Graves often felt 'very nervous', and suffered a recurrence of nightmares connected with his war experiences. Riding was equally nervous. They were neither of them any happier than they had been before, but were nevertheless driven along, and kept afloat, by their activities. Both shared enjoyment in planning the gardens of the Posada and Canelluñ (much of the planting was done by Graves personally), in making improvements to both houses, and in the behaviour of their dog and cat. The cat, called Alice, was observed by everyone with great interest; she is the subject of an Aldridge painting, 'Alice in the Grotto'. Solomon the dog lived in a barrel and was fed on sheep's heads. Riding told Graves that he looked better through taking Solomon for walks. Alice had a 'war' with Solomon lasting for months, and at one time put the corpse of one of her drowned kittens into his barrel in order to 'make us think its death was due to his violence. He got greatly excited over the corpse but did not maul it' (16 June 1935). The animals made things less unpleasant than they might otherwise have been.

There were visitors; plans for the 'university'; a good deal of wasted effort put into a 'book of the film' of *Claudius*; serious consideration about requests from anthologists; and poems. Money became a worry because of the ambitious plans for the road, and Riding was concerned to get her hands on the large sum of marks (in April 1935 16,800 marks were due) which had accumulated in Germany on sales of *Ich, Claudius*. Eventually it was obtained through German connections of the British literary agents Curtis Brown, who took a commission. Graves had not yet found a permanent agent in A. S. Watt.

The visitors included the novelist Louis Golding, who had known Graves slightly at Oxford: 'L. & I rather severe but he didn't behave badly' (8 May 1935). On 23 May Honor Wyatt and her then husband Gordon Glover (who became a well-known broadcaster) arrived, with their friend Mary Phillips. Mary was a practised typist, and did all the typing that Karl could not manage, including drafts of Graves's poems. Other visitors in 1935 were John Aldridge and Lucie Brown, Ward Hutchinson and his wife Dorothy, and, from 31 October until 13 December, James Reeves.

James Reeves, a schoolmaster, was a reticent but tough-minded Cambridge man, whose quiet poems – despite their echoes of Pound and Aldington – were particular favourites of Laura's. More than any of the others in the group, he defied her judgements of his poems, and a number of interestingly argumentative letters between them exists. She liked his toughness but did not tell him this. She did tell him, shrewdly, that 'in you fear is golden': his very best poems, when not overtly satirical, did have a Schubertian quality of fright.

At this time Michael Roberts was compiling his *Faber Book of Modern Verse* and W. B. Yeats his famously disastrous *Oxford Book of Modern Verse*. Both Roberts and Yeats wanted poems from Graves. Graves and Laura liked and respected Roberts – who also wanted poems from Riding – so much that they invited him to Mallorca, and made the rare exception of allowing their poems to be included in his anthology, though making it a condition that Reeves also be included, to which Roberts rather reluctantly agreed. Later he made a note to exclude him from future editions, and this was acted on by future editors.

Yeats they loathed. Riding had written of him in a letter to John Cullen: '. . . the pleasure Yeats gets out of "Lake waters" etc. is a loathsome pleasure of a poet possessing his poem'.

On 20 October Graves noted in his diary that Yeats had written to request poems, from him (not Riding), and noted his 'threat to come to Mallorca this year'. On the next day he replied to Yeats, careful to include Riding in the 'refusal' to what had never been a request:

I was rather surprised at your request for four poems of mine for your anthology. In 1928 Laura Riding and I wrote *A Pamphlet Against Anthologies* which stated the arguments clearly enough. Neither of us has since had a request from any anthologist which did not recognize our objections and ask whether a special exception might not be made. In a very few cases we have made exceptions; the anthology which Michael Roberts is now doing for Faber & Faber – it covers the same ground as yours – is the most important of these: and the exception was made because

a) he worked out the choice of our poems *with* us.

b) he told us specifically who the other poets were to be and in some instances took advantage of certain objections and suggestions of ours so that we could feel that there was a cooperative attitude and not merely that we were being thrust into his book at his own discretion or caprice.

c) he sent us his introduction before hand and was most sensitive to our marginal comments. There was the further inducement that to an extent he shared our feelings about anthologies; and also that he conscientiously tried to present a good block of the work of each of us – sufficient to act as introductory indications of what we are respectively doing. So that there is no feeling on our part that in his anthology we are being labelled or treated against our knowledge or feelings. I myself only became strict in this way after my association with Laura Riding, but my experience before this had already begun to give me a distaste for anthologies. . . .

I do not know whether a letter from you to Laura Riding is on the way from some forwarding address. But if so, the answer for both of us, your anthology being what it seems to be (from the indication of those four poems of mine and from the absence of any awareness in you that we do not lend ourselves to any but cooperative activities), would have to be, I think, No.

We are both very watchful in our relations, whether in literature or in neighbour-ship: never casual, and least of all here in Majorca where we live permanently in hard-working privacy. With the many foreigners who visit the island we have, as a rule, nothing to do – unless they are friends of ours, who come here purposely to see us. Certainly we like to get to know new people and especially those with whom there may be something in common; but we are not sure what there might be in common between you and L.R. (someone in a press-cutting a few months ago said that you and she had both learned things from each other – but certainly L.R. does not go about 'learning' from people) and between you and me; and we hate the mere literary-name fraternizing – but perhaps you feel the same about that.

Later, at Christmas, Yeats did visit Mallorca, but there was no meeting. It was, however, suggested that Yeats should include James Reeves in his anthology, but Yeats responded by calling him 'too truthful, too sincere'; the Muse, he said, preferred 'the gay and warty lads'.

Plenty of money was coming in during this time, including what Graves described as an 'astounding cheque for £500 from Korda' (£150 of which he sent straight off to Nancy); but he still refers to money troubles. These were again due to Riding's plans. By this time the hotel idea had been transformed into the university project – it seems she even contemplated starting a school as well. A house by the beach was on offer for 15,000 pesetas, and she was seriously considering buying it. Riding had early succeeded, through John Aldridge, in getting Mrs Lloyd (John's mother) to advance money for the hotel project from which Norman Cameron had withdrawn; but – political considerations apart – the affair was badly planned from start to finish. Nothing came of it. But a large amount of time was consumed studying educational systems in all parts of the world and at all periods of history – though from a collection of books nothing like large enough to permit of this being done properly. They bought books from England but had no access to libraries. On 17 June 1936 Graves recorded

Laura gave me job of going on with *Schools* [as this project had been called] by myself. Last night worked on Chinese, this morning on Indian school systems.

There are countless other references to work on 'Schools', which, as Graves later admitted, he loathed doing.

By 1936 yet another project was under way. First called *Poetry and Politics*, it developed into *The Left Heresy in Literature and Life*, which was published by Methuen in 1939 as by 'Harry Kemp, Laura Riding and Others'. Graves's only contribution was a revision of his essay 'Politics and Poetry', which first appeared in *Epilogue III*. So far as Graves was concerned, the project, on which he put in much work, was not anti-left, but a statement of the case for not involving poetry with political doctrines. (He would always consider serious-minded Tories as 'politically misguided', though he never felt strongly about it.) Such rightist fire as was in this work came from Harry Kemp, a Cambridge contemporary of James Reeves who wrote overfluent poetry in the style of Graves, and who was then as devoted as the others to Riding. One of his distinctions is that he was the only man to get his name in before Riding's on the title page of a book.

Meanwhile, in the middle of all this, and of endless discussion with Gelat, often difficult correspondence with his children – particularly Jenny – and work on four other books, Graves was still labouring at the very difficult detail of *Antigua, Penny, Puce*. Certainly, whatever he said, he did not regard it as only a potboiler, even though he recorded that he had initiated it 'during money-shortage as a means of extracting higher royalties from Harrison Smith for C. the God' (25 February 1935). Riding insisted on going over every word of this comic-nasty tale of a feud between a brother and sister over a valuable stamp, although her influence, probably because she went through it quickly, is nowhere evident. What is evident in the book is some harsh satire on John Graves – but John ('certainly *not* a sensitive man' says one of his family in a letter to me) remained unaware of it. The book did well, and as a Penguin (1948) sold 60,000; it is still in print in a library edition, and still much read.

IV

I mentioned above that Graves was working on four other books besides *Antigua, Penny, Puce*. One of these was Frank Richards's *Old Soldier Sahib*. He had received two-thirds of the script of this from the modest author on 10 July 1935: Richards said he would stop it if it was no good. But Graves found much in it 'just the thing', and agreed to do it up as he had his previous book, for a third share of the royalties. He worked very hard on it; it was published by Faber on 2 April 1936, and sold even better than *Old Soldiers Never Die*.

Another book, upon which he spent all of April and May 1935, was the abortive film version of *Claudius*, for which he did, however, receive £50 as advance (not enough to justify the time he spent at it). Then in addition there was Schwarz's *Almost Forgotten Germany*, a labour of love.

The fourth book upon which he started was the result of a tragedy which made world news. On 13 May 1935 T. E. Lawrence was fatally injured while riding back to his Clouds Hill cottage from Bovington Camp, where he had just sent a wire to the dementedly fascist novelist and war-veteran Henry Williamson asking him to lunch on the following day. (Williamson wanted Lawrence to 'guide Hitler' along the right path; there is no evidence that Lawrence would have agreed, although Graves told me that he believes Lawrence was not wholly uninterested.)

On Sunday, 12 May (post arrived in Deyá on Sundays in the thirties), Graves received news from Edward Marsh that he had won the Hawthornden Prize: 'If I *can't* come, cancel ceremony. Replied, couldn't.'

Two days later he received a wire, and recorded: '. . . news of T.E.'s accident believed fatal. Undertook to write obit. notice for Ass. Press.'

For the next five days he felt anxious and ill. He kept going to the cafés in the village to try to obtain news on the radio, but could not make out what was being said. On Sunday, 19 May, the morning Lawrence died, he 'felt rotten. Wrote to Mother. . . . In afternoon locked up and slept till 5.' On the Friday he received a wire from Marsh: 'Almost no hope: sinking.' But not until the Monday did Gelat pass on the news, obtained in Palma, that Lawrence had died.

He was upset. And the more so because things had not been well between him and Lawrence for some years.

Even before the window incident they had had a not wholly friendly correspondence on the subject of the sexual act. In 1928 Lawrence finished his account of life in an RAF barracks called *The Mint* (it was first published in a trade edition in 1955). He had a few copies privately printed, and one of these he sent to Graves. In the book Lawrence made clear, as he had to most of his close friends, that he had never 'tried it [the sexual act]'. Graves challenged his views on it. His own letter is not available; but from Lawrence's reply of 6 November one can easily infer what kind of jocular yet sharp letter Graves had written him: his last page, 'about fucking', he said wholly defeated him. 'I haven't ever and don't much want to. . . .'

He went on:

However, your positive, comparative, superlative (we make it fucking good
bastard good
f. bastard good)
defeats me wholly.

Clearly Lawrence was irritated. The man–woman subject was to become the most serious bone of contention between them – though it would eventually take the form of the Lawrence–Riding question. When Riding tried to kill herself he had been the most loyal of Graves's friends, and had taken the trouble to go to see her in hospital – though his time was very severely restricted. But when Graves asked him to give a scholarly look over the proofs of *I, Claudius* in autumn 1933, he met with an unexpected outburst of irritation.

Lawrence had by this time become a good friend of Frederic Manning, an Australian poet and author who had written a still neglected classic of the First World War, *Her Privates We*. He liked and confided in Manning, believing him to be an 'exquisite' man. He told Manning that he thought the tone of *Claudius* 'sickening'. He had done as Graves asked him: sent to Barker for a copy of the proofs, and had been disgusted. Graves told him:

> I don't want any too great howlers. The book is largely guess-work & imagination but I want it to hold water & have done a great deal of reading to get it passable.

Lawrence criticized the book fairly severely. He was by this time unhappy about his own literary abilities, and may have envied Graves's fluency; much more likely, though, is that the sense of brutality and repressed sexual urgency which runs through the book upset him. He had by this time reached the peak of his own masochistic problems, had evolved a most elaborate (and infantile) framework of fantasy in which to experience his floggings from Bruce – he even required a witness to them. Perhaps also his Irish purity – something he had in common with Graves – was offended or disappointed by the idea of a poet writing a popular book. He was himself at this time flat broke.

Graves replied, in detail, in early December 1933:

> Your remarks are of two kinds, those about Claudius & those about me and I shall answer them separately....
>
> About the crime: yes, it's a crime story. But the facts are unescapable and I have at least made Postumus a decent fellow against the prejudice of Tacitus, Suetonius etc, and Germanicus & Agrippina, and Acte and Calpurnia the hetairai ... & Medullina Camilla, and Cocceius Nerva and Drusus Senior and Nero Senior and there are others. I have white-rather than black-washed. And then there is Claudius himself – surely he's a good specimen? ... Tacitus hated him.
>
> About the middle part dragging. I purposely slowed down the writing in the later Tiberius period because it was necessary for a fuller appreciation of Caligula's insane liveliness. It makes Caligula 'quite a relief' instead of 'such a monster.' It drags but one is kept going by interest in the fate of the few surviving decent characters and a premonition of the old He Goat's sticky end.
>
> Next, remarks about me & Claudius. 'I, Claudius is not an essential book.' Did I say it was? 'I can't say why, exactly, but I feel unsatisfied.'

You read it looking for things that I had no intention of putting into it. I chose Claudius for a number of reasons: the first was that he was a historian before he was anything else and because he lived in an age in which every moral safeguard of a religious or patriotic or social sort had gone West – things were just disintegrating. He realized this and found it impossible to reintegrate them. The best he could do was to be a historian & keep historian's faith. The more he tried, as Emperor, to interfere with the process of disintegration the madder things got. But that's for the sequel. Claudius hadn't the courage to give up, as Nerva did; his naive optimism & curiosity kept him going. Well, it all fell to pieces in the end & there was a new, false reintegration with Christianity. That's the point. I prefer Claudius's post-Augustanism to your post-medievalism. What you're really saying is 'This is not an idealistic, hopeful book and it isn't even a portrait of a heroic "minority" character resisting tyranny bravely: Claudius is no Brutus.' No, indeed he wasn't. But you and your Englishry ought at any rate to have the greatest respect & sympathy for Claudius as the first Romanizer of Britain. I wrote the most popular book I could write while keeping within the limits of personal integrity: that is, Claudius is an old story but I identify myself with him as much as with any other historical character I know about, even including Skelton. I identify myself with him historically, but merely historically. That was what leaves you unsatisfied. . . . I agree it is a pity that *Claudius* books have to be written because people won't pay a living wage for the essential works, but at present it is so. The essential work is always, of course, going on. Claudius is only the most stupid side-activity, like eating and dressing & going up & down stairs for fire-wood for the stove. It takes time from the essential work, but not much. . . .

But what beats me in your letter is your suggestion that I should come 'home' at least for a while & meet people who don't care enormously about my 'subjects' (Roman history do you mean?) and don't value my work: what sort of picture have you of my life here? Do you imagine me surrounded by an adoring band of literary admirers? What would I be likely to meet in England?

No I don't think you Victorian, but you place yourself as an Edwardian in your literary vocabulary – Edward VII, reaching back longingly to Edward I – and you oughtn't to involve me in superb's and masterly's. The writing is definitely *not* high-pitched but the sort of writing to be expected from the man we know Claudius was. It is a very *modest* book, & full of anecdotes because people like anecdotes; and the only, to me, really horrible thing is Tiberius's striking out Agrippina's eyes. I can't help feeling bad about that, but after all, that was what happened & she & Tiberius can't be cut out of the story.

The book will be valued if it is valued, because it is a good crime story. That is not a 'wrong reason.' People are today predominantly interested in crime. The *essential work* that is being done here by Laura, a few others & myself takes in the subject of crime and explains why people are now so interested in it. But you are not really interested in the essential work, as you have made perfectly plain, so you have no right to feel unsatisfied with Claudius.

Lawrence replied to this letter in a more friendly tone, and Graves's own reply is more friendly: they didn't want to quarrel over *Claudius*. But Graves's last letter to Lawrence, written not long before Lawrence was killed, makes it evident that things had gone seriously wrong – although Graves and possibly Lawrence still wanted to be friendly.

I wrote to you at Cloud's Hill the same day as you wrote to me here: you will have got my letter, I hope. You answer me one question that I asked, about your cottage etc. I am so sorry that your reserve has fallen so low. 20/– a week is comfortable living in Majorca but very little indeed in England whatever your capacity for going without. I should very much like to bring your income back to £2.2/– for a year or so: may I? I don't think you'll refuse me that. I could find the money in March when I begin to cash in on Claudius: so far I have been 'riding on dead horses' & only just keeping pace with debt. By the end of the summer I expect to be quite unencumbered again: it has been a rotten two years in that way and at one time I thought I was sunk altogether. My mother has been supporting my children meanwhile. A great help has been Korda's decision to do a Claudius film. (Funny, he didn't know about my book about you & I think he'll find it useful in the film he's doing: it's better for studio purposes than Liddell Hart & handier than the 7 Pillars. I told him that there's no copyright in it.)

I am sorry you have to leave the R.A.F. because you suited it & it you; but it has probably done its job of slowing you down – I only hope not too well. I am hoping for a recovery of mental speed in you – for quite selfish reasons. I have felt very unhappy about the breach between you and Laura and would give a great deal to have it healed. But reviewing the facts it seems entirely your show, and I can only say that it is a great loss to me that Laura who is my best friend & you for whom I have always felt more closely than for any other man should be not even on terms of greeting distantly. If I could be sure that it was just your slowed-down mind that was responsible & not any active bad feelings that would be something. The fairest way would be to restate the case. . . .

Laura and you were on good terms & personally she liked you, I think very much, & was grateful especially for your visit to her in hospital. We met last in London four years ago for a moment. That was all right, too. Then one day she asked you to join in a sort of informal collaboration of several ordinary nice, not particularly clever people in expressing liking for some characters in history in an uncritical way. E.g. 'I like Rubens because he always painted such nice fat women' or 'I like Torrigiano because he broke Michelangelo's nose' or 'I like Lady Hester Stanhope because she once rushed at some Druses with an umbrella (they were trying to intimidate her) opening it in their faces & shouting "Avaunt".' That sort of thing. You made heavy weather of it, and if you didn't feel capable of doing anything so superlatively simple as expressing an uncritical liking for someone, anyone, in history, you had only to write to Laura & excuse yourself. Instead, you wrote a long chatty letter to *me* and as a sort of afterthought made some light-hearted reference to Laura's obscure style. The protest I registered did not convey anything to you. You merely wrote to *me* again, and your whole tone conveyed the sense of Laura as a sort of intellectual freak and worse than that, of Laura as having no status of her own but as being some sort of appendage of mine. This was reflected in an earlier letter when you asked how to address Laura on an envelope. As though you did not know her surname & the name of this village. As though her address, forsooth & pshaw, was perhaps 'care of Robert Graves'! No, T.E., you must 'brake your feathers' as the Gym instructors say. Granted you and I are very old friends, & that you have not been able so far to see Laura more than occasionally & as a friend of mine, & you have not felt capable of the concentration that reading her more concentrated work demands, you should not have made such a graceless error; which I feel more strongly than Laura who merely dismisses from her mind people who attempt to treat her as you have done; because I feel responsible in introducing you to her as a friend, and you behave like . . . I don't know . . . but the nearest I can get to a comparison is the junior partner in a third-rate New York publishing firm, & I mean this literally as a counter-insult. I am writing this letter without Laura's knowledge, because I don't want her to feel that I am trying to work anything that seems to her a hopeless job. . . .

A postscript suggests that Lawrence might like to earn a few pounds by writing his own obituary for *The Times* 'morgue': 'no one need know: 2000 words.' He sent this to Graves.

This was not perhaps the letter Graves wanted to write. It is perhaps true that he never felt closer to any other man than he did to Lawrence in the early twenties. He knew that Lawrence felt lonely because he (and certain other friends) was out of his reach, living abroad. He had already made it clear that he would be prepared to risk having Lawrence out to Mallorca – this was foolhardy, for Riding could never have lived near any true celebrity, as T.E. was, without quickly quarrelling with him.

The letter Graves wanted to write was more personal: he wanted to sympathize with Lawrence's difficulties over women, with his flagellation problem, with his difficulties over what he should do with his life. But his fierce protectiveness towards Laura forced him to write, instead, an unhelpful and arrogant letter.

Graves wrote a lengthy obituary of Lawrence, which appeared in the *Evening Standard*; the draft typescript has a number of unimportant corrections in Riding's hand, but is mainly the work of Graves, who took careful precautions that the literary agent Pinker, who had asked him to write it, should not publish it until Lawrence had actually died. His final public verdict he published in *The Long Weekend* (1940):

> T.E. sent Robert Graves an obituary notice on himself just before his death, in which he remarked, with some satisfaction, that being a mechanic cut him off from all real communication with women – there were no women in the machines, in any machine – no woman could understand a mechanic's happiness in serving his bits and pieces. . . . The chief difference between the two Lawrences [the other being of course D. H.] was that T.E. had a healthy mind and body and deliberately fell short of the best from a proud Irish scruple against perfection.

It is good to know that T.E. understood his old friend's state of mind well enough to reply to the letter, though his obituary on himself is intended at least to tease, if not to wound. Graves did complain bitterly, much later, that towards the end of his life Lawrence 'had gold fillings put in his teeth and took to talking garage English' – but this genuinely upset him. He now admits, however, that Lawrence committed no offence against Riding at all. He retained affection for him always, even though he regretfully concluded that there had been less to him than he had hoped; but in any case he could have done nothing to help – Lawrence was at the end of his tether, had threatened suicide, and had on a few occasions hinted that he would die on his motorbicycle. His death was probably not suicide; but he rode his machine at dangerous speeds, and seems to have made no serious effort to avoid the accident.

Lawrence's death resulted in Graves being asked to produce yet another book on him. After many difficulties with publishers and agents, and complicated negotiations with Lawrence's brother A. W. Lawrence, this became *T. E. Lawrence to His Biographer*, published in 1938 – Basil Liddell Hart's book of the same title forms a second volume in uniform format. A good deal of work and a good deal of reticence were needed. It was a very busy time for Graves, and he felt the strain, even though the hard work was a relief.

V

Towards the end of 1935 and for the rest of 1936 Riding became ill increasingly often. Graves complains in his diary that she will neither see a doctor nor give up smoking. On 25 November 1935 she half fainted at the gate to Ca'n Torrent; often she spent days in bed. She was working mainly at her historical novel about Troy, for which Graves had to supply her with copious notes.

One good thing resulted from the Lawrence project. Basil Liddell Hart wired that he was putting the book into the hands of the highly respected literary agent A. S. Watt. Thus Graves placed all his literary affairs permanently with the firm of Watt. This association was to be extremely happy and fruitful for many years.

While James Reeves was visiting, an enormous amount of work was done. Graves was going over Lawrence's letters 'cutting out personal parts', working over *Antigua, Penny, Puce*, writing the *Claudius* film novel, and going through Blake's and Browning's poems 'dismissing those which failed. . . .' Riding was 'going over' Reeves's novel (he soon destroyed it on the grounds that 'it was no longer his own'), 'doing education – India and Japan', and planning a '5 years hence world-itinerary for Epilogue people – Holland Denmark Siberia Cochin China, Rumania California New York Cyprus & Turkey'. Both part-ners were 'discussing part-time activity of J[ames]', and Riding told Karl to take up humorous writing – which annoyed him. There was 'serious talk about dancing': Riding found real music 'poetic crime', so these discussions were probably about how the prospective university people would be taught to dance to 'honestly perverse' music, of which she approved.

On 20 December Graves recorded 'Laura writing to Hodge'. Alan Hodge was then in his second year at Oriel College, Oxford, had become interested in *Epilogue*, and had written to say so.

By Christmas Eve he was on the island: '20, young, blonde good head', Graves noted. This visit would in due time make more difference to Graves's life than he could possibly have dreamed. Meanwhile this gifted young man made an excellent impression:

> Hodge very decent & sensible: said about Claudius had read it while ill – liked it, lot of work: I said 'written to make money' – said, 'yes, he thought it read like that' I liked that – first time I have heard it.

Hodge was with them until early January.

On 23 January 1936, as the Spanish political crisis became daily more serious, Reeves's *The Natural Need* and Riding's *Progress of Stories* were published. The next day the partners heard that 'James & Mary Phillips are to be married at Easter'. Laura decreed that Mary continue to be called Phillips (she took no notice), a situation to which Graves was already used. They heard that the *New Statesman* had carried the first notice of *Epilogue I*: 'not a review, nasty & long'. But they were surprised a day or two later by 'a long eulogy' of it by Rebecca West in the *Sunday Times*.

On 16 February an election was held in Spain. It resulted in a landslide victory for the Left – and spelled eventual doom for it, and for the partners' prospects in Deyá. But Gelat was delighted; he had campaigned for the Left.

In March Graves decided that he could not deal with the legal aspects of *Antigua, Penny, Puce* without the help of a lawyer. He had written to various people asking if they knew one. Fortunately Mary Phillips did: a solicitor, an ex-boyfriend of hers called William Fuller. Fuller gave Graves much expert advice – and the book is dedicated to him 'in gratitude'.

At the end of March 1936 Graves recorded: 'can't feel well these days'. Doubtless his health was not improved when he went to Palma a few days later and 'saw worst film ever filmed'. This was *Vanessa*, Hugh Walpole's story, starring Robert Montgomery and Helen Hayes. The night before he had stayed in a hotel and had been kept awake from '1 to 2.15' 'owing to French couple honeymooning entirely. . . . No word spoken, only activity and [indecipherable]'.

By April he thought that he had got *Antigua, Penny, Puce* into shape: 'apart from obvious jacking-up corrections'. This was a relief, because for a comedy of manners the book had taken up more time than he had anticipated. Yet he spent two more months tinkering with it.

The Leftist successes in Spain led Gelat to see his prospects as local factotum as rosy; he began to speak of the power he might achieve. On 11 May he was made mayor of Deyá by the governor general. Riding became excited, and even spoke of becoming a Spanish citizen. She seems genuinely to have believed in the possibility of some sort of community in which, through Gelat, she could exercise political powers. She wanted, too, to adopt her favourite child, Francisca – which would in itself have obliged her to become a Spaniard.

But the political situation was worsening, though none of them noticed this. They both hated German and Italian Fascism, and there are many references to this in Graves's diary. But at the same time they were working on the 'Left heresy'. This was consistent enough; but they were at a certain disadvantage in keeping 'outside history'. More important in that hot June were the jobs on the Posada and the sacking of a maid called Catalina for 'insolence in not listening to Laura speak'. It looked as though Gelat had finally obtained his way over the water, for Graves heads his diary entry for 29 June 1936: 'Water Affair Solved'.

On 1 July they were getting Ca'n Torrent ready for Alan; on that day Graves 'got lunch again' (he did more of the cooking than anyone else – except for the servants), went over some of Honor Wyatt's novel *The Heathen* with Laura, and did some household chores. On 2 July Alan was met in Palma, where Graves did some shopping; later he had to go over a chapter of *Antigua* with Laura and, he tersely notes, 'She came on a contradiction & we stopped'. On 3 July Alan was set work by Laura: '"Poets" (subject of knowledge)' – the *Epilogue* plans were rapidly merging into the 'university' ones. For the whole of this time education was being studied, especially that of girls: Moslem, Jewish, 'medieval'. Plans were being made for the Graves children to visit. On 9 July, at last, *Antigua* went off to Constable.

Then, on 18 July, comes the first mention of a sinister name, a man whose death would be celebrated in Canelluñ with champagne – but not, alas, for over forty years: Francisco Franco. They heard on the radio that there had been a 'military insurrection at Melitta & Seville and the degradation of Franco and 5 generals'.

They took little notice. But Graves felt obliged to confess, on the next day, 'Could not bring myself to work on schools – revulsion against education.'

The troubles soon spread to the island. The Baleares were claimed to be one of the '13 Fascist provinces', or so they heard. Gelat and the other mayors were ordered to hand over to 'some non-political'. There were shooting incidents. By 21 July Mallorca, Graves recorded, was 'isolated'. But they heard on the radio of government victories, and almost until the last they thought the insurrection would be quickly put down. On the day that Fascist thugs passed through Deyá yelling their slogans Graves 'painted Posada lavatory' and Alan worked on the well there.

Gelat was in deep trouble: his enemies were calling him a Communist. His enemy the doctor was mistaken by Fascists for a Communist (but he thought them Communists sent by Gelat) and chased off into the mountains; he reappeared later: 'in drawers and alpargatas [Spanish rope sandals]' in 'a lamentable state'.

Graves records all this laconically. He had seen such things before. Riding was not much interested in the politics of the situation, but Gelat was associated with the Left, and she was therefore anti-Fascist. The village was in a panic, Graves wrote, but immediately beneath it: 'Schools'. That was 23 July, the day before his birthday; when he went into the village, which had quietened down by nightfall, he found it divided into two camps. The 'Rights' were jabbering; the 'Lefts' were silent.

His birthday was 'blank'; they worked on 'Schools'; but there was now an impression that the Fascists would surrender. The government was said to be making progress on the mainland. Few foresaw the reign of terror about to be unleashed on the island, in which thousands were murdered.

By 26 July, although the news from the mainland still sounded good, the Fascists controlled most of the island. They were eating and drinking free, letting off their guns when they felt like it, and tarring 'Communists'.

Graves remained calm. He wrote in his diary of 'normal working', the progress of the flowers. But Palma was now being bombed, and the Fascists were consolidating their position.

On 30 July Riding finished her Trojan novel, and Graves was able to record that 'No fascists have come forward in Deyá.' They decided to stay on, 'for the present at least'. But events moved very rapidly. They thought they might have to leave because of 'interrupted communications'. Graves stated that the 'British radio ha[d] a F. Tinge' (which it did). He was going over Riding's A Trojan Ending chapter by chapter, putting some of her historical errors right, and rewriting dull passages, in as tactful a manner as he could.

Then on 2 August they were told that their last chance had come:

they could leave by destroyer from Palma, that evening, or they could stay. They knew that they would have to go.

> We had just had lunch. Packed hurriedly and at random. Gelat came & undertook to do everything. He said 'sinverguenzas' and wept. . . . Gelat took keys, will keep everything for us, 'don't worry', will take Solomon for walks. Everyone weeping as we went off. Skirted Palma – saw broken windows no other damage. Today 60 bombs dropped. . . . Short [the pro-Fascist English agent in Palma who looked after the affairs of English and American residents] confident Fascists will soon win.

And so in the end they left within a couple of hours: Riding, Alan Hodge, Karl – and Graves. They thought they would soon be back. But, as he was to learn a few years later, Graves's (alleged) 'debt' to Riding was 'probably paid' at that very moment. Her rule in Deyá, where she is now remembered as a bossy eccentric who wore strange clothes, was over for ever. Their unhappy relationship had less than three more years to run.

But at this traumatic moment Graves, as the one old soldier in the group, was – if reluctantly – in his element. He had to get everyone through safely to London. He took charge, as if it were second nature to him, and for once Riding, bemused, allowed him to do so.

Chapter Eighteen
1936–37

I

The destroyer that picked them up was HMS *Grenville*. Graves soon got on good terms: 'Lt Comm. Evans asked me to sign Claudius which he had with him. Made an exception.' By 4 August, having been to the neighbouring island of Ibiza to pick up more refugees, they were at Valencia. Here they transferred to the *Maine*.

There were difficulties at this point: Karl carried a German passport. Graves records:

> The surgeon commander [of the *Maine*] who took passports carried on generous trad. of *Grenville* which allowed Karl to stay with us instead of handing to German boat which would have meant concentration camp for him.

He is modest in this entry, for it was only by his vigorous intervention that Karl was not handed over to the Germans. The evacuation arrangements were that all refugees were to be sent back to their own countries. It was the surgeon commander's duty to hand Karl over. But it was by a combination of the surgeon commander's decency and Graves's old-soldierly and stubborn insistence that Karl was able to continue to England.

By 8 o'clock on the morning of 6 August they reached Marseilles, after an uncomfortable journey. Graves noted the unpleasant behaviour of a certain 'awful English fascist, who gave Fascist salutes to passing ships'; and how two titled English sympathizers with the Fascist cause, who had none the less chosen to leave Mallorca, 'queened it' on deck. In Marseilles they had to draw money from the bank, obtain a British visa for Riding (whose passport had expired), and make further and exceedingly difficult arrangements for Karl's safe passage. They spent the night in a hotel, and on 7 August 'Just got train 10.19 (Laura protesting)'. From Dieppe they wired their old friend Maisie Somerville, who arranged for them to stay at a friend's house in York Terrace, near Regent's Park.

On the ferry they met Roy Campbell, who had written a line about them in his satirical work *The Georgiad*. Campbell was later to fight for Franco, and to celebrate, in his Catholic-Fascist *The Flowering Rifle*, the piles of corpses of dead 'reds', whom he called 'Charlies'. Graves records:

> Roy Campbell on boat: full of coloured lies. Apologised for libel on us in 'Georgiad' or something.

Although he found Campbell a 'half-crazy schoolboy', he liked his daughters, who were with him: 'fine stuff; poor girls'. He certainly never took to Campbell, for when, on the eve of his return to Mallorca in 1946, Campbell sent a message, 'God speed', Graves's answer was: 'Tell him to go to hell: I can do without his good wishes.'

Once in London, they made contact with Graves's mother, with Jenny ('very sweet'), and with old friends: James and Mary Reeves, Ward and Dorothy Hutchinson (in London at the time), Len and Jane Lye, and with various publishers – Constable, Barker (now forgiven), Cape, Faber. Graves also saw A. S. Watt, his new agent, and Liddell Hart, whom he had got to know well by correspondence over the increasingly complex ramifications of Lawrence's affairs. He immediately liked him, and they became good, and lifelong, friends. He found his sister Ros 'unchanged'. He wrote little about Laura in his diary at first, beside noting that she 'has got a lot of grey hair from all this'. She was unusually quiet, resting, and gathering up her energy for new projects. Graves sold some Lawrence material for £1000 ('£884 clear') on 13 August, thus setting them up financially for the time being.

On that same day he visited Denham Studios. Korda had promised that he would be making the film of *Claudius* by the autumn. He was now finishing *Rembrandt*, which also starred Laughton. He was planning a film on the life of T. E. Lawrence – it was not made – but as Sassoon had been chosen to do the scenario Graves was not as keen about this as he might otherwise have been, though he was prepared to act as an advisor. His diary reads:

> Mad day at Denham . . . Watched Rembrandt being filmed: only Laughton and Elsa Lanchester on set. Same passage 8 times or so. Laughton discussed Claudius. Korda promised money, wanted to send car for Laura, wanted to give Jenny a part. Saw Vincent [Korda] the decor chap

who wanted to be an artist again. So did Laughton. Mad restaurant meal filled with costumes of Elizabethan film, Swedish police & Russian refugees, English waiters etc. Vivien Leigh supplying dirty rhymes. . . .

On 14 August he met Jenny, who delighted him by telling him: 'I like clothes and I like jewellery and I'm not ashamed. The only thing I am ashamed of is keeping in with your brother Charles' – she had to do this, as one of his great, and genuine, pleasures was 'putting' people in the press, and effecting introductions to influential people.

Then Graves and Laura went to stay with John Aldridge and Lucie at their 1564 house, The Place, at Great Bardfield, where they enjoyed the cats – Courtney and Osset, each of which caught birds. Graves noted with pleasure that John had not changed; he always regarded him as the most stolid and stable of his friends. He was all this time going over *A Trojan Ending*, doing what he could to rescue it, with Laura. (This, too, had been offered to the overburdened but invariably courteous Korda.)

At The Place they were able to start work again: still on *A Trojan Ending*, and on the proofs of *Antigua*, which had arrived shortly after they came to London. They listened eagerly for news from Spain, hoping to hear that the Fascists had been defeated and that they could go back. Alan was still with them, and joined in the work. He also enjoyed 'kicking a coloured ball about the garden' with Robert – who was to do a great deal of this kind of thing, including shooting with bows and arrows, for the next two or three years. He chiefly enjoyed playing football (he still watches it on television in Mallorca), and soon had everyone (except Laura) 'goal-shooting' and trying 'ball-touch and grab hankie'.

On leaving The Place on 21 August they took John Aldridge's mother's flat for a limited period. On their first day there they saw Norman Cameron again, for the first time since he left Mallorca in 1932. All was now forgiven.

They dined out a great deal – with the Constable people, with Maisie Somerville, Tom and Julie Matthews (who were visiting London), Vyvyan Richards, Rebecca West and her husband, and many others. Graves notes carefully in his diary what Laura wore (her clothes were still as exotic as she was neat).

Graves saw and made friends again with all his children. He was delighted with Sam's good looks, liked David but found him harder to understand, and eventually won over Catherine – who was, at first, the most adamantly opposed to Laura Riding and her influence. He did not yet meet Nancy. He spent much of his time taking the children to films and restaurants, and to places such as Madame Tussauds, and buying them presents. He records the purchase of more than two hundred small antique items in this period. Many were for Laura, but others were for the children, friends and sometimes himself. He bought prints, jewellery, snuffboxes, bowls, horn whistles, a gold bean and a first edition of Borrow's *The Bible in Spain* which he gave to James's brother David Reeves – who, he records, 'had never heard of it' (this would have been explained by his Cambridge education).

But it was Jenny he saw most of, and although he generally enjoyed her company, she caused him some anxieties. She had career problems, partly because although she could dance well she could not sing. But she did obtain a three-month engagement at the Dorchester Hotel, which pleased Graves (even though he does not enjoy cabaret). He was less pleased about having to apologize to her landlady, a Mrs Bishop, for her 'staying up late and breaking a light bulb', although he did not take this seriously; nor did he bother too much about having to lend her money from time to time.

Jenny was a friend of the Churchills' daughter Sarah. Sarah was, as Graves noted, 'running off with Olivier [*sic*: he meant Vic Oliver] the Cochrane Follow the Sun humorist'. The Churchills did not keep their fury about this a secret; it was known to the nation. Jenny wanted to buy her a wedding present and Riding went to Selfridges to get it for her. This was on 14 September. On 16 September Graves records that he 'found Jenny in trouble with Churchills about her part in the Sarah business. Helped her write to Mrs & enclosed a covering letter to Winston.' Soon afterwards he had a pleasant acknowledgement from Mrs Churchill exonerating Jenny.

In early September Graves was able to speak, for the first time (by telephone), to Catherine. This was effected by his mother. Catherine wrote him a charming letter soon afterwards, from Harlech, incidentally observing:

> Last night it was very funny when the wireless was switched on to very vulgar comedy. Grandmother [Graves's mother] looked up suddenly and said 'Is that English?' thinking that we had got on to a foreign station.

For the first time for at least ten years Graves was, by his standards, unoccupied. He saw a huge number of films, mostly comedies – and took to visiting newsreel cinemas to try (vainly) to discover the realities of the Spanish situation. Work on 'Schools' was still going on, but had become rather mechanical by this time. As autumn began he became restless. He felt cut off from his home, from his work, from the progress of the unhappy but self-purgative adventure he had undertaken with Riding. He suffered from sore throats, headaches and boils, worried endlessly if he would ever get back to Deyá, and started to have bad dreams and premonitions of disaster. They talked of renting a houseboat in the Southampton area, where old friends from Deyá, the McCormacks, were living. His poetry became more haunted and premonitory. Sometimes he felt that he was going mad. But only his closest friends noticed his bad state. Riding was less ungenerous to him than of old; but she also took less notice of him. He missed Deyá much more than she did.

His only consolation was the new relationship he was building up with his children, for Riding's attitude puzzled him. Although she was for ever instructing him to jerk Constable into action over the Seizin project, and in particular *A Trojan Ending* (they did not want to publish it, but he persuaded them to – 'not enough enthusiasm', as he reported), she was directing her severities onto others and was often more relaxed and pleasant with him. This was unfamiliar. Were her attentions spreading into 'history'? Had the self-discipline he had practised been worth it? In late autumn he wrote 'A Jealous Man', intimating his doubts and fears. It is a very personal poem, powerful but only fully comprehensible in the context of his other poems arising from the Riding relationship. It is not a study in 'jealousy' as this is ordinarily understood, but of the state the word 'jealous' properly connotes: 'ardent, amorous, devoted to a cause, vigilant, zealous for the preservation of someone esteemed'. To understand a Graves poem, one has quite often to go to the original, or earlier (one might even say, poetically proper) meanings of its key words.

> To be homeless is a pride
> To the jealous man prowling
> Hungry down the night lanes,
>
> Who has no steel at his side,
> No drink hot in his mouth,
> But a mind dream-enlarged,
>
> Who witnesses warfare
> Man with woman, hugely
> Raging from hedge to hedge:

ROBERT GRAVES

The raw knotted oak-club
Clenched in the raw fist,
The ivy-noose well flung,

The thronged din of battle,
Gaspings of the throat-snared,
Snores of the battered dying,

Tall corpses, braced together,
Fallen in clammy furrows,
Male and female,

Or, among haulms of nettle
Humped, in noisome heaps,
Male and female.

He glowers in the choked roadway
Between twin churchyards,
Like a turnip ghost.

(Here, the rain-worn headstone,
There, the Celtic cross
In rank white marble.)

This jealous man is smitten,
His fear-jerked forehead
Sweats a fine musk;

A score of bats bewitched
By the ruttish odour
Swoop singing at his head;

Nuns bricked up alive
Within the neighbouring wall
Wail in cat-like longing.

Crow, cocks, crow loud,
Reprieve the doomed devil –
Has he not died enough?

Now, out of careless sleep,
She wakes and greets him coldly,
The woman at home,

She, with a private wonder
At shoes bemired and muddy –
His war not hers.

Less than a week before starting this poem – which is loaded with distressing sexual imagery – Graves noted in his diary 'Ate apple – felt poisoned. . . . Very sick.' His love was not being fed with any apples now: he was aware of the allusion. A day or two after that, visiting Southampton again, he went to Old Burseldon (just north of Southampton Water), and wrote of it:

> Remarkable contrast of old and new graveyards and dignified stone squares, & awful celtic crosses white marble and red sandstone (?) obelisks and things.

Later he said that he found that part of the country strangely haunted in atmosphere; but it was his state of mind rather than the depressing area. He could sense in Riding that his own 'war' was no longer hers, that she was now looking for someone or something else. The twelfth stanza indicates the atmosphere in which he felt he was living; and what added to his illness (he was increasingly plagued by ill health) was the horrified conviction – rigidly repressed – that behind the mask of what he had taken to be a true rectitude there was 'bricked up' a caterwauling 'longing'. He began to see things as they were, the past as wasted, 'His war not hers', virtue as 'ruttish'. This emerged in his poems, but only occasionally elsewhere; there is a tone midway between amusement and exasperation in this note about a dinner party on 27 November 1936:

> Dinner: Eddie [Marsh], Douglas West, O.K[yllmann of Constable]., Maisie, Laura, me . . . & Laura started woman-power talk, Eddie challenging, Douglas doubtful, O.K. helpless – till about 12.30 Douglas staying last.

Riding was now writing a large number of letters speaking directly of women seizing power – many are extant – in terms so unrealistically literal that it is hard not to see them as comic. The partners were certainly for the time being less close, with Riding at work on influencing such notables as Rebecca West (who remembers her, affectionately, as earnest and sincere) rather than supervising Graves. Riding had visited doctors and been 'reassured' about her heart – but told to stop smoking, which she could not.

They heard from Deyá from time to time, and were not yet unduly perturbed. Often they heard through Gelat's daughter, Anita, who lived at Rennes, in Brittany. Their view of the general situation varied from day to day. They regarded the Italo-German aid to Franco as what it was: practice for a world war – and, of course, their own future and all their property depended on the result. On 24 November Graves saw Churchill, to whom he had been introduced by Lawrence many years before. He presented an edited version of his diary entry for that day in *The Long Weekend* (published just after Churchill had taken over the leadership of the country). It reads:

Saw Winston. Told him of the importance of his commitment. . . . He said: 'Both sides imbrued with blood' – country wouldn't stand intervention. I referred him to cinema audiences. He asked 'Do you wish for intervention?' I said 'Not in any sense of taking sides in Spain but of defending British interests in the Mediterranean'. He said '7 French Deputies have just been making frantic appeals to me to urge intervention – best brains in country.' Lamented British military weakness. All Baldwin's fault – Most pessimistic. Equal chances of victory or defeat at war. Thanked me for coming. Will make a speech tomorrow that hopes will please me.

But I had got him into a state – rushing up and down the room. 'What can we do? – Baldwin is in power & parliament is lethargic'. I said 'not so lethargic as you think. Speak out and you'll have an overwhelming popular following. Everyones waiting for it'. I said 'Press propaganda does not represent the country's feelings – look at Roosevelt. 2–1 victory when press 3–1 against him.'

On Sunday 4 December he wrote to Mrs Churchill

about Jenny [who had by now got embroiled in boyfriend trouble] and to Winston suggesting the prophetic application of the *Ass in the Lion's skin* fable [an allusion to the fable about the ass who put on a lion's skin but gave himself away when he brayed: a fool who apes a wise man] – Baldwin the Ass being the traditional name, like Reynard the Fox, Bruin the Bear.

Graves followed the Mrs Simpson scandal with some interest. Having heard that Mrs Simpson was 'beastly' to shop assistants, and disliking her for what he considered to be her go-getting vulgarity, he hoped Edward would give her up. But on Friday, 11 December, he listened to Edward 'broadcast his message in an angry, tragic, vulgar voice'. As his and Alan Hodge's account of this affair in *The Long Weekend* demonstrates, he was not at all taken in by the hypocritical nonsense about Mrs Simpson being a divorcee, and so forth. He did not think anyone came well out of the crisis.

Because of the difficulties Jenny had got herself into Robert at last met Nancy; between them they extricated her without quarrelling. But the notion (once or twice canvassed) that at this, or any other, time Graves considered taking up life with Nancy again is quite wrong: this was simply wishful thinking on the part of Robert's mother – and officiousness on the part of certain other members of the family.

Graves felt he was only working 'a bit'; he had repeated injections for his recurring boils, and also tried homeopathic remedies. He was acutely unhappy – and anxious about Canelluñ, about the new direction Riding's activities had taken ('woman-power') and about the casually long leash she was holding him on; and he was sickened by the film world, though he liked Korda personally. He suddenly found himself involved in films, for Paramount had expressed an interest in *Antigua, Penny, Puce*. Also Korda had commissioned what is referred to in the diary as a 'Spanish refugee' script from Riding and Graves: he gave them the impression that he seriously meant to make a film of it. They wrote part of it, and received some payment – but it was never filmed.

II

On 15 October the *Claudius* movie troubles started. Had that film been completed, it would have been a success; the clips that exist show great promise. The erratic director, von Sternberg, had already made *The Blue Angel* and was still at the height of his powers.

On 15 October Graves went to Denham Studios, where he met Carl Zuckmayer, who had written the script, and the translater, June Head. Zuckmayer was a German, an anti-Nazi friend of Bertolt Brecht's. He had already written some good plays, and was to become internationally famous with *The Devil's General*. He was also, unknown to Graves, a graceful and genuine minor poet, one of Germany's best. But on 16 October Graves was

Reading script [in the translation]: absolutely cheap nonsense strung on historical absurdities. . . . Wrote angrily to Korda.

'Zuck', as his friends knew him, had indeed nodded over this job. On 18 October Graves 'told [Korda] how awful it was. Persuaded him to recast [the script] entirely. . . . I had a bad headache & schemed it out.'

At least he now had a job: to rewrite the screenplay himself. In fact von Sternberg, in compromising between the more experienced filmwriter Zuckmayer and the Graves version, which he had 'cinematophized', stuck more closely to the latter. But to Graves the job was not a pleasant one. He had to force himself to stick at it, working late at night even when feeling ill – and hearing Riding hold forth on woman power. He looked and felt depressed, events began to overwhelm him. The Italians were moving into Mallorca; the Catalan invasion of the island had been repulsed; the war might well drag on; he and Riding had seen Franco proclaimed dictator on 10 October on a cinema newsreel – and even though the Generalissimo's prospects were at that time far from certain, this must have depressed them both. He took solace from the fact that some newsreel audiences cheered the government troops – but gloomily noted the attitude of the press, in particular of the *Telegraph*, which nauseated him.

The excellent reviews of *Antigua*, published on 15 October, cheered him a little. In early November John O'London's referred to the printing activities of 'Mr Robert Graves'. He was obliged to make a quick retort:

> Mr Robert Graves has for the last eight years been partner to Miss Laura Riding in the Seizin Press, of which she is chief manager. . . .

He went on to say that the printing of the Seizin books was now done by commercial firms, and that the partners had the intention of returning to Mallorca 'as soon as the situation has cleared up'.

It was in this gloomy November that he fictionalized his position in the poem 'The Halls of Bedlam', at first entitled 'Before Bedlam'. If 'A Jealous Man' is a very 'private' kind of poem, then the Bedlam poem is equally 'public'. It is like the bare essentials of a novel, stripped of dialogue (always Graves's weakest point in his fiction) and detail:

> Forewarned of madness:
> In three days' time at dusk
> The fit masters him.
>
> How to endure those days?
> (Forewarned is foremad)
> ' – Normally, normally.'
>
> He will gossip with children,
> Argue with elders,
> Check the cash account.
>
> 'I shall go mad that day –'
> The gossip, the argument,
> The neat marginal entry.

His case is not uncommon,
The doctors pronounce;
But prescribe no cure.

To be mad is not easy,
Will earn him no more
Than a niche in the news.

Then to-morrow, children,
To-morrow or the next day
He resigns from the firm.

His boyhood's ambition
Was to become an artist –
Like any City man's.

To the walls and halls of Bedlam
The artist is welcome –
Bold brush and full palette.

Through the cell's grating
He will watch his children
To and from school.

'Suffer the little children
To come unto me
With their Florentine hair!'

A very special story
For their very special friends –
They burst in the telling:

Of an evil thing, armed,
Tap-tapping on the door,
Tap-tapping on the floor,
'On the third day at dusk.'

Father in his shirt-sleeves
Flourishing a hatchet –
Run, children, run!

No one could stop him,
No one understood;
And in the evening papers. . . .

(Imminent genius,
Troubles at the office,
Normally, normally,
As if already mad.)

This is far from being a mere '*jeu d'esprit*', as one critic calls it. It combines a horror story with satire on mass-media responses, and expresses a mood of tense premonitory despair. The horror story is of a man, a 'normal' 'business' man, who realizes that in three days' time he will become insane and kill or try to kill his family. The madness is so irresistible that it has, so to say, already happened. He goes about his business neatly and 'normally, normally' until he resigns to become an 'artist' – because 'artists' are regarded as more suitable for Bedlam than business men. The satirical element is aimed at the excited, yet mechanical, stock responses of the media to such incidents. Underlying 'The Halls of Bedlam' is a powerful sense of the real action, and its real consequences. The fiction and the incidental satire modify this unease: they act 'normally, normally', as neat marginal notes. There is no doubt that Graves is nasty; but then so is the public world. He is the most self-consciously poetic of the poets of this century, and there is a direct connection between 'The Halls of Bedlam' and the pre-Riding poem, 'The Cool Web', which ends:

> But if we let our tongues lose self-possession,
> Throwing off language and its watery clasp
> Before our death, instead of when death comes,
> Facing the wide glare of the children's day,
> Facing the rose, the dark sky and the drums,
> We shall go mad no doubt and die that way.

It was the loss of self-possession, of poetry, that Graves now feared. It was to threaten him, and he was to 'die' in his own poetic sense of death; but he was to be rescued and survive. But this lay three years (not days) in the future. Thus his diary reads 'normally, normally'.

On Armistice Day he and Riding moved to a new flat, at 10 Dorset Street, which crosses Baker Street just before it reaches the Marylebone Road. During the loading of their baggage they observed the two minutes' silence. He wrote that everything 'was frozen still' except for one 'loud angry voice' from a garage; and one senses that he resented this. The next day he felt ill and troubled by his boil, and stayed in bed after visiting his doctor, who, he remarks cryptically, told him that he had 'no sugar' – and recommended 'oranges and rest'. He half read a Sayers thriller ('arch, complicated, boring'), and then had a nightmare about rats or mice on his bed: there were mice in the flat. He was in bed for a few days after this, and enjoyed a Wodehouse (a favourite from Deyá days) more than the Sayers. On 14 November he did get up for a while: to hear Stephen Spender talk about 'Modern Poetry' in a 'gloomy, sissy voice'.

Of the new friends or acquaintances they made in this period the one they liked best was Sally Graves, Philip's daughter, whom they had known as a child in the late twenties. She surprised one of the Constable people, Kyllmann, 'by knowing everything', and when she visited the partners on 4 December Graves noted 'Sally came, was lovely'.

All through November and December he was taking various treatments for his boil, which refused to disappear. He was troubled about his general health, and felt sure that sexual abstinence was causing it. He confided this to his doctor and to one or two others, such as Norman Cameron. Still, even in the midst of feeling 'rather hopeless' about everything, he managed to retain his sense of humour. He met two professors, one of whom, he wrote, was 'the ugliest man in London including W. Rothenstein' – both had 'bad voices and bad manners', and they showed each other 'a field-work film' 'leaving everyone else in the dark': 'low-grade talk about traffic problems'. He found himself in this situation owing to Laura's desire to convert these traffic experts (if this is what they were) to woman power. Her new plans were forming, but had not yet reached fruition. She said that she hadn't done much work, but then she'd been fighting so hard in Spain.

Riding, invited by Alan Hodge, had been to Oxford to deliver a talk in the Taylorian Institute about the end of the world. Unfortunately no reports of this event are obtainable. While there she and Graves met Kenneth Allott – and a girlfriend of Alan's called Audrey Beecham ('restless nice girl', observed Graves), who was for a short time after the war quite well known as a poet and eccentric Oxford character. Alan began to write an excellent novel, *A Year of Damage*, occasioned by his experience of and with Audrey Beecham – it was most unfortunate that this was never published, as it was better than all the Seizin Press novels, barring *Antigua*. Graves liked the novel while Alan was writing it, and has continued to do so. In the end Alan destroyed it, to everyone's regret.

On New Year's Day 1937 Graves felt that they must return to Deyá 'after all, if in any way practicable'. The previous months had been regarded as an interruption; if there were more delay then he saw the whole edifice of his life collapsing. He saw deeper into Laura Riding's state of mind than she did herself. For him it was exile; for her, though she had no conscious notion of it, escape from too limited regality. The German situation in Spain was getting more 'sinister', and Graves was getting more desperate-minded. On 9 January he read Kafka's *Castle* (he makes no comment about it, but has since said that he felt and feels thoroughly at home with it), but then could not sleep 'with semi-aches and angry thoughts of Charles' (who had been behaving outrageously over Jenny's troubles, which were just then causing extreme anxiety).

He remained ill throughout January, which saw the *Claudius* confusion apparently deepening: he heard on 8 January that von Sternberg was making his own, personal version of the script – not yet knowing that this was, on the whole, nearer to his own than to Zuckmayer's. This made him 'feel stupid' – and the news that his old American publisher, Harrison Smith, who had joined Random House, had now left it, depressed him. It meant that Random House might drop Laura, which would lead to frustration for her, more financial outlay for him. There was little enthusiasm at Constable over *A Trojan Ending* – in fact, as records show, they dreaded publishing it as much as they dreaded Riding's 'end of world' talk – and this upset Riding, who was for ever at them to advertise the Seizin activities more vigorously. In the end she had to settle for a 'cynical wrapper' by Aldridge for *A Trojan Ending*. Graves wanted to go away somewhere for a couple of months – London was becoming increasingly oppressive to him – but Laura, herself unwell, at first opposed the idea: there was too much work to be done – on people.

Several other factors were pressing him to wish for a change. Riding was still writing to people about forming a new group to resist evil, and (though unconsciously) he wanted to get away from this, as he did not really think that he could save the world – and he knew that it would cost him money to fail to do so; and by now the accursed film version of *Claudius*, which he sometimes now referred to as the 'bookstall version', had reached them from Deyá through the good offices of a diplomat, and so he had to go on with that, too. He often felt too ill for work. All that really interested him was writing poetry.

He began to feel decidedly unpleasant, and when a bad review of *Antigua* appeared in the obscure *Colne Times* he wrote the editor this letter – which he did not, however, post:

> Only four unfavourable notices of my *Antigua, Penny, Puce*, out of more than 100, have hitherto appeared in England. This includes the one in your Jan 15 issue. By a queer fatality the publication of the first 2 – in the *News Chronicle* and *Observer* – was in each case followed by the

sudden death of the reviewer. In the third case, the *Schoolmaster*, the notice appeared posthumously two days after the reviewer's death. As a student of coincidences I should be much interested to hear of any untoward accident that may have overtaken your Mrs Halliwell, who has awarded the 'prize of the worst novel of 1936' to my book.

But his spirits lifted when Riding agreed to a vacation in Switzerland. Karl arranged for the tickets on the day of Sally's marriage to Richard Chilver, a civil servant and gifted scholar. Robert noted that Sally 'will not change name'. He went about pleasedly saying 'goodbye' to everyone.

His diary shows his spirits rising as the days pass by towards his departure from London. A publisher asked him to contribute to the popular 'In the Steps of . . .' series, which H. V. Morton's historically improbable and vulgar *In the Steps of St Paul* had established as a going concern. He was asked to do *In the Steps of Hannibal* for £2000, for publication in 1941: 'I said I didn't go in anyone's steps – H. V. Morton's, Christ's or anyone's.'

There had been talk, going back to Mallorcan days, of a project which, in his diary, Graves simply refers to as 'dictionary': Laura was now talking about this to Constable and Watt. This project was to play a big part in Graves's life and then, continually transformed, to take up the rest of Riding's. But the plan had not crystallized as yet.

Riding finally packed up to go to Switzerland almost as willingly as he. Although both had apparently innumerable dental appointments (some of which they forgot to attend), and scores of people to see, they managed to prepare *Epilogue III* for the press (it was published in April 1937). They saw three of Len Lye's films at the GPO Film Unit on 2 February, and made arrangements for David Reeves to write a book on furniture – Laura would supply the articulation, Reeves the knowledge – which appeared under the Faber imprint. The book is a standard work and still in print. For some time Riding had also been helping Norman Cameron with his Rimbaud translations, which appeared in 1942.

Korda promised them that things would soon be once again in full swing. They worked and visited incessantly until 4.30 p.m. of 5 February 1937, when they left Victoria for Lugano. Karl accompanied them. They had chosen the destination because their old Deyá neighbour Schwarz, author of *Almost Forgotten Germany*, and his companion Emmi Strenge, had gone there. They missed the connection at

Basle, and therefore missed Schwarz and Emmi. Eventually they located them and checked in, at Schwarz's recommendation, at the Hotel Rive Ziefort: '10fr a day – 21 to £1/–' noted Graves.

III

They were in Switzerland until 8 June. Here they got more work done – on the preparation of their respective *Collected Poems*, on Riding's new project, which was now gathering momentum, of forming a group of 'inside people', and on a collaborative novel called *The Swiss Ghost*. This last was never completed; what there is of it is feebler than *No Decency Left*, and is probably the worst piece of work Graves ever had a hand in.

'The First Protocol of the Covenant of Literal Morality', which is what Riding's first sally into world politics came to be called, spelled the beginning of the end of the Graves–Riding relationship, though not (so far as is known) the beginning of any morality, alas, literal or otherwise. In Switzerland Riding was still working it out. It would not reach its final form until *The World and Ourselves* (1938), in effect *Epilogue IV*, went to press.

In 1933 Schuyler Jackson, Tom Matthews's friend, and Laura Riding had agreed to differ. On 18 June 1933 he had written to thank her for her last ('not harsh') letter, and for her help in maturing their argument (over, in effect, his notion that her poetry was 'philosophy') 'to the point where it . . . goes to seed'. Perhaps, he suggested, they would stop arguing and begin 'understanding'. However, he now refused to endorse her 'Covenant of Literal Morality', when it went, at Tom's suggestion, to him. But he did restart their correspondence, in spite of having received (according to Tom Matthews) one of her 'rebukes'. It would not be too long before she would become as interested in the notion of him as she was in literal morality: the two might even be said to have been merged by her. His untutored and uncouth mind began to fascinate her, and Graves sensed the slow growth in her of something he had always, except involuntarily in his poems, denied was even there. Although he had written of them in 'A Jealous Man', the bricked-up nuns still wailed with cat-like longing, and his boil continued to trouble him. It burst, several times, but always formed again. And her bladed mind began to pull through his hopes rather than through time. Ravaged by guilt, she would later accuse him of

280

having a wrong sense of time: i.e. one not hers (though she did not feel it necessary to add this). But that was to come later. Now he continued, with characteristic doggedness, to support her efforts, morally and financially. No one else was yet in sight – for her or for him.

Chapter Nineteen
1937

I

They had moved into a house, or rather a 'half-house', by 10 February: the Villa Guidi, in Paradiso, a district skirting the lake itself. Riding's bed was not comfortable, and so Graves changed with her; but this was not good enough either. He had to hire one in Lugano. Graves was still sweating out the 'Claudius F.V.' – the film version. But he was held up without the Sternberg script, 'promised so often'. He wrote to Korda for it, and for more money (which had also been promised). On 13 February he ends his entry with an irony characteristic to the very colon: 'Feeling well: still have boil.' Having on 13 February been depressed by the Blackshirts and 'aggressiveness' while on a short trip to Italy, on the 15th he 'Worked all day' on an answer to Laura's 'Letter on International Affairs' (which became the 'First Protocol'). His own and others' 'answers' were eventually printed, and commented on, in *The World and Ourselves*. (In certain cases the answers were revised so that the comments could be sharpened up: Riding was adept at pointing out to people what 'they really meant'.) Graves went on working on his answer all the following day; Riding, going over some of Harry Kemp's work, got an attack of migraine. On this occasion Graves read her Kierkegaard interspersed with *Huck Finn*, an odd mixture. He finished his answer – 'about 2500 words – at 11 p.m.' Or he thought he had; but on the next day he recorded: 'Once more over my answer, gave it to Karl to type.' There follows one of his cryptic entries: 'Laura not well, did not go out. ("Schools").'

In the following days he went on with the *Claudius* film book – and began once more to buy *objets*: 'another silk Italian blanket . . . nacre buttons. . . .' For some time he had been controlling his smoking, but by 20 February he was 'Smoking again, carelessly'. His stomach was bad. They were correcting the *Epilogue* proofs, and those of Honor

Wyatt's novel; they were also enjoying the typescript of Alan Hodge's *Year of Damage*, which seems to have afforded them and Karl a good deal of consolation. They loved the background of snowy mountains, as a contrast to dirty and noisy London. Karl remarked with the wit that is typical of him: 'You'd expect God to come forward, hat in hand: All my own work!'

Riding went over *A Year of Damage* in great detail (later she denied that it had ever 'passed through [her] hands'). Otherwise it was anxiety about not hearing, or not getting money, from Korda, 'Schools', walks, and, for Graves, trying nobly but failing to be able to read Michael Sadleir's romance *These Foolish Things*.

Then on 1 March bad news came. They heard via Short that Gelat had been imprisoned. It later turned out that his old enemies the priest and the doctor had denounced him, had commandeered his bus, and generally settled old scores. Graves had a bad headache and felt desperate; he was shocked when Schwarz 'did not take the . . . news at all personally'.

He heard that shooting of *Claudius* had begun, but then received a script (it was an out-of-date one, not the shooting script) which upset him: 'more and more dreary as it goes on'. He was so depressed that by 6 March he was reduced to reading Nat Gould (a once highly popular producer of pulp fiction about horse-racing). He felt sympathy for the drunk man he heard (as he walked home from a café evening with Karl and Laura) shouting: 'Mussolini. Brutto uomo senza cuore! Ecco! La difficultá della civita. . . . Noi altri. . . .'

One or two 'constructive' replies, among many, had come in in response to Laura's 'I.L.' (International Letter). Graves's natural robustness and realism, and his first-hand experience of war and its total uselessness (Riding saw war as merely schoolboyish), had caused him to suspect her idealism. But for the time being, at least, he began to revive hope in her. He knew that the arrest of Gelat meant the encroachment of a new era of evil in Spain: he had seen the Blackshirts, saw that they resembled the Fascist thugs who had torn through Deyá, had heard about conditions in Germany from people who had been there. He felt sickened by the atrocities committed by the Left elsewhere in Spain, and refused to sign a petition against the Fascists: both sides, he pointed out, were guilty. Mainly, though, he did not want to put any English nationals at risk.

Riding's plan was at least consistent. As she later summarized it in a document called 'To the Endorsers of the Covenant of Literal Morality' (February 1939), which was not commercially published, she wanted from those to whom she addressed her 'letter' a pledge to 'a recognition of the relation between personal values and outer events', and a belief that 'by their power of distinguishing between good and evil in all the contacts of life, they had a further power of arresting evil works'. The 'First Protocol', the 'Letter', is published in *The World and Ourselves*.

For Riding there were 'inside people' and 'outside people'. As Tom Matthews comments: 'Laura herself, by common consent, was as inside as you could get.' He and his wife Julie regarded her as a witch, but a 'white witch'. Others reached the same conclusion, independently, though some left out all mention of colour.

All she was saying, in effect, was that the public acceptance of public factoids was a useless activity.

> We cannot allow ourselves to be deceived, when we hear the activities of the international disturbers being denounced as 'immoral', 'a disgrace to civilisation', into believing a lively private sense of values is at work.

Such people did recognize that international events affected their privacy, but had no 'sharp realisation that the laws of events are crude counterparts of the inner laws that govern their own personal reality'.

This is very traditional fare, though stated more crisply than in the usual standard texts. The difficulty she spoke of was hardly new: all are very well known to be ignorant of the 'inner laws that govern their own personal reality'. Graves, when he had been able to love her wholeheartedly, had genuinely believed that she embodied the truth of these 'inner laws'. But those who are sure of what inner laws govern *others* are deeply disturbing influences on others. This Graves refused to see, though he knew it.

None the less, he at this time added 'four new verses' to his 'A Country House' poem, and one of them was

> A smell of mould from loft to cellar,
> Yet sap still brisk in the oak
> Of the great beams: if ever they use a saw
> It will stain, as cutting a branch from a green tree

– some of the loveliest lines of hope written in this century. And they came from a temporary resurgence of hope in Laura, a forgetting of what disturbed him in her – of his premonitions of how she would relentlessly apply her 'knowledge' of the 'inner laws' to justify her own behaviour. He would continue, for more than two years, to waver between his loyalty and commitment to Laura's anti-physical 'holiness' and his own tough, old-soldier sense of reality and instinct that the needs of the flesh must be satisfied, though at a high price.

One of the charges levelled against Graves, both in private discussion and occasionally in print, is that in his poetry he ignores 'central realities' (politics, 'why are we here?', and so forth). But, being a true 'inside man' (though naturally sceptical about the exact nature of all 'inner laws'), he has consistently allowed his personal anxieties and problems to coalesce with his feelings about international events (for which one may safely read, and certainly in the twentieth century, 'stupid', 'wicked', 'destructive' or 'illusory' international events). This approach is a more honest one than that of an over-self-consciously direct concern with 'international events', and is less crude than the now familiar philosophy of 'commitment'. Where Riding and Graves really differed is that the one was uncertain, whereas the other was absolutely certain. So that Riding turned out to be Graves's experiment, in the end, in faith, and in that sort of deliberately self-inflicted suffering which is taught, significantly, by some Sufi schools of thought. And he was cast as her chief Judas.

Thus, Auden's poem *Spain* (the original version) is a moving and sincere effort to express indignation and pity – but is ultimately rhetorical because its language is devoid of any personal reality, or any sense whatever of the poet's exploring what he meant by his own pity. In Switzerland Graves wrote a poem that is quite as political, in its way, as *Spain*, but he eschewed the temptation of trying to attract a wide public by connecting it with topical events.

The story of the Tower of Siloam is only found in Luke (xiii, 1–5). Its point is that, according to Jesus, the eighteen who perished were not worse offenders than those who escaped ('Nay: but, except ye repent, ye shall all likewise perish'). The poem is written as if by one of those who escaped.

> Should the building totter, run for an archway!
> We were there already – already the collapse
> Powdered the air with chalk, and shrieking
> Of old men crushed under the fallen beams
> Dwindled to comic yelps. How unterrible
> When the event outran the alarm
> And suddenly we were free.

Free to forget how grim it stood,
That tower, and what wide fissures ran
Up the west wall, how rotten the under-pinning
At the south-eastern angle. Satire
Had curled a gentle wind around it,
As if to buttress the worn masonry;
Yet we, waiting, had abstained from satire.

It behoved us, indeed, as poets
To be silent in Siloam, to foretell
No visible calamity. Though kings
Were crowned and gold coin minted still and horses
Still munched at nose-bags in the public streets,
All such sad emblems were to be condoned:
An old wives' tale, not ours.

Behind its deliberately provocative 'cynicism' the poem is about guilt
and innocence, as is the passage in Luke to which it directly refers.
The attitude it reveals is ambivalent: it seems ostensibly to recommend
staying 'inside' oneself, remaining a private person with private values
– a poet; but it is at the same time blandly ironic in its tone. The
ultimate attitude is clinched by Jesus's own comment, to which the
poet, however, here remains uncommitted: that everyone will perish
unless they repent (change their ways). The poem also records the
failure of Christianity: this is, again with 'nasty' irony, seen as the very
tower itself – its European side fissured, its Hellenistic rotted. It reveals
the Christian religion as resting on a bad compromise – a theme Graves
would take up again. This is the least ambiguous element in the poem.
It is interesting that Riding's poem 'March 1937' is, in contrast to this,
weak and wearied, as though her poetic powers were in temporary
decline.

When their friends the McCormacks visited them *en route* to England from a holiday in Yugoslavia they took Riding, Graves and Karl
for a trip to Italy: 'Italy lovely, but the Duce's apothegms stencilled or
engraved everywhere.'

Then on 18 March news came that Merle Oberon had been hurt in
a car smash and that 'the I Claudius film is likely to be scrapped'.
Graves makes no further comment in his diary, but continued with the
work on the nearly completed film version. On 20 March they talked
'of a visit to America to write a book if Spain does not clear up'. But
on 22 March he underlines the better-than-worse news that he has

heard from Short that although Gelat was still in prison '*no charge yet*'.

Pasted opposite Graves's diary entry for 23 March is a newspaper picture of Charles Laughton captioned

Fate of £100,000 'I, Claudius' was in his hands. Though he had other plans, Laughton agreed to finish the film in spite of delay caused by injury to Merle Oberon.

But he felt indifferent – in spite of the financial difference that the final *Claudius* decision would make to him. He read two Leonard Merrick novels (Merrick was a popular, accomplished bitter-sweet writer), played cards with Karl, bought more and more small articles – and worked at poems.

The news from Spain was mixed. The Italians had been doing badly. But news of the first Mallorcan atrocities, unleashed by the ferocious clerics, were coming through: any of their friends might well have been murdered. His boil remained 'much the same as before', while Laura corresponded about literal morality with Christina Stead and Storm Jameson and some others. They finished going over Alan Hodge's novel, now complete, and were still thoroughly delighted with it.

By this time *Claudius* had brought him in £8500 altogether. But he was still short of money, for he noted on 1 April that he had £650 in Paris, £250 in London, and £200 with him. The next day was 'bad', and the partners did nothing but gloomily discuss 'the hopelessness of carrying on any decent writing or publishing business in face of the dark age opposition to anything good'. Laura had been having bad dreams, which they attributed to the fact that her room had 'had a lot to do with death at one time or another'. They heard for the first time that the accusations against Gelat were 'the water, the road, his being mayor'. Then, confusingly, they received news that Merle Oberon was out of 'nursing home & that Korda is likely to finish the film later in the year'.

On 16 April there is another mention of the 'dictionary'. Graves was by now feeling better and cheered up, perhaps because just then Franco was regarded as 'definitely beaten' even by his numerous British supporters. He writes:

Ox. Univ. Press turned down dictionary as 'too individual and personal . . . words cannot be put into strait jackets.' Another example of tolerance of illiterates (for the sake of Lexicographical richness).

OUP were to turn down the same book, utterly transformed, forty years later. What they turned down in 1937 was simply an outline.

The dictionary was first conceived as a 'thesaurus of related meanings', and Riding had written a draft of an essay with this title in 1935. It was offered to OUP as a working English dictionary and thesaurus: some 20,000 (in the first instance: the number grew) words were to be dealt with; they would be given a *distinct* definition ('or set of definitions'), and would be grouped into categories of meaning.

The notion of the dictionary had grown from a casual remark Graves made one day to the effect that he wished that the *Roget* groupings were more satisfactory. He wrote to me in 1975 saying that he thought that, if completed in the form originally intended, it 'would have been quite a useful thesaurus'. But for Riding it was to be the final escape from language confusion: her (and eventually Jackson's) definitions of words would be accepted by the English-speaking world, and confusion would thereupon cease.

But the ultimate collapse of the enterprise into an unreadable and overlong essay of Heideggerian density should not distract attention from the powers of intelligence which Riding still possessed in 1937, before she had met Jackson. A new *Roget*, to anyone interested in words, was (and is) a reasonable notion. Graves was interested in the *grouping* of the words; Riding was really interested in their definition – the groupings were for her only a corollary to the definitions. For Graves, as a practical poet, believed in 'Lexicographical richness': he might deplore it as much as he deplored sexual desire, but he knew it existed, whatever he might write in his diary about OUP. Nevertheless, he went along with Riding, supported her, and was as loyal to her intentions as he was able to be. He brought his knowledge of words (much greater than hers or Jackson's) to the work he put into the dictionary.

But really serious work on this was not to start for some time. Now Graves worked at poem after poem: 'To Evoke Posterity', 'Largesse to the Poor', 'Hotel Bed', 'Act V, Scene 5' – and others which he destroyed. All of these were 'read and passed' by Riding, as he dutifully noted.

She was working on revisions of her earlier (and, in general, best) poems, as he was working on his new ones. On 21 April a note of irritation crept into his diary entry: 'Checked Laura's poems after typing: found two small ones left out, *not* Karl's fault'. There were times when, privately – out of sight of other people – he resisted her rages, particularly when these were unfairly directed. Another way in which he resisted her tyranny, and preserved his own integrity as a person, was by unconscious self-defence: he indulged in what she later called in a letter his 'poor Laura talk'. He would commiserate with her lack of success (quite sincerely), and this, of course, distressed her.

By the last day of April, having registered the 'general horror' at the Guernica massacre ('even by *Morning Post*') and the German threat to Czechoslovakia, Graves wrote: 'Curse pronounced generally – on all but the true' (the last word is substituted for a very heavily crossed out but still just legible 'poets'). On the same day Graves wrote 'The Laureate' (first published as 'The Wretch'). This tells of the 'wretch' who is like 'a lizard in the sun' but who was once a poet: 'It was no natural death, but suicide.'

> Arrogant, lean, unvenerable, he
> Still turns for comfort to the western flames
> That glitter a cold span above the sea.

This poem does very well as a description of any written-out poet, any Wordsworth, who persists. 'I suppose it could be Masefield,' he admitted to me in 1943; but he still had an affection for Masefield, and the specific poet he may have had in mind is Bridges: 'His time and truth he has not *bridged* to ours'. He passed James Reeves's suggestion that this was an intended pun when the latter printed the poem with a note in an anthology – but there is a difficulty in that he never thought Bridges was a poet at all. Chiefly, though, the poem is an expression of his premonitions about Riding's apostasy (as he saw it) from poetry; he could not suppress his fears in face of her new activities. To write a poem directly on this subject would have been impossible for him just then; but in this poem he was able to disguise the subject in one of his neat quasi-biographical modes. He did, however, have unusual difficulty with it. For the whole of that last day of April he 'did nothing' – a most unusual course for him to take. On 1 May he 'tentatively' finished the poem in 'eight drafts'. He continued to tinker with it until it went to press in his *Collected Poems*.

They kept in as close touch as possible with Deyán events, their chief concern being the well-being of Gelat, of whom they could get no certain news. They were in constant communication with his relatives at Rennes, and there was much depressing talk of who might have denounced whom for this or that uncommitted 'crime'.

But Laura was by now planning a revolution herself, and, on the back of one of the envelopes in which they received a letter from Spain via Italy and Rennes, she made a note of a book she wanted: Raymond Postgate's *How to Start a Revolution*. A sea-green incorruptible, she was looking for tips from any quarter, even ones as leftist as Postgate. Graves received from Frank Morley of Faber (Morley had recently pleased him by diplomatically agreeing with him in a London pub that Auden was a 'thief' and 'magpie') a copy of David Jones's *In Parenthesis*: this interested him, since Jones had been a Royal Welch Fusilier and had fought in some of the same places in Flanders as he had. But he disliked it: 'a war-book by Joyce out of Eliot'. This is critically imprecise; more interesting is his real objection to the book, that the author does not communicate himself properly to the reader: 'I know what he's talking about because I was there', he once said indignantly to me of one passage, 'but how could you or anyone else know?' What Graves's attitude reveals is his own dislike of attempting to mix poetry and prose.

Having dealt with the death of poetry three days before, Graves dealt with 'The Poets' (later 'Any Honest Housewife') on 4 May: 'a new one, soon written'.

> Any honest housewife could sort them out,
> Having a nose for fish, an eye for apples.
> Is it any mystery who the sound,
> And who the rotten? Never, by her lights.
>
> Any honest housewife who, by ill-fortune,
> Ever engaged a slut to scrub for her
> Could instantly distinguish from the workers
> The lazy, the liars, and the petty thieves.
>
> Does this denote a peculiar sixth sense
> Gifted to housewives for their vestal needs?
> Or is it a failure of the usual five
> In all unthrifty writers on this head?

He was not officially, and had not been for many years, 'allowed' to write poems 'about himself'. This was discouraged. He tried not to do it. But none the less his poems were (of necessity) about himself. (Riding's poems are also, of necessity, about herself – even if cast in the form of not being so.) So it is again interesting that here, imagining himself not to be writing 'about himself', he is looking for an 'honest housewife': Riding was no housewife, even though he might sometimes have felt like a 'slut' who 'scrubbed' for her.

He still worked at 'Schools' ('reached typed page 85') with Riding; much of the rest of the time he spent on *The Swiss Ghost*, at resolutely buying *objets* whose prices he might lower by a little (or, sometimes, by a lot) when recording them in his diary – and on walks, when he would observe the names and peculiarities of the many flowers he encountered. In these days he noted sensitively and unsentimentally the solace he found in nature. These entries dispel the myth of his 'dislike' of nature: those earlier, apparently 'anti-nature' poems, such as 'Nature's Lineaments' ('Nature is always so: you find/That all she has of mind/Is wind . . .') are records of his honest attempt to accommodate himself to Riding's distinctly Manichean suspicion of 'beauty', which she painfully threw out because of its association with sexuality and matter.

By 10 May, when Lugano was no more than 'already a pleasant memory to L & me', they had 'a strange letter from Maisie [Somerville] accusing Laura of judging by hearsay' (no details are given in his diary). The accusation was in no way 'strange', because, 'judgement' being Riding's overriding passion, she would judge on whatever 'evidence' she had to hand. Graves wrote gloomily that this 'meant long letters to her [Maisie], practically breaking things off'.

On 13 May Barker wrote to tell him that the *Claudius* movie was, after all, 'almost certainly being abandoned'. He felt relieved rather than disappointed; Riding was the more upset, since this threatened her plans financially. He was more interested in what they would do when they got back to England, for the Swiss trip had not after all made him feel any better. Almost every day he was waking with sick headaches. His chief consolations were his long walks, the flowers and working at poems. He was glad to hear that Harry Kemp had arranged to rent a house for them outside London, at Ewhurst, in Surrey. This is midway between Horsham and Guildford, near Cranleigh.

As their days in Lugano drew to a close, they felt heavy and depressed, at heart 'loathing', to take a phrase from a later poem by Graves ('The Beast'), 'each other's carrion company'. Maisie Somerville had offended Laura by not answering her letter, and she complained bitterly; Graves worked on his gloomy poem 'Or to Perish Before Day' and on finalizing his *Collected Poems*.

Feeling the weight of exile more than ever. Discussion of next step: money, publishing, friends etc.

he wrote on 19 May. Two days later 'very nice' letters 'about Maisie' arrived from Alan, David Reeves, and Honor Wyatt. Things were somehow patched up, for they met as soon as Graves and Riding were back in London. He could not get the foreword to his *Collected Poems* right before they left for London on 8 June; but he did write the last poem for it, 'Leaving the Rest Unsaid'.

II

When they returned, at first to London, Graves continued his visits to dentists and his buying up of what seems to have been the entire stock of small antique objects in the city; he saw the movies *The Ghost Goes West* and *A Man Only Dies Once*, and heard one 'Left Book Club poet' saying to another: 'I met you first at the Socialist Club. You had long hair: you were rather beautiful.'

On Tuesday 15 June he discovered that his boil was a fistula: 'must be cut out. Will take at least three weeks to heal. Arranged for Monday.' It was a positive relief. He could stop trying for a while: he was physically down, emotionally exhausted, and lost.

On 18 June comes the first mention of Beryl – a girl with whom Alan had become friendly at Oxford, and who was now his girlfriend. They met a few days before 8 June 1937. It was to be some time before Graves noticed Beryl, although she noticed him. They had dinner with boring people that night: 'Gramophone records & insincere conversation.' On the following day he went, alone, to see Korda at Denham studios. Korda told him that he might make *Claudius* in 1938, although it would have to be without Laughton. He 'complained bitterly of [Laughton] and his intellectualism. It was worse with Sternberg, who did not humour him.' Korda offered Graves £100 – with a promise of a further £750 'if accepted' for the 'Margaret Catchpole modern film, for L and me'.

Graves had read Richard Cobbold's Suffolk classic *Margaret Catchpole* (1845), the partly true story of the author's father's servant, who got involved with smugglers and was sentenced to transportation for stealing her master's coach and horses – and had decided to give it a modern treatment. They wrote part of it, but it came to nothing.

On the Sunday he went into a private room in St Mary's Hospital for his operation. Riding suddenly became especially solicitous of him, and made a visit to see if he was comfortable. He spent the day listening to the radio, writing eight lines of what would become his

'Leda' poem ('Heart, with what lonely fears you ached'), read Philip Macdonald's *The Rasp* ('bad'), and was starved all day (which he disliked intensely, although it made him feel 'mystical').

After the operation had been successfully performed he was visited by Riding, and then by Nancy; the pain was relieved by four-hourly draughts of opium. He was to have nothing but fluids for four days. The day after the operation he read Cook's *Voyages* and finished 'Leda', for the time being, in 'five drafts'. On 23 June he had to endure – having just heard that it would be inadvisable to return to Deyá – the shallow chatter of a 'Fascist doctor's wife' who spoke of 'how quiet things were in Franco Spain'.

But that was soon forgotten: for on the next day news came through that Gelat had been released on the preceding Thursday: a telegram from Anita at Rennes read 'PAPA LIBRE BUENAS NOTICIAS ABRASOS'. 'Feeling weak, I wept for about ½ an hour: restored with tea.'

Three days later Riding came in at lunch time with serious news:

> ... we discussed the Alan–Beryl position. Apparently Beryl was rather rude to Laura last night: and then Alan spoke coolly about her to me yesterday.

One would like to have been there 'last night'.

After this, Graves had an interesting experience. His own doctor brought with him, to visit the patient, a man who was both a notable doctor and (by common consent) a madman on the subject of women: Sir Almroth Wright. Wright it was who had said, many years ago, with perfect seriousness, 'Peace will come when surplus women shall have been removed by emigration': 'Then Sir Almroth Wright. . . . Anti-feminismo. An awful row: frightened him. Then Alan, soothing.' Riding came to tell him that her meeting with Naomi Mitchison had been 'hopeless'. After a series of visitors that day Graves read E. Arnot Robertson's *Four Frightened People*, but was unsoothed: 'a bad minded woman'.

The figures for the Seizin Press were 'hopeless', too, he learned from Laura on 30 June – while he was working on the retrospective 'Certain Mercies' and on 'The Florist Rose' – but she told him that although the Ewhurst house Harry Kemp had taken for them was 'rather depressing', it was in nice countryside. But at least they both had projects planned, for money was again scarce. Riding was outlining her *Lives of Wives*, her only book to show a profit to its publishers, and Graves had contracted to write a novel about Belisarius, the sixth-century

Byzantine general. This was, in one way, a prophetic choice: Belisarius, just as the Allies were to do within a few years, fought a hard campaign in Africa and then used Sicily as a springboard to take Italy. Graves got valuable help from Sally for this book, as it had been her 'special period' when she read history at Somerville a year or two previously. Sally visited him, and he got news not only of Belisarius but also of his other niece, (the now late) Diana Graves, the actress and journalist, daughter of Graves's brother Richard.

The Seizin Press now broke with Constable. With the help of Watt they went over to Cassell, who would eventually become Graves's regular publishers. The partners were now becoming friendly with A. S. and A. P. Watt, father and son, and particularly with one of their assistants, Patricia Butler – who was one of the few to stay on good terms with both Graves and Riding; A. P. Watt himself remained Riding's agent until Patricia Butler's death in the sixties.

On Sunday, 4 July, he got up for the first time; Laura came, 'with contentment about Seizin plans now'.

As soon as he got back, on 6 July, to 'frantic scene of packing' at their temporary flat in Nottingham Street, he 'lay on sofa and wrote letters for Laura, who was over-tired'.

The next day they left in a car they had just bought (neither could drive, but Harry Kemp could) for Ewhurst. Graves 'could not help much' with the arrangements, but found the house less depressing than 'Laura had described it'. Harry Kemp, a schoolteacher, and his wife Alix – who owned a cheese business – shared Highcroft, the Ewhurst house, with them.

Graves soon became overactive, forgetting that he was an invalid (as he put it), and thus made himself feel ill. Promising news came: Doubleday was interested in the dictionary. Laura insisted that he stay in bed all day on 10 July: he read Wodehouse's golfing novel *Heart of a Goof* and played marbles with Harry Kemp. A visit to Charterhouse made him tired, and so on the 12th, while Laura 'trained' a quarter-Persian kitten without a name ('yet'), he 'took peas and gooseberries to my bedroom to top and tail, and shell': 'I get easily tired but cannot be idle easily. . . .' He had that morning written 'out prose account of my poems [i.e. the introduction to the *Collected Poems*] in a fairly final draft'.

He was now spending most of his time reading up for his Belisarius novel. Marbles became less attractive on 13 July as 'Harry now beats me at our marble game every time: studies each move for 5 minutes, which bores me'; but on 14 July, triumphantly, he records that he has 'recovered prestige at marbles'.

Games distracted this prophet of kitsch from the question he had asked himself in his diary on 15 July:

¿How to deal with the ineluctable mauve carpet & the irremediable yellow-brown fire-place tiles?

Beryl came down to stay with Alan – who was already there – a few days later, while Graves read Procopius (the principal source for *Belisarius*) and played various games with golf balls on the lawn outdoors and with thread on the carpet indoors. He could never relax (except for very short and deliberate intervals), and here he was as bored as he had ever been in his life. Having to carry on with the *Swiss Ghost* novel, which neither he nor Riding ever really believed in, did not make things more interesting. Money was a constant worry, and there seemed nothing to look forward to. He also had toothache. He was being treated by a local dentist called Trace, and believed himself to be coming out of the wood; but on 18 July it was discovered that he had an abscess under an eye tooth. He had to make an urgent appointment. Trace

found an anaesthetist to gas me and removed most of [the tooth] without difficulty. It was rotten and fast in the bone. Afterwards I wept & went home to bed: removed a piece of casing with a pair of forceps & felt better. . . . I said, on coming out of the anaesthetic, that the way wisdom teeth were fitted into the mouth made one a Manichean, sceptical of a wise personal benevolent God.

The next day he felt 'lacerated', and, although he worked, he 're-introduced' a German card game, which Karl knew, into the Ewhurst household, and even got Karl making a papier-mâché mask. The 19th was the anniversary of the Spanish revolt, and was a 'dull, sweaty, awful day'.

Two days later, despite news of the war starting in China and a still painful gum, he felt better. He wrote the first six pages of *Count Belisarius*. Meanwhile Karl's mask had been dressed up 'in an old dress of Laura's' and was 'a witch hanging on the wall'.

For his forty-second birthday many preparations were made. Among the presents he received were 'an old English bow and a quiver of arrows'; this was to give him great pleasure in the ensuing weeks. But in spite of the balloons, fireworks and the dreadful fireplace 'disguised with greenery', he finished the first chapter of *Belisarius*. Anyone who has lived with him for any length of time will have experienced a sense of wonder at how he can participate in social affairs, do chores, be ill (that day he still had bad toothache, and even had to retire to bed temporarily with it), and yet turn out substantial quantities of work. Few writers have worked so hard; yet the working itself has been oddly unobtrusive – no Balzacian nights on coffee – a matter of quiet persistence. That birthday in Surrey ended with a serious discussion of 'the condition of poets when not writing poems'.

He continued with *Belisarius*, getting at this time valuable help from Alan Hodge – who, like Beryl, had just left Oxford – and 'found surprising accuracy with bow and arrow'.

All his children visited him there, too: Sam and Catherine camped in the meadow by the house, and a day or two later – mid-August – David and Jenny came to stay at a nearby guesthouse. Jenny was now getting on better, though she found life as a chorus girl trying. She complained of having no friends, and even discounted her father as one because, she said, he did not trust her. He tried to make it clear that he did, but that she was still young. He discussed David's future with him: 'has 1½ years to get Univ. schol. Will specialise in English & French.'

He was glad about the progress he was making in his relationship with his son David, and delighted when he received this letter from him, written from Harlech:

> The atmosphere up here is rather strained – Uncle John, Clarissa, Grandmother – all at loggerheads with each other and with us. The only thing I can do to amuse myself during mealtimes is to make Sam [who was very mischievous at this time] giggle, which brings forth mouthings from John & dignified silences from the other two.

This implied a new confidence between them, and although there were to be a few tiffs caused by Riding's complaints of David's disrespectful treatment of her, they became good friends.

Graves's spirits went up and down with the nature of the news about the war in Spain. He felt 'really well' on 4 September when the newspapers of the previous day had printed reports of an important government victory.

As well as carrying on with *The Swiss Ghost*, Riding and Graves made a serious start on the *Margaret Catchpole* scenario, which they called *The Smuggler*. The amount of time they were now wasting may be put down mostly to their enforced ignorance of where they could go: must they reorganize their lives, or would they be allowed back into Spain? They decided to stay in England for the time being, 'despite Income Tax'. Graves noted on 9 September, after a medical examination made on behalf of an insurance company, that he weighed 'just under 14 st.' and that he was physically perfectly well: he had '*low* blood pressure', which he was told accounted for his occasional giddiness when standing up. On the next day, though, he went to bed in the afternoon, and was forced to listen to what Riding had 'worked on all day': 'recommendations . . . for dealing with misbehaving countries.' The veteran of the trenches repressed his dismay, got up, walked to Cranleigh, and bought some fish.

On 24 September, suddenly, and after they had decided to go back to London, 'we decided to get some money together and start a school in Deyá.' This hastily reversed decision may have been a reaction to further bad news about Seizin Press sales, which were negligible but for *Antigua, Penny, Puce*.

The 16th of October was Alan Hodge's birthday, and he came to visit with Beryl – they both stayed at a nearby guesthouse. Alan was bought presents, including two toy soldiers. In his first personal reference to Beryl in his diary (apart from the one about rudeness to Laura) Graves noted, on the day after Alan's birthday, that Beryl hated her job 'because too many people about'. She was just then working in Woolworths, and was indeed what Alan called his 'Woolworths girl'.

One day Graves, with Riding, James Reeves, Norman Cameron and Harry Kemp, wrote a spoof sonnet ('The courage of the Dog no man denied/Who had not heard the ghostly bugle blow. . .'), which Graves sent to the *Times Literary Supplement* as the authentic newly discovered work of T. L. Beddoes (the editor was not taken in). More seriously, he and Riding arranged for Alan Hodge to write a letter to the same paper complaining of Auden's plagiarisms from Riding.

Just before leaving Ewhurst Graves decided or was instructed to write a book about Riding – after talking with her. He even wrote half a page of it, and much more later; but none of it was published. He also read in the *Daily Express*:

> Robert Graves, the English writer, is mentioned with others in the Swedish papers as one of the leading candidates for the Nobel Prize in literature. . . .

But the prize for that year went to the French novelist Roger Martin du Gard, who was duly vilified, neither Graves nor Riding ever having read a word by him.

On Monday, 15 November, they moved to 31 Alma Square in Maida Vale, very close to Lord's Cricket Ground: 'by far the best place we have been in since we left Deyá.' They did their duty to the landlord at Ewhurst (whom they disliked) by 'restoring the place to its original sordidness', or, as Graves put it another day, they 'restored it to awfulness'.

Harry Kemp and Alix went to another flat in London – only Riding and Graves went to Maida Vale. And the cat, which despite several disappearances had survived and was now much loved. Her name was Solace.

Rosaleen, Clarissa and Robert Graves, c. 1899–1900

Graves at Charterhouse

For permission to reproduce the photographs
included in this book the publishers
would like to thank Beryl Graves,
Thomas Hinde, Freya Edwards,
Mrs. J. Vinogradoff and the Headmaster of
Charterhouse School

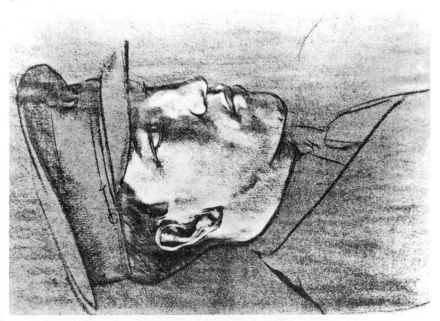

Graves (second left) with fellow-officers of the
Royal Welch Fusiliers, September 1917

Drawing of Graves in uniform by Eric Kennington

Deya – oil painting by John Aldridge, 1933

Siegfried Sassoon at Garsington

Laura Riding, *c.* 1930

Graves and William at Galmpton, 1942

Graves, Beryl and guest, Galmpton, 1943

Graves working in bed, as he frequently did,
during the Second World War

In the kitchen at Galmpton, 1944

Graves with the author and others
at a Palma bullfight, 1952

Chapter Twenty
1937–38

By mid-November Graves was so well on with *Belisarius*, now to be called *Count Belisarius*, that he agreed to deliver it to Random House by the end of January. Although he liked Alma Square, London soon began again to encroach on his nervous system. Riding flourished there, however: she could be on the telephone all day with all sorts of people on the subject of literalness and inside people. One evening at Ewhurst, when she had been unwell in bed, Graves read to her from a life of St Francis of Assisi. In it the Saint's Holy Conscience was reported to have enjoined his followers to follow a severe new Rule 'literally, literally, literally, without gloss, without gloss, without gloss'. This had much impressed her, and she was to quote it in the aggressive note 'To the Reader' which prefaced her *Collected Poems*.

Alan Hodge and Beryl were now living in what Graves called 'Alan's mad flat' at 88 Adelaide Road, a long street in the Chalk Farm district. On 28 November he walked all the way there in thick fog, and brought them back to a cold supper at Alma Square. He was still immersed in Riding, and it is doubtful if at this time he noticed Beryl as any more than Alan's girlfriend.

He had at present the serious problem of selling Riding's *Collected Poems*. On 29 November he went to Watt with 'L's poems, & promise of mine & of Int. Letter book'. Heinemann had already turned the poems down; the ease with which he could sell his own work and the difficulties he had in selling Laura's proved greatly embarrassing to him, and on some occasions he had to represent the publishers' resistance to hers in a much modified form.

He continued to buy up necklaces, buttons, pieces of glass and other objects – and became popular with the dealers he visited, and whose stories of provenance he believed.

At Ewhurst Laura had made a friend of an Irish woman called Mary Lucy, who wrote poetry which both she and Graves liked. Mary Lucy had a husband who knocked her about ('homicidal and violent', he could not comprehend long letters about the niceties of his and his wife's 'relationship-positions' with Riding), and she and her problems became a nuisance – even if hardly through failings of her own – though the partners tried to help her. She had been about for most of the time since they came to Alma Square, and she now tried to take Graves aside to complain about 'being ordered about' (by Riding). Whatever Graves thought, he did not say it, 'but . . . gave her a plate of tongue & sent her to bed'. By 12 December she had been passed over to the care of two old friends, and arrangements had been made 'to get a Catholic priest to make [the husband] make peace with the Church'. This obscure affair delayed *Belisarius* a little. So did the matter of a broadcast about poetry made by Michael Roberts: it had been arranged by Maisie Somerville, who worked for the BBC. There had been a cut of 'two mentions of Laura's name'. Did Maisie do it? Why? Her 'explanation' was accepted, but no details are given in Graves's diary.

Riding went to see Bosman at Dent 'about the Dictionary' on 16 December. She later told Graves that she had not mentioned his name to Bosman on that occasion so as to identify him as, in any sense, an author of it; but Dent's interest was in fact based on his connection with it, to the extent that partners in the firm spoke at the time of having probably acquired a book 'by Robert Graves' – without mentioning Riding's name.

A week before Christmas they had to ask for protection from an Inspector Thompson of St John's Wood Police Station: Mary Lucy had fled, with her two children, from her husband in Ireland. He was in hot pursuit: 'threatened to kill us as well as Mary.' They had to wire her £10. Graves himself did not mind being 'gunned' for, as he put it; he worked for fifteen hours at *Belisarius* 'feeling half-ill only', not because of Mary Lucy's husband but because of boredom. There was talk of getting Mary Lucy's husband certified as insane, and as this drama proceeded, and people came and went, Graves began to feel physically ill and oppressed again. His bedroom was Riding's workroom, which created difficulties when she wanted to work and he to sleep. Three days before Christmas, struggling with *Belisarius* (the only thing in sight that might bring in real money), he made his bed up in the dining room:

Very bad cough, handle-expenditure, sweats. Listened to L's telephone talks from the extension at my bedside. . . .

It was not a happy Christmas. He had fits of weakness and sweating ('but on my feet'), Riding was taking charge of Mary Lucy's complex affairs (the mad husband was still in Ireland) and issuing just as complex diktats on when and how who should or should not communicate with whom on the matter; the news from Spain – and from Mallorca particularly – was bad; and there was the 'worst fog ever'. He was exceptionally anxious to fulfil his contract for *Belisarius* with Cassell, and said so on Boxing Day: 'Working very hard to complete contract.'

The 'chief event' of 27 December was 'a long talk with Alan and Beryl – Beryl having abstract doubts about the success of the marriage'. The prospective marriage was her own, to Alan.

On 7 January 1938 Graves met Desmond Flower, who was to be his publisher for so long, for the first time: 'Good impression . . . very decent and intelligent.' Cassells had agreed to do Riding's as well as Graves's *Collected Poems*; but on this occasion they talked mostly about *Belisarius*, which was all ready except for Riding's checking. She had made a helpful suggestion earlier, causing Graves to shift the narrative viewpoint: the story is told by Eugenius, the educated eunuch and slave of Belisarius's wife. This improved the novel, which Randall Jarrell too hastily described as a 'G. A. Henty book' without (apparently) recognizing that Henty had his considerable if limited virtues. *Count Belisarius*, which has been translated into seven languages, and which has sold some 250,000 copies, is not one of Graves's best novels – not in the class of *Claudius*, *Wife to Mr Milton*, *The Golden Fleece*, *King Jesus*, *Seven Days in New Crete* – but is a sound historical work, conscientiously done. The accounts of the battles and the strategies underlying them are superb, and the fallen Rome – which the Romans do not realize has fallen – is presented in vivid and cruel detail; but Belisarius himself is a little stiffly noble – the narrator has the more lively personality.

The 'Letter' book had now acquired its published title, *The World and Ourselves*; on Laura's birthday (16 January) he went over this while she went over *Belisarius* ('lots of corrections'). The problems over *The World and Ourselves* were particularly pressing just then, and *Belisarius* was further delayed because of this. This was frustrating.

But some good news did come. After very long and difficult negotiations with the Lawrence trustees and with various publishers, it had finally been decided that Faber would do *T. E. Lawrence to His Biographers* in two volumes: one by Graves, the other by Liddell Hart. Morley of Faber came to Alma Square to talk about it, and was also

> good on subject of Auden who knows how to take care of himself and his sales. His point: 'a dreadful & tedious task digging up his plagiarisms: he will find his own level at the end'.

They had not yet been murdered by Mary Lucy's husband, but had received a letter pleading 'forgiveness between threats'; now they had one calling them 'you cruel shits'.

It was taking – he half-complained in his diary – Riding '2½ hours to correct, I 4 hours to adopt her corrections for each chapter' of *Belisarius*. On 23 January they both went to supper at Maisie Somerville's. Maisie gave Laura 'a large Elizabethan stage ring' – but neither this nor the supper enabled her to escape a royal dressing-down:

> A row: Laura spoke sharply about the way M. treated her talk on poetry [a talk Riding had written for broadcasting and which was unusable]. M. was hurt.

As January drew to a close he was delivering *Belisarius* to Desmond Flower bit by bit, and felt able to begin a dramatization of Riding's Troy novel – this had had a few good reviews, but had sold only a few copies. This was a collaborative effort, to which Riding committed herself – much to her regret later. They worked on it alternately.

On 29 January

> Alan & Beryl married today. Papa Pritchard [Beryl's father] very rude to Alan (not a word) & Mama told her she was throwing her life away.

Later they went to the wedding party, where, Graves wrote, 'the elements did not mix'. The poet Kenneth Allott was present, and Graves noted that he spoke only to him – not to Laura.

It is evident that Riding was exasperating him with her complex talk ('a talk with Laura in which key word was "revive"'), so much so that he went out to Kilburn at night and bought some artificial flowers. And he permitted himself to repeat that she was very 'tired' (as she was). Laura being 'tired' or 'very tired' means, in his diary by now, 'trying, nit-picking'. A day or two later: 'Artificial flowers giving great pleasure.' This is an ironic remark from the author of the recently written 'The Florist Rose':

This wax-mannequin nude, the florist rose,
She of the long stem and too glossy leaf,
Is dead to honest greenfly and leaf-cutter:
Behind plate-glass watches the yellow fogs.

Claims kin with the robust male aeroplane
Whom eagles hate and phantoms of the air,
Who has no legend, as she breaks from legend –
From fellowship with sword and sail and crown.

Experiment's flower, scentless (he its bird);
Is dewed by the spray-gun; is tender-thorned;
Pouts, false-virginal, between bud and bloom;
Bought as a love-gift, droops within the day.

Graves's diary at this point becomes blandly non-committal, covertly punning and sarcastic: 'Solace is unwell – heat and constipation & worms. (Principal cloud over house.)' The list of objects bought continues, a substitute for the bored entries about games of marbles, archery and golf. Among other things are a pair of pinchbeck bell earrings, a butter press, an ostrich egg stand, a silver cloak-clasp, several frames for pictures, a pearl headdress, a scarf ring, a shawl pin, an Indian jug, late Georgian cut-glass vases. . . . These are only a few of the items bought within a period of two weeks – and they mean that Graves (even though he does enjoy buying such objects) was not happy but was trying to tell himself as best he could that he was. 'Feeling well, but fat,' he wrote on 5 February.

In the middle of Riding's efforts to bring 'inside people' together in time to prevent the war, of financial anxiety, illness and despair over the increasing number of threats of total war (casually noted in the diary, but often asterisked) – in the middle of all this there was still time to laugh. Much of the laughter at this time came from Norman Cameron, who was now quite free of Laura. It was in 1938 that he described Stephen Spender as 'The Rupert Brooke of the Depression', and wrote a poem about him in which he is called 'King Sensitive the First'.

On 1 March Graves discovered one of the physical causes of his unease: he had an impacted wisdom tooth, and it had to be removed surgically as soon as possible. This was done at the Duchess Nursing Home on Monday, 7 March. The dental surgeon cut out the tooth next to the Manichean wisdom one, for good measure. On the next day he felt a bit 'jarred', but, stuck at *The World and Ourselves*, heard that *Count Belisarius* would be the April Book Society Choice and that 'Cassells may do Dictionary'. Norman Cameron came to tell him that he had given up a girlfriend because 'of intervention' of someone with the splendidly caddish name of 'Gerald Fox-Edwards' (he invented this, to cheer Robert up). On 10 March he was forced to write: 'Depressed at Belisarius atmosphere of success.' The money could be used to set the world in order, but the success required to bring it in – being his – always led to repercussions, and his diary was open to inspection.

Just after the invasion of Austria, which 'clouded' 12 March for Graves, Maisie Somerville again got into trouble with Riding, who was still struggling to resolve the paradox between cash-in-hand and her disgust at Gravesian worldly success. Maisie, a tough character, 'accused L of changeableness about people'; but she apologized later. Many of those who apologized for their erroneous criticisms of Riding did so because they wanted to remain friends with Graves, who would not speak to them if they didn't. It was in his presence (as many have remarked), nervous though it often was, that they felt at ease.

Despite the jokes from Norman, by 19 March, in the midst of chatter from Len Lye about his prospects as film-maker, talk of protocols, and visitors who bored him, Graves 'became hysterically over-tired'. On 23 March he complained that he had not read a book or written a poem 'except in the course of work' 'for weeks'.

On Saturday 26 March a meeting of twenty-six people was held in Alma Square. It was 'to decide moral action to be taken by inside people: for outside disorders.' Graves lists who was present (and 'Sally absent'); not one was in a position of political power, since these were 'inside people'. Some were privately sceptical then and there (Maisie Somerville, Beryl – who has said that she always felt less awkward at these affairs when Sally was present); others seem embarrassed about it now, perhaps because they were not then. After Riding had talked for half an hour 'then nearly everyone did' – but, Graves added, 'no arguments', not even from Maisie. What was the point? It was agreed that a 'moral protocol' would be drafted on the Sunday week.

This has its farcical side; but it must be remembered that what Riding said (the pith of it is in *The World and Ourselves*) made good sense as historically marginal comment, and, although not original, was so pungently and lucidly stated (owing not a little to Graves's help) as to appear so. During the first four months of 1938 Riding wrote some 400 letters and made three times that number of telephone calls.

On the day Riding gave *The World and Ourselves* to A. S. Watt – who came to get it and was given sherry – she, Alan Hodge and Graves had a discussion which lasted 'for hours'. It was about trying 'to find words for the inside way of doing things: all good words either stiff or tainted.' What they were talking about is commonplace: words such as 'good', 'decency', 'virtue', and so forth have been subjected to so much misuse by 'outside people' – politicians and so forth – that they have become clichés, dead. The assumption that goodness – 'the good' in Plato's sense – is locked up in words is less commonplace. This discussion marks the beginning of the real work on the dictionary.

Graves himself could accept that in *poetry* words should be restored to their proper use. It was part of the line he had been following since the early twenties – a line which has been pursued, curiously enough, more in those non-English poetries of which he takes so little notice, than in English: in Italian and French especially, and in perhaps its purest form in the heartrending Spanish-language poetry of the Peruvian Vallejo.

Riding was still eagerly awaiting the reception of her *Collected Poems*, which she was urging Cassell to publicize to the greatest extent – and to which she had supplied an introduction which (she hoped) would explain her position. Her fervent desire that poetry – by which she meant her own poetry – could become 'international' carried her to the very edge of sanity. She had naively grand expectations of Tom Matthews, whose power at *Time* (as Graves noted in his diary) had suddenly increased: he had been made an executive editor.

Graves's reaction to all this is summed up in 'The Great Grandmother', which he began on the very day Watt collected *The World and Ourselves* from Alma Square, and on which the discussion about words took place. This portrays a sour, dissembling old woman who has 'outlasted all man-uses'; the reader is exhorted, however, to

> Hear her, therefore, as the latest voice;
> The intervening generations (drifting
> On tides of fancy still) ignore.

In biographical terms, this is almost the last poem he wrote in which an unambiguous faith in Riding herself is expressed. He is candid enough about her apparent unpleasantness (the great grandmother is assaulted by the 'false-innocence' of 'music, sighs and roses'), yet still recognizes her as the one voice to listen to; she has no misconceptions about the nature of men.

At this time they were both correcting the proofs of Riding's *Collected Poems*, which were arriving in batches – and he was helping her 'compose a letter about publicity' for them. He hoped that at last she would be acclaimed, that she would find some consolation in this. But his poem about her has built into it certain conditions, best expressed in the line 'She has outlasted all man-uses'. Her solution to the 'lust problem' had been to cut it out; though this had troubled him he had fully accepted it.

None the less, the beautiful weather that March ('the best March there has ever been in England'), and the agreement of many other serious people (for example, Liddell Hart) with the principles expressed in *The World and Ourselves*, put him in a better mood. Moreover, there was a good chance – in the form of an excuse – of getting himself (and Laura) out of England. He went to an accountant on 3 April, and was told that he could only spend three more months in England to avoid tax (the advice he was given was bad, as he later discovered).

But then, one by one, their friends began to withdraw from the project, one on the grounds of 'Christianity': Maisie Somerville 'withdrew, God being Love' (8 April). When he and Laura went to see Len and Jane Lye in early April they met a 'Manchester U history don who believed that the Good Should Differ'. This was A. J. P. Taylor, a friend of Norman Cameron's. Although Laura did not agree that the good should be allowed to differ, she did allow Taylor to drive her and Robert back to Alma Square.

Count Belisarius was published in early April, in a first edition of 20,000 copies. It sold well, and received satisfactory notices, although many of the reviewers complained that Belisarius himself had been presented as 'altogether too noble' in what Graves himself described as his 'highly coloured, evil, dirty' age. He wrote to the *Sunday Times* complaining that he had not falsified history, and that it was

a shocking comment on twentieth century literary taste that when . . . a really good man is shown . . . it must be said that he does not come to life.

At Easter he was correcting the proofs of his own *Collected Poems* and of part of the T. E. Lawrence book, and rewriting the play based on *A Trojan Ending*. He was also devilling for Laura, for her *Lives of Wives*, to which he made a substantial contribution. Too much of his energy was being deflected into 'recommendations' and protocols and 'preambles to protocols'; there is even talk of Riding's working on an advertisement for a shop window. Both were sickened by tne fact that the accounts of atrocities committed on Jews were printed without comment. Riding wrote to the *Telegraph* about the dangers of anti-Semitism, but the editor of the day was no more interested in printing her letter than he was in the plight of Jews.

On 21 April Graves went to Canada House to see a 'mischievous' man whom, as a corporal at Oxford in 1917, he had recommended for a commission. This was Mike Pearson, now better known as (the late) Lester Pearson, Canadian premier. Graves made the visit because he was worried about Karl, and thought that he might be able to find safe refuge in Canada. He had no luck with this plan, although Pearson himself was 'disgusted' with the situation – and with Chamberlain.

It was on that day, too, that Solace – who had been sent to a cats' nursing home in Knightsbridge with bronchitis and other ailments – died.

Through May they worked on the 'Protocol', and (to Graves's private horror) 'rediscovered' 'Universities'. They were up until the early hours almost every night with all this. Often they went to the Café Royal, where on one occasion Graves 'succeeded in not knowing Hugh Walpole [whom he had previously met]. . . .'

On 4 May he records: 'Agreed to let Dent do the dictionary.' For the past ten days everyone who met Riding, or Graves when he was with her, had to talk about 'literal', attention having suddenly been directed to this word. So when John Aldridge came to lunch (4 May) he talked about a 'literal' way of painting pictures; and when (7 May) the poet, critic and (later) detective-story writer Julian Symons called he, too, was subjected to 'literal criticism'.

Symons (*Critical Occasions*, 1966) records that Graves opened the door to him, genially but 'I thought a little nervously'. He took him into a large room, gave him some beer, and said, 'Miss Riding will be here in a moment.'

> She came in, wearing a dark dress reaching almost to the ground, and using a stick to help her lameness. She was . . . beautiful in a ferocious way: sharp nose, thin lips, eyes dark and snapping.

Symons was doing a special American number of his magazine *Twentieth Century Verse*, and had the perspicacity to try to ensure that Riding should be included in it. But she made difficulties: she was, she said, a 'special case'. However, the evening was devoted not to a discussion of her sought-after contribution, but to an anatomization of his poetry.

> 'What you really meant to say in this verse', she would say, 'was . . .'. Had I meant to say just that? I did not feel sure of it, but her own certainty was impressive. When I raised objections she was ready for me. 'But don't you see that what you are saying now is inconsistent with your opening lines'. . . .

She began to have 'the effect of the Wicked Queen in "Snow White"' on him, and he was relieved when Graves, who had gone away to 'finish a chapter' (probably of *The Swiss Ghost*) returned. The subject got around to Auden, whom Symons said he admired. 'There was a good deal of head-shaking', and it was suggested that he have a talk with 'a young friend' of theirs (Alan Hodge) who was writing about Auden. There was 'not much room for disagreement' with Riding, Symons writes.

Symons did go to see Alan Hodge (whom he considerately calls 'X' in his essay), and was indiscreet about his account of Riding. 'There ensued a tremendous correspondence,' Graves recorded, sympathizing with Symons but unable to say so.

Of that evening Graves wrote:

> Laura went over a poem of his with him. It was the first time he had been subjected to literal criticism of his poems and he behaved very decently.

On 15 May he recorded:

> Julian Symons found L *oppressive & wearing* and told Alan so: he told Laura & so a thing started.

On 19 May Desmond Flower wrote to him about Riding's *Collected Poems*. He began by saying that he was sending a proof copy (complete), carefully adding that he, in conjunction with Random House, felt 'privileged', but

> Though Laura Riding's poetic work is regarded with high respect . . . poets and critics of poetry have had some difficulty in characterising the unfamiliar quality which differentiates it from the work of every other woman poet of her time. . . .

He told Graves that on account of this he was writing to a limited number of poets and critics, 'asking them to signalise the appearance of this book with a considered statement' – and he asked for 'yours'.

This was embarrassing to Graves, but he spent a long time on a letter to Flower; part of it was eventually incorporated into the jacket blurb.

About six weeks before this they had decided to leave England for Rennes. On 11 June Alan Hodge went ahead of them, to report on its suitability. They thought they had managed to finish the 'Protocol' ('all but'), but so far had found no publisher for *The World and Ourselves*, which Watt was having difficulty in placing. They also helped Harry Kemp finish what they called 'his book': *The Left Heresy* ('read last chapter of Harry stuff').

On 15 June Alan came back with messages and fruit from Anita at Rennes, and told them that he liked it there and thought they would.

On 20 June Graves's mother came to see him 'in purple silk', he restored the flat 'to its original barbarity', and received 'bright news' to the effect that Little, Brown in America might do the dictionary. On the 25th he was taken by car, with Jenny and his mother, by his brother John to Sam's school, St Christopher's at Letchworth:

Rather a Peace Pledge & eyewash atmosphere but nice children & nice grounds. Turned a picture of Krishnamurti back to wall. . . .

Later he had dinner with René Jean Pleven – 'Breton, Unanimiste, sells telephones' (Pleven, as managing director of the International Cable Company, might have put it differently; he was to be French premier twice after the war). The popular writer Joan Evans (author of *Winged Pharaoh*, dictated to her by spirits) was present; it was a 'difficult even hostile evening', possibly because Graves did not like Madame Pleven, about whom he made unpublishable remarks in his diary. Anyway, on 27 June they 'rejected the Plevens' introduction to Rennes people, as incorrectly phrased in regard to us'. The rejection was ordered by Riding: the introduction had put Graves first. Pleven kindly revised it a few days later, putting Riding first.

Two days previously they learned that Ian Parsons of Chatto & Windus, 'startled by lowness of [a printer's] estimate, agreed . . . to print *World and Ourselves* if L [i.e. Graves] paid half production costs (£50)'. In the end Graves had to pay off a somewhat larger debt, of about £100.

On the morning of 30 June they arrived at St Malo from Southampton. Karl was left behind, though his interests and safety as an alien were being carefully looked after. The secretarial work would now fall on Beryl. But, as 'she was not a writer', she was not apparently considered as either suitable or mature enough to write 'answers' to any questions about how to deal with misbehaving countries – and so forth. She privately felt as competent as some of those who had 'answered' (the crypto-fascist poetaster Lord Gorrell, for example), but kept her own counsel. Quite unexpectedly, and especially to Laura, she would soon make herself noticed, for, although unobtrusive, she had as strong, and unusual, a character as any of the members of the party who put up at the Hotel Centrale, Rennes, that night.

Chapter Twenty-One
1938–39

I

At first they took separate flats in the town: one for Robert and Laura, one for Alan and Beryl. They found the place 'lovely' – according, at least, to Graves, who was clearly delighted to shake the dust of London from his feet. They heard unhappy news of Deyá from Margarita, the doctor's sister, who had by now made her way to Rennes. Everyone, including Gelat and the doctor, were 'friends now at Deyá – for fear of the outcome'. There was 'compulsory mass', and the Germans and the Italians were in full control. Gelat's goods had been seized. Such was the impact of the Franco terror on this small Balearic community: to force enemies (except for the Church Triumphant in the shape of the priest) together, in fear. As the good Spaniards then said, 'after the war no man would be honoured who had not been in prison'.

The flats proved unsuitable, and within three days they were looking for a country house in the surrounding district. On 5 July they discovered the Château de la Chevrie at Montauban de Bretagne (thirty kilometres from Rennes), to let furnished at about £40 (Graves's estimate) a year. It was 'seemingly perfect', and they agreed to take it. This was to be the last home Riding and Graves would share.

While they waited to sign the lease (with Mme La Comtesse de Kerellouan, the owner) Graves worked at Riding's *Lives of Wives*; meanwhile she went over the fourth section of his *Collected Poems*, which had not yet gone to the printer. On 14 July they moved in, finding the place well ornamented but filthy with rat dirt, and dust, and with unaired beds. They got Laura's room ready first.

By Graves's birthday on 24 July they had the place clean, and had settled in; a kitten, doubtless at Beryl's insistence (or by her stratagem), had been acquired; the postman turned out to be a drunkard. Riding was 'very tired', but starting on Aristotle's wife. The cook, called

Modeste, used 'her deafness strategically so as not to cook the way I told her'. Graves started riding a bicycle for the first time since 1928.

On his birthday Dorothy Simmonds, a sculptor they had known from London days, arrived; the kitten-gave him a present of a packet of Gauloises. They began to settle into a routine, fighting battles with bats, which kept getting into the house, and with a swarm of bees which lived in one of the chimneys.

Graves, preparing his *Collected Poems*, had now given up working on any project that would bring in real money except (he hoped) the dictionary. On 1 August he and Alan spent a long time on 'Dictionary Americanisms for Laura's report'. On 4 August he wrote: 'Started real work on dictionary.' He regarded this as a prospective source of income, a rival to *Roget* which readers would find better arranged. Had he not done so, he would have engaged himself, simultaneously, on a commercial project.

They had a number of Spanish friends in the district; some were exiles from Deyá, others, all in the fruit and vegetable trade, had settled in Rennes long before the beginning of the Civil War; they saw a good deal of them, and were helped by them in their battle with the bees. Norman Cameron visited them over the bank holiday, and Dorothy's husband Montague Simmonds joined them as a guest shortly afterwards (he was soon instructed, by Laura, to write a book on seasons). David Reeves, who was still working on his furniture book with Laura, became a resident for some months – James Reeves and his sister Ethel came only for one short visit.

On 11 August Graves's last entry reads: 'We are getting very fond of Beryl.' This 'We' may confidently be read as 'I'. Graves had started to notice her as a person. The next day he worked hard at the dictionary, finding himself 'staring at a word-group – *minutiae* & *smithereens*', and late at night while in the kitchen

> answered 'yes' unthinkingly to a voice that addressed me as Marthe. This kitchen ghost Beryl already knows. It left an old-fashioned poker on the stove; which disappeared when she touched it.

This was his characteristic way of bringing Beryl into focus. She begins, from now on, to be mentioned regularly in his diary; and it was at Rennes in fact that they fell in love. There was a sense in which, as Graves said to me many years later, 'neither of us wanted it to happen'; but it proved irresistible to both – which was really the point he was making. They discovered that a rapport existed between them; they knew what each other was thinking without having to speak.

Beryl Hodge was born Beryl Pritchard, on 22 February 1915, in Heath Drive, Hampstead. Her father, Sir Harry Pritchard, was a distinguished solicitor who did not retire from practice until some time after his ninetieth birthday. In 1935–36 he was President of the Law Society. The lawyer who wrote his obituary notice began by remarking: 'The passing of Sir Harry Pritchard cannot go unnoticed by those who have experience of the machinery of Parliament,' and went on to praise his skill and integrity as a parliamentary agent. He was wholly responsible for the exceedingly complex Kent Water Act of 1955: 'there was no moment at which Sir Harry was not in complete command of every detail and every problem.'

I met him in 1949, when he was eighty-one, and took him for sixty. He had the extreme dignity – which is by no means pomposity – of the (now) old-fashioned honest lawyer, and sometimes a faintly sardonic look which suggested that he was more aware of what was going on than he was prepared to admit. His favourite book by his (eventual) son-in-law was *Seven Days in New Crete*. I think it appealed to his humour – the kind of humour that becomes highly developed in solicitors because they inevitably get to know how odd life really is. Like Beryl – who was one of five children – he was unobtrusive but possessed of great character. At the age of ninety he was rushed to hospital to be operated on for acute appendicitis – he was carried from his house in a chair but refused to leave without his hat. He was home in a few days.

From school at Queen's College in Harley Street, Beryl went up to Oxford, in 1933, to the Society of Home Students (now St Anne's), and read PPE (Philosophy, Politics and Economics). She overlapped with Graves's niece Sally, but did not meet her at Oxford – Sally being a year ahead of her, and in a different school. Her friends were either left-wing Socialists or Communists, although she herself never joined a political party. She is too naturally humane to attach herself to any specific doctrine; but she has never been known to express any strong sympathy for full-blooded Toryism as such – for although Alan Hodge was always a Tory, he was not one of the Colonel Blimp variety. One of her chief interests is in the ordinary lives of ordinary people; this has been mistaken as a 'liking for the drab'; but she knows that what looks ordinary is not, that it is on the contrary extraordinary.

She met Alan Hodge at Oxford, and recollects that he was even then struggling with his *Year of Damage*; but she was only a friend until just after both left the university in 1936. Now she found herself in this strange situation, as typist for (mostly) Laura, whose treatment of Robert she had quietly registered, and whose scarcely qualified hatred of him she had discerned long before any of the clever people who had been asked to answer the 'Protocol' questions. At times she would take as many as twenty letters at a time from Laura's dictation. What she thought of them she did not say: she was not expected to. Her job was typing – and, as Graves had put in his diary, 'groceries and provisions'. With Graves once more becoming distraught, Riding increasingly engaged in stopping the war, and her husband Alan going into a state of vagueness, she was the only one completely sensible, sane, practical person among them; David Reeves was never truly involved – his presence was an accident resulting from his youthful lack of direction, and because he was James's brother. Beryl began (Riding later wrote in a letter) exchanging glances with Robert across the table at meal times. They both knew; and if they had arranged to leave then and there they, and Alan Hodge, would have avoided a terrifying experience in America. But they could not; it was as if Graves and Alan Hodge were under some kind of spell. The Rennes months were like the prologue to a sixth act tacked onto an Elizabethan tragedy – a sixth act which would end in madness, cruelty, evil and above all in pretence: a microcosm of the Fascist explosion which was just then nearing the point when even the wormlike Chamberlain would have to turn.

Graves's mood is reflected in a poem he wrote on or just after Assumption Day, Monday, 16 August – when Hitler was expected to invade Czechoslovakia, and when everything went wrong at the house: 'a bad day. Cold and cross.' He made jam, got interrupted and spoiled it; Alan was annoyed when Riding teased him; a guest who had amorous problems was 'hanging around like a skeleton at a feast'; 'everyone crossly peeling mushrooms'. . . . The poem, 'Assumption Day', is not important as a poem, but rather as an indication of how he felt as he awaited Nemesis – whatever form that might take – in that summer in Brittany. For he dared not acknowledge to himself that he had fallen in love, for the first (and only) time in his life, with a person – rather than with someone who represented something he needed, such as a wife, or a Muse. A man already in love with love, treated like dirt ('a little boy'), his work derided or patronized at best, his health not then good, even he could hardly stand the strain. The feast that 'nobody could welcome' at the beginning of this poem is primarily this love – but he quickly allows this aspect of it to die out. Not for some time would he be able to write the truest of all his love poems.

But 'Assumption Day' has another and sourer dimension. Assumption Day is a Roman Catholic festival: it celebrates the assumption of the Blessed Virgin Mary into heavenly glory (a belief unknown in the early Christian Church). The poem, admittedly *mal réussi*, is pasted into his diary in typed form.

> What was wrong with the day, doubtless,
> Was less the unseasonable gusty weather
> Than the bells ringing on a Monday morning
> For a church-feast that nobody could welcome –
> Not even the bell-ringers.
>
> The pond had shrunk: its yellow lilies
> Poked rubbery necks out of the water.
> I paused and sat down crossly on a tussock,
> My back turned on the idle water-beetles
> That would not skim, but floated.
>
> A wasp, a humble-bee, a blue-fly
> Uncooperatively at work together
> Were sucking honey from the crowded blossom
> Of a pale flower whose name someone once told me –
> Someone to be mistrusted.
>
> But, not far off, our little cow-herd
> Made mud-cakes, with one eye on the cattle,
> And marked each separate cake with his initials.
> I was half-tempted by the child's example
> To rescue my spoilt morning.

The third stanza is cryptic: who or what was sucking honey 'uncooperatively' from a pale flower – and what is this pale flower, whose name he had once been told, but by 'someone to be mistrusted'? It is not hard to guess what represents whom. This was as near as he could come to expressing his true feelings, and it is necessarily enigmatic. But the disgust and hopelessness that were forming in him are perfectly evident. All he has to say about it is: 'A poem about being cross' (16 August) and 'I finished a poem in 3 drafts about Assumption Day' (18 August).

Apart from housework, Graves was mostly working at the dictionary – work later to be acknowledged by Riding as 'extensive sorting'. On 26 August he worked on the dictionary all day; but the 'chief event' was the receipt of a letter from Norman Cameron telling them that 'he could not continue as Protocol secretary', a position which he had been persuaded to take on, against his wishes, by Riding. He was just then on the verge of a marriage that was to prove his shortest and least happy – and he felt that he could not continue to serve a cause in which he did not believe. He was deliberately keeping his distance, and was the only person – except Beryl – who understood the extreme gravity of Graves's situation with respect to Riding, to whom he would have been more outspoken had it not been for his friend.

The next day, depressed by this, Graves was

> Working all day on Laura's proofs of World & Ourselves. With a headache.

On 31 August they telephoned an old friend

> to inquire if anything can be done to rescue Norman from this disastrous marriage. She replied 'Nothing: & says he's happier than ever in his life – in spite of [his prospective wife's] having quarrelled with all his best friends'. . . . She prophesies some sticky disaster: as Laura does too.

On top of this there came more news from Deyá: Graves described the circumstances there as 'horrors'; the fascist priest was now 'rampant'. But he invented a new marbles game with Beryl, and was finding more and more consolation in her company. On 3 September he writes:

> Norman's wedding-day: God help him! (Ill-omened cries of screech-owl last night reminded us of him.)

Their friend, who was intimately concerned in Norman's affairs, wrote them an anguished letter from London, which Graves put into his diary.

In early September everyone was engaged on the correction of the proofs of *The World and Ourselves*, but on 8 September Graves 'had short break at 4 o'clock to do a little of my own *Poems* proofs' – and, on that day, too, there was a 'contretemps about the black kitten: Beryl became possessive'. But there was something he liked about her possessiveness, since on the next day he recorded:

> Proofs all day: only ½ an hour's break till 12.15 a.m. Beryl had Eileen [a friend of hers who had turned up on a short visit] fortunately.

He wrote the same on the next day. Both had the same feelings, without needing to describe them, about the bleak oppression of the times – and of the circumstances of that place. Graves, who had had no woman to turn to for human sympathy for the whole of his life, was now turning irresistibly and with a natural ease, astonishing to him, to Beryl.

She won her battle over the black kitten, since by 11 September it was well established, and named Bellamy.

II

On 15 September, the day Riding's *Collected Poems* were published, Chamberlain made what Graves called his 'fantastic visit' to Hitler; the drunken postman fell off his bicycle. Two days later Beryl felt unwell; Graves described this as 'notable'.

Proofs done, it was back to the dictionary. Graves noted his disgust at the Anglo-French surrender to Hitler ('more and more depressing and shameful', a 'Rogues' meeting'); but work at the dictionary was 'habitual already'.

A comic note intruded into the sombre gloom of that autumn: Mary Lucy's husband wrote from Ireland to apologize to Graves and Riding, and to say that his wife had been ill, and that the psychologists said 'he isn't mad but madly jealous; and the cure would be for her to sleep with him'.

Graves now found an excellent opportunity of attending to Beryl: he found that she had made '33 mistakes in 24 pp.' of Laura's *Lives of Wives*; a little later (14 October) he had

a little tiff with Beryl because I noticed the typewriter was dirty in her attic & brought it down to clean – but all right.

This tells us that he had now reached the stage at which he could have a 'tiff' with Beryl, and could record that he had made it up with her – an important stage in any relationship. (He knows nothing about typewriters and cannot operate one.)

Riding's *Collected Poems*, which sold few copies in England or America, got off to a bad start with a hostile review in the *Times Literary Supplement*; the editor refused to print Graves's letter of reply, and Riding cancelled her subscription 'after ten years'. But correspondence over the matter dragged on. Everyone worked on making jams and other preserves, and there was much housework and playing of games; but mostly it was, as Graves put it on 23 October, 'Dictionary, headache, aspirin, fine weather, more aspirin.'

At the end of October he started the poem that was to end up as 'The Suicide in the Copse' (which first appeared in *Work in Hand*); here he successfully distanced himself from his predicament. The poem asks whether a suicide, staring down at his shattered skull, had meant 'this': he was not contented, and had failed to 'liberate himself from duns and dolts/By change of scene', which had been his purpose. He now found himself with nowhere to go, and hearing from somewhere a 'roll of laughter': 'He had looked so on his wedding day/And the day after.' He had nothing whatever to do but read whatever blew into the copse where his body lay:

> A year-old sheet of sporting news,
> A crumpled schoolboy essay.

In other words, however bad life is, it is worth living because there are things in it better than mistaken marriages, out-of-date sports news, and boring essays. . . . The sense of hope is felt here only obliquely, but it is pointed at; its source was, certainly, not Laura Riding but Beryl. One of her attributes he was learning to love was her peculiar wit, very different in kind from that of Riding, in that it did not claim to come from the ultimate.

When tasks are being performed, Graves is a terror: he does not (cannot) take a rest himself, and is therefore caustic towards those who do. If one is performing a task with him, and stops off for a cigarette or a sit-down, he will bark out some such question as: 'Are you a bad life?' or 'Got a weak heart?' Beryl early saw this in him. He records (29 October 1938) that while they were jam-making (it is a mystery who ate all the jam and preserves made at La Chevrie) she had been set to stir. Presumably she was looking bored, for he asked her: 'Frankly, are you bored with the stirring?' 'No, not frankly,' she answered.

By the end of October they had almost finished the specimen pages of definitions through which they hoped to clinch the deal about the dictionary. Most of the real work had been done by Graves and Alan Hodge.

Alan was also feeling the strain, for on the evening of 5 November he 'came home very drunk [or: Pernod] & saying that whatever he said was true.' There may have been an element of mockery of Riding in this; or perhaps his long sessions at defining words had exhausted him. Any temporary loss of inhibition in the presence of Laura Riding would almost inevitably have led to such imitativeness – with or without a mocking element.

On 8 November Graves contented himself with simply listing the present incumbents of La Chevrie: 'Laura, Alan, Beryl, David [Reeves], Dorothy [Montague Simmonds had left], me', and he added the names of the two servants they had engaged. The next day was David Reeves's birthday, and in the evening they played a word game: someone asked a silent question, and it was answered 'with a composite sentence, a word each'. To Alan's silent question 'What is wrong with Montauban?' the answer came out as: 'Rather hesitantly she said: I undertake no responsibility for this wretched circumstance in which we find you placed.'

On 21 November he worked all day at a poem; but at midnight he gave it to Beryl and asked her to burn it. In his diary he wrote: 'I destroyed' but deleted this and substituted 'I asked Beryl to burn it, which she did.' One can guess what he was doing; and Beryl did not have to guess.

Good news came at the end of November: Karl, with help from Robert, had 'got permanent leave to live and work in England'.

The entries in his diary for December are perfunctory. He mentions the first (bad) review of his *Collected Poems*. The Lawrence book, issued in a limited edition of 500 signed copies, was published in America (in England a few weeks later), and he was well satisfied with it. All his working time was taken up with the dictionary and with *The Swiss Ghost*; on 5 December he is unusually casual about Riding, who, he says, is 'writing something about poets'.

On 10 December a new name is suddenly mentioned in the diary: Schuyler Jackson. His was one of the bunch of letters received that day which gave it, Graves wrote in dutiful echo, 'a lovely colour'. Riding's interest in him was now quite open – even though he had refused to endorse the 'Protocol'. She believed, erroneously, that he was securely in the position of a 'contributing editor to *Time*'. She has since called him, variously, 'poet', 'farmer', one 'learned in English and American poetry', 'critical author', and a 'scholar of poetry'. Farmer, though financially unsuccessful, he surely was: he had a true feeling for the proper use of the earth. It was his greatest gift. At this point it is necessary only to examine the realities of Jackson's post on *Time*: Riding, it seems, was deluding herself – though she was led astray by

Tom Matthews, who was confusedly anxious for her to meet his old friend in whom he had so much doubt.

In 1938 Matthews actually had found Jackson a place on *Time*. He was attached to the Books department – but his name did not appear on the masthead, and he was scarcely ever to be seen in the office. (Riding's assertion, made in 1973, that he had been 'Poetry Editor of *Time*' is incorrect.) Matthews, however, could cover for him. Jackson was known by sight to only two or three members of the staff. But he did receive all the volumes of verse sent in to *Time* by publishers, and on these he made 'painstaking', but never printed, reports. But as Christmas approached he had an idea: he would write a review of the year's poetry. *Time* – under Matthews's vigorous persuasion – tried it out.

The review divided the authors under notice into three categories: poets, poetasters and poeticules (a word Matthews remembered from Swift). The review was not written by Jackson alone, who, when the time came to put his ideas on paper, found that he was unable to do so. Matthews, by now a practised journalist, gave up an entire weekend to producing it with him. The result was a hybrid: Matthews, who was responsible for the writing, praised the Riding *Collected Poems* in terms he knew Riding would approve, but incorporated the hardly original notion which Jackson had formed on his own – that words 'should make sense'. When the review arrived in Rennes early in the year Graves described it as 'daring', and, unequivocally, as by 'Tom and Schuyler Jackson'. (He had himself been writing – as he records – to Matthews, and any suggestion he may himself have made about the review would have been gratefully taken up; some sentences in it are actually by him.) There is nothing whatever unusual about the piece itself except that it takes pains to praise Riding's *Collected Poems* in terms near to those in which she, in her notice to the reader, 'defines' them; but it does not go into the same sort of detail as she does. 'I have learned from my poems what, completely and precisely, the scope of poetry is. . . . Antagonism to the large claim is generally of an animal kind. . . .' The *Time* treatment was not (and could not be) critically adequate; and other reviews (there were not many, though extra payment was offered by Graves to the publisher, Desmond Flower, to give the book wider publicity than poetry is usually accorded) were either unsatisfactory or downright rude.

But Riding wanted the attention of more than the poetry-reading public, and in this she was unrealistic. (When in December 1938 Graves wrote, as Riding's mouthpiece, admonishing Desmond Flower for having been 'sarcastic' both about Graves's own protest at being described as a 'significant artist' and about Riding's 'active interest in the sale of her books', he qualified the last remark by the parenthetic, and partly conciliatory, 'I am myself lazy in this respect, I confess'.) She tried altogether too hard, and her efforts to publicize herself looked and were both frenetic and pathetic. Besides, the *Collected Poems* is too long: she had, by the time she came to compile it, reached a certain exasperation with poetry, largely on the grounds that it had not got her (overstrained) ideal anywhere at all. Certain of the longer, self-proselytizing poems tend, in the context of the large volume, to overwhelm the lucid beauty of the shorter ones. The notice 'To the Reader' completed the disaster: the tone of the third century AD sounds awkward in the twentieth. Rigorously tactless immodesty looks unseemly.

Graves, by contrast, while he would, and did, struggle with the given, with the 'world he never made', always knew better than to try to outwit it, or destroy it. He knew he was human, a mixture of good and ill. Riding would not thus robustly accept that she was human. She insisted that she was *not* a stranger, not afraid (though there is no record of her having claimed to make the world, and I don't think she believes she did: she merely claims to understand the workings of the Universe).

III

At the beginning of 1939 Graves summarized the position:

> *at* La Chevrie Montauban: rented from Countess de Keroullan at £40 a year furnished. Present: Laura, me, Dorothy, Beryl, Alan [David Reeves had returned to London]. . . .
> Relations: good.
> Health: good.
> Work: *Dictionary of Exact Meanings*: contract not yet signed but general understanding with *Dent* & *Little Brown*. Laura generally supervising, Alan & I sorting out (about 25,000) words for definition – have about 17,000 so far – arranging them in groups. *The Swiss Ghost* Constable has option. Laura and I have done all but 3 chapters, thoroughly. Of these three I have written out rough draft of 2½. . . .

This entry conceals his financial anxiety, and his worries about the difficulties posed by life at La Chevrie, where the atmosphere was too tense to allow of proper work. *The World and Ourselves* had incurred a debt of £125 to Chatto & Windus 'less sales'. He felt himself gradually being excluded from Riding's most serious intellectual projects; his faith in them was ebbing, despite the last violent throes of his habitual protectiveness towards her.

Robert Graves is not interested in hedgehogs. But the fate of a hedgehog allowed him to console himself. He was able to record it in his diary, and thus direct his attention where he wanted to. The black farm dog found it first, by following a track of blood on the snow. Beryl took it up to her attic. It was hibernating; but gradually it began to uncurl. She gave it milk and it 'walked about her attic'.

One of their maids, Léonie, who slept in the attic next to Beryl's, was disturbed by its scratching in the night. In Beryl's absence she put it into a grandfather clock. This clock had stood in the hall, but had been 'punished', for falling on Graves on several occasions – as though 'attacking' him – by being exiled to one of the many outhouses. And on 3 January Graves wrote:

> Beryl's hedgehog when it wakes up from its interrupted hibernation will say: 'I had the craziest dream – something about bread and milk and a typewriter and a grandfather clock'.

He knew, in the words of one of the poets whom he loved unreservedly (Hardy), that Beryl was a woman 'who noticed such things', one of whom it might truly be said that she 'strove that such innocent creatures should come to no harm/But . . . could do little for them. . . .' The understanding that was growing between them was disturbing them both, and both took to dissolving it in jokes and play – and glances. He was to draw on this experience of tacit and telepathic understanding between lovers in *Wife to Mr Milton*, in his account of the relationship between the unhappy Mrs Milton and her lover Mun.

On 6 January Graves noted that Laura 'wrote to Chamberlain'. She was ill for most of this time, and planning to move to America. But whatever Graves's thoughts about Chamberlain's possible reactions and about Laura's now visible disintegration of health, he worked hard at a poem called 'The Beast':

> Beyond the Atlas roams a love-beast;
> The aborigines harry it with darts.
> Its flesh is esteemed, though of a fishy tang
> Tainting the eater's mouth and lips.

Ourselves once, wandering in mid-wilderness
And by despair drawn to this diet,
Before the meal was over sat apart
Loathing each other's carrion company.

This poem is as much testimony to his *desire* to keep good faith with Laura Riding's 'point of view' about sex (as he had once described it) as to his newly awakened feelings for Beryl.

The position was complicated: Alan Hodge now began to suspect that he was wasting his time with Riding's work, although he continued to believe in her; Beryl was scrupulous as to his feelings, but was unable to remove herself from Robert's company – and Robert himself was hanging at the edge of an abyss, a fact of which she was fully conscious.

The 'First Protocol' had been printed and sent out in early autumn. It had been 'endorsed' by some seventy people. Now, in the midst of work on *Lives of Wives*, leaving much of the 'supervision' of the 'dictionary of exact meanings' to Graves, Riding was frenetically writing letters to these endorsers, taking each of them with great seriousness. She had on 7 December 'started a system of letters to people who get in the way'; she had begun this process with 'Michael Roberts & [his wife] Janet [Adam] Smith'. That 'system' immediately cut down the number of endorsers, or at the very least offended them – and thus caused her further frustration. Some dared to argue with her. She reacted with bad headaches, fainting spells and weakness. On 11 January she wrote to the endorsers 'about active friendship', and everyone present at Rennes discussed such matters as 'obligations of friendship' – even out of Laura's presence. Still no one dared to challenge her authority, and probably only Alan and Beryl would have seen any point in such a challenge. The enforcer of her authority was Graves, still maintaining his role as the lion guarding her. His persistence was obstinate; but Riding, who hated and resented this protectiveness, who yearned to be disciplined (so odd is human nature), had put herself into the difficult position of having availed herself of it. In this as in many other ways his 'influence' over her far outweighs hers over him.

Because of his onrush of new feeling towards Beryl, and in a brave attempt to dispel the nightmare he was being sucked into, Graves suddenly forced himself into a false posture of gratitude towards Laura Riding, which expressed itself in rather pious diary entries, and much talk about her goodness to others. It was almost as if he were willing her to fulfil her potentiality for good.

The increasingly bad news from Spain – Franco was by now clearly winning – 'somehow' (he said) did not affect them. Sally wrote to them of the imminence of war, 'but this makes no real sense'. It was his last effort: now there was serious and open talk of their all going to America to stay in 'Pennsylvania for a few months near the Jacksons & Tom & Julie'. He walked with Alan near the lake and talked desperately of Laura 'as focus of love amongst us'. Alan said nothing, but thought to himself 'focus of disease amongst us'. Graves was strangely happy because he had fallen in love; but sublimated his new feelings into an intensity of devotion to the old cause. He wrote of having received a 'very good letter from Schuyler Jackson.' He went along with Laura's new discovery, whose virtues had first been transmitted to her by Tom Matthews, of whose opinion he had nothing but contempt.

On 22 January difficulties over the dictionary presented themselves. McIntyre of Little, Brown wrote to Riding 'throwing I. A. Richards & semantics at Laura'. She found his letter so hard to answer that she had to seek Graves's expert help. It was only thus that a contract was obtained.

The 4000-word answer resulted in a cable from McIntyre announcing that all objections raised 'by so-called experts' were now met. Graves and Alan Hodge regarded themselves as participants in the dictionary, and Riding regarded them as such: money to come on signature of the contract would go into the 'joint finances', and Alan would get his share.

By 7 February, largely because of what Graves described as a number of 'disciplinary Letters' that had gone out, the number of endorsers of the 'Protocol' had been reduced from seventy to forty-five.

Laura Riding said to him, 'I write so well anyone might mistake me for a hypocrite' (diary).

He was going more and more often for walks with Beryl, alone; and after one of these he wrote 'Feeling thoroughly happy, somehow'. It was in these days that he wrote 'The Thieves' and 'A Love Story', the one ('Lovers in the act dispense/With such meum-tuum sense') suddenly recognizing a 'single heart' that 'grieves' for the greed inherent in the sexual act, and the other for the first time looking at his relationship with Riding in long perspective, and with an end to it in mind. He felt so good, in fact – despite everything else – that on 11 February he, Beryl, Laura, Dorothy Simmonds and Alan went off to Rennes and had a lunch 'in honour of demise of Yeats'. Only a day or two before he had had the chance to get in a crack at brother Charles in the *Daily Mail*:

> My brother Charles Graves and I are not avid readers of each other's works. Hence it is not surprising that he is under the impression that I have deserted poetry 'for the more profitable medium of prose', and for all I know he may lately have been taking a contrary course.
>
> But for myself: Though I have now and then written novels or biographies on the side, my principal work has always been poems; and my Collected Poems, condensed from a dozen or more volumes, were published this winter.
>
> As for the late W. B. Yeats, from a mention of whom in 'I See Life' [a regular gossip feature in the *Mail*] this point arose – his father told our father some 40 years ago: 'Willie has just discovered a very profitable by-path in poetry.' This remains a just criticism.

By 2 March the decision to go to America had been made, although they did not yet know exactly where they were going to stay (but Laura herself had fixed notions on the subject). They asked Tom to suggest somewhere, and he and his wife Julie thought hard about it. By 7 March reservations had been made on the *Paris* – the boat which had brought Laura Riding to Europe at the end of 1925. Early the next morning Riding called Graves into her room to say 'sleepily "Love is a beautiful insincerity; & true".' She, too, had premonitions, perhaps even faint intentions.

But Graves was more concerned, in his heart, about Beryl's only apparently more commonplace predicament: by this time there were two cats, Bellamy and Nono. The plan then was that Bellamy was to be left behind, but Nono taken. Graves consoled Beryl by telling her 'that Bellamy had been given too much love. He does not appreciate it being French: he is just a "beau chat" for a serious établissement.'

Laura, who had suddenly decided to give up smoking (she soon resumed it), was 'very nervous indeed', suffering from bad headaches, and wrapped up in dreams of America. On 13 March a friend, the artist Joän Junyer, arrived from Paris with his wife Dolores: he was a refugee from Franco, and had had a very bad time escaping from Franco Spain, which Chamberlain had by now been happy to recognize.

> Glad there was no political talk: but they told us of the dreadful conditions in the Spanish refugee camps and the brutality of the French police.

On 16 March there was a 'long talk about relations of L. A. B. & me'. Riding was trying to make sure that she remained in control. Unfortunately Graves stuck to his old Laura-protective habits, so that nothing really got said. He might as well have written: 'Instructions from L about relationships.'

Mid-March was 'very difficult', although on 20 March, after a 'queer day' a 'letter from Schuyler. . . made things less strange' (this has two meanings; but Schuyler and Laura certainly now had a good idea of what they were going to be up to, though they had not set eyes on each other). On 28 March Graves recorded, in very shaky handwriting, that 'Norman counted himself out.' Norman was always very dear to him, and this sensible decision of his weighed heavily with him: he respected it, though he could not say so. Two days later David Reeves, who had turned up from London, announced that he, too, would come to America. Everyone, including Riding, was apprehensive about money. But she had hopes of one thing: ironically, it was called *Time*. She did not realize that Jackson's 'career' at *Time* had virtually ended with the one review of her poems which he had half-contributed to it. It is true that he had suggested to Matthews that he would 'perfect' *all* the copy before the magazine went to press, but nothing had come of that – and he did, with Riding's considerable help, write one more clumsy poetry review for the paper. But by now she had convinced herself that Jackson and Jackson alone had written the piece saying that her *Collected Poems* was the 'book of books of the mid-twentieth century'. This reviewer's cliché excited her out of her habitual intellectual acuteness. (That Jackson had or would have an important place on a paper with a circulation of (at that time) 700,000, and a readership of several times that number, was, while not to his discredit, an impossibility.) *Time*, she convinced herself, would provide the scope she needed to stop war. (At present there was no threat of war in America: why should she stay in Europe and, her letter to Chamberlain unanswered, watch her failure to discipline 'misbehaving nations'?) Jackson was soon to persuade her that her long visit to Europe had been a great mistake. All Graves could do was to write down that the imminence of war seemed to make no sense. He knew that what Sally had written to him was right; but what could he say – unless he abandoned Laura? But he could not allow himself to entertain such thoughts. Had he known for certain what was to come, then he would have cut his losses, and left then and there. But he was still infected with Riding-esque hope; he had to see into the darkness and ruthlessness of its depths before he would accept the truth. Although he made such statements as 'Everyone very happy', he was far from happy, except for a few moments – such as this:

> Nono smelling plum blossom on the red tiled top of the peach-wall in the garden: against the blue sky watched by Beryl & me. Then the others came out. . . .

On 3 April he heard that *Count Belisarius* had won the Femina Vie Heureuse Prize; but this gave him no relief from his stiff back – or Laura from her rheumatism. But despite pains and tiredness, and an annoyance that had been caused by Dorothy Simmonds's alleged behaviour towards Laura (the details of this are highly complex and tedious: fundamentally it came down to a 'judgement' that Dorothy was modelling herself 'awkwardly' on Laura, an especially serious form of lese-majesty), work on the dictionary went on – until on 9 April Alan and Robert sorted out their words into boxes. Everyone was confident that they would shortly be sailing on the *Paris*; and Laura instructed a temporary guest on how to, and how not to, 'talk'; Bellamy went to the Hotel Ouest.

On 16 April Graves closed his diary entry with ' "Nimrod": bond of immediate intelligence between L & B.' This was typical wishful thinking apropos of 'B'. But it again demonstrates how important she had become to him.

Tom Matthews had been obsessed by Schuyler Jackson and Laura Riding ever since he met them. They puzzled him; and so he was excited at the prospect of bringing them together. He and his wife Julie and their children lived in Princeton, in Mercer County, New Jersey. Jackson and his wife Kit and their four children lived about twenty miles away, just over the border, at New Hope, in Bucks County, Pennsylvania. On the Jacksons' farm there stood the ruin of an eighteenth-century farmhouse, still a shell, which a builder said could be repaired for the then very large sum of $25,000. Matthews had, some time before this, generously tried to give some money to Schuyler – who had refused him in sullen silence. He had also told Matthews that whereas his own excessive drinking was 'destructive', his, Tom's, was 'disgusting'. A fine distinction. But now, for the sake of what he would soon call the 'now dawn of human innocence' (and so on), he allowed himself to accept the loan of $25,000 from Matthews – who agreed to take repayments at the rate of $50 a month in 'rent'. It was not a practicable arrangement (it was in fact crazy), and Matthews actually got only $200 back from his 'investment' – nor was he the only 'investor'. Graves, too, was to lose money on this. The house was to be called Nimrod's Rise, although it was later referred to by Riding as simply 'The Rise'. Nimrod (*Genesis* x, 8) is the first to be 'a mighty one on earth', a 'mighty hunter', the founder of the Assyrian Empire – a counterpart of Gilgamesh of Babylonian mythology. 'Nimrod' in those last days in Brittany meant the future community on the Jacksons' farm in the house called Nimrod's Rise. Whether Jackson fancied himself as a new Nimrod (whose literary reputation is as a hunter of men), or as co-founder of à new Assyrian Empire, is not clear. However, Nimrod or not, his own miserable marriage was on the verge of breaking up, though at his own and not at his wife's wish. A year before he met Riding this generous but wholly irresponsible man told Tom Matthews that he was going to leave his wife – that he was in love with an ice-skater, who loved him in return. But he did not – unfortunately for his wife as it turned out – leave her at this time.

The visit to America, however, was understood by Graves (and by Alan and Beryl) to be of only a few months' duration. On 17 April Graves wrote about the kitten Nono: 'he is to go *en pension*. . . . waiting for us to take him to Deyá.' The ostensible plan was to return to Deyá as soon as things settled down: Mallorca was, after all, remote from the centre of government, and Deyá even more so. Graves at least was mesmerized by Riding's apparent refusal to consider war as inevitable (possibly he did not realize that she was thinking in terms of America), although it is quite clear that by now he knew, in his heart, that it was.

The plan was for Robert and Laura to go to America on the *Paris*, while Alan and Beryl would follow on via England. But 'DERNIERE MINUTE: TERRIBLE INCENDIE A BORD DU PAQUEBOT "PARIS"', Robert and Laura read in a newspaper bought *en route* for Le Havre. So, having already left Alan and Beryl and Dorothy Simmonds, they were ferried to Southampton, from which they sailed on 21 April 1939, on the *Champlain*. David Reeves joined them at Southampton.

Graves was making a journey to the underworld with Riding; but he would return without her, and, luckily for him and for literature, into the care of someone quite as remarkable – though in no way as spectacular – as the returning exile.

Chapter Twenty-Two
1939–40

I

Graves spent much of the voyage to America writing a 'long chronicle letter to Beryl & Alan'. They arrived at New York on 28 April, where they were met by 'Tom, Julie, Schuyler, Katherine'. Jackson drove them to Princeton in his truck. 'I sleep in Tom's study in basement, Laura next door.' Not much, wrote Graves, was said. David Reeves took lodgings along the street, '5 doors from Einstein'.

On the next day Graves at last knew for certain that it was all up. He headed his diary entry, 'Ten years ago Laura fell.' He certainly meant that, in his terms, she was about to plunge again, and this time to greater depths. Laura and he saw what Graves referred to as 'the Ruin', to be rebuilt 'by June 1st'. He added gloomily, already disliking Jackson and his crude speech habits: 'Only history of Ruin: "A nigger once lived there and the roof caved in".' 'Schuyler', he wrote on that day, 'rather dumb, Katherine not.' On 30 April 'L. & S. got things clear.' And he must have seen what was clear between them.

On 2 May: 'Schuyler will work on Dictionary.' He began to put the word 'work' into inverted commas, but thought better of it and deleted the first inverted comma. He was, however, 'getting to know Katherine better'. They had dinner with Tom's father, the awful bishop, and his wife: 'they froze,' wrote Robert. Laura was 'happy but thinner and not sleeping well'.

On 3 May: 'Katherine came over in the morning for her first talk alone with Laura.' This was the beginning of an inquisitorial (or 'holy' – as the reader wishes) process that was to end dramatically; and Graves foresaw it. On 4 May it seemed 'queer' to him because they did not see the Jacksons; but they did discuss the role of the 'book-page on *Time*: how it would be made closer to what a book-page should be.' This all came from Riding, who could believe that Luce –

owner of *Time* – could be brought to her point of view, which would be embodied by a Schuyler as fluent and as efficient as Graves. She now dreamed of having an audience of millions; but 'had a temperature and seemed thinner'. She was in fact going into a moral convulsion: the essence of what she had preached about sex for some ten years had been destroyed by the sight of Jackson; her desires were reciprocated. It was a simple matter of very violent sexual chemistry. There were obstacles: evil people might thwart the new New Order. And so, on 6 May, Graves ends his diary:

At this point the diary seems graveyard; so I stop it.

But the final entry in the diary is a poem, which did not appear until 1975, when, in an issue devoted to Graves, the *Malahat Review* printed a holograph of it. It is not, therefore, at all well known – though Graves used parts of it in later poems. It is called 'The Moon Ends in Nightmare' (*Malahat* dates it 'May 1939', but it did not reach this form until June).

> I had once boasted my acquaintance
> With the Moon's phases: I had seen her, even,
> Endure and emerge from full eclipse.
> Yet as she stood in the West, that summer night,
> The fireflies dipping insanely about me,
> So that the foggy air quivered and winked
> And the sure eye was cheated,
> In horror I cried aloud: for the same Moon
> Whom I had held a living power, though changelesss,
> Split open in my sight, a bright egg shell,
> And a double-headed Nothing grinned
> All-wisely from the gap.
>
> At this I found my earth no more substantial
> Than the lower air, or the upper,
> And ran to plunge in the cool flowing creek,
> My eyes and ears pressed under water,
> And did I drown, leaving my corpse in mud?
> Yet still the thing was so.
>
> I crept to where my window beckoned warm
> Between the white oak and the tulip tree
> And rapped – but was denied, as who returns
> After a one-hour-seeming century
> To a house not his own.

From this time onwards, until he was altogether rid of Riding, it was nightmare for Graves, and pretence, and 'helpless terror'. It seemed (to him) that he was an unwilling accomplice in evil-doing. But for the time being he stayed – and even paid lip-service to what Jackson was to call 'the now-dawn of human innocence'.

II

A cloud hangs over the happenings at New Hope, Pennsylvania, in the year 1939. No one likes to talk about them. Laura Riding (so it would appear to an outsider) came to England in 1926 and broke up a family consisting of a wife and husband and four children. When she came back to her own country (a prophet, and as yet honoured only by a few lines in *Time*, which she apparently did not repudiate when it had an initial capital), she broke up another family also consisting of a wife and husband and four children. But it is possible that she has been misjudged, that she acted for 'the general good', a phrase which, like 'the general honour', she is fond of using. For in *Epilogue III*, in a public piece called 'From a Private Correspondence on Reality', Graves had written (to and of Riding):

> I accept your statement of the crucialness of the present moment, not only because it appeals to me emotionally and then seems a historically inevitable conclusion, but also because it is your statement. That is to say: I concede that you have the right to speak with such certainty because I am aware that you do indeed perceive human history with eyes trained on it from some point outside. I am aware that your consciousness is of a final quality and that you are yet someone immediate and actual. How do I know this? By a process of elimination, I should say: I have always had a blind but obstinate will to discover a consciousness of this quality and a realist's conviction that it was to be found in my time, and a painful frankness with myself that it was not my consciousness, and a physical intuition that it would be a woman's. And the process of elimination points to you, with a fantastic kind of logic. But there is nothing fantastic in my conviction that you think finally: because the recognition your thought invokes in me is not blind, but becomes clearer at every step. . . . But there does remain, if not for me, at least for others, the question of practical authority: how is one to be sure that what you say is so? . . . the fact must be faced that the problem does arise for people habituated to more formal titles of authority.

He does not offer a solution of this 'problem', and makes it clear that he cannot, except in his own ('physical') terms; but, in this dialogue, she states in her answer that 'the question of modesty does not arise' and, by implication, identifies her claim to 'general authority' with 'general goodness'. It was a bad habit in people, she believed, to fail to accept her authority: were not she and her works demonstrations that this was indeed an authority directed to the general good?

The Graves statement to Riding from *Epilogue*, made of course much earlier in their association, has been seen as 'abject'. But it is not that; it is simply indiscreet. For it is two things: a love letter (and are not many love letters, made public, apparently 'abject'?), and a dutiful description (carefully revised by her) of Riding as the Supreme Being. She was the chief editor of *Epilogue*, and the decision to print this piece was hers. It was what most people would call a vulgar decision. But with refinement vulgarity can go hand in hand.

However, Graves now no longer believed this. Once he had been prepared to finance the publication of his own revised love letters; once he had been prepared to accept Riding's 'point of view' about sex. But now he had to acknowledge that his worst premonitions were coming true – and that he was himself involved. As his poem 'The Moon Ends in Nightmare' shows, the scales fell from his eyes all at once; but he still could not entirely separate himself from the habits of nearly thirteen years. He struggled with his intense dislike of Schuyler Jackson; he had already had practice in this, with Phibbs.

In 1960 Matthews published his autobiography, *Name and Address*. Graves wrote of it (to me): 'He couldn't face the Laura thing. Good on *Time*, though.' And to Matthews himself he wrote what is perhaps still the best summing-up of the problem of the 'story' of that summer of 1939: he tactfully congratulated him on not having tried to

> put down the Schuyler story in full: one that couldn't be told intelligibly and fairly in cold print. It would have to be told from all angles; but two are incommunicable; and for myself, I prefer to let it go into the bottomless gulf where Laura knowingly cast herself, and into which she nearly dragged me and indeed, all of us.

Matthews says that Graves's 'humble adoration' of Riding had turned to 'hate', and quotes this passage to justify his judgement. But Graves never came to hate her. On the contrary: she came to hate him, perhaps mostly because he knew so much about her.

Who was Jackson? We have to know, for he broke up the Graves–

Riding association, and is the key to Riding's much vaunted 'renuncia-tion of poetry', as well as to her sudden change to what she called the 'common plane'.

Schuyler Jackson was at Princeton with Matthews, whose nostalgic memories of his own youth have caused him to overrate Jackson's youthful verse, an archaic magma of Miltonian and Wordsworthian pastiche, some of which Matthews unkindly quotes –

> Let us remember this wild day and all
> The glory:– how we stood in ecstasy
> On that wild summit; saw the swirl and rise
> Of atoms in the womb of air –

and so on. Outside Princeton ephemera Jackson published only two or three sets of verses – his widow has not seen fit to publish his poetical remains, and so these and Matthews's quotations are all we have to judge him by. To write poetry as dreadful as his is no discredit; but no one who wrote it could under any circumstances have been 'learned in American and English poetry', as Riding claims.

Kit Jackson, née Townsend, was a perfectly 'nice', unextraordinary, hospitable American woman of good family. Her marriage to Jackson (1924) had not been a happy one. He was a good but financially impractical farmer. He was also, according to Matthews (and other accounts), a mostly sullen and boorish man, but one who could be genial, 'folksy' and vastly generous when he felt like it. He had a serious drinking problem to which he freely admitted, but was probably never an alcoholic. Graves's final feeling about him (contrary to what Matthews says) is that the unintellectual Jackson was sucked into a vortex, a 'gulf'; but Graves could never muster up any admiration for his intelligence, or find him 'learned' in poetry. Certainly he did not like him; but he hated him for only a few weeks. He soon forgot him. In 1943 he felt sorry for him.

Before becoming a farmer Jackson had had high literary ambitions – which explains a great deal about him. He was not unlike Riding in certain important respects, although his intelligence was minuscule compared to hers. When he wrote his contribution to *Time* (for ex-ample), he expected letters to pour in by the sackful: the nation would be alerted. Here were two who could subsist on hopes never to be fulfilled. Riding had Graves as her backer; Schuyler regarded Matthews as his. Matthews was to be blamed by both him and Riding for cheating Schuyler (and America and the world) of its rightful heritage:

'a conspiracy of silence', Riding wrote to him, meaning that he had jealously smothered her husband's brilliance.

When Jackson came to England (at the same time as Matthews) he was all set to start a triumphant literary career. J. C. (Jack) Squire was a beery Georgian – essentially a nice man – who edited the *London Mercury*; as the twenties wore on he became an increasingly incoherent literary reactionary, an indiscriminate attacker of all he took to be modernist, much of which was not. Graves knew him pretty well. Squire took a slight interest in Jackson, accepted one or two of his verses for the magazine, and (so Jackson claimed) commissioned an article from him – on Yeats, who was at that time Schuyler's favourite living poet. Jackson told Matthews that he went to Ireland to see Yeats, and found 'great attunement' with him; this must be taken, if it is to be taken at all, on trust, as there is no record of the meeting; nor did any article appear.

Schuyler's real enthusiasm was reserved for C. M. Doughty (1843–1926), the explorer of Arabia, whose huge epic poem (30,000 lines) *The Dawn in Britain* (1906) was in intent an operation mounted to rescue the English language, and its values, from the corruption of Latinity and 'un-Englishness'. Curiously, Graves knew a great deal about Doughty, through T. E. Lawrence, one of the true English heroes to the mind of the author of *Arabia Deserta*. Doughty, whose best poetic work is in the short 'drama' *Adam Cast Forth* (1908), is an interesting writer who has never had adequate treatment; but he did not get it from Jackson, whose lifelong project was to provide a glossary and notes for *The Dawn in Britain*. He never did this. That he had any understanding of Doughty's complicated English patriotism, which was intimately related to his sense of Arab tradition, is not credible.

Jackson suddenly left England for America in early 1923. A garish book by Waldo Frank (*Our America*, 1919), and some other excited piece of journalism, had convinced him that there were scores of young and unknown American writers to be discovered, and he went off to discover them – and himself.

He returned to America, announced the inauguration of the Open Road Press in a short, undistinguished and lavishly printed *Manifesto*, and enlisted a few names in support of it. Then he travelled throughout most of the States of America. He accomplished nothing literary, but did meet his hapless future wife.

After his marriage he started farming in earnest. He never had any money, but was skilful in borrowing – first from banks but then from individuals, since, like Ezra Pound, he objected to usury. He seemed 'to draw a smudged line between a loan and an outright gift'. His father distrusted him so much that when he made his will he made the money he left to Schuyler what Matthews calls 'Schuyler-proof': he couldn't get at the whole of it, or raise more money on it.

Suddenly he left farming and became an antique dealer; but he was too generous, unmethodical, crooked and inconsistent to succeed. It was after this failure that Matthews tried to help him by giving him the 'job' at *Time*. When Graves and Riding arrived he had taken up farming again; but it is plain that both his abilities and his contribution to *Time* (and possibly his 'position' on it) had been exaggerated by Matthews for Riding's benefit. However, the speed with which Graves concluded his diary after his arrival in America makes it clear that Riding and Jackson were well and truly ready for each other from the moment they met – or even some months before it.

III

In due course Alan and Beryl arrived. By that time The Rise was ready for occupation, and Graves was living at New Hope – although he would sometimes go over to Princeton. David Reeves was also at New Hope.

In the first weeks Riding took over the Matthews's house for the ostensible purpose of holding meetings about their 'Second Protocol'. There was no longer any 'Second Protocol'. But all the open talk was of saving the world from war, of the general good. Everyone was kept busy, kept running errands, kept confused. . . .

Katherine Jackson underwent her 'talks' with Riding, alone or with Jackson, each day. This resembled an inquisition, the victim inexorably being driven into insanity (of which she had no previous history). Graves was as one mesmerized; both the Matthewses marvelled at their own inability to act; Alan Hodge felt helpless and nauseated. Only two people there, perhaps, besides Jackson and Riding, knew precisely what was going on. One was the Jacksons' twelve-year-old daughter Griselda, who could not be reached by Riding's authority, and who showed a defiant loathing of her; the other was Beryl, who did as Graves was doing – ran here and there at beck and call – but who shrewdly waited for the inevitable end to come. There was nothing more she could do. Had it not been for her sympathy and understanding Graves would have broken down.

What was really happening? First, Laura Riding was deferring to a man. Schuyler Jackson became her master – and she revelled in it. Later she would fight back, but always within the framework of her thoroughly folksy adoration of 'her man', whose slippers she would warm before the fire. The female mind was no longer the judge. When at last they went to bed together ('bodies have had their day') they locked the door; but apart from that they made almost a public spectacle of it. For two days they were incommunicado. Then Riding stated to all present that she was aware that some knew that she had been against sexual activity, and that for this reason she thought she should make the following announcement: 'Schuyler and I do.'

Still Graves failed to protest openly – though he now began to mutter. He pretended to agree with the new arrangements. He was incapable of asserting himself, though eventually he began to argue about his new position vis-à-vis the dictionary. He had been supplanted by Schuyler. He did not resent being supplanted as lover – though Riding's lapse into crass vulgarity ill-disguised by high talk shocked him – but he did resent being supplanted as intellectual collaborator by an idiot. He could not accept that Jackson's half-articulate obstinacy, and his roughness, were much more to Riding's liking than his own self-confident literacy. And he did not – how could he? – like to see her, as someone who knew her well (and who lived with her and Schuyler for a time) put it a few years later, 'treated like dirt and liking it'. For her subservience to Schuyler was obvious from the beginning, even though they sat as equals at the head of the inquisitorial table, and even though he allowed her to take charge of the household for the time being.

At these sessions there were oppressive silences. Matthews began to feel that someone was going to be a 'victim'. He was slower than Graves and the others (he was often away for days at *Time*; but he later wrote that he had been 'stupid' not to 'see which one . . . was the intended victim'), who knew perfectly well that something quite other than the planning of the 'Second Protocol' was in process.

> Schuyler and Laura were falling in love. What a way to do it! . . . I thought of two basilisks, motionless and staring, the rest of us . . . immobilised into cramped stone until the predetermined affair was ready

writes Matthews, and it is a fair description.

Kit Jackson soon went mad, became violent, was taken to an asylum ('Katherine is going into an asylum,' Laura told Beryl, 'you must pack for her as if she were your child'), stayed there for a few weeks, returned to New Hope, and was then taken off again (after a 'horrible struggle', in the course of which she got herself savagely beaten, by Jackson for one, about the head, which was 'the size of a football') for a long period. She is said to have recovered completely only after twenty years, and to have become a convert to the Roman Catholic Church. In the earlier stages of her illness, 'bewitched' (the word is Matthews's), she spoke of Riding with great admiration.

On Jackson's death in 1968 she said to Matthews that he needed 'our prayers', and had a mass said for him; she also said: 'I firmly believed that those two extraordinary people would come to their senses!'

She was in London in the early fifties, and seemed perfectly normal to James Reeves. She then asserted, to him and others present, that Laura and Schuyler had driven her mad, and that they had intended to do so. She dismissed as nonsense the notion that she, Katherine, was a 'witch'.

But why should she refer to witches? This is explained by an accusation made by Riding. According to Matthews (and many others: his account is confirmed, and could be very considerably augmented), Riding spent much time in trying to persuade him and his wife Julie that Katherine was a 'witch' who had been 'unmasked'; Riding told him that she was purifying the house of Katherine's 'cabalistic relics' (this is interesting, since Katherine Jackson had never heard of the Cabala, whereas Riding was writing about it – and about the question of her 'being a magician' – years before, in a letter that is still extant), and she told him to throw away a small china figure that had belonged to Katherine. This Matthews, although feeling a fool, did. She claimed that all the others were 'in accord' with her pronouncements on Katherine's wickedness. So they seemed to be. They did as Riding told them, fetched and carried, and did not question her and Schuyler's decisions. She made it clear from early on that she loathed Katherine Jackson. 'Schuyler and I are going to lie down and rest,' she told the distressed woman, and, turning to Beryl: 'You must sit in the room!'

Graves has never made any public pronouncements about the events of 1939, and has talked about them only rarely. He and Beryl made a point of not discussing the past. In The Long Weekend, written with Alan Hodge (and Karl) in 1939–40, there is a long and generous tribute to Riding. Contained within this tribute are two remarks. The first is that she achieved an 'unshakeable synthesis' – 'Unshakeable, that is, if the premise of her unique personal authority were granted' (he had for some years granted it). The second describes the end of her European career: 'At the very end [of the interwar period] . . . she returned to the United States, surprisingly rediscovered her American self, and wiped the slate clean again.'

In *The White Goddess*, in speaking of the phenomenon of women turning into 'Bassarids' (terrifying ivy-wreathed female orgiasts indulging in Dionysian rites) he says

> the archives of morbid psychology are full of Bassarid histories. An English or American woman in a nervous breakdown of sexual origin will often instinctively reproduce in faithful and disgusting detail much of the ancient Dionysiac ritual. I have myself witnessed it in helpless terror.

He had Katherine Jackson specifically in mind here; but when it was later suggested to him that in this passage he was conflating two aspects of a similar process, manifesting itself simultaneously in two contrasting ways in two people, he readily agreed. He was genuinely terrified at what he saw going on in Riding.

When someone really goes mad – as Katherine did – a situation is created in which everyone who happens to be about has to lend a helping hand. The atmosphere is charged, fairly or not, with suppressed temporary resentment against the mad person. It is not pleasant to be chased with an ice pick (as Beryl was). So it is hardly surprising that the people who were at New Hope at the time rallied round Laura Riding, and seemed to be in agreement with her 'judgements' on the wife of the man with whom she had fallen in love. Afterwards, no longer in the difficult situation of dealing with a deranged person, they were to see it differently.

> A healthy suppressor in my consciousness has blotted out most of the details of life at Nimrod, except the Inquisition manners of Laura and Schuyler and the martyrdom of Katherine Jackson

wrote the gentle Alan Hodge, positively an anti-sensationalist in his attitudes and behaviour, in a letter to Graves ten years later.

Of Riding's accusations one may say nothing except that they were somewhat old-fashioned in style ('witch'; 'wicked woman'); and that they were odd, for was it not unnecessarily melodramatic to raise the question of sorcery at all?

Of the Jacksons' life together one who knew them well for many years after 1939 wrote:

> they were too bogged down in their own past, from which they could not struggle free, to give out love or happiness to anyone else. . . . people respected them, but did not like them. . . . almost always you felt the hate of what was foreign to them far more strongly than any love of their own things and ways. . . .

Matthews writes that Griselda felt 'wrongness in the house', and that it seemed to her 'like bad air . . . a miasma which . . . [Riding] generated and spread'. It could not have been pleasant for Jackson to feel (as he did, 'at naked sensation-point', wrote Riding to Graves) that his own daughter disliked the new lady her father loved, and who had hissed furiously at her 'Don't call me Laura in front of the servants!' as she awaited her breakfast in bed. Riding complained to Graves in a letter that 'her language about me is a mixture of queer-vulgar artful. . . . Don't comment on this in answering'; she hoped the child would soon be free 'of this clutch'.

Katherine's children did not grow up under Riding's care. They went elsewhere within a year. Katherine Jackson divorced her husband. Schuyler and Laura left the farm – they sold Nimrod's Rise, and presumably someone (but not Matthews or Graves) got the money – lived in New York in an apartment whose doorbell bore the legend 'Mr and Mrs Jackson' (literally, literally, literally, without gloss, without gloss, without gloss?), married at Elkton, Maryland (a 'Gretna Green' of its area), and ended up at Wabasso, Florida, where they failed to 'sustain themselves' (Riding) in a citrus-fruit venture 'in spite of low prices and unpaid labour' (Matthews). But, though Nimrod had not risen, they were not too poor to keep up another house in New Mexico. From their bedroom in Wabasso they could see in large letters the name of the firm which shipped out their citrus fruit: 'R. GRAVES INC'.

IV

At New Hope Graves became increasingly insistent about a settlement of the practical affairs between him and Riding. His position was now wholly undefined – and 'joint' affairs are always impossibly complicated. *The Swiss Ghost*, the dramatization of *A Trojan Ending*, other smaller projects: what was now to become of them? Riding allowed Graves to assume that they would all be pursued. But it was clear that he had been ousted from the dictionary – into which he and Alan and Beryl had put most of the work – by Jackson.

So a verbal deal was made: he should have all the rights in the collaborative works he had done with Riding. In return he would hand over, to Schuyler Jackson, his already considerable interest in the dictionary.

Robert and Alan left for England, together, at the beginning of August, although it was firmly stated that Graves would return. Beryl had to hang on until war had been declared, because everyone pretended that Graves really would return (work was supposedly continuing on the 'Second Protocol'). She finally left on 6 October 1939. Tom Matthews got her a ticket for a ship which took an indirect route round the Azores: the straightforward crossing was now unsafe.

The break between Graves and Riding did not 'officially' occur until 17 February 1940, which is the date of her last letter to him (except for two of 1949); in this she said that she would not write to him again. The actual break occurred when she first set eyes on Jackson. It did not occur when Graves and Beryl fell in love at Rennes, because despite his premonitions of disaster, and his capacity to write prophetic poems, he was doggedly prepared to continue working with and for Riding. Jackson may have hoped, even while Beryl was crossing to England, that Graves might return: he would have been useful as a writer of historical novels or other 'potboilers', a subsidizer of the dictionary – a useful meal ticket living somewhere at a convenient distance.

There were some rows, half-rows and bad atmospheres before Graves left. Riding had an acute and uncomfortable sense of Alan Hodge's disgust with her; she later referred to it as 'hatred', and called it 'rebellious'. But Alan, an undemonstrative man, did not want to show his disgust; he wanted to be elsewhere. Intense emotion was disagreeable to him. Graves publicly maintained, for the most part, his old attitude towards Laura; but he displayed anger towards Jackson and, most particularly, when Laura seemed to allow Jackson to speak for her in matters which had originally concerned only Graves and Laura. He then took his fury out on Jackson.

One day he would make himself unpleasant to him (he could run rings round him in the matter of verbal malice), but would be conciliatory the next. His behaviour was confused and inconsistent, so at one moment he would sympathize with Schuyler about his problems with Katherine, but at another make woundingly sarcastic remarks about them. Riding's hatred for Graves increased as she saw the blockish Jackson continually worsted in their verbal battles.

Katherine's illness (or wickedness) was costing money. Jackson had no money, had never had any, and never would have any. His general habit had been to make use of other people's. In the few letters he wrote to Graves in England, he spoke of his 'problems'; but he never had these in clear perspective. Graves was later to describe him as one who 'always wants the right word even if he has to wake one up in the early hours of the morning to bumble it alcoholically in one's ear. . . .' He had a touching yearning to be a good man, and was full of fine intentions ('Believe me, Robert, I have been and am your sidekick in what you have been through,' he wrote on 8 November 1939, and believed himself). He had a conscience. The putrid and isolated condition of this in 1939 led him to attack when attacked. He was then still drinking (he kept the extent of this from Laura) and alcohol played its part in his maladroit moves. Since he felt himself to be guilty of bad poetry, cruelty, drinking and adultery, he would, whenever he felt himself attacked on these grounds (and Graves bitterly and cleverly made him feel that for most of the time), launch out into moralistic attacks on these faults in others. It was around this time that he seriously lectured Matthews on his 'loose attitude towards women'. He worked at Riding until he forced her into her notorious 'repudiation of poetry' – which, for all her later convoluted elaborations of it, is really no more than a genuflection towards his own inadequacy in that medium. He even criticized Graves for his relationship with Beryl, which was now openly admitted. That relationship was convenient for him, as was Riding's consignment of Beryl to the role of one 'not grown up'. When Alan Hodge recollected the 'inquisitorial attitude' of Riding and Jackson he was referring, in part, to the manner in which they tried to beat Graves over the head with his, Alan's, own feelings. This injured his *amour propre* considerably more than what was going on between Graves and Beryl, for they sat in solemn judgement on Graves's new feelings. Riding later summed it up in a letter to Graves (26 September 1939): because she wished herself and Schuyler well in their relationship, she informed him, that was not good reason for them to wish him well in his with Beryl. Graves, she said, was being 'unfair' to Beryl; his behaviour was 'unworthy'. He was making Beryl into a 'pseudo-Laura'. She rebuked him for writing things to Beryl which should have been written to her. Had she not warned him of this in an earlier letter?

She assumed and exercised the authority to read all that was written to everybody. She collected sufficient information to be able confidently to tell Graves that, by misguidedly trying to protect Beryl from herself and Schuyler, he was in fact depriving her of their 'good feelings'. How could they help her out of 'the mess' she had got herself into since 'she first began shooting intense glances at you across the Chevrie table' if he would 'interpose' himself between Laura and her? Only a few days earlier (15 September) she had, for Graves's benefit, analysed and defined the nature of his feelings for Beryl. Of Beryl's own behaviour she wrote: 'she holds on, but frequently hates me': she was afraid to let any feeling for Schuyler 'pass through her eyes. . . .' Beryl was perhaps less 'afraid' than polite – and certainly she was well advised to keep her own counsel. One notes that while Beryl was in a 'mess', Laura and Schuyler had 'difficulties'.

Yet Beryl does not recollect those tense days when she was left alone in the Jackson household as being ones of unmitigated gloom. There was, she recalls, a kind of pleasant light-heartedness that would often keep breaking through. She couldn't dislike Laura – and preferred to leave others to discuss her qualities, though she has always agreed with Graves about the astonishing beauty of her best poetry – and she maintains this attitude.

Riding's first letters to Graves on his return are full of instructions as to which people he must contact about the 'Second Protocol'. This is odd, because no work was being done on it – and Riding had in any case changed her mind about it. She eventually wrote stating that the 'First Protocol' had been wrong in certain ways – ways which she related to the conflict between herself and Graves. She appears to relate the troubles of the world to this conflict, her definition of which drastically alters as Graves becomes more argumentative. The general sense of her talk is that she is right and he (and everyone else) is wrong; but her tone remained, on the whole, friendly.

At one point she launched into a page-long parenthetical disquisition on the difference between 'dear' and 'dearest' at the beginning of letters. Graves is indeed addressed in a varying number of ways in these letters: 'Dear Robert', 'Dear loving Robert', 'Dear Truer Robert', 'Now, dear Robert', 'Dearest Robert', 'Dear Robert (dear means dear here . . .)', 'Dear Robert Graves' and (in 1949) 'Robert Graves!'

Before Graves left with Alan Hodge he felt sure (as Hodge recollected in a letter – 12 March 1949 – to him) that 'something had been salvaged from the wreck'; Alan remembered that they both assumed it throughout the voyage home. What was 'salvaged' was, Graves believed, Riding's resignation to him of her rights in all their joint works – to which I have already referred. In a letter to the vice-president of the Creative Age Press in 1949 Riding did confirm that this had been the case; but she firmly rejected whatever she may then have told Graves.

The matter of these 'rights' seemed important to Graves as he sailed homewards – occupying himself, characteristically, by writing a play for children, *Horses* – because he badly needed money. He was not then thinking about reprinting any of their joint critical work, which would bring little money in. The joint works (novel, play and other smaller projects) in which he and she had more recently engaged might, however, he then hoped, bring in some money.

He kept asking her about them from England. She kept procrastinating. Yes, she would eventually be able to get on with this or that; yes, work on the 'Second Protocol' was going on (she revealed her changed attitude to it only after Beryl had left America and it was clear that Graves was not returning – no work was going on on it at all). And so on. There is plenty in the earlier letters – those written before Beryl left – that is affectionate enough, although nothing that shows respect for Graves as a person; where the tone is not pedagogical it is gushing. She clung on to her tutorial role for as long as he allowed her to.

She cared less about Graves's state of mind than about 'talk', in England, of her affairs. She kept asking him not to say anything about the change 'here', or to be careful. 'I have a feeling that you have been over-talking.' If he sees Rebecca West then he must 'be careful to avoid saying anything that will give her temptation for public talk of me, of a kind to make confusion.' At one point, frightened, she sensed a 'new confidence' in him. She told him that she was not 'attacking' this, but she thought that 'over-talking' might be 'over-enjoyment' of this 'new confidence': she reminded him of the 'proprieties of enjoyment'. There were also, she reminded him, proprieties 'for the non-reporting of things of private pain'. She does not say whose pain; or that acute shame is pain, too.

Naturally, Graves was 'talking'. He always does. The impression he gave to those he saw in England, particularly to James and Mary Reeves, was of a man distraught. Laura, he told the Reeves, had suddenly transformed herself from poet and critic to the devoted wife of a folksy, ignorant American farmer with literary pretensions. She actually thought she could do the dictionary in collaboration with this man – why could she not see that she was deceiving herself? It would never appear. She now seemed to enjoy being physically bullied. Yes, Laura! She had even at one point 'ordered' him to go back to Nancy. Graves broke into tears as though (Mary Reeves said) he had just come back from another war. He hinted at strange pressures having been brought to bear. The farmer's wife had not been able to take it: she had undergone a breakdown horrifying to behold. He never wanted to see anything like that again. Laura and Schuyler were alienating all their friends, one by one; the Matthews already had their grave doubts, and soon, certainly, they would sever relations. They had been 'foul days' over there; he could not really bear to think about them. Only Beryl's sweetness and strength had saved him. Meanwhile he was flat broke. He knew he loved Beryl and believed that she, he and Alan would work out a fair arrangement. But Laura was being impossible about even that, too.

However, he wanted to save something from the wreck. Would they therefore please, when writing to her, pretend that nothing strange had happened. She might come to her senses, even yet. It was unlikely that she would leave this awful man ('He's *bald*,' he sobbed); but at least she had given him the use of all the rights in the stuff they had done together over the years, and in several joint projects now under way.

Mary Reeves had been charmed by Laura, but she was not surprised. She felt for Graves now just as she had felt for him over the press-cuttings incident.

Riding meanwhile 'repudiated' all the 'wrong talk' that was going on about her in England. She explained to Graves (26 September 1939) that the 'perplexed feelings' of John and Lucie Aldridge, 'and Schuyler's being an enigma to everyone', were the results of his – Robert's – failure to tell people of 'his own irritations'. If he had mentioned these, then people wouldn't have been puzzled by the fact that Tom and Julie were also 'irritated'. But, she added, it would all be all right; when all her friends in England had recovered from 'all those years of special pleading for them and me in a hierarchy of utmost hopes', they would begin to know Schuyler, her – and (she could not even now resist this) themselves.

V

When he returned Graves first went to Harlech, to see his mother and children. He was still so dazed, in such a state that he could not think clearly about the international situation – he did not expect (could not face the notion of) a 'real war'. He later wrote to Alan Hodge admitting not only that he had 'underestimated the inefficiency of the government', but also that he had been plain wrong in his optimistic assessments. Alan went to Riga, travelling through Poland, on a journalistic assignment almost as soon as he returned, and told Graves that, judging from what he had seen, real war was on the way; that Poland was no 'tough nut', but ready to collapse – and that Hitler knew it.

At first Graves wrote letters to Riding implying that he was returning to America; he was still blotting out his knowledge that everything between them was over. He even deceived himself into hoping that, by behaving suitably, he could get back in on the dictionary again. Neither of the contracts for it had actually been signed by him; but he knew that both publishers – Dent in England, and Little, Brown in the States – had drawn them up, and paid advances, on the understanding that he would be collaborating on it, that his name would appear on the cover. Both publishers were to lose money: there was never any 'dictionary'.

As the nightmare of Nimrod's Rise began to fade, so he became aware of his own position. Although even now he continued to send money to Riding in America, he began to work out a scheme by which he could extricate himself from a situation in which his and Laura's affairs were 'joint' – and in which Schuyler was a factor. Matthews had warned him of Schuyler's financial habits. There was a joint account at a Westminster Bank in London, and other accounts in Trenton, New Jersey – one, it seems, in his name, another in Laura's. What about royalties on his past work? Might Schuyler get hold of these? And what about the Spanish properties? These were in Riding's name; but his money had bought them, and he felt that, since she had recommitted herself to the New World and Jackson, then he had some right to them. She had after all told him, before he left New Hope, that she regarded her long stay in Europe, as well as all her collaborations with him, as a 'great mistake'. Yet even after war had been declared, and Beryl had returned, he found it hard to put out of his mind the possibility of renewed intellectual collaboration with Riding – perhaps first in America, but then in Deyá, which (he occasionally fantasized) might be reachable from there. If Riding wanted personal *use* of the properties there, he told her, then perhaps something could be worked out. But he was extremely nervous lest Schuyler should take it into his mind to try to raise cash on them.

John and Lucie Aldridge, meanwhile, were pleased to allow Robert to live at The Place at Great Bardfield until he could find somewhere of his own. When Beryl returned she returned to Alan; but she had already made up her mind that she was going to join Robert. She did so in the late autumn of 1939, at Great Bardfield.

But they needed somewhere to live. Robert had been seeing a good deal of Basil Liddell Hart, and when he and Beryl went to Bishop-steignton to stay with his sister Ros, Liddell Hart drove him around the countryside looking for a suitable home. One afternoon they found a farmhouse in Galmpton, near Brixham, to which they moved in May 1940. Their first child, William, was born on 21 July 1940 in the hospital at nearby Paignton – three days before his father's forty-fifth birthday.

By late October 1939 matters were happily settled between Alan and Beryl, as Alan's long series of letters to her, written throughout the war, amply testify. The two found they were happier as friends than as husband and wife.

Graves wrote to Alan, from Great Bardfield, in October 1939:

> I am asking Beryl to come here on Saturday unless you two have pressing business together. I hope that she will be able to come.

He went on to ask if Alan wanted to do 'this research job' on his newly projected novel about the American War of Independence (*Sergeant Lamb*), and asked him what money he needed. He ended:

> Dear Alan – I think that since this has had to be, it will end happily for us all; you know how I have always felt towards you. And how to me the only painful thing has been when it seemed you were fighting me.

Alan made another marriage, shortly after the war, to one of Conrad Aiken's daughters (the novelist, Jane Aiken Hodge), and they had two daughters. He died in May 1979. He divorced Beryl as soon as the then archaic laws allowed; but Graves was unable to get a divorce from Nancy until many years later.

The two men soon agreed to collaborate – along with Karl, who could do much of the necessary research – on a social history of England between the wars, eventually called *The Long Weekend*. This was to be the first of two very successful collaborations, both of which they enjoyed doing.

On 10 November Graves received a long letter from Riding, unusually friendly in tone, which defined their past as unsatisfactory because their 'technique for that long-seeming time of uncertainties' was not one that could be shared with everyone. Now, she said, they could be friends 'in truer wish for the same good everywhere'; there need be no 'strain of joining personal meanings that could never be the same'. She even admitted that he had been 'more consistently generous' to her than she had to him. Everything he had 'arranged' about money had been very helpful.

Could he get Watt to send out another instalment of 'dictionary money'? She suggested that he consider the idea of her making a transfer of the Deyá houses to him. She made it clear that she did not foresee any possibility of a resumption of a working partnership between them, but told him that he would be welcome as a friend.

Graves was relieved to hear of her intentions about the Deyá properties, since the prospect of losing these haunted him continually. At this point he decided, therefore, to help her in the matter of the dictionary. For she was in trouble over it. She had written earlier (5 October) telling him that she hoped McIntyre of Little, Brown would not 'lose confidence because of the decrease in personnel' (i.e. the loss of Graves), and that she hoped that when she and Schuyler saw McIntyre in Boston in a few weeks they would be able to convince him of 'the undamaged integrity of the work'.

By the time Graves received the letter, they had seen him – and had got 'an extension of writing time'. Jackson had written to Graves about it in a letter dated '2–8 November', telling him that McIntyre had also been '*thoroughly* convinced about the permanent validity' of the work. In that letter Jackson had also spoken of Katherine's 'third breakdown', of its difficulties, and of how he thought

> we are storing up enough new treasure to take care of whatever payments we may be called upon to make. (I don't like this last sentence, but won't cross it out).

Graves had no money with which to respond to this invitation, but surmising that McIntyre's conviction might not be as 'thorough' as Jackson believed, he wrote the publisher a tactful letter saying that, although he himself could not for personal reasons return, after all, to the States, he had every confidence in Miss Riding's capabilities – and so forth. On 10 December (the posts were now slowing up because of the war) Riding sent him a letter beginning 'I thought you wrote well to McIntyre about your not returning.' She acknowledged that there was *The Swiss Ghost* to 'finish', his play (*Horses*) to read, his poems to reread. It was again unusually friendly, and ended by saying that the financial position there was very 'sound', in spite of 'great pressure'. If something happened 'outside our calculations' then Schuyler would ask 'for what help you can give us'. Meanwhile, could Robert settle her debt to John's mother, Mrs Lloyd, in 'private between you and me', and could she draw £75 from the Westminster account? (She had a few weeks before that spoken of 'paying back' yet another £75.)' They were sending him a book on early American material that he might find useful for his War of Independence book.

All was still friendly, more so than it had recently been. Yet all ended, at least for Riding, in poisoned feelings. This first becomes apparent in Riding's letter of 31 December 1939 (dated 31 December 1931 in error). Her tone now reverts to the severe. She apologizes for not sending manuscripts back to him sooner. She says that she will not go on with *The Swiss Ghost*; he could publish it as his. 'My life is now all to Schuyler, and in him to everyone, everyone of you. . . .' Graves's last letter to him had been 'like a literary treatise', 'too well-aimed in style to reach him', for both she and Schuyler now belonged to a larger audience than the one he reckoned on in his language. They were, she had already explained, on the 'common plane'. She would see about transferring the Deyá properties to him. 'In return, give us what you feel happy in giving from your American monies.' The letter ends by telling him that a poem of his called 'Manifestation', which he sent her and which she has just read, is 'personal', 'a violation of decencies common to life and poetry'. (This may have made him feel unhappy about parting with any of his American monies; but she acknowledged her part in the processes which led to its composition.) And Graves was to regard all the property that they have stored with a firm in England as his.

She interrupted this long letter (sent later than 31 December) by one of 4 January 1940. It was in answer to one of his written on 11 December. She had received from Random House in the autumn 'cheques for $2,169.53'. She had 'assumed that this was O.K.', but 'can only *be* sure of having thanked you for your allotment of the money to me in prospect'. She thought a letter must have gone astray, 'but there is against me the evidence of these royalty statements not yet forwarded to you. . . .' But into this complex statement she injects the remark that she had received 'no Claudius royalties'. If her first two paragraphs are muddled, then the third is not: 'No, Robert, I can't pay any of this back without bringing insolvency upon us.' That letter ends by telling him that Schuyler feels that in the 31 December letter 'too much' is left to the 'mercy of your understanding'.

Graves now had Karl and Alan to pay for their research, and a wife who was expecting a child. He was also some £1500 in debt to the Inland Revenue.

In fact, although Riding did not choose to realize it, the $2000 odd from Random House was a mistake. Graves explained the affair to Alan Hodge in a letter of 2 February 1940, with which he enclosed the contract for *The Long Weekend*, and a cheque:

> I don't know if I told you that Random House overpaid Laura & me about £500 in Nov. Laura now says that she can't pay me back anything without insolvency. (Also that she is doing the Dictionary in a new way with Schuyler, making any further cooperation impossible – which puts me in a very false position with the publishers.) So I shall have no more Lamb money till May because of Random House recouping but can manage all right without using Faber [*Long Weekend*: Faber had contracted to publish their social history book] money, which is for you.

Evidently he had asked for some of his money back from Riding; but he did not seem particularly upset about her refusal to pay. It might be said that her indebtedness to him villainized him in her eyes.

On 6 January 1940 Schuyler did write, to comment on Graves's 'literary treatise' letter: 'Laura has got it a bit wrong . . . about my reasons for not answering your last.' He was not answering it because it made him feel bad; Graves had been concerned to attack his personality rather than to evaluate (for his own 'personal use') Jackson's 'judgements' of his, Graves's, personality. Doubtless this is true; probably Graves's letter was elaborately ironic, and deliberately above Jackson's head. He then damned Robert's relationship with Beryl, and its future, and referred to 'the miraculously held-together heap of human wreckage that Laura became in attempting to save your soul with words'. Graves, he pronounced, was now in the same position as his wife, Katherine: 'as one who has been the beneficiary of somebody else's holy words.' This is reminiscent of Riding's remark that Katherine's 'deviance' is seen 'by some' as 'rational opposition'. Laura's words, explained Jackson, were holy because 'entirely meant'. Now 'hardly a crumb of those words' uncorrupt meaning has escaped to salute the now-dawn of human innocence'. (The reader will note how well Schuyler's own pseudo-Doughtyese combined, for at least the time being, with Laura's infectious grandiloquence.) The last sentence of the letter is: 'I'll write the Doughty letter when I've finished *The Dawn in Britain.*'

Probably Graves had earlier rashly told him that he would help with the selling of his projected edition of Doughty. He had also been actively helping with a book, to be called *The World Has Changed*, of which Methuen had asked to see an outline – but it never materialized, perhaps because the world did not change. With this Schuyler faded for ever from Graves's life. 'A generous man, but violent. We never came to blows,' Graves would say thirty years later, on hearing of his death.

Riding's letter of 17 February liquidates all their affairs. She says that she has received five letters from him, and that the first two are 'entirely unanswerable'. She will not, after this, write to him again. He could have the houses in Mallorca and 'everything in them' (this, she later forgot to take into account, included the Seizin Press). She would make a declaration to this effect.

She did this promptly, through an attorney; but she ignored the fact that she had given Gelat her power of attorney. Graves wrote to the American attorney asking him if his client would, in these circumstances, care to leave the matter as it was until the situation in Europe became clearer. The matter was left in abeyance until 1947.

Riding listed items which she said she would return to Graves. A few she said she would keep. She wrote: 'I have no wishes about anything at Deyá except that you burn all papers of mine found there.' She went on to thank him for paying her debt to John Aldridge's mother, but said that she was sorry if he had told any 'lie' about it:

I do not regard my share in our once joint finances, and the properties literary [an allusion to his sole rights in their joint publications, and to the Seizin Press] and real *I am handing over to you* , as so illusory as not to allow of my regarding this repayment as my own [my italics].

Riding accompanied this written 'handing over' with a justification of her change of attitude towards the dictionary (her use of him had been 'an experiment' she now maintained), asked him to accept her 'assurance' that he had not been 'put in any hole with' the publishers, and warned him that if he communicated with them on the subject she would be obliged to 'explain to them your reasons for questioning my authority to do what I think best. . . .' Graves did not understand what this, which sounds like some form of *chantage*, meant, and it remains obscure.

At the very end she defined their past together; this definition differed from the previous ones – clearly this goose was now tin. She said that at the end of 1925 she made a mistake which 'put you in my debt and me in your protection': she thought that the debt had been 'paid' by the time they left Mallorca. He had paid it 'in the form of a protracted apology for calling on me originally as someone in true need of me'. (She first wrote the interesting word 'summoning', but crossed it out and substituted 'calling'.) She had accepted the apology – by accepting his 'protective interest' in her. She found it hard to thank him for anything at all now; but she could say that in 'settling with Random House' (that is, in forfeiting his own £500), she thought he was behaving well. He had never been one to face things with a bad conscience (she told him). In her acceptance of this 'final protective offering' she felt she was helping him to forget what he needed to forget: 'in order to hold your head up'. She did not mention the money he had put into Nimrod's Rise.

Graves held his head up without difficulty. He was no longer bogged down by the knowledge that they had once been lovers; and he could forget about the money by making more. When he was planning *Work in Hand* (1942) – a shared volume of poems by Alan Hodge, Norman Cameron and Graves – he treated her with the greatest consideration. He wrote to Alan Hodge:

> About the mention of Laura in the book: I have thought about that. But she would not like her name to be heavily stressed: we do not want to advertise ourselves as a 'Broken Pleiad', or 'Five [James Reeves and Harry Kemp were going to be included, but the publishers rejected them] Poets Widowed of their Muse'. We can, however, say that some of the poems have appeared in *Epilogue*, edited by L.R. and R.G.: no longer published since L.R.'s return to America, but collaboration in which was the tie which originally bound us together as poets. [18 February 1941]

There is no trace of ill feeling, or of bad conscience, here. Nor was there in his letter of 2 July 1941, to Alan:

> [Had] a letter from Laura's sister Isobel, very decent: she says there is a 'miraculous change' in Laura since New Hope days, she is gentle, sweet, patient. . . .

ROBERT GRAVES

So this was the end of an association as famous as it had been – for most of its duration – unhappy. Indeed, the name of Laura Riding is better known amongst the reading public for her 'scandalous' association with Robert Graves than it is for any of her own work. Graves continued to feel that her poetry transcended any 'irritation' she might have caused him. Although his experience of her remained etched on his heart, he forgot the woman herself, and her affairs, within a few months. He missed her intellectual companionship for some years; but in that time he also learned that the capacity for such companionship no longer existed in her. If asked by acquaintances about Jackson he would invariably say little more than that he was a farmer, or, sometimes, a 'literary farmer'. People had to know him very well to discover his real view, for he seldom spoke of it. He had a new life to lead, new work, a new family. The next twenty years were to be the most serene of his life.

Chapter Twenty-Three
1940–46(I)

I

Until his forty-fourth year Graves had had an outwardly, as well as an internally, eventful life. His schooldays had been unusually eventful. He had undergone a long period of active service, as well as being 'killed' at the end of it – and he had gone back to France when he wasn't well enough to do so, which in itself did much to delay his return to normal health. Then ten years of acute neurasthenia, and an unsatisfactory marriage, had followed. His nerves had just started to settle down when the Phibbs affair exploded. He had then saved himself from going crazy only by writing 'a reckless autobiography... with small consideration for anyone's feelings' (as he calls *Goodbye to All That* in *The Long Weekend*). The Deyá years had been the happiest; but happiness is a comparative word. He had loved, there, more than anything else, his isolation from the 'goddawful', existence in a truly rural community. In his six years on the island, however, he had failed to provide happiness to the person he believed most deserved it, and had suffered from increasing helplessness and terror; but there, in Deyá, was an atmosphere in which he could find happiness – even if at bottom he was unhappy. There was nothing, now, he wanted to do more than to take Beryl there. This prospect, and Beryl herself, and three new children, were what kept him cheerful throughout the war, though this too was to cause him personal suffering. He worried, like everyone else, about its outcome – but most often took the optimistic view, the one which is natural to him.

Now at last his situation had become more tranquil. From 1940 until well into the fifties his external life was quiet, a period of sustained work, with little stress imposed from outside. To those years belong his most substantial prose books (with the exception of *Goodbye to All That* and the *Claudius* novels).

Graves is a necessarily dramatic and ritualistic man. So the drama eventually continued; but for long it was internal. His poetry acquired a new and more positive quality, his prose a new, adventurous urgency – an urgency which reached its climax in *The White Goddess*.

Behind all this was the unobtrusive figure of Beryl. She had had to stand by helplessly, watching him both invite and receive bad treatment. Hostility is not in her nature, and she felt no hostility towards those who had made him unhappy. It was enough for her practicality that his affairs were in disorder and needed restoring, that only work could make him whole again.

She eventually exercised a more profound effect on Graves than Riding. He never 'invented' her as he invented Riding. His letters to her before they began to live together are unlike any of his other letters, to anyone. They are not addressed to a capricious and unpredictable Muse, but to a woman wholly trusted. None of his later, voluntary, adventures with the Muse would have been possible without Beryl's understanding of his nature, without his certain knowledge that he could always depend on her. He has said more than once to close friends: 'Only Beryl could have stuck by me.' He has been fully aware of this since 1939.

In 1940 he was probably nearer to disintegration – as those who saw him at that time testify – than at any other time. In the exhausting years with Riding he had always felt himself to have one consolation: he could draw support, gain instruction, from Riding's intellect, if not from her heart. Now even that had been withdrawn and transferred to another. He soon put Jackson and Riding, as people, out of his mind; but Riding's gesture, as the abandonment of a poet by the Muse in favour of 'corpse-flesh', so impressed itself upon him that eventually he felt impelled to re-enact it, with others – and to try, yearningly, to change it.

But not now, or for many years hence. Before they joined their lives Beryl could only try to hold the shattered pieces of him together by her unassuming placidity. Now she was present this was easier. He had grown so used to being 'judged' that acceptance on equal terms was a new experience to him. Beryl had no conditions. Except a cat. There was always a cat. In 'The Thieves', written at Rennes and inspired by Beryl, he had at last made a cerebral acknowledgement that there could be a 'single mind' between lovers. In 'Despite and Still', first published in *Work in Hand*, the acknowledgement is emotional. This, which belongs in the tradition of Donne's 'Sweetest Love, I do not goe', sounds a new, lucid note.

> Have you not read
> The words in my head,
> And I made part
> Of your own heart?
> We have been such as draw
> The losing straw –
> You of your gentleness,
> I of my rashness,
> Both of despair –
> Yet still might share
> This happy will:
> To love despite and still.
> Never let us deny
> The thing's necessity
> But, O, refuse
> To choose
> Where chance may seem to give
> Loves in alternative.

Intimations of this note had always been present in Graves's poetry, first in the guise of pastoral, whimsicality, or nursery rhyme; then, more grimly in the poems of the Riding years, as a lyrical element guyed by irony, guilt or melodrama. The straightforward love theme in the early poems is prettified at worst, objectivized or made wistful at best – as in the 'Richard Roe and John Doe' poem. The most light-hearted of the poems about love in the Riding period is 'Down, Wanton, Down!' – and how far that is from being a tender love poem. Now, for the first time, the love theme is able to emerge uninhibitedly and robustly. The old theme of guilty lust vanishes, to be replaced by one of serene and shared confidence: 'Never let us deny/The thing's necessity.' 'Despite and Still' is one of Graves's great simple poems. We feel the presence of an actual woman very different from Laura Riding or Nancy Nicholson. Knowing himself fully loved at last, Graves is at last able to both love, and feel happy that he loves.

Two other poems in particular, 'To Sleep' and 'Through Nightmare' – the first published in *No More Ghosts*, a retrospective selection of fifty poems published by Faber in September 1940, the second in *Poems* (1945) – reflect his new and happier situation. 'To Sleep' is more complex and more substantial than 'Despite and Still', but it is not superior to it; rather, it is complementary.

> The mind's eye sees as the heart mirrors:
> Loving in part, I could not see you whole,
> Grew flesh-enraged that I could not conjure
> A whole you to attend my fever-fit
> In the doubtful hour between a night and day
> And be Sleep that had kept so long away.

> Of you sometimes a hand, a brooch, a shoe
> Wavered beside me, unarticulated –
> As the vexed insomniac dream-forges;
> And the words I chose for your voice to speak
> Echoed my own voice with its dry creak.

> Now that I love you, now that I recall
> All scattered elements of will that swooped
> By night as jealous dreams through windows
> To circle above the beds as bats,
> Or as dawn-birds flew blindly at the panes
> In curiosity rattling out their brains –

> Now that I love you, as not before,
> Now you can be and say, as not before:
> The mind clears and the heart true-mirrors you
> Where at my side an early watch you keep
> And all self-bruising heads loll into sleep.

Here the old lust guilt is at last transformed into love. 'To Sleep' records the process, and in doing so expresses a loving gratitude that is rare in Graves's poetry – and rare in English poetry. It is the poem of a healed man, one at last able to sleep without bad dreams.

In 'Through Nightmare' Graves recognizes that there is as much poetry in the gentle and unassuming as in the militantly literary, or aggressively intellectual, woman:

> Never be disenchanted of
> That place you sometimes dream yourself into
> Lying at large remove beyond all dream,
> Or those you find there, though but seldom
> In their company seated –

The untameable, the live, the gentle.
Have you not known them? Whom? They carry
Time looped so river-wise about their house
There's no way in by history's road
To name or number them.

In your sleepy eyes I read the journey
Of which disjointedly you tell; which stirs
My loving admiration, that you should travel
Through nightmare to a lost and moated land,
Who are timorous by nature.

This thanks Beryl for her intuitive understanding of all he has been through, and for her gift of love for one who could attract such a fate. And at the end of 'Mid-Winter Waking', which begins 'Stirring suddenly from long hibernation,/I knew myself once more a poet', he affirms this:

Be witness that on waking, this mid-winter,
I found her hand in mine laid closely
Who shall watch out the Spring with me.
We stared in silence all around us
But found no winter anywhere to see.

Bearing in mind lines from yet another poem of this time, 'The Oath' – 'early emblems/Prognosticated,/Fulfilled here' – it is interesting to go back to one day in Rennes: 21 March 1939. Graves wrote in his diary:

Walk with Beryl down . . . lane and picked primroses. . . . Beryl said 'first day of Spring: no need to feel guilty about good weather'.

The placid poems of this wartime period – the first truly placid poems he had written – are collected together in what is perhaps the most satisfying of all his volumes: *Poems 1938–1945*. The tension of the earlier, haunted, self-reproachful or ironic poems is here perfectly resolved. The whole process is best seen in the *Collected Poems* of 1947, which include *Poems 1938–1945*. (The *Poems and Satires* of 1951 contain the beginning of a new cycle.) Of all Graves's poems, those of 1938–45 may well be the best remembered and best loved. It is in any case these, and the experience which prompted them, that underpin the later love poems, which are diluted by comparison. In 1940 Graves learned that love could be real and unadulterated, because he discovered that it could be returned: indeed, he learned that it could simply 'happen'. It was no one's fault that it had not happened to him before; but he was more than well aware of his good fortune when it did happen.

Beryl astonished him by not disappointing him, even to the extent that eventually he had to create disappointments for himself – to test his empirical nature, and thus to write more poems. She, however, did not idealize him: she knew from the beginning exactly what she had taken on, and never regretted it.

II

Arthur Barker failed in April 1939, and Methuen took over the rights in the *Claudius* books. Watt therefore offered them the forthcoming *Sergeant Lamb* and its sequel *Proceed, Sergeant Lamb* (1941). They sold 10,000 copies of the first title during the war years; there was a small second impression in 1945. Eventually both books went into large paperback editions. Random House also did well with both novels. *Wife to Mr Milton* (1943) – rejected by Random House but published by Creative Age Press – followed. And while Graves was exercising his imagination on early America and then on the survival of the poetic in Puritan England, he was simultaneously doing two jobs with Alan Hodge: *The Long Weekend* (1940) and *The Reader Over Your Shoulder* (1943), 'A Handbook for Writers of English Prose'. The rest of his time in south Devon was spent in writing *The Golden Fleece* (1944; *Hercules, My Shipmate* in America – not his choice of title), the first draft of *The White Goddess*, and *King Jesus* (1946). He was able to pay off his income tax; and, as always, he and his dependants did not go in need. But by the time he was halfway through *King Jesus*, which proved very difficult, he described himself as 'broke'. Fortunately royalties on previous books saved him. He no longer felt obliged to write for big money – though he was able (jokingly) to call himself 'affluent' by the late fifties. He and Beryl and their family never lived badly, though they have worried about money ('Have seen the parallel red-ink lines drawn/Under their manic-depressive bank accounts'); for most of the time they have lived well.

Vale House Farm lies at the southern end of the small village of Galmpton, a few miles from the little south Devon fishing port of Brixham. Brixham, which looks out over Torbay, is a busy and picturesque place. Its inner and outer harbour are distinctive. The coast in those parts is impressive, with red cliffs; much of the earth in the area is also a rich red. Inland the countryside is, by Devonian standards, dull. From Galmpton it is a short walk to the wide estuary of the River Dart. This is where Graves used to take his long afternoon walks, often carrying William – and later the other children – perched on the back of his neck.

Vale House Farm, which had a small front garden, and a rather larger one at the back – where the Graveses grew vegetables, and where visitors who were not disabled were set to work for not too unreasonable periods of time – was a typical nineteenth-century farmhouse, not quite rambling, but spacious. The Graveses did not spend much on furnishing it, but it was comfortable, they were comfortable, and they made their many guests feel memorably comfortable.

The house was, for the whole time of their occupancy of it (1940–46), a hive of activity. Beryl's first three children were born while they were living there: William on 21 July 1940, Lucia three years later on 21 July 1943, and Juan in December 1944. Considering the circumstances – Graves's temporary lack of funds, made worse by Riding's inability to 'Pay ... back' and by his indebtedness to the Inland Revenue; the difficulties caused by the war – they were lucky to find such a suitable house. Its chief fault was that it was damp. In addition to its stone-floored farm kitchen, with a large range, and its conveniently numerous upstairs bedrooms, it had two front rooms. In one there was a radio, and little else – though it could serve as dining room if there were many guests. This radio was switched on for the news, Churchill's speeches – and for 'ITMA' ('It's That Man Again'), the comedian Tommy Handley's show which helped to keep English people cheerful in the war years.

The other room served as workroom, had a dining table which was used when the Graves did not eat from plates on their knees – and was also the sitting room. Quite often Graves would work with William – or, later, one of the other small children – sitting on his shoulders. It was not unlike the earliest years of his first marriage, with the important differences that Beryl did not display the hostility towards him that the misandrous Nancy had exhibited from very early on, and that there was no overt evidence of poverty. So he got a great deal more work done. Beryl typed many of the drafts and final versions of his books (work went out to local typists when she was unable to do them).

They had plenty of visitors from other parts of the country, and these increased during the course of the war. As Graves put it in 1943,

'I am gradually reconciling myself with most of the people with whom Laura made me quarrel.' He was selectively de-isolating himself. Alan came down whenever he could spare time from his exacting work under Brendan Bracken at the Ministry of Information. James and Mary Reeves came from Slough, where James was teaching at the grammar school. John Aldridge was in the army, at first in the ranks. Norman Cameron was also for some time away on war service, although he too called whenever he could.

There was another more famous caller. As Graves put it to Alan (11 November 1940):

> A large, impressive Mrs Mallow or Mellon or something [it was Mallowan] 'from Greenway House' walked in to call with an archeological little husband. After 20 minutes Beryl & I realised that she was p57 (or whatever) of the L.W.E. [*Long Weekend*] – Agatha Christie herself. [They had written: 'Agatha Christie remained true in her detective novels to the romantic-cumbersome English style of the early Twenties.'] I asked her why if she never noticed anything (as she confessed) she had become a writer. She said, very simply and fairly, that she had been an only child and told herself stories, all plot & no characterisation.

She called fairly often, and even dedicated one of her novels to Graves, who became much fonder of her archeologist husband Max Mallowan than of her.

The most important new contact Graves made while living in Devon was his future collaborator Joshua Podro. He has described how it came about:

> I once went to a typewriter shop at Paignton in 1941, during the Blitz, to buy carbon paper, and the shop man was being rude to a nice girl of eighteen or nineteen who wanted to rent a typewriter. 'There's not a typewriter to be had in the whole of Devon,' he told her. So I said 'You're a liar!' and asked the girl what she wanted one for. She said: 'To type out a list of all the El Grecos in existence'. This seemed to be a hopefully paradoxical sign; so I at once offered to lend her our spare typewriter, and we made friends. It turned out that she lived opposite Joshua, whose press-cutting business had been evacuated to Paignton, and who went to play bridge with her father. As a result. . . . [*Quoz*]

The villagers, especially the constable, were slow to accept Graves – though they finally warmed to him. He helped them fill in the dreary forms applying for food ration books, coal and other commodities, which everyone in wartime had to complete, but which few understood.

But at first it was more difficult. The constable knew about Graves's always troublesome middle name, and spread this about. The result was that someone wrote HEIL HITLER on a vegetable marrow in his garden; the HEIL HITLER grew with the marrow. But that the constable was to blame for the 'von Ranke' getting about did not emerge until 1942, when Graves – who had already become an air-raid warden – was invited to join the Special Constabulary. The constable refused to forward his name. Graves had his revenge a few months later, when his age group was called for medical examination. The policeman, whose view of Graves was by this time not shared by the other villagers, triumphantly brought Graves an order to appear before a medical board at Exeter, and gave him a third-class ticket. But Graves was a pensioned officer, and knew his rights.

> I refused to travel except first-class . . . he [the policeman] and I might find ourselves in the same compartment, and it would never do for us to mix socially.

Graves became even more popular in the village. They addressed him as Captain, deprecated the constable's prejudice, and respected him as the old soldier he was. They liked it when he introduced Beryl to the vicar as 'my wife by courtesy', and when he told them that he was writing *King Jesus* 'to convert the Church of England to Christianity'.

Beryl was able to obtain a divorce quickly. This led to an inconvenient situation for collaborators on a book, since, as Graves put it to Alan (9 October 1942):

> I am very sorry that the absurd divorce laws will now prevent any but surreptitious junketing together until the courts eventually do their duty; but there is always the post.

But Graves himself could not get a divorce. The reasons for this must be unique. Nancy did not object to granting him one, and announced her willingness for proceedings to begin. He appointed Brixham solicitors to get in touch with her solicitors.

But she regarded her name not as Graves, but as Nicholson – and, legally, it *was* Nicholson. Now the law required that the suit take the form of Graves *v.* Graves. Nicholson *v.* Graves just would not, legally, do. And so, Nancy decided, there could be no divorce. The letters from Graves's solicitors to him explaining this are amazed and commiserating documents. Many thought that Nancy must have been using this as a reason to spite her husband. This is not so. She simply would not go through the formality of calling herself 'Graves'. It was not until he had been back in Mallorca for some years that she relented and, persuaded by Jenny and her first husband Alex Clifford, let Graves have his divorce.

Meanwhile he continued to renew his friendship with his children. David had entered Jesus College, Cambridge, in October 1938 – at first much to his father's disgust, for Graves's antipathy to Cambridge, if not to all Cambridge men, is more than skin deep. In fact David had had to write to him from his school back in 1938 in firm, angry terms:

> I am sorry you are so against me going to Cambridge [a later letter, this time from Sam, begins with the identical sentence]. I don't see any reason for my not doing so. Apparently you think it would be nice for me to go to St John's and be received with open arms, just because some of my relations happened to have made a name for themselves. I think there could be nothing more loathsome ... my recollections of Oxford are unhappy and sordid – I'm sure I don't know why, but there it is. . . .

But his father did not pursue his anti-Cambridge line, and was touched when David chose to do his war service with the Royal Welch Fusiliers. For himself David would certainly have liked to know his father better, to have dissolved some of the constraint that remained between them. Although he came to Galmpton as often as he could, he could not bring himself to show his father his poems. As with his choice of university, he was determined to go his own way.

Both Catherine and Jenny joined the WAAF (Women's Auxiliary Air Force), Catherine as a radio operator and Jenny as a war correspondent. She would have married the writer Anthony Cotterell (brother of the novelist Geoffrey), to whom she became engaged, had he not been killed. Towards the end of the war (22 February 1945) she married her fellow war correspondent Alexander Clifford, whom she had met in the front line. This prompted Graves's poem 'At the Savoy Chapel' ('Family features for years undecided/What look to wear against a loveless world/Fix, as the wind veers, in the same grimace').

But they saw the most of Catherine during the war years. In 1941 she married a scientist, then a squadron leader, (George) Clifford Dalton; later, after working at Harwell at the same time as Fuchs and Pontecorvo, he became Engineer-in-Chief to the Australian Atomic Energy Commission. Graves wrote to Alan Hodge on 9 October 1942:

Catherine is discharged honourably from the Waafs and is doing a real civilian flop with the brooding eyes of the mother to be.

Catherine was at Galmpton until the summer of 1943; and she and her husband (who died in Australia in 1961) were frequent visitors thereafter.

III

Since Graves had abandoned the so-called 'main stream' of English poetry in 1929 there had been few critical discussions of him as poet. But he gathered a small but devoted body of readers, and his volumes of poetry did not do badly in terms of poetry sales (which are usually very small). In the forties, however, his poetry was badly reviewed (if at all), and he was known primarily as a novelist. He was certainly a part of literary history, but during the war years he did not attract the attention of journalists – or even literary journalists – and there is only one published account, based on a flying visit, of his life at Galmpton. This is by Tom Matthews; it appears in *Jacks or Better* (in England, *Under the Influence*). All that needs to be said about this is that it is misleading, especially on the subject of Beryl. To correct it would be to give it an attention it does not deserve. It is dated by Matthews as having occurred in the autumn of 1941; in fact it was a year later. Mathews quite fails to convey the impression that, in this period, Graves was happier than he had ever been in his life. Nor are his more detailed impressions of the situation accurate; the visit doubtless faded in his memory.

Thus happy in his domestic life, Graves remained sanguine about the outcome of the war. When Churchill was taken into the War Cabinet as First Lord of the Admiralty in September 1939 Graves immediately wrote to congratulate him, and received a prompt reply (10 September 1939) from Chartwell: 'Thank you so much for your kind letter of congratulation.' Some two years before this Graves sent Churchill *Count Belisarius*, and received the following reply:

I have delayed thanking you for the copy of 'Belisarius' which your publishers sent me, at your kind request, until I was able to read it. This, I have now done with the very greatest pleasure and profit.

I most heartily congratulate you on this brilliant piece of work. You have 'rolled back the time-curtain' in a magical way and made all this strange epoch young again. I daresay some of your readers will have felt there was too much war, but the vivid accounts you give of those long-forgotten campaigns, in my mind, only enhance the value of the work.

I delight also in the theological discussions which blend so amusingly with the easy morals.

Once I began the book, I could not put it down.

Again thanking you,

Believe me,

On 28 December 1942 Graves wrote to Churchill asking him if he might make use of this letter in the promotion of a new edition of *Belisarius* (it was postponed, though the novel has been reprinted several times since). Churchill told Graves through a secretary that 'there would be no objection to your using his letter ... as a foreword as you propose'. But he 'would, however, be glad if you would omit the paragraph which reads' – and he went on to quote the third paragraph of the letter about 'easy morals'.

Although he never concerned himself with politics, Graves unequivocally detested Fascism. Back in 1937, on 1 June, he had written to Alan – then still at Oxford – from the Villa Guidi saying:

There is a slight letter I should like to send to the *Sunday Times* but can't, for reasons of having books published in Germany & also being Karl's official guarantor in Anglo-German passport situations. Would you honour me by being its author?

The letter read:

Mr Desmond MacCarthy in his interesting review misses two other close points of resemblance between the Protector [Cromwell] and the Führer: the voices of both were remarkable for a peculiarly harsh timbre, and both added greatly to the prosperity of England by their attitude to the Jews.

The letter ends with a joke then current amongst Italian anti-Fascists: 'Why is the Duce like a chamber-pot?' and is illustrated with a Gravesian drawing of both the Duce and a chamber-pot.

But Graves had tended to underestimate the dangers of Fascism, and was surprised (and dismayed) when Franco won Spain. Work on *The Long Weekend* (which did not get its title – Jenny's choice – until the last moment) caused him to consider the matter more deeply. On 16 May 1940, when Churchill went to Paris, perhaps the lowest point of the war, he wrote to Alan:

This is to thank you for the second lot of typescript and to reassure you that I feel capable of filling out the parts you have left a bit sketchy with a thesis & further detail. The preliminary thesis is that there were in Oct 1918 two Englands, the revolutionary but apathetic Fighting Forces, and The Rest. The latter included all the schemers in the Law & Order interest who side-tracked the promised social revolution; and so the rebels degenerated into mere Lefts. The Conservative Party used Lloyd George as a Liberal buffer to take the preliminary shock; & then, when they felt their position secure, threw him over. The Liberal Party had been knifed by Lloyd George himself. Naturally: these violent terms would not appear in the book [*The Long Weekend*].

Title still simmering. I think *Lull* ought to come into it. *Lull Between Wars* – A record of happenings in Great Britain between 1918 and 1939.

As for May 1940, you were right when you came back from Poland about real war being on the way. . . . The whole question as to whether we win or lose the war depends on the comparative rate of wastage in Allied and German planes. If the alleged 4–1 proportion is true [it was not; but Hitler never, despite assertions to the contrary, achieved decisive air superiority], and maintained, we are all right. But if not, o dear! Our fighter pilots and the French are on average better than the Germans, it is thought: though the Germans have a few stars, just as in the last war. . . .

In the autumn of 1942 the Germans began to handcuff British prisoners; the British retaliated in kind, although with reluctance. Graves told Alan he had an altogether better idea (in fact it came from Beryl):

This reprisal business is most depressing; the Cabinet should never have competed in that crude way. The obvious retort courteous would have been to announce that while our people will not return evil for evil, they propose to treat their prisoners three times a day so long as our men are handcuffed, to recorded speeches of the Führer given through a loud-speaker. The Germans couldn't object.

Just before this, in July, he commented both on the impending arrival of the Americans, and on his response to a leaflet asking him why he shouldn't join the Home Guard.

The authoritative rumour here is that the Americans will take over Southern Command on August 1st & hold the fort while our brave boys invade France; and will woo their disconsolate widows & sweethearts with Spam Teng & Born, and re-educate the rest of us psychologically.

Today I am asked in a leaflet whether there is any reason why I should not join the Home Guard. I am answering rather pompously that I am not Mr R. Graves, but Captain Graves, a retired officer, Pensioned List, who did not have a temporary commision; & that I am ready to answer any orders addressed to me in my rank but cannot be called up as a private soldier, since I was not cashiered; & that I have important literary contracts to complete.

This is the poem (printed only in a limited edition) he wrote at the time:

> July the twenty-fourth, a day
> Heavy with clouds that could not spill
> On the disconsolate earth.
>
> Across the road in disconsolate chorus
> School-children raised their morning hymn to God
> Who still forgot their names and their petitions.
>
> 'What an age to be born in!' cried old Jamboree.
> 'Two world wars in one generation!'
> 'However,' said I, 'the plum crop should be heavy!'
>
> What was the glass doing? The glass was low.
> The Germans claimed to have stormed the town of Rostov.
> Sweden dismissed the claim as premature.
>
> Not a single painter left in the neighbourhood –
> All were repainting ruined Exeter.
> We had no earthly right to grumble . . . No?
>
> I was reading a book about bone artifacts
> In the age of the elk or woolly rhinoceros.
> Already, it seems, men had a high culture.
>
> A clerk wrote from the Ministry of Labour
> To ask what reasons (if any) would prevent me
> From serving in the Devonshire Home Guard.
>
> Soon the Americans would be here: the patter
> Of their rubber heels sounding like summer rain.
> So pleasantly passed my forty-seventh birthday.

When the war inflicted a cruel personal blow on him, he was characteristically reticent. His letter of 7 April 1943 to Alan Hodge begins by telling him that, whenever he came down to stay, he couldn't expect 'the sort of service' he needed and deserved, as they would be 'overwhelmed' with visitors:

It isn't to be wondered at that you're so tired and depressed: it is saturation in one sort of Information [Alan was at the Ministry of Information] which is necessarily Information about the war-effort or the subsequent peace-effort.

He went on to say that the many letters he had received about his Milton novel, which appeared in England that January, proved 'how charmed people are to get away for a few hours into another sort of world even though a war was going on in it just the same.' And he added,

The war has just given me a body-blow: the usual horrible telegram has arrived saying that David is missing since March 19th. I imagine that he's been on the Maya River with the 2nd Div. Of course 'missing' may mean a whole lot of things, just as 'died of wounds' in my case meant 'unconscious'; but it's no place to be missing at the best of times, and the Japs aren't too good to prisoners.

David was killed – one of the 120 members of his college to die on active service – on the Arakan peninsula under what were described as 'circumstances of great gallantry'. As one newspaper put it (1 June 1943):

The story of how he fell while attacking single handed a Japanese strongpoint during the final big Allied attack in the Donbaik area on March 18 was told by those who saw Graves in action.

The company ahead was held up by heavy automatic mortar fire and grenades. Carrying on with a sergeant and a Bren gunner he bombed his way to the first position, where the sergeant and Bren gunner were put out of action.

Undeterred he returned with a new load of grenades, and, crossing the open ground swept by heavy enemy fire, attacked single-handed a new strongpoint which the Japanese were defending with grenades. He charged and captured the post alone, and was continuing to advance when he was shot [in the head].

Graves continued to hope that he might have been taken prisoner, and still be alive. He didn't give up this hope until the Japanese were defeated – but he always knew that there was only the slenderest of chances. When he sent Alun Lewis's poems, *Ha! ha! Among the Trumpets* – for which he wrote the introduction – to General Wavell at the India Office in the late summer of 1945, Wavell thanked him, and added that, while he would like to wish him good news of his son, 'I am afraid that, as you say, the hopes of his being alive are very slender.'

Graves now saw the poems which David had refused to show him; it seems that he may have contemplated publishing them, though they never appeared. One, though, was printed in the *Cambridge Review* of 25 May 1946. It was called 'In Conclusion':

It will be small loss, never to return.

The summer-house will be cobwebbed,
The plaster flaked;
The nets over the unpruned fruit-bushes
Holed and torn.

Wild grasses dropping seeds on the sundials
And the penny-farthing and the saddlery
Grown dusty in the stables,
And mildewed the embroidered
Dressing-up clothes in the chest,
The artificial lake stagnant and undrained,
The hedges unclipped, the boarding rotten,
The lawn rough-floored under the cedar-trees,

And the pigeon-cot stairs will be broken,
The swing hanging broken.
The engine in the boiler-house will have ceased its beating,
The known voices will no longer be heard about the house,
There will be weeds and crumbling and desolation only.

We should be sorry we returned.

He was very deeply affected by David's death, but wrote no poem about it. Perhaps he felt that the extreme bitterness of his old and now discarded David and Goliath poem – it is a bitterness which still sears, despite its youthful uncertainties of diction – was adequate. In any case he does not 'take advantage' of occasions of grief to advertise himself as a poet. But he regretted that the failure of his marriage to Nancy had cut him off so long from at least this one of their four children, although Laura had always shown scrupulous regard for him in this matter. The other children he did get to know very well.

He gave Nancy all the information and newspaper cuttings he had received about David, and news that he had been recommended for the VC (turned down by a clerk based in London because the attack failed). She replied (5 July 1943): 'Thanks for the things about David. As far as his life goes this leaves it as it was? . . .'

Graves found only one young 'war poet' he could wholeheartedly admire. This was the Welshman Alun Lewis, who was born in 1915 and died in an accident while on active service in March 1944. Graves was not much impressed by the poetry of Sidney Keyes; he liked better that of a Canadian airman, Bertram Warr – who was also killed – but felt that there was not enough of it to make a confident judgement. The work of Keith Douglas did not come to his attention until many years after; he appreciated the quality of this, but thought Lewis the truer and more certain poet.

The work of this love-obsessed and, at his best, very powerful poet consoled him a little for the loss of his own son, who died near where Lewis died. Lewis chose Graves to select the poems which would be included in *Ha! ha! Among the Trumpets*, his second collection. (His first book was *Raider's Dawn*.) He was impressed, he told Graves, by the quickness with which he spotted 'punk poems'. They had a long correspondence (they never met), and Graves responded warmly to the young poet's insistence on writing, and publishing, his 'personal love poems'. He was most moved by this passage from one of Lewis's letters to his wife, with which he ended his short foreword to the posthumous volume:

> ... I'm more engrossed with the *single* poetic theme of Life and Death, for there doesn't seem to be any question more directly relevant than this one, of what survives of the beloved.... Acceptance seems so spiritless, protest so vain. In between the two I live.

Graves felt his death deeply; he has always been proud that Lewis should have written to him in the first place, and should have asked him (subject to his wife's Gweno's final veto) to make the selection for his last book.

IV

Settling down with Beryl and raising a new family, and the death in action of David, were the chief things that 'happened' to Graves in the years he spent in England – although the birth of his first grandchild, Catherine's (David) James, a few days after David's death, should not be forgotten. All this time he dreamed of peace, and of the return to Mallorca. He often told Beryl about how much better the conditions of domestic life were in Deyá. He went to London very seldom. It was in London that he had written in almost helpless misery, in 'Idle Hands', that 'the pavement-coloured dog befouls/The pavement-kerb'.

The Brixham area he preferred infinitely: it was rural and remote. But even so England was still connected in his mind with that 'god-dawfulness' he had discovered in the twenties. He has always preferred to love England at a distance. He had no confidence in its capacity to improve itself, as a country to live in, after the war. He thought that if Churchill were returned in 1945, it would 'put the country back thirty years' (both he and Beryl voted Labour). The notions he had in the forties about what England would eventually turn into have proved right. 'Everything good is being taken from us,' he said in the early seventies.

Before he started on *Wife to Mr Milton* he carefully reread Milton's poems, and found them, by his own standards, corrupt. He considered him to be a true poet (as distinct from Pope, whom he saw as 'a prose man' − a phrase he frequently used at that time) only in *Comus*. In this he considered that Milton had dealt honestly with his 'chastity problem'. But he found Milton a false poet in his 'posterity-conscious set pieces' (as Graves, in conversation, rudely described such poems as *Paradise Lost* and *Lycidas*). Embarrassed by the derivative poems of a friend, he wrote to Alan Hodge (18 February 1941):

> The pity is his [the friend's] poems *are* so nice: people unaware of the sources would think them marvellous − perhaps more marvellous than the originals. As has happened with Milton, of course, in his cribs from Giles & Phineas Fletcher, Browne's Pastorals etc etc. − I prefer the originals always.

He was always genuinely shocked by 'cribbing', though the present-day academic fashion is to call this 'poetry of allusion'. The question is in itself a difficult one to resolve, if only because it can almost always be shown that no one is as original as he or she might seem. Graves had himself used a couplet by John Gay to begin one of his own poems:

> Lest men suspect your tale untrue,
> Keep probability in view
> [Fable XVIII]

and the poem as a whole, 'The Devil's Advice to Storytellers', owes rather more than only the opening lines to Gay's Fable, 'The Painter Who Pleased Nobody and Everybody'. But he 'covers' himself by inserting 'some say' (having substituted a decasyllabic line for Gay's octosyllabic one):

> Lest men suspect your tale to be untrue,
> Keep probability – some say – in view.

Graves might, if reluctantly, accept that all poetry is less original than it seems; but he would always insist that the poet's response – made in what he has consistently described as a 'trance state' – be authentic, 'his own', 'unmanufactured'. His attitude is best summed up in one of his *Oxford Addresses on Poetry*, 'The Anti-Poet', who is in that instance Virgil (but might well have been Milton, Pope, or the later Wordsworth), represented as a writer for cash or fame, who 'never consulted the Muse' but 'only borrowed Apollo's slide-rule', and was guilty of perpetrating 'deliberately contrived rhetorical horripilations'. The portrait of Milton, though unfair, is not more one-sided than the one painted by the regular classicists.

In 1941 Graves had not formulated the vocabulary of his criticism. This evolved – and not really satisfactorily, as criticism – only after the writing of *The White Goddess*. But his preliminary study of Milton, in fictional form, was important to him as an examination (and demonstration) of poetic bad faith.

He remained devoted to Skelton above all. He chose him as his example of 'The Dedicated Poet' in his Oxford lectures. His view of other poets was to become increasingly severe, as this letter of late 1945 shows:

> .... Yes, I was severe on Coleridge and Keats [in an *Epilogue* essay]; but Keats should have been content to be wet without that 'mannikin' maleness which shows in his 'Give me women, wine and snuff', and his ambitious 'Cap and Bells' nonsense. And darling old Coleridge should have kept up his end better against his dreadful stuffy pious friend Southey and that old soul-ruptured tyrannical humourless Wordsworth. I don't think it's worth saying that Keats would have shaken off his badness; the fact is, he didn't. And yet, of course, he was an awfully nice person in his letters especially to his younger sister. He just needed somebody to tell him where he was going wrong; a woman. Perhaps that girl he saw at Vauxhall one day. Yes, one *is* sorry for Keats.
>
> I think poets can die, or commit suicide, before their natural deaths. In fact, most of them do. Wordsworth was probably a decent chap until he turned ecclesiastical anti-Jacobin and murdered his moral conscience because he could not face its accusations of treachery. [To M.S.-S., December 1945]

371

When I first got to know him, in February 1943, Graves was harassed by the need to complete *The Golden Fleece* ('I am having a terrible time with a book about the Argonauts, the most complicated historical novel I have yet attempted', he wrote in a letter), and much absorbed in it – but thoroughly happy in his routine, which was running quite smoothly.

At fourteen I was full of brash questions, all of which he answered sympathetically, at length and with genuine interest. He seemed to have no doubts about the total validity of his opinions, but rather to assume that all 'saved' people ('necessary for salvation' was a phrase he often then used about poems, or poets he loved – and even about Defoe's *Colonel Jack*) automatically shared them. His regally held convictions were perfectly in tune with the man he was: some were based on false premises or on hearsay – but not one was held in deference to his own convenience. Everything was for poetry. He told me that he was glad I was

> getting to the stage of realising that there are hardly any poets or ever have been: this is the only decent excuse for writing poems oneself, because after all there *is* such a thing as poetry. . . .

Just before I met him I had, or so I believed, 'discovered' a poet I liked better than Auden, Eliot or other idols of the time: Norman Cameron. I did not expect Graves to have heard of this unfashionable Scotsman, and so took my copy of *The Winter House* to introduce him to this poet. This created a rapport which made it easier for Graves to talk at length about poets, poetry – and its problems. He showed no interest in the contemporary novel, and told me that all plays were written by 'rascals' – but that Shakespeare and Ben Jonson were exceptions (though rascals). 'Jonson wasn't really quite mad enough, but splendid nevertheless.' He loved, he said, the sweeping, exclusive, *unfair* statement. Things could be factually untrue and yet 'philosophically true'. (This is the only occasion on which he uses the word 'philosophical' in a non-derogatory sense.) Thus, while Dylan Thomas might not actually have syphilis ('at present'), *philosophically* he was riddled with it.

L. A. G. Strong? Yes, a very nice chap, Leonard, who had written a few decent minor Irish poems. But he had a hernia, and he suffered this mentally as well as physically – did I see? Charles Madge? He had overheard him being 'stupid' in the Café Royal before the war. No good. And so on about many others.

Each of his strictures was particularized by a concrete occasion: in the Café Royal, and so forth. These particularizations gave an air of validity to pronouncements which others might consider preposterously unfair. But had the gentle Madge, at least, turned up in person, he would immediately have revised his view. His prejudices were neither set nor rancorous, though some were slanderous and untrue (I have, with great reluctance, not quoted these, though some are 'philosophically true').

T. S. Eliot: a marvellous satirist with a true poetic sense who had sold out to institutionalized religion – and blotted his copybook by publishing Auden. But always a poet, and 'a very decent chap really'. As for Auden, no one could possibly like Auden (this remained a very strongly held conviction, undispelled when he finally met him); he was the kind of man who borrowed a flat for the weekend and then left it in a filthy mess. He was unoriginal, synthetic. Graves showed me examples of his thefts from Laura Riding: the Auden texts were in an American anthology he had been sent because he was included in it – he wouldn't have Auden's own volumes on his shelves: 'bad for the soul'. When it was rumoured that Auden, who had left England in 1939, might return in 1945, he wrote to me: 'Ha ha about Auden: the rats return to the unsunk ship.'

Spender? A nice chap, but better as a greengrocer than a poet. Beryl suggested that a dentist would be more appropriate. 'Yes, we'll give him that. He wouldn't hurt his patients.' MacNeice was probably the most honest of that group, but should not have kept a Borzoi – and should not have thrown back the plates which Nancy Coldstream (with whom he lived for a time) allegedly threw at him: 'It's all right to duck, but you must never offer violence to a woman.' Dylan Thomas was a latterday Swinburne whose early verse, which he had sent to Graves, had been 'very badly accomplished – really very badly accomplished indeed.' But 'The Hand that Signed the Paper' was all right. George Barker had seemed better than most when he had last had a look at the young English poets, and was certainly better than Thomas, who was nothing more, really, than a Welsh demagogic masturbator who failed to pay his bills.

What about Richard Church's essay on him, reprinted in a volume called *Eight for Immortality*? 'O God!' Had he read Sir Edward Marsh's autobiography, *A Number of People*, in which he figured? 'I haven't dared.' But he didn't mind Marsh having left Edward Thomas out of *Georgian Poetry*: had never been able to see what the fuss was about (this continued failure of Graves to see the virtues of Edward Thomas is surprising; but I don't believe he ever read him carefully). But, pressed, he admitted that Frost had admired Thomas; and if Thomas had started Frost off, then there must have been something to him. Frost's best poems, he believed, were in his first two books – but these were very good indeed. The two other good American poets, apart from Laura Riding – who was not really of any 'nationality' as a poet – were Ransom and Cummings. Ransom had gone back on his poetic excellence by becoming a prescriptive critic; but while he had been poetically alive he had been very good indeed. Cummings was a marvellously funny, bawdy satirist, but his love poems were too 'wet'. Tate was wholly artificial – and a bit of a beast with women, though 'Laura forgave him'. Red Warren (Robert Penn Warren) was all right, from what he had heard; but he hadn't read anything by him. Pound? He wouldn't like to say that Pound hadn't got a sense of rhythm, but the sense of rhythm he did have was unpleasant, and Graves disliked it as much as he disliked Pound's anti-Semitism. Eliot should never have got mixed up with him. Yes, he had met Pound once: in T. E. Lawrence's rooms at All Souls. He'd had a wet handshake and was clearly crazy.

I asked him about a certain Irish writer (who is still alive) whose work I had been reading. He told me that he thought he had read two or three good early stories – 'but' (with a giggle) 'he's a frightful man: when he quarrelled with a mistress he wrote "Prick", "Cunt", "Balls" and so on in all the copies of the privately printed, valuable books he'd given her – so that she couldn't sell them.'

He asked me about my public school life. I told him. He suggested that I write a book analysing my schoolmasters' personalities (I completed about two-thirds of it: it was a scarifying and libellous document), and that to remedy injustices I should consider starting a mutiny 'with due regard to the rules'. He lent me *The Floating Republic: An Account of the Mutinies at Spithead and the Nore in 1797* by Bonamy Dobrée ('my successor at Cairo University, very decent chap, humble, doesn't know what literature's about, but good on mutiny because he wouldn't dare to do it') and G. E. Manwaring: this would give me the general picture. I did not follow up the suggestion, but felt encouraged.

When Graves later became fully recognized as a poet, people without vested interests hugely enjoyed his forthright way of expressing himself. He made no compromises, and in his lectures and addresses said exactly what he felt. But back in those wartime days, when his poetic reputation was eclipsed, some were offended or even appalled by what they regarded as his arrogance. A bald account of the way he spoke then may indeed give an impression of an eccentric dogmatism. But this would be misleading, even though the 'method' does sometimes recall Churchill's retrospective description of his dealings with his war-time Cabinet: 'All I wanted was compliance with my wishes after reasonable discussion.' The Gravesian *hauteur* and *morgue* had been well known since his Oxford days. But these characteristics were displayed only when he found himself in hostile circumstances, or when he was quarrelling.

His authority as a romantic poet is now accepted in the public mind. But in those days it was not. He nevertheless possessed it. So those who were not prejudiced against extreme individualism, or were not overtimid, bureaucratized souls, were delighted to hear him talk, and recognized that he spoke from convictions which had been reached through much suffering and work.

He listens courteously to what others have to say, but he will not agree with them for the sake of politeness. He has never changed his views to please anyone (except Riding), though he has tried not to be rude to his friends or acquaintances. I don't think he meant to be when he told a certain young man with temporary poetic aspirations that typing – of Graves's poems – was his forte. Once when an alcoholic he liked quoted certain fervent lines by Edna St Vincent Millay, he commented: 'Well, she meant it.' He always knew that he was provocative (he enjoyed teasing Tom Matthews in particular), but did not form his personality around the need to be so. When in his role of protector of Riding, he shared – or felt himself to share – her hope that what seemed provocative now would be recognized as true tomorrow.

Without her he kept faith with himself: it simply did not occur to him to modify his opinions in order to gain either poetic fame or money. He gave the benefit of his convictions only to those people whom he felt shared his view of the world. They knew how he thought, even if they did not agree with all his opinions. If people were present who weren't poets, or who weren't interested in poetry, he would quickly sense that they felt 'left out', and would turn the conversation to whatever subject he believed they were expert in (I recollect a Canadian coffin-maker). He was not, in fact, what he called his old Oxford neighbour Tolkien (whose books he refused to read, and Beryl loved), a 'monologist'. He would listen to whatever anyone had to say

ROBERT GRAVES

– although when he was especially wrapped up in his work, as he usually was while living at Galmpton, he could not always absorb the sense of what was said, though he tried to. So happy in his personal life that he could not get used to it, he was for the first time able to concentrate wholeheartedly on his work. During this period he got as hopelessly absent-minded as he ever has been. 'It was terrible,' Beryl recollects. When he was doing chores he would be thinking about the work, often muttering about it. Once when laying the table he put down knife, fork and glass for Sergeant Lamb. He did not do this, however, for Jesus Christ when he was work'.ing on *King Jesus*.

Chapter Twenty-Four
1940–46(II)

I

Before the *Sergeant Lamb* books Graves had written, on his own, five novels (and the short novel *My Head! My Head!*). From the *Lamb* novels onwards his prose style became more self-consciously careful. Beryl, though she knew that he was a poet first and foremost, did not take the simplistic view that his prose books were mere potboilers. Her attitude influenced him, and he began to take his prose more seriously, confidently and conscientiously. This is why he first thought of *The Reader Over Your Shoulder*.

But he never pretended to have a capacity for writing novels set in contemporary society. 'Pure fiction is beyond my imaginative range,' he wrote when introducing his *Collected Stories*. His attitude to his fiction is revealed in a letter (of 1952) to an inquiring stranger:

> . . . I make no attempt to assess myself as a novelist. I have a large family and every now and then I have to write a novel to pay for schools or dentists or holidays, and I do so: but nowadays the historical side tends to overshadow the fictional. . . . In writing *I, Claudius* I did not know as much about history as I do now; and needed money more desperately, so it is more readable.
>
> Frankly, all I really care about is poetry – that is my life, not novel-writing. My next interest is history. . . .

And he goes on to demonstrate how 'there is always an excuse for these novels': Lamb was in his own regiment; his 'direct ancestor' had charge of King Charles I's person in *Wife to Mr Milton*; *Count Belisarius* 'is a military manual . . . tactics interest me', and so on.

But the themes of Graves's novels are always revealing. The *Lamb* books had two antecedents. First, he had, for a few months in 1939, the notion that he might soon be again involved in active fighting: he was going to volunteer – until he discovered that he would be put behind a desk, not in the field. Secondly, he had bad feelings about 'the New World'. About the loss of the American colonies he felt, with due allowance for the passage of time, very much as Dr Johnson had before him. The Welch Fusilier Sergeant Roger Lamb had his sympathy – as a good-soldier victim of corrupt and stupid politicians and bad generals. He formed an intense dislike of George Otto Trevelyan's Whiggish and disingenuous accounts of the American War of Independence; he continued for some time to express himself ferociously on this subject. The real Lamb was a stolid, self-educated Dubliner, a reliable man. The subject was just what Graves needed to absorb him in this period of transition. He wrote it quickly. On 2 February 1940 he told Alan Hodge, who (with Sally) had been helping him with the research, that he was writing two chapters a week; it was published as *Sergeant Lamb of the Ninth* by Methuen in the following September; its sequel *Proceed, Sergeant Lamb*, which he thought 'a nicer book' (because he was in a happier frame of mind while writing it), appeared in February 1941. *The Long Weekend* had meanwhile been published in November 1940.

So this was an exceptionally busy time. He worked not in sporadic bursts, but relentlessly, persistently and regularly. And despite the fact that he had to pay out money for research – with only a part share in the royalties for *The Long Weekend* – he was solvent enough by the end of 1941 to be able to take *Wife to Mr Milton* and *The Reader Over Your Shoulder* at a slightly slower pace. By the time he came to write *The Golden Fleece* he had more time to concentrate. The result is a more complex and closely argued book.

The *Lamb* novels are solid and workmanlike, but are his stodgiest work. Their function was to bring solvency – and to guard their author against the kind of self-pitying introspection that he hates. Of ennui he knows nothing. 'What is this bloody *néant*?' he once asked apropos of Sartre.

Wife to Mr Milton is a very different matter. One of the best of his novels, its themes are more relevant to his deeper concerns. His imagination here is altogether more *engagé*. In his personal life he had by now adjusted himself – and with some relief – to the absence of a strict mentor. But he had still to relocate himself poetically. His poems were, mostly, ones of gratitude. If the work on *Sergeant Lamb* helped keep him from disintegrating – giving up poetry in disgust – then *Wife to Mr Milton* had the more important function of helping him to redefine his poetic position.

Graves's disgusted attitude towards the poet who seeks fame in posterity has its source in his conviction that experience, as distinct from thinking, is primary in poetry. Since no one can plan his experience, his fate, how can anyone *plan* to be a 'great poet'? For Graves everything in Milton, except some early poems and *Comus*, is artificial and 'classical' – and 'classical poets try to transcend the true Muse'. But Matthews's suggestion that he based his portrait of Milton on Schuyler Jackson is nonsensical: he respected Milton's gifts too much for that. Besides, he had forgotten Jackson.

Wife to Mr Milton is the story, narrated by her, of Marie Powell, the Oxfordshire girl of Royalist parents who married Milton in 1642 (to save her parents from financial disaster), at the age of sixteen, and then left him precipitately. In 1645 she returned to him, bore him three children, and died in childbirth in 1651. The academic view of Marie Powell is that she was 'a flighty young girl'. Milton's pamphlets on divorce, prompted by the failure of this marriage, are respected – although the academic view is that they are more successful in proving that marriage must be 'true companionship in every sense' (or dissolved) than they are in showing that this is 'true Christian doctrine'.

Graves felt that Marie was lively rather than flighty; he thought Milton's solution to his 'chastity problem' 'ugly'. But all he did in the novel was to present the case from Marie's point of view, and to cause her to be in love with a young Royalist, Mun. The result was a very fine, commercially successful historical novel. The Cassell edition (January 1943) of 10,000 sold out immediately, and a new impression of 3000 was needed within two weeks; the American edition (1944, Creative Age Press) sold more than 20,000 copies. The 1954 Penguin edition of 40,000 copies sold out quickly, as did another American edition of 1962.

But reviewers were appalled; they failed to allow that Marie Powell's view of her husband could be granted status as a fact. Random House, although they published Graves's *Collected Poems* and the two *Lamb* novels, would not take it on. As Graves said in his letter to Alan Hodge of 9 October:

> Random House turned down my Milton book ... the reason quoted
> was that their [reader] Professor Kelly of Princeton objected to it, not
> because he could find any anachronisms etc in it but because it destroyed

the idealistic figure of Milton which scholars have patiently built up these last fifty years! Joke.

Graves has given an account (in his lecture 'Moral Principles in Translation', an address given to the Institute of Linguists in 1962) of how the theme crystallized in his mind:

> The theme of my novel *Wife to Mr Milton* came suddenly with the realisation that Milton was what we now call a 'trichomaniac' (meaning, that he had an obsession about hair – his own, and women's). This discovery gave me the key to his lamentable marriage to Marie Powell ... truly a ghost with a grievance. Yet to keep any hint of modern psychology or sociology from intruding, I wrote the book in pure mid-seventeenth-century style, avoiding all words of later occurrence than 1651, the year in which she died. The language had to vary greatly from character to character – Marie Powell's associates being Royalists and rural; John Milton's Roundhead and urban. Worse, she wore a dark blue favour, he a light blue – miscegenation between the Senior Universities can be dangerous in the extreme ...

Whether Milton's trichomania (if he suffered from it) was as important as Graves thinks hardly matters; it is made convincing in the novel.

For his source material he used the massive life by David Masson, the standard work until Parker's dull, diligent, updated work appeared in 1966. No one caught him in an anachronism; nor did they fault him historically.

It is obvious that Graves himself agrees with Marie's picture of her poet, or 'anti-poet'. He may be accused of lack of sympathy for Milton. But whether or not his view is wrong-headed, his portrait of Milton is a refreshing contrast to the pious – and incredible – one constructed by academics.

Eddie Marsh's reaction is fairer than the reviewers'. Acknowledging the novel on 1 March 1943, he wrote:

> Thank you for yr. distressingly interesting letter – of course your spate of knowledge sweeps me off my feet & I can't possibly argue against it – but I shall continue to believe in my heart of hearts that the man who wrote L'Allegro & Il Penseroso can't have been the *unredeemed* monster you have depicted – and that the elegance of mind which shines in the Lawrence Sonnet wasn't merely assumed to curry favour with an eligible pupil [as Graves suggests]. . . . I know the brutality that M. was capable of – there's no doubt that there was a horrible side to his character. I still think there must have been another side. . . .

Possibly Marsh is right. But Graves wasn't the right man to discover the 'other' and pleasanter side of the personality of an 'anti-poet', and supporter of puritanism. That other side is, in fact, hard to find.

II

The Reader Over Your Shoulder, published by Cape in England in May 1943 and by Macmillan in America in November of the same year (an abridged version appeared in 1947; this is the one that has been reprinted in paperback) was another collaboration with Alan Hodge. After the success of *The Long Weekend*, Graves thought yet another book with Alan would be a good idea. He wrote to him on 30 October 1940:

> ... this new book of mine is not a grammar, but intended to help people like Jenny & B. Liddell Hart who have never learned to write but who have a lot to write about and know that they could do better; and also ... to draw conclusions from errors in English about the minds of the Prominent People who make them. I have already about fifty departments in my shoe-box file: such as tautology (though I won't use the term in the book) *Cruelty to Metaphors, Reckless Statement* and – most populous of all – Utter Confusion. In the 'Utter Confusion' section each entry has pinned to it what I think the writer meant.
>
> Now, Alan, wouldn't it be a good plan if we followed up *Long Week End* with another collaboration? If you would like to help me with this book – Basil [Liddell Hart] calls it 'A Short Cut to Unpopularity' – I should like that too very much: we have worked so long together now and disagreed so little and are such good checks on each other. ... I get more & more self-conscious and that raises the point about the difference between spoken English – letters being spoken, really, not written – and written English. Hansard's record of speeches isn't fair on the Hon. Members unless they are allowed ... to hand in their own accounts of what they said. ...
>
> I should not expect you to do as much work on this collaboration as myself, because you have a full-time job at the Ministry and I have no other job but a little housework; and I should expect you to take whatever share of the royalties you think you have earned when the book is written. If you need money there's no reason why you shouldn't have some out of any advance we get – 'without prejudice' as they say. ...
>
> About clichés. I am not *against* clichés: they are inevitable & rather

charming in drowsy parish meetings, addresses by colonels to their regiments, & so on. But in cases where a really strong effect is intended ... they are useless. ...

Alan agreed – he did, by Graves's rough estimate, about a fifth of the work – and together they elaborated the original scheme.

The basic rationale of the book is that people ought to say what they mean. The authors, unlike Jackson, who – it will be recalled – had formulated a similar notion, set out to show how this might be achieved. Since they decided to make 'examinations' of passages by eminent people, and give what they called 'fair copies' of them after correction and discussion, this gave Graves the opportunity to have a certain amount of fun. He had to obtain permission to quote, but met with little difficulty. Eliot cheerfully submitted himself. Others whose prose was quoted, dissected and rewritten included Baldwin, Hugh Dalton (the Labour politician), Daphne du Maurier, the fascist military historian J. F. C. Fuller, Halifax, the popularizing philosopher C. E. M. Joad, F. R. Leavis, Cecil Day Lewis, Ezra Pound, J. B. Priestley, Herbert Read and Stephen Spender. The last named paid a wartime visit to Graves, who showed Spender his 'fair copy': 'I showed Stainless his bit, and he promised to do better and was very pleased,' he recalled.

'He didn't, and was very embarrassed,' Beryl rejoined.

'Well, philosophically.'

The Reader Over Your Shoulder is one of the most sensible guides to the writing of clear English. The authors wrote as realists, not to reform the world. As Graves was to put it, some quarter of a century later, in a lecture called 'Five Score and Six Years Ago' (*The Crane Bag*, 1969):

> The craft of writing good English is based on a single principle: never to lose the reader's attention. Since the most obvious ways of losing it are to offend, confuse or bore him, good writing can be reduced simply to the principle of active care for sensibilities.

This aptly combines the pragmatic and the moral attitudes evinced in *The Reader Over Your Shoulder*, the book which shows Graves at his most straightforwardly sensible. It helps to demonstrate why the hyper-romantic poet is one of the best craftsmen in English poetry.

III

Graves had always been wrapped up in mythology. His classical background familiarized him with the Greek and Roman myths, and since he was brought up on the less well-known Celtic ones, it came naturally to him to examine and compare the relationships between the two groups. He has read in mythology all his life: first and foremost in Homer, then in the other sources. In his Oxford days he became acquainted with the works of James Frazer and Jane Harrison.

But until the end of 1942, when he began to write *The Golden Fleece*, he had never tried his hand at a purely mythological work – creative or critical. (Only the remarkable but small-scale excursion into biblical history *My Head! My Head!* anticipates his later concerns.)

The Golden Fleece, finished in July 1943, was published by Cassell in October 1944 and by Creative Age Press in September 1945. In his 'postscript' to the last revision (1960) of *The White Goddess* Graves implies that he was still working on *The Golden Fleece* in 1944, and that he interrupted it to write the first 70,000 word draft of *The White Goddess*, then called *The Roebuck in the Thicket*. This is a misrecollection, understandable because he was in a state of continuous excitement from about two-thirds of the way through the *Fleece*. He did write the first 70,000 word draft in three weeks – his mind 'running at a furious rate'; but what his 'sudden overwhelming obsession' interrupted was not the writing of the *Fleece* (then finished) but 'four very difficult, and very full, maps ... of the Argo's voyage' (to M.S.-S., August 1943). It was indeed in (early) 1944 that he wrote his frenzied first draft of *The White Goddess*; but the 'overwhelming obsession', the sudden urgent feeling that he had an enormous amount to say, that he was bursting with a new discovery, came upon him in late August 1943. From then onwards until he left England for Mallorca his mind was on the Goddess theme; the subject of Jesus Christ bore so directly upon it, for him, that he had to get it out of the way – by writing *King Jesus* – before he could finish *The White Goddess*.

As soon as, or even a month or two before, he finished the *Fleece*, Graves was thinking about a new project: a history of poetry. At first it was just another book. Then his mind began to race. One could see it happening:

> ... I have been, and still am, extremely busy with domestic what-nots caused by the birth of Lucia [21 July 1943] a month ago; she and Beryl

383

are all right, but the easier things can be made for the two of them this first four months, the sooner the household will be able to run normally. And since finishing *The Golden Fleece* I have had four very difficult maps to do of the Argo's voyage; and my correspondence is behindhand; and I am reading proofs for Basil Liddell Hart of his *Thoughts on War* [published in 1944] which has gone to press far too soon – he should have worked another four months on it. . . . This projected book on poetry is for people of good sense who have shelved the consideration of poetry because it is too muddled a study, and also for people who have themselves written a little; and for anyone else who is interested. It is going to be exciting to write because of the discoveries I have already made, in the course of the Golden Fleece researches, about Apollo and the Muse and the tenancy of Mount Parnassus. This sounds nonsense; but isn't it queer that English poets have always owed loyalty to the Muse rather than Jehovah? The Muse is – well, she's the mouse-aspect of the Moon, and it all starts with that, i.e. with Big Medicine under the Moon on Mount Parnassus in matriarchal days. The connexion has never quite snapped. [To M.S.-S., August 1943]

He had not, by then, got far in his quest, although the foundations were already there. By September he was writing longer and longer letters about it. He had at first considered doing it in collaboration with Alan; but Alan's letter of 22 September 1943 makes it clear why he pulled out early: he saw that Graves was going off on a highly individual tack. The book had originally been conceived as a historical discussion of poets and poetry. Alan wrote:

Second, our Orphics. I am most interested in your epitome of early poetic history, but I cannot much help you to write it out – at least, the historically early part of it, because I know so little of Latin and Greek literature and religion. I should regard your epitome as a kind of myth (in the sense that Jason's story is a myth), needing telling and interpreting as only you can do it. I think it is a good myth – that is, it has truth, and it is not necessary to ask whether it is entirely factually true.

Anything I may write towards this Orphic book would be based on later poetic happenings. I should like to see your first chapter when it is written and work out how what I have to say can be fitted in.

The next four or five months were difficult, and Graves did not get a great deal of work done. The household was not fully geared to the arrival of the new baby until the beginning of 1944. Money was tight. Readers were avid for fiction in the war years, but the wartime economy put a restriction on the number of copies of novels that could be printed. The demand for Graves' books was high enough for Methuen to reprint the 4000 copies of *Proceed, Sergeant Lamb* which had been destroyed by Nazi bombs in 1942. He could count on very little money from the translations of his books into foreign languages in wartime. Indeed, *I, Claudius* was in Germany, in 1944, being used for a purpose quite other than entertainment: it was the plotters' codebook for the abortive *coup* against Hitler led by Count von Stauffenberg (a distant relative of Graves on his mother's side). No royalties were due on that.

Graves, not too far from the familiar insolvency, his bank account in a 'depressive' phase, struggled on with the 'book on poetry' with mounting excitement. At the beginning of 1944 he produced his astonishing first draft, *The Roebuck in the Thicket*. The foundations of *The White Goddess* were well and truly laid.

Then, quite suddenly, the whole project was 'usurped'. On 10 February he wrote:

> This is to say O is K here, but I've been dreadfully busy (still am) on housework, garden & a hopelessly difficult book that has usurped the place of the one I began about poetry – a historical reconstruction of the whole Jesus Christ story, on which I have a rather startling new line. I had never realised how hopelessly corrupt the O.T. & N.T. texts are; hardly a single straight strand in the whole tangle – parables, lies, half-truths, miscopyings, mis-editings, mis-datings, mystification. Yet if one is patient a story emerges clearly: one gets it by the same means that one finds hidden arms in an African village, by grabbing an obviously dis-honest text and going in exactly the other direction from the one in which it pulls you. [To M.S.-S.]

He needed money. He was scared of what he had started ('Ought I to publish this?' he asked several people).

IV

The Golden Fleece is the story of the Argonauts: of the loss of the Fleece by King Athamas (through his worship of patriarchal Zeus), and of its recovery. Graves consulted all the available classical sources – including the late ones, of which he is especially fond because they afford him more speculative scope – and provided a complete roster of the crew of the *Argo*. It is a thrilling and well-told story, Graves's finest novel of action; but it has another dimension, one of which the author himself only gradually became aware in the course of writing. He discovered that there was a basic theme underlying his narrative: that of the struggle between a Goddess whose authority had, until about the fourteenth century BC, been unchallenged in the Mediterranean countries, and a new, patriarchal religion. In *The Golden Fleece* the Goddess triumphs over the Olympians. He later developed the thesis that the Olympians supplanted her, though he added that this was only because she 'allowed' it. In the novel the Goddess is represented by her priestess at Colchis, Medea – who enables the Argonauts to get the Fleece back. Jason is protected by the Goddess of Pelion.

Graves has stated his 'matriarchal' thesis most concisely in the introduction to *The Greek Myths* (1955; revised 1960):

> Ancient Europe had no gods. The Great Goddess was regarded as immortal, changeless, and omnipotent; and the concept of fatherhood had not been introduced into religious thought. She took lovers, but for pleasure, not to provide her children with a father. Men feared, adored, and obeyed the matriarch; the hearth which she tended in a cave or hut being their earliest social centre, and motherhood their prime mystery. . . . Not only the moon, but . . . the sun were the goddess's celestial symbols.

Graves's anthropological and mythological theories are most important as the background to his poetry, and the suggestive and ingenious details he gives in his exposition of them are frequently of independent value. A few regard him as an important anthropologist, others as a propounder of idiosyncratic or even pernicious nonsense. Both views are wrong. It is essential to view his beliefs from an anthropologically informed point of view, which has never been done.

It must be stated at the outset that there is *no* evidence for the existence of true matriarchies, in the past or in the present – but much against. It is often assumed in newspaper articles, even books, that there is such evidence – sometimes even existing isolated societies are described as 'matriarchal' – but this is not the case.

However, the belief that matriarchy had existed in the past was easily assumed by many, in fact most, anthropologists and classicists of the late nineteenth and early twentieth centuries. And, as Robin Fox puts it in his *Kinship and Marriage*, the

> debate between the 'matriarchal' and 'patriarchal' schools of thought proceeded with mounting acrimony for . . . fifty years, and is not quite dead yet, as readers of Robert Graves . . . will know.

Part of the confusion in the minds of the early 'matriarchalists' arose from their belief that lines of descent which were not patrilinear, but (in one way or another) matrilinear, implied that 'power and authority were in the hands of women in such a system'. This, as Fox says, is 'just not true'. But Graves had formed his ideas long before the matriarchy theory was finally laid to rest – and his belief in it makes little or no difference to the value of *The White Goddess*. That there were, and are, no matriarchies – in an anthropological sense – does not invalidate the *essence* of Graves's thesis. That thesis is, in general terms, that the feminine has been so trampled upon as to make life artificial and intolerable for the whole of mankind. This is indubitably correct.

Graves's debts to Frazer (of *The Golden Bough*) and to Jane Harrison – author of *Prolegomena to the Study of Greek Religion* (1908), a more sensitive and able writer than Frazer – have been noted by most commentators. Some have even gone so far as to suggest that he must certainly have been indebted to Johann Jacob Bachofen – they can hardly believe it possible that he was not. 'His debts to the theories of Bachofen and Briffault seem indisputable,' writes Patrick Grant. But the debt to Bachofen does not exist.

Bachofen was a Swiss ex-judge and amateur archaeologist who published a book called *Das Mutterrecht* (*Mother-Right*) in 1861. This armchair thinker, falsely described as an 'anthropologist' by those who should know better, believed that the memory of the 'matriarchal' stage of human development was so intolerable for humanity that it had to be repressed; he therefore regarded everything as a symbol of it. Bachofen has become a hero of modern (mostly male-run) Women's Liberation, and his book was translated, as a rediscovered classic, in America in 1967. This is ironic, for he believed that the patriarchy which succeeded his 'matriarchy' was vastly superior to it. His book is tedious but ingenious; it anticipated a few developments in what turned out to be the worthy but false anthropology of the later nineteenth century, and is quite interesting as a collection of certain specific instances of Goddess-worship (which he confuses with matriarchy) or relics or memories of it. But Graves had never even heard of Bachofen in the forties.

A more impressive collection of ethnological facts was put together by a French Marxist lawyer (not anthropologist), Robert Briffault, in a book called *The Mothers*, which was translated in 1927. This book became known to Graves after he had formulated his own thesis – and he did not agree with its argument. Briffault was attempting to strengthen the contention of Engels (in *The Origin of the Family*, 1884) that 'the great historical defeat of the feminine sex' coincided with the rise of private property. Graves is no more of a Marxist than he is a Tory, and would have none of this. Yet he became one of the heroes of the Women's Liberation movement of the sixties in America because he was seen as a poet-Bachofen! This is unfortunate, because it is misleading.

Graves the anthropologist, however, is not as important as Graves the poet. Had he himself believed otherwise, he would have fully documented *The White Goddess* – and kept himself abreast of modern anthropology. His system, however, is a poetic metaphor; and those who make poetic metaphors cannot afford to disbelieve in the foundations upon which they are based.

Thus, in conversation in about 1965 with two anthropologists – one of whom was E. R. Leach, certainly (after the death of Evans Pritchard) Britain's most distinguished practitioner – who were trying to persuade him that the matriarchal theory was simply 'not on', he remained obdurate; he even floored them with erudite irrelevancies. Both anthropologists had the greatest respect for his poetry, and were sympathetic to the tenor of his theory. But he was not prepared, at the age of seventy – both *The White Goddess* and *The Greek Myths* revised for the last time – to rethink his position. Why should he?

He could, and would, have accommodated his conviction to any set of facts, in any case: it was a poet's theory, and it functions as a poet's theory. It is subjective. His 'age of the Goddess' is the expression of a state of longing in him, in his poetry, in ourselves. One must add, too, that, while it is not true that Goddess worship was the earliest form of Western religion, none the less there was and is such a phenomenon as Goddess worship – even though it has not and does not take place in 'matriarchal' societies. On the spirit of this worship Graves is the most illuminating writer ever.

Chapter Twenty-Five
1946–47 (I)

I

The imaginative findings of *King Jesus* were a necessary step towards the formulation of the poetic theory embodied in *The White Goddess*. In *Wife to Mr Milton* Graves had dealt with the consequences of the demise of 'Merrie England'. Marie Powell was named after Charles I's Catholic queen, Henrietta Maria, and is dedicated to the old country customs and to the 'merry' (the same word as Mary) ways of an England still able to find peace and heartiness in the representation of the Virgin Mary. Her family's financial predicament (commerce) caused her to sacrifice herself to the miserable and amorously disgusting hair-fetishist Milton. Her relationship with Edmund Verney, Mun, murdered by Puritan policemen, was represented as 'magical', irrational, and victimized by 'puritan reason'. But this 'puritan reason' is seen as defeated by the magic of their love: their telepathic awareness of each other's feelings.

Then, in *The Golden Fleece*, Graves found that he had gone right back to the source of the trouble: the conflict between the irrational and once almighty Goddess and the obstinate and ambitious patriarchs bent on setting themselves up as the controllers of a masculinized world.

But still he had not touched on the Christian religion, the system which supplanted paganism. This had, though long ago, been his own religion, seriously and sincerely held. It was high time to come to terms with it.

He had been feeling aggressive about official Christianity for some time; not a few of the animadversions on *The Reader Over Your Shoulder* had criticized him for 'sneering' at Christianity – and he had stoutly defended himself. He was telling his correspondents, sometimes to their discomfort, that 'we make a monster of [Christ] in the name

of Belief'. But he had no doubts at all about the historical existence of
Jesus Christ (such now entirely discredited doubts were fashionable
until some years after the end of the Second World War), and the
question of his identity, character and purpose began to obsess him.
Like almost all poets, he is at heart a religious man – though not at all
in the sense (all too often taken as synonymous with 'religious') that
he believes in an afterlife or in the infallible goodness of priests. Such
notions strike him as irrelevant, and he hardly thinks about them.

The path he took was, then, a lonely one. Biblical scholars had long
been prepared to admit that there were inconsistencies in the Canonic
Gospels; but *falsifications, lies* . . . ? Few were at that time prepared to
listen to such claims. He was not inclined to be tactful in this matter.
There was something in Christianity which he felt was alien to mankind's true needs; yet he was not disposed, at all, to believe that Jesus
Christ himself was any kind of monster. But as he pursued his inves-
tigations he began to see Jesus as the antithesis of the genuine, the
poetic hero: as patriarchal, fanatic rather than devoted – and terribly
vulnerable to betrayal and deceit.

For many years he had regarded his very early poem about Christ,
'In the Wilderness', as 'wet' (his word). It had been written when he
was a believer, and he rejected it out of hand when he lost his own
belief. But now he reconsidered it carefully, and decided that it was
valid; he reinstated it in his next *Collected Poems* (1947), and it has
remained as the first poem in the canon ever since.

> He, of his gentleness,
> Thirsting and hungering
> Walked in the wilderness;
> Soft words of grace he spoke
> Unto lost desert-folk
> That listened wondering.
> He heard the bittern call
> From ruined palace wall,
> Answered him brotherly;
> He held communion
> With the she-pelican
> Of lonely piety.
> Basilisk, cocatrice,
> Flocked to his homilies,
> With mail of dread device,
> With monstrous barbèd stings,

With eager dragon eyes;
Great bats on leathern wings
And old, blind, broken things
Mean in their miseries.
Then ever with him went,
Of all his wanderings
Comrade, with ragged coat,
Gaunt ribs – poor innocent –
Bleeding foot, burning throat;
The guileless young scapegoat:
For forty days and nights
Followed in Jesus' ways,
Sure guard behind him kept,
Tears like a lover wept.

It is a very individual poem, making Christ seem rather more like St Francis than his traditional self. But Graves now felt that he had written the poem in the right spirit: he respected the Christ of his invention, even if he attributed his downfall to motives different from those taught by the various churches. In reinstating 'In the Wilderness' he was even prepared to overlook what he considered to be a serious anachronism. A lady researching 'the subject of "Goats in History"' wrote to him in July 1945, to inquire if he was author of some lines about the goat in 'In the Wilderness', which she had seen attributed to him, and to ask him would he mind telling her if there was any tradition about a goat's having accompanied Christ: 'Our local Parson was also very interested when I asked him about it but he has not been able to find any legend connected with it.'

Graves replied:

Dear Madam:

What a subject! The Goat is the oldest animal in European religion, so much so that even Zeus had to admit being suckled by the 'Goat Amalthea': and this is substantiated by pre-Zeus Cretan works of art.

The Scapegoat of my juvenile poem (1915) was my own unhappiness' invention. In point of fact the Azazel Scapegoat of Jerusalem could not possibly have gone into the Galilean wilderness of the Temptation, which is a great distance away. Of course Jesus was 'with the θηρια.' or wild beasts, but as your local parson will be able to inform you these did not include goats.

And he went on to tell his correspondent that the oldest of the European goats was the Triple Goddess of Libya who appeared to Jason:

'she was really Amalthea, and also the original aegis-bearing goddess Athene'.

For Graves there is, for poets, one 'Theme', 'one story and one story only': he summarizes this in *The White Goddess* (chapter 24) as 'the single grand theme of poetry: the life, death and resurrection of the Spirit of the Year, The Goddess's son and lover'. Immediately after this he asks the question: 'Then is Christianity a suitable religion for the poet?'

His answer is negative. Of Jesus himself he writes:

> [Jesus] denied the Theme by his unswerving loyalty to the only contemporary God who had cast off all association with goddesses, and by declaring war on the Female and all her works.

This is what he believes characterizes Christianity at its best (which it is seldom at); and he believes it to be fatally in error.

In *King Jesus* he presents us with a Jesus who is the son of a temple virgin called Miriam. She is secretly married to Herod Antipater; because of this her son inherits the right to the throne of Israel. Herod the Great had been appointed King of the Jews by the Romans in 40 BC.

Jesus becomes a fanatical devotee of the God of Israel, to the extent that he wants to end, once and for all, the cycle of life on earth. He returns from Egypt to Israel to claim his inheritance. There he is accepted as King of the Jews – but not all 'his' people want to welcome the Kingdom of Heaven (i.e. the final break-up of the cycle of birth and death). A bride, Mary of Cleopas, is found for him; but he refuses her – and warns the kingdom to observe celibacy.

Jesus makes his position plain, particularly when he meets Mary Magdalene. The old matriarchal mystery cults (anthropologists would call these goddess, rather than matriarchal, mysteries) he denounces: if the female (who generates) is defeated, then death is defeated; thus the Kingdom of Heaven will be at hand. That the historical Jesus and his disciples believed and worked for the immediate coming of the Kingdom of Heaven is now accepted by many scholars, including not a few Christians; in those days it was still a bold view to take.

When Jesus realizes that Israel will not hear his message, he knows that he must – in accordance with a prophecy of Zechariah – arrange for one of his own disciples to kill him by the sword. Only in that way will the Israelites be made to heed his message.

Judas devotedly but misguidedly tries to save his master. Having got wind of his plan, he arranges with Nicodemus to have Jesus arrested – thus to avoid his being done to death. But there is a confusion: Jesus's disciples think that the swords he has given them are to protect him, whereas they are to kill him. The result is that Jesus is crucified. The terrible irony of this is that by dying a ritual death – a maimed and hanging god, of the waxing year – he becomes a 'matriarchal' hero. And the White Goddess herself presides at his death in her triple aspect as Mother, Lover (Mary of Cleopas, who was to have been his bride) and Crone (Layer-out: Mary the Hairdresser, Mary Magdalene). Thus Jesus is sucked back into the scheme which he has fought to end: his whole career had, indeed, been instituted within it.

King Jesus sold some 100,000 copies in thirty-five years; it has proved most fascinating to those who are not bigoted, or who are agnostic. It did not cause the sense of outrage that the later *The Nazarene Gospel Restored* caused; but that was because it was cast as fiction – which can always be forgiven.

It is a remarkable feat of imagination, and is not made less so by the fact that Graves believed what he was writing to be the historical truth. It was at this time that he formulated his notions of 'proleptic' and 'analeptic' thinking, which he defines in *The White Goddess*. Proleptic thought he defined as 'the anticipation, by means of a suspension of time, of a result that could not have been arrived at by inductive reasoning', analeptic thought as 'the recovery of lost events by the same suspension'. He would occasionally claim in conversation that he had recovered the lost facts about Jesus in 'an analeptic trance'. Any scepticism he encountered was soon dealt with: the doubters were 'prose men', who did not understand poetic thinking – none the less, they ought to know better, since (as he put it) when 'J. W. Dunne's *Experiment with Time* has prosaicized the notion that time is not the stable moving-staircase that prose-men have for centuries pretended it to be, but an unaccountable wibble-wobble, the prose men too will easily see what I am driving at.'

It is easy to make fun of this. And Graves himself intends us to be amused when we see him on television, asked how he knows for certain that something happened five thousand years ago, answering with a modest smile: 'I was around!' But few who have seen Graves at work care to scoff. And even fewer scoff who have read him. Graves's absorption in his subject matter was so intense as to be unique. When he laid a place for Sergeant Lamb while writing the second novel about him he had to be told about it by Beryl. There was no affectation in this absent-mindedness. His imagination had taken him over; it hardly matters if we call this 'proleptic' and 'analeptic' – or something else. This state reached the peak of its intensity in 1945, when he was expanding the text of *The White Goddess* – the act of creation was authentic and authoritative; it impressed because it had nothing at all about it suggestive of an 'act'. A good many madmen behave in the same way, and what they write is nonsense. But Graves was obviously not mad. He was perfectly conscious that he could be led astray, and make mistakes. He checked his work constantly. Wartime conditions, and the comparative remoteness of south Devon, made it difficult to get hold of essential books. He got many volumes from the London Library, and from booksellers who were old friends – Sanders at Oxford, Francis Edwards near Marylebone station, and Harold Edwards; for very difficult books he would turn – he continued to do so until the late fifties – to my father, a bibliographer and librarian. He wrote to him (29 April 1945):

> Really, I don't know how to thank you for your kindness in getting hold of these volumes for me. . . . The [Clementine] Recognitions are amusing as apparently the moral which Voltaire satirized in *Candide*; I expect that has been observed before but I have never met it.
>
> There are a lot of very welcome bits of information in it, one of the ones that pleases me most – you'll laugh – is that the father of the first Sibyl of Delphi was a Lapwing [see *The White Goddess*, 1961 edition, p. 53]. It proves a beautiful point for me. . . .
>
> I am still working on my book about Jesus – now called *The Power of the Dog* (a quotation from the Psalm Jesus quoted from the Cross). I can't afford to get too many things wrong.

Nor, though so intensely preoccupied with his work, did he neglect Beryl or the children. On the contrary. While he was still struggling to familiarize himself with the complex material for *King Jesus*, at the end of 1944, Beryl was in hospital: Juan was born on 22 December 1944. He was looking after William and Lucia as well as working on his novel. On the last day of the year, she being still in hospital, he wrote her a note:

> Darling
>
> This is just so as not to miss the post and to remind you of me. We went to the other side of the Creek [of the River Dart] and all the way I had to explain to Wm how one makes houses, and farms and shores and whether one had to dig a place for rivers to run & so on. They have

been very sweet today. There have been no callers or helpers, but everything smooth. I am reading another long scholarly Life of Jesus – each
of which contains some small point I need but which are all exactly the
same in outline of the story and take the wrong turning like sheep at
each place where the original sheep got it wrong. I had a nice letter
today from you & the post car was 2 hours late, so it didn't spoil
breakfast for the insistent children. I must begin to prepare for your
home coming with one thing & another – Ever your dear love

Now that Graves had (for the time being) set his mind right about
Christianity and what it represented, he was ready to complete his
work on poetry: his 'historical grammar of poetic myth', *The White
Goddess*. This is certainly his central prose work.

II

Graves tried the 1944 draft (which he then thought would expand to
only some 160 printed pages) on Dent. It was promptly returned. The
earliest chapters, in their first form, appeared in the magazine *Wales*,
edited by Keidrich Rhys, in 1944 and 1945. This, apart from a draft
of the chapter called 'Conversation at Paphos – A.D. 43' (which
appeared in *The Windmill* in 1946) was the only chance Graves had
of testing out his strange new book on the public. He never had more
difficulty in placing a book with a publisher than he had with *The
White Goddess*.

No publisher was more friendly to him than Jonathan Cape. But his
letter of 16 June 1944 was not encouraging:

My dear Robert,

The Roebuck in the Thicket

When you first told me about this and mentioned that some of it would
appear in *Wales*, we got in touch with Keidrich Rhys, and he was good
enough to let me see a proof of the piece that he was printing ['Dog,
Lapwing and Roebuck']. I have to say that it was beyond me and failed
to stir any spark of interest. And this being the case, there is nothing for
me to do but send the material [Graves had presumably sent him the
whole as it stood: Cape did not want to read it] back to A. S. W[att].

A publisher frequently publishes many books which are too good for
him; i.e. they transcend his individual taste and scholarship, but at least
he has some inkling of what the author is aiming at and can see that
there is some reasonable ground for publication. Here it seems to me

that the interest is so obscure and so limited. . . . You need for this book
a publisher who is humble enough to take it ex cathedra. . . .

Cape went on, tartly, to recommend two publishers (recently deceased!). Clearly he thought Graves had gone temporarily off his head.
It did not help much, either, when Cape genially added, in writing to
him three days later on another small matter:

> If you will come to town I will buy you as good a lunch as can be found
> when 'The Roebuck' is published; so we can drink to its success. The
> better success it has the better pleased I will be!

But Graves was not too disappointed: he recalled what Cape had
written to him over a year before:

> And so you and Alan Hodge are proposing to write a book about poetry
> which will end books about poetry! As a tradesman I ought not to
> favour such a publication. . . . Personally, I think books about poetry are
> largely futile. . . .

Nevertheless, Cape was a literate publisher and this was financially
bad news for Graves – though he was well aware that he could not
excite his readership up to quite his own pitch. Yet Cape's judgement
could not have been more wrong: *The White Goddess* continues to
reprint, and to sell in quantity, more than thirty years after it was first
published.

Although Cassells, under the directorship of Desmond Flower, were
now well on their way to becoming Graves's regular publishers, they
did not feel that they could take on *The White Goddess*, and gave as
their reason the need to conserve all the paper (desperately short in the
war) they could get in order to keep his other books in print. There
was nothing Graves could say to counter this. In addition, *King Jesus*
– which they were publishing – was itself a difficult subject, open in
those days to charges of 'blasphemy'; and Flower, most helpfully, had
all along been markedly enthusiastic about it: '. . . a grand piece of
work . . . easily the finest book you have given Cassells' (his verdict on
reading it in June 1945).

Graves wanted to get on with what he still thought of as *The
Roebuck in the Thicket* as soon as he had finished his *Jesus* novel,
about which he always felt a trifle uneasy, if in spite of himself ('scares
me a bit at times' was what he often wrote or said); he did not want
to write another historical novel – though he would do so if it proved
necessary. There are some respects in which he did not want to write

even *King Jesus* – he fought against the compulsion to start on it. This may, perhaps, be inferred from his answer to a request, made in October 1943, from Korda for an option on the film rights of his next five novels: Korda would pay £500 a year for five years, just for the opportunity of considering each script. If he liked a novel then he would pay £5000 for it. Graves wrote to Watt:

> I have a warm personal feeling for him, especially since he helped me over the bad years 1936-37, after I had to leave Spain, by giving me commissions on several occasions. This feeling makes me the more scrupulous in not wanting to get 'something for nothing' from him ... novels are *gifts* to me; either I suddenly feel the need of clearing up a particular historical obscurity or I don't write at all. ...

But he did accept an arrangement by which Korda would pay him £500 for the first option on any novel he did write; he could not, he said, allow himself to take any money in advance because 'I have no immediate sense that I will be writing any historical novel for some time.' But he was writing *King Jesus* within three months. 'He did it partly against his own better judgement,' Beryl now confirms, 'although of course he was excited about it. Something about it worried him.'

Anxious to find a home for *The Roebuck*, he remembered that Charles Williams, of the Oxford University Press, had written sympathetically of his early poetry in his critical book *Poetry at Present* (1930). He did not much like the essay, or Williams, who wrote verse very different from his own, and who combined an unhealthy interest in occultism along with a soapy Anglo-Catholicism. He asked Watt to send the material to the Oxford University Press, and meanwhile wrote a strategic letter to Williams – whom he suspected might also dislike Milton's puritanism – who replied cordially on 23 June 1944:

> This is very kind of you. I shall do my utmost, if it is needed, for your book here, though our straits are painful at the present time. But I can wish for nothing better than to be involved in anything of yours. And of course I look forward very much to reading it myself.

But Oxford University Press would not take the book, even when Graves suggested that they might simply distribute it, if he himself found the paper and had it printed. There is a letter from Keidrich Rhys asking Graves how many pages he thought would be needed, and telling him that the cost of 2500 copies would be around £200 'without binding' 'unless Charles Wms can knock the Western Mail down somewhat'. (The printer was to be the *Western Mail*, who did *Wales*.)

Nothing came of this, and Graves became frustrated. Later he blamed Williams for not pushing the book – and attributed his premature death to this failure.

> I sent it to two publishers [OUP and Macmillan]. . . . One of these rejected it politely, saying that he would not venture to persuade his colleagues of its merit, though convinced himself. He died three weeks later. Another [American] rejected it impolitely and almost at once was found hanging from a tree in his garden dressed in a skirt, blouse, nylon knickers and a brassière. I saw the White Goddess's terrible hand in that, but never found what sort of tree it was. Yew? Elder? [*Quoz*]

Eventually it was T. S. Eliot, at Faber, who came to his rescue; which is to his credit – as an impartial critic, and as a publisher with a nose for an eventual *succès d'estime*. ('Then Eliot accepted the book with enthusiasm and within the year had a Nobel Prize and an O.M. "Makes you think, doesn't it" ' – *Quoz*.) When Eliot saw the material his interest was immediately and genuinely aroused; and he saw, too, that Graves would have problems completing such a complex project.

While still struggling with the final chapters of *King Jesus* (completed at the end of May) he wrote to Eliot telling him of some of the difficulties which lay in the way of completing *The Roebuck*. Eliot replied (8 March 1945):

> Thank you for your very interesting letter of February 21st, which I have shown to Geoffrey [Faber] and discussed with him. Your letter makes me all the more anxious to see the book in its final shape.

Thus the matter of an English publisher was settled, Eliot being a man of his word; but no American publisher could yet be found; and Macmillan (USA) were to refuse it.

While in London he went to see Eliot. They still respected each other, for all their differences. But Graves made no attempt to modify his views in Eliot's presence. The subject of Rossetti came up. Eliot said that he felt that Rossetti's techniques may have been just a little bit 'too good'. Graves stretched out his feet, looked at them, and muttered: 'A wop, of course.' A momentary spasm crossed Eliot's face, but he made no further comment.

They warmly commiserated with each other about ungrateful writers to whom they had given money and who had turned out badly – but mentioned no names. Eliot again made his interest in and enthusiasm for the book clear. It was obvious that he not only expected but wanted to publish it. The formal contract was drawn up in the autumn.

At the end of the discussion, as Graves was about to leave, Eliot somewhat awkwardly raised the matter of Ezra Pound's predicament. Pound was then in some danger of being tried for treason – and even executed – because he had made broadcasts, for money, from Rome in wartime. He was very well aware, he said, that Graves did not care for Pound or his work, but he thought he'd ask him if he would like to sign a petition that was being got up.

Graves declined: he was very sorry for Pound, but he could see no reason to sign the petition himself, as he had never valued Pound's poetry – and wasn't the poetry one of the grounds of the petition? He wished Eliot the best of luck. Eliot, who had not expected to succeed, was gracious. On the way home Graves told me that he thought it would have been dishonest to sign a petition for Pound, since he didn't think he had any more literary merit than other traitors. (It has been stated that he spitefully hoped that Pound would be executed; but this is not so: he hoped he would be let off as insane; he has never been a proponent of capital punishment.)

In the next months he worked intensively and excitedly at *The White Goddess*. At the end of August 1945 he wrote that the final typing was being done; and (4 September) 'Have nearly finished my Roebuck chase'. But on 24 November he was still 'working away at *The Roebuck in the Thicket*, now called *The Three Fold Muse*'. In those months he felt driven and obsessed; yet he continued to confess (to more than one person) that he wondered if he ought really to publish 'all this'. And he was often at pains to point out that it was all 'only a way of speaking'. For very many people, when they read the book, were to ask the question: 'Does he *literally* believe all this?'

III

The White Goddess, which had acquired its final title by the time it went off to Faber in January 1946, is the product of a highly sophisticated, independent and uncompromising mind. The simple answer to the oft-asked question as to whether Graves believes its thesis in a literal sense is that *The White Goddess* is a gigantic metaphor – although it is at the same time an idiosyncratic 'key' to, not all, but some, mythologies. It is, as well, the lively and stimulating expression of an outstanding and unusual temperament, a temperament which loathes and distrusts machinery, which hates the development of technology, and which needs to live as near as possible to nature, in accord with the seasons. 'The study of mythology . . . is based squarely on tree-lore and the seasonal observation of life in the fields.' Graves, like Wyndham Lewis, disbelieves in 'human progress'. He accepts change, and is no Luddite or anti-banausic fanatic; but it has never occurred to him that this is progress. He regards life as cyclic, not linear – but there are many differences between his and more familiar 'cyclic' attitudes.

What happened after 'patriarchy supplanted his postulated matriarchy' is, for him, all bad. But it is temporary. Behind and inspiring *The White Goddess* lies a highly charged vision of the past: a golden age of the Goddess. Though Graves's postulated matriarchy never existed, it none the less stands for something that both poets and others yearn for.

He was fifteen years ahead of his time. His yearning for the end of masculine domination was to manifest itself, though in a very different form, strongly in the early sixties. At the time he wrote *The White Goddess*, Graves's poetic stock was as low as it had ever been; he showed courage in backing his own hunch, and in defiantly continuing to write poetry in the way he believed it ought to be written. Much to the dismay of many old-fashioned academic critics the book has had an immense influence; but this was not fully felt until Graves's own mastery of lyric poetry was recognized. *The White Goddess* is above all the testament of a practising poet. There is no more fascinating guide to a certain kind of romantic poetic thought. (Riding admired it greatly, and claimed that it was based on her notes, which is, however, absolutely impossible.)

The book is as unashamedly romantic as it is unashamedly self-confident in its tone. Yet, romantic though it is, it is also ultra-sophisticated – to the point of extreme, humorous, cunning. Pure reason is scoffed at, throughout, as inadequate to solve any worthwhile problem. Yet the author teasingly asserts that the 'mystical Bull-calf formula and the Tree-alphabets', which he introduced into *King Jesus*, were 'logically deduced' from 'reputable ancient documents'. He also teases his orthodox reader by telling him that he will answer such questions as 'Who cleft the Devil's foot?' and 'What secret was woven into the Gordian knot?' He does answer them, too. He believes in something he calls magic, but (again) teases his 'scientific' reader, the 'prose man', by telling him – at the end, in the 'Postscript 1960' – that he is 'no mystic', and that he avoids participation in 'witchcraft, spiritualism, yoga, fortune-telling, automatic writing, and the like'. He did not eschew facts, but believed them to be insufficient. In a letter written while he was putting the final script into shape he said:

> Anthropology is the key science of the 'humane' ones and it is most important for a poet to get his facts right. As I say in *The White Goddess* facts are not truth, but have a power of vetoing untruth by saying 'This is not in accordance with fact'. [To M.S.-S., 29 March 1946]

He asserts his independence by calling himself 'the fox who has lost his brush', his 'brush' being his 'contact with urban civilisation'. He is 'nobody's servant', and has chosen to live where 'life is still ruled by the old agricultural cycle'.

Yet, for all his belief in the Goddess and in her magic, it is obvious that what Graves is talking about is *not* a theologically conceived meta-human 'external spiritual authority', but rather a factor in the structure of the poetic personality. Many have therefore tried to compare his work with that of Jung, but he himself has refused to take Jung seriously. When asked to write on him, he rudely dismissed Jung as his own self-styled 'wise old man' ('Jungian Mythology', *Hudson Review*, 1953). In conversation he has always shown the utmost contempt for him.

Graves could in the mid-forties have become a 'dull easy writer'. That was the phrase he used in his autobiography when he recorded his refusal to consult a psychiatrist in order to get 'cured', to be less of a 'drag' on Nancy. This argues not only a well-justified lack of faith in psychiatrists to help with that kind of problem, and a strong and proud sense of self-reliance, but also an absolute determination – come what may – to avoid a 'dull easy' life. As he now struggled with the material that flooded into his consciousness, and which became the central dogma of *The White Goddess*, he was storing up enough interesting unease to last most men two lifetimes. He felt himself to be undergoing a revelation of religious intensity – even if he did obstinately and consistently refuse to include within the range of his subject matter the questions (ridiculous to him) of who created mankind, and what for.

The Goddess thesis in itself is simple, though its detail is complex. The language of 'poetic myth', which is in honour of the Moon-goddess or Muse, was a secret and magical one, 'bound up with popular religious ceremonies' in honour of the same deity. The language of true poetry is still bound to this myth, which dates from the 'Old Stone Age'. The early Greek philosophers opposed this magical language, and the myth upon which it was founded: it threatened their 'new religion of logic'. Myths are now wrongly relegated to the nursery as 'quaint', for those early Greek logicians prevailed. The original Goddess is Mother, Lover and Crone (Layer-out). But the language of myth in which she was honoured persisted: in Mysteries such as those of Eleusis and Corinth – and countless others less well known. Poetry 'of a magical quality' is still written, but in the modern context seems 'almost pathological': 'a wild Pentecostal "speaking with tongues" '. The true modern poet is 'mad' in the best romantic manner: he cannot be bought with money, and he is 'truth-possessed'. He – to use a metaphor Graves was fond of in the forties and fifties – 'puts down his last halfpenny'. Graves's definition of his own function is quite different from that put forward by any other poet (or critic): it is 'religious invocation of the Muse, the experience of mixed exaltation and horror that her presence excites'.

In 1944 and the following years, while Graves was working on the elaboration of this thesis, it seemed a hopeless cause; but he affirmed his sincerity by showing that he, at least, could not be bought for money. Writing this book made Graves relatively poor. As Beryl now recalls, money was tight until well into the fifties. Nor in his foreword to *The White Goddess* was Graves at all encouraging, even to his few penurious fellow poets. He offered them no help:

> my brushlessness debars me from offering any practical suggestion. I dare attempt only a historical statement of the problem; how you come to terms with the Goddess is no concern of mine. I do not even know that you are serious in your poetic profession.

When in 1946 he published his short, forty-poem collection *Poems 1938–1945*, he put before it a curt note to the effect that his poetry was for poets, that he was content to be known to the general public as a novelist, and that (as he plainly implied) he was the most dedicated poet alive. This last point was made with exquisite grace and irony. The Scilly islanders took in one another's washing, and 'nowhere else was washing so well done'. His readers pretended to be scandalized, but they liked it; only reviewers were outraged.

His quest for the Goddess, *his* Goddess, involves ravishingly ingenious disentanglements of apparent nonsense; by no means all of his arguments about tree alphabets, and the Battle of the Trees, can be – or seem – wrong. His insistence that poetry is written in a special sort of trance-like state is fully supported by modern research into brain states; much else he asserted has been confirmed.

Yet he took no note of the 1929 translation of *The Mabinogion* by T. P. Ellis and John Lloyd (he hadn't heard of it), which is more scholarly, though less well written, than Lady Charlotte Guest's familiar one; nor did he consult Loth's useful nineteenth-century translation. He did not incorporate O'Rahilly's Irish *History and Mythology* (1946) into his final or his revised texts. Very many more criticisms could be, and have been, made.

But more source books would have made no difference. Had he studied more works, he would have simply absorbed them, assimilated them, into his own grand scheme. For Graves this *is* no 'theory': it is, and it has been, his whole life, his experience. It is the autobiography of his soul.

The mind that becomes sometimes dubious – rather than frantically angry – about some aspects of the 'theory' is the kind, naturally sceptical, which dwells in those uncertainties recommended by Keats. This is a mind with which Graves finds it hard to come to terms; but he respects and understands it. He teases those who angrily, boldly, state that he is wrong; and he knows he can disarm them because the thesis is related to his poems – far too accomplished, powerful and assured to be dismissed.

But the possessor of 'negative capability', the sceptic, is a different case: all Graves can say to him is that he should join the team and await the punishment that is coming to him – from the Goddess.

The true nature of the Gravesian scheme is best seen in its famous (even notorious) culmination. It comes in the chapter called 'War in Heaven', in *The White Goddess*. It begins gently enough, but then turns into a truly alarming pronouncement.

The main theme of poetry is, properly, the relations of man and woman, rather than those of man and man, as the Apollonian classicists would have it. The true poet who goes to the tavern and pays the silver tribute [cf. 'the last halfpenny'] to Blodeuwedd goes over the river to his death. As in the story of Llew Llaw: 'All their discourse that night was concerning the affection and love they felt one for the other and which in no longer space than one evening had arisen.' This paradise lasts only from May Day to St John's Eve. Then the plot is hatched and the poisoned dart flies; and the poet knows that it must be so. For him there is no other woman. . . . As Blodeuwedd she will gladly give him her love, but at only one price: his life. . . . Poetry began in the matriarchal age, and derives its magic from the moon, not from the sun. No poet can hope to understand the nature of poetry unless he has had a vision of the Naked King crucified to the lopped oak, and watched the dancers, red-eyed from the acrid smoke of the sacrificial fires, stamping out the measure of the dance, their bodies bent uncouthly forward, with a monotonous chant of: 'Kill! kill!' and 'Blood! blood! blood!'

For it is the doom of the poet to be ousted by his rival: 'The theme is the antique story . . . of the birth, life, death and resurrection of the God of the waxing Year. . . .' The poet, the God of the Waxing Year, fights against himself, the God of the Waning Year, for the love of the Goddess. Thus the 'naked' (apparently a word of considerable *frisson* for Graves) Anatha of Ugarit was fought for by the twins Aleyn (Baal) and Mot. Aleyn murders Mot. 'The twins were . . . gods of the Waxing and Waning Year.'

The 'Goddess system' *à la Graves* arose from something very much more particular than the extension of a mere Oedipus complex, as alleged by Randall Jarrell in an interesting but misleading article. We have in Graves a man very sharply divided, a man more obviously two-sided than most. The officious, moralistic, cautious, puritanical, 'regimental' side of Graves is inherited from his mother, whose purity was as obstinately irritating as it was genuine. The 'Irish', 'romantic' side is inherited from his Celtic father. His 'system', far from being the result of an attempt to resolve an Oedipus complex (the Randall Jarrell view), is a highly sophisticated and courageous coming to terms with his own experience (which includes a full knowledge of the Oedipus complex).

The manner in which this system served him after his sixtieth year may be less impressive, less admirable. It may even be that there were good reasons why he should not (as he himself occasionally felt) have published *The White Goddess* at all. But Graves's accommodation of himself to himself was not a glib or easily achieved one. Randall Jarrell implies that we read *The White Goddess* for the same reasons as we read Yeats's *A Vision*: for the sake of the poems 'it enabled' the poet to write. But *The White Goddess* is very different from *A Vision*.

Yeats's poetry is more widely read and translated than that of Graves; but *A Vision* is far less widely read book than *The White Goddess*. *A Vision* is self-consciously 'occult'; it is extraordinarily unsophisticated; it is vulgar (though Auden, an admirer of Yeats, found it full of the 'wisdom of the mysterious East'); clearly it is not the work of an educated or an informed man. It is a compound of very unsound astrology and 'esoteric wisdom' culled from sects such as the Theosophists; it reads like a third-rate mystical treatise. It is an embarrassment to Yeats's admirers – as Auden frankly admitted.

The White Goddess, however, is genuinely learned, although it is based on now outdated anthropological models. It is read by people who are not interested in Graves's poetry (as his correspondence testifies) but in religion, Women's Liberation, psychology, and other allied matters. Graves, unlike Yeats, is well aware of the effect he is creating. He is cunning, ironic and funny, concluding one chapter:

> The proleptic or analeptic method of thought, though necessary to poets, physicians, historians and the rest, is so easily confused with mere guessing, or deduction from insufficient data, that few of them own to using it. However securely I buttress the argument of this book with quotations, citations and footnotes, the admission that I have made here of how it first came to me will debar it from consideration by orthodox scholars: though they cannot refute it, they dare not accept it.

Had Graves been accepted for military service in the Second World War, there would surely have been a case for making him a general: his strategy is impeccable.

In a 1955 letter (to a stranger) he wrote, about *The White Goddess* and its lack of footnotes and scholarly apparatus:

> *The White Goddess* is about how poets think: it's not a scientific book or I'd have given it notes and an immense bibliography of works I hadn't read. . . . Some day scholars will sort out the White Goddess grain from the chaff. It's a crazy book & I didn't mean to write it.

This is modest and sensible enough, and we are bound to allow Graves the assumption that a book about how *he* thought was really about how all poets thought.

Graves has always been in search of chastity, about which he has said that he possesses an 'Irish thing'. Revulsion at physical lust is an old theme amongst poets. Graves knows, however, that he cannot 'deny/The thing's necessity'. So he has also known that he could not actually have chastity (monkish solutions do not appeal to him). There is no doubt that Graves's mother's own purity left a powerful impression on him. He says that although she was extremely puritanical and 'disapproved deeply' of his actions, he 'never resented her attitude in the least' ('Miss Briton's Lady Companion' in *The Crane Bag*). He inherited the same tendency; and despite the fact that she 'did not understand irony, sarcasm, or jokes about other people's misfortunes' she was the perfect mother for him; she was, in her own way, a shining example of the ideal of perfection, the pursuit of which is absolutely necessary to her son.

Here we need to return to Graves's earliest sexual experiences: the understanding of these, and his attitude to them, is essential to an understanding of his development as a poet, of the wildness of his idealism, of his need for the impossible.

He felt greatly ashamed of ever having experienced what he took to be 'homosexual' emotion. The function of the attacks of homosexuality which he makes in the course of *The White Goddess* is to relieve his feelings about this. His implication that 'Apollonian' or 'classical' poetry is in some way homosexual fulfils this same function. But the aggressive heterosexuality of the White Goddess system is not a classic defence against homosexual impulses (as one or two critics have implied: the notion has certainly gained currency). Graves is too sophisticated for that.

Why should Graves be so fearful of homosexuality, since he is not himself a repressed homosexual?

We must revert to an important incident in his past. His relationship with Dick (G. H. Johnstone) had been wholly platonic. Then had come the terrible shock of hearing that Dick had been caught making a *homosexual* proposal to a soldier. Graves himself doesn't underestimate the extent of this shock; nor should we. But has he ever fully understood it?

He wrote the following letter to Dick on 5 August 1915 (a long time before he received the *John Bull* cutting). It demonstrates the remarkable innocence and purity of Graves's attitude towards him (noted, it will be remembered, by his headmaster). It was written at a time when he had given up any real hope of surviving the war.

This is just in case I die, it'll be young & happy & in splendid company without fears of Hell or anxious hopes for Heaven. I leave all that to God: no good building on doubts. I should have liked to write something fine & lasting by which nice people hereafter might remember my name but childlessness loses its sting when I think that you who mean infinitely more to me than myself are going to be a greater poet than I would ever be & that perhaps I have sometimes helped you to understand & love,

& so in a sense may live in you when my body is broken up, & have a share in all your doings.

I leave you all my friends & my books & wish you all the happiness from them that I have had. God bless you always. My favourite hope is to be remembered by the future as your friend – Really, old thing!

Robert Graves

Give my love to . . . George Mallory & Eddie Marsh if you can ever.

It is a moving letter of idealistic friendship – not at all of homosexuality. A repressed homosexual would not have written of the 'sting' of 'childlessness'.

The shattering of this dream by such squalid news was a decisive event in Graves's life. Johnstone's 'lapse' is nothing to us; to Graves it was the end of a whole way of life. In one sense he never got over the disillusion it aroused in him. His reaction was of anger and shame. He felt: 'So I am tainted with this horror! He did that, so that's what I was! I was impure, a *homosexual*!'

It is notable that he did not feel at all sorry for his friend: as he records in *Goodbye to All That*, he was glad to be able to regard him as mad or dead. It seemes a vicious reaction – until one remembers the fierceness of Graves's purity, and its immense vulnerability. 'Never again homosexuality!' we can hear reverberating through his battle-numbed mind, robbed for ever of its ideal.

But he never was homosexual. He mistook his youthful idealism, friendship, for the thing that sullied it – the adolescent homosexuality of G. H. Johnstone. Always women in the future no matter what!

We can now readily understand why Graves's involvement in his own 'Goddess system' (he invented it in order to be involved in it) causes him to be punished for both lust *and* idealism. Sensitive men struggle, in one way or another, with their lust: it is, no doubt, a part of the tragicomic destiny of being male. To want to be punished for idealism – which is in part to want to be punished for stupidity – is less usual; in Graves's case it is a component of his defensive sophistication. While married to Nancy he had existed in a postwar world which none the less seemed, at least at first, to be haunted by war; marriage had not proved Utopian, and he entertained bad thoughts about his wife. 'All that' was to him an aspect of the destructive terror of war; disappointed, he remained haunted. But when Laura Riding came into his life he was able to respond to her absolutely. She haunted him continually. She manipulated him to brilliant advantage.

Riding saw that his purity craved a mentor – but his mother, from whom he had inherited this purity, was wholly unsophisticated, 'absurd'. The antinomian Riding was as sophisticated as Amalia was unsophisticated. She, too, claimed to regard homosexuality as a sin against the Holy Ghost. She combined militant femininity with what she claimed was absolute, non-conventional, 'poetic' virtue.

It was difficult at first, because he had been troubled by feeling divided between his duty to Nancy and his love for Laura. Doubtless he was recalling this when he wrote in 1956:

> My divinatory little finger . . . must not be out of touch with my logical index finger. Being in love with two women at once used to be the most troublesome of my inconsistencies. . . . Fortunately this has not happened for a long time. [*Quoz*]

It became easier when Nancy went away. And in one way even easier – though painful – after the Phibbs affair, when Laura repudiated him as lover. For this put him in the extreme position of being sympathetically (as he saw it) taught to be non-procreative, chaste, subordinate to the female. But in the end he escaped being sucked into the maelstrom of her total subjectivity.

So the Goddess is by no means simply a 'transmogrification' of Riding (the Jarrell notion), whose behaviour was in large part adapted – it is important to realize this – to provide the Gravesian needs. To a large extent she was his own creation; the model suited her needs at the time. Certainly it was Riding's treatment of him that led him to emphasize the cruel side of the Muse at the expense of her gentler side. In that respect Graves's portrait of the Goddess really is one-sided. He makes no allowance for the poet who experiences not the cruel and capricious Muse, but the gentle one. But woman as deceiver and inconstant lover does after all fit in well with a vital tradition in poetry – and indeed with the notion of true romantic love, which is squarely based on the premise that it will end unhappily.

As a critic has written, *The White Goddess* is 'tendentious as historical mythology', but it 'cannot be faulted as a coherent, cyclical vision of the relation between the life process and imaginative existence'.

The book was formed in the crucible of both original need and individual experience. But the test of the value of any 'system' is its relevance to general experience, not in its 'truth'. *The White Goddess* may not be very relevant, except in the matter of certain details, to mythography, or to anthropology; but it *is* relevant to the male experience of women, to the 'way poets think'. It slips into the wholly idiosyncratic only when it overemphasizes the cruelty of the Muse. But even here it illuminates the practice of a major poet.

One element in the Gravesian portrait of the Muse is extremely interesting. This is her appearance. His poem 'In Dedication' (entitled 'The White Goddess' in the *Collected Poems*, but first published in *The White Goddess*) has an undeniable authenticity, a quality of genuine vision. Graves's mother had black hair. Nancy was dark. Riding was hebraically dark – and her skin could not be described as white. Beryl is dark. I quote the version of the poem printed in front of *The White Goddess* (1960 edition) because the Goddess is really *his* Goddess, and his later change of voice – to the first person plural – does not do justice to the power of his vision:

> All saints revile her, and all sober men
> Ruled by the God Apollo's golden mean –
> In scorn of which I sailed to find her
> In distant regions likeliest to hold her
> Whom I desired above all things to know,
> Sister of mirage and echo.
>
> It was a virtue not to stay,
> To go my headstrong and heroic way
> Seeking her out at the volcano's head,
> Among pack-ice, or where the track had faded
> Beyond the cavern of the seven sleepers:
> Whose broad high brow was white as any leper's,
> Whose eyes were blue, with rowan-berry lips,
> With hair curled honey-coloured to white hips.
>
> Green sap of Spring in the young wood a-stir
> Will celebrate the Mountain Mother,
> And every song-bird shout awhile for her;
> But I am gifted, even in November
> Rawest of seasons, with so huge a sense
> Of her nakedly worn magnificence
> I forget cruelty and past betrayal,
> Careless of where the next bright bolt may fall.

But Beryl, certainly the one true love of Graves's life (as he has plainly, although privately, acknowledged), was not the Goddess, nor even *the* Muse (the one we are so used to as being 'Graves's'). This was to have consequences.

I

As soon as the war ended Graves was in a frenzy to return to Spain, but he had to restrain his impatience for some eight months. There were serious obstacles, at that difficult time, involved in going abroad to live. Spanish residence visas were hard to get; the formalities of obtaining permission to transfer sterling were tedious and time-consuming. He spent much of his time dreaming about his return. He sent off *The White Goddess* in January 1946:

> I have at last got off that complicated book, now called *The White Goddess*, to Faber's, & Macmillan in U.S.A. If I hadn't it would have stayed and stayed and swelled for another few years. I went on inserting things up to the last moment: e.g. an equine description of the Nightmare, which would have served for a 'Lost Stolen or Strayed' advertisement in the Times – answers to the name of Rhiannon.
>
> And King Jesus is page proofing and looks very nice.
>
> And now I'll have a big tidy-up, including tidying-up my Collected Poems definitely for the new edition. It will be fun watching the reviews of my Poems [1938–1945] to see which way the wind of fashion is blowing. [To M. S.-S., 30 January 1946]

As it happened, Macmillan 'rudely' refused *The White Goddess* (with apparently dire consequences to one of its presumably transvestite staff, as already reported), and he did insert more material. On 29 March he wrote that he was 'soon having back' the typescript from Faber 'to incorporate new material'.

Meanwhile, having discovered that the necessary arrangements could be made, he took the decision to return to Spain. He even offered his services to the British Council, on the advice of his daughter Jenny and her husband Alex Clifford, now both well known in their journalistic profession. (Nothing came of this bizarre project, although it might have done had he been planning to live on the mainland.)

His small volume of poems appeared in November 1945 in England (not until June 1946 in America); he resigned himself to their obtaining a hostile – or, worse – indifferent reception. He guarded himself against the expected by his defiantly arrogant foreword – and by telling everyone that, as he put it to Alan Hodge:

> if I have a good review [in the *New Statesman*] I would know I was a failure & my friends would find me lying dead with a smoking revolver by my side in a public *pissoir* like the hero of a decadent French novel.

Reviews were slow to come, but in the event he did get an irked little notice in the *Statesman* ('Mr Graves's poems are like the knots in wood') from the assistant literary editor, G. W. Stonier.

But despite the reviews his readership remained loyal. The book went into a new impression in April 1946. It sold altogether 7500 copies in Britain; Creative Age Press quickly sold out their edition, of 5500. Many poets then more fashionable were selling fewer copies of their collections.

At Easter 1946 (it fell in late April) James and Mary Reeves and their children, and Alan Hodge, visited the Graves at Galmpton for the last time. On 29 March Graves had written 'Can't seem to make any progress about getting to Spain', but by 5 April they were 'dreadfully busy settling up, and packing, and planning'; they had heard that they would be granted residential visas. 'Unless some snag arises, as snags do' – he was feeling superstitious, since he felt that his life had reached another watershed – 'we are flying to Mallorca by specially chartered plane on May 15, spending our last week in Town' (to M.S.-S., 5 April 1946). He was now busy sorting out a vast quantity of papers, drafts and letters. His own manuscripts he took with him. Some letters were thrown away, others sent back to the writers, still others stored with his niece Sally (where they remained until late in 1979, when they were rediscovered). Early in May they were at Browns Hotel in Dover Street, waiting to make their journey from Croydon – then still Great Britain's main airport. After hectic meetings with friends and relatives, and a send-off party, they got off according to schedule. Their plane, a specially chartered air-taxi, put down at Rennes, where they had a grand reunion meal with Anita. Then the pilot had to land at Lyons for fuel, which was at first refused him. When they reached Barcelona they were told that they had no permis-

411

sion to proceed to Mallorca; but after some hours of telephoning they continued safely to Palma airport, where, Graves has said, he and his family 'had the distinction of being the first civilian passengers to alight'. The journey had taken three days. His return was reported in the press.

He was overjoyed to find Canelluñ just as he had left it, Mallorca just as he remembered it: 'It was Paradise, and I . . . could take it.' British austerity had been hard on everyone: cigarettes difficult to obtain, dull food and little of it, no choice of alcoholic drinks, strictly rationed sweets, a general atmosphere of bureaucratized gloom. This explains the pleasure in food and drink, and general sense of relief, expressed in the letters written to friends back in England.

. . . we now have the air-mail *Times*, and a Phillips radio set which gets England rather more clearly than we got it down at Devon, so are *au courant* with all your latest . . . disasters [i.e. English austerity]. And yes, there is such freedom of speech here and absence of any sense of constriction or restriction that I don't feel in the least cramped about writing to you. The Terror of the Civil War times is now ancient history, . . . life is certainly very hard for the labouring class, but no revolution is talked. They have had it.

Thank goodness the children go nicely brown instead of that horrid red, or freckling. They love the heat & have escaped new-arrival stomach, as Beryl has not. It laid her low on the very morning of San Juan, when the . . . feast of arroz paella, roast kid, ensaimadas [a kind of light-textured whorled bun peculiar to Mallorca] etc had been spread with no unlavish hand. I count as an old-arrival and have been spared. The great thing is to be able to drink as much as I like of any drink I like except whiskey (which I don't like) and of course vodka which I have never sampled. Pimientos and aubergines are now in the market, and this is when they catch salmonetes – Beryl says they have too many bones.

. . . King J will be out in Sept on both sides of the Atlantic and I am now revising my early essays on poetry. I am still in 1926 and the style doesn't mature until about 1934. . . .

Gelat has undertaken that while there is any food left on the island we shall eat it: he and I are so mutually (or is it reciprocally?) grateful to each other for past services that it is almost uncomfortable. . . . I am getting a private bank a/c in the U.S. which should help a bit. My stock has gone up among the señores of the island since I have had my novels translated into Spanish: three more are being translated this year, but *not* K.J.! [To Alan Hodge, 27 June 1946]

He goes on to say how he has destroyed Laura's 'loose papers' as she had wished:

> Fulfilling Laura's wishes I have destroyed all her loose writings – several half-finished or ¼ finished books & bundles of scrawled notes. She left a lot of unhappiness behind her but we are clearing it off gradually: unhappiness breeds clutter.

About a month later he wrote a more general description of how he had found things on his return:

> Well, we arrived very safely and everything was ten years older but just the same: for example, all my shirts and trousers & socks wearable; and five jars of green tomato chutney, eatable; and cigarette tobacco in my tobacco jar, smokeable. And the Encyclopaedia Britannica & Times Atlas ten more years out of date. But it is wonderful to be here & will be still more wonderful when the traffic jam breaks and our friends can come out. . . . Apart from the British Vice-Consul and his wife we have seen no English-speaking people since we left. I am feeling thoroughly relaxed now. Beryl is becoming acclimatized and bolder with her Spanish & the children are able to cope a bit better with the weather and change of food (we are all very well indeed and the heat is intense). My first writing job was to make final amendments in The White Goddess, which are now being typed by Karl [still in England] and sent to Creative Age Press in U.S. (they are definitely publishing it; and will do it before Faber's.) [The English edition appeared in May 1948, the American on 26 August 1948.] Then I set myself to revise and see what was worth keeping of my early essays. They are very badly written & inaccurate, but . . . I daresay they'll make a book if I'm ruthless enough. . . . I found a lost poem of mine here among my papers, quite nice . . . but not written anything new: not feeling settled enough for poems. That will come, I hope. There don't seem to be many, or indeed, any books that I feel I want to read: in U.S. or England. I hope this does not mean that I am getting stupid; it is more likely that nobody has much to say . . . really it *is* nice not to worry about coupons, points [part of the British rationing system], and to drink what one likes and not to have to fill in a single form. . . . Now waiting for September to know whether King Jesus is going to be a financial success, and to what degree. It doesn't really make much difference, because I will always work, except that it will determine what books I will be able to afford to write, and whether we can give ourselves a bit more liberty by getting a car, etc. . . . The evening lizards are on the netting of our windows catching moths, so pretty to watch that it's difficult to work. I have not seen a bull-fight yet,

being perfectly content with bathing and picking greengages off the trees.
[To M.S.-S., 25 July 1946]

The revised essays became *The Common Asphodel*, published in
1949. *The White Goddess* did not see the light of day for more than
two years – and so Graves could not resist adding to it until the last
moment, and then the next last moment. No book of his was written
with less regard for the money it might bring in. He never anticipated
the small but respectable and regular income that it would eventually
bring him.

Graves's work now began to creep back into the periodicals. In 1946
he made five contributions to magazines, in 1947 eight, in 1948 six;
in 1951 there were seventeen; and the number grew until it reached a
steady average of about thirty throughout the sixties. The *New Yorker*
paid him for first option on all his poems, from 1950 onwards. The
first poem they published by him was 'The Death Room', with which
he struggled for five years. He wrote it in the middle of the batch of
mythological poems associated with *The White Goddess*; but it did
not fit in with the mood of these. It is the kind of stark, uncomfortable,
charming-remorseless little poem – unrelated to his current preoccupations – which Graves is always liable to produce. It was not collected
in volume form until 1955.

> Look forward, truant, to your second childhood.
> The crystal sphere discloses
> Wall-paper roses mazily repeated
> In pink and bronze, their bunches harbouring
> Elusive faces, under an inconclusive
> Circling, spidery, ceiling craquelure,
> And, by the window-frame, the well-loathed, lame,
> Damp-patch, cross-patch, sleepless L-for-Lemur
> Who, puffed to giant size,
> Waits jealously till children close their eyes.

This poem was mostly worked at in the early period of Graves's return
to Mallorca, before he had settled; it does not have the weight of such
mythological poems as 'To Juan at the Winter Solstice', in the interests
of which it was temporarily put aside; but it has other and different
kinds of attraction, which may give it greater appeal for some readers.
With all but the very best of the mythological poems there was, even
from the beginning, the danger of oversystematization. This was to
emerge more strongly in the early fifties in such decidedly less success-

ful, indeed embarrassingly oversystematic, poems as 'Dethronement' (which he recognized as highly artificial, and suppressed after 1961).

Graves derived great pleasure from his postwar reunion with Gelat, who did all he could to make life easier in Deyá for the family. But although genial and helpful, he was not as friendly as he seemed. It was Graves's mother who had the most accurate notion of him, though she had met him only once (in 1934), and had not been able to speak his language. She had long showed anxiety that her son should have possession of the properties he had bought with the money he had earned; and she had not been taken in by his prevarications about whose name it was in. He tried to reassure her that Gelat was 'all right', and absolutely trustworthy. That he idealized him is clear from his euphoric short story 'Está En Su Casa', in which Gelat is Pedro. On 15 November 1948, soon after Gelat had had an operation, Graves's mother wrote with prophetic tartness:

> How good that Gelat survived . . . as you think he is a friend of yours. I hope he is. Will he help you to pass on to your own children the possessions you have got in Mallorca?

II

Fortunately *King Jesus* was financially quite successful. It aroused much interest, though not everyone in those days could acknowledge this in public. Graves now had enough money to bring Karl to Mallorca, and in 1947 he did so. Karl settled in at Ca'n Torrent, with his new wife, Irene (previously married to an army major who had been a frequent guest at Vale House). Karl stayed at Ca'n Torrent for eighteen years, during which he acted as a highly critical, tensely devoted and loyal secretary. The extent of Karl's influence on the detail, though never the content, of Graves's prose work can hardly be overestimated, even though he modestly refuses to acknowledge it. He learned his job from Graves (and Riding), and so he held Graves's own standards – often as a pistol aimed at their originator's head. He did so with extreme conscientiousness and capability. 'Robert, this just will not do!' became a well-known saying, as did the sight of Graves sighing and making off shamefacedly to correct his script. Karl would often insist, with great emphasis, on quite long passages being entirely rewritten (which they were). One feature of his annotations of Graves's drafts was his marking of undesirable repetitions of vowel sounds. These were extensive, sometimes too much so ('This is going too bloody far!'); but in general Graves found that the search for other words helped him to express his meaning more clearly. No writer has had a more constructively capable secretary – or one who so studiously avoided trespassing on creative ground.

Graves sent Churchill a copy of *King Jesus* in August 1946. He began to think that it would not be acknowledged, on account of its subject. It seems likely however that Mrs Churchill, who had fond memories of Graves from ten years back, felt that some kind of clandestine acknowledgement should be made. She therefore sent Graves the following note, in a four-page card of one of her husband's paintings, 'Island of Choisi':

January 7. 1947.

My dear Mr Graves, I'm writing to you on this card as I think you may like to see this tiny reproduction of a picture Winston painted last September on the shores of the lake of Geneva.

I know that he would like to read your new book; he is always deeply interested, indeed engrossed in anything you write.

I'm glad that altho your island is subdued you still have sun and oranges. We have tangerines at 3/9d each!

We both send our wishes for 1947.

Yours sincerely,

Clementine S. Churchill

The title of the book is not mentioned: nor is Winston said to have read it. There is a lesson here for anyone who wishes to learn the art of diplomatic letter-writing.

1947 is one of the few years in which Graves published no book – and there were only eight magazine contributions (four of these to the Creative Age Press quarterly, *Tomorrow*). 1948 saw the publication of the new *Collected Poems 1914–1947* (in Britain only), his third such retrospective collection – and of *The White Goddess* at last.

The White Goddess emerged quietly. The first reactions to it in Great Britain, as well as America, are aptly summed up in a letter to Graves (17 January 1949) from the vice-president of Creative Age, H. D. Vursell, who, although no literary man, was admirably shrewd and intelligent:

... you might have been much amused to see the diffidence and fright with which the reviewers approached the book. They were obviously (even as I) scared out of their pants at the thought of saying something stupid so they circled round Hecate making tentative and, they hoped, acceptable salaams. The book started off with a very small buy on the part of the booksellers. One had to tell them truthfully that it wasn't easy reading. However, the sales are now 2,837. And I think it will sell quietly for at least some years. The book has terrific admirers and also detractors. Prescott of *The [New York] Times* loathed it. He is an anaemic man and spiteful as a toad. Katherine Anne Porter and Thomas Sugrue . . . think it a very great work. I wonder if you know Porter's writing [he did]. She is quite something.

Creative Age were – as the cordial tone of this letter shows – exceptionally generous and understanding to Graves about *The White Goddess*, and he was duly grateful to them. For he had, and knew he had, given them cause for offence.

Although Graves was happy, and could even write immediately after his return that it 'was a wonderful land for people with money, and I feel rather ashamed of ranking as such' (to M.S.-S., 25 July 1946), he soon found himself once more in a familiar state: anxious about money. He already knew that *The White Goddess* could not be considered 'as an extremely desirable commercial undertaking' – as Creative Age had told his agent Watt (16 January 1948). None of the books upon which he was currently working could be expected to bring in an immediate, substantial amount.

Fortunately he did remarkably well with a new project, eventually titled *The Isles of Unwisdom* (*The Islands of Unwisdom* in America). Although the least well known of his novels, it sold 52,000 copies in hardback and the same number in paperback. The book was originally to be called *The She-Admiral*, and was based on the (historical) exploits of one Isabelle de Barretto, discoverer of the Marquesas Islands.

It is not clear who thought up the idea for a historical novel based on the exploits of the fierce Isabelle de Barretto, but the scheme, or the first part of it, was cooked up by Graves and an Austrian called Otto Kubler, 'a dreary man' (Beryl Graves, and others), who visited Mallorca in 1947. At first the book was intended as a collaboration, and was contracted for as such. As a novel it probably meant less to Graves than any other; but he nevertheless became interested in the subject, as he usually does. However, when about six chapters had been completed, Kubler became temperamental and dissatisfied with the way Graves was handling the material. He took himself off, received adequate payment and 'that was the end of him'. Graves completed the novel in 1948.

But he had, with some twinges of conscience, kept Creative Age in the dark about this project. For Kubler's incursion into his life (the episode was brief and unimportant) had coincided with a shy inquiry from Doubleday, a much larger American publisher. It had occurred to Doubleday that Graves, a potentially 'big name' published by a small firm, might like to join their list. Had he not needed money he would have refused their offer; but Doubleday could afford to give him much larger advances than Creative Age, whom Watt was already pressing for better terms. So he agreed to sign a contract with Doubleday for this one novel; he instructed Watt accordingly.

When Creative Age heard the news through *Publisher's Weekly* they were distressed. On 13 January 1947 the vice-president wrote:

> We are very astonished to hear you have contracted with Doubleday for the publication of a novel about Isabelle de Barretto. I trust and hope that this is purely rumor. . . . MCA [US agents who acted for Watt] knew nothing of any book except a translation of Apuleius' *The Golden Ass*. . . . We feel, rightly or wrongly, that we are your American publishers. . . . Occasion might arise when it would be impossible to bring out all your books as quickly as you might want them done, but we surely feel that we have first claim on you.

Creative Age felt, as they told Watt, that since *The White Goddess* was a 'prestige' book, they ought to have 'a right to Mr Graves's more readily saleable works'. Their feelings are understandable; but Graves knew that Doubleday could bring him in more money. They also had more money with which to 'push' him.

He wrote honestly to Creative Age explaining the position. He pointed out that he had told them they could publish his 'Utopia novel', *Seven Days in New Crete*, of which he had already written an outline. The firm, with exemplary good will, let the matter drop:

> . . . the confusion and bewilderment of finding someone else publishing you has been considerable. This has in no way been lessened by the friendly notes of condolence which we have received from many people in the publishing business who know of our long association and who are admirers of your best work. For example, one of your best reviewers here wrote as follows, 'I can't tell you how bad I feel to see that Robert Graves has gone to the big boys. Too often that is the way it is. . . .' etc. . . . We are, I think understandably, disappointed that you did not

make your appeal for an advance on this collaboration project to us. Whether or not we could have satisfied your needs is something that neither you nor we have now the opportunity to know, for you did not approach us. As a publishing house, however, we have no wish to belabor that point nor to disturb, in any way, our cordial relations with you, so, as far as we are concerned, the . . . matter is finished. [3 March 1948]

And Creative Age went on to discuss *The New Cretans*, the provisional title of the new novel on which Graves was now suddenly working. They had had a sample from MCA, but though they found it 'provocative and fresh' it was not yet substantial enough for them to make an offer:

We are doubly sorry to take this point of view on the heels of the Barretto matter for fear that either you or Mr Watt might construe our action as arising from disappointment and a desire to be difficult. Please believe us that such is emphatically not the case.

Creative Age, which did eventually publish the 'Cretan' novel, *Seven Days in New Crete*, as *Watch the North Wind Rise*, was never a distinguished house, even though it published Graves; but it was tough, impeccable in its business ethics, and knew its own mind. However, it turned out to be fortunate that Graves had found himself a new publisher, for although Creative Age did the *New Crete* novel and, subsequently, the miscellany *Occupation Writer*, both in 1949, they went out of business in the following year, and Farrar, Straus and Cudahy bought up their stock.

But Graves found Eileen Garrett (an American, but born and raised in County Meath, Ireland – which gave her a lifelong dislike of the Catholic Church), who owned Creative Age, great fun, and told me that the two of them got on together 'like two oysters on a plate'. He studiously avoided comment on the more garish of her occult pronouncements and beliefs, but knew that she had been and was a genuine psychic. She was very well known in this role. Although inclined to accept overextravagant claims made on behalf of the supernatural, Eileen Garrett was intelligent, matter of fact, practical, shrewd and a lively letter-writer. Like her vice-president, she never wrote to flatter her not unflatterable correspondent. She was intensely interested in *The White Goddess* because, as she told him soon after receiving the typescript in 1946,

I have in my psychic way been preoccupied for years with thoughts and studies concerning the origins of religions, and I spent ten years of my life in the British College for Psychic Science in London searching for objective meanings to the great pattern of subjective language.

Eileen Garrett was puzzled by Tom Matthews. It was always desirable for Graves to get a review of his books into the book pages of *Time* when he could manage it. Soon after his return to Deyá he wrote to Eileen Garrett suggesting that it would be well worthwhile, for both their sakes, for her to contact Tom Matthews about a review of *King Jesus* in *Time*. She did what she could, and then wrote (8 October 1946):

I think that you will be happy to know that the salesmen were pleased with the space that Mr Matthews 'ordained' for us in *Time*. They went on the assumption that in this particular instance quantity was as good as quality. I gather from my lunch with Mr Matthews that he was still suffering from a 'hang-over' or 'guilt complex' from being in love with a lovely European lady who evidently stirred him up so badly that hers was the first name he mentioned! You, who are a student of mankind, will probably sense that he saw in me some kind of danger, for upon telling him a little about the White Goddess (which was very fresh in my mind) and how much I would like to sit at your feet and discuss it with you, he flushed rather red and told me what dire consequences would result if I ever 'tried that on'. . . . I must confess that if I had a little more time on my hands I would like to weave a little spell or two for Mr Matthews. . . . I think it is rather a pity that the church and Mr Luce [Catholic owner of *Time*] has such a frightening effect upon nice people who otherwise could be charming and happy. I need hardly add that Mr Matthews is not happy.

Graves enjoyed this, and immediately replied giving her some pertinent and not uncompassionate information about Tom's problems. Eileen Garrett answered promptly (29 October):

I was interested in all you had to say about Mr Matthews, but please rest assured that my life is too busy and a little too full to trouble any more about him.

Graves eventually met her in London in the summer of 1949 (before there was any question of her giving up her publishing house). She lived up to her letters, and it was obvious from their encounter (which took place over a lunch at Claridge's) that *The Isles of Unwisdom* affair was completely forgotten. In certain respects she was the most suitable publisher he ever had, at least since his association with Cape in the twenties.

But always more important than individual publishers was his relationship with his agent, first A. S. Watt ('a very wonderful man', Graves called him during the war), then A. P. Watt, and then, sadly only for a few months, because of his unexpected and early death, Peter Watt. This never went wrong: Graves was never tempted to question their opinions, and they managed him with extraordinary skill and tact – which sprang from their genuine respect and liking for him and his work. To all three Watts Graves had a profound debt, of which he was fully conscious.

III

In August 1947 William met with an accident, serious enough to disrupt affairs for several weeks. Bicycling round a dangerous corner in the village with one of Gelat's grandsons, his machine was knocked down by a taxi. His leg, dragged along the road, was so badly injured that he required a skin graft. He was rushed into the insurance hospital, Mare Nostrum, in Palma. But when he was discharged his leg was still in urgent need of treatment. At first he was taken in by friends of Graves, Archie and Cicely Gittes, who lived in Palma. Robert and Beryl were grateful, since they had no car, and the frequent journeys into Palma would have proved an almost impossible undertaking.

But the treatment William was receiving in the Mare Nostrum, though the best they could give, left room for improvement. Robert heard of a doctor, Gabarro, who had worked in Oxford, and who was a step ahead of anything Palma could then offer. Gabarro worked in a clinic in Barcelona; so Graves had to take William there with him until his treatment was completed.

Nothing ever stops him from working – but he had no books with him. So, having an outline of the Utopia novel in his mind, he began work on it. This was how it came to be finished before *The Isles of Unwisdom*.

Seven Days in New Crete is a futurological novel. Although he was to say of it, casually, 'Don't like it, really, it smells too much of the Barcelona clinic where I wrote it,' it is one of his most revealing books.

The hero (who tells his own story) is a poet called Edward Venn-

Thomas who has distinctly Gravesian characteristics. At one point he says:

> 'I can't love a woman unless I can convince myself, in spite of all my previous failures, that I'll love her for the rest of my life. So I try to see her always as I saw her first. A self-deception, perhaps, but that's my way.'

This Gravesian self-dissection was never done so openly or thoroughly, in prose, before or since. The novel as a whole is a self-fulfilling prophecy. Its importance as a key to Graves's personality cannot be overestimated.

One vital question for the student of Graves is how much, in the revelation of his own intensely romantic and idealistic desire-nature, he manages to illuminate the nature of other people's, of his readers', sexual psychology. In the sixties he gave the impression of believing that his own way should be that of everyone else. Yet he did acknowledge the difference, at least in private – as when he wrote (1971) to a poet friend who had just published some unhappy and decidedly anti-romantic poems:

> You seem to be the only one who gets down to work on the art of; and it is not your fault that you are born into such a filthy world that you have to castigate yourself for being a part of it. I escaped by a whole puritanical generation and a half.

The self-insight apparent here, as late as 1971, when he was complaining of 'loss of memory and giddiness' after a debilitating operation, is remarkable. (At the top of that letter is written 'Love from splendid Beryl'.)

One joking passage from *Seven Days in New Crete* prompted a hurt letter from a famous and influential woman. Venn-Thomas is answering inquiries about his era (he has been transported into the future). He is asked if he ever met God. He says no, though he has met two people who claimed to have done so. One of them was

> an English woman scientist who met God in a wood. . . . She was an authority on coal – and God told her to write a message to the Bishops of England on his behalf: they were to advocate the use of contraceptives by married people. . . . She couldn't give any clear description of God's appearance but said that he treated her very kindly.

On 18 April 1950 Marie C. Stopes, pioneeer of contraception and herself a purveyor of verse, wrote to Graves:

Your father knew my mother, & as a young girl I remember him singing 'Father O'Flynn' in my mother's drawing-room more than once – 'Oh you can't go without singing it again' we always used to say.

I have just bought 3 of your books, & read them with great interest & much appreciation. Your essays on the technicalities of poetry [in *The Common Asphodel*] make me want to have a lively discussion with you. Are you ever in England? & if so would you let me know & come & stay a few days?

You ought to be shown the dark yew wood where I *heard* not 'saw' God as you say on p. 223 of your 'Seven Days in New Crete'. All but the line no. 23 ['said that he treated her very kindly'] is fair enough if you put 'heard' instead of 'saw', but line 23 is mean & unworthy both of you & the subject [presumably God] & is a lie. I never said any such thing.

I have had several other strange experiences of the super-normal, but my work for the world is devilishly hindered by Roman Catholics.

Poetry is & always has been my most fundamental interest, of my free-will activities. As you do not seem to know any of them I am enclosing one small book. I hope you will enjoy it.

Chapter Twenty-Seven
1947–50

I

When Laura Riding said in 1940 that she would transfer the properties of Canelluñ and Ca'n Torrent to Graves, he was not in a position to accept; nor was she in a position to make the transfer. Riding had communicated with him through a lawyer, Nathan N. Schildkraut, of Trenton, New Jersey. Schildkraut wrote to Graves to tell him that 'a Miss Laura Riding' had called upon him that morning, and had asked him to prepare the 'necessary papers' for the conveyance.

Graves politely asked Schildkraut to remind her that she had vested her power of attorney in one Juan Marroig Mas (Gelat), 'of the village of Deyá' in '1934 or 1935'. She could hardly, in fact, have forgotten this. Could the lawyer please arrange for Miss Riding to give him 'instructions' which he could hand Gelat on his return 'requesting him to "sell" me the property, but making it clear that no money would in effect change hands'. This, for various legal reasons, and because of conditions imposed by war, would be 'by far the simplest method'. Such a document was prepared.

But when he did return Graves found that the document was not, legally, effective. However, so far as the houses went, all was finally well. As he wrote to Alan Hodge on 4 May 1947

> I have at last got the houses under my own name. I had a half-fear that Laura would refuse to play ball at the last moment, but since Gelat did the letter-writing she was not tempted.

What passed between Riding and Gelat in this correspondence is not officially known. But Graves did get his two houses.

Alan Hodge was at this time doing a good deal of editing and other part-time work for the London publishing firm of Hamish Hamilton. Alan was enthusiastic about Graves's *The Common Asphodel*, his collected essays, and Hamish Hamilton were as pleased to have him on their list as he was to be on it. In view of the firm and unequivocal undertaking Riding had given him about his right to make whatever use he wished of their joint writings, which she confirmed in writing, he assumed that he could publish. Watt, who continued to act as agent for Riding, informed him (27 January 1949) that 'Laura Riding has surrendered all her rights in the books which you wrote together'. Hamish Hamilton, satisfied with the position, were anxious to sell sheets to Creative Age, who also wanted to publish the book. But both Eileen Garrett and her vice-president felt that Riding's 'ethical' position should be considered. They were unwilling to 'rest on legal rights alone', although they knew that they could publish without fear of legal consequences: Watt had her letter (which I saw). So Riding was able to go back on her word and ditch the American publication. She wrote to Creative Age:

> Regardless of anything I may have said or written to Mr Graves in 1939, I have an attitude to the inclusion. . . .

She made certain bizarre proposals, such as that the joint material could be printed at the back in small type; but none of these was practicable. So Creative Age had regretfully to refuse to publish the book:

> Personally I think Riding is being tiresome, petty and vindictive, but whatever her motivation the effect of her emotion would fall on us in a way which would be most disagreeable

wrote the vice-president; and Mrs Garrett (who sensed a badness in the Wabasso air) could not in any case agree to it, he added. Obviously Creative Age did not want to go through the long horror of a detailed argument with Riding by letter, particularly since they found the utmost difficulty in translating her circumlocutory and stilted style into plain English. At one point the vice-president wrote to Graves:

> Here is a labored, unsigned letter by Laura Riding Jackson. She is determined to go down with her ship. What a commander of a submarine the lady would have made! I really can't see how either to get through her or around her. Up to this point it has been rather amusing to read her letters. . . . I tell you again that what I think she really wants is to get her horns into you. . . .

At the request of Creative Age Graves himself wrote to her; she wrote

425

ROBERT GRAVES

back two extraordinary letters, in the first of which she offered him
'two pounds ten shillings' in respect of a classical dictionary 'once of
joint use'. He refused this, much to her displeasure. He was annoyed
at losing American money on *The Common Asphodel* (in which the
fullest acknowledgements and credits are given to her), but sadder at
the deterioration of her epistolary style. Others to whom he showed
the letters laughed, but he did not join in. He had been tempted to
fight her, for a time, but felt it would depress him. Besides, Alan, while
sympathizing ('What a witch Laura is! I think we should ignore her
caterwaulings'), reminded him that 'Schuyler is an unscrupulous man'
who might easily ' "fix" a local judge. . . .'

Thus all communication between Graves and Riding ceased. Later
she would mount attacks on Graves in various periodicals, most of
them obscure. These are of no interest, and have no factual value; she
forgets, for instance, that she deeded him the Seizin Press along with
the contents of Canelluñ – and much else. But she believes what she
writes.

The Common Asphodel was published in England, where it sold
well. It would have been turned into a Penguin, and reprinted, but
neither Graves nor Hamish Hamilton wanted to offend Riding. When
someone suggested to Graves, in 1949, that he might try to act as
mediator between them, he replied, 'Leave her alone.'

II

The seventeen books Graves published between *The Isles of Unwisdom*
and his last work of fiction, *They Hanged My Saintly Billy* (1957),
consist of six translations, one fairly short essay about Genesis in a
special illustrated edition (*Adam's Rib*), two miscellanies, three volumes
of poems (one of these a *Collected*), his Clark Lectures at Cambridge,
a short historical work (*Jesus in Rome*), two very long works about
Christ and Greek myths – and only one other novel, *Homer's Daughter*
(which did not do well financially). Three of the translations he undertook were for Penguin, and these brought in excellent royalties over a
very long period – though little immediate cash. This was for most of
that time in short though sufficient supply.

Graves's agents could get him the best advances on royalties for his
fiction, and he knew this; he none the less showed an increasing
disinclination to write it. Therefore money remained tight until he

began to earn it by giving lectures and writing for the glossy journals, which paid him top rates. He did not like giving lectures, or doing journalism, but he preferred it to doing novels.

This is why the decade of the fifties is marked by efforts to make a big killing through films of his novels, by musicals, and by filmscripts. Sometimes he seemed to be very near this goal – but every attempt failed in the end. His efforts resulted in a great waste of energy, often (though not always) with the kind of people with whom Graves would not normally have associated. He was continually encouraged in his showbiz hopes by his daughter Jenny, and this was very unfortunate: she meant well, and was intelligent – but was not as intelligent as her father.

However, he had seldom really enjoyed writing fiction. He was happiest working on what he wrote during the war – when the poems, though probably the most breathtaking of all, were few and far between. In the mid-fifties he was pressed by various acquaintances to write a popular 'Roman novel': a successor to *Claudius* – preferably about Nero. He could have done it, but refused: 'I do not like ancient Rome or the Romans, and Nero is a bore.' He did however write *Homer's Daughter*. He also planned – and obtained many of the books necessary for – a novel about the Island of Tonga. His attention was first drawn to the island by the colourful figure of Queen Salote. He discovered that in its early history there had figured an interestingly loathsome missionary and hypocrite called the Reverend Shirley Baker. There was much talk about the remarkable exploits of this Rev. Baker; he spent a fair time on preparation, and it seemed certain that the book would be written; but it came to nothing. His splendid treatment of the notorious Palmer poisoning case (*They Hanged My Saintly Billy*), in which he characteristically 'puts the story right' in the most controversial manner possible, he much enjoyed. He did not write another novel after this one – which he took light-heartedly, and wrote quickly.

Of his translations, two, the Dominican novelist Manuel de Jesus Galván's *The Cross and the Sword* (published by Indiana University Press in 1955 and by Gollancz in England in the following year) and Pedro Antonio de Alarcon's *The Infant with the Globe* (also published in 1955), were done by Beryl; he polished the texts. *Winter in Mallorca* (1956) was a translation of George Sand's diatribe against Mallorca and the Mallorcans after her unhappy stay there with Chopin; Graves added his translation of a refutation of Sand by a Mallorcan journalist, and a commentary of his own. The three other translations, all from the Latin, were for Penguin Classics: *The Golden Ass* (1950), Suetonius's *The Twelve Caesars* (1957) and Lucan's *Pharsalia* (1956). He loved doing *The Golden Ass*, enjoyed the Suetonius, and hated the Lucan. Of the Lucius Apuleius he wrote to Alan Hodge, in 1947:

> I am still translating my *Golden Ass*: nearly at the end. I found that why he wrote such extraordinary highfaluting Latin was (like Rabelais with his French) that he was parodying the popular storytellers who used to hold their audience's attention by oratorical flowers of this sort.

There was much in *The Golden Ass* that he found, as he used to say in those first heady days of his discovery of the Goddess, 'central to the story'.

Unfortunately from the financial point of view, the book he was determined to write in 1949 was to expand into what was certainly the biggest single project he ever undertook: *The Nazarene Gospel Restored*. It is an erudite and physically massive book (one thousand pages). It never earned its keep. Eight thousand copies of it, in all, were printed, and these sold slowly. (Only 756 copies of the shortened edition, containing the Graves–Podro *Nazarene Gospel* alone, were printed.)

Some books that are expensive to write still bring in money indirectly by the interest they create, and the projects they prompt. For example, Graves as author of *The White Goddess* has been invited, over the years, to write journalism or to talk, for very high fees. Graves as the author of *The Nazarene Gospel Restored* has never been invited to do anything. Readers have always preferred *King Jesus*, and have wanted it reprinted. But Graves has not: the longer, non-fiction book supersedes it, since his view of Jesus is changed (as he once explained) from a third century AD one to a 'fully accurate' one ('Joshua and I have got it about ninety per cent right', he would say).

Joshua Podro, a fast friend since they first met in 1941, had been fascinated by *King Jesus*. He was a gifted and knowledgeable scholar of Judaism, as well as an extraordinarily good and kind man. He was humble and self-effacing, quite the opposite of Graves; but Graves took much notice of what Joshua told him. Joshua never suggested that *King Jesus* was historically misconceived; he took the sensible view that it is fiction. But he began to tell Graves, first in conversation in Devon and then, later, by letter, of his conviction that Jesus was first and foremost a Jew – and of his belief that the Pharisees had been gravely libelled in the Gospels. He convinced Graves. The thesis of a wholly Jewish Jesus, operating in a world in which people firmly believed that the end of the world was nigh, is now a more familiar one that it was in 1950 – as is the notion that Jesus survived the Cross; orthodox Christianity was then still *de rigueur* for conventional public men. Today few bishops would object to *The Nazarene Gospel Restored*. Then no bishop, whatever his personal view, could have dared to do other than condemn it as blasphemous. Podro, as a practising Jew, incurred no wrath. But the apostate Graves, who had always been a bounder anyway (consider his disgraceful remarks about the consolations of the Church as well as about senior officers in that dreadful war autobiography!), took the full weight of the official opprobrium. This invigorated him; but he was sorry that book was taken in that way, rather than considered seriously and on its merits. By the time such theologians as Reinhold Niebuhr were praising it, and the atmosphere had become less repressive, it was too late: the book was out of print, and the publishers (Cassell in England, and Doubleday in America) did not care to risk a reprint. He kept asking them to: he rightly felt that, in a less prejudiced atmosphere, it stood a better chance. It has not yet received this, although it is not really very far, in certain respects, from the so-called 'Form Criticism' of the Gospels pioneered by Bultmann and others from the twenties onwards.

Like many very big books, *The Nazarene Gospel Restored* had small beginnings. In the early summer of 1949 Graves, while in London, wrote in a letter to me: 'Had a wonderful evening with Joshua who's enthusiastic about working with me on the Sayings of J[esus].'

The idea at first was to do no more than extract from the literature (including the Gospels) what Graves and Podro thought that Jesus, as a devout Jew, had really said. It was, from the start, a typically Gravesian exercise in 'getting it right': the falsifications of the corrupt editors were to be explained and corrected.

The modest project grew into the enormous task of providing an outline of the situation in Palestine at the time of Christ, giving an explanation of the views and the attitudes of the various Jewish sects – and explaining all the sayings of Jesus, which included radical and, to many highly offensive, reinterpretations of parables in terms of Jewish law. Finally an entirely new, 'correct' gospel, in an English based on that of the Authorized Version of the Bible, was given. The great villain and falsifier, in the Graves–Podro view, is Paul. Graves denied that Paul was a Jew at all. Hostility, or at least suspicious feelings, towards Paul has been one thread running throughout the history of Christianity; but no book of comparable learning incorporates such a violent attack on him.

When the book appeared in 1953 Graves was attacked from all sides. One reaction, from a canon, was that he was trying 'to put out the light that millions live by'. The *New Statesman* reviewer, a theologian who knew nothing of Jewish history, challenged Graves on scholarly grounds. A vicious public correspondence ensued, which Graves delightedly ended by himself anticipating the editorial 'This correspondence is now closed'.

The Nazarene Gospel Restored is the hardest going of all Graves's books, and is so largely because Jewish law, as embodied in the Talmud, could not be made light reading by any writer. But, though very specialized, it is one of the most interesting. Its interpretations of some of the parables are extremely ingenious. Podro's contribution was crucial. His caution acted as a brake on Graves's natural bent towards the idiosyncratic, and *The Nazarene Gospel Restored* is thus his least idosyncratic book – given, of course, that he has rewritten the sacred history.

He got the book off to press in June 1951. He was then obliged to set to work on another massive project: a Penguin two-volume *Greek Myths*. This took two and a half years, and he had to employ (and pay) a part-time assistant in addition to Karl, to get it done in that time. Again, the advance was not huge; but the book has sold steadily since its publication in 1955.

III

From 1948 Graves and Beryl were able to visit London each year. In May 1948 they stayed at the large house in Clifton Hill owned by his neice Sally and her husband.

In the summer of 1949 they were in London again, this time staying at the Victoria house of a Labour MP friend of Sally's. By now responses to *The White Goddess* had started to come in regularly. These varied in quality. Kathleen Raine, one of the most distinguished of modern English women poets, was deeply affected by it. Graves told her to 'move from the navel shrine to the head'. She answered that he accept the responsibility of his own 'divinity': 'I wish I could send you any wisdom that would enlighten you as your words enlighten my way.' Meanwhile the ideas put forward in *The White Goddess* were being taken with the utmost seriousness by the Church of Aphrodite in New York. One Warren Keith, unable to be a member of this, as he was 'not wholly able to agree with the founder, Rev. Gleb Botkins', was going to found a new movement, Gymnosophy, which would assimilate and extend the principles of the Church of Aphrodite, incorporating those of *The White Goddess*. From this time onwards Graves's files became increasingly filled with zany correspondence. For example:

> Eruditissime proffesor:
>
> I beg of you to excuse the extraordinary temerity of this missive. . . . I find it scarcely creditable that I am at last now doing the deed. May I find it benign that you will offer to operate my brain pan at eleven Goddess time on the Isles Silly that shrine fortissimo. . . .

This kind of material pours in to this day, together with telegrams, pamphlets, cassettes and even film.

Graves saw Eliot again that summer. It was their last meeting. He took William with him, and Eliot had prepared himself for this: he had obtained a game called 'Photo-Finish'. It consisted of transfers. You made a bet, with counters, on which of a number of horses would win. You then did the transfer, which showed the winner. Eliot demonstrated the rules of the game to William, kneeling down on the floor – with a jam jar of water. He won; William lost. He thereupon had another go, and won again. This delighted him – but bewildered William. Someone had to remind Eliot that Mr Graves was awaiting him, whereupon he reluctantly left his horse-racing.

When in his office Eliot immediately expressed his amazement at the power he found in *The White Goddess*, and praised the poem 'In Dedication'. He seemed anxious to turn aside any discussion about Graves's forthcoming Jesus book (Graves had actually come to sell it to Faber), commenting sardonically that he would of course be interested to read it – and that he hoped it might be rather 'dry' 'if the Faith were to survive'.

They discussed Housman's puzzling poem

> Her strong enchantments failing,
>   Her towers of fear in wreck,
> Her limbecks dried of poisons
>   And the knife at her neck,

> The Queen of air and darkness
> Begins to shrill and cry,
> 'O young man, O my slayer,
> To-morrow you shall die.'
>
> O Queen of air and darkness,
> I think 'tis truth you say,
> And I shall die to-morrow;
> But you will die to-day.

Eliot said that he understood it better than before: Graves had in *The White Goddess*, he presumed, succeeded in identifying the 'Queen of air and darkness'. But why would *she* die? What did that mean? Graves replied that Housman had 'got it wrong' because he had been a homosexual – but that this was 'all right' because he'd hated being one.

Eliot also expressed his admiration for the poem in *The White Goddess* which is used to 'demonstrate the peculiar workings of poetic thought':

> Circling the circlings of their fish,
> Nuns walk in white and pray;
> For he is chaste as they,
> Who was dark-faced and hot in Silvia's day,
> And in his pool drowns each unspoken wish.

He rose from his chair, exclaiming: 'That's certainly real poetry, the real thing! But what does it mean, and how on earth did you do it?'

Graves, pleased, shrugged his shoulders modestly and muttered, 'Don't know, don't know. It's there. I saw it'.

Obviously Eliot regarded Graves as someone extremely odd – but as extremely gifted. It is as obvious, for all that Graves has said and written about Eliot, that he respected him. It was a moving meeting between two very different sorts of poet, puzzled by each other – but trying hard to understand each other. Graves said, warmly, in the underground on the way back to Victoria (William clutching the rest of his photo-finish transfers): 'He knows an awful lot about poetry you know; an awful lot. Pity he ever got mixed up with that man Pound.'

The Graveses continued to come to London each year – most often to Clifton Hill. They also went quite often to Portofino, in Italy, where Jenny Nicholson lived in a castelletto which she and her husband, Alex Clifford, discovered and lovingly restored. (Alex died of Hodgkin's disease in 1953; she subsequently married Patrick Crosse of Reuters.)

From Portofino Graves, in 1952, was able to go to see Max Beerbohm. When Beerbohm died in 1956 he wrote:

I've just heard, sadly, of Max Beerbohm's death. I now know nobody of the generation older than myself whom I can unreservedly and affectionately admire as a writer; which makes me feel orphaned. (Or nobody in my own country; there's Robert Frost in America, of course. . . .) When I was supposed to be dying of influenza in Feb. 1918 just after I got demobilised, my then father-in-law . . . read me *Zuleika Dobson*. Zuleika and an unconquerable resolution to complete a poem ['The Troll's Nosegay'] kept me alive in spite of the doctors. Afterwards, I sent Max a message, saying that the death of the Laird by falling from a window (before the communal drowning of the whole university) was one of the most tragic events in English literature [incidents from *Zuleika Dobson*]; and he answered that he agreed – it had brought more tears to his eyes than even the demise of Little Dorrit.

When I recovered, I hung up in Nicholson's studio at Appletree Yard, St James's, my steel helmet as an ex-voto offering on the peg next to a superbly glossy top hat. I had the curiosity to look at the lining. Inside was Max's visiting card with a verse commemorating his abandonment of London club life when he went to live in Italy:

> Once I used to perch on Max Beerbohm's pate,
> But now he's become Italianate;
> So here in contempt and disregard
> I moulder for ever at Appletree Yard.

So in 1920 I met Max at last: at Nicholson's house in North Wales. And what were they doing that afternoon? Libellously embellishing a copy of *The Illustrated London News*: shading the photographic portraits giving the bride of the year an imbecile squint, giving a group of visiting royalty crapulous simpers which recalled Goya's portraits of Fernando VII and his frightful family. They were working very seriously and methodically with a delicate precision worthy of an even nobler cause. And it was only the other year [1950] that I discovered with a shock how long ago it was that I had first fallen under Max's spell: I came across a bound collection of 1901 *John Bulls* – my father had been one of the editors. Every issue contained a fantastic drawing by the same hand; the plague of my childish imagination: I had enrolled them as members of my private nightmare life along with Jack the Ripper, Old Kruger, Og King of Bashan, and the Great Agrippa of Struwwelpeter. Though fifty years had passed, I turned again to them with an involuntary shudder: then suddenly I began to laugh. They were Max's caricatures of politicians and big-wigs of the day, and how admirably economical they were! I don't know whether early Edwardians wore the same self-satisfied smirk as late Georgians did when they boasted: 'I have been done the honour of a caricature by Max'; but if Balfour, Campbell Bannerman, Lord Rothschild, and the rest of the early victims did not go about with their thumbs complacently thrust into the armholes of their waistcoats, beaming to find themselves immortal, then they were ungrateful. It is one of my chief claims to fame that I was once included in a caricature group with Nicholson, Hardy and (I think) Orpen.

When I saw Max last, at Rapallo, in 1952, he was very proud of a limerick he had just composed:

> There was a young lady of Hythe
> Who said: 'I am lithe, I am blithe'
> But Old Father Time
> For the sake of the rhyme
> Simply mowed her away with his scythe.

and we had a long talk about Charterhouse where the fiery young masters of his day had become crabbed old fossils in mine; he had disliked his time there almost as much as I did. They say it's a splendid school now; but I wouldn't like to send any son (or grandson) of mine there, in case 'they' are wrong.

IV

Between 1949 and 1951, when he began work on *The Greek Myths*, Graves was writing *The Nazarene Gospel Restored* and putting together his miscellany *Occupation Writer*, published by Creative Age in February 1950, and by Cassell in September 1951. Financially disappointed by his failure to get *The Common Asphodel* published in America, he tried to make up for it by collecting as many of these old pieces as were entirely his own, and making them up into a volume. He did well with it: sales were 15,000 in hardback, and another 30,000 in the American paperback (of 1951). He included in it everything revivable: *Lars Porsena*, *Mrs Fisher*, *The Shout*, the children's play he had written on the way back from America in 1939 called *Horses*, a few occasional pieces (several hitherto unpublished) – and the play *But It Still Goes On*.

He was enjoying himself even more than he had in Galmpton; his status as a well-liked foreign visitor in the place he loved best in the world suited him well. Deyá had no telephone, just a telegraph office:

the only distractions in those days before the tourist invasion (which began in about 1960) were the noise of sheep bells tinkling and the occasional camion winding its way through the village. There were few visitors, and fewer still that he had not personally invited. He didn't encourage them. There was a daily bus to and from Palma – and one could reach by taxi, or even walking, the port of Soller along the coast in the other direction (a useful shopping place). Soller was amusing if one did not go there too often: besides boasting a cinema, it was frequented from 1950 by myriads of painters of all nationalities, none of them proficient in their craft, but many of them charming or at least diverting. One of these, a Mallorquín, described himself, *ad nauseam*, as the 'amigo de todos': he was so entertaining a shark that he almost persuaded several people to buy his pictures, which would have presented the problem – much discussed, if only hypothetically – of 'what to do with a picture by the *amigo de todos* if one possessed one'. Graves himself provided an answer he felt highly appropriate: give it to the University of Cambridge in general, and to Frank Leavis in particular.

He no longer complained of bad eyes, stomach aches, headaches and the other ailments of the Laura years. He bathed on most days, from early spring until late autumn. Until he was seventy years old few people, however young, could match his speed on the tortuous and rocky way down to and back from the *cala*, the beach.

He enjoyed the company of such visitors as did come: Norman and his new wife Gretl, Alan Hodge, and above all his daughter Jenny, who stayed with them in 1947. Norman he found happy but looking tired and unwell, which worried him. But Alan, who came out in 1947, was in excellent form, and full of interesting tales of the junketings at the Ministry of Information (and elsewhere) during the war. He was now coediting the monthly magazine *History Today* with Graves's old friend Peter Quennell; in 1948 he made a happy remarriage. And Graves found himself delighted with Jenny, who had now carved out a career for herself in her own right, and who was full of advice. His warm relationship with her made up a lot for the loss of his son David.

He was saddened by the death of old Gelat in March 1949. Although he wasn't quite the loyal friend that Graves thought him to be, he had always been helpful and amusing, and their friendship dated back for many years. His son, also Juan, was not at all the same kind of man.

Graves was writing often and dutifully to his mother, who retained all her clearness of head and shrewdness until the end. At the age of eighty-eight, in 1948, she was told she had cancer. She was too old for an operation, but survived by taking 'electrical treatment' at Exeter Hospital three times a week (she was staying with her doctor daughter, Ros, who lived at Bishopsteignton in Devon, and who drove her). All the doctors, she told Robert, thought her 'wonderful for her age'. Robert sent her dried figs, from Soller, and everything else he could procure in the way of luxuries.

She was cured of the cancer; but the treatment enfeebled her. She began to grieve for her son's moral state. In 1949 she wrote saying that she thought her 'end very near'; and, speaking of her stepdaughter Mary ('Molly'), who had recently died, she said that it would be her 'first Easter' 'when she will be beginning to get used to the New Life beyond the grave'. She begged Robert, in writing to his brother John, '*please*' not to 'give him any title' (he had been mischievously addressing him as 'M.A.', 'Dr' and even 'Sir John'). She sympathized when she heard of Gelat's death, but asked Robert: 'Who will act as landholder for him [Gelat] now?'

He wrote often to her. She told him that his children by Beryl were 'yours in heart, though not officially'. However, she had hopes here: in 1948 she had had to inform the always slightly scatty Nancy that she must not try to see her husband if he should be in England, as she had instructed solicitors (on Nancy's behalf) to take proceedings for divorce. It was Jenny and Alex who persuaded Nancy to take this step – and in that she acquiesced, even to the point of styling herself 'Nicholson alias Graves'. Perhaps she did so because of her mother-in-law's old age and state of health.

So at long last the divorce did take place, on 18 November 1949. Norman Cameron wrote to Graves (30 January 1950):

> Your giving me news of the divorce makes me think you can't have received a letter in which it was I who informed you that the event went off smoothly. I was the only witness, and I took Nancy out to tea afterwards, when she asked me to let you know, as perhaps the legal notification would take some time.

Beryl's father, Sir Harry Pritchard, in writing to Graves (5 January 1950) about *Seven Days in New Crete*, which he enjoyed, added a postscript: 'I was glad to see the law report in the Times on 19 November. . . .'

Robert and Beryl were finally married, at the British Consulate in Palma – followed by a party on a boat in Palma harbour – on 11 May

1950. (Norman Cameron and his wife Gretl were the witnesses.) This was convenient, but made no difference to their relationship. The chief advantage was that Graves could now tell his mother, of whom he was extremely fond, that his union was legitimized and that the children were his 'officially'. This pleased her very much. She had for years deeply admired Sir Harry Pritchard's family as being a 'rare example of propriety'. It made a great difference to her state of mind at the end of her life. She did not restore Graves to her will, out of which she had cut him when he left Nancy; but she remembered his children instead – which pleased him just as much. He saw her for the last time in July 1949, and found her well – and delighted with her three new grandchildren and with Beryl. But her death, in 1951, he felt, was 'sad'. As he put it:

> One of her many descendants . . . got involved in a libel action which threatened crippling damages, and came to her for help. The worry caused a nervous breakdown, the local doctor could not deal with the case, and my . . . elder sister . . . a good doctor . . . happened to be holidaying in Austria and got back too late to save her life.

Until this catastrophe occurred she had been as lively and sharp-witted as ever; as late as 28 December 1950 she was writing to Robert about his father's books, and telling him of her activities, many of them charitable. He remembers her chiefly for a piece of advice she gave him which stuck in his mind: 'Robert, this is a great secret, never forget it! *Work is far more interesting than play.*'

> Being ill never stops me [working] and on holidays I take my work along

he wrote when he had just taken a week off, in Madrid, in early December 1955, in 'a deliberate attempt to break the habit':

> all I did was to go Christmas shopping, meet people, put on unneeded weight, and read four or five modern novels. [*Quoz*]

He has always been thus, and the 'habit' was not broken until his eightieth year.

It was in the early fifties that his friendship with the thriller writer Selwyn Jepson ripened. *Homer's Daughter* was dedicated 'to Selwyn Jepson of course'. Jepson was a well-balanced and knowledgeable man, who had held a position of high responsibility in Intelligence in the 1939–45 war. Graves came to describe him as his 'business advisor' – and with justice, for in 1969 he was to prove a godsend in time of difficulty.

The children were now growing up: in 1951 William was eleven, Lucia eight and Juan nearing seven. Deyá had a village school, and the children had picked up both languages spoken in Mallorca – Castilian Spanish and Mallorquín, the local dialect of Catalan. So they had no linguistic difficulties. But this school, excellent though it was for children of the locality, could not offer enough – most especially in the case of William, who now needed to be prepared for Common Entrance examinations, obligatory in England for boys and girls who were to enter public schools. In 1950 Robert decided that Oundle was the best place to send William: a school with high standards and an enlightened approach; and he had friends living nearby.

The problem for the Graveses was how to prepare William for the very English Common Entrance examination (which demands a reasonable standard in Latin, Mathematics, History and English) in an off-shore Spanish island. Not even Palma could offer anything helpful. But it could do so, for a few years anyway, for the two younger children – who in any case needed a dash of less rustic company than they were getting at Deyá.

In 1950, as a first step, Graves decided to engage a suitable private tutor for William: this could not be left any longer. The man he found – he lived with his (first) wife in the Posada in Deyá – was the American poet and translator, W. S. Merwin. Merwin was a twenty-two-year-old Princeton graduate whose verse was highly thought of: his first book, *A Mask for Janus* (1952), won the Yale Series of Younger Poets Award. Graves used to say, 'Bill and I agree on a lot of things about verse, but not on so much about poetry.' He respected Merwin's technique, and admired his capacity as a translator. Considering that Merwin was young, had marital problems, admired Dylan Thomas and (at that time) wrote verse in the 'New Critical' style, influenced mostly by R. P. Blackmur, his stay in Deyá was not unsuccessful. At all events, William got the required rudiments from him.

Merwin's chief legacy to Deyan talk was that he received a telegram from a girl who had returned from Deyá to Africa beginning 'IF YOU WERE A MAN YOU . . .', which for a time became a catchphrase.

So as Graves worked at *The Nazarene Gospel Restored* all was well; these were his happiest years. This period of relative happiness was to continue for at least a decade: but, as Graves had written, he held that 'every Muse-poet must, in a sense, die for the Goddess he adores'. He also held that the true Muse poet distinguishes between the Goddess as manifest in the supreme power, glory, wisdom and love of women, and the individual woman whom the Goddess may make her instrument for a month, a year, seven years, or even more.

A poet, having once known her, might (he had written) know her again. That meant, of necessity, knowing 'in a sense' death. Beryl, though he loved her fully, refused to have anything to do with 'killing' him. She knew that married couples are 'separate people', as her counterpart in *Seven Days in New Crete* put it. He, in search of the impossible, was determined to make it possible. And how better to do this than to conjure up the notion of individual women temporarily made the instrument of the Goddess? Another might have said that the essence of the feminine manifests itself only in certain aspects of certain women. But not Graves: the 'obsessed' Muse poet is obliged to combine the absolutely empirical with the resolutely idealistic. That was 'madness'; not the madness of the lunatic, but the madness of the poet.

In 1950 an instrument of the Goddess turned up in Mallorca. She was the most 'Muse-like' of all Graves's four Muses (although the fourth comes, in most respects, into a different category from the others) of the fifties, sixties and seventies. She began a process which did not end until Graves stopped writing in 1975.

Chapter Twenty-Eight
1950–52

I

Her name was Judith and everyone thought her a nice girl. Of Graves's four post-Riding Muses, she was the least neurotic, the least ambitious, and the most effortlessly graceful. But her life at that time was complicated enough, if in no unfamiliar way.

She was an American, whose parents had long ago separated. Her father had done a little writing at one time; but her friend and confidant was her mother, who came to Mallorca (where she still lives) in 1951.

Graves announced Judith's presence, in 1950, by uninhibitedly telling his English correspondents that the Muse had turned up on the island – 'unmistakable, wielding a Cretan axe'. He did not mean to be taken literally; but that figurative axe became the central feature of his poem 'Darien', written in 1950. It opens:

> It is a poet's privilege and fate
> To fall enamoured of the one Muse
> Who variously haunts this island earth. . . .

The theme of the poem is that the Muse must cut off the head of the poet, who is watching 'the curved blaze of her Cretan axe' with a 'cold shudder', so that her son Darien may be born. The poet knows that Darien will be 'the spell of knowledge', 'A tear streaking the summer night,/The new green of my hope'. If the Muse is reluctant, the poet is not. He ends:

> 'Sweetheart,' said I, 'strike now, for Darien's sake!'

'Darien' does not have the power of Graves's best poetry: he was expounding a theme he already knew by heart, and the language lacks energy because of it. It is even a little stilted. He was not trying to find something out about himself, but rather to justify his new state – of being in love.

The type of union with Judith that Graves sought, and may for a time have believed he had achieved, recalls the paradoxical practice of his New Cretan poet-magicians in *Seven Days in New Crete*, who 'merged' while 'sexually quiescent'. It was telepathic (like Maria's and Mun's in *Wife to Mr Milton*), transcendent, and 'impossible'. The peerless Darien, the Goddess's son and hero, who will bring her back to cure human evil (' "Mistress," I cried, "the times are evil/And you have charged me with their remedy",' says the poet, who is about to be beheaded), will be engendered by a marriage of eyes:

> . . . If I lift my eyes to yours
> And our eyes marry, what then?
> Will they engender my son Darien?

asks the Muse, of her poet.

Graves did not, in his relationship with Judith, show many signs of the inordinate nervous strain he displayed with the later manifestations of his Muse. Beryl liked Judith, and was as interested in her wellbeing as Robert. At first both Robert and Beryl were kind to her, and helped advise her on the emotional difficulties she was experiencing with her fiancé, which she was relieved to be able to confide to them. This was indeed a precondition of the relationship: Graves would not have discovered the Muse incarnate, at that time, in any woman who bored or irritated Beryl. Judith, on her side, was flattered to have attracted the interest of a distinguished poet – though this never went to her head, for she was a fundamentally sensible girl, who had little desire to be the centre of attention. She was artistic rather than literary, and had good aesthetic taste – and she behaved outstandingly well (for example, none of Graves's hundreds of letters written to her is in any public collection). She came to Deyá just at the time of the first influx of postwar visitors to the island, and during the whole of the time Robert was involved with her, he made a point of speaking to her as 'we', including Beryl in everything he thought or felt. But Beryl, when things warmed up, was not the initiator of the pressure Graves put on Judith: she did not believe such an approach was practical.

The essence of the events which occurred is usefully summed up in a letter which Graves wrote to Judith's mother on 10 September 1953 (although it will be necessary to fill in a few gaps, where Graves has made omissions through 'tact'). Judith's mother had been taking her daughter's part.

Yes, I agree that truth is needed, but I don't think we should dispense with tact unless we conceive ourselves injured. So these are the facts which please quote verbatim to Judith; I have tactfully omitted the more emotional ones. Judith has never injured us; but only herself.

When Judith came to stay with us at Deyá in the spring of [1951] to recover her health, and have breakfast in bed, and be loved, she had already agreed to illustrate the *Genesis* book (for which I said I would do rough sketches) as a way of showing her gratitude for our help to her when she was in trouble during the previous winter. [The '*Genesis* book' became *Adam's Rib*, and was illustrated by James Metcalf.] A month later, when she had completed nine or ten drawings of the 36 series, her fiancé . . . turned up, and insisted on her breaking with us, but made her say in his presence that 'as a matter of business' she would finish the book. I answered that between J and us there were no business conditions, only love. Two days later she decided to go away & decide whether she really loved him. But she had no money. So we lent her £50 to go direct to England . . . where she would work on the book until we came, and then either resume life with [her fiancé] or return with us to Mallorca. In fact, she delayed at Paris until [the fiancé] went there, broke with him then went briefly to [England] . . . did no work on the book, & when we turned up, said that she had no time to work on it because she had arranged to go with friends to France & Southern Spain. But she would, of course, finish the book with us that winter.

When she eventually came to Soller last year [i.e. 1952] the question of the book came up again. She then said that 'as a matter of business' she would finish it by correspondence. I reminded her that we had agreed that it could be done only if I were at hand to check the drawings, and asked her whether the words written in quotes ['a matter of business'] were her own; she blushed & said no, & retracted them. She knew that she was still morally bound to fulfil her original obligation, whatever difficulties might be put in her way, and I made it as easy as I could for her to delay the decision though it had eventually to be faced. The matter came up again the other day when Arnold Fawcus said that he would publish Beryl's & my translation of the *Nino de la Bola* if he could also have the Creation. [Fawcus was director of the Trianon Press, who published both *Adam's Rib* – 'Creation' – and the translation.] So you wrote to her for me.

Her answer no longer acknowledges her moral obligation, or even a business one. She is so far from remembering what kind of people Beryl & I are that she has been persuaded – the words once more do not seem to be hers – that I would give her drawings to a commercial artist and say 'please do another 27 in the same style'. All I am asking, since it seems that she cannot keep her word, is that she either returns me my original drawings or lets me have her drawings to reduce to squiggles again – because I spent a good deal of time working out the set-up, & do not want to have to do it again. She has our continued love, and remind her that Beryl & I will always tell her the truth.

Although Judith was not in the position of Queen Elizabeth I of England, Graves was being as 'tactful' to her as the Earl of Essex was to his monarch – and Graves seems to have been looking for a some-what similar fate (if only figuratively). For, to quote from 'Darien' again (the poet is speaking):

> I knew then by the trembling of her hands
> For whom that flawless blade would speak:
> My own oracular head, swung by its hair.

But, in contrast to later episodes with the Muse, a casual visitor to Deyá would not have been likely to guess that anything dramatic was going on; Graves had not yet re-formed the habit of talking incessantly about his affairs. Certainly he was living his private life in the open (this was always necessary to him), in the sense that everyone who visited Canelluñ would know that he *and* Beryl were very fond of Judith; but that was about as far as it seemed, to strangers, to go. His chaste love for Judith he expressed in poems – and to a few intimate friends, to whom he would describe her Goddess-like rather than her personal qualities.

However, the real trouble lay not in Judith's recalcitrance about executing the drawings for Graves's version of the creation myth (this was a minor irritation), but, in his view, in the character of her fiancé, with whom she took up again – after having made the break with him recorded by Graves in his letter to her mother. Here is another poem written by Graves in 1952: 'The Blue-Fly':

> Five summer days, five summer nights,
> The ignorant, loutish, giddy blue-fly
> Hung without motion on the cling peach,
> Humming occasionally: 'O my love, my fair one!'
> As in the *Canticles*.
>
> Magnified one thousand times, the insect
> Looks farcically human; laugh if you will!
> Bald head, stage-fairy wings, blear eyes,
> A caved-in chest, hairy black mandibles,
> Long spindly thighs.

The crime was detected on the sixth day.
What then could be said or done? By anyone?
It would have been vindictive, mean and what-not
To swat that fly for being a blue-fly,
    For debauch of a peach.

Is it fair, either, to bring a microscope
To bear on the case, even in search of truth?
Nature, doubtless, has some compelling cause
To glut the carriers of her epidemics –
    Nor did the peach complain.

A critic says that this, 'an attack on the male lover', is 'morally' weak: it 'expresses little more than an uncontrolled physical revulsion for him'. 'The motive is wholly vindictive.'

This is based on a careless reading, and on ignorance: the line beginning 'It would have been vindictive . . .' is discounted. The critic believed that the object of the satire had 'displaced' Graves in the affections of the beloved. That was not the case. The fiancé was in existence before Graves was ever aware of Judith, and when she came to them in 'trouble', that trouble – confided to Beryl as well as to Robert – was being made for her by him.

Certain critics may feel that such nasty poems ought not to be addressed to anyone – or even written. That is why they are not poets. A poet, and especially a poet as dedicated as Graves, is obliged to accept the less obviously pleasing aspects of human nature, such as the feelings of intense dislike which overtake men when other men possess some hold over the woman they love. A poet cannot begin to be any kind of moralist – or not in his poems – until he has made such acceptances; a critic can be what suits him or his academic ambitions, at any stage.

The fiancé, regrettably, was not as unlike the bluefly as he might have wished; the resemblance was not accidental. Judith became involved with him because she felt sorry for him, not because she loved him. Graves's 'moral' error consisted not in writing 'The Blue-Fly', a variation – if a savage one – on the old theme of why nice girls waste themselves on unsuitable men, but in putting too much pressure on Judith, thus making her feel trapped. It is true that 'The Blue-Fly' lacks charity, that had Graves been more charitable towards the fiancé he might well have achieved his aim of separating Judith from him. But it is none the less a mistake to take the poem to mean that Graves wants the girl for himself.

His action had the effect of driving Judith further into the arms of this unfortunate man. When they were all sitting together in a small London flat, in the summer of 1951, Judith and her fiancé were looking through a book of portraits of saints. Judith came across Esdras, and muttered: 'Why, that's just like — [the fiancé]!'

'Yes, yes,' said Graves in his most mincing tone. 'Rather a *boring* saint, Esdras, I've always thought!'

The fiancé, never stood a chance in this sort of contest. But instead of admiring Graves, Judith pitied the fiancé the more. She confused her pity with love, and so her confusion was reinforced.

The situation, however, was potentially dangerous and painful: Judith became a victim. She was a young woman, under the powerful and yet puzzling protection of a poet, who was not sure that she required any protection from anyone. She had a character of her own; she would work out her own problems, make her own choices. But nothing that either Beryl, or her mother, could do could prevent Graves from maintaining an emotional pressure on her. To him, it was a situation that must be 'put right'; he set to work to do just that. However, he was working this time not on an attempt at 'pure fiction', but on real people – and even 'Pure fiction is beyond my imaginative range'.

Some eight of Graves's poems to Judith were included in *Poems and Satires* of 1951. 'Darien' was one of them; but there are others both better and more revealing. The remainder of the Judith poems, with the exception of 'The Window Sill' and 'Spoils', are in *Poems 1953*. Best of all these are the laconic 'The Foreboding' (the drastic revision of an unpublished late thirties poem written to Beryl), 'Prometheus', 'The Portrait' and 'The Sea Horse'.

'The Foreboding' is 'classic Graves': he looks in upon his 'own self' through the window; his corpse-like figure begins to write 'a name, yours, in printed letters:/One word on which bemusedly to pore. . . .' He does not know when the vision will come into effect, except that it will do so sometime – and he turns away from it 'Aghast at you':

> Was never a warning, either by speech or look,
> That the love you cruelly gave me could not last?
> Already it was too late: the bait swallowed,
> The hook fast.

'Prometheus' has the overriding virtue of detachment. It is mistaken to consider 'The Blue-Fly' without considering this much more important poem:

> Close bound in a familiar bed
> All night I tossed, rolling my head;
> Now dawn returns in vain, for still
> The vulture squats on her warm hill.
>
> I am in love as giants are
> That dote upon the evening star
> And this lank bird is come to prove
> The intractability of love.
>
> Yet still, with greedy eye half shut,
> Rend the raw liver from its gut:
> Feed, jealousy, do not fly away –
> If she who fetched you also stay.

'The Portrait' was to be appropriated (so to say) by Ava Gardner.

'The Sea Horse' was written one spring day in 1952. Wandering the Palma streets in search of bargains, as he often did, Graves came across a seahorse nicely mounted on a small plinth, with a neat lid to the whole. He brought it home, put it on his desk, and began to think about Judith. For just that hour or two, while he drafted the poem, he recognized that all the misery and the confusion were hers, not his; that he was, although unwillingly, bullying her. How to make up? He looked at the seahorse, and decided to pack it up and send it to her, with this poem:

> Since now in every public place
> Lurk phantoms who assume your walk and face,
> You cannot yet have utterly abjured me
> Nor stifled the insistent roar of sea.
>
> Do as I do: confide your unquiet love
> (For one who never owed you less than love)
> To this indomitable hippocamp,
> Child of your element, coiled-a-ramp,
> Having ridden out worse tempests than you know of;
> Under his horny ribs a blood-red stain
> Portends renewal of our pain.
> Sweetheart, make much of him and shed
> Tears on his taciturn dry head.

Although Judith's arrival set an important precedent for Graves's future life, and although she was the inspirer of some of the best of his later poems, she created no great external commotion. She did not interrupt his writing, nor did it then occur to him that he would under any circumstances allow it to be interrupted. Between the summers of 1951 and 1952 she was in touch with him only by correspondence. He remained placid.

Then, in the late summer of 1952, someone saw her, her mother and the once-rejected fiancé walking in the street in Palma. When spotted she looked annoyed; but, since her mother had settled in Soller some months earlier, and had herself become a friend of the Graveses, she cannot have seriously expected to be able to avoid Robert indefinitely. He was immediately told of her reappearance, and of the presence of the 'blue-fly' – and lost no time in establishing contact.

II

By that time Graves's life had changed considerably. Merwin gave up his tutorial job in June 1951. This meant that William had to have another tutor by September. By now Lucia, too, was in urgent need of a Palma rather than a Deyá education. The same applied, though to a lesser degree, to Juan. So the Graves decided to take a flat in Palma. They planned to live there during school term time, and to spend the rest of the year – as well as all weekends – at Deyá. Neither of them liked living in towns, or wanted to; but they felt it unavoidable.

It happened that Graves had just signed a contract to undertake the vast task of *The Greek Myths*. This was to be a fully comprehensive work, and he knew that he would need help in assembling, and sifting, the huge amounts of available material. An assistant would need facility in Latin and Greek.

My wife read Greats at Oxford, and was willing to do the job. If she could do the myths job, why shouldn't I teach William? The arrangement killed two birds – if not with one stone, then with two that were tied together. We stayed in Mallorca until 1954, when William went to England for his education.

So the Graveses had to take not one but two flats, one above the other. They chose an area of Palma known as the Ensanche. This was neither central nor fashionable; but it was near good shops, and adequate schools; the centre was only ten minutes' walk. It was also cheaper than central Palma – though life in Mallorca was cheap anywhere in those days.

The street was called Guillermo Massot (the name of a Mallorcan musician so obscure that he was unlisted in any available biographical dictionary): it was narrow, dusty, featurelessly urban – and yet somehow not unpleasant. One could reach the countryside (and, alas, the many wretched thrush-trappers with their nets and lime) on the outskirts of Palma within ten minutes, and there were many pleasant walks.

The flats were newly built ('in Belgian style,' said Graves), and were scarcely ready to inhabit when, in September 1951, they were needed. The Graves had a first-floor flat (then 73 pral 2: the number is now 45), and we a smaller second-floor one directly above it. Graves had his workroom in our flat: a large room overlooking the street which, being very narrow, never (in those days) had any traffic in it.

When he arrived at the newly completed building Graves found that the sitting rooms of both flats had been furnished with huge vulgar glittering chandeliers. He explained that the superintendent of the building would like anything *cursi* (the approximate Spanish equivalent of *kitsch*), and that getting them taken down would prove a delicate matter. The superintendent, a harassed-looking, underpaid, plump, puffy-faced young man with a pretty, servile wife (he had a Latin glare in his eyes which said, 'If-I-catch-you-with-her-I-approve-your-taste-' Señor-but-that-doesn't-mean-I-won't-kill-you'), was duly astonished; but Graves explained that the English could not live with such things, just as the Jews could not eat pork: pork was very nice, like those chandeliers, but. . . . More ordinary fittings were procured.

The Graveses had no car (they did not acquire one until 1955), and the bus service between Palma and Deyá was infrequent. They came into Palma, from Deyá, early on Monday mornings with the three children (these mornings were difficult and fractious occasions); they stayed until Friday afternoons. There was a fixed arrangement with Karl for the transport of work backwards and forwards. Fortunately there was a bus which came in at 8.30 a.m., and left at 2.30 p.m. Karl would send back whatever he had typed (with heavy annotations) in a battered old briefcase (it got the name of 'the diplomatic bag'), and Graves or his representative would put the new work in its place. This worked perfectly.

The Graveses discovered that this new style of life, about which they had been highly apprehensive, was pleasant. Lucia was getting a much better education than before, and had moreover been able to find a good dancing school to attend – which delighted her. She was much happier.

There were many diversions in Palma. Some, like attendance at cockfights, were tried and rejected; others such as bullfighting were found enjoyable (though not by Beryl). Like most Mediterranean cities, Palma is (or was then) pleasant to stroll around at night. There was a greyhound-racing track near the flats. In Spain (at least at that time) one could not place a bet, to win, on a single dog: one had to forecast the order in which the first three dogs would come in. This is a difficult bet unless one is prepared to invest money in permutations. No one was. Only one person was consistently successful with three-dog forecasts: Juan. His skill was uncanny, and the odds against his successes being due to chance alone must have been astronomical. Some spectators thought that we had fixed, or even that we owned, the track – until they saw that a small, blond-haired seven-year-old boy was responsible for the placing of the successful bets.

Although the Graveses liked their new way of life more than they had anticipated, it was costing them more money. They therefore still had financial worries. Graves was experiencing difficulties with the marketing of *The Nazarene Gospel Restored*, about which Cassell were nervous and Doubleday near to despair. He badly needed to make money from this long expenditure of effort, and was determined not to allow the publishers to be coy about the book. Do you, he asked Ken McCormick of Doubleday,

realise the sales potentiality of the book? Agreed, it's a very long book, but it could not be shorter and still solve all the outstanding historical problems that the theologians & Higher Critics have hitherto disregarded or by-passed. Joshua Podro ... and I do not anticipate any serious criticism on the score of factual irresponsibility either from Christians or Jewish critics. By pooling our complementary stocks of knowledge – mine the Graeco-Roman, his the Hebrew-Arameo-Syriac side of the matter, we have got results which Christians or Jews acting independently have hitherto failed to get, & in every case quote our sources. Yet though many of our less uncontroversial findings will be quietly adopted by the Protestant & even the Catholic clergy, we foresee an attempt by active minorities to boycott the book or to ridicule it as one more presumptuous attempt to explain the inexplicable. With any smaller or poorer firm than yours, they might well succeed, but if you break the boycott, the success will be all the greater. Your main problem is to provide sufficient detonation to explode the bomb – and it *is* a bomb of great power – despite the attempts to smother it. It is NEWS, not merely another book about Jesus. . . . There are always three publics when any revolutionary book is published. First: the small public who understands all its implications, second the middle public who pretend that they do so & like to have the book lying on their library table, third the greater public who want to know in general terms what it is all about & demand an 'Einstein Made Easy' or 'Freud for the Millions'. To secure the middle and greater publics you will have to persuade one or two prominent members of the small public to approve the argument as new, serious and watertight. Who these people are you will know better than I, & Joshua Podro will be able to give you a list of Jewish names – he is well known in U.S. Jewry – among whom do not forget Dr Raphael Patai. . . . To feed the larger public, once the excitement begins, you will be well advised to publish Part III separately. . . . This gives the *results* in easily assimilable form, and might sell in very large numbers. . . .

The Nazarene Gospel Restored did not fulfil Graves's hopes: it was too long, too controversial and too serious. Many of its findings have since been incorporated (unacknowledged) in less serious, shorter books written in a more popular style. It remains a valuable contribution to the historical problem of Jesus Christ, and it is regrettable that it is no longer in print.

The loss of money from the failure of this book to create the 'excitement' that Graves hoped for led him to pay increasing attention to the approaches of the cinema industry, in which Jenny had more faith than he.

III

Graves had already had experience of the world of the cinema. This had proved disappointing, and in 1952 he had no wish to repeat it. But when he was approached by two Hollywood people, Forrest Judd and Will Price, early in that summer he did not feel in a safe enough position to turn them down flat, though he was tempted to. They sent the usual excited telegrams, and expressed willingness to come to Deyá; he allowed this, feeling that he had nothing to lose and – just possibly – something to gain.

Neither man was well known in the film world, but both had what looked like promising credentials. Forrest Judd had just come from

India, where he had been working as assistant producer to Jean Renoir on *The River*. Will Price had had what he called 'a youthful hand' in *Gone With the Wind*, had been married to Maureen O'Hara – this marriage, of which there was one daughter, had just broken up – and had directed one or two low-budget films. Price was most interested in becoming a producer or co-producer, and a scriptwriter. He knew a great deal about his craft, but had not yet struck it rich. He was looking for backers.

Judd was the 'money man' in the sense that, although he had no money of his own, he was sure he could obtain backing. What he proposed was that Graves, guided by Price's cinematic expertise, should write a script based on an *Arabian Nights* story. He offered what was then a handsome sum in dollars – half now and half when the script was delivered – and suggested that Price and Graves get together and do the writing by the end of September. This was almost too good to be true: the money offered was worth it to Graves even if the film was never made, and, what was more, he could afford a relatively short time off from *The Greek Myths*, as this was well up to schedule.

But the factor that most influenced his acceptance of the offer was that he liked Will Price. Will was indeed likeable – even lovable; but over the next few years he was to be more of a hindrance than a help to Graves in his attempts to extract money from the cinema. Yet Graves stuck to him through thick and thin.

Will turned up again, ready to write the script with Robert, in June. He set himself up in the best hotel within walking distance of Deyá – Lluchalcari. It was expensive. He brought with him a young girl he had encountered in London: called 'Kitten' by him, she was the scion of an ancient and noble family, more than one of whom had lost their heads (but to English, not Cretan, axes).

Kitten became a problem. She drank triple brandies, and many of them; often she would order them by house telephone while lying stark naked on the bed in the room she shared with Will, causing considerable agitation to the waiters (most of whom were young men unfamiliar with such matters). She was genial and pleasant, but needed to be watched – which was difficult when Will was away working with Robert in the Posada. At first they tried to work at the hotel, but Kitten kept interrupting them. When she became bored she might decide to concentrate her attention on a male guest, or even a male waiter – and this caused commotions.

'Kitten must go' became an urgent axiom: from Graves, from Beryl, from those who watched over her – and finally, even from Will himself, who would have liked to have her there, but who was more practical than the waiters.

But Kitten would not go. She would, she said, go in three days; no, she would go tomorrow; no, she would stay a week. But eventually, with some assistance, she did leave. She had been there for some five weeks.

Then a new problem emerged. Robert's instincts about Will Price had been right: he was a man of true quality, who had had a very bad war (in the Marines in the Pacific); but he was mentally and physically ill. He had not been doing well in Hollywood recently – had in fact got himself a bad name, through his drinking. He was by now an incipient alcoholic, perhaps worse. The break-up of his marriage and the loss of his young daughter's company had affected him deeply. He felt an increasing grievance because (as he wrongly interpreted it) Maureen O'Hara denied him access to her. Later this became an obsession.

He drank by fits and starts; sometimes he would go dry for days or weeks at a stretch. But eventually he had to stop work, be put to bed, and 'take a cure'. Then he recovered – and did an excellent spell of work. Then he collapsed into drinking again, and took another 'cure' (shorter this time). In his last weeks in Mallorca in 1952 he did not drink at all – and he and Robert were able not only to finish their *Arabian Nights* script, *The World's Delight*, but also to write a play based on a pet idea of Will's, the story of Susannah and the Elders.

After 1952 he continued to decline. At one point he got back into movies; he made some TV films. But eventually he succumbed to drink. He died, a sweet soul – guilty and alone – in a veterans' hospital in the early sixties. Robert continued to have faith in his negotiating abilities until almost the end.

The script finished, Graves could not get hold of the second instalment of the money, now due. Judd was elusive. Will was broke – and owed over £500 to the hotel at Lluchalcari (this included Kitten's and her guests' brandies) and a large dentist's bill. Graves quietly settled these.

Eventually the second instalment of the money due on the script was obtained; but, after much fuss and bother, nothing came of the project – though it was good enough for Alec Guinness to say he wanted to play the lead, and, later, for Fernandel to be seriously considered for it.

IV

When Judith returned to Mallorca she based herself in Soller, where her mother was living. She was accompanied by her fiancé; and Graves was still determined to separate her from him. No one questioned the reasons for his intentions; many questioned the wisdom of his actions. Judith's mother, in particular, was hoping that if she said as little as possible, and merely sympathized, her daughter would recognize for herself that the prospect of life with this man was an unhappy one.

One of the chief topics of conversation at Canelluñ that summer was a consideration of who would be 'the right man' for Judith. Graves took more interest in this than in anything else. One man was chosen as highly suitable; but I am uncertain if he ever knew this, or even that he met Judith.

Picture Post, Edward Hulton's illustrated British weekly, wanted to do a picture story on Graves. The editor suggested that Robert Kee, the novelist and reviewer (and later telecaster and historian), then working for *Picture Post* as a journalist, should come out to Mallorca for about a week, accompanied by John Chillingworth as photographer. These two had very recently done a story on Oxford, and I had helped show them around. When Graves was about to turn down the proposition flat, I mentioned that they were not at all an ordinary journalistic team, but well worth knowing for their own sakes. On the strength of this he gave them the go-ahead.

Kee duly arrived – but with him as photographer he brought a then unknown Cambridge graduate, the young Daniel Farson: Chillingworth was unable to come. Graves and Kee (a pre-war Oxford graduate) got on very well together. Farson at that time seemed unhappy and awkward in company, and could not stand up to the often outrageous Oxonian jokes which were made (though not so much by Graves) about his Cantabrian origins – of which he felt, perhaps understandably, entirely innocent. On one occasion, at a dinner under the stars at the Lluchalcari hotel, after undergoing a preposterous barrage of in-jokes about the propensities of Cambridge men – the novelist Thomas Hinde and his wife, both Oxonians, were present – he banged the table and shouted impressively that he had never in his life encountered such intolerance, cruelty, lack of the ordinary decencies, and so forth. He then silently munched nuts for over an hour.

At the end of the meal Graves, who had been as amused as anyone else, took him aside and pointed out that the chief culprit – the man who had been making most of the jokes – did not fully mean them, and that Farson should not take them seriously, or as directed at him (as they had been). Kee said that he found this gesture moving and deeply courteous. Certainly it marks a capacity for kindness and tact in Graves which is sometimes ignored. Farson was comforted, and eventually became a popular entertainer.

It was Robert Kee, whose first marriage had recently broken up, who was chosen by Graves as the most suitable companion for Judith. Kee was assuredly a nice man, just as Judith was a nice girl; but that is about as far as it went. He had a pleasing date to fulfil on the Spanish mainland.

Since the fiancé had been urging her to break with Graves – except over the drawings for the Creation book 'as a matter of business' – she felt herself to be in an intolerable situation. She did not put as much emphasis as Graves would have liked on his ability to provide her with a real man; possibly she simplified the situation, and felt that whereas the unmarried fiancé could at least provide her with marriage, the married Graves could not. All this made things even more difficult for her mother.

At this point Graves turned the pressure on too high. He began to worry Judith about her 'obligations' to him, and even the £50. The work on the drawings, he was sure, would 'cure' her of her feelings – whatever they were – towards the fiancé. Her mother asked Graves to desist: to leave her daughter alone. Hence his letter quoted at the beginning of this chapter. The fiancé felt able to tell Judith that Graves had now put himself wholly in the wrong: she no longer had an obligation to him. He advised her to avoid him. But they stayed on in Soller: Judith still had her doubts.

One afternoon Graves went to Soller to 'have it out': ostensibly about the drawings, but really to settle matters with the 'blue-fly'. Will Price went along with him 'as Sancho Panza' on the Graveses' donkey, Isabella; he was less serious about the matter than Robert, and was delayed in a bar. Graves tracked the couple down to the town's small cinema, where they were watching a matinée performance of *Cry Havoc* (called by James Agee 'a sincere fourth-rate film made from a sincere fifth-rate play'), in a version very badly dubbed into Spanish. Possibly they had heard that Graves was in Soller, and wanted to find a place where they would not be disturbed. If so, they were in for a disappointment: Graves entered the small foyer and demanded that two of the audience, whom he named and described, come out on urgent business. They sent out a message: no. Graves thereupon demanded that at least 'the pock-marked señor who looked like a preying insect' come out: it was a matter of *honor*.

The fiancé, who could not speak a word of Spanish, unhappily emerged. Graves began to berate him: he had interfered in a matter of love beyond his comprehension, had called it 'business', thus damning himself in matters of the heart for ever, had taken the wrong course in his life, must discover his *raison d'être* (if he had one) elsewhere, was a liar who treated his mother disgracefully, might be forced by destiny to leave not only the civilized world, but also the earth itself: . . . The fiancé was terrified by Graves's drily delivered fulminations: seeing a policeman patrolling nearby, he called, 'Police, police.'

The policeman did not like the situation. He asked the fiancé, in Spanish, why he had cried out.

'Este embustero tira asalto. Un poltrón Americano,' said Graves – whose Spanish is not elegant – calmly. ('This liar is making an affray. An American idler'.)

The fiancé's confused explanation, given in English, cut no ice with the policeman, who promptly led him away to gaol. Graves went home. When he told the story, he ended it with the observation: 'People who love one another should stick together.' When someone suggested that he might at least have got the fiancé out of Soller gaol he replied that this was where he naturally belonged.

That was, virtually, the end of Graves's relationship with Judith. Graves's last poem to this Muse was 'The Window Sill':

> Presage and caveat not only seem
> To come in dream,
> But do so come in dream.
>
> When the cock crew and phantoms floated by,
> This dreamer I
> Out of the house went I,
>
> Down long unsteady streets to a queer square;
> And who was there,
> Or whom did I know there?
>
> Julia, leaning on her window sill.
> 'I love you still,'
> She said, 'O love me still!'

I answered: 'Julia, do you love me best?'
'What of this breast,'
She mourned, 'this flowery breast?'

Then a wild sobbing spread from door to door,
And every floor
Cried shame on every floor,

As she unlaced her bosom to disclose
Each breast a rose,
A white and cankered rose.

Chapter Twenty-Nine
1953–59

I

On 27 January 1953 Tomas, Robert and Beryl's fourth and last child ('eighth child of an eighth child' wrote his father in a celebratory poem published only in a magazine), was born in the large bedroom of the upper of the two Guillermo Massot flats. Unlike William, who went to an ordinary English public school, or Lucia and Juan, who went to the same Swiss school, Tomas eventually went to Bedales, a well-established English coeducational school in Hampshire which operated, in a sensible way, on as free a basis as possible. 'Schools are for different sorts of boys,' Graves told James Reeves, an authoritarian in matters of education, who had vigorously objected.

> Knowing Tomas well, I am sure that Bedales will be better than any public school. He likes work, and wants to get on, unlike . . . the usual Mallorcan boy. [To James Reeves, 29 January 1963]

Tomas, born not long before William was due for an expensive education, made one more mouth to feed. So the blow that fell not long after his birth was peculiarly unwelcome. It came to light by an accident.

The Graveses were friendly with one of Gelat's sons-in-law called Marcus, who lived in Palma. Marcus one day let slip that 'Señor Graves's land' in Deyá belonged to his brother-in-law Juan. It had never occurred to Graves to question his rights: the land, a wide strip more than halfway to the sea, together with another separate piece at the bottom, went after all with the houses – and every year he had been getting his due share of olive oil. He assumed, naturally, that he let the Gelat interest use the land, and that in return he received his 'tribute'. Marcus explained: 'That's not your land. That's our land. Who do you think's been tending it?'

Graves immediately went round to protest to Gelat's widow – now living in Palma. But she confirmed it. She was ashamed, but asserted that her late husband had lovingly looked after Graves's houses in his absence of ten years, and that it was his land because of 'his sufferings in the war'.

Graves could do nothing, and so made the best of a bad job. He decided not to think badly of old Gelat: let him rest in peace. It went against the grain, though, to have to buy half the land that was morally his own 'back' from the Gelats; but this was the best even a business friend could do for him. He did not let it worry him for long, and did not brood about it. The land had been in Riding's name, in any case – to whom, if anyone, had she transferred it?

Not long after this affair came news of Norman Cameron's early death, in April 1953. He had had an operation, and was feeling some benefit. But he still suffered from high blood pressure, and he refused to treat himself as an invalid. A few days after spending a weekend with James and Mary Reeves, he collapsed from a stroke and died without regaining consciousness. Graves said little, but was subdued and sad for some time.

From 1953 until 1959 Graves had no Muse, official or unofficial, and wrote fewer poems. But these years marked his emergence into world fame as a poet; America, in particular, began to take notice of him. Readers of the *Nation*, the *New Yorker*, the *Hudson Review* and the *Atlantic Monthly* became used to seeing groups of his poems at regular intervals; in England the *Statesman*, the *Spectator* and the *Times Literary Supplement* took anything his agents sent them. Most of the poems he thus published come into the 'occasional' category, and he reprinted few of them in book form. Jarrell's two-instalment article on his work in the *Yale Review* attracted attention; and in England, in 1956, there appeared the first full-scale monograph devoted to him – in a standard series distributed worldwide. Suddenly editors everywhere were asking for his work; his correspondence doubled. Wryly observing this growth of his reputation, he wrote:

> I, an ambassador of Otherwhere
> To the unfederated states of Here and There
> Enjoy (as the phrase is)
> Extra-territorial privileges.
> With heres and theres I seldom come to blows
> Or need, as once, to sandbag all my windows.

And though the Otherwhereish currency
Cannot be quoted yet officially,
I meet less hindrance now with the exchange
Nor is my garb, even, considered strange;
And shy enquiries for literature
Come in by every post, and the side door.

It was Graves's consistent integrity that first led to the sharp rise in his reputation. This rise was consolidated when the Master and Fellows of Trinity College, Cambridge, decided to invite him to give the 1954–55 Clark Lectures. He appreciated the irony of this, and decided, for his part, to hold nothing back: he would tell them what was what at Cambridge, for they were very Here and There – even though he had nothing personal against them.

This annual series of six lectures, delivered in the Michaelmas and Spring terms, is among the most prestigious that a writer can be asked to give in the United Kingdom. The text of the lectures, in slightly revised form, was published – along with some other material, and sixteen poems – in *The Crowning Privilege* in September 1955. This provided a useful opportunity for yet another volume of 'bits'; later (1959) an unexpected bonus came in the form of a Penguin edition of 25,000.

By 1954 he had finished *The Greek Myths*; William went to Oundle in September of that year. The other children, for the time being, continued their education in Palma; the Graveses continued to commute between there and Deyá as they had been doing.

The Greek Myths had to be made into a more profitable venture than *The Nazarene Gospel Restored* – a financial failure he could not afford to repeat. It was more promising material, especially as no one believed in the myths any longer; but Graves still had difficulties with the book, owing to his unconventional approach. He had both English and American paperback editions – it went into two substantial volumes – securely tied up with Penguin. The first printing totalled 70,000 in all. But more money could be earned by issuing the book in a hardback library edition, on both sides of the Atlantic. He had no trouble in England: Cassell printed, as they had agreed, 3000 copies in hardback, in 1958 – and this was followed by two more impressions.

In America the case was different: he had a long, hard struggle to find a publisher for a hardback version.

At first he thought he had this sewn up well before publication. The critic and writer Malcolm Cowley, who worked as an adviser to Viking

Press in America, and whose opinions carried considerable weight, had both conceived and commissioned the book. He had even persuaded Graves (against his will, for he was worried about Creative Age) to agree. Viking advanced $2000 (which they later took back: 'they want their pound of flesh,' Watt commented).

But on 19 March 1954 Graves had a disquieting letter from B. W. Huebsch, then managing director of Viking Press. Huebsch, who had once had his own, very literary, firm, and who had even taken a risk over so unconventional a writer as Sherwood Anderson, had become conservative and stuffy. Huebsch told Graves that the directors had been discussing the matter 'without the benefit of Cowley's views since he has for several months been engaged on a special task in the West'. He wanted to withhold a final decision until figures for the first year were available from Penguin – and until the book had been 'examined by scholars'.

This was too long to wait, and Graves reacted by immediately offering the book to Doubleday; on the same day (27 March 1954) he wrote to Watt:

> If Huebsch & his associates are half-hearted there is no earthly point in continuing with these blighters at all; Cowley has been put out of the way to spare his feelings, I suppose. Huebsch has been made a coward by his weak heart and New England surroundings.
>
> I think you will approve of my decision to offer the book to Doubleday; but this means that it can't be published for a year, I suppose because Doubleday don't want to publish too much of my work, & are already committed to *Homer's Daughter* & the *Collected Poems* [1955]. But there are means of securing an interim copyright. . . . You should mention to McCormick frankly that though the Classical Faculties cannot complain about the narrative part of the book, they will complain about the explanatory part. . . . But the book is (as Penguin realises) . . . for the general public which wants to know what the hell this mythical nonsense is all about, rather than for Classical students at Universities. . . . Once more (as in the Naz. Gosp.) I have come up against vested interests. Professors Tush and Bosh of Harvard & Cornell Classical Faculties resent an outsider throwing light on their subjects.

He asked Watt to press Doubleday to bypass Professors Tush and Bosh and sell straight to the general public – 'Besides, all nice women will love it.'

But so far as Doubleday were concerned, well though they served Graves in general, Professors Tush and Bosh had their way. He encountered hostility from some reviewers – not, in the main, classicists – but, as he had hoped, grateful acknowledgement from the general public. His main English-language rival was H. J. Rose's *Handbook of Greek Mythology*, which had gone through several editions since its first appearance in 1928. This is useful, sound, worthy – and dull. Rose himself reviewed Graves crossly, in the *Classical Review*, mentioning a few howlers. But there is little doubt which book makes the more interesting and lively reading; and Graves puts in much more material than the conformist Rose.

Ultimately the American firm of George Braziler published the hardback edition of *The Greek Myths*. In 1957 they made it available in both a one- and a two-volume format. This soon sold out its 5000 copies; but it did not reprint.

Graves expressed what he aimed to do in the book most succinctly and reasonably in a letter of 14 June 1954, written to a friend who was an amateur anthropologist (he described this person, characteristically, as a professional 'out of a job'):

> I am just indexing my dictionary of *Greek Myths* for Penguin. . . . I am not a Greek scholar, or an archeologist, or an anthropologist, or a comparative mythologist; but I have a good nose and sense of touch, and think I have securely connected a lot of mythical patterns which were not connected before. Classical faculties will hate me, and I will get a lot of sniffy reviews. But people like you . . . will, I think, know that a good deal of it makes sense; and anyone is welcome to take over where I leave off and make even better sense. Unfortunately one can't be on sure ground in a culture so long dead. . . .

He did get some sniffy reviews, of course; and this was understandable, since his method violated tradition. The classical scholars of those days, however, were not as lively – or possibly as good-humoured – as they are now (they had not read Lévi-Strauss; and knew no anthropology), and they gave no credit to Graves's poetic powers – or, indeed, to his achievement in making the old stories so readable.

In *The Greek Myths* we encounter the two sides of Graves, the empirical and the romantic-magical, working side by side. On the one hand we have, in the explanatory part of the text, in the detail, countless examples of Graves's insistence on his 'matriarchal' thesis; but on the other, we find the following statement in the introduction:

> A true science of myth should begin with the study of archeology, history, and comparative religion, not in the psycho-therapist's consulting-room.

Though the Jungians hold that 'myths are original revelations of the pre-conscious psyche, involuntary statements about unconscious happenings', Greek mythology was no more mysterious in content than are modern election cartoons. . . .

The 'sniffy' reviews did not worry him much; and the public bought – and buys – the book.

Meanwhile Graves's daily life went on much as before, except that he began to travel more. In 1955 he acquired a Land Rover, which Beryl drove. At just the time he completed *The Greek Myths* he gained a new friend and companion, with whom – for seven years – he was to be on the closest of terms. But the relationship was to end – at least for him – in disaster; and that result was owing to his habit of putting, as Emily Dickinson has it in a poem, 'pewter on [his] silver shelf'.

In the summer of 1953 a Scottish journalist and poet called Alastair Reid came to the island with his first wife. Reid, born in 1926, the son of a parson, was a graduate of St Andrew's University, Scotland. From 1950 until 1955 he was teaching at Sarah Lawrence College in New York. He had published one book of verse, *To Lighten My House*, with a small American firm called Morgan and Morgan.

Reid was easily able to accommodate himself to Graves's habit of regarding everything that happened to himself as significant coincidence – but as easily (privately) to dissociate himself from it. For the reader who likes clever, playful verse, Reid provides a genuine service; but he is not, and does not usually try to be, serious. As companion he is witty, intelligent, sharp, entertaining, sophisticated, teasing and courteous; he possesses considerable charm.

There was nothing equivocal about Reid in Graves's eyes, at least. He soon came to trust him implicitly, and showered him with his usual generosity, including the use of a house in the village.

During his first visit to the island, in 1953, before he knew Graves well, Reid gave the impression of studying him from a distance; he asked several people questions about him, and about his tastes and habits. It was in the next year, back on vacation from Sarah Lawrence, that he made fast friends with him. Reid seemed to have decided to take to him, although his own tastes in poetry (as he had expressed them in the previous year) were not at all like those of Graves; he deeply admired, for example, Dylan Thomas, Auden, Pound and Yeats. But he did not give the impression of holding his convictions with any great tenacity, as he showed in his contributions to *Quoz*. *Quoz* was an exchange of letters, intended for publication (an American publisher made a firm offer for it), in which (in effect) Reid acted as foil to Graves – who set forth such details of his autobiography, and of his tastes, as he wished. It was written, but never published.

Reid, who made his 'privacy' something of a special, even mystical feature of his public personality, found Graves's habit of living out his private life in public something of a strain; but until 1959 he acted out his role of companion and loyal supporter without giving his feelings away. Graves became increasingly convinced of Reid's loyalty to the Gravesian cause, as well as to Graves. This was a mistake: Graves is and has to be a deeply committed man, whereas Reid does not give that impression to others. For him reality quite rapidly keeps breaking in. He does, like Graves, seem to exist in order to be ensorcerized; but, unlike Graves, for the sake of mere 'moments' which give him 'odd' 'omens' and inklings. When Graves is ensorcerized it is until he hears the familiar 'kill! kill!' – or until his own oracular head is swinging by its hairs. Reid's head is not oracular, because he makes sure that it is never really swinging by its hairs. This attitude is easily understandable; but it was unfortunate that Graves gained a different impression.

So Graves proceeded to build up a false picture of Reid's personality. When Reid mortally offended him – if few others – it was by an action which everyone but Graves himself regarded as entirely in character. None of this, of course, was Reid's fault.

Graves had no Muse during all but the two last years of his association with Reid – who became his confidant in poetic matters. He would become excited over new discoveries, or objects which had magical properties for him, and Reid encouraged him. The atmosphere between the two men became overintense – overexcited on Graves's part, possibly confused on Reid's. The latter would, from time to time, confide to third parties his disbelief in the Gravesian universe. He was in a position others had been in, though to a greater extent; and it is a dangerous position. (Only Beryl took care never to put herself into it – by her insistence, acknowledged by Graves in *Seven Days in New Crete*, upon the necessary 'separateness' of people.) Reid yielded to Graves's excitements, and pledged devotion to the Gravesian cause. This was not insincere, indeed it was all venial enough; but it was laying up trouble. Reid is not the first man to have yielded to Graves in this way.

However, Reid, by nature a wanderer, was not in Mallorca all the time. He travelled a good deal, and was often in America. During the latter part of the fifties he and his first wife – a dancer – were divorced, and he married again; by this second marriage he had a son, Jasper. ('I'm not at all surprised he dislikes matrimony, but likes parenthood,' wrote Peggy Glanville Hicks – the composer who made *Homer's Daughter* into an opera – 'he's an odd boy . . . his real anchor is in himself. . . .')

Graves came closer – although nothing like as close – to another friend during 1955. He began corresponding with R. Gordon Wasson in 1949, first met him – in Mallorca – in November 1953, and remained friendly with him until the mid-sixties. At first Wasson, vice-president of J. P. Morgan & Co., the bankers, was referred to as 'the mushroom man'. He was a student of rare hallucinogenic mushrooms, and published several books on the subject. His *chef d'œuvre* was *Mushrooms, Russia and History*, which he wrote with his wife Valentina.

Wasson, as an amateur, felt insecure, but he was wholly committed to his subject. His style of letter-writing was curiously stilted and formal; he was awed by Graves's fame, but determined not to be overinfluenced by him. Sometimes his letters sound a slightly petulant note, perhaps arising from a resentment that he was a rich business man rather than a scholar – and thus forced to turn to qualified professionals and poets.

Wasson's interest in the psychological effects of hallucinogenic mushrooms and allied substances synthesized in the laboratory was to have a considerable influence on Graves towards the end of the fifties. And Graves meanwhile helped build up Wasson's reputation.

In 1956 Ava Gardner made a visit to Mallorca – Graves's fictionalized account of it first appeared in 1958, as 'A Toast to Ava Gardner'. Both he and Beryl found her exhausting, but as Beryl puts it, 'a film star with a heart'. Before he wrote the story (originally for the *New Yorker*) Graves gave a more revealing account of her visit. (The visit came about through friends of the Graveses, the Sicres, who lived in Barcelona. Ricardo Sicre was a Catalan who had fought against Franco, then left Spain, joined the US Services, fought in the war – and taken American nationality. He wrote a novel about his experiences, *The Tap on the Left Shoulder*, with which Graves helped him. Graves first came across him at Great Bardfield in 1939. While in America he married an American, Betty Lussier; after the war he returned to Barcelona – as an American he was of course immune from Franco's vengeance – and made several fortunes by buying and selling.)

Graves wrote:

'She speaks only in her own voice' ['The Portrait'] – odd that you should have quoted that, because. . . . This new anecdote begins with Betty Sicre ringing us up from Madrid, about ten days ago, to say that she was sending Ava Gardner to us, and we must take good care of her, and see that she ticked off all the items on her list of resolutions. This we promised to do. She arrived in the late afternoon at the airport. . . . Ava came rushing across the tarmac to us taking good care to get wrapped in a close family embrace – which was her only way of throwing off the Spanish wolf who was pursuing her with amorous yelps. . . . Ava had used the Ladies' room in the plane, to escape from this wolf, and then gone to sit in the only other unoccupied seat, next to what she hoped was a sheep. But he was a wolf, too. . . . Poor Ava wasn't pleased at all. And the other wolf attacked her as soon as she landed. . . .

It was a most fantastic experience, getting caught in Ava's spotlight for the next five days. Among the items in her list were a visit to Deyá; resting up; seabathing; reading Spanish grammar; and asking me about poetry. She didn't find time for Spanish grammar, or resting up, but came out to Deyá, and we took a picture of her . . . and though the weather was far too cold for bathing, bathe she did. She also asked me about poetry, and how she could start reading it. I reassured her that there was so little really worth reading, and so much that was wrongly supposed to be worth reading, that she had better not start without being sure she wasn't wasting her time. . . . I asked her about the monstrous legendary self with which she had been saddled, and she said she does her best to get out from under it . . . it isn't what she does that creates her solitary reputation, but what she says. She can't control her tongue at times. . . . [The autographed poem I chose to give her] was: 'She always speaks in her own voice' ['The Portrait']; because Ava does, when not on screen. The verse beginning

> She is wild and innocent, pledged to love
> Through all disaster. . . .

went straight to her heart, as I had expected. It wasn't written about her, but no matter – the cap fits. [*Quoz*]

There are several rather splendid letters from Ava Gardner to Graves, one as late as 1966. They are not always quotable, by virtue of her accurate pronouncements upon certain of her famous colleagues – directors, actors and producers. It is clear that Graves made a deep impression on her; and while both the Graveses remember the exhaustion of entertaining her – they and others had to take it in turns to sit up until the small hours – they better remember the quality of her personality in its struggle to remain intact and uncorrupted in the sea of publicity and vulgarity in which it was unhappily suspended.

While Ava Gardner was in Mallorca, Beryl and Graves were just putting the finishing touches to a novel they had translated: *El Embrujo de Sevilla*, a bullfighting story by the Uruguayan novelist Carlos Reyles (1868–1938). They did not know that it had already been translated, in 1929, as *Castanets*, and they never could find a publisher for it, excellent story though it is. But Graves did do a 'film-treatment' of it for Ava Gardner, who sent it enthusiastically to her agent – who turned it down flat. She expressed willingness to play a part in any film from a book or script by Graves, but she never did fulfil this ambition. Being able to write to Graves, and to confide in him, always meant a great deal to her.

II

Graves's opinions in the mid-fifties did not change, though he broadened his interests. He did not dwell too much on the fact that the quantity of his poetic output was directly related to the quantity of amorous unrest going on within him. He was, in fact, making an attempt not to repeat the Judith experience with another woman.

> Few poems this summer [1956] and those few sedately written – a good sign when that happens. If there's need to write the wilder and more poignant sort, there's trouble about for sure. I've had enough trouble in my life and feel glad not to be plagued, if only for a summer. Poems, of course, if they match the trouble in intensity, and record a decent facing of the trouble, do provide some solace to unhappiness, but I should never deliberately court unhappiness. . . . [*Quoz*]

At Cambridge, where he gave the Clark Lectures, he went out of his way to treat his hosts with courtesy; and the undergraduates, and some (only) of the graduates, thoroughly enjoyed listening to someone who was prepared to give his views directly and unequivocally, unqualified by any respect whatsoever for conventional academic opinion. Graves is not a brilliant orator: distrusting all forms of rhetorical performance, he concentrates on saying what he means. He has been accused of 'standing to attention' both when reading poems and lecturing. Why, then, without the usual skills of the orator, does he impress so much?

Mainly because what he says has the conviction of his experience, and is therefore interesting, so that his audience is eager to follow what the dry Oxonian voice is saying; and because they are awed by the presence of a dedicated poet. Few English-speaking poets of the century have possessed this poetic 'presence'. The exception, though in a different and much more theatrical way, is Yeats.

The Clark Lectures for 1954–55 were a sustained, deliberately provocative attack on the literary academic conventions, with a few sideswipes at the then still flourishing school of Leavis. As lectures they were successful in their purpose; but the text reads disappointingly, since it was conceived to be spoken. In printed form, the Clark Lectures do not show Graves at his critical best, since his approach is biased, even if deliberately so. This is what led reviewers such as Herbert Read to attack the book: they failed to appreciate that in dethroning Wordsworth for his Cambridge audience Graves had had no time to pay proper tribute to the early Wordsworth – a true poet, whom he fully recognized as such. Read himself, who deeply resented the attack on his fellow northerner, had in fact taken a somewhat similar line in his own early study of Wordsworth. Graves was believed, by many of the more solemn academics, to have inflicted what they called 'serious harm' on the appreciation of poetry.

In *The Crowning Privilege*, which begins with the text of the lectures, he included some of his reviews for the *New Statesman* and other magazines, and sixteen poems. The most memorable of the essays are an appreciation of E. E. Cummings, a comic and effective demolition of Ezra Pound as classicist, and, above all, an account, with some translations, of the Mexican poet-prodigy Juana de Asbaje (for which Rebecca West wrote him a letter of gratitude when she later read it in the Penguin edition).

While in Cambridge Graves came across Siegfried Sassoon, strolling in King's College Chapel. They discovered that their sons were both at Oundle, though William had only just started there, whereas George Sassoon was about to leave. 'We have mellowed,' wrote Sassoon to him soon afterwards (7 January 1955), with a copy of *The Tasking* (poems by Sassoon printed by Geoffrey Keynes in a private edition of one hundred copies), in a friendly letter; it was followed up by one more, beginning 'Dear Mallorcan' (dated 1562), in 1962. But the reconciliation was a superficial one only.

Though now more comfortable financially than he had ever been, Graves could still never put money out of his mind, as he desperately wished to do: 'it has been years since I could look more than half a year ahead for income' (6 February 1956, *Quoz*). He had therefore toyed with the idea of allowing himself to be put up for the Professorship of Poetry at Oxford, the elections for which were due to be held in February. This in itself would bring in no money – but it would make money easier to earn. In this context he wrote:

Well, recently there was a movement to get me the Professorship of Poetry at Oxford. . . . The only serious opponent, they told me, was W. H. Auden, and he had very decently told my daughter Jenny in Ischia this year that he would stand down if I were nominated. Anyhow there has been a good deal of opposition to him in academic Oxford . . . so someone nominated G. Wilson Knight . . . as a rival candidate. . . . Then Sir Harold Nicolson, who has never made poetry his profession . . . wondered, it seems, why shouldn't he get those extra few hundred pounds a year. . . . So on the strength of two short studies of Verlaine and Tennyson published a year or two before you were born he persuaded 'Six Valiant Heads of Houses Six' [a joking allusion to bullfight announcements] to nominate him, while politely conceding (according to *The Daily Express*) that 'Auden is undoubtedly the greatest poet this country has seen during the last twenty-five years'.

When I'm asked why my name doesn't figure in the *Times* list of nominations, I say that the Statutes demand a B.A. diploma from the Professor of Poetry, and I haven't such a thing on me. I'd got a B.Litt at Oxford in 1925, and was then deemed to have achieved a B.A. because no one can win a B.Litt without one. But there can be no Professorship of Poetry for me, without a further act of deeming that I took the degree they once deemed me to have taken! That's my story. The honest truth is that the appointment would be hopelessly uneconomical. Had there been real money involved, my friends would have found a loophole in the Statutes and nominated me; however, I explained that I couldn't afford the job, which would have meant breaking my overseas domicile. A pity, because Beryl and I have always wanted to show the children Oxford. . . . [*Quoz*, 1956]

The consideration of taking up the Professorship of Poetry at Oxford made no difference whatever to Graves's views, or to his expression of them. Genially answering a stranger who had sent him two books, he wrote (10 March 1956):

Yes, isn't everyone awful? . . . Yes, and isn't sex awful? And pubs? Me, I'm past the age of pubs, and am what they call an escapist: having gone abroad in 1929 and never come back. I have nothing against love, though, which makes sex less awful; and if I tie my life neatly together, and am happy, am I a bloody fool? Or even insensitive? *I* don't know. God give you good riddance.

Asked by George Scott, at that time editor of the (now defunct) weekly, *Truth*, whether he would like to review Stephen Spender's *Collected Poems*, which appeared in January 1955, he returned Scott's letter with the following written at the bottom:

Dear George Scott: Forgive me; I like Spender too much as a person to want the job of reviewing his poems.

On Yeats and Housman he was more illuminating, and much more explicit, in his deliberately informal letters in *Quoz* than he had been about any of the poets he dealt with in the Clark Lectures:

Yeats's posturings: I can't find them true, just as I can't be convinced by a stage actor who throws himself, body and soul, into an obviously false part. There's a puritanical resistance to Yeats in me – I see him as a 'dirty old man'.... But A. E. Housman never preteneded to be a Shropshire Lad; if he had done so, he would have written in dialect ... and bought a cottage at Clun. All he did was to say: 'If this flabby self-tortured Classical scholar, myself, could be magicked into a vigorous Shropshire ploughboy would his troubles be in any way mitigated thereby?' It's a dramatisation of an *if*, not a lie. You'll find the torture of being a homosexual, in an age that did not licence, far less extol, it bitterly described in his 'Shot? so quick, so clean an ending?'... I think poor Housman had a passion for soldiers.... I find no vain posturing in Housman; the verse is almost painfully clean and in perfect good faith.... Yes, I gratefully accept Morgan Forster's dictum about good faith – he was another haggard scholar when I knew him thirty years ago, but he's grown old, gracefully and plumply, and come to terms with the world. The point seems to be that Yeats can't really have believed in the Brocken Spectre Yeats [a dramatic optical illusion on the Brocken, highest peak of the Harz range in Saxony: the shadows of watchers are seen, monstrous, on the mists swirling around the top of the opposite peak] he conjured up; or he'd have won my acceptance of it. [*Quoz*]

The Suez adventure of 1956 made a strong impact on Graves, particularly so since he usually ignores political events. This one, however, was different:

A pity [about] the Suez trouble; the only comfort being that, against all comers, we protested wholeheartedly that Eden had acted with all the folly of a weak man who puts his foot down in the wrong place. It really is extraordinary how the country has split on the Suez question: not by party or income group ... but by moral sensibility. The last time I remember being thoroughly ashamed of my Government was in the Munich Crisis. . . . [*Quoz*]

He was disappointed that James Reeves, alone of his close friends, fervently backed Eden. When Graves wrote asking him, 'I wonder if you feel as shocked by Eden as we do?', James even protested that the British forces had been pulled out too early. Graves would have been less surprised, though, had he known the identity of the person who influenced the impressionable James: it was none other than Jacob Bronowski. (Later James freely admitted to having made an error of judgement, and to having been taken in by the Government's lies.)

Yet Graves still rejected any form of political action, despite 'god-dawfulness', explaining:

> I certainly like things to happen dramatically, short of bloodshed or broken hearts, but when times are fruitful of evil – say, the recent Thirties, with Nazism and Stalinism – I wish myself back in the 'good' old days of my childhood when the newspapers seldom printed anything more than 'Small Earthquake in Ecuador: Few Casualties'. Am I losing my elasticity of mind? I don't think so. As a child I never could have joined the 'Baddies' against the 'Goodies' and I couldn't now; which shows perhaps that my Protestant conscience has impaired my sense of humour. [*Quoz*]

There were the usual crop of visitors in 1956. The meeting Graves enjoyed most was with the composer Ralph Vaughan Williams, an old Carthusian whom he had last seen in 1912 – when he had visited the school as a distinguished old boy. His wife, Ursula, wrote to Graves (7 October 1956), 'The *Carmen* [the Charterhouse school song] sung by you & Ralph in a thunderstorm is a splendid memory.'

Another visitor, or pilgrim, of 1956, was John Wain – then still teaching at Reading University – who had received a note from Graves telling him off for misquoting one of his lines in the title of a book of his poems. Wain, already armed with a letter of introduction (from me) to Graves, though he did not say so, suggested (23 June 1956) that he might come to Mallorca, and send him up a copy of the book 'with a note of my lodging in case you wanted me to come and answer your wrath in person'. He apologized for the misquotation: he had thought of writing to A. P. Watt, but since Graves did not know him felt obliged to explain what those who know him 'would not need to be told,' that

470

in the end I thought it seemed unpleasantly like trying to bring my book to your notice – literary careerism is a thing I abhor. . . .

He did call; and the two, both of St John's, Oxford, have maintained an up-and-down acquaintance ever since.

III

Throughout 1955 and most of 1956 Graves still wanted to avoid going to America, although Mount Holyoke, America's oldest college for women, had offered him $4200 for three lectures – whenever he liked to give them. He was relying too heavily on hopes of income from the cinema. Both Beryl and his agent Watt ('many writers have been deluded . . .') warned him of the danger of allowing his hopes to be raised, but he persisted. He wanted to spend as much of his time at home in Mallorca as he could, and to stop having to depend on grinding out prose for a living.

His friend Ricardo Sicre had been talking to Ava Gardner about a role in a Graves film for some time before she went to Mallorca. He wrote to Sicre – his confidant, at this time, in financial matters – in late August 1955 to ask him to tell Ava Gardner that he would be glad to 'help' her. The details of what she was planning are now obscure; but they involved working with a certain famous director ('a nice earnest old queen who thinks women are wonderful because he'd like to be one,' Graves told Sicre) on a film tentatively entitled *The Female*. By the time she came to Mallorca in early 1956 this had been dropped and forgotten.

He was then, however, pinning his hopes not on Ava Gardner, but on the interest shown in *Homer's Daughter* (the book had been published in February 1955) by Roberto Rossellini and his (then) wife Ingrid Bergman – and on Will Price.

With Price he was, in mid-1955, working on a 'TV "spectacular" film script for N.B.C. . . . who has another job with me of the same pending sort' (to Sicre, late August 1955). But neither this, nor the other script 'of the . . . pending sort' ever saw the small screen. Jenny, who was in a position to keep her ear to well-informed ground, warned him that Will Price's name was 'poison' in the film world; but to his credit, as well as to his financial embarrassment, Graves would not give up working with him.

He had met Rossellini and Ingrid Bergman while visiting Jenny in Rome in 1954; soon afterwards he sent them a proof of *Homer's Daughter*. He told Sicre:

Ingrid Bergman whom I know and like is dead set on playing *Homer's Daughter* & working on the script with me & her husband. But she can't come here until the New Year. . . . [It] is very odd; so far no contract has been drafted but it all looks probable, & I certainly could do with some real money.

He had good reasons for optimism. On 3 July 1955 Jenny wrote to him from Rome:

About Ingrid: we drove along the coast to lunch with her and the children . . . yesterday. She lives in a concrete boat-box on the main road. It's no worse than Cannylun [*sic*] of course on the outside!! Inside – alas, no sign of your taste. Homer, she is one of the most charming women presently on the face of the globe and she is absolutely determined to play Nausicaa if she and Roberto can rustle up the money. . . . Rossellini has suddenly run out of ideas, she says, which means he can now make other peoples'! . . . She wants you to come over and write (with Roberto technically advising) the script. . . . She is a little sad not to have had a personal answer from you to her two letters. . . . Ingrid just telephoned to say a wonderful letter came from you this morning. Roberto returned late last night from Paris and they were up early discussing Homer's Daughter and she wanted aid for the drafting of telegram to Watt in reply to his saying £5000 for film rights!

'Agree in principle grateful you send urgently draft contract.' This, Roberto needs for rustling up the money-lenders. So far, so good.

On 30 June Watt had wired Bergman, on Graves's instructions:

ROBERT GRAVES HAS SENT ME YOUR LETTER JUNE TWENTYFOUR ABOUT HOMERS DAUGHTER STOP SUGGEST FIVE HUNDRED POUNDS FOR OPTION FOR THREE MONTHS TO BUY FILM RIGHTS AT FIVE THOUSAND POUNDS FOR TEN YEARS

But after all this excitement no more was heard. Jenny's judgement was no more dependable than her father's. So Graves went to England in the late April of 1956 in a somewhat perturbed state. He and Beryl travelled through France, she driving the Land Rover; one of their purposes was to 'take William back to school':

He'll soon be sixteen. Whereupon I'll be allowed to claim for his education on my income tax returns. . . . I'm still taxed in England as though

472

I were living there and enjoying all Welfare State benefits. . . . I have to earn another £500 to pay the taxes. . . . No wonder I have to write too many books. . . . I expect everyone thinks I'm a millionaire. . . . It's not even as though I gambled or kept a cellar, or a mistress, or collected first editions. I haven't hit a jack-pot since 1936 (with *I, Claudius*) and only jack-pots count in this dying profession of literature. Battling on is a sort of proud game with me, and I think I'm what anyone would call a thoroughly happy man. Still, having reached the age of sixty, with a large family to support, I shouldn't, I suppose, go on playing the game: I should sell my soul to the Devil, or the next highest bidder. . . . [*Quoz*]

In Paris he met, once again, Alexander Korda's film-producer brother Vincent, who spoke to him of a remake of Claudius, and of paying him 'good money' ('God knows I need it, good or bad'), whether he was legally entitled to it or not. Korda had a particular actor in mind for the name part: Alec Guinness. Graves wrote from Paris telling Will Price, who – repentant over the television scripts – got to work (not to Graves's advantage) on his own account.

While in London he was given tickets to see Guinness in the farce *Hotel Paradiso*, at the Winter Garden, and 'went round to his dressing room afterwards, and he is mad keen to play Claudius'.

This was the most promising project yet. But Graves is prey to showbiz gush.

When he returned to Mallorca in mid-May he found a letter from Will Price telling him that he had recovered the full rights in the old *World's Delight* script: Film Group Inc., which originally commissioned it, had gone bankrupt. He wrote immediately to Guinness:

It was great fun meeting you . . . I do hope your subsequent accidental meeting with Vincent Korda was a good sign. . . . [He] wants me to rewrite the Claudius script as soon as ever production is assured; so when he gives the all clear I'll do it with an eye to your particular talents, giving Claudius a dry, comic but generous wit. . . . The *World's Delight* script, sent under separate cover [is sent] partly as a reassurance to you that I can manage the technical side of the Claudius script . . . chiefly in the hope that you may get excited by it. . . . If you decide you're interested, there are no strings attached . . .

By 1 June Graves was sure that a *Claudius* film was in the bag, though he had earlier recorded that

Beryl, never fooled by golden dreams, says she won't believe a word of all this until the money is safely in the bank. [*Quoz*]

He wrote:

> I'll go to lecture in America briefly next year, but only if the ... film isn't made and if nothing else happens to fill my purse. [*Quoz*]

His spirits were raised even higher when, on 13 June, he received this telegram:

> VERY MUCH WANT TO DO WORLDS DELIGHT IF CONTRACTUAL DIFFICUL-TIES CAN BE OVERCOME WHICH I THINK POSSIBLE LETTER TO YOU IN POST ALEC GUINNESS

The contractual difficulties to which Guinness referred in his telegram were explained by Graves when he wrote to Will Price on 14 June:

> It's a sort of phobia [Guinness] has got himself into of large-scale American film production; he wants everything to be very cosy and English and he has this friend Peter Glenville with whom he really enjoys working and who has been directing the ... success at the Winter Garden [*Hotel Paradiso*]. ... My immediate hunch, and Beryl's, is that a single misplaced word or gesture would send him scurrying away into the shrubbery, and all would be lost. It is clear ... that he doesn't want to do anything on a great and glorious scale, that he wants to make this a real stay-at-home treat for himself. ... He feels just the same about Claudius – doesn't want any Ben Hur or Quo Vadis stuff, just the domestic Palace drama. And why not?

He pointed out to Will that they 'mustn't *insist* on anything, but only *suggest*':

> He is generous. The situation is peculiar. Dazzling prospects of riches mean nothing to him. ... And he doesn't want to go to America if he can help it.

But Graves had another, and more delicate, point to lead up to. For even he was by now coming to realize that Will was only erratically reliable – that if he went on a drinking spree, and then overconfidently began to ask for too much money, he might wreck the project for both of them.

> The job of getting back the copyright of World's Delight was essential and only you could have done it. The job of treating with Guinness until the contract is signed is essential and only I can do it.

And then the last and most difficult question of all:

Would you be content with a paid advisory job in the production? I think that to insist on directing or co-producing, as a sort of package deal with the script, would be most unwise. There are lots of other scripts for him to choose from. . . .

And he went on to remind Will, delicately – in case he should rebel, the *World's Delight* script being as much his property as Graves's – that 'we are down to a pretty low level in money'

and we know that among your greatest wishes in the world is repaying us the money we lent you in the confidence that you would make a come-back.

This referred to the old hotel bill of about £500 – and to more, which was lent afterwards.

But by the end of that summer he was writing:

No, none of those golden dreams came true. Ingrid Bergman has now made her come-back in films but says not another word about Homer's Daughter – I suppose she is no longer making films with Roberto Rossellini [they had parted], and Twentieth Century Fox would doubtless not consider the book as script-worthy even if Ingrid went down on her beautiful knees to plead for it. Nobody has shown the least interest in filming *The Infant With the Globe* or *Bewitchment of Seville* (. . . remember that Ava would gladly have played in either . . .). Not another peep or cheep from Vincent Korda about *I, Claudius*. The nearest I got to success at the cokernut [*sic*] shy was with Alec Guinness and that *World's Delight* script I wrote with Will Price: he loved it, and tried his damndest to get a backer for it . . . but found none. . . . I got the last rebuff, from Sir Michael Balcon of Ealing Studios, for whom Alec is making four pictures next year, and who says that the script, though charming, is unlikely to interest Alec Guinness. . . .

Anyhow, I'm glad I didn't count on any of those dreams; but took my old-fashioned wooden penholder with its old-fashioned steel nib and earned my next year's money the hard way, scratching laboriously on the back of old typescripts. As you know, Palmer's alleged poisonings provided me with a very amusing summer's work [*They Hanged My Saintly Billy*], and I finished the book in three months. . . . The chances are that some fool of a film magnate will send me a long excited telegram offering to buy a three months' option on the Palmer book, for $1000, which I shall accept gratefully – and that will be the last I shall ever hear of it. [*Quoz*]

But the dreams were not yet quite over. Will Price urged him to keep up his hopes that Ingrid Bergman would make *Homer's Daughter*; he also vigorously revived the *Claudius* venture; and there were other projects. But for the time being there was no option but to go to America:

> There's a solid core of extraordinarily sensitive, intelligent, open-minded and golden-hearted Americans; but the activities of the more ignorant and unbalanced ones who come here on holiday often makes one forget them. If only I could be sure of meeting the right sort on a lecture tour; but you know what lecture tours are. [*Quoz*]

However, he was in this matter rather luckier than he hoped.

IV

Throughout the last months of 1956 he reconciled himself, but never actually looked forward, to his visit to the USA. When he had finished *They Hanged My Saintly Billy*, he polished (as he privately put it, 'Englished') *Battle for the Mind*, to which he contributed the chapter about brain washing in ancient times, for its author, the psychiatrist Dr William Sargant (he took a third of the proceeds, Sargant two-thirds).

He was also carefully following Wasson's progress, since he had suggested to him where he might find the mushroom oracle he was after:

> My mushroom man is very elated since he actually found the mushroom oracle I sent him after in Mexico, and ate the sacred mushrooms and had them analysed – and there's the next wonder drug to watch out for. He thinks they were what the worshippers ate at the Eleusinian Mysteries to get such terrific visions. . . . [To M.S.-S., 24 December 1956]

Wasson's discovery became famous, though Graves's original part in it is not. Later the Wassons took Roger Heim – the real expert – to the same place; Heim cultivated thirty-two species of the Mexican mushrooms, and sent them to Dr Albert Hofmann, at Basle, who discovered the potency of some of them.

Graves was continually thinking about the visit to the States, but tried to dismiss it:

> On Feb 4 I go to the U.S.A., for a fortnight (or a day less) to lecture:

and I'm going to mince no words neither. It's just a smash-and-grab money raid. [To Janet Seymour-Smith, 24 December 1956]

He was now working on the text of the three lectures – 'Legitimate Criticism of Poetry', 'The White Goddess' and 'Diseases of Scholarship, Clinically Considered' – he was scheduled to give at Mount Holyoke, and on a revised version of *Goodbye to All That*, which Doubleday had suggested he do for a reissue, in their Anchor Paperback series. He had not, he wrote, looked at it

> since 1929 since I published it. . . . I find it a very compelling story, and though I recognise the incidents by memory it really seems extraordinary that they happened to me. To write one's autobiography at the age of thirty three is a good way to stop thinking about the first part of one's life, and to insure that nothing further occurs in the remainder that will be of any great public interest. . . . I could never rewrite a sequel to *Goodbye* – which by the way is very clumsily written.
>
> Here's another problem: how far is a man of my age justified in rewriting his earlier books? Some would say that they have passed out of my jurisdiction. But because I dictated most of *Goodbye*, late at night, hurriedly and in a state of great emotional tension, I have now taken the liberty of cutting out dull passages, repetitions, and an unnecessarily mysterious epilogue; and of tidying whatever sentence my reading eye stumbles over. [*Quoz*]

He finished the revision on 5 November: 'very badly written, but a good story when the nonsense is cut out', he told James Reeves (5 November 1956).

Most unfortunately, as it turned out, the 'golden dreams' returned just before he left for his short trip to the States. They were, of course, irresistible golden dreams – and ones which Graves by now badly needed to turn into a reality. The *World's Delight* scheme had for the time being foundered, though Will Price was hopefully offering it to backers – with an apparently willing Fernandel, instead of Guinness, in the lead. But Will had also pre-empted Vincent Korda, who was still saying nothing, and who may have been annoyed. Having failed with Rossellini's second wife, Ingrid Bergman, Graves now contacted – at Will's behest – his first, Anna Magnani. This great actress of the ferocious school, having defiantly shot her own *Volcano* – while Bergman–Rossellini were shooting their *Stromboli* across the same bay (both films were disastrous, and both were ignored by the public) – had gone into business for herself. She wrote to Graves on 23 January 1957, from Rome:

Your letters are always welcome and I was looking forward to seeing you in New York. I have your address in New York [the home of the Wassons], and will call you when I arrive ... we will keep in touch. I am happy and excited at the idea that some day I might play 'Messalina'.

I will be in Rome until February 2 in the morning, if you have something to tell me write at once, otherwise as we have decided, I will meet you at New York.

She changed her travelling plans, and they were unable to meet. But Will Price was meanwhile overoptimistically preparing a grand 'confidential' document to tempt backers. If he obtained a backer, United Artists had pledged (he maintained) to make the film. Graves wrote, a few days before he left for the States:

The raid on the States will be in aid of funds, not glory. Somehow or other I must raise enough money [to educate Lucia and Juan in 'decent schools' in Switzerland] – and if I hadn't been a fool and lent about £2000 to indigent friends in the last few years, I wouldn't need to work so hard. The golden dream situation is that Vincent Korda [who had now been in touch again] wants to do the I, Claudius film and Alec Guinness is very anxious to play Claudius with Anna Magnani as Messalina; and she to play Messalina with him as Claudius and both want me to write the script. But Vincent is being mysterious and cagey and doesn't seem to welcome such a trinity of talent – maybe his backer has made difficulties – but if Vincent doesn't make up his mind quick, both Alec and Anna will have signed other contracts. Maybe he's cross because I [i.e. Price] have got to work behind his back. This golden dream seems already on the fade. [Quoz]

It took over a year to fade, in fact, which was unlucky for Graves, who – although he received some money – never covered his costs over the affair.

On the day before he left for America, 3 February, he remarked, in a letter:

Why am I writing so small? Probably because at 7 a.m. tomorrow I fly to the States, and am not feeling particularly extrovert at the prospect. But the money's all right, if I can stick it out for a fortnight. [To M.S.-S., 2 February 1957]

He delivered his three lectures at Mount Holyoke (at South Hadley, in Western Massachusetts) with great success. He worked harder at them than he had at the Clark Lectures, and did not seek to be so provocative. He was more at pains to explain himself; and certainly the predominantly female audience suited him better. Their reception boded well for return trips to the States – of which he made many. He was learning to take full advantage of his unrhetorical manner. After going to Boston, where he met Robert Lowell and his then wife Elizabeth Hardwick, he came down to New York to stay with the Wassons.

He was finding America more agreeable than he had anticipated. He liked the genuinely classless society, 'with "Sir" used only as a mark of respect for the aged' – and that he and the wealthy Wasson had gone down to the kitchen in the mornings and 'got our own breakfasts as a matter of course'. The black woman who came in to help 'was treated as a friend of the family and naturally included in the conversation, in so far as it might interest her'.

He was fascinated by and absorbed in, although he distrusted it, the 'orderliness and smoothness of life'. He was astonished at a place where 'out of date' meant 'ten years old'.

But he had criticisms, although 'not a formidable list'. He summed them up under three heads: vegetables and milk did not taste real; because only 'card matches [sic]' were sold, one could not tap one's pocket to listen for a rattle, to find out if one had a light; the lecterns in the auditoria were too low – 'so tall chaps like me have to sprawl when they perform'.

He met, and was impressed by, the linguist Roman Jakobson, and by Moses Hadas: 'profoundly wise men'. The 'most exciting occasion' was an evening at the Wassons, when the sacred mushrooms were put on show and a tape-recording played of the *curandera*'s (local priestess's) chanting at Oaxaca, where they had rediscovered the cult of psilocybe (*teonacatl*, 'God's flesh', the 'divine mushroom'), and had participated in what they rather gushingly called the 'soul-shattering' ceremony.

Alastair Reid was in New York at the time, and amused Graves at a party by arguing law in an authoritative way with Francis Biddle, whom he did not know to have been US Attorney-General at the Nuremberg Trials – and immediately following this by asking Huntingdon Cairns, Director of the National Gallery of New York, whether he liked pictures.

Graves's 'most memorable' meeting was with E. E. Cummings, whose *Enormous Room* he had introduced to the English public over a quarter of a century earlier: a meeting longest looked forward to, and even happier than I expected. Nothing was said, of importance, but little needed to be said; we weren't doing business together, just humorously communing. [*Quoz*]

As soon as he returned he wrote telling Cummings how much he had enjoyed seeing him; and received this reply (28 February):

> Robertus –
> hearty thanks for a fine letter!
> as you correctly surmise, our unhero
> 's not much of a reader (in fact
> quite the reverse) but since he's
> allowed more than one book, how about
> – in addition to the "crime novel" –
> your opus exposing Xianity (King
> Jesus?)? I'm assuming that an American
> edition of The revised&enlarged White
> Goddess will soon appear
>
> Marion sends greetings
>
>   – bonne chance
>
> eec

'Our unhero' is of course Cummings himself, the 'crime book' is *They Hanged My Saintly Billy*, and 'Marion' was Cummings's photographer wife Marion Moorhouse.

It was during this busy fortnight that Graves first appeared on American television. He had been relieved not to have it 'shown' to him, or be asked to talk about it; but he did not mind appearing on a show with John Mason Brown and the famous Gipsy Rose Lee: the subject was 'the meaning of English words'. The first word was 'lady'; and he was (he said) a little too scholarly, slow-speaking and 'intellectual'. He began to tell the audience that the word had originally meant 'a woman who kneads bread', and was just about to ask Gipsy Rose Lee if she had ever kneaded any, when 'the eloquent John Mason Brown' 'robbed [him] of the ball'.

He had badly wanted to meet another old friend by correspondence – one who had, if in an indirect way, had a profound influence on his life: John Crowe Ransom. But he lived in far away Ohio, and Graves could not find the time. As soon as he returned to Mallorca he wrote to him, warmly. Ransom replied promptly (11 March 1957):

It is wonderful to hear from you after all these years. . . . I think the

American couple you talked to about me were Mr and Mrs Robert
Lowell [Lowell's poetry left Graves cold], in Boston. At any rate Elizabeth
wrote me that you had been there, and they were quite taken with the
affectionate tone in which you spoke of me. You have always been high
in my affections too. I wish we could have got together during your late
trip over, but maybe there will be another chance.

Graves had for long felt, strongly, that Ransom had spoiled some of
his best poems when he reprinted them in his *Selected Poems* (1945),
and, even more strongly, that he should have retained certain of those
from *Grace After Meat*, the Hogarth Press collection of the early
twenties. He modified his feelings but did tell Ransom that he regretted
that he had left some out from the *Selected Poems*. Ransom ended his
letter:

> The great trouble with those poems which I omitted from the 'canon',
> they were the ones which seem muddled and ambiguous in style; they
> were the 'literary' ones. I didn't like them, and don't. But we'll talk that
> over some time.

It is a pity that they never did – though they were to correspond again
briefly fourteen years later.

V

When he returned he had much work on hand. Penguin wanted a
selection of his poems made by himself for their Penguin Poets series.
Doubleday, who had published his *Collected Poems* in 1955, wanted
the same thing – only with more poems. The two selections, which by
no means resemble each other – Doubleday's is twice as long – were
published on 27 August 1957 and 5 June 1958 respectively.

He found that he had enough essays, articles and reviews from
periodicals to make up, together with the Mount Holyoke lectures, yet
another miscellany for America. Cassell had published *!Catacrok!*, all
stories, in 1956; in *5 Pens in Hand* (published by Doubleday in March
1958) he was able to put a selection of these stories from *!Catacrok!*.
Steps, yet another miscellany, was published in England by Cassell in
November 1958; this in turn drew on *5 Pens in Hand*, and added new
material, including some poems. He had finished his Lucan and Suetonius translations, and *Jesus in Rome* (published on 11 April 1957 in

England by Cassell, but never in America), 'a mighty odd book'. He wrote this in collaboration with Joshua Podro.

Subtitled 'A Historical Conjecture', it takes as its point of departure the thesis of *The Nazarene Gospel Restored* that Christ survived the Crucifixion, and conjectures his subsequent life. It is a short book, of ninety pages, and is an ingenious and stimulating piece of speculation; but, like its predecessor, it was published at the wrong time – before conjecture about the life of Christ (especially from the rewriters of the Gospels) became respectable. An agreement to publish a good-sized American paperback edition was scotched by a pious publishing director. It appeared in one edition, of 3000; and it has never been reprinted.

Instead of taking up the Tonga novel, which he again considered before finally rejecting it, he began a new task: the translation of the *Iliad*. This would be nearer to poetry. He had long felt that the only viable way in which to translate Homer was 'as if it were an ancient Irish epic: prose laced with lyrics'. Since he has never believed that a narrative poem can sustain a high poetic level, but since he also loves the *Iliad* (alone of long poems), he interpolated the lyrics at what he called the 'points of greatest stress'. As he was not 'plagued' with poems of his own at this time he found the exercise of writing the lyrics congenial.

He had not long been at work on the *Iliad* when he had to go to London to make recordings for the BBC, and to be interviewed by the film scriptwriter and journalist Paul Dehn on the programme 'Frankly Speaking' (9 May 1957). While there he heard from 10 Downing Street (10 May 1957):

Sir:

I am asked by the Prime Minister [then Sir Harold Macmillan] to inform you that he has it in mind . . . to submit your name to the Queen with a recommendation that Her Majesty would be graciously pleased to approve that you be appointed a Commander of the Order of the British Empire.

Before doing so, the Prime Minister would be glad to be assured that this wish of Her Majesty's favour would be agreeable to you. . . .

He was asked, to his amusement, please to quote 'reference . . . B.E.3' in his reply. He wrote back declining the honour, for reasons which are made apparent in the rather flustered reply he received from 10 Downing Street (13 May 1957):

The Prime Minister is sorry not to be able to include your name in the list. . . . Fortunately we have been able to enjoy the results, or some of them, of your private pursuit. I suppose it is in the recognition of the pleasure, in the widest sense, that is given by the communication of poetry . . . that honours are offered, and accepted. This seems to me to be reasonable – and all creative art . . . is primarily a private pursuit.

But you know best what is right for you as a poet.

He was not tempted by the offer. He does not really believe in the honours system, and felt that he might compromise himself by accepting. Besides, he blamed Sir Harold (quite unfairly, as it happens, though doubtless in the proper 'philosophical' spirit) for Macmillan of New York's turning down of *The White Goddess*.

Meanwhile he found that the *Claudius* affair was still alive and kicking. Will Price was busy with his promotion of the project – now without Vincent Korda. Apart from the elimination of Korda, there was another alteration in the plans: the script was to be written by Graves and Bridget Boland, rather than by Graves alone.

This was Guinness's idea, and it was less because he lacked confidence in Graves's expertise than because he had once greatly admired Boland's, and wanted to give her the chance to excel again. She had written a sound and competent middlebrow play, *The Prisoner*, in which he had starred with enormous success in the West End. Based on the ordeal of Cardinal Mindszenty, Roman Catholic Primate of Hungary, when he was charged by the communist government with treason in 1948, this performance helped to consolidate Guinness's reputation as a serious actor. Both he and Boland were Roman Catholics, and the subject had therefore been close to their hearts. A film, also called *The Prisoner*, had been made of this play (1955), with Boland as scriptwriter and Peter Glenville as director. Glenville was not as good as a film director as he was in the theatre – and the film, which failed, is no more than an uninspired filmed stage-play. But Guinness believed in Glenville, and in Boland's capabilities. So he tactfully suggested Boland as co-scriptwriter for *Claudius*, with Glenville directing; and Graves as tactfully agreed. Guinness's desire to do the film was Graves's and Price's ace, and they did not find him at all unreasonable in his demands. Unfortunately the cinema moguls had no reason to regard Glenville highly as director, or to be bothered in the least by Boland's needs (she was not considered to be very proficient in the art).

Will Price had by now cooked up an impressive-looking document as bait for a certain fish called Mr Youngstein. It began:

(1) PROPOSED CAST INCLUDES

Claudius – Alec Guinness
Messalina – Anna Magnani
Calpurnia – Ava Gardner
Germanicus – ?

EXECUTIVE PRODUCER – To be nominated by United Artists when the rights have been purchased and first draft screenplay has been completed and approved.

PRODUCER OR CO-PRODUCER – Will Price

DIRECTOR – Peter Glenville

SCREEN PLAY BY – Robert Graves and Bridget Boland

To be filmed in Rome in the spring of 1958 in colour.

THE paragraph numbered (2) dealt with 'RIGHTS', and stated that although the estate of Sir Alexander Korda owned the rights, the rights 'to the original material' could 'in all probability' be 'purchased or optioned thru Will Price and Robert Graves'. The sum 'should be' 'under $25,000'. Other paragraphs dealt with the merits of Miss Boland, who was currently adapting Daphne Du Maurier's *The Scapegoat* for Mr Guinness; with Mr Guinness's desire '*not*' to do the picture for the Korda interests; and with the willingness of Mr Glenville, now rehearsing *Hotel Paradiso* for its New York opening on about 3 April, to see Mr Youngstein at any time. There was a mention of 'current confusion and lethargy in the Korda organisation'. But Mr Youngstein did not buy. Graves had this letter, from Jenny in Rome (7 March 1957):

Oh *dear* – you tell Alec Guinness that *he* had given the impression of *not* believing in Will Price. . . . The mention of Will Price's name in *any* film circle produces a glazed look, usually an actual rumble of disgust. Nowadays we are a lot with film people. . . . The John Huston, David O'Selznick crowd and other crowds on that level. If they've heard of Will Price it's rather the same reaction as with Vincent K— 'Oh *him*' or 'Poor old drunk Will – hasn't been associated with a picture since . . . *God*, since before you were born'. I protect him for your sake and they look at me like a fool. *Has* he had any successes in recent years? . . . Is he *really* such a trusty of Youngstein's? etc etc? . . .

So when Youngstein failed to buy, the golden dream faded again. But Bridget Boland wrote a script, and Graves revised it. He continued to hope. Late in the following year Graves heard again from Jenny:

she told him that Alec Guinness and his wife had been in Rome for 'the Pope's last audience' – and that he was 'on Claudius business'. Graves already knew that he had interested a backer, Rizzoli. But Jenny, surprisingly, reported him as saying: 'The only thing we haven't got is a script.'

Guinness had now lost confidence in Bridget Boland, whose *Scapegoat* script had turned out to be unsuitable. The film was not released until 1959, but Alec Guinness was apprehensive about it (it was in fact a total flop, despite the presence of Bette Davis as co-star), and fed up with Boland. He seemed to Jenny (who liked Boland, but thought her *Claudius* script very 'common') to be 'fearfully disloyal' to her, 'says how rotten all her scripts have been since Prisoner. . . .' So the *Claudius* script still did not appeal to Guinness, who nevertheless retained his confidence in Graves. Jenny wrote:

> He told me, however, that one of the points of his contract in making Claudius will be that *you* will be connected with the script. He said that your Bridget-revised script was not good enough but he seems determined – not only to have you on the script but also determined that you should play Tiberius. Now he may be saying all these things to sweeten ME. But. . . . I think we can start counting on a British-Italian production here next summer . . . the Italian is Rizzoli very rich and powerful in Italy and backs the Socialist party which is to his credit. . . . We don't know him – yet. But that leaves Bridget. . . . Can you not offer her something? Perhaps out of your first earnings here?

However, Rizzoli did not buy the rights, no new script was written, Graves never played Tiberius (which might not have added to his reputation), and no film was made: Claudius had to wait eighteen years to see any kind of screen. It could have been a relief, almost, to watch the last possibility of the film vanish – but the gushing gods of showbiz had by no means finished their sport with Graves. Within a few months he received yet another dazzling proposition.

VI

The rest of 1957 was uneventful, though there were the usual visitors. In 1958 he went to America again. In May 1958 he received an invitation, sent to him via his brother Dick (ex-Mayor of Jerusalem), to Israel – on behalf of the government. He was as pleased to take this up, for January 1959, as he had been to turn down the CBE. Then, at the very end of that year, not long before he was getting ready to set out for Israel, came the dazzling new proposition. It was for something he had never tried before – and he was not sure how he would set about it. But he knew that he would have to get the *Iliad* sent off very soon after he returned from Israel if he was to manage it.

A Broadway producer, Alexander H. Cohen, commissioned the text of a musical on the subject of Solomon and Sheba from him, 'as a wild shot' (in Graves's phrase). The reason he chose Graves was simply that he liked Graves's poems ('Who says poetry don't pay, eh?' he asked James Reeves, 10 March 1959).

When he set off to Haifa from Marseilles on a ZIM line ship, on 11 January 1959, he was excited about his prospects, less because he was writing a Broadway musical than because 'if it comes off I'm rich for life' (to James Reeves, 17 February 1959).

He was in Israel from 15 to 28 January. It was the happiest of all his visits abroad. While there he joined Ben Gurion in his usual early morning walk (the only time one could join him), and both he and Beryl were impressed and excited by the country. Ben Gurion gave him a rug from his own kibbutz, which he still uses. 'Tomas [then five] behaved beautifully, even at breakfast,' he told Reeves. He wrote an article about his visit (not reprinted), 'I Discover Israel', in *Holiday* in the same year. Tyrone Guthrie, commissioned to direct the musical, was in Israel at the time doing a play for the Habimah; the two of them had discussions about it.

They returned via Genoa, met Jenny, and went on to Rome. At a Rome lunch with Jenny he caught a very bad stomach infection, which did not manifest itself until he got back home; the antibiotic used in the treatment cured him but left him 'as weak as a kitten'. Lucia, in Geneva, went down with a 'really bad' appendicitis – and so they had to go on to Geneva, where she was operated on. When he reached Deyá in early February, his illness (a typhoid-type virus) laid him low – but he managed to get his Homer off to Watt, who was pleased with the translation but profoundly disliked the work of the chosen illustrator, Ronald Searle (an old friend of Graves), and said so.

He had thought hard about how he could possibly tackle the script – of all things – of a Broadway musical, and sensibly decided that the girl he needed was his daughter, Jenny, who had, after all, been in show business, and was a writer, and had had ambitions in just that direction. Jenny, as agreed in Rome, arrived in Mallorca on 18 February 1959. When she left, after only fifteen days, *A Song for Sheba* was finished.

> We worked for a fortnight, ten hours a day, at the ... material, and sent it off three days ago, complete with lyrics. Tyrone Guthrie comes here on the 17th [of March] to discuss its stage possibilities – he is directing. I get 4½% (less agent's fees, tax, etc) of the weekly takings: if it only runs for three days, too bad. If for two years, much too good: I shall have to wear mink bedsocks. [To James Reeves, 10 March 1959]

Cohen wired his typical Broadwayman's wild reaction: MAGNIFICENT, BRAVO, BRAVO, BRAVO.

The outlook was rosy. Guthrie (with his wife) duly turned up, was lodged in the Posada, and made some 'useful emendations'.

But then things hung fire. Robert and Beryl both went to London for a fortnight, from 20 April:

> I have to meet Cohen and his partner – also his Money Bag – ... & be taken around the shows. [To James Reeves, 19 March 1959]

Before they left for London 'Huw Wheldon (B.B.C. T.V.)' arrived in Mallorca with his 'gang'

> to interview and televise me – did I tell you? – in honour of my Collected Poems, 1959 [published 23 April 1959]. The programme will be shown on Ap 29th when the book comes out [*sic*]. ... [To James Reeves, 17 February 1959]

This was the most extensive of all the television programmes on Graves; among many other things, it showed him shaving – with his 'voice over', reading 'The Face in the Mirror':

> Grey haunted eyes, absent-mindedly glaring
> From wide, uneven orbits; one brow dropping
> Somewhat over the eye
> Because of a missile fragment still inhering.
>
> Crookedly broken nose – low tackling caused it;
> Cheeks, furrowed; coarse grey hair, flying frenetic;
> Forehead, wrinkled and high;
> Jowls, prominent; ears, large; jaw, pugilistic;
> Teeth, few; lips, full and ruddy; mouth ascetic.
>
> I pause with razor poised, scowling derision
> At the mirrored man whose beard needs my attention,
> And once more ask him why

He still stands ready, with a boy's presumption,
To court the queen in her high silk pavilion.

The meeting with Cohen and his colleagues went well enough; but
a serious blow fell very soon after their return from England. It had
been decided that, whoever wrote the music for *A Song for Sheba*, the
main part would be offered to the immensely popular Black star, Lena
Horne. All that was necessary was that she should see the script. She
had not had it long before she announced that she wouldn't be playing
in any production of it, with any music: she did 'not dig the lyrics'.
This meant that Graves, having written the script – for which he did
receive a substantial fee – was saddled with the miserable business of
marketing it himself. For a time he persisted. Jenny spoke to Sir William
Walton – who lived on the island of Ischia – about it. He told her that
he would have loved to write music for it, but that he was already
four years behind with his (commissioned) Second Symphony. He
recommended Malcolm Arnold, whose music he told Jenny was 'very
good'. She had not heard of Arnold, but passed the message on to the
Graves household, where there was someone who had both heard of
Arnold and had heard Arnold's music. Meanwhile Graves sent the
script to yet another producer, Leyland Heyward, who replied (15
October 1959):

> I am very sorry that I have taken so long to read your play ... the
> reason being I have been in rehearsal with two plays, one entitled 'The
> Sound of Music', and the other entitled 'Goodbye Charlie'. . . . *A Song
> For Sheba* is a wonderful play, and a great piece of writing. However,
> I believe it poses a problem at this time for production. . . . In any case,
> it is a great script. . . .

He thought that it might have a chance in America if it could first be
put on successfully in London; but his prose style inspired little confidence in either his opinion or the sincerity of it.

The next year, having heard from Jenny that James Mason was 'very
enthusiastic' about it, and – more to the point – that she had managed
to get the gifted and lively American choreographer Jerome Robbins
interested in it, he decided to try Benjamin Britten, who had already
set a poem ('Lift-Boy') by Graves, and who replied very cordially (11
April 1960):

My dear Robert Graves:

As my secretary explained to you, I was abroad when your letter arrived, and I am only just back. I am extremely interested in the idea of your 'musical', and very flattered and – I must admit – rather surprised that you and Jerome Robbins thought of me in connection with it. I have never associated with this world at all, and would have thought my ideas rather remote from it; but I presume you and Robbins would not have approached me unless you felt my gifts might be suitable. Anyhow, as I said, I am extremely interested, and would much like to see your script. . . .

By the way, time might be a slight problem because I have a great deal on my plate at the moment. But if we all are agreed on wanting to work on it, I am sure we can sort something out.

But the project simply petered out, and not even the lyrics which Lena Horne, whose tastes were not those of Ava Gardner, did not 'dig' have been published.

It must again be emphasized that the ambition to succeed in 'show-biz' was always Jenny's, not her father's. He just wanted the money and the security it would bring. To a certain extent he got tied to the apron-strings of Jenny's own creative aspirations, which were very different from his own.

But other things were looming on the horizon. There were to be about ten times as many poems, and infinitely more real excitement. 'I've had enough trouble in my life and feel glad not to be plagued . . .' Graves had written not so long before. But that summer of 1959 a visitor came to Deyá, a young woman called Margot. Graves was soon plagued again. As he had said,

If there's need to write the wilder and more poignant sort [of poem] then there's trouble about for sure.

Chapter Thirty
1959–60

I

In a quieter time Graves had said that he would never deliberately 'court unhappiness'. And now, indeed, he did resist swallowing the bait, tried not to allow the hook to become fast. Yet, during that same quiet period when he was writing of having had 'enough trouble' in his life, he wrote 'Woman and Tree' (first published in the *New Yorker*, 9 June 1956):

> To love one woman, or to sit
>   Always beneath the same tall tree,
> Argues a certain lack of wit
>   Two steps from imbecility.
>
> A poet, therefore, sworn to feed
>   On every food the senses know,
> Will claim the inexorable need
>   To be Don Juan Tenorio.
>
> Yet if, miraculously enough,
>   (And why set miracles apart?)
> Woman and tree prove of a stuff
>   Wholly to glamour his wild heart?
>
> And if such visions from the void
>   As shone in fever there, or there,
> Assemble, hold and are enjoyed
>   On climbing one familiar stair. . . ?
>
> To change and chance he took a vow,
>   As he thought fitting. None the less,
> What of a phoenix on the bough,
>   Or a sole woman's fatefulness?

In this partly premonitory poem – or perhaps it is an unconscious

490

intention – Graves separates himself from the practice of womanizing (being like Don Juan) with what his detractors would call an impudent, or at least disingenuous, aplomb. He has sometimes been taken by his enemies – and occasionally by his friends, if only while they have been impatient with him – as a man who conceals a straightforward 'Don Juanism' under a pious system.

No judgement could be more mistaken. Graves differs from most other men in his feeling that any sort of resistance to romantic love is in itself a kind of sin: a refusal of the Goddess, of what the Goddess means to him. But it is hard for those who know only the public Graves, bent on explaining his devotion to the Goddess (whose genuine manifestations he feels that he must under no circumstances ignore), to realize that although he has the compulsion to fall in love, he also hates to do so. He does not enjoy suffering more than anyone else. Moreover, so far is he from being a Don Juan that his fallings-in-love-with-a-Muse have presented him with the serious problem of reconciling them with his permanent love for his wife. He never convincingly worked this out in intellectual terms – although it seemed to some, from his Oxford lectures, that he had found a formula to solve this problem. Beryl is genuinely 'inscrutable', as he has himself called her. Yet his readers have always taken it for granted that when he referred to the kindly Vesta, the 'wifely' woman, he meant Beryl. On several occasions in his private correspondence, however, he angrily denied this – and he always exempted his own marriage from the generally sour remarks he made, during the sixties, about the institution of marriage. Nor could anyone who knew Beryl regard her as any kind of Gravesian 'Vesta'.

When Margot first attracted his attention in 1959 he was preoccupied with the problem, as his affectionate poem 'Joan and Darby' shows; it contains a rueful acceptance of the fact that he and Beryl were 'separate people':

> My friends are those who find agreement with me
> In large measure, but not absolutely.
> Little children, parasites and God
> May flatter me with absolute agreement –
> For no one lives more cynical than God.
>
> As for my love, I gifted my heart to her
> Twenty years ago, without proviso,
> And in return she gifted hers to me;
> Yet still they beat as two, unyielding in

Their honest, first reluctance to agree.

Other seasons, other thoughts and reasons,
Other fears or phases of the moon:
In loving kindness we grow grey together –
Like Joan and Darby in their weather-lodge
Who never venture out in the same weather.

This love poem was written, in fact, just after what Graves himself later called an 'emotional crisis'. It concerned his vain struggle, which he thought for a short time he had won, to resist his love for Margot.

Margot was an intelligent though not literary Canadian girl who was of just the sort to attract Graves's attention: she was striking to look at, had sensibility, was much sought after – and was encountering difficulties in her emotional life. She was different from Judith: more inclined to experiment, wilder, more dramatic, more ambitious, more flamboyant, less reluctant to hold the centre of the stage. She was also more obviously flattered than Judith to be the object of the attention of a famous love poet.

The old friend who was most open in his criticism of Graves during the Margot affair was James Reeves. Some others muttered behind his back: James made no secret of what he thought. He was both blunt and exceedingly irritable about it throughout – and Graves reacted. Their exchanges are instructive.

James and Mary Reeves were on holiday, staying in the Posada, for a month in the summer of 1959. James formed a bad impression of Margot; but, more to the point, he thought he saw his old friend in a state of self-delusion. Graves had a direct answer to this, which he expressed a little later in 'Troughs of Sea', which begins:

'Do you delude yourself?' a neighbour asks,
Dismayed by my abstraction.
But though love cannot question love
Nor need deny its need,

Pity the man who finds a rebel heart
Under his breastbone drumming
Which reason warns him he should drown
In midnight wastes of sea. . . .

James Reeves's hostility to Graves's relationship with Margot (he would mouth the first line of 'Troughs of Sea' with the most withering scorn) is revealing for two reasons. First, he was only saying aloud what a number of Graves's other friends (often the older rather than the newer ones) thought but would not say. Secondly, Graves's own response demonstrates his need to satisfy his oldest friends – and, indeed, as many others as possible – that he had not changed, was the 'same Robert still', and was not, as he often humorously put it, 'mad', which in fact he was not. The wiser amongst his friends saw that his unhappiness was necessary to him as a poet. But they were none the less irritated with him.

The affair started in the same way as that with Judith: both Graves and Beryl took an interest in, and formed an affection for, Margot. Beryl was not following her husband's lead – she had already formed friendships of her own, on several occasions, with other women. When she saw that Margot was becoming a Muse, she had no objection (though many people, including those who should know better, have assumed otherwise): she knew, as she had known all along, that one woman alone could never fairly handle the poet she had married. Her role was a protective one; so far as Margot, at least, was concerned the bargain was never, for long, a bad one from Beryl's point of view. She is an excessively tolerant woman (if tolerance can be excessive), and understands better than most that youth is a time when people appear to behave badly, although their motives are often not as bad, or as selfish, as they appear. She always remained attached to Margot, who travelled with both the Graveses after the affair was over, and who has stayed in Deyá in 1978 and in 1979.

In his lectures as Professor of Poetry at Oxford for Michaelmas Term 1963 – combined, in the printed version, into one essay called 'Intimations of the Black Goddess' – Graves said that

> Only during the past three years [*More Poems*, which contains the first of the group of poems addressed to Margot, was published by Cassell in May 1961; *New Poems 1962* appeared in October 1962; *Man Does, Woman Is* in April 1964] have I ventured to dramatise, truthfully and factually, the vicissitudes of a poet's dealings with the White Goddess, the Muse, the perpetual Other Woman. Whatever may be said against her, she at least gives him an honest warning of what to expect – as it were, tying a poison label around her own neck. . . .

About half the poems in *More Poems* are uncommitted (in this book, as in the editions of *Collected Poems* that gathered up most of its contents, the poems are not arranged in the precise order of their composition). So (perhaps this will be surprising to some) the resistance was coming from Graves – and from no one else. It turned out to be a vain resistance; but it was a resistance none the less, and one which is recorded in the poems. Resistance, as Graves would say, 'is part of the story'.

More Poems concludes with the poem '*Song*: Come Enjoy Your Sunday', in which the poet treats himself to a holiday:

> On a warm sand dune now, sprawling at ease
> With little in mind, learn to despise the sea's
>   Unhuman restlessness:
> Come, enjoy your Sunday
> While yet you may!

he ends it. He thought he had won his struggle. As he later put it, in his final lectures as Oxford Professor,

A few years ago, after an emotional crisis, I wrote a poem advising myself to be content with the mild pleasures of old age and inaction.

He quotes the poem, and remarks: 'But it was already another Monday morning; the moon being insistent in her demands.' However, that was how *More Poems* ended. When he sent it off to press in early 1961 he did not foresee the events of the next May, which would concern Margot – and he did not anticipate publishing another volume of love poems, *New Poems 1962*, so soon. For just a short time, he seems to have believed the episode to be over. What had passed so far had enabled him to 'dramatise', as he put it, a theme that had been at the centre of all his poetry. In 'The Starred Coverlet' he resolves the turbulence of 'The Death Grapple' – and by the *Collected Poems* of 1965 he had arranged these in their proper order, 'The Starred Coverlet' immediately following the 'The Death Grapple':

> Lying between your sheets, I challenge
> A watersnake in a swoln cataract
> Or a starved lioness among drifts of snow.
>
> Yet dare it out, for after each death-grapple,
> Each gorgon stare borrowed from very hate,
> A childish innocent smile touches your lips,
> Your eyelids droop, fearless and careless,
> And sleep remoulds the lineaments of love.

This only temporarily relieved restlessness he resolves in 'The Starred Coverlet':

> A difficult achievement for true lovers
> Is to lie mute, without embrace or kiss,
> Without a rustle or a smothered sigh,
> Basking each in the other's glory.
>
> Let us not undervalue lips or arms
> As reassurances of constancy,
> Or speech as necessary communication
> When troubled hearts go groping in the dusk;
>
> Yet lovers who have learned this last refinement –
> To lie apart, yet sleep and dream together
> Motionless under their starred coverlet –
> Crown loves with wreaths of myrtle.

II

The last four months of 1959 were busy ones for Graves. They began with serious illness: a prostate operation in St Thomas's Hospital, London, in September – and a longer stay there than he had anticipated. Graves's operation did not go well. He has put it best himself, in 'Surgical Ward, Men':

> Something occurred after the operation
> To scare the surgeons (though no fault of theirs),
> Whose reassurance did not fool me long.
> Beyond the shy, concerned faces of nurses
> A single white-hot eye, focusing on me,
> Forced sweat in rivers down from scalp to belly.
> I whistled, gasped or sang, with blanching knuckles
> Clutched at my bed-grip almost till it cracked:
> Too proud, still, to let loose Bedlamite screeches
> And bring the charge-nurse scuttling down the aisle
> With morphia-needle levelled. . . .
>
>   Lady Morphia –
> Her scorpion kiss and dark gyrating dreams –
> She in mistrust of whom I dared out-dare,
> Two minutes longer than seemed possible,
> Pain, that unpurposed, matchless elemental
> Stronger than fear or grief, stranger than love.

The cause of the trouble was diagnosed and successfully treated, and Graves was discharged on 12 October. But, as one of his doctors explained to him when answering a letter from him complaining of 'giddiness and pricking sensation' in the arms, 'After the trouble you had ... I would have thought it would have been some three months before you really began to feel fit again' (19 November 1959). He did not feel really well again until the following year. While in St Thomas's he met, as fellow-patient, Lord Woolton, Minister of Food in Churchill's war government, and then Chairman of the Conservative Party and Chancellor of the Duchy of Lancaster; Graves liked talking to him, but thought him 'politically misguided', in particular because he defended the Suez adventure, and denied collusion between Israel and the British and French.

But even severe illness did not allow him to rest. A figure from the past intruded once more into his present: T. E. Lawrence. In 1955 he had joined in the defence of his old friend against the hostile biography by Richard Aldington (this is now only a curiosity piece, with little bearing on Lawrence); but unlike some of Lawrence's other friends he was less interested in the attack itself than in the reason for it – which he claimed was a slighting remark Lawrence made about Aldington in a letter he wrote in the early twenties. He had not at the time cared to be identified, too closely, with what a journalist called 'the ageing members of the Lawrence Bureau'. He himself had not, after all, much liked what T.E. had become by the time of his discharge.

While he was lying ill, however, he had two more personal matters to attend to, both pertaining to Lawrence. One was Terence Rattigan's play *Ross*; the other was Sam Spiegel's project to make a film about Lawrence for Columbia – a project which had been under way for some time. Rattigan had written a script for it, which had already been rejected. A. W. Lawrence sent Graves *Ross* to read, while David Lean, scheduled to direct the Lawrence film, came to see him, to inquire if he would accept an advisory role (or to pick his brains). The star Spiegel then had in mind was – astonishingly – Marlon Brando.

T.E.'s brother, A. W. Lawrence ('Arnie'), in charge of the Lawrence Trust, would have nothing to do with the play, since he suspected Rattigan of portraying his brother as a homosexual (on the rather poor grounds that Rattigan himself was homosexual); but, as he told Graves a month later, 'I liked Spiegel. . . . If they make good in my eyes I'll help them actively.'

Graves was interested in helping with the film, for obvious reasons;

but he was irritated by the play, and reacted negatively to it. He thought that it did portray Lawrence as a homosexual – though Liddell Hart, to whom he passed on the script for his opinion, disagreed with him, and thought it a sympathetic and effective play (though he admitted that some of it jarred on those who had known Lawrence).

Graves wrote to Rattigan immediately he had read it, suggesting that the play gave a wrong view of Lawrence, and that A.W. might well be able to persuade the Lord Chamberlain to refuse it a licence. This, he knew, was what A.W. was considering. He also wanted to use his influence with the actor cast to play Lawrence, who was none other than Alec Guinness – but, as he was in America, wrote to his wife Merula instead. (The Guinnesses had been staying in Deyá in the previous summer, while Reeves was there.)

From Rattigan Graves had what Liddell Hart – to whom he passed it on – called a 'curiously emotional letter'. What it said, in so many words, was that if A.W. succeeded in having the Lord Chamberlain bar the play, then he would put it on in America, and thus, as Liddell Hart put it, 'force the issue here in a lurid way'. However, Rattigan hated nastiness (he had put in much work on the play, which was close to his heart), and he generously offered to make such 'changes, cuts and emendations' as Graves suggested – so long as these were 'compatible with the play's theatrical life'. Liddell Hart urged Graves to take this course, and implied that he should urge A.W. to take it, too.

Guinness, writing from America, was very unhappy. He began by saying that he wished that Graves had written to him direct, as his wife, who took no part in theatrical goings on, was 'a bit distressed'. He had been 'pretty shocked' by Graves's letter, as he had assumed that Rattigan's portrait was 'fair'. But he wanted no part in denigrating a great man – he *must*', he said, know that it had the approval of A.W., or at least of people 'delegated', as he put it, by him.

A. W. Lawrence was still testily annoyed; but he had been persuaded by Liddell Hart not to try to get the play barred. On 30 November he wrote to Graves asking if he knew Guinness well enough 'to butt in, pointing out that you are the only intimate friend to have written a report on the play'. This Graves had already done; and in any case A.W. seemed resigned, though he did hint that Graves might like to write a 'blasting article' to coincide with the first night. In the event the play did Lawrence's reputation no harm.

Graves had, as usual, too high hopes of the Lawrence film possibilities. But here he had good reasons for his hopes. What he could never realize was that the film people – or at least those among them who controlled the money – wanted something far more vulgar from him than he could give, even if he tried. Lean had come to see him in hospital to find out what use he could make of Graves, doubtless with the best of intentions. But it should have been obvious that a project which began with the plan to miscast Brando would end up as a lovely-to-look-at but characterless charade, with a mechanical script (eventually put together by Robert Bolt).

David Lean sent Sam Spiegel, the producer, along to see Graves; on 27 October Lean wrote to him, from Bombay, telling him that he had 'contributed towards a small miracle in a big way'. He could not tell him how excited he was. . . .

Since Korda had bought an option (long since lapsed) on the film rights to all Graves's Lawrence material – *Lawrence and the Arabs*, his part of *T. E. Lawrence to His Biographers* and the relevant parts of *Goodbye to All That* – Graves optimistically assumed that Sam Spiegel (who, like many other film people, was a friend of Ricardo Sicre's) wanted to do likewise. But he did not: he did not need to pay for any of this material. Graves had done what Spiegel most needed: he had made A.W. look agreeably in the direction of an 'epic' on the subject of T.E. In any case, Bolt provided a script for a 'spectacular' – not for a movie that tried (it is to be hoped) to provide an insight into Lawrence's character.

So Graves had to be content with the role of 'adviser'. His tart letter of 14 August 1960 to Spiegel speaks for itself:

> I'm sorry I couldn't come to Burgenstock, but as I told you long ago I can't move from Deyá in the summer, where my children all come for their holidays . . . also great numbers of my friends. Until recently I believed you would be on a yacht and would come here, so kept my desk free of work.
>
> Another thing: I can't think in Switzerland; I've tried it.
>
> If my advisory function, as I see it, is to say: 'Lawrence could not have done or said this or that; he would have done (I think) the other thing'; or 'this could not have happened for such and such a reason' – then all I need is a semi-final script; and you are not, of course, compelled to take my advice.
>
> Can't I be given something to read here, as soon as you have got it from London, so that I can discuss the points with you either in London, where I arrive on Sept 24th, or by letter, or both?
>
> By the way, your agreement with me about this advisory function is

vaguely worded, and should now be made more definite in terms of money, credits, etc.

By the way, Alec Guinness in a broadcast about *Ross* made last week paid me the very handsome compliment of saying that he had been anti-Lawrence until I had given him a slant on Lawrence's character. . . .

In the end Graves's chief contribution – apart from making the film possible at all – was a useful one, in as much as any contribution to such a film could be useful: he helped Peter O'Toole (who later acknowledged it in a broadcast) in his own characterization of Lawrence, which is as intelligent as the script allows. He cannot be 'credited', even by his worst enemies, with any other aspect of the film. As befell him always with the film world, his hopes were falsely raised, and his time wasted. But Spiegel did introduce him, in 1961, to a financier called Tom Roe, who (as we shall see) represents a most appropriate gift from show business to this uncommercial man.

Meanwhile things in 1959 were not going as well as they had been with Alastair Reid.

Since 1956 Peggy Glanville-Hicks, an Australian composer, widow of the English composer Stanley Bate, had been working at her opera *Nausicaa*, based on *Homer's Daughter*. She finished composing it in 1959. (She had written two other operas and a quantity of orchestral music. She had trained in England, and regarded herself as 'as high as any save perhaps Menotti here [USA] and Britten *chez vous*'.) The libretto of *Nausicaa* is now credited to Graves; but this is not quite accurate. When the idea of the opera was first floated Graves wrote to Alastair Reid (1956) – who had written libretti, though there is no record of them being used – that he would not 'insist' on his aid; but he suggested that Reid and Peggy Glanville-Hicks might 'fix up something together'. They did, and about half the libretto is by Reid, though it was also worked at by Graves. However, Reid mysteriously insisted on withdrawing his name from the credits, well before the opera was given its premiere in Athens in the late summer of 1961.

The row first broke out in the autumn of 1959. Peggy Glanville-Hicks wrote to Graves on 15 September 1959 to say that she was 'completely at a loss' about a letter he had sent her 'concerning a "falling out" with Alastair'. However, she could not see why, if Reid wanted his name to be left out of it, it should not be – even though he had 'done a great deal of work on the libretto'. 'I'm not going to oppose him, naturally.' The trouble dragged on for some months. Graves wrote to Peggy Glanville-Hicks and 'explained' why Alastair had withdrawn his name; he added that Reid would put it back and that – as Alastair (not Graves) put it in an infuriated (undated) letter – 'love will vincit absolutely omnia'. 'This makes me so angry,' Reid complained to Graves, 'I don't know what to say'.

He told Graves that he must understand that his reasons – which he said concerned his (second) wife – were *'private'*, and must remain *'private'*. 'My name is not on this opera because I say so. I do not need to explain why to anyone.' Previously he had told Graves that because he lived his 'own private life so openly' he (mistakenly) 'claimed the same openness for others'. Graves had been told this before, and not without good reason.

The reasons for Reid's not wanting his name to appear as co-librettist are now obscure; perhaps he did not want to appear as a junior partner to a famous figure, which is understandable. He may have disliked the music (he accused Peggy Glanville-Hicks of writing 'greenish bilge', though whether this alludes to a letter or to her music is not clear). This episode – in which Reid had his way (even the Higginson bibliography credits Graves alone with the libretto), and in which he accused Graves of 'explaining' him to other people, and bitterly upbraided him for it – was the prelude to a much more serious quarrel.

III

In May 1959 Graves was invited by the National Poetry Society of America to accept its gold medal, the Prince Droutzkoy Memorial Award for Services to Poetry, at a dinner to be given on 21 January 1960. Acknowledging his reply, Clarence R. Decker, president of the organization, wrote:

> We are delighted to have your letter . . . accepting. . . . We assume that Robert Frost will be present. . . . I am taking the liberty of passing on to him your good words about him and your hope that he will attend.

He had recovered sufficiently from his operation (unforeseen when he accepted the invitation) to go to America in time. He accepted partly because it was the society's golden jubilee (they were almost pathetically anxious to give the medal to him), but mostly because he would get a chance to see Frost. Frost did come up from Florida especially for the occasion, and did not fail him.

> Robert Frost, the Society's Honorary President, sat near me, making mischievous *sotto voce* comments

he said in 'Poetic Gold', an address to the Oxford University Philological Society – but for 'mischievous' we should certainly read 'malicious'.

As Graves said, this award was an 'alarming experience', despite the presence of Frost: 'I have always considered poetry as a private and, indeed, almost anti-social obsession. . . .' 'Poetic Gold' (reprinted in *Oxford Addresses on Poetry*) is a prime example of Graves genially exploding a much cherished illusion – in this case the true value of awards. In it he tells of how his speech of acceptance was on the theme of pure gold in poetry, and of how he said in the course of it that he was

> glad to know, by this gift, that the Society considers my work to have attained a certain karat-fineness.

The medal had, in fact, a fourteen-karat stamp – but he was told when he got back to Palma, by a jeweller who asked to see it, that it was not 'gold of any sort'. He wrote an ironic letter to Decker, decided not to post it, then sent it to Robert Frost, to forward or not 'as he thought fit' ('the demon of plain speaking has always plagued Robert, as it plagues me . . .'). As Graves anticipated, Frost 'gleefully' forwarded the letter. Decker, embarrassed, answered that he would 'look into it'. But Graves, as he says, never received his 'report'. He ends by pointing out that several dignitaries, including 'Prince Philip in 1957 for his not-too-perilous world tour', have received *real* gold medals – but that the Key of the City of New York, 'last presented to the Honourable Sir Hugh Stephenson', was, like his own medal, of 'electroplated bronze'.

It was ten days after this occasion, on 31 January 1960, that Graves took – in the company of Wasson and four others – psilocybin. On this occasion he took an extract of the real mushroom, not a synthesis. (In the following May, accompanied by Beryl and others, he took pills synthesized in Basle. The result was disastrous, and everyone – including Graves – felt very ill.) He described his experience in his lecture to the Oxford Humanist Society, 'The Poet's Paradise'. His account of the actual experience, a rather self-conscious one, is not among his best writing. It is probably impossible to describe a mystical experience (which is what these hallucinogens usually, for want of a better word, induce when they do not induce insanity) with anything approaching accuracy – but it is characteristic of the empirical Graves that he should make the attempt. He 'saw' what he expected to see, and, when confronted with 'lovely ... naked Caryatids'

> hesitated to indulge in erotic fancies, lest the Caryatids turned into filthy, deformed devilkins, like the ones in Flemish pictures of St Anthony's Temptations. Blushing, I dismissed them too. ... What I had been taught at school and in church proved true enough, though the truth enormously transcended the account.

For a short time he was excited by the possibilities presented by the hallucinogens; but in May 1962 he wrote to Wasson to tell him that he didn't want to take them any more. As he had said in his original paper:

> The natural poetic trance ... means a good deal more to me than any trance induced by artificial means. ... Tlalócan [the Eden of the Mushroom God], for all its sensory marvels, contains no palace of words presided over by the Living Muse, and no small white-washed cell (furnished only with a table, a chair, pen, ink and paper) to which a poet may retire and actively write poems in her honour – rather than bask sensuously under her spell.

He put 'the natural poetic trance' above the induced one, and so was never a wholehearted adherent of the 'psychedelic experience'. He was greatly put off by all the slick talk about 'contact with the Greater Reality' which was going on in America in 1961 and 1962. Later he turned more intensely against all drugs, and wrote to a friend in 1968 (28 September):

> As for *pot*; it is only for the down and outs, poor creatures, and for the wretched GI's in Vietnam. The worst trouble is that it makes one vulnerable to suggestion; I like to keep my own mind clear. The Greeks used it, in sweat baths, and had a word for it.

It was in 1960 (6 May) that Graves published another miscellany with Doubleday: *Food for Centaurs*. In it he reprinted a piece originally published in *Atlantic Monthly* called 'Mushrooms: Food of the Gods'. Wasson wrote to him, in July, to acknowledge the gift of the book, saying that he had read it (during a plane flight), and enjoyed it. Thereafter his letters to Graves became a little more distant in tone, although he did write to him in early January 1962, telling him how much he was looking forward to retiring. After 1965 they ceased to correspond. The silence began on Wasson's side. He may have felt guilty. Graves explained in a letter of early June 1973 to two Swiss writers who had sent him a copy of their article refuting Wasson's account of the death of Graves's own, so to say, Claudius (the very subject on which Wasson had first written to him):

> I suggest you read my *Food for Centaurs* a piece published by Doubleday 1960 in a book of that same name. . . . Wasson has been curiously abstemious in his mentions of me, considering that I first sent him the mushroom source in Mexico; introduced him to his sole European predecessors there; & sent him to another mushroom source in New Guinea, and so on and so on.

However, while he regretted Wasson's unexplained silence, he said no more, since he had valued his friendship.

As soon as he returned from America on 1 February – on the morning following his psilocybin experience – Graves heard from his brother Charles:

> I think I have fixed for you to receive the £250 Foyle Poetry Award. If you had only telephoned me when you were in London on your way back from the States, it could have been fixed there and then.
> The Award can be given either for your last collection of poems or (better still in my opinion) to coincide with the publication of your Iliad. It would mean, of course, your receiving the cheque personally at some public dinner in London. . . . Any day now you should be getting a letter from Christina Foyle about all this.

Graves had already heard from Christina Foyle 'about all this'; his brother Charles had had nothing to do with it. He quickly wrote to Charles to tell him so; Charles replied:

> All right, all right.

> Ramasse-toi la chemise.
> So I didn't fix it. All that happened was that Christina came up to me at Kettner's the other night, asked me dubiously about the idea, wondered how to broach the subject to you, and asked for your majorca [*sic*] address. . . .

The occasion itself was somewhat grotesque, as these affairs often are. Graves was introduced by the Tory businessman Lord Mancroft, who described Lord Alanbrooke (Chief of the Imperial General Staff from 1942 until 1946, and present at the function), as 'one of our leading historical novelists' and Helen of Troy as 'the Lady Lewisham of the Levant'. 'Mr Graves', one newspaper report runs, was 'wearing a striped waistcoat of old-fashioned cut . . .'; he 'combined the features of a saintly pugilist with an expression of perpetual surprise'. In his speech, decidedly a light-hearted one, he said that he was 'only a peasant', and called the Gods of Olympus 'a bunch of lecherous old squares'. The award was not only for his *Collected Poems 1959* but also for his *Iliad* – called *The Anger of Achilles* – which appeared on 10 March (the American edition had already been published, on 5 November 1959).

He was at this time generally in the news. Not only did *The Anger of Achilles* gain a good deal of attention, but he was also embroiled in a battle of letters with the former pilgrim-to-Mallorca John Wain. Wain had attacked all Graves's critical views in a piece in the *Observer* – 'in the name of orthodox literary opinion', as he explained afterwards in a private letter (2 August 1960). Graves, who had no respect for any 'orthodox' literary opinion, wrote to the *Observer* complaining that he had had no apology from Wain for calling him 'an absurd eccentric'; he also denied that he had tossed off

> any irresponsible statement that Ezra Pound got his Latin verbs wrong. . . . I showed that his Latin was distinctly below O-level in *all* parts of speech.

Most of the reviewers liked *The Anger of Achilles*, and in 1964 he turned it into a successful radio script; in this form it won the coveted Prix d'Italia (awarded exclusively for radio drama). It was a good popular translation, which sold nearly 18,000 copies in hardback – and many more in the American paperback edition. But some of the classical scholars did not like it. Adam Parry, son of the great American Homeric scholar Milman Parry, angrily accused Graves of producing a translation 'unworthy of a distinguished man of letters', and attacked him for his explanation that he had been writing for 'a hypothetical proletarian audience (surely a romantic notion)'.

But the fact is that a translation both scholarly *and* popular, of a work that is nowadays accessible in the original to only a very few, even among well-educated people, simply cannot be produced. Graves provides an in many ways more acceptable alternative to the best-selling version of this century, the one by Rieu, in Penguin. He agreed with his friend Robert Frost, that poetry is what gets lost in the translation – but could not resist the challenge or need for money.

There was a useful spin-off from this task, and from the earlier *Greek Myths*: *Greek Gods and Heroes* (*Myths of Ancient Greece* in

England), written for children, which sold over 50,000 copies in hard-back – and at least 75,000 in the Dell paperback edition.

Another best seller – in terms of poetry – was his first collection of poems for children, *The Penny Fiddle*, published in England on 10 November 1960 (and in America on 8 September of the following year). *The Penny Fiddle* was illustrated by Edward Ardizzone, who liked the poems so much that he offered to change his usual terms. Only the illustrations in *The Penny Fiddle* are new; all the poems in it had been published before, and most are early. But in this new form it makes a pleasant book for children; it sold some 20,000 copies. In 1964 he published another (briefer) book of poems for children, *Ann of Highwood Hall*. This was also illustrated by Ardizzone.

Meanwhile, he was preparing for his next substantial task: to do for the Hebrew myths – this time in collaboration with the American Hebrew scholar Raphael Patai – what he had already done for the Greek. This was published as *The Hebrew Myths* by Doubleday in America in March 1964, and as *The Book of Genesis: The Hebrew Myths* by Cassell in England in October of the same year. It is not as big a book as *The Greek Myths*, but nevertheless runs to over 300 pages. This was respectfully reviewed, although some of the commentators could not resist mentioning that the authors had failed to take into account the work of Claude Lévi-Strauss – but that was put down to Patai, who was an anthropologist of sorts, rather than to Graves. The main weakness of this book is its assumption of the existence of a past 'matriarchal culture', and even of a 'semi-matriarchal' one, whatever may have been meant by this. But it was Patai who should have known better, since the real importance of Graves's beliefs does not depend upon their anthropological credibility.

Except for a return visit of ten days to America, to read poems and lecture, 1960 was generally quiet. He did not begin to publish the poems which were to form the bulk of the content of *More Poems 1961* in magazines until January 1961 – when a group of twenty-one appeared in the *Observer* (almost the same group appeared in the *Atlantic Monthly* in June).

However, he did in 1960 meet two brothers who were to become influential friends: Idries and Omar Ali Shah. Some of his other friends have been critical of their influence. The Shahs are Afghans – and were reputed among some to be experts in Sufism. Later Idries Shah established himself as an authority on the subject with the general public, especially with his book *The Sufis* (1964), to which Graves contributed an introduction (and which he helped Shah to get published). There are some experts, including Sufis, who say that Idries Shah's picture of Sufism – which may best be described as the mystical (and ritual-eschewing) branch of Islam – is misleading. But this is, no doubt, an area in which conjecture is free. Whatever the case may be, Graves found much that was sympathetic to him in Idries Shah's account of Sufism; indeed, it contains elements to which he was particularly responsive at that time.

He gained one formulation from Sufism which exactly matched views he had arrived at independently: this was contained in the word *báraka*. He gave a lecture about it, first to the American Academy and Institute of Arts (as the Blashford Address), and then (in expanded form) to the Oxford University Poetry Society; this is reprinted in *Oxford Addresses on Poetry* (1962). Graves compared it to the Elizabethan English word 'virtue', in its meaning of 'act of blessedness'. Essentially, however, the word means – in his words – 'the sudden divine rapture which overcomes a prophet or a group of fervent devotees'. He assimilated the concept into his own scheme of thinking and feeling. In his hands it becomes more familiar and understandable than it is in Shah's. Thus, durable goods that have been used with loving care, until they disintegrate, possess *báraka*, as do handmade objects, with their 'glow of care'. '*Báraka* will never become a scientific term.' In literature *báraka* means 'quality of life'; and, like religious ecstasy, is attained by 'self-hypnosis'. The poem – the true poem – that has *báraka* has an 'inspirational quality' which defies critical analysis. *Báraka* came to mean, to him, 'love', while 'anti-*báraka*' meant 'lovelessness'. The concept figured strongly in many of the poems he wrote after 1960; but its essence had always been an essence in his poetry.

Graves did have one piece of financial good fortune in 1959–60: one which made all the theatrical failures less hard to take. He was asked by Charles Abbott of the University of Buffalo if he would consider selling to the university all his poetic manuscripts, drafts and notes (Buffalo never wanted prose). (Some Graves material was already at Buffalo; he and Laura Riding had given some drafts and holographs to Abbott in the thirties.) Karl sorted out all this material – there is much of it – in 1959, and it eventually arrived safely at its destination. The money Graves received came from the Lockwood Memorial Fund, administered by Mildred Lacey. This money was jointly 'locked up', invested, in Switzerland, and never had to be drawn upon even when Graves was desperately short in the sixties.

Chapter Thirty-One

1961–63

I

As Auden's term as Professor of Poetry at Oxford drew to a close he made no secret of the fact that he thought Graves should be his successor. The two men had eventually met – at a party in London in late 1957. Tom Matthews wrote to Graves (16 March 1958) about this:

> So Auden got to you at last. I'm glad his hands trembled, and that you behaved gently and affably. I don't like him. There's too much Caliban in his Ariel, or too little Ariel in his Caliban.

One would have expected Auden's hands to tremble in view of what he well knew Graves thought of him; but he certainly never went back on his admiration (although he did, at the party, take Graves's niece Sally aside, point at Beryl and ask, 'Qui est cette femme?'). Graves remained genuinely repelled by him and by his poetry, but allowed that he could be 'decent' and 'generous'.

Graves easily won the election, which was held in February. He was up against Enid Starkie – who was not popular, and who was not a poet – and F. R. Leavis. He was elected because the university believed him to be the right person for the post, and because it wanted a poet. They granted him an MA by decree (which is what he had wanted), and allowed him to concentrate his three lectures into the Michaelmas Term (as Auden had done), so that he could preserve his foreign domicile. He had rooms in his old college, St John's, what he described as 'a Charles Addams flat' on Boars Hill, and sometimes he would stay at Sally's house in London at weekends.

He was now at the height of his fame, and in 1961 and 1962 his name was mentioned once more in connection with the Nobel Prize. Little that is reliable leaks out about the machinations that go on behind the scenes concerning the Nobel Prize for Literature; but he came closest to it in 1962, when it went to John Steinbeck (who, as it happens, was a fervent admirer of Graves, and often sent messages via friends telling him so). In 1963 he was asked, in his capacity as Professor of Poetry at Oxford, to whom he thought it should go. 'All sorts of cracks' occurred to him, but he reminded the committee, fruitlessly, that Robert Frost was 'still just about alive'.

When he heard the result of the election Auden wrote to him from New York:

> I was so delighted to read ... about your victory. ... I would have sent a telegram but don't know where you are. ...

and he recommended the 'ghost' he had employed for the obligatory Latin Oration (of whom Graves had no need).

The appointment in itself cost Graves money, as he explained in his last lecture:

> You may be unaware that the salary, once irrecoverable income tax and forced benevolences to the University Chest have been deducted at source, and my return fare from Mallorca and a term's living expenses have been paid, amounts to an impressive minus figure, each lecture costing me around £150.
>
> I am grateful for being thus acquitted of mercenary ends; and even more grateful for the licence to say whatever comes into my mind so long as I avoid obscenity, blasphemy or provocations to breaches of the peace. ... I would always rather be a Court Fool than a Laureate.

But he welcomed the opportunity to go to Oxford, of all places, to put the poet's side of the case about poetry. His lectures became more and more popular, and were attended by many who were not in the English School. This is just what he wished, since he wanted as many people as possible to hear a poet talking about poetry – rather than a critic instructing students in academic niceties, which (as he made abundantly clear) he believed to be irrelevant.

His attitude to the honour remained, however, detached:

> This Oxford job involves me in too much correspondence: I go up in October. They have given me an M.A. by decree! ... I've been plagued by poems lately: one of those awful periods that come every seven years ago [sic], and sear the heart while gilding the name. But all's well. Deyá is still Deyá. Beryl is wonderful. ... The garden has never been so fruitful. ... In August I go to Greece to do a T.V. programme for C.B.S.

on Greek Myths: have to pretend I have been there before. [To M.S.-S., 22 June 1961]

This particular TV project actually did come off: he wrote his own part in the Esso-sponsored programme 'Greece: The Inner World', and it was telecast in America on 19 April 1964.

The poems he mentions appear in *New Poems 1962*, a book he had not anticipated publishing, and about which he had some anxiety. He had always had to resist the temptation to write what he felt were 'unnecessary' poems, and he worried about whether these were necessary or not. He felt that they were; but was none the less defensive about his conviction. Only James Reeves, who knew the inspiration behind them, attacked him openly. He had already told him that he disliked the group of poems that had appeared in the *Observer* at the beginning of 1961. In May Graves wrote to Reeves:

> Have written several more poems. . . . I know you did not like the Observer lot; but why should you? Too highly charged, too personal or something. . . .

Reeves, as we shall see, kept up the attack – which prompted some interesting answers from Graves. He did not really resent this attitude in an old friend, for he appreciated that Reeves was, as a fellow poet whom he respected, keeping him on his toes – and he took the trouble to tell him so when they met in the summer of 1962.

In May 1961 he was looking forward to going to Oxford, and to the visit to Greece just before that. But suddenly there was a catastrophe – at least in his terms.

First, bad feelings between him and Alastair Reid (who was living in Madrid with his new wife and son) broke out afresh.

Something trivial Robert 'explained' to Sicre about him angered Alastair greatly. He told Graves in a letter written from Madrid some time in April that he (Graves) never hid anything ('*Hide* is not the word'), whereas he himself 'had a sacred regard for privacy'. Things that passed between him and another person, he added ominously, 'concern me and that person'; 'you must respect that privacy'. He suggested that Graves did not perceive people, but rather invented them – and afterwards came to believe in his own inventions. After this unusually aggressive – but not untruthful – blast he ended, genially enough, that he would 'certainly' come to Deyá sometime, that his wife Mary was 'writing her book'; and that he and Margot, who was

ROBERT GRAVES

living in Madrid and apparently (at least in Graves's estimation) under
Reid's protection, were playing tennis in the mornings.

However, he and Margot were not only playing tennis. Or if they
were then it was while playing tennis (and, in Alastair's word, 'improving') that their love for each other overcame them with what
Alastair later dramatically described as 'terrifying suddenness'. They
ran off together, at the beginning of May, to the Basses-Pyrénées.
Graves, adding mythology to drama, later described Margot's action
as 'feasting on corpse-flesh in the land of the dead'.

Outside the Gravesian context this was – and should be regarded as
– no more than a private escapade. It was, at least as far as Reid was
concerned, entirely predictable. Alastair liked his freedom as much as
he liked his privacy, as Peggy Glanville-Hicks and several others noted.
'Why shouldn't he?' – as Graves himself, under other circumstances,
was fond of saying.

Although he had ended his *Poems 1961* with the poem about enjoying his Sunday, Graves had, for some months before May 1961,
realized that it was 'already another Monday morning'. He had started
writing poems to Margot again, and the still-trusted Alastair had even
finished a script for 'a *White Goddess* film' in which (naturally, at least
from Graves's point of view, if not from that of the Hollywood agent
to whom he sent it) she was already cast for the main role.

He had had, yet again, to restate the theme of 'Joan and Darby', in
'Ruby and Amethyst', which further explores the contrast between the
Muse, 'the Other Woman', and the 'Vesta' figure:

> Two women: one as good as bread,
>   Bound to a sturdy husband.
> Two women: one as rare as myrrh,
>   Bound only to herself.
>
> Two women: one as good as bread,
>   Faithful to every promise.
> Two women: one as rare as myrrh,
>   Who never pledges faith.
>
> The one a flawless ruby wears
>   But with such innocent pleasure
> A stranger's eye might think it glass
>   And take no closer look.
>
> Two women: one as good as bread,
>   The noblest of the city.

510

Two women: one as rare as myrrh,
  Who needs no public praise.

The pale rose-amethyst on her breast
  Has such a garden in it
Your eye could trespass there for hours,
  And wonder, and be lost.

About her head a swallow wheels
  Nor ever breaks the circuit:
Glory and awe of womanhood
  Still undeclared to man.

Two women: one as good as bread,
  Resistant to all weathers.
Two women: one as rare as myrrh,
  Her weather still her own.

It is clear that in most respects, in respect of the peaceful and quiet life most people want, Graves 'prefers' the woman 'good as bread' – and even wishes that, like her, he were 'resistant to all weathers'. But, as he had observed in 'Symptoms of Love', written almost two years earlier, 'Love is a universal migraine,/A bright stain on the vision/ Blotting out reason . . .'; in 'Under the Olives', written at about the same time, he said, 'We would never have loved had love not struck/ Swifter than reason . . .'. It was certainly another Monday morning.

Beryl, as well as Robert, felt that to go off with Alastair Reid was, for Margot, a mistake. Graves, just off to America, wrote to James Reeves:

Just off to USA for ten days. . . . Am on an Aviaco plane for Brussels via Barcelona: haven't been to Brussels since 1912 – sent there to learn French. Thence by Pan American. Arrive New York 9 p.m. which is really 2 a.m. if you get me. There I read poems, the new ones, plus some newer ones, completing the series, to three audiences in Pennsylvania, New York & Washington, & address to the American Academy and Institute on – well, the word is Baraka – it means all sorts of things in Arabic but is whatever makes a poem a poem – holiness, rapture, love, virtue (from the word Barak lightning). Then I've got to see Fred Friendly about a tv narration on Greece in August when I go to see the Homer's Daughter Opera (am taking Lucia), and Decca Co. about a recording [of poems], and Bill Morris [William Morris, the Hollywood agent] about the White Goddess film – though I think that won't come off without a miracle – and Jerome Robbins about a ballet. . . . I am well and have lost about a stone of weight and swim every day. This ridiculous professorship makes me feel like a prize cat at a show: i.e. it means nothing at all. Am still Robert. . . . Beryl and I will miss each other a lot these ten days – no twelve – but it's worse to be left behind than to go, I always find. She was a week in hospital having [an operation]. . . . There's a lot more news that won't go into letters: rather horrible, but no damage done – discovery of treacherous behaviour in an old friend known to you. I don't invite guesses. Anyhow, being more perspicacious and less credulous than I you wouldn't be surprised. [16 May 1961]

Immediately he returned he followed this up:

Can't tell you the treachery story by letter – but Beryl and I equally surprised and horrified . . . a close friend of yours and mine. Anyhow, no hearts/bones broken. And probably Mary [Reeves] will say: 'I always warned you. . . . Do you mean to say you trusted him?' etc. [She did.] . . . Have written several more poems, including one beginning 'Beware, Madam, the Witty Serpent' – that will make the hair rise on some lovely necks. . . . [29 May 1961]

He soon wrote to Alastair; and Alastair wrote back thanking him for writing. He told Graves that the Margot he, Graves, knew would remain 'constant': 'that' Margot he, Reid, would never know – because he was not Graves. Growing confident in this vein, he added that what had passed between him and Margot was 'nothing that either of us did'. He did not feel 'the least differently' about Graves, he told him: 'just as I have long left jealousy behind, when once I realised fully that no relationship replaces any other.' 'What is is always more than what is said. And of this, I say nothing, it being to me utterly private.'

Graves was genuinely anxious about Margot; and in 'Beware, Madam!' made no bones about how he now rated Alastair:

> Beware, madam, of the witty devil,
> The arch intriguer who walks disguised
> In a poet's cloak, his gay tongue oozing evil.
>
> Would you be a Muse? He will so declare you,
> Pledging his blind allegiance,
> Yet remain secret and uncommitted.
>
> Poets are men: are single-hearted lovers
> Who adore and trust beyond all reason,
> Who die honourably at the gates of hell.

The Muse alone is licensed to do murder
And to betray: weeping with honest tears
She thrones each victim in her paradise.

But from this Muse the devil borrows an art
That ill becomes a man. Beware, madam:
He plots to strip you bare of woman-pride.

He is capable of seducing your twin-sister
On the same pillow, and neither she nor you
Will suspect the act, so close a glamour he sheds.

Alas, being honourably single-hearted,
You adore and trust beyond all reason,
Being no more a Muse than he a poet.

But for a time he saw Margot's status as a Muse as unchanged; she had just made a terrible mistake. When he visited Greece ('wonderful ... unsentimental', he told James Reeves in a letter of 25 September 1961) he met a young woman with whom he found he could exchange confidences (she never threatened to become a Muse). As soon as he returned from Greece he wrote to her:

> Before answering the stack of about 100 letters piled up here I want to enjoy myself by writing to you and telling you how much ... but you know that already.... No letter, no news, of Margot for a month.... But I have decided not to worry, or take any more steps to bring her where she wants to be.... Poor girl: how she injures herself! But I suppose it has to be got through.... In the plane I wrote a poem – I don't yet know if it's right – it may have to be cooked again, perhaps, but here it is....

I give the poem, called 'Ouzo Unclouded', as it appears in the letter:

> Here is ouzo (she said)
> Better not mixed with water,
> Better not chilled with ice,
> Nor sipped at cautiously,
> Nor toped in secret –
> Drink it down (she said) unclouded,
> At a blow, this tall glass full,
> But keep your eyes on mine –
> Like a true Arcadian acorn-eater.

On 1 September Reid wrote to him from France: 'The misunderstandings have become murderous.' But he loved Margot 'utterly and truly', and was completely committed to her. Time would show Graves that it was 'true and clear' between them.

In one of his 1961 lectures as Professor of Poetry Graves quoted 'Beware, Madam!', 'a message to would-be Muses'. He continued:

A poet may likewise be mistaken in his Muse; she may prove unworthy of his continued trust. I have written about this, too.

And he quoted the poem 'In Her Praise', in which he speaks of women 'sinking' beneath the 'weight of majesty' of the Goddess.

Yet he was soon writing in a different vein – in, for example, 'A Restless Ghost':

> Alas for obstinate doubt: the dread
> Of error in supposing my heart freed,
> All care for her stone dead!
> Ineffably will shine the hills and radiant coast
> Of early morning when she is gone indeed,
> Her divine elements disbanded, disembodied
> And through the misty orchards in love spread –
> When she is gone indeed –
> But still among them moves her restless ghost.

II

Graves enjoyed his first series of lectures at Oxford. Soon after his first lecture ('The Dedicated Poet', about Skelton) he wrote to James Reeves:

As I warned the University authorities, 2000 came and there was room for only 650. The ones that got in were mostly rubber-necks and 1st-year medical students – a bad audience. Never mind.

Tonight I lecture the London Jews on their Myths (will be reported in the Times tomorrow) – have I a nerve?

Am behaving with extreme courtesy & have a close haircut and a brand new gown. . . . Apart from a great number of new poems (which the Listener will print and which must be carefully distinguished from those of Petrarch etc. . . .) I have been remarkably unbusy these last few months. . . . Having a wonderful holiday with Beryl. . . .

The sarcastic joke about Petrarch was prompted by another shot fired by James Reeves in his war with Graves over the recent poems. He had suggested that Graves's attitude in them was not at all new, but simply an instance of *amour courtois*, courtly love. This faintly annoyed Graves, who had more to say about it later.

He followed his first lecture with an attack on Virgil as 'The Anti-Poet'. The third lecture, 'The Personal Muse', was the one in which he quoted 'Beware, Madam!' – and was in all respects more personal.

About the time he was due to return to Spain a book of correspondence between Herbert Read and the American novelist and scatologist Edward Dahlberg, called *Truth is More Sacred*, was published. In this book Graves is discussed (mainly by Dahlberg) in terms of extreme (indeed, self-defeating) hatred. Most of his friends thought that he had been libelled, and urged him to consult a solicitor. But he had seen the book:

> I saw Truth is More Sacred when it came out in America and let it go: a dirty damp squib left over from last year's wet Guy Fawkes night. But England is different and I am writing to Watt asking him to let his lawyers read the book for libel and act accordingly. Dahlberg was [in Mallorca] five years ago: behaved disgracefully and was mortified that I did not accept him at his own valuation [Dahlberg got himself known among Alan Sillitoe and others in Mallorca in the fifties as 'The Great Insufferable']. Read is a bloody fool to get mixed up in that; but he seems vexed with me for my piece [in the *New Republic* in 1965, and subsequently reprinted in two miscellanies] as an 'Eminent Collabora-tionist' – the reference being to his alliance with crook-psychology, though a self-styled poet – and I suppose owes me a kick for my plain speaking. [To M.S.-S., 20 December 1961]

Watt's solicitors felt that Graves should not draw attention to the attack, which, on Dahlberg's side, all too obviously referred to his own 'mortification'. They advised Graves that the authors might be able to defend themselves on the grounds that they 'really believed what they said'.

He was still quite busy:

> As usual I am publishing too many books. In 1962 there'll be Oxford Lectures (3 public and 3 ordinary): Terence's Comedies [this is a revision of the seventh edition of the eighteenth-century translations collected by Laurence Echard]; New Poems; The Trojan War (juvenile); and a privately printed More Deserving Cases of revived or revised poems I suppressed and which have been pleaded for [this was printed by some of the boys at Marlborough College, where Graves had a great-nephew] . . . keeps me fixed to my table for ten months of the year. No films of mine made despite so many options. The only exception is the Golden

Ass!! – the money boys to whom someone sold the idea hadn't heard of Apuleius, but had heard of me, so I was cut in on it. The film will be made in Spain this coming Spring & I get 1½% of the takings. Isn't it odd? [The *Golden Ass* film was not made.] All those attempts to make Claudius came to nothing. . . . Now I'm working at a Hebrew Myths. . . . The village is very much the same. So, oddly enough, is Oxford: surprising. . . . I met two or three undergraduates who had something *to* them.

It is embarrassing the way my stock has soared in the last two or three years, but I am doing my best to treat it as a joke; which in Deyá is easy. I am also a little embarrassed by the spate of poems forced on me by what is called personal preoccupations, meaning really a new vision of Isis-Caridwen-Belphoebe. But they were all undodgeable so there I am landed with them and by the end I think I got through to something so old it reads like new. [To M.S.-S., 20 December 1961]

This obsession with whether one is writing poems or not is so natural in a poet that it actually amounts to a test of genuineness – even C. H. Sisson, a poet more than somewhat antipathetic to Graves and his aims (yet oddly like him in certain respects: his collected essays have the title *The Avoidance of Literature*), has written with some irony about the time spent 'between writing poems'. Graves's fame always made him feel uneasy, and above all made him afraid that he would attract *bad luck*. Fortunately such instincts led him to 'speak plainly'. But there was, even in this habit of plain speaking – as even more in this habit of loving – a problem. Casting about for a means of defining it, one cannot fail to be reminded of his brilliant quatrain (1922), called 'Epitaph on an Unfortunate Artist':

> He found a formula for drawing comic rabbits:
> This formula for drawing comic rabbits paid,
> So in the end he could not change the tragic habits
> This formula for drawing comic rabbits made.

III

Graves's three Oxford lectures for 1962 concerned themselves with vulgarity and technique. He discussed a recent poem, 'A Time of Waiting', 'the theme of which was a resolve not to prejudice the future by hasty action'. This was his state of mind as he waited to discover how Margot would move. So the series of lectures was less personal than those of the previous year. Together they comprise one of his best pieces of practical criticism. The first lecture quoted instances of vulgarity in Browning, Kipling, Byron, Swinburne, and concluded that 'nine-tenths of what passes as English poetry is the product of either careerism, or keeping one's hand in: a choice between vulgarity and banality.' Although he was unfair – by any standards – to Browning (he should at least have implied that Browning had other, compensatory poetic virtues – particularly as he believes this to be the case), he was saying something that no one else had said publicly in a university for fifty and more years. It prompted Geoffrey Grigson to write, in the *New Statesman*:

> He speaks as a poet, who writes and publishes poems, not as one of the innumerable dons who have taken to literary journalism ex cathedra, from every mean little salaried cage between Aberdeen and Brighton – or Harvard.

The other two lectures were about technique and craftsmanship, and offer many insights into how poems get written. They are also refreshingly informal (and non-academic) in tone, distinguishing for example between 'truly beautiful' women and 'mere lumps of handsome flesh'. The Oxford audience was fascinated and gratified to hear from someone who really believed that 'any jewel a woman wears is not mere ornament but a chosen extension of her inner loveliness'. That is a good example of Gravesian idealism. He is as aware as any that this is not strictly true – that it attributes motives altogether too unsullied to women who may not even exist – but he none the less insists upon the paradox of its truth, and in his poems, of course, this paradox is illuminated.

Graves had invested a good deal in trying to enjoy his Sunday; and when he found that he could not, had invested even more in trying to achieve the maximum *báraka* from his relationship with Margot. In 1962 he was in rueful mood: he thought a good deal about whether his dedication to the Goddess was real or illusory, whether it was 'all worth while'. But his obstinate idealism asserted itself: he saw the situation as one in which it was his duty to wait, in the hope that Margot would be able to become her full self (that is, be worthy of the Goddess, of woman). 'Give, ask for nothing, hope for nothing', he begins one poem written at that time; but ends it by asserting that 'the lonely truth of love' is *somehow* being 'honoured, and her word pledged'.

He had now removed himself from the reality of the situation, in as much as he believed Margot to be more actively engaged with the problem not only of their relationship, but also of her role as Goddess, than she actually was. It is unlikely that she understood it very well. But, like all the girls with whom he had relationships after 1950, she was a *Muse* and not a mistress: so he could and did feed his own reality, as poet, into the situation.

The next year, 1963, he spoke to the university only about a new aspect of the White Goddess, the Black Goddess. It was an entirely new concept for him, and a surprising one. He never formulated it properly, and it came to nothing.

In his lectures on the subject, combined into one essay in the printed version ('Intimations of the Black Goddess', in *Mammon and the Black Goddess*, 1965), he speaks of the poet's 'disappointment that she [the Muse] cannot behave like Vesta' — Vesta being the 'wifely woman'; and he quotes 'Ruby and Amethyst' in this connection. He then speaks of the myth in which the Muse 'always' betrays and murders the poet, 'for the sake of his twin, the anti-poet', and quotes 'Horizon', with its haunting refrain:

> On a clear day how thin the horizon
> Drawn between sea and sky,
> Between sea-love and sky-love;
> And after sunset how debatable
> Even for an honest eye.
>
> 'Do as you will tonight,'
> Said she, and he did
> By moonlight, candlelight,
> Candlelight and moonlight,
> While pillowed clouds the horizon hid.
>
> Knowing-not-knowing that such deeds must end
> In a curse which lovers long lost weeping for
> Had heaped upon him: she would be gone one night
> With his familiar friend,
> Granting him leave her beauty to explore
> By moonlight, candlelight,
> Candlelight and moonlight.

And, thinking not only of James Reeves but of other friends, he says:

Though the poet's friends may descry his Muse as a vixen, a bitch, a bird of prey, he is pledged to accept what he would refuse from any other woman; and suffers most when she uses the light of glory with which he invests her, to shine in an anti-poetic and even criminal world. Is she, in truth, his Muse, his love? Or is she acting a part with sardonic humour? His test will be: which gives the greater pain – belief or disbelief? Many poets break under the strain. . . .

And he quotes 'To Beguile and Betray', about those women who 'make private to their mysteries/Some whip-scarred rogue from the hulks. . . .'

He was indeed living out his private life openly, though few in his fascinated audience at Oxford realized how fully. On 27 August 1962, some time after he heard that Margot was on her own again, he wrote to James Reeves:

> Margot is coming here next month; she is no longer with Alastair who now accuses her of ruining his life (I hear from people who have seen him lately). But he was warned. . . . The strange thing is that I can find nothing to reproach Margot with, and owe a great deal to her, & that all the family (including Beryl) remain deeply attached to this strange primitive being. She's been on her own for about three months, clearing her mind: though unpredictable, she's neither impossible nor evil and I now expect a lot from her in a constructive sense.
>
> This is private for you and Mary. I don't in the least blame you for mistrusting her of course; nor have my feelings for her ever been *amour courtois*. It's easy to see why she can be treated as . . . heartless . . .; that is a natural social interpretation; but I see her in a different context where she makes better sense. The fever has ended, I hope & believe; but the bond between us remains.

And again, in a letter written soon afterwards:

> About Margot: such things are incommunicable and it's nice that you don't like some of those poems [*More Poems 1961*], because you're the only dissident voice of any consequence (except Alastair's, who tried to persuade her that she was having a bad effect on my poems, and quoted you!) and this has removed the curse of general praise. Also, the whole course of the sequence is what matters: love begins with a blind innocence which has to be recorded. Anyhow: to be undignified is to lose one's self-respect, and forfeit one's family's respect. Neither of these things has happened and the whole family, from Beryl down to Tomas, are solid in their love of her. . . . My grey hairs are inconsequential (though it is hard for people to see that) because this isn't a love-affair in the usual sense: so many strange, far-reaching events have already sprung from it. If I told you them in a brief summary you'd think me bonkers or put it down to coincidence. . . . I know generally what it's all about, but can't

519

predict particulars; all I mean is, don't worry about my dignity. All's well; we don't disagree really, you & I.

His Sufi friends, at least, seem to have encouraged him to believe in the 'strange, far-reaching events', just as they encouraged him in his 'Black Goddess' theorizings (black being the Sufic colour of wisdom). Before he gave his obligatory Latin oration, *Oratio Creweiana*, he wrote in another letter:

> Have just passed the page proofs of New Poems 1962: feel rather embarrassed by them – they gave me such a shock on reading them all together. And me 66; or is it 67?
>
> Am now in the curiously euphoric state in which cosmic coincidences abound and startling discoveries are made. Don't worry; I remain practical and there's no trouble around.
>
> On June 27th I give my Latin Oration at Oxford to all the Doctors, including the Honoris Causa ones: Dean Rusk, Graham Sutherland & Charles Spencer Chaplin. I wrote it myself what's more. [To M.S.-S., 22 June 1962]

Graves exercised an iron control over even the more startling of the 'cosmic coincidences', and did 'remain practical'; but they served their purpose, in the context of his relationship with Margot, in that they invested in her the power of the Goddess. Even now all this was, emphatically, only 'a way of speaking', but those who did not know him might be forgiven for supposing otherwise.

But what of the *Black* Goddess? What he had gathered of Sufism from the Shahs (mainly from Idries) was the main inspiration here. Here is how he introduces her in his lectures:

> A poet who elects to worship Ishtar-Anatha-Eurydice, concentrates in himself the emotional struggle which has torn mankind apart: that futile war for dominance waged between men and women on battle-fields of the patriarchal marriage bed. He rejects the crude, self-sufficient male intelligence, yet finds the mild, complaisant Vesta insufficient for his spiritual needs. Renascent primitive woman, the White Goddess, to whom he swears allegiance, treats him no less contemptuously than she does anyone else in this man-ruled world. . . . There can be no kindness between Ishtar and Enkidu [her lover in the *Gilgamesh* story, and subject of his ballad-poem 'Inkidoo and the Queen of Babel'], despite their perverse need for each other. Nor does a return to Vesta's gentle embraces – though he may never have denied her his affection – solve his problem. . . . Nevertheless Ishtar, though the most powerful deity of her day, did not rule alone . . . she acknowledged a mysterious sister, the

Goddess of Wisdom. . . . Call her the Black Goddess. . . . This Black Goddess, who represents a miraculous certitude in love, ordained that the poet who seeks her must pass uncomplaining through all the passionate ordeals to which the White Goddess may subject him. . . . The Provençal and Sicilian Black Virgins are Sufic in origin. . . . The Black Goddess is so far hardly more than a word of hope whispered among the few who have served their apprenticeship to the White Goddess. . . . It is idle to speculate . . . whether the same woman can, in fact, by a sudden spectacular change in her nature, play two diverse parts in one lifetime. . . . The Black Goddess may even appear disembodied rather than incarnate. . . . Does it matter?

Graves was already hopefully casting Margot for the part of the Black Goddess. He meant every word of what he told the students at Oxford. He ended the printed version of his lecture thus:

Poets . . . will no longer be bullied into false complacency by the submissive sweetness of Vesta, or be dependent on the unpredictable vagaries of Anatha-Ishtar-Eurydice.

This is as near as he ever came in public (or for that matter in private) to making a complaint about women in general – but even then, characteristically, it was only in the context of a new image of woman. The Black Goddess was, at first, no more nor less than what Graves hoped Margot would become – this embellished with a few of Shah's Sufic notions about blackness. She was never of true importance in his thinking, and no woman succeeded in permanently representing her. But some critics insist, not unnaturally in view of the fact that he put her in the title of a book, on attaching undue importance to her.

After she and Alastair parted, Margot eventually returned to Deyá, for a number of visits; she was also in America when Graves was there in 1962 and 1963 – and they met briefly. She had her own life to lead, and her own problems; unfortunately these oppressed Graves quite as much as they oppressed her, which made them all the more oppressive. For every letter that he wrote and actually sent to her, he wrote some twenty that he did not send. Quotations from some of these unsent letters will make the situation between them in these years clearer than any general description could.

The background to what he has to say to her is in no way an unusual or a remarkable one. To recapitulate: first she is with Reid, then she finds him wanting and is 'thinking things out for herself', then she is in America trying to be free to form her own relationships (but at the same time receiving help from Graves, and never wholly denying him a part in her life), and finally she decides to marry. It is as well to remember that Graves's statement, made to Reeves and to many others, that this was not 'a love affair in the usual sense', was justified. It was, essentially, the discoverer of the Muse as White Goddess pursuing the consequences of his discovery, and recording them. In the foreword to *Man Does, Woman Is* (1964) he writes:

> *Man Does, Woman Is* closes a three-book sequence dramatising the vicissitudes of poetic love. Because such love walks on a knife-edge between two different fates, Parts XV and XVI – these numbers stand for additions to my *Collected Poems*, 1959, and to the 1961 and 1962 supplements – supply alternative endings to the sequence. . . .

As we shall see, the first 'ending' is one in which Graves honestly gives way to despair (that is, is dependent on the vagaries of the White Goddess, as he put it); the second is one in which he fantasizes that he discovers the 'Black Goddess of Wisdom', who is tawdry nonsense by the side of the old White Goddess of his own imagination and vision. But he was now an old man, and his belief in the capacities of an Idries Shah is fully understandable – Idries Shah possesses notable attributes.

What Graves wrote to Margot in letters, sent or unsent (most of what he said did reach her, though sometimes in a recast form), probably bewildered her, and made her feel under an intense and often mysterious pressure or obligation; but it certainly reflects, very faithfully indeed, what he wrote in his poems to her – and it is the poems, really, that are the only important, and the only universal, thing.

While she was still with Reid he wrote to her:

> I have never said a word against you, and never intend to. You are inevitably yourself.
>
> But after six months silence from you I think it only fair to us both to say that the situation between us ought to be cleared up. If you never want to hear from me again or see me again because you are too closely committed to a partnership with what I know to be wholly ———, I must obviously accept it. . . . In either case you can always call on me for help, without any strings attached.
>
> If I don't hear before the end of this month, I'll assume that you have finished with me; and withdraw myself; the result to you will be soon felt in a loss of the magic protection that our love gave you.

After the Reid episode was over, he tried to explain to her the situation as he saw it – and as he felt she ought to see it. In his Oxford lectures he spoke, specifically, of the Palestinian version of the 'twin myth' – that of the Goddess Anatha and the rival twins Aliyan and Mot – and he spoke of the 'secret passion' of the Goddess for 'serpents . . . corpse flesh, a need to spend seven months of the year consorting with the sly, the barren, the damned'; he wrote about these things to her, too.

> I don't know if this helps, but this is how I see it. You sought me out and before I said anything about it identified yourself with the Love Goddess, throwing the remark over your shoulder one day. . . . You thus securely tied yourself to the most ancient theme in the world (which I wrote about in the *White Goddess*) and faithfully played the part of the Love Goddess and the twins. The performance was exact, and admirable in the closest detail. In fact: it showed up the *White Goddess* script [by Reid] which was sent to Bill Morris, as utterly inadequate. If you hadn't accepted this part and acknowledged its implications, you'd not have had to go through the horrors of the last year & a half; nor would I. . . . After betraying Aliyan, the Goddess entertains his murderer Mot for awhile, then aware of Aliyan's suffering in the Underworld grinds Mot to pieces in the Mill, and goes down to suffer in the Underworld herself, then returns with Aliyan's soul and restores life to the world. Mot was the twin of drought and nothingness and cunning destruction, and tried to destroy her; but overreached himself.
>
> As I see it, you had a long battle with the forces of destruction and are slowly emerging from Hell. The strength of the situation is that the betrayal was a real one, you had to go through with it because you must . . . my love and undefeated trust in you has kept my soul alive: yes, I had natural ups-and-downs of despair that you could not recover from the drain of báraka to which you had subjected yourself. . . . Male love is different from female; founded on honour and generosity. I don't expect either from you, as I would from an ordinary wifely-conditioned woman. But I do know that your happiness and recovery depend on your awareness of the indissoluble tie between us and your readiness to give again as you once gave; without practical considerations. . . . Being a poet makes me a prophet.

To some people this kind of thing would simply confirm the oft-met and facetious view that all poets are 'insane'. In fact it is an instructive demonstration of the sort of idealism from which love poetry must, initially, spring. The stress self-consciously set up between this 'blindly innocent' idealism, and Graves's extreme sophistication, was over-whelming – and there is no doubt that it exhausted him. He was nearing seventy, and he had never taken off more than a month – if that – at a time. Yet his life – and letters – are every bit as dramatic as his poems. Such is very rarely the case; it certainly wasn't in the case of Yeats. But it was a matter of principle with Graves that this should be so. He had said that as a poet he 'mistrusted the comfortable point of rest', but that the 'demon' does come and 'all's well' (this in his lecture 'Sweeney Among the Blackbirds' reprinted in *Steps* and then again in *Food for Centaurs*); but finally he needed to write the poems rather than to have the peace. Readers who value his poems must accept that these love poems are not factitious, or the results of a pose, even if they find them uneven in quality, or inferior to the ones to Beryl.

But Graves undoubtedly did force – or if he could not force, exhorted – his Muses to behave like *his* Goddess. It is interesting that in the rather drearily formulaic 'The Young Cordwainer' (a poem of the early fifties suppressed by Graves) it is the *victim* who first leads his lover to the place where she will destroy him. If his Muse is destructive to him, then, with an almost Panglossian zeal, he will praise her for her splendid performance. Yet still he casts light for all of us on the obstinate habit of romantic love, as well as on the cult of perfection. He could not have done this by staying at home and writing a script for himself, or by indulging in what academics call 'poetical exercises'.

Thus, full of vain faith in that telepathic communication between lovers he first illustrated in *Wife to Mr Milton*, he could write to Margot:

I write this for your sake, not mine, and I hate writing it. . . . I may not post it; but you will get the message nevertheless.

And:

I need not explain the reasons except the main one: that I don't want you to lose your beauty and neither do you. . . . I trust you to trust me.

This became the poem 'All I Tell You From My Heart', which begins:

> I begged my love to wait a bit
>   Although the sky was clear:
> 'I smell a shower of rain,' said I,
>   'And you'll be caught, I fear.'
> 'You want to keep me trapped,' she said,
>   'And hold my hand again. . . .'

> But not ten minutes had she gone
>   When how the rain did rain!
>
> *'Alas, dear love, so wet you are –*
>   *You should have trusted me!*
> *For all I tell you from my heart*
>   *Is sure as prophecy.'*

In the last stanza, after the heedless girl has for the third time made the complaint that he wants to keep her 'trapped', she loses her maidenhead 'scarce a hundred yards from home':

> *'Alas, dear love, it is too late –*
>   *You should have trusted me!*
> *For all I told you from my heart*
>   *Was sure as prophecy!'*

There was very little that he did not see, including even the fact that he was exasperatingly insistent, was compelled to try to force his Muse into the perfection of womanhood (at that time misconceived, in his almost pathetic confusion, as the Black Goddess) – and consequently was misunderstood by almost everyone except Beryl. Yet he tried very hard. Writing (in frantic pencil) on 6 May 1963 he said:

> I'm glad you didn't decide to be finished with me. As a Muse you need a poet; as a poet I need a Muse. I don't know which is the hardest to find. The poet is obliged to love whatever happens, and to tell the truth however unacceptable. The Muse is under no obligation to him at all; but all I tell you from my heart is sure as prophecy. Your private life is your private life, but I am at pains to make my own private lives ['life' is deleted] wholly clear and reconcilable. . . . it was [the] sense of not being trusted that sent my weight down – as it had sent my weight down on two previous occasions. Eventually this distress of mine always angers you, & you accuse me of wanting to chain you down [to Deyá]. That is not so. 'Seldom Yet Now' is how I have always seen our love, and the poem is explicit in this sense. [Her husband's] goodness and directness and simplicity are outstanding, especially in his profession, and his understanding of you – well, you need no talk from me about that. But I know both sides of the axe, and my love for you has been an almost wholly foul-weather one; so I am your poet and fated to love you despite everything. No one can ever fill my place and Time, love's gaunt executor, will record that.

The poem he mentions, 'Seldom Yet Now', comes from the earliest group that he wrote to her:

Seldom yet now: the quality
Of this fierce love between us –
Seldom the encounter,
The presence always,
Free of oath or promise.

And if it were not so
But birds of similar plumage caged
In the peace of every day,
Would we still conjure wildflower up
From common earth, as now?

Yet four days before writing that letter to Margot he was writing to James Reeves:

As a matter of record, I have never been so happy in my life as now: all the unhappiness of three years has peeled away. I wrote a poem two days ago beginning 'Not to sleep all the night gone, for pure joy . . .' which is one of the few poems of utter happiness ever written. There's 'Sally in her Alley' & 'Fain would I change this' and the tear of pure delight that ran down heaven's cheek, and Bill [W. H.] Davies's rainbow and cuckoo; but this is mine, & may it excuse all the dark ones. [2 May 1963]

Reeves crossly said (though not to Graves) that he did not believe that anyone *could* stay awake all night through pure joy, thus usefully summing up the views of those friends of Graves who felt that he was wasting his time, and deluding himself. They missed the point: even if his mood was highly volatile, he remained faithful to the familiar condition of the lover – which is nothing, after all, if not volatile.

But even Graves could not continue to cling to the situation as it now stood. The poems of *Man Does, Woman Is* therefore finish it, though they allow two conclusions, two 'fates'. The poem of pure joy (a very poor one) is, of course, one of those which 'ends' with the 'knowledge' of the Black Goddess. That sequence finishes with the poem entitled 'The Black Goddess':

Silence, words into foolishness fading,
Silence prolonged, of thought so secret
We hush the sheep-bells and the loud cicada.

And your black agate eyes, wide open, mirror
The released firebird beating his way
Down a whirled avenue of blues and yellows.

> Should I not weep? Profuse the berries of love,
> The speckled fish, the filberts and white ivy
> Which you, with a half-smile, bestow
> On your delectable broad land of promise
> For me, who never before went gay in plumes.

The alternative fate he prescribed for himself is stark by contrast –
and his summing-up of it ('I Will Write') is a more powerful poem
than 'The Black Goddess' because it is nearer to psychological reality
than to allegedly Sufic-style mentation. At this point he is beginning to
emphasize what might be called the necessity of the 'impossible' –
about which he had a good deal more, perhaps too much, to say after
1965. But in this more realistic sequence of poems, which acknowledges
simple loss and defeat, he fully acknowledges the human cost. 'I Will
Write' is the last of the series:

> He had done for her all that a man could,
> And, some might say, more than a man should.
> Then was ever a flame so recklessly blown out
> Or a last goodbye so negligent as this?
> 'I will write to you,' she muttered briefly,
> Tilting her cheek for a polite kiss;
> Then walked away, nor ever turned about. . . .
>
> Long letters written and mailed in her own head –
> There are no mails in a city of the dead.

In May 1963, a few days after he wrote his poem about staying
awake all night out of pure joy, Graves went to America for two
weeks. He was to give the Arthur Dehon Little Memorial Lecture to
the Massachusetts Institute of Technology. The lecture, 'Nine Hundred
Iron Chariots' (reprinted in *Mammon and the Black Goddess*) is one
of his best. He knew that he was speaking to a group of the most
advanced scientists in the world, and he made no attempt to tell them
what he thought they might like to hear. He began by announcing
that, now he had been elected to the Chair of Poetry at Oxford, he
was often mistaken for a 'respectable public figure'; he told his audience
that he would, for once, pretend to be one – 'and investigate'. The
poet, he said, was 'on the whole, anti-authoritarian, agoraphobic and
intuitive rather than intellectual'; a poetic trance, he told the scientists,
was 'no more predictable than a migraine'. He also gave what is
perhaps the most succinct account of his final view of poetry:

All poems, it seems, grow from a small verbal nucleus gradually assuming

an individual rhythm and verse form. The writing is not 'automatic' as
in a mediumistic trance . . . but is broken by frequent critical amendments
and revisions. And though the result of subsequently reading a poem
through may be surprise at the unifying of elements drawn from so many
layers of consciousness, this surprise will be qualified by dissatisfaction
with some lines. Objective recognition of the poem as an entity should
then induce a lighter trance, during which the poet realises more fully
the implications of his lines, and sharpens them. The final version
(granted the truthfulness of its original draft, and the integrity of any
secondary elaboration) will hypnotise readers who are faced by similar
problems into sharing the poet's emotional experience.

He ended by telling them that the true scientist would not have to be
afraid to recognize 'magic': that he would 'follow [the Goddess's]
irrational instructions. . . .'

Just before he delivered this lecture (14 May), which was a great
success, he was engaged in a violent struggle of wills with Margot.
Writing from the Hotel Continental in Boston, he told her that he had
had

> lunch with —— who began talking about you & Reid: how coolly
> you had destroyed him and how utterly destroyed he was. He had
> charged him with —— some time before I did, and with ——
> treatment of women. (All I tell you from my heart is sure as prophecy.)
>
> The effect of you on me has been fantastic in transforming the thought
> of the people here. Be angry with me if you must: my utter love and
> trust of the real you makes a sort of flame that eats away metal and
> stone; because I am uninterested in my own fame or powers. . . . And
> you will never need to destroy me: you are essential WOMAN and I am
> a MAN. . . . I char in the furnace, but survive.
>
> Yes, you could do without me but. . . . Three years of intense love for
> you can't be cancelled as easily as you gave away my . . . hat [which,
> evidently, she had done].

But Margot was now unmoved; or, if she was moved, dared not
show it. He saw her only on his last day in America, in New York.
When he got back to Mallorca he felt (unprompted) that he was being
unfair on Beryl – both in being himself distraught, and in continuing
to support what she might well feel was an unworthy, unnecessarily
unhappy cause.

> It is wrong to tell Beryl lies. . . . She is ready to love you as much as
> ever; she doesn't want to interfere with your life in the least but there
> has to be a settlement of Truth. . . .

He went on to detail some of the ways in which he had helped her (his aid had been considerable, as it always was to his Muses).

> Now between you and me all these things are understood; but since you have not once written to Beryl since [we all met in] London, and from her point of view you have failed me . . . there is a breach of love to be healed. She loves me wholly . . . and she has always welcomed this and never said anything against you except that the Reid business lasted too long. . . . She can't be interested in your hopes of fame and riches. Beryl is the noblest and most understanding woman alive; she doesn't grudge you or me anything and is incapable of jealousy. But she does expect truth . . . when you say: 'You're married to Beryl' that implies a sacred bond between you of respect and love: to which she has always been faithful.

The damage was now irreparable. Margot faded out – though in time she returned, to become a friend. But as Graves's Muse she was finished. He wrote, in *Man Does, Woman Is*, which went to press shortly before the end of 1963, that the poems in the third section were 'miscellaneous' – 'mostly written under less emotional tension'. Some certainly were occasional and relatively light-hearted, such as the wry one about his broken neck –

> 'Some forty years ago or maybe more,'
> Pronounced the radiologist, 'you broke
> Your neck. . . .'

He was prescribed (as he says in his poem) 'a Swiss analgesic/Which should at least . . .' (an '&c' is implied), but

> I laugh it off
> And all Swiss mercenary alleviations,
> For although I broke my neck in God's good time
> It is in yours alone I choose to live.

This is an excellent Gravesian minor poem, and perhaps better than most of the poems written 'under emotional stress': here he is being less dutiful to the course of his love as prescribed by his own theories, and more spontaneous.

Although he went on optimistically and cheerfully, he was inwardly distraught. Once again love had failed him. He was growing old, and he was very tired. But still he could not prevent himself from continuing to try to rehabilitate the image of the Goddess more fully and yet more fully.

Chapter Thirty-Two
1964–69

I

After *The Hebrew Myths* Graves did little more substantial work in prose. For the most part he drew on work he had already done. He published his *Collected Stories* in 1964. There were four more collections of essays: *Poetic Craft and Principle* (1967), consisting of his final lectures as Oxford Professor, with other material, *The Crane Bag* (1969), *Difficult Questions, Easy Answers* (1972) – and *On Poetry* (1969), a large selection of all his more substantial essays on poetry, which appeared only in America.

He translated the *Rubaiyat* and the *Song of Songs*. He lectured a good deal, both in America and, later, in communist Europe. He travelled to Mexico twice, in 1965 – and in 1969 for the Olympics. He suffered a serious financial crash through no fault of his own.

But his main work became, at last, what he had always wished it to be: poetry. In 1965 he published his penultimate *Collected Poems*; between that and the final *Collected Poems*, of 1975 (published in America in 1977, with a surprisingly inappropriate introduction by a nonentity), he put out no fewer than ten collections of new poems (not including two more books of children's poems, and a large, useful anthology culled from his own work called *Poems About Love*, 1969). He was more (and too) prolific in the ten years separating his last two collections than he had ever been before. The poetry of these years was – with occasional exceptions – markedly inferior to what he wrote in the years 1929–50.

In 1962 he had refused yet another honour: that of Companion of Literature, which is in the giving of the Royal Society of Literature. Writing to the (then) Right Hon. R. A. Butler, the president, he explained that 'membership would put me under a certain moral constraint if I ever felt tempted to blot my copy-book.' He may have been put off by hearing that one of the aims of the society is 'to further literature', an aim which, in the worthy sense intended, he does not share – believing as he does that a literature thus 'furthered' lacks the *báraka* (as he calls it) of real (living) literature.

Not long before he declined the CLitt he had been introduced, by the film-mogul Sam Spiegel, to an international lawyer, operating out of Lausanne in Switzerland, called Tom Roe. T. W. C. Roe, who advertised a CBE on his notepaper, had for some years been operating a company 'International Authors' (sometimes referred to as 'Roturman', his telegraphic address in Lausanne). This handled the financial affairs of authors, businessmen, actors and 'celebrities' who were domiciled outside their own countries. In the case of the authors he bought their copyrights from them – then paid them the money whenever they wanted it. Among Roe's clients were Noël Coward and James Hadley Chase, whose Swiss residential permit he had 'fixed'. He had in fact acquired the nickname of 'Mr Fixit'. Roe knew a large number of American film stars; and he preyed over more pies than he had fingers. One of these became well known: the Scottish Cadco Pig Project, in which he was up to his neck.

From 1962 until 1965 Graves's books were copyrighted 'International Authors', and for most of the time the arrangement ran well. But there were a few early warning signs. Roe's signature did not inspire confidence: an enormous 'T', curling far up into the text of his letters, was followed by a minuscule, pasty, furtive 'om'. There was a little trouble early on, too: a large amount of money failed to reach Graves's agents, and in autumn 1962 he wired Roe to ask why. Roe replied (6 October) with a letter typical of an 'international financier': he had been 'very conscious of the delays in monies', had been away on a short holiday when the telegram ('not received as Reply paid') had come in, and was sorry. 'As soon as I get the money in from Curaçao . . .' the letter ended. Anyone might have been excused for smelling a rat at the mention of money coming in through Curaçao; but the matter was quickly put right, and, as Graves later commented to the press, 'My fees came through in perfect order until June [1965].'

Then, in December 1964, the Cadco Project, supposedly worth £1,300,000, collapsed – with only £45 in its accounts – and created an international financial scandal. A co-director was a British 'businessman', Denis Loraine. Both men avoided prosecution, though there was a subsequent inquiry in which they, and the movie star George Sanders – a Roe client – were heavily criticized. When the Cadco site in Scotland was visited there was nothing there at all: not a solitary pig, fence or outhouse – let alone sty.

In August 1965 Swiss police arrested Roe, and kept him in gaol; within a matter of days the FBI and Treasury agents had flushed out Loraine in Las Vegas, where he (and others) were charged with being in possession of forged dollars, and with distributing them.

The Swiss were after Roe because they discovered he had passed fifty-eight forged $100 dollar bills in Swiss banks. In the boot of his Mercedes sports car they found 200,000 more forged dollar bills – and the same amount in his office.

It seems that Roe had agreed (for a cut) to place the counterfeit dollars in Swiss banks for a group of American movie actors, who had somehow acquired them; but he found he had bitten off more than he could chew, and began to steal from his authors' monies. The sufferers, besides Graves, included the administrators of the estate of the recently deceased Arthurian fantasist T. H. White (worth a great deal because of the Hammerstein musical *Camelot*), and the Guernsey-based *persifleur* Cyril Northcote Parkinson. Graham Greene also suffered.

It was a serious setback for Graves, who lost at least 65,000 Swiss francs. This amount, however, is only an estimation. The blow was cushioned by the fact that in that year, at almost the same time as the crash (of which Graves was informed while in residence at St John's), the Commissioners of Inland Revenue decided to agree with his accountants' view that he was not eligible for British income tax.

None the less, he had to pay money towards the fees of both a Swiss and an American lawyer – and no royalties could be paid in, anywhere, until the affair was settled. He had to sell a large number of his manuscripts: mostly of worksheets of poems, and letters written to him by other authors. He also had to pay a lawyer to regain the copyrights he had signed over to Roe, who, being held incommunicado in gaol while the forgery affair was being investigated, could not have helped even if he had wanted to. Eventually Roe was tried, found guilty of passing counterfeit money, and imprisoned.

Over a year before this (2 February 1964) he had had to endure a far worse blow: his daughter Jenny, not yet fifty years old, suddenly collapsed and died. It was a cruel surprise. She had made no pretence of agreeing with him when she didn't – but he appreciated her for this, and always felt that they were getting closer to one another. He missed her advice, too. But most of all, he – like Beryl – missed her lively company, and her shrewd and mostly tolerant concern for his welfare.

As always, he seemed outwardly unaffected – to a point which some mistook for callousness.

II

Graves survived his financial difficulties just as he had all the others. It would have been impossible for him – by this time – not to have a Muse.

The third one he acquired, in 1964, 'on the rebound'. She had been in Deyá, on and off, since 1959, and Graves, if few others amongst his friends, had noticed her favourably. She, too, had taken note of him. When she first arrived on the island it was as the wife of a deep-sea diver (a 'nice chap', he soon vanished from the scene). Subsequently she sported a bewildering variety of names: the one the public knows her by, because she illustrated a book of Graves's poems, is 'Aemilia Laraçuen' (which was a concoction), or Aemile, or Emile, and variants. She was Mexican-American, and her face, though not beautiful, 'had a knowing, impish stamp that some men, and some women, found alluring'; others did not find her at all 'prepossessing'. She could put on an excellent, 'gipsy-type' 'I'll-tell-your-fortune' act and, as one who knew her well put it, could 'pass as socially acceptable for substantial periods of time'. But that elderly judgement would be dismissed as old-fashioned, uninformed and snobbish by any member of the set to which she naturally belonged. It is a set that used to be called the poorer end of the 'international jet set', though it contained bohemians, untrained artists, drug addicts, musicians, and workshy people of all sorts.

She treated old men like, and thought of them as, sugar daddies – which was her privilege. But Graves was never a sugar daddy – he suffered greatly from her treatment of him. But it was he, rather than anyone else, who suffered. He began by trusting her implicitly; but she gave no signs (except ones he imagined) of understanding what he meant by trust, the Muse – or by anything else. That had not applied to either Judith or Margot. The impression gained by those who knew Graves best – it may have been a wrong one – was that whereas his other Muses had valued him as a poet and as a man Laraçuen neither did so nor knew how to do so.

But she certainly should not be called a 'vulgar adventuress' or a 'semi-literate opportunist': the University of Victoria think her important. And there can be little doubt that she found being his Muse 'psychedelically exciting', thus giving him – for a year or two – the illusion that she might be 'in tune' with him. Idries Shah enthusiastically supplied Graves with 'magical' Sufic information on the relationship, as he had refrained from doing throughout the Margot affair (he disliked Margot) – and Graves thought it all fitted in. Laraçuen was also pleasant and sportive; and was fairly devoted – during the years of her association with Graves – to a musician who underwent much psychoanalysis. Some of Graves's woman friends used to say that he was a 'poor fellow', but Graves wrote (in a 1968 letter to a friend) that not only had he three times broken his word to him, but also that he was

> no *man* (after eight years on the Freudian couch) and is not *poor*: except to women who are sorry for men who. . . .

Having a Muse always involved, for Graves, having a 'rival'. The rival must always be either a bluefly, or a lily that had festered. The musician was a bluefly – though for Graves he lacked the horrible fascination of such a creature. Rather he caused him to plead:

> Grieve for the loveless, spiritless, faceless men
> Without alternative but to protract
> Reason's mortmain on what their hearts deny –
> Themselves – and owed small courtesy beyond
> The uncovered head, as when a hearse goes by.
> ['Dead Hand']

Graves's fastidious attention would certainly not have centred itself upon this particular girl – with whom, for some five years, he had conducted a playfully 'magical' relationship, and to whom he had acted as confidant – had he not found himself suddenly deprived of a Muse, and thus incapable of writing more than the odd occasional poem. She was in the right place – New York – at the right time (when he felt abandoned by Margot); ignorant of poetry, she lacked neither shrewdness nor genuine desire for some guru. But Graves was above her intellectual level.

Readers of Graves quickly became aware that Laraçuen possessed a talent for doing fanciful little designs and drawings when he published (on 16 July 1965) *Love Respelt*. (Most of his closer friends thought them repulsive.) This was a signed edition (limited to 280 copies) of thirty-two poems, reproducing Graves's own MSS – with illustrations by Aemilia Laraçuen. All the poems were published in printed form in Graves's *Collected Poems*, which appeared two months later.

Long ago Randall Jarrell had shrewdly if not quite accurately said that Graves 'became his own Laura Riding'. But at this stage Graves may fairly be said to have become 'his own Muse'. What drove him to this behaviour – which was not intended to make him happy – was the need to write poems; but he did not see it in that way.

Margot had been a disappointment to him. But for all that, he continued to respect her as a person, to retain the confidence he had always had in her as a decent human being. The 'impish' semi-hippie Mexican-American was not in her class, or not by Graves's standards. She could be relied on to be capricious (and so forth), because that kind of behaviour was as natural to her as it was to the sorts of people with whom she mixed. Such shallow people – and Graves became acquainted with a number of them during the association with Laraçuen – made a habit of what they elegantly called 'blowing their minds'; their attitude towards drug-taking was very different from his own; and their many letters to him are inarticulate. Many of them professed to be, in one way or another, 'artists', and it was of them, among others, that he was thinking (bitterly) when he wrote 'Wigs and Beards', in 1967. This poem is about the 'beards', the 'Latter-day bastards' of the old wicked bewigged squires long ago, 'ploughed . . . under' by taxes and wars (' "And serve the bastards right" the Beards agree,/Hurling their empties through the café window'). The beards remain true to the 'same hell-fire code':

> Their ancestors called themselves gentlemen
> As they, in the same sense, call themselves artists.

But by the time this poem was written Graves had reached a stage of disillusion that he had never reached before.

For all had, at first, gone well. Laraçuen was more than willing to take over what was for her the fun-role of Muse; and Graves, with that 'blind innocence' which he insists on believing marks the beginning of love, thought himself 'ecstatic'. Love, he felt too hurriedly, was truly 'respelt'. Yet the best of the earliest poems he wrote to Laraçuen – the ones in *Love Respelt* (though 'La Mejicana', in *Man Does, Woman Is*, refers to her) – do not fully reflect his overt mood at the time.

By the mid-sixties, more famous as a poet than he had ever been before, Graves was diffusing his poetic power. The second half of his final *Collected Poems* (1975) would be better for the sort of pruning he had repeatedly given the first half – and more relentless pruning at that.

In 'Batxóca', from *Love Respelt*, he might be said to be rationalizing certain of the current Muse's habits (such as living from hand to mouth) as 'disguised wisdom' (a Gravesian ploy with all those he loves); and 'Who are more to me than any woman upon this earth' is, for Graves or anyone else, an absurdly weak line, quite unrescued from banality by its courtly tone. Yet can the poem, as a whole, be said to be wholly the product of self-deception?

> Firm-lipped, high-bosomed, slender Queen of Beanstalk Land,
> Who are more to me than any woman upon this earth
> Though you live from hand to mouth, keeping no certain hours,
> Disguising your wisdom with unpracticality
> And your elusiveness with hugs for all and sundry,
> Flaunting green, yellow and scarlet, suddenly disappearing
> In a whirlwind rage and flurry of skirts, always alone
> Until found, days later, asleep on a couch of broom
> And incommunicable until you have breakfasted –
> By what outrageous freak of dissimilarity
> Were you forced, noble Batxóca, to fall so deep in love
> With me as to demand marriage, despite your warning
> That you and I must on no account be seen together –
> A Beanstalk Queen, no less, paired with a regular man!
>
> Did you wistfully, perhaps, expect me to say 'no'?

Other poems to Laraçuen demonstrate a similarly extravagant indulgence of feeling, as well as an unfamiliar linguistic awkwardness. But Graves was never really happy in the role in which this Muse had cast him, and his diction shows it, even though his technical proficiency and fancifulness try to conceal it.

At this point he reached his final, and (at least by his standards) quasi-mystical, view of poetry. This is expressed in his final lectures as Professor of Poetry, which he was writing, as he awaited the publication of *Love Respelt*, in July 1965. He was thinking, too, of Laura Riding – which he seldom did. In a letter of 8 July 1965, replying to a request for a poem from a newspaper – whose reluctant poetry editor had been asked to prepare a 'symposium' of poems by well-known poets accompanied by short statements – he wrote:

But at least I am still free of Laura. The moral is that one can't use

——— for private ends and expect to remain a poet: and that to deny poetry and supply its place with a new religion only inflames the wound.

I wish I could convey a blessing on her, but it would be . . . useless. . . . The trouble is that she once wrote me love poems, and that she ——— me as a goodbye . . .

Dearest Martin, forgive me if I don't join your symposium: I can say only that:

A poem is a miraculous, unpredictable and unassessable event in non-history. It is foolish to claim that we have ever written poems worthy of this definition; but pardonable to believe that one day it will happen to one of us if we abide by poetic principle – however we care to define *that*.

So I don't think that, after this, I can send a poem. . . . My *Love Respelt* . . . comes out on my birthday. The poems (!!??) will be reprinted in a new *Collected Poems* for September. . . . Maybe I am . . . quite, but quite, mad. It often happens to the elderly. [To M.S.-S.]

In his opening lecture at Oxford that autumn, his sad experience of Margot's merely independent ways now reinforced by matters that more thoroughly 'plagued his scruples', he found himself obliged to pronounce:

Musedom cannot be measured by [the Muse's] ethical virtues, or by her intellectual powers. . . .

and:

Despite the elegiac 'true love' concept of domesticity, to which my poems have returned time after time, I am drawn to the conclusion that though a poet must experience this before understanding the full perils of his profession, there can be no solution in time, to the problem of love; only in timelessness.

This attitude is the argument of the poem 'Between Hyssop and Axe':

> To know our destiny is to know the horror
> Of separation, dawn oppressed by night:
> Is, between hyssop and axe, boldly to prove
> That gifted, each, with singular need for freedom
> And haunted, both, by spectres of reproach,
> We may yet house together without succumbing
> To the low fever of domesticity
> Or to the lunatic spin of aimless flight.

By this time Graves was asserting that monogamy was a patriarchal invention (with the implication that it had been one of the institutions by which matriarchy had been superseded), and that 'There is no domestic poetry'. This was too extreme or at least too unsubtle: an extrapolation from a temporary and overexcited experience, denied by the best of his own past work.

Many of the poems in *Love Respelt* are about the 'oath', or the 'vow', taken between him and his Muse. He now felt that he had good reason to be very serious, very hopeful, about this 'vow'. There was, certainly, a series of disappointments – but in March 1965 he made quite a long visit to Mexico with Laruçuen, and found the surroundings there as conducive to a positive judgement of her Musedom as was her behaviour, then, towards him. For a short time, at this stage, his feet left solid ground altogether – for the first time in his life.

Over twenty years ago he had memorably demonstrated, in *Wife to Mr Milton*, his notion of the sort of telepathic communication that could be achieved between lovers – in the doomed relationship between Marie and Mun. This kind of communication only ever existed between him and Beryl; with others he wished and so invented it. As a scrutiny of the group of poems in the privately issued *Seventeen Poems Missing from Love Respelt* (1966) shows, however, he believed, while in Mexico and for a time thereafter, that this sort of communication existed between him and Laraçuen. Did he ever suspect that her acknowledgement of such communication, so seemingly astonishing to him, was part of an act, that he was deluded? Probably he did, and probably it made him suffer greatly.

There is a sense in which he knew, in any case, almost from the beginning, that the fullness of his experience with her was illusory. It emerges from a superb, sour poem, 'A Shift of Scene', which is not included in *Love Respelt*, but is added to that sequence in the *Collected Poems* of 1965. This seems like a shining sliver of the old concentrated Graves embedded in the, for the most part, diffuse, soggy matter of the poems to Laraçuen.

> To lie far off, in bed with a foul cough,
> And a view of elms and roofs and six panes' worth
> Of clear sky; here to watch, all the day long,
> For a dove, or a black cat, or a puff of smoke
> To cause a shift of scene – how could it do so? –
> Or to take a pen and write – what else is there
> To write but: 'I am not dead, not quite, as yet
> Though I lie far off, in bed with a foul cough

> And a view of elms and roofs and six panes' worth
> Of clear sky'? Tell me, love, are you sick too
> And plagued like me with a great hole in the mind
> Where all those towers we built, and not on sand,
> Have been sucked in and lost; so that it seems
> No dove, and no black cat, nor puff of smoke
> Can cause a shift of scene and fetch us back
> To where we lie as one, in the same bed?

In this claustrophobic, dry poem – all the better for being oblique and far removed from the euphoric mood of the sequence in which it was eventually placed – Graves records his undergoing of that acerbly melancholy experience familiar to most of us: the moment of certitude that an affective project is doomed.

Otherwise, though with certain exceptions, the poems to Laraçuen apply the Gravesian 'Goddess formula' to the situation, rather than take it as it really was. As a generalized account of this particular poet's obsessive love for his Muse the sequence as a whole – the last poems appear in *Poems 1965–1968* – is of great value; but psychological particularities are lacking, as they were not in, say, 'Through Nightmare', where the actual personality of the woman addressed is a factor in the poem.

Graves's love poems to Beryl are his most powerful because they are prompted by a strong-minded individual who is committed to loving him, and whose personality therefore emerges in them. The 'rural' side of Nancy, too, comes across in the earliest love poems, though little else about her does; Riding comes across as superior being, tester of the male, cruel and capricious paradigm of the Muse. Beryl, more 'human' and less ideological than either (and very much more devoted to and interested in Graves himself), emerges as a whole person. One cannot think of the lyric beginning 'Have you not read/The words in my head' as being addressed to anyone but a real woman who has the qualities of lovingness; they could not be addressed to an abstraction, or even to a woman to whom some set of abstract qualities is attributed, such as Judith or Margot.

In the poems to Laraçuen, though, Graves appears to evade the issue of her personality altogether. The poems to her are wholly idealistic. They insist that she is, that she will be made into, the Goddess – whether she is in fact the Goddess or not. An investigation into whether she was or was not 'the Black Goddess' would be fruitless.

She had no wisdom of the sort Graves values. When he could endure no more, he wrote of the 'fire-eyed guardians' who said:

> 'These two have learned to love,'. . .
> 'But neither can forget
> They are not worthy of each other yet.'

And of 'Our Self':

> When first we came together
> It was no chance foreshadowing
> Of a chance happy ending.
> The case grows always clearer
> By its own worse disorder:
> However reasonably we oppose
> That unquiet integer, our self, we lose.

He insisted, still, that there was a single 'self', a merging. But this existed only in his own mind; it had never existed in hers at all: he had mistaken an amateur actress for a 'real woman', in his special sense.

She caused him, from time to time, acute embarrassment with his close friends. On 3 September 1968 one of these (a well-known folk-singer) wrote him to say that Laraçuen and a male companion had left her flat – which she had lent them, on Robert's recommendation – 'in a filthy mess'; this had made her feel hurt and 'plain bloody angry'. Graves immediately wrote back a contrite letter, with a cheque for the expenses of clearing up the mess – and for the bills left unpaid. His friend returned the cheque on 18 September, but could not help adding: 'I find dirt neither artistic nor pleasant.'

But, as noted, there had been intimations long before this – even while the *Love Respelt* poems themselves were being written, and before the Mexico trip. Writing to a woman confidante on 15 January 1965, Graves said:

> As for Aemile. After a lovely reunion in Paris, and my fitting her out again in London for painting in Spain & our meeting again in the New Year, she got tangled up with ——— [the man who had spent years 'on the Freudian couch', not the one who failed to clean up the borrowed flat] again at Paris: broke free, came back to London, another lovely meeting; got her ticket for U.S. and was going to spend Christmas in Mexico & then have her mother to stay at 108 [Clifton Hill, Sally and Richard Chilver's house in London], & then I'd join her there – but [she]

540

invited ——— to London – and there we go again! Whenever she does these things guilt keeps her from writing to me or even disclosing her whereabouts. Evil, evil, evil!

I don't know where she is now – probably back with him. The terrible thing is she *knows* he's no good for her and that she is hurting me; and so pretends that I'm the one to blame. And all this hurts so many people who love her & me . . . it's a true madness, when I'm the most important love of her life as she constantly confesses. . . . Patience. . . ! We must depend each on his or her own moral strength, not on others. I don't yet know if I'll be well enough to come in Feb. [to New York]. This has knocked me sideways.

This kind of thing went on for most of the time; only the Mexico trip revived Graves's wild hopes (easily revived by the slightest sign) of the relationship. Yet in the above letter, as in many hundreds of others he wrote (there were at least 406 letters from 1959 to 1968 to Laraçuen herself, which she preserved), there is a strong element of wilful self-delusion: the question of Laraçuen's 'guilt' (embarrassment?), in particular, stands out – as does that of her constant 'confessions'.

Graves, now old and tired, his natural vigour sapped, was often made nervously ill by her unpredictable movements, and by her failure to keep in touch. He talked incessantly about her to everyone who came to Deyá (many did). He worried incessantly about her when she was not there. He waited, usually vainly, for her to turn up when she said she was coming. Had his great vitality and compulsion to work not kept him going, he might have become a permanent nervous wreck. His life was further complicated by the fact that no one in Deyá who had his interests at heart liked her – and although he pretended not to notice this, he felt it keenly.

Ava Gardner continued to value her own friendship with Graves:

. . . so often when I'm sad I write to you – I almost never send them to you – but still I feel better. . . . Robert, I tried to explain to [a friend] today that getting your letters makes up for [a famous film tycoon] and all the motion picture crap. Instead of feeling dirty and useless I felt very strong & worthwhile – It's very nice to know someone I love & admire so much takes the time out of a very busy life to say good things to me.

She then sympathized with him in his situation, but told him:

Please try to be happy with or without Emile – give her a kiss for me – but to you I send a big big love.

What he was told about Laraçuen by her acquaintances was not so helpful, nor in any way revealing. Thus, one inarticulate musician, who headed his New York notepaper with his name in capital letters but gave no address, spoke of her as being 'all warmth and spontaneous delight'. Having seen her in late 1966, he reports that she looks even better than before, 'more succinctly Mexican stone'. She spoke, he told Graves, of 'rebirth and LSD' (meaning, of course, no more than that she was interested in the concept). Graves – who had the greatest contempt for the Leary-inspired LSD cult – would not normally have been encouraged by this, nor by the tone of his correspondent's praise ('. . . you are an ancient poet-reverend acting out a ritual as contemporary as light . . . it is still beyond our habitual reflex-arc'); but he had been so captivated by Laraçuen on those occasions when she did attend to him that he was, for some two years, unable to maintain a sense of reality about the sort of person she really was. It was this fact, one may be sure, rather than the American musician friend's remark that he had 'felt principally awe at the regimen you develop out of your acceptance of the recognition of the creative principle in [Laraçuen]' that influenced him: he was after all the co-author of *The Reader Over Your Shoulder*. Was this sycophantic hocus-pocus much better, was it perhaps even worse, than the letter he received from an unknown admirer, a woman, at about this time?

May I please be your Mysterious Benefactor? A Mysterious Benefactor sends small things – stone [increasingly succinctly Mexican?], flower – from time to time, even prps [*sic*] only a word. . . . I can't send flowers, but I send a sunset.

Just before going to Mexico in 1965 he wrote to his friend James Metcalf, a sculptor who had lived in Deyá for some years but who was by now remarried and living in Mexico:

Aemile had already written to me about your visit [to see her]: how much she regretted that [a male companion] was tagging on, so that she couldn't really talk. . . .

I'll arrive, I hope, soon after this letter: am giving some lectures and readings [in the USA] – but the main object is to be with Aemile quietly for a while: for as long as necessary. We got somehow out of touch on the ordinary level: the *strange* level remains, necessarily, because it can't be avoided even if one wished. Too many alien pressures and tensions. I think these can vanish, now that she has broken with her late nightmare. What our practical life will be or can be we will find out: but separation has been tried & has failed lamentably.

And Deyá means too much to both of us to keep away long from
... there's liquid fire or liquid gold in Aemile; when she has properly
harnessed it (and she will) that will be something! ... [c. February 1965]

It was his experience in Mexico that led him to believe, for a short
while, that this relationship had a future. He was confused by it all,
and sometimes even spoke as though he might leave Mallorca –
although, as his remark in the above letter shows, he did not really
intend this at all, and would not have done it.

While he was in Mexico, apparently urged on by Laraçuen, he
wrote to Karl to tell him that he no longer required his services. Karl
expected nothing of this sort, at least in this manner; and on receiving
Graves's letter went to consult Beryl – who knew nothing about it and
could tell him nothing – about what to do.

This was a graceless move on Graves's part. It was true that, now
he had reached seventy, employing Karl was no longer economic. But
afterwards he felt guilty about the way he had dismissed him, and felt
obliged to explain it, in roughly these terms, to most of his old friends:

I had no more work for him, being on strike so far as concerns books
for him or anyone to type. ... [To M.S.-S., 8 July 1965]

People began to worry that he would do no more work at all in this
thraldom. When Roe was arrested a few months later, he found it hard
to raise the money that Karl was due after his long service, though he
did so; fortunately, however, Karl was able to find a job as Curator of
the Poetry Collection of the Lockwood Memorial Library of the State
University of Buffalo.

By 1967 a good deal of the 'magic' of Laraçuen had worn off. Had
the trip to Mexico not taken place, it might well have done so earlier.
In the late summer of that year he was, it is true, still helping her
friends: a letter from the New York musician thanking him for permission to set some poems reads:

Thank you for the permission and peppercorn contract, transmitted in
spirit, received in spirit, glorify us both, you have the forms of the sun
and the moon. ... How can I ever return more than I've received? [9
July 1967]

But even if he did not yet experience a shudder of nausea at the
language, Graves was certainly getting tireder of this gush than he had
been a year before. For he was feeling unwell, and confided both this
and the reasons for it to everyone. One guest, not even a close friend,
wrote to him, on 20 August 1967:

Couldn't help remembering our conversation in your kitchen about your ill health related to disillusionment about [Laraçuen] – it certainly isn't easy to shake the obsessive confusion connected with someone in the grip of dark or destructive powers – it poisons one's life. . . . Your comment that one must eventually realise that this kind of exhaustive battle prevents one from caring for others who are more deserving and more appreciative really hit home with me. . . .

In his poems, instead of recording his disillusion – which would have seemed ungallant – he turned, for a time, to what he described to James Reeves as 'Songs of obsessional perfectionism'. He had to have something to distract him from the personality of this Muse (the previous one, Margot, had disillusioned him in a way he could feel was at least worthy of a Muse), and so he turned to a lapidary type of love poem – quite as 'classical' in form as anything he ever wrote. 'Song: Though Once True Lovers' is typical:

> Though once true lovers
> We are less than friends.
> What woman ever
> So ill-used her man?
> That I played false
> Not even she pretends:
> May God forgive her,
> For, alas, I can.

He was, as ever, resourceful: he knew that he did not at the time possess the energy and the concentration required to articulate a disillusion that was quite different in nature to anything he had previously felt, and so he confined himself to perfecting a form almost entirely neglected in twentieth-century poetry. The break with Riding had been traumatic. But when it came he was already in love with someone else; the trauma was that of breaking with a Muse who was no longer loved, only intellectually respected above all others. He had admitted (to James Reeves and others) that the 'social image' of Margot might well seem, to those who did not know her, to be one of a nomad – but he had been confident that she wasn't what they thought her to be. Now he had no such confidence – as his conversation in his kitchen with a casual visitor (and there were hundreds more like it) amply demonstrates.

As early as *Love Respelt* ('Change') he had already half-heartedly tried to deal with the problem:

'This year she has changed greatly' – meaning you –
My sanguine friends agree,
And hope thereby to reassure me.

No, child, you never change; neither do I.
Indeed, all our lives long
We are still fated to do wrong.

Too fast caught by care of humankind,
Easily vexed and grieved,
Foolishly flattered and deceived;

And yet each knows that the changeless other
Must love and pardon still,
Be the new error what it will:

Assured by that same glint of deathlessness
Which neither can surprise
In any other pair of eyes.

This is a grim poem, as essentially disenchanted as are almost all of
the 'obsessionally perfectionist' *Songs*; but it still allows Laraçuen the
quality of what he calls *báraka*, deathlessness – and it stands fast in
its faith in their fated love. By 1967 that faith was broken. His choice
of her as Muse had been mistaken: he could no longer make sense to
this woman in the light of his image of Woman. When he came to
publish *Poems 1965–1968*, in which the final poems to Laraçuen are
in section XXI (the same numbered section as in the final *Collected
Poems* of 1975) – and are followed by poems to another and different
kind of Muse – he wrote:

> Once more, my theme is metaphorical of experiences, which as in clas-
> sical Persian poetry, transcend ordinary physical circumstance. . . . When
> I sent *Love Respelt* and *17 Poems Missing From Love Respelt* to the
> printers I twice deceived myself into thinking that this particular poetic
> battle had ended; in each case another charge was needed.
>
> Now, I can withdraw my forces awhile and see whether 'Respelt'
> should have read 'Mis-spelt'; for the battlefield seems deserted for a
> while. Perhaps, though, in Theocritus's words, misquoted by Coleridge
> in his introduction to Kubla Khan, 'And henceforth I shall sing to you
> even more sweetly?'
>
> 'Who knows?'

The reference to 'Love Mis-spelt' is an acknowledgement of his error, as is the song 'Dew-Drop and Diamond' in which the qualities of a different kind of Muse are praised:

> The difference between you and her
> (Whom I to you did once prefer)
> Is clear enough to settle:
> She like a diamond shone, but you
> Shine like an early drop of dew
> Poised on a red rose-petal.
>
> The dew-drop carries in its eye
> Mountain and forest, sea and sky,
> With every change of weather;
> Contrariwise, a diamond splits
> The prospect into idle bits
> That none can piece together.

But not all was quite over. There were practical matters to attend to, and these were not finally settled until late 1969. As I have mentioned, Graves had, through the years, written Laraçuen at least 406 letters (consisting of 1350 pages), which she had preserved. These, whatever their intrinsic interest, are the letters of a famous poet, and – Laraçuen's tender sentiments apart – had high financial value.

Letters are legally the property of the person to whom they are addressed, and there is nothing whatever to prevent that person from selling them. But the copyright in the letters remains the property of the sender.

Graves's personal attitude to the sale of his letters written to his Muses, or of his private letters of any kind, is summed up in a letter he wrote to an old friend who was faced with a blackmailing request for sale of some letters to do with her family's private affairs, and who had asked him for advice:

> What can I say?
> All that collecting of letters by or to famous characters is a dreadful bore and also highly embarrassing when the letters are private and intended to remain so. But it can't be stopped, only discouraged.
> Me, I'm in frequent trouble when women with whom I have been in love sell their collections of my letters. Not that I have anything to be ashamed of – except my choice of women who would do so. . . . [c. July 1972]

By 1969 the London dealer Bertram Rota Ltd, managed by Anthony Rota, had collected a large amount of Gravesiana from various sources, and he knew where he could obtain more: batches of letters of literary interest sold with their author's permission, drafts of manuscripts, some early editions and the like. Rota, with Graves's approval, was trying to find a market for this material, and was looking for a university interested enough in Graves to pay a proper price. He offered the University of Victoria, in British Columbia, Canada, the opportunity to start a Graves collection – and, in the words of the special collections librarian, Howard Gerwing, the university accepted 'with very little hesitation'. Gerwing goes on, in his short account of the transaction, to say:

> [The] first purchase established a happy relationship and through the good offices of Anthony Rota and Selwyn Jepson, business advisor to Robert Graves, the University of Victoria has continued to add extensively to one of its more significant research collections.

In 1975 there were (apart from that 'first purchase', to which we shall return), eighteen lots 'available for research through the permission of Robert Graves'. The chief item is the 1935–39 diary. Graves did not really want to let this go, even though he was not displeased that some of his worksheets, first editions and letters about poetry should find their way into the hands of a university a number of whose members were keen students of his work (the *Malahat Quarterly*, the magazine of the university, published several works of his, and devoted a special number to him in his eightieth birthday year). But there were heavy pressures on him.

Selwyn Jepson went to extensive trouble to maintain Graves's good relations with Rota (who had been the publisher and distributor of all his limited editions of poems) in an effort to build up a representative collection at Victoria. He more than justified Graves's confidence in him as a friend.

The 'first purchase' made by Victoria seems to have helped. Gerwing writes of this:

> The collection of letters between Robert Graves and Amelia Laraçuen dated 1959 to 1968 was purchased, and a legal agreement between the contracting parties gave the University of Victoria the right to publish the letters. But, this valuable [sic] correspondence collection is restricted against all private and public research and will not be made available until ten years after the death of Robert Graves or until the death of Mr Graves's present wife, whichever is the later.

This makes the collection of letters sound as if it were worth studying in depth – and might even mislead people into believing that it contains all Laraçuen's letters to Graves (which it does not by any means). As it stands, there are 406 letters from Graves to her (not all those he wrote), sixty-two of hers to him (which he supplied in order, he told a correspondent, to 'let the full story be known if it must ever be'). Under this arrangement both parties on the selling side of the contract (Graves; Laraçuen) had to make an assignment of copyright (under the conditions stated) to the University of Victoria.

Selwyn Jepson, who was sympathetic and practical throughout – and a great comfort to Graves in his difficulties – wrote to him on 15 August 1969:

> I was very relieved to hear from you. But never keep from me anything that is so horrid you can't bear, even for a moment. I can generally ease it for you by listening, by reading what you write about it, if only because you know this is true.
>
> ... I have prised the assignment of copyright out of Aemile; she either pretended there was a catch in it or some illiterate fool told her there was, and I had to write firmly if not sternly to her, crossing 'i's and dotting 't's, as though to a backward child of five, and in the meanwhile you and I and everybody else on this side of the sale got close to bad names from the University because the assignment wasn't being carried out. She is quick with suspicion and no less so in accusations of cheating. I suppose in truth there are few people one can try to help who won't react in some way to avoid feeling simply gratitude – and fewer whom one has succeeded in helping. Never mind, it's all over and done with now. ...

The sum paid for the letters was $12,000, and, as Graves wrote in a letter to a collector of his work:

> I never made any money from selling the Laraçuen letters: she had it all [including the proceeds accruing from her own letters to him]. [15 May 1972]

Anyone who has had the experience of having their intimate letters fall into the hands of strangers, let alone sold to an institution for future publication, will understand how Graves felt. And by now he had several brief terms he did not mind using of Laraçuen: those used by everyone except him and her friends since 1959.

But although the deal with Victoria marked the end of the Laraçuen episode, there is a sort of sequel. Graves reported it wryly, in a letter written on 23 March 1972:

The last I heard from Emilia [*sic*] was that she had gone to Nepal with an American called ——— & then visited Turkey where she ran out of money and appealed to me for help. Spain cannot send money to Turkey, and in any case when we were 'together' she ——— but never mind – I got back somehow and I expect she has done the same.

And I am very fond of the Mexicans. . . . [To M.S.-S.]

Chapter Thirty-Three
1969–81

I

Although during all this time spent in agonizing about Laraçuen Graves did little work in prose, 'being on strike' as far as prose books were concerned – as he deserved to be at seventy – he was far from inactive. He gave more poetry readings (in Australia, America and Europe) than he had ever done. In 1967, after a painful gall-bladder operation, he went to Australia to see his daughter Catherine, and to give poetry readings. He arrived on 4 October, and on the same day as landing was surfing – something he had never done before. He returned to Mallorca on 16 November. In 1968 he took a long journey behind the Iron Curtain. On 3 May he made his first stop, at Budapest, where he had been invited by the PEN Club. There he met, for the first time since 1938, Ian Parsons of Chatto and Windus, the firm' which had published *The World and Ourselves*. He gave readings, met many translators, and made good friends of the Hungarian poet whose work he most admired, Gábor Devecseri – a friend of Patai, with whom he had worked on the Hebrew Myths. Devecseri, a Jew born in 1917, was a classicist and was best known for his translations – particularly from Homer and Catullus. He also translated some of Graves's poems, which he first read during one of two long prison spells served before the war. But Devecseri, though in favour with the regime and holder of an important cultural post (to do with army publications), was (discreetly) a poet in his own right, and the last part of the judgement given in a French directory, that he was

> plus connu pour ses belles traductions . . . que pour ses recueils person-
> nels, dans lesquels il essaie, après 1945, d'utilise une inspiration socialiste

is somewhat misleading, since he was the author of some wholly non-political poems of great beauty and power, as well as some regular

Marxist ones. (Devecseri sympathized with Nagy at the time of the Hungarian uprising but was unable to do anything about it.) Graves's translation, 'Women and Masks', which he included in his *Collected Poems* (1975) – he made other translations – exemplifies Devecseri at his best. In 1969 Graves set up a prize, called the Graves Prize, in Hungary. This was unique in the communist world: the only prize named and set up by a living Englishman.

From Budapest, on 14 May, he flew on to Moscow – his first visit to Russia. Beryl had already been there, during Graves's last Oxford stint in 1965. While there Graves tried to meet someone in whom he took a slightly morbid interest: the fluent Russian poetaster Yevtushenko, who was for some time regarded in the West as Russia's finest poet – until better informed sources demonstrated his essential flashiness and tawdriness, and his time-serving nature. Graves had devoted a substantial part of the second of his last trio of lectures at Oxford to him. He attacked him, though gently by his standards, for encouraging 'a personality cult of poets' – and for his rhetorical public readings:

> Either the listener must allow himself to be enchanted [by his 'rabble-rousing eloquence'], or he must fight the enchantment.

A few months after returning from Moscow he wrote in a letter:

> Yevtushenko tried to see me in Moscow, but he couldn't come to the rendez-vous. He is a very interesting character & his visit to this island was hilarious. He was bedded up with a capitalist Banker's wife when cornered by the Press, but offered to write a poem in honour of Mallorca. He & I are at opposite ends of our common profession but I do not intend to quarrel with him. I only require that poets tell the truth; and he doesn't always try. He was a centre forward in football; I was a full back. See? [To M.S.-S., 28 September 1968]

In July Graves received an honour which pleased him more than any other in this year of events and honours: he had been a citizen of the village of Deyá since 1929, and the inhabitants decided to make him an 'adopted son', the only one ever. It was a splendid occasion: there was free sherry for everyone. The event confirmed Graves's natural citizenship of the place – watching him there, one cannot imagine him belonging anywhere else.

Then, in late September, he set off (alone) for Mexico once again: he had been invited to the Cultural Olympic Games there, to read poetry. He received his second Olympic medal for poetry on this occasion – officially styled 'Gold Medal for Poetry, Cultural Olympics, Mexico City, 1968' – for being, it was stated, the only one invited to attend who was 'fearless of fire' (students riots were rife at the time). He had a good time, saw old friends (in particular Jimmy Metcalf and his Mexican wife), and cheerfully quarrelled with the British press for inaccurately reporting him. He returned, very tired, on 24 October. But he was happier than he had been for a long time; and his family and friends were happier because he was.

He found awaiting him a letter from the Poet Laureate, Cecil Day Lewis, asking him if he would accept the Queen's Medal for Poetry for 1968 (to be presented in the following year). Day Lewis had previously been more than a little irritated with him, to the extent of addressing him in a letter as 'Graves' instead of 'Robert', and signing himself with his full name. The occasion of this disagreement was the quality of a recording of Edmund Blunden's poems – done as a birthday present to the poet. Graves had been sent a copy, and asked to subscribe. He refused, provoking Day Lewis to write:

> Eric White [then literature director of the Arts Council] has passed on your letter about the Blunden record. I'm sad. . . . First, the poems are not, I think, misread: they are read by Carleton Hobbs, my wife [the actress Jill Balcon] and myself. . . . I do hope you will change your mind. It would be sad for Edmund not to see your name on the . . . list. [Undated]

Graves didn't change his mind: as he had said in one of his Oxford lectures, 'personally, I cannot stand' the 'trained-actor' method of reading poetry, and this was the way he felt Blunden's poems were read on the record (with the best intentions, and delighting Blunden). But all was forgiven, and Day Lewis was as pleased to get Graves's acceptance of the medal as he had been to have the duty of asking him.

The award of the Queen's Gold Medal for Poetry seldom makes news. It had gone (as the King's Gold Medal) to Auden in 1936 (his Marxist friends objected to his acceptance), and in more recent years had been awarded to Philip Larkin (1965). Auden, Larkin and one or two others apart, the medal goes to nonentities. And Graves was in his seventy-third year.

But he was attended by his usual luck in such matters. It so happened that Richard Cawston was at that time making his television film about the royal family: a propaganda exercise aimed at presenting the 'human' side of the monarchy. Cawston chose to show the award of the medal, because it was going to a more than usually distinguished recipient, as part of his film. It was one of the highlights of the show, and Graves was thanked for assisting in it so effectively. (They had to film the ceremony three times.)

When Graves's term as Professor of Poetry at Oxford came to an end in 1965, he immediately turned his attention to his old friend, Edmund Blunden. It was at first calculated that Graves's successor would be elected unopposed: a pressure group in the university had decided that Robert Lowell should have the Chair. But neither Graves, nor a number of others, felt happy about this. Graves did not dislike Lowell personally, but he thought that he was a 'personality cult' type of poet – and one whose technical virtuosity had been, moreover, much exaggerated. Enid Starkie, who had stood last time against Graves, decided this time not to stand but to organize a movement against Lowell. Blunden was persuaded to enter the lists at a very late stage – and at the election he won by 477 votes to Lowell's 241. Starkie's success enraged John Wain, who wrote an article attacking Blunden's victory as a result of 'the sheer brute weight of the herd instinct'. (He was taken in by one of Starkie's jokes: she had given out that Wilfred Scawen Blunt had told her, 'We must stop this Americanisation.' Wain dutifully reported this, sneering that Blunt was 'aged'. Indeed: he would have been 126, but had died in 1922.) He singled Graves out for special attack (a habit he had got into), for his letter to *The Times* (16 February 1966) speaking of a 'modernist revolution . . . directed mainly by American expatriates in London and Paris against the English poetic tradition'. Actually Graves only wrote this letter to annoy, because he hoped it would tease people such as Wain. He, as well as the more moderate critics of Blunden's victory, believed that Blunden had been poetically moribund since the early thirties; but he did not think that Lowell's 'iambic narcissising' would much provoke the Oxford students – and, chiefly, he wanted to show an old friend that all was forgiven and forgotten. He heard from him on 20 February 1966:

> I . . . was, I need scarcely tell you, moved and gladdened by a letter from you. That I was so 'editorial' ages ago about your war chronicle has not pleased me much in later days; but I must beg for one thing – do not finally condemn your war poems of the 1915–16 vintage. . . .

Graves had another cordial letter from him in April. But Blunden's frail health did not stand up to the Oxford job, and he resigned in 1968. On the occasion of the new election Graves was one of those who nominated Starkie, for she had decided to stand against Roy Fuller – already nominated by Auden and Day Lewis. Fuller was elected. Graves could not very well speak publicly about Starkie's merits, since she had few critical ones, and was not a poet; but he supported her because he had disappointed her hopes in 1961, because she was in very bad health, and because several of his friends and relatives liked her and urged him to do so for sentimental reasons. He also found her the most suitable nominee amongst the other serious contenders, namely Yevtushenko (nominated by the eccentric Richard Cobb, of Balliol), Alfred Alvarez, Kathleen Raine, Alan Bold (who received not a single vote, though he was one of the better of the younger candidates), and Barry MacSweeney, described by Graves as 'the lout from Newcastle'.

He was still writing vigorous letters to those of whom he did not approve. In 1968 Tambimuttu, editor of *Poetry London* during and just after the war years, returned to England to try to make a comeback. He wrote to everyone he could think of for testimonials, including Graves, who replied:

> I am sorry but I can find no reason at all to give you any testimonials for your former literary politics in England.
>
> I never published anything in your magazines and kept clear of the whole crowd of your then associates, and you know it. And I heard a good deal about your private life: I hope it was all lies.
>
> Please do not visit me here. . . . I am [not] interested in what any critic writes about my work, ever. [8 August 1968]

He was kinder to strangers with whom he disagreed – but just as firm. One who tried to engage him in a polemical correspondence received a letter interesting for its incidental insights:

> . . . There's a fundamental difference in our vocabularies. I don't, for example, admit the term great in art or literature; as for Prime Ministers of England – what a list! And 'sophists' is a bad word: invented by the official school of philosophy to discredit whoever didn't agree with them. . . . Ah, those 'universal' men! Goethe and Milton and Ben Franklin and dear muddled Coleridge!
>
> You have had bad luck with your 'personal' people if they are concerned only in rejecting what is unlike them; for me 'personal people' are ones with completely different skills from my own, but absolute integrity.
>
> I have never had any ambitions except to do my own job as well as

possible: the reward being acceptance by friends whose motive is the same, but with whom no rivalry is possible.

If you and I met there would be an immediate explosion, so let's not.

As we say to the owls here when they begin hooting: 'Good luck to your hunting, leave me to mine!' [18 July 1968]

II

The influence of Sufic thought, or of what he was informed was Sufic thought, on the poetry of Robert Graves will inevitably be the subject of earnest future theses. More to the point may be the exent to which his friend Idries Shah, upon whom he placed great reliance, encouraged him in his own thinking and behaviour, and the extent to which he reinforced this with Sufic lore.

One thing is quite certain: any friend who had tried to discourage him in his own thinking and behaviour – especially towards his Muses – would not have remained a friend for long. James Reeves was so close a friend as to be an exception, though Graves took no notice of his objections.

Graves took exactly what he wanted, and no more, from the version of Sufism presented him by Shah. There are some who say Shah encouraged Graves in the wrong direction; but could anyone? Others say that he is a superficial man with a gift for popularization. But a man's decision is always his own if he is not at gunpoint. Idries Shah is not of interest, at least in the context of Graves's poetry.

But Sufism or what passed for it did have a direct effect on Graves's reputation as a translator. While in the throes of his affair with Lar-açuen, Graves did what he thought Edward Fitzgerald had failed to do properly: render an *accurate* translation of the *Rubaiyat* of Omar Khayyam. He did not do this in collaboration with Idries, who is a loquacious although cautious man, but with his more taciturn and less cautious brother, whom he called, with his usual wild generosity, his 'fellow poet', Omar Ali-Shah. The new version was published in 1967 (in 1968 in America). It met with considerable hostility: from sentimentalists who wrongly believed that the Fitzgerald version was being in some way slighted, and from Persicologists who were enraged by the claims made in the two introductions – one by Graves and one by Shah (but completely rewritten by Graves).

Fitzgerald's version comes into the difficult category of 'good popular' rather than of serious poetry. It is certainly an achievement, but its inspiration is not Persian. So there was still room for a new and more accurate version. Major J. C. E. Bowen had already provided an interesting one in 1952, though this would have been more valuable had it been cast in the form of prose. Had Graves simply taken Shah's literal version, and made his own from it, and said nothing, then he would probably have been praised for making an 'accurate and effective enough' translation (as the anonymous *Times Literary Supplement* reviewer called it). As he wrote in 'Translating the "Rubaiyat" ' (in *Steps*, 1969):

> I am . . . no Persian scholar and therefore followed closely an annotated English text with which Omar Ali-Shah had supplied me; and made the first draft of my verse-rendering in the corner bed of St Thomas's Hospital, London [where he was having his gall-bladder operation; he produced his version very quickly]. . . .

However, too much was said about Ali-Shah's credentials and about the *Rubaiyat*. Graves got himself into serious trouble on two counts. First – and this was the less important charge – his version was called 'prosy'. This, by comparison with Fitzgerald's, it does seem. The rhythms, contrasted with Graves's own, in his original poetry, are oddly flat. However, he succeeds in achieving the concentration of Khayyam – a quality which all Persian scholars allow this poet – far better than Fitzgerald. He was clearly being very conscientious: he sacrificed technical fluency to a sense he was persuaded was sacred.

But his worst fault, in the eyes of the public, was that he denigrated Fitzgerald – and stuck blindly to what Shah told him, which got him into trouble. It is obvious that he 'Englished' both Shah's own introduction to the translation, and then the letters Shah wrote to the press in answer to the critics – before suddenly giving up and leaving Graves out on a limb, as he did. But the views expressed were Shah's alone; and Graves, characteristically, never doubted him for one moment. So he found himself, as he put it in the foreword to his miscellany *Steps*, 'accused . . . of resorting to literary forgery in Classical Persian'.

Shah told Graves, and the public, that Omar Khayyam was by no means an anti-Sufic hedonist, as Fitzgerald (unconvincingly) presents him, but a great Sufic teacher. He much annoyed the Persian scholars; but even this was not as grave as his other claim. This was not merely that the AD 1259 manuscript in the Chester Beatty Library, and the AD 1207 one in the Cambridge University Library, were both probably forgeries, but that the Shah text upon which Graves's translation is based is an authoritative one, of the twelfth century, in the possession of Shah's family. Now the first part of this claim was not too dreadful since several scholars had already questioned the authenticity of the thirteenth-century manuscripts, and that of 1207 has since been exposed as a forgery (Graves was by then too ill to draw attention to this – Shah, to his discredit, kept silent, which has led some to assume that his manuscript does not exist).

But the scholars became very suspicious when Shah told them of this hitherto unheard of text, going back even earlier in time, which he claimed was authentic. Fired by their annoyance at the translator's insistence that Omar Khayyam was 'the Sufi voice' (this was quoted from what was described by Omar Ali-Shah as the 'standard work of Sufism', by Idries Shah), the Persicologists began to ask questions about this 'Jan Fishan Manuscript', upon which Shah's attempt at a ' "standard" edition of . . . Khayyam's original *Rubaiyat*' was based. He had been a little coy about this in his own introduction, stating only that the

present translation is made from a twelfth-century manuscript of uncontradictable authority, whose existence has been known for centuries. I cannot claim that its one hundred and eleven verses form the complete corpus . . . only that these are poetically the most important ones. . . . Finally, that Khayyam's Sufi connections form part of the oral tradition which has been handed down in my family for the last nine centuries.

Graves opened his own introduction by telling the reader that this manuscript belonged to Shah's family. Later it was claimed that it had been given to his 'princely Afghan family, senior in descent from the Prophet Mohammed [Graves himself, as he states in *Steps* and elsewhere, was led by Shah to claim descent from the Prophet – through his Irish connections], when a contemporary Sultan presented it to them'.

Now Ali-Shah had already stated that every one of the verses in his 'Jan Fishan' manuscript appeared 'in one or more of the earlier MSS', and that 'none of them are blasphemous, atheistic or anti-Sufi' (as Fitzgerald's 'boozers' version', certainly wrongly, implies Khayyam was). So the 'Jan Fishan' version could have been a concatenation from various manuscripts, made by Shah: a selection from those verses of the *Rubaiyat* which could not be taken as anti-Sufi. However, such a charge seemed preposterous: besides, all that Ali-Shah needed to do was to show that the 'Jan Fishan' manuscript 'had been available to Sufic scholars in Afghanistan since shortly after Khayyam's death' – this is what he had told Graves, and was what Graves had written – and all would be well.

But no trace of such a manuscript has been found, no evidence of its existence produced. Doubts have therefore been cast upon it, and even upon the princeliness of Shah's family; and upon the integrity of Omar Ali-Shah and his motives in providing Graves with the 'authentic' *Rubaiyat*.

All this, though by no means conclusive, was unlucky for the good name of Omar Ali-Shah (whose brother, strangely, as he was Robert's trusted friend, kept right out of the affair). The controversy continued, with delighted Persicologists weighing into Graves for all they were worth. Eventually in late 1969, the *Sunday Times* published what appeared to be a conclusive hatchet job, by a clever journalist, on Shah's claims. Unfortunately it involved Graves, too – and he could not answer the charges without Shah's help. An acquaintance wrote asking him why he had not answered. He replied ('shortest day of the year', 1969):

> The *Sunday Times* piece about Omar Ali-Shah & me came out very soon after the death in a car crash at Tangiers of his father Sirdar Professor Ikbal Ali-Shah who was very soon going to let fall his block-buster on the *Khayyam* controversy.
>
> I said that I had 'not been deceived' (as was suggested) 'by a bunch of crooked orientals': they are men of honour and of the most direct line not only from the Prophet but from the last real King of Persia. . . . So I did not answer that . . . fantasist in the *Sunday Times*, out of respect for the dead.

And so there the matter has rested. When the Cambridge manuscript was finally exposed as a forgery (1978), no word came from Shah. Perhaps Graves's faith will be justified in due time, the manuscript found. Meanwhile it seems sensible to treat his version of the famous poem as an interesting – and more concentrated – alternative to Fitz-gerald's adaptation, and as his own possibly intuitive tribute to the subtleties of Sufic thought. His treatment of the complex argument of the original will prove a more fruitful subject for research than will the truth about the 'Jan Fishan' manuscript – which is for the investigator of the career of Omar Ali-Shah to puzzle out.

III

The Khayyam controversy was the last in which Graves was publicly involved. And this was more a matter of his loyalty than of his judgement – for in this case the facts were not at his disposal to judge, except at second hand. Throughout his life he had been involved in controversy, partly owing to his being plagued 'by the demon of plain speaking', partly owing to the fact that he was a natural odd man out, occasionally (as now) because of his loyalty to his friends. When the establishment took him up – as one might put it – in the early sixties, he did not change his ways. And he did not now. But he was seventy-five; even his enemies thought it time to leave him alone.

He had certainly made many enemies. A few people he had melodramatically misjudged. But most, the ones who didn't know him (or who knew him only glancingly), were the people who resented their academic positions as critics of poetry being undermined by a poet the quality of whose work no one could dismiss. He had often been careless as a scholar, and he had sometimes relied on doubtful sources of information. He had, with only a few exceptions (such as Rilke, Lorca, Rimbaud and Villon), too easily dismissed poetry in languages other than his own – a hangover from the days spent with Laura, whose own language was English and for whom (naturally enough) the only viable poetic language was English. He did not completely perform the service to criticism that, as a poet, he might have done – but he had been too busy earning a living, and writing poetry, to achieve the required level of scholarly meticulousness. Nor would such a role have suited him.

But he had shown a whole generation of young people how real poets worked. For that it was said of him, in *The Times* (2 January 1968), that 'his periodic identification with the hippier end of the poetic spectrum would have brought him enemies'. That was written as an explanation of why Day Lewis got the Laureateship rather than Graves. It is an inadequate and misleading remark; but is certainly interesting as applied to one who has so frequently been accused of being a 'traditionalist' and even a 'Georgian'. What the writer must have meant is that Graves did not treat young people as a professor should. But this is not 'hippy' – and in any case no hippy who writes verse writes it in any recognizable *form*, upon which Graves has always insisted. The *Times Literary Supplement* also called him (in 1968) a 'reactionary medievalist'. This was on the grounds that he claimed that science was no longer 'a Humanity' as it had once been, that scientists were 'dependent for support on Governmental or institutional finance, and therefore dedicated, in the main, to findings which can be industrially exploited' – and that 'popular love lyrics' were 'highly expendable'.

Yet all these are now wholly acceptable views, even if ones still loathed and feared by the holders of the purse strings, and therefore discouraged by the pliant and mediocre clerks they put in to keep culture apathetic, banal and acquiescent of the destruction of nature in the interests of commerce – all processes Graves has passionately fought against for the whole of his long life.

Graves's sort of modernism seeks a return to some, although not to all, of the features of the remote past. Hatred of the 'modern', of the technological, the banausic, the commercial, the materialistic, the featureless, is no longer quite as unfashionable a stance as it was twenty years ago. 'Human progress' is not so popular. 'Barbarians' are no longer simply from the past. And if Graves seems to have been mistaken in his anthropological assumption of the existence of matriarchies, what he *meant* by this (and that is what is important in his work) is neither wrong nor, as we are well aware, any longer unfashionable either. So, paradoxically, Graves's special form of traditionalism has always been, in its way, 'modern' and anticipatory.

In 1970 he was happier than he had been for some years. His children were all doing well. William, an oil consultant, had married a shrewd Spanish girl, who was expecting their second child. Lucia, after taking first-class honours in Spanish at Oxford, had married Ramon Farrán, a Spanish musician, and was expecting her second child. Juan had settled down in Deyá; and Tomas was enjoying his late teens without giving anyone cause for concern.

Graves was not so happy about the situation in Deyá itself, although affairs there straightened themselves out in time. As he put it in a letter:

The hippies here were all right until they started stealing from the villagers & making too much noise at night. They have been *chassé* and a big group which tried to rent [a large house in Deya] for 100,000 pesetas a year have been turned down – there's a rule 'no renting without running water and electricity' to keep things quiet. It became last year so that I couldn't visit the café.

I have nothing against the students who are rioting against the imposition of academic logic on all thought and action; but I do like good manners and respect for other people.... Maybe I'll be able to go to parties again [in Deyá] without meeting crooks murderers and C.I.A. men. [To M.S.-S., late 1969]

Nor was he happy about a scheme by which the Mediterranean Institute of Dowling College (USA) was located in Deyá in 1969–70. He had repeatedly told the irresolute progenitor of the scheme, one Bob de Maria, that it was a bad idea; he begged him not to go through with it. But de Maria persisted. The institute was located in a large house called Ca'n Gelat, then administered by Graves's son William. He had been in correspondence with de Maria for some time – in 1967 the latter even asked him: 'Would you be terribly offended if I wrote a novel in which the main character resembled you somewhat?' Graves's answer is not on record, but there is no novel of this kind.

The Mediterranean Institute had a number of regular instructors, of whom the least undistinguished and certainly the least drunken (he was not drunken at all) was the over-credulous but personally likeable occultist, Colin Wilson. As almost always, people forgave Wilson his wild ideas because he is such a nice man.

Graves's nephew Simon Gough began in the early sixties to build a little open-air theatre (it is not an amphitheatre, as it has been called) on the land opposite Canelluñ. He had the help of Tomas, and others whom he roped in. By the end of the sixties it was complete. It is a charming place, and is frequently used for plays, music, singing, poetry readings and other spectacles. Graves lectured to the institute students there on Mallorcan history; and later gave two readings of his poems, and another lecture – this time on poetry and myth.

Graves travelled more extensively than ever – despite bad health – in 1970–73, though for shorter periods than before. He went with his daughter Catherine, who had left Australia for a time to live in Deyá, to Budapest for a poetry congress on 1 and 2 May 1970. Here he met a Russian poet greatly superior to Yevtushenko, Andrei Voznozensky. But as always when in Hungary he most enjoyed talking with Devecseri. He was back in Mallorca on 11 May. On 6 September of the same year there was held 'Poetry: an Evening with Robert Graves', at the Mermaid Theatre in London. From 18 to 24 October he was in Yugoslavia for the 7th International October Meeting of Writers in Belgrade. He joined Beryl, already there, from London.

By now, however, he was feeling distinctly unwell, with frequent headaches and dizziness. Back in January 1970 a doctor who was staying in Palma examined him, and told him that his trouble was originating from somewhere connected with his nose. The old botched operation of 1916, which had left him unable to breathe properly through one nostril for the whole of his life, had caught up with him at last. He underwent a serious nose operation in University College Hospital in March 1971; but he still felt unwell and low-spirited. This did not prevent him from going to Budapest again, from 20 May to 1 June. He had been invited once again by the PEN Club – but he accepted, really, because he had learned that Devecseri was dying of cancer. He saw him for the last time; and in the next year he published, in *New Hungarian Quarterly*, a record of his 'poetic friendship' with him. On 28 May he lectured to the PEN Club on 'Crane and Horse' (this lecture, much loved in Hungary as a beautiful response to their country and folklore, is reprinted in *Difficult Questions, Easy Answers* (1972). By the beginning of June he was back in Deyá – and still feeling the symptoms caused by his sinus condition.

The hospital treatment did not relieve his condition for long, and in March 1972 he had to return to London for a third, major operation. He wrote soon after this:

Am recovering from a marvellous Wimpole Street nose operation to right the mess made in 1913 when I played rugger with soccer men, and in 1916 when a military surgeon nearly killed me in King Edwards Hospital. My nasal *antrum*, an attic full of fossilised mucus and a huge colony of virus types, has been cleaned out and I hope to be free from

nose,

throat,

ear,

eye

and stomach aches and

so no longer have to be a saint. [To M.S.-S., 3 April 1971]

But in September of the same year he wrote again:

the operation on my nose last March ... kept me ten hours under the anaesthetic [an overestimate]. This was successful but led to a virus infection in my antrum which has shown no sign of leaving me. Bad effects on general health plus earache stomach & throat aches.... Worst is loss of memory and giddiness. Meanwhile I write poems (they are going way out into the fifth dimension).

He did not wholly recover from this trouble, but was able to visit Hungary for two weeks in October 1973, Poland and Budapest (yet again) in the following October, and Poland again – after his eightieth birthday – in July and August of 1976. He came to London most recently in 1978 – and while he was there saw the film of his story *The Shout*.

In some ways 1971 was the most depressing of his more active years of old age, for he felt his powers of memory and concentration slipping slowly away; but miraculously he managed to continue to write poems. He was much cheered, too, to hear from John Crowe Ransom – who was by now getting very old – again in early 1971. He had read, at the request of the publishers Holt, Rinehart and Winston, a book by Ransom on English grammar that they were thinking of reprinting. Ransom wrote:

> What a dear kind man you are! ... It has been many years since we corresponded, but I have three or four of your books of verse that I can turn to.
>
> I venture to include in this note half-a-dozen of my poems which are in their most finished state, just waiting to replace the *Poems* in the present *Third Edition*. I'm glad to have cut out some horrors of diction, and hoping for a much better show.
>
> I read and hear of you in these U.S.A., as of recently, and anyhow [*sic*].
>
> How I regret the entrance of Laura Gottschalk into our colloquy of five or six years! I still read you in the letters I've saved. . . .

Graves's final miscellany, *Difficult Questions, Easy Answers*, appeared in 1972. He gave interviews to magazines, and wrote a few articles – but he was still concentrating almost exclusively on poetry. Between *Poems 1970–1972* (1972) and the last *Collected Poems* of 1975, he published three private, limited collections – and he remained as obsessed as he had been throughout his life with 'getting it right'. What he now had to get right was solely and simply love, and for this he needed – and had found – yet another Muse.

IV

The experience with Laraçuen had been shattering to Graves – almost as shattering as that with Laura, with the important reservations that Laraçuen lacked the intellect and the power to clothe her private morality – whatever that was – with rhetoric, and that he was now almost fifty years older. Little need be said of the qualities of his final

Muse, except that – in the words of one of his closest friends – 'everyone gave a huge sigh of relief when she came along'. She was called Julie, and was the child of friends of very long standing. She was still in her teens when he saw in her what he had so devastatingly failed to find in Laraçuen. Just how deeply he felt his failure is aptly illustrated in his reply to an angry letter he received from an American stranger accusing him of being a 'square' – of not being a rebel and not wanting to rock the boat. Even though he didn't bother to post his reply, or forgot to, it affords a good answer to that foolish journalist who thought he was part of the 'hippie spectrum'; and it shows how, deep down, he connected his own private struggle with the struggle for a decent world.

> *You* have not fought in a real war. None of your generation has. . . . 'Police-actions' with mass murder of civilians, defoliants, poisoning of the earth, shooting practice on prisoners, rape and infanticide, breaking all the sworn rules of the United Nations, are not wars but *obscene* outrages – your word – and in the original Latin sense of obscenus ('unlucky', 'inauspicious', because of breaking human and divine law). This implies divine punishment.
>
> The 1st World War was started by the German invasion of Belgium, without excuse; we fought to rescue Belgium & our French allies, and we fought honourably throughout.
>
> Why glorify 'the human being with deplorable habits'? All people are not poets and you know it.
>
> *Maxima debetur senibus reverentia*! [Juvenal wrote in his Satire XIV 'Maxima debetur *puero* reverantia', the meaning of which Graves has reversed.]

But it is the last sentence of this indignant letter that is of interest in connection with love, and with Laraçuen. He wrote:

> And you do not know how far I have risked my neck recently for what you most value (or not enough). Nor will I tell you.

He by now connected the practice of love directly with the observation of decency in human affairs. There was no other way left for a man of his temperament. But although the poems of his final years of writing poetry do not rest on any new premise (a poem was still a 'miraculous, unpredictable and unassayable event in non-history'), there is a distinctly new – and somewhat calmer – attitude apparent in them.

It would be untrue to say that he did not suffer at all in his last affair with the Muse. It is a part of Graves's nature to fret if everything is not quite right with his Muse, and to interfere in her life (for her own supposed good). But his episodes of anxiety, his dramas over small incidents, were as nothing to the comparative serenity he was able to achieve through this new relationship. The whole series of poems to Julie still suffer, by comparison with the poems of the early forties, from a degree of diffuseness, and an overspreading of poetic energy. Nor does he convey any strong sense of her individuality. But he does convey a sense of youthful sweetness – and of the triumph of transcending physical desire. In one of the poems to Laraçuen he had written of the 'blood sports of desire'. Now he had passed this stage, and could write

> With you for mast and sail and flag,
> And anchor never known to drag,
> Death's narrow but oppressive sea
> Looks not unnavigable to me.

He put his new feeling best himself, when he wrote in the foreword to his *Poems 1970–1972*:

> Little need be added to my *Foreword* in the *Green Sailed Vessel* [published in a limited edition only, 1971 – the poems are all collected in the *1970–1972* volume]. I wrote there that, now well into my seventy-sixth year, I had been increasingly concerned with hidden powers of poetic thought, which raise and solve problems of advanced mathematics and physics. The word 'poetry' meant in Greek the 'act of making' – a sense that has survived in the old Scottish word for a poet, namely 'Maker'. . . . The poetic power to make things happen, as understood for instance by the early medieval Irish master-poets, and by their Middle Eastern Sufic contemporaries, raises simply love-alliances to a point where physical absence supplies living presence. These experiences occur not only in the fourth dimension, where prison walls are easily cheated . . . but in the fifth, where time proves as manipulable as is vertical or lateral space in the usual third dimension, and where seemingly impossible coincidences and so-called 'Acts of God' occur almost as a matter of course. In poetry, the fifth-dimensional coidentification of lovers is truth rather than idealistic fancy. . . .

And so even in the last poems he was bent upon insisting that his idealism, his search for the miraculous and the impossible, was no dream, but 'truth'. Thus he elegantly ends as he clumsily but doggedly began:

When you are old as I now am
I shall be young as you, my lamb;
For lest love's timely force should fail
The Serpent swallows his own tail.

But serenity for Graves is a comparative state: he has remained true, to the end, to the unrest of romantic love. The very last poem he wrote contains both serenity and unrest: the joy of having, and the restless and disturbing joy of not having.

Let the weeks end as well they must
Not with clouds of scattered dust
But in pure certainty of sun –
And with gentle winds outrun
By the love that we contest
In these green woods of unrest.
You, love, are beauty's self indeed,
Never the harsh pride of need.

V

Graves's eightieth birthday came – an occasion for a gathering of many of his friends – and went. He found that by now he remembered events long past with sometimes piercing clarity, but that yesterday was often a blur. He lost altogether the concentration needed to write poems, though he said as late as November 1976 (to me) that he quite often felt that a poem was 'on its way'. But none came, and he lives now mostly in the past – and often in that of the war in which he so nearly lost his life.

When he was very tired and almost too ill to care, news came through that the BBC were actually shooting a version of *I, Claudius* scripted by the late Jack Pulman. Graves gave his last interview on television (1976) just before the first episode of this long serial was transmitted. He had been on the set – there is a picture of him, with George Baker, who played Tiberius – and enjoyed watching the filming until he became exhausted, which he now quickly did. After all the vicissitudes which this, the most famous of his books, had been through, the event should have been a triumph. But it was clear that he had now 'retired'.

The first critical reactions were tepid; but the serial soon became one of the most successful the BBC has ever put out. He saw only the first two episodes in English – specially shown to him before he had to go home. He enjoyed them, but was still unwell; he could only be as enthusiastic as his health allowed, and at this point his health was bad. Contractual problems, involving options sold many years back, meant that he at first received little from the screening – though the Penguin reissue was on the best-seller lists for months at a time, and this brought in welcome royalties. After his return to Mallorca from England in late 1976, he began to be preoccupied with his old war experiences. He seemed indifferent to *Claudius*. But he much enjoyed it when Beryl read it to him at nights, and would sometimes ask, surprised, 'Did I write that?' Eventually this period of preoccupation passed over, and he attained more serenity. While it lasted it was painful. In early 1977 he declared, as he quite often did, that he had murdered a lot of men. His interlocutor politely demurred: 'That's hardly murder,' and Graves answered emphatically, in his confident and authoritative voice of thirty years back: 'It is, you know.' It was a strangely moving moment, and reminds us that his adult life began with sudden and unexpected slaughter. Since then he has made as long a journey – through nightmare – as most of us would wish to take, and one in which the baleful figure of Laura Riding stands out, a bleak and still enigmatic landmark.

Claudius continues to be transmitted all over the world; one feels that he could say something about it if he wanted to, and that his mind occasionally wanders back to the days of its genesis. He writes no more poetry – he ceased to talk about it at all in 1977, though he still enjoys having his poems read to him, and still praises Hardy. Nor does he write letters. But now he 'enjoys his Sunday', and will often suddenly interject a sharply appropriate remark into any conversation that may be going on around him.

But there is another figure, most important of all, without whom all of his poetry since 1938, *The White Goddess*, what peace of mind he has since then had, his Muses, the comforts of his old age, and much else good and happy besides, could never have been. This is his true muse, the one who never expected or wanted a capital letter.

Often he has talked of a poet's ending his life, if he is fortunate, in the secret garden of a woman. There is no doubt in whose secret garden he now lives: that of the woman to whom he wrote – to use an adjective he hates – his greatest love poems:

In your sleepy eyes I read the journey
Of which disjointedly you tell; which stirs
My loving admiration, that you should travel
Through nightmare to a lost and moated land
Who are timorous by nature.

Notes

As I have mentioned in the introduction, many of those people and institutions who kindly gave me information, or supplied me with copies of letters and documents, did so only on the condition that their anonymity would be preserved. They are referred to in these notes as 'anon.' – whether singular or plural.

Chapter One

The material for this and the four chapters that follow is drawn, mainly, from Graves's own autobiography, *Goodbye to All That*, from his father's *To Return to All That* (1930), and from many conversations with R.G.; also from general family history and other matters related to me by the late John Graves – R.G.'s brother – and by anon., a member of the family and a close friend of R.G.'s from early childhood.

p. 4   *The Graves family pedigree . . .* : there has been some fierce argument in the family over this. Certainly R.G. made many careless errors, but his brother John, self-styled 'guardian of the family honour', was not more accurate. I have relied mostly on anon., also a member of the family.

p. 9   *Amy . . . was not shocked . . .* : I have preferred A.P.'s version over R.G.'s here.

Chapter Two

p. 13   *What he felt about Charterhouse . . .* : this is one of the first things he told me when we first met (March 1943) – I suppose because I was at a public school, a situation he (and I) regarded as horrible at the time.

p. 18   *But he knew his wind was not good enough . . .* : both Beryl Graves and I believe that it was cherry *brandy*, and so he inadvertently told me in 1943. But I have stuck to his 'whisky', as when I spoke to him about it more recently he was insistent about it.

p. 21   *He told Edward Marsh . . .* : O'Prey, in *In Broken Images* (Hutchinson, 1982), prints the letter, and this reveals that Graves put back the *John Bull* revelation by almost two years in *Goodbye*. This was not deliberate: it arose from his tendency to synchronize the shock of his physical wound with the shock of this mental one.

Chapter Three

Graves did not talk much about his war experiences until he was past eighty, but he described some of them to me in detail in the fifties and then again in 1977, when he was going through a painful process of reliving them. Many of his letters to Marsh, and Marsh's letters to him, are printed by O'Prey, whose selection is excellent.

Chapter Four

p. 49   *The first letter . . .* : R.G.'s account is confused; I have followed A.P.'s chronology.

p. 50   *To an inquirer . . .* : the letter, to a stranger, did not get posted.

p. 50   *He suffered no permanent injury . . .* : his lung wound continued to seep lymph whenever he had a chest infection; I have seen this myself in 1953.

Chapter Five

The letters of Owen, and to Owen from Graves, are in *Wilfred Owen: Collected Letters* (OUP, 1967).

p. 55   *Then in July a letter arrived . . .* : Sassoon's version differs from R.G.'s. It is now impossible to sort out the true sequence of events. Probably Sassoon's is more accurate.

p. 66   *He has explained . . .* : memorably, to an angry Cambridge undergraduate who visited Palma in 1952. But he has not been as generous about Owen as he might have been.

Chapter Six

Much of the material for this chapter is drawn from Graves's autobiography, but is supplemented by the information he gave me in the years 1951–54 about his feelings at that time. John Graves gave me some information from which confirmatory inferences could be drawn, although his attitude was one of continued disapproval.

p. 76   *Quennell* ... : in his *Sign of the Fish* (Weidenfeld & Nicolson, 1964).

p. 79   *Nancy impressed those who knew her* ... : this is the unanimous verdict of those who knew both at the time. Edith Sitwell reported that Nancy told her that Robert was exceptional among men (Geoffrey Elborn, *Edith Sitwell*, Sheldon Press, 1981); but this is the only instance I have been able to find.

Chapter Seven

The sources for this chapter are mainly derived from anon. friends, from R.G. himself, from sporadic conversations with Edmund Blunden, and from James Reeves's reminiscences in letters to me of his many conversations with Blunden and with F. W. Bateson. The relationship with Blunden is well brought out in the letters O'Prey prints.

p. 80   *(his brother was ... so upset ...)*: Blunden to Reeves on several occasions. He seemed obsessed by the incident, which is perhaps understandable, since R.G. could occasionally be exceedingly offensive in this manner. It disappeared as he grew older.

p. 81   *It was Simpson – of whom he wrote* ... : to M.S.-S.

p. 82   *She disapproved* ... : Graves began his habit of 'finding shoulders to weep on', as his brother John put it with malicious accuracy, at about this time. He was now surrounded by intelligent people, and he never really learned discretion (although, as particularly with Riding, there are important exceptions).

p. 82   *Not long before his death F. W. Bateson* ... : in that part of his entry in *World Authors* (H. W. Wilson, 1975) contributed by him.

p. 83   *W. H. R. Rivers*: by a coincidence 'Dick' had come under his care after the Canadian soldier incident; Rivers pronounced him 'cured', and fit to enlist. In his entry in *Who's Who* as Baron Derwent, after the Second World War, he listed as his recreation 'Just loving the twentieth century'. It was as much his being an awful little squirt as anything else that embarrassed R.G.

p. 87   *Of the reading ... Graves ... wrote* ... : I cannot identify his correspondent. Evidently someone sent him a quotation from his own letter, but not the letter. It is among his papers, but with no identifying names.

p. 88   *Graves was privately unenthusiastic* ... : he told me he knew it would be a 'bloody disaster'.

p. 97   *Graves knew Freud* ... : R.G. has always been markedly anti-Freudian in his public utterances. But in private, when pressed, he is a little less hostile. What he dislikes is Freudian dogma. He had a perfectly good understanding of the Oedipus complex as Rivers expounded it to him, but later insisted that it was really a hippopotamus complex (on learned grounds). His final position on the way poetry comes into existence does have an affinity with Freud's views. For Jung, despite the 'Eternal Feminine', he has nothing but contempt – much to the disappointment of many.

Chapter Eight

p. 107   *Monro . . . experimented 'with too long lines'*: to M.S.-S., 1943.

Chapter Nine

The material for this chapter, and for much else on Riding in this book, is based on mainly anonymous information. I am sorry this should be so. Riding's capacity for generosity and good fun has been acknowledged by many. The standard works on the Fugitive Movement are: J. M. Bradbury, *The Fugitives* (North Carolina Press, 1958); L. Cowan, *The Fugitive Group* (University of Louisana Press, 1959); J. L. Stewart, *The Burden of Time* (Princeton University Press, 1969). The author of the last book had access to a great deal more information than the others. T. S. Matthews's *Jacks or Better* (Harper, 1977; in England *Under the Influence*, Cassell, 1978), speaks for itself. I have used it only with care. In two sentences about my wife and myself Matthews makes six errors! None the less, it is valuable as a chronicle of impressions, even if certain of these are wayward. Joyce Wexler's *Laura Riding's Pursuit of Truth* (Ohio University Press, 1979), has been described by Riding as 'malignant drivel'. It was started with its subject's approval, but finished without it. It reads as though it has been heavily cut; it is without malice to a fault. I wrote a book about Riding's poetry in the fifties, but threw it away recently. I had a correspondence with her in the early sixties, in which I whined in an unseemly way about Graves (I told him about it later); she dismissed me with a few fairly accurate epithets, for which I hold no grudge – but her 'judging by hearsay' (see p. 291) was wrong. I should say, since she inevitably comes into this book a great deal, that I doubt if anyone has ever written more astonishing poetry – but I wish that she could be more friendly and less prone to believe that people wish her ill. I have good reason to know what the real situation is. Her accounts of her time with R.G. are more copious than his with her (he has said hardly anything, and written less), and I cannot marry some of her assertions with what I know to be true. Despite what she may imagine, she has almost everyone's good wishes. My attitude towards her in this book reflects, I find, the sort of exasperation often felt about respected people who make 'large claims'. Of the anonymous material sent me, mentioned at the beginning of this book, I have used only a fragment; I have shown it to no one. I have not been able even to form a guess as to the sender, but he/she must be a collector, if only of Ridingiana. The only suspect, if he can be called even that, recently died. Riding's second husband, Schuyler Jackson, obviously had, or developed, remarkable qualities; but they could not have been literary, or have pertained to literature.

p. 123 *Louis Gottschalk* . . . : Gottschalk had more to say of his first wife in private than he had in public.

p. 127 *'Mrs Gottschalk and Hirsch quarreled* . . .': she and Hirsch had certain characteristics and interests in common, and it is possible that their encounters – always unfortunate – provide a valuable key to her subsequent history.

Chapter Ten

Material for this chapter is based on reminiscences by several anon., and on letters from and telephone conversations with John Graves. The only good interpretation of T. E. Lawrence is *A Prince of Our Disorder*, by John Mack (Weidenfeld & Nicolson, 1976). Mack visited Graves in Mallorca while he was writing it. I am much indebted to it. There are a few things about Lawrence that Mack could not say in the book, owing to the threat of libel action by a known blackmailer.

p. 135 *Edith Sitwell*: the book is now in the library of the University of Wisconsin, where I encountered it quite by chance while I was there in 1971–72.

p. 136 *In any case, as she told a friend* . . . : John Graves to M.S.-S.; and the friend, anon., to M.S.-S.

p. 141 *Ironically, he was educating her* . . . : Riding had a fair grounding in philosophy, and seems to have read Leibniz – to whom she is indebted – although not Russell on Leibniz. She read and wrote French very well, but she disapproved of French poetry. For her work on Nietzsche she relied on wholly inaccurate translations into English, as Graves did, though he had read Nietzsche's poems in German. Undoubtedly Graves was her chief educator, though he did not think of it in that way.

Chapter Eleven

The late Norman Cameron and others told me many of the details and subsequent history of the Seizin Press. The Press and its imprint certainly belong to Graves, as Riding gave them to him, in writing, in 1939. A few misinformed commentators have stated differently. He used the imprint to publish poems by Jay MacPherson and Terence Hards, in 1952 and 1964.

p. 151 *Graves and Riding lived* . . . *together* . . . *even though Riding later* . . . : I have a copy of this puzzling letter, and have seen the original.

p. 151   *On one occasion John Graves...*: John Graves in a letter to M.S.-S., 1977.

Chapter Twelve

The material for this and the following chapters comes mainly from a series of documents, including the 'Précis', now in private hands. There are notes of conversations, letters by Graves and Riding and Frank O'Connor, and the inimitable letters of Phibbs. Further confirmatory details come from Cameron, R.G. and anon.

p. 153   *'I knew something ... frightful was going to happen'*: he told me this in 1949 when the row with Riding over *The Common Asphodel* was going on. Receiving a letter from her made him unusually reminiscent on the subject for a few days.

p. 155   *'Précis'*: I have quoted from this throughout. It was written by R.G. (though not typed by him), though there are one or two small corrections in Riding's hand. All the quoted material is from this document unless otherwise indicated.

Chapter Thirteen

p. 172   *'awful bastard'*: to M.S.-S. several times, most recently in 1977; but good-humouredly and with some pity for Phibbs.

p. 174   *She later told one of her children...*: Catherine Dalton, who told me in 1977. This is recorded as her impression. I do not think it comes near to being the case: as will be seen, she took responsibility literally as soon as she could.

p. 174   *Towards the end of her life she said...*: to John Graves.

p. 184   *'he wanted children of his own'*: Catherine Dalton has fond memories of him, and told me he was 'a good substitute father'.

Chapter Fourteen

O'Prey prints a very good selection of the Graves–Sassoon correspondence, as well as some of the Graves–Stein correspondence, including Stein's final and not, I think, accurate aspersions on Riding. These were based, I am told, on a row they had about rescuing a Jew from Nazi territory: Stein was for, Riding against, but on practical grounds. But Riding quarrelled with Stein before this, and 'the quarrel was of her choice', I am told by someone who was with Riding at the time. I had great difficulty with the facts about the quarrel about rescuing someone from the Nazis, because a witness insisted that he/she was present at the quarrel in England – but this meant, chronologically, that Stein had made a visit to England which has gone entirely

unrecorded by any of her biographers. It has been much bandied about that
Stein said of Riding, 'She always thought she was Jesus Christ'. Someone did
say this, but not Stein, or a person of her calibre.

Chapter Fifteen

Sources for this and the following chapters include Cameron, R.G., testimony
of people associated with R.G. and Riding at this time (anon.), Matthews's
Jacks or Better (quadruple checked), and local people. There also exist the
unpublished typescript memoirs of one who was very close to R.G. and Riding
in these years; I have been allowed to read the relevant parts of these candid
and curious memoirs, and am most grateful to the person who made this
possible. They confirm the general accuracy of my account.

p. 213   *By the time Laura had made the novel* . . . : she has several times
         stated that she had nothing to do with *No Decency Left.*
p. 218   *At one point* . . . : Cameron to M.S.-S.; and in the unpublished
         memoirs referred to above.

Chapter Sixteen

The sources for this chapter are the same as for the last; I am also grateful to
Eirlys Roberts, who kindly gave time to talk to me, and who was full of good
humour and kindly reminiscence about all those concerned.

p. 232   *Perhaps he had been indulging in* . . . : Mary Reeves (née Phillips)
         to M.S.-S.

Chapter Seventeen

Sources for this chapter include R.G.'s diary, James Reeves, John Graves, the
late George Ellidge. I ought to say that George Ellidge and Graves at first got
on very well. George Ellidge, who struggled against a grave illness with great
courage, was a most agreeable companion. He was eventually 'expelled' from
Deyá, by Riding.

p. 242   *Riding, John wrote* . . . : to M.S.-S., January 1977.
p. 259   *The letter Graves wanted to write* . . . : R.G. to M.S.-S.
p. 259   *Graves did complain* . . . : to M.S.-S., for one, at great length. He
         was genuinely disappointed with Lawrence, and perhaps rightly.

Chapter Eighteen

Sources for this chapter, and the following, include the diary, Alan Hodge,
Cameron, James Reeves – and many others who met R.G. and Riding while
they were in England.

Chapter Twenty

p. 300   *Riding went to see Bosman . . .* : Bosman and other partners in Dent
told both my father and Richard Church – who told me – that Riding
had sold them the dictionary 'on Graves's name'. But they may have
misunderstood, as she told R.G. later that she never mentioned his
name. It is unlikely that she did, though they may have done.

Chapter Twenty-Two

The chief sources for this chapter are anonymous. Alan Hodge contributed
greatly to my understanding of the American episode: he was the perfect
impartial witness, since he never twisted facts to suit himself. Certain
Americans, not literary people, have confirmed details.

p. 340   *So a verbal deal was made . . .* : there is no doubt about this. But it
must be said that for some time R.G. himself paid lip-service to
Jackson's excellence, which was unwise. He did not take the advice
he gave me in 1943: 'Always say what you think.' Nor have I dared.
I think Riding's idea was to set R.G. up at some conveniently distant
place, say the house next to Einstein's, and draw on the royalties she
presumed he would make from historical novels. He would not have
given her, at least, any impression he would not have been willing to
do this for the common good (etc.) until after he returned to England;
he pretended to himself that he would return, though he knew in his
heart he would not.

Chapter Twenty-Three

p. 359   *As Graves put it in 1943 . . .* : to M.S.-S.
p. 360   *Quoz . . .* : this was the projected title of an exchange of letters,
never published, between R.G. and Alastair Reid in the mid-fifties.
The letters were not spontaneous. It was a scheme by which R.G.
could tell as much, or as little, as he liked about his life and opinions.
Reid acted as foil. I have quoted from this extensively later in the
book. It was not published because of the quarrel with Reid.

Chapter Twenty-Four

p. 385   *Indeed,* I, Claudius *was in Germany . . .* : I cannot confirm this, but
believe that it was one of the code books used by the conspirators.
p. 388   *Thus, in conversation in about 1965 . . .* : information from one of
the anthropologists.

Chapter Twenty-Five

p. 393   *King Jesus sold* . . . : he did not want it reprinted for some time after
writing *The Nazarene Gospel Restored*, but later relented, telling
himself that it was written as fiction. It was reprinted by Cassell and
1960 and 1962.

Chapter Twenty-Seven

p. 424   *When Laura Riding said in 1940* . . . : the complexities of this property transfer are impossible to unravel, not least because Gelat acted
crookedly or at least unstraightforwardly. J. Matthias's statement in
Poetry Nation 14, 1980, that Riding 'deeded' R.G. the property
simply does not cover the case. Anyhow, Riding could legally have
taken everything; she did not.

Chapter Twenty-Nine

p. 457   *On 27 January 1953* . . . *of the two Guillermo Massot flats*: my
wife and I had moved to another flat in a nearby street.

p. 458   *Not long after* . . . *came news of Norman Cameron's early
death* . . . : on the day the telegram (from Alan Hodge) arrived, he
sat around, unable to work. I heard the news from Beryl and went
to him and said, 'So Norman's dead?' (We knew that he had been
very ill.) He answered: 'Oh, yes, he's dead all right. Never played
safe, Norman. I've always played it safe.' As usual, he refused to
display his real feelings; soon he was back at work again.

Chapter Thirty

p. 492   *James made no secret of what he thought*: I was then working with
him, two days a week, and he seemed obsessed with the matter.

Chapter Thirty-One

pp. 507–8   *Little that is reliable leaks out about* . . . *the Nobel Prize for
Literature*: my information from a Swedish anon. is that in 1962
R.G. was 'beaten' by the merest whisker – owing to the objections
of a member of the committee who was convinced that his work was
not 'avant garde'.

p. 515   *Watt's solicitors* . . . *'really believed what they said'*: I should be
obliged if any lawyer amongst my readers could tell me if this defence
has ever been used, and, if so, whether it was successful. If so, I could

make a fortune. The attacks on Graves in the book in question seemed and seem to me plain libellous, in the technical sense.

Chapter Thirty-Two

p. 532 *He had to sell a large number of his manuscripts* ... : he did not sort these out himself.

p. 536 *In a letter of 8 July 1965 ... poem from a newspaper* ... : the *Scotsman*, of which I was acting as poetry editor: the literary editor had asked me to produce the 'symposium'.

Chapter Thirty-Three

p. 553 *He heard from him on 20 February 1966*: Blunden was genuinely surprised and a little ashamed (of his previous spiteful talk) by R.G.'s advocacy of his cause, as he told James Reeves.

p. 555 *He did not do this in collaboration with Idries* ... : I am reliably informed that Idries Shah would never have anything to do with or make any comment upon this matter. Whether this was friendly or not, I cannot say. Certainly he could — and still can — cast light on it if he chooses to do so. Let him confirm or deny his brother's claim.

p. 567 *His interlocutor* ... : M.S.-S.

Books by Robert Graves

Poetry

Over the Brazier, Poetry Bookshop, London, 1916; St Martin's Press, New York, 1975.

Goliath and David, Chiswick Press, London, 1916.

Fairies and Fusiliers, Heinemann, London, 1917; Knopf, New York, 1918.

The Treasure Box, Chiswick Press, London, 1919.

Country Sentiment, Secker, London, 1920; Knopf, New York, 1920.

The Pier-Glass, Secker, London, 1921; Knopf, New York, 1921.

Whipperginny, Heinemann, London, 1922; Knopf, New York, 1923.

The Feather Bed, Hogarth Press, Richmond, Surrey, 1923.

Mock Beggar Hall, Hogarth Press, London, 1924.

Welchman's Hose, The Fleuron, London, 1925; Folcroft Editions, Folcroft, Penn., 1971.

(Poems), Benn, London, 1925.

The Marmosite's Miscellany (as John Doyle), Hogarth Press, London, 1925.

Poems (1914–1926), Heinemann, London, 1927; Doubleday, New York, 1929.

Poems (1914–1927), Heinemann, London, 1927.

Poems 1929, Seizin Press, London, 1929.

Ten Poems More, Hours Press, Paris, 1930.

Poems 1926–1930, Heinemann, London, 1931.

To Whom Else?, Seizin Press, Deyá, Mallorca, 1931.

Poems 1930–1933, Barker, London, 1933.

Collected Poems, Cassell, London, 1938; Random House, New York, 1938.

No More Ghosts: Selected Poems, Faber, London, 1940.

Work in Hand, with Norman Cameron and Alan Hodge, Hogarth Press, London, 1942.

(Poems), Eyre and Spottiswoode, London, 1943.

Poems 1938–1945, Cassell, London, 1945; Creative Age Press, New York, 1946.

Collected Poems (1914–1947), Cassell, London, 1948.

Poems and Satires 1951, Cassell, London, 1951.

Poems 1953, Cassell, London, 1953.

Collected Poems 1955, Doubleday, New York, 1955.

Poems Selected by Himself, Penguin, Harmondsworth, 1957; rev. 1961, 1966, 1972.

The Poems of Robert Graves, Doubleday, New York, 1958.

Collected Poems 1959, Cassell, London, 1959.

The Penny Fiddle: Poems for Children, Cassell, London, 1960; Doubleday, New York, 1961.

More Poems 1961, Cassell, London, 1961.

Collected Poems, Doubleday, New York, 1961.

New Poems 1962, Cassell, London, 1962; as *New Poems*, Doubleday, New York, 1963.

The More Deserving Cases: Eighteen Old Poems for Reconsideration, Marlborough College Press, Marlborough, 1962; Folcroft Editions, Folcroft, Penn., 1978.

Man Does, Woman Is 1964, Cassell, London, 1964; Doubleday, New York, 1964.

Ann at Highwood Hall: Poems for Children, Cassell, London, 1964.

Love Respelt, Cassell, London, 1965.

Collected Poems 1965, Cassell, London, 1965.

Seventeen Poems Missing from 'Love Respelt', Stellar Press, Barnet, Hertfordshire, 1966.

Collected Poems 1966, Doubleday, New York, 1966.

Colophon to 'Love Respelt', Stellar Press, Barnet, Hertfordshire, 1967.

(Poems) (with D. H. Lawrence), Longman, London, 1967.

Poems 1965–1968, Cassell, London, 1968; Doubleday, New York, 1969.

Poems about Love, Cassell, London, 1969; Doubleday, New York, 1969.

Love Respelt Again, Doubleday, New York, 1969.

Beyond Giving, Stellar Press, Barnet, Hertfordshire, 1969.

Poems 1968–1970, Cassell, London, 1970.

Advice From a Mother, Poem-of-the-Month Club, London, 1970.

The Green-Sailed Vessel, Stellar Press, Barnet, Hertfordshire, 1971.

Corgi Modern Poets in Focus 3 (selection), Corgi, London, 1971.

Poems: Abridged for Dolls and Princes, Cassell, London, 1971; Doubleday, New York, 1971.

Poems 1970–1972, Cassell, London, 1972; Doubleday, New York, 1973.

Deyá, Motif Editions, London, 1973.

Timeless Meeting: Poems, Rota, London, 1973.

At the Gate, Rota, London, 1974.

Collected Poems 1975, Cassell, London, 1975.
New Collected Poems, Doubleday, New York, 1977.

Play

John Kemp's Wager, Blackwell, Oxford, 1925; T. B. Edwards, New York, 1925.

Fiction

My Head! My Head!, Secker, London, 1925; Knopf, New York, 1925.
The Shout, Matthews and Marrot, London, 1929.
No Decency Left (with Laura Riding) (as Barbara Rich), Cape, London, 1932.
The Real David Copperfield, Barker, London, 1933; as David Copperfield, by Charles Dickens, Condensed by Robert Graves, ed. M. P. Paine, Harcourt Brace, New York, 1934.
I, Claudius, Barker, London, 1934; Smith and Haas, New York, 1934.
Claudius the God and his Wife Messalina, Barker, London, 1934; Smith and Haas, New York, 1935.
Antigua, Penny, Puce, Seizin Press, Deyá, Mallorca, and Constable, London, 1936; Random House, New York, 1937.
Count Belisarius, Cassell, London, 1938; Random House, New York, 1938.
Sergeant Lamb of the Ninth, Methuen, London, 1940; as Sergeant Lamb's America, Random House, New York, 1940.
Proceed, Sergeant Lamb, Methuen, London, 1941; Random House, New York, 1941.
The Story of Mary Powell: Wife to Mr Milton, Cassell, London, 1943; as Wife to Mr Milton: The Story of Mary Powell, Creative Age Press, New York, 1944.
The Golden Fleece, Cassell, London, 1944; as Hercules, My Shipmate, Creative Age Press, New York, 1945.
King Jesus, Cassell, London, 1946; Creative Age Press, New York, 1946.
Watch the North Wind Rise, Creative Age Press, New York, 1949; as Seven Days in New Crete, Cassell, London, 1949.
The Islands of Unwisdom, Doubleday, New York, 1949; as The Isles of Unwisdom, Cassell, London, 1950.
Homer's Daughter, Cassell, London, 1955; Doubleday, New York, 1955.
They Hanged My Saintly Billy, Cassell, London, 1957; Doubleday, New York, 1957.
!Catacrok! Mostly Stories, Mostly Funny, Cassell, London, 1956.
Collected Short Stories, Doubleday, New York, 1964; Cassell, London, 1965; as The Shout, Penguin, London, 1978.
An Ancient Castle, Peter Owen, London, 1980.

Other

On English Poetry, Knopf, New York, 1922; Heinemann, London, 1922.

The Meaning of Dreams, Cecil Palmer, London, 1924; Greenberg, New York, 1925.

Poetic Unreason and Other Studies, Cecil Palmer, London, 1925.

Contemporary Techniques of Poetry: A Political Analogy, Hogarth Press, London, 1925; Folcroft Editions, Folcroft, Penn., 1977.

Another Future of Poetry, Hogarth Press, London, 1926.

Inpenetrability; or, The Proper Habit of English, Hogarth Press, London, 1926.

The English Ballad: A Short Critical Survey, Benn, London, 1927; revised as *English and Scottish Ballads*, Heinemann, London, 1957; Macmillan, New York, 1957.

Lars Porsena: or, the Future of Swearing and Improper Language, Kegan Paul Trench Trubner, London, 1927; Dutton, New York, 1927; revised as *The Future of Swearing and Improper Language*, Kegan Paul Trench Trubner, London, 1936.

A Survey of Modernist Poetry (with Laura Riding), Heinemann, London, 1927; Doubleday, New York, 1928.

Lawrence and the Arabs, Cape, London, 1927; as *Lawrence and the Arabian Adventure*, Doubleday, New York, 1928.

A Pamphlet Against Anthologies (with Laura Riding), Cape, London, 1928; as *Against Anthologies*, Doubleday, New York, 1928.

Mrs Fisher; or the Future of Humour, Kegan Paul Trench Trubner, London, 1928; Folcroft Editions, Folcroft, Penn., 1974.

Goodbye to All That: An Autobiography, Cape, London, 1929; Cape and Smith, New York, 1930; rev., Doubleday, New York, 1957; Cassell, London, 1957; Penguin, Harmondsworth, 1960.

But It Still Goes On: A Miscellany, Cape, London, 1930; Cape and Smith, New York, 1930.

T. E. Lawrence to His Biographer Robert Graves, Doubleday, New York, 1938; Faber, London, 1939.

The Long Weekend (with Alan Hodge), Faber, London, 1940; Macmillan, New York, 1941.

The Reader Over Your Shoulder (with Alan Hodge), Cape, London, 1943; Macmillan, New York, 1944.

The White Goddess, Faber, London, 1948; Creative Age Press, New York, 1948; rev., Faber, London, 1952, 1966; Knopf, New York, 1958.

The Common Asphodel: Collected Essays on Poetry 1922–1949, Hamish Hamilton, London, 1949; Folcroft Editions, Folcroft, Penn., 1971.

Occupation: Writer, Creative Age Press, New York, 1950; Cassell, London, 1951.

The Nazarene Gospel Restored (with Joshua Podro), Cassell, London, 1953; Doubleday, New York, 1954.

The Crowning Privilege: The Clark Lectures, 1954–5, Cassell, London, 1955; Doubleday, New York, 1956.

Adam's Rib, Trianon Press, London, 1955; Yoseloff, New York, 1958.

The Greek Myths, 2 vols., Penguin, London and Baltimore, 1955.

Jesus in Rome (with Joshua Podro), Cassell, London, 1957.

Steps, Cassell, London, 1958.

5 Pens in Hand, Doubleday, New York, 1958.

Food for Centaurs, Doubleday, New York, 1960.

Greek Gods and Heroes, Doubleday, New York, 1960; as *Myths of Ancient Greece*, Cassell, London, 1961.

Selected Poetry and Prose (ed. James Reeves), Hutchinson, London, 1961.

Oxford Addresses on Poetry, Cassell, London, 1961; Doubleday, New York, 1962.

The Siege and Fall of Troy, Cassell, London, 1962; Doubleday, New York, 1963.

The Big Green Book, Crowell Collier, New York, 1962; Penguin, London, 1978.

Nine Hundred Iron Chariots, MIT, Cambridge, Mass, 1963.

The Hebrew Myths (with Raphael Patai), Doubleday, New York, 1964; Cassell, London, 1964.

Majorca Observed, Cassell, London, 1965; Doubleday, New York, 1965.

Mammon and the Black Goddess, Cassell, London, 1965; Doubleday, New York, 1965.

Two Wise Children, Harlen Quist, New York, 1966; W. H. Allen, London, 1967.

Poetic Craft and Principle, Cassell, London, 1967.

The Poor Boy Who Followed His Star, Cassell, London, 1968; Doubleday, New York, 1969.

The Crane Bag, Cassell, London, 1969.

On Poetry: Collected Talks and Essays, Doubleday, New York, 1969.

Difficult Questions, Easy Answers, Cassell, London, 1972; Doubleday, New York, 1973.

Editor

Oxford Poetry 1921 (with Alan Porter and Richard Hughes), Blackwell, Oxford, 1921.

John Skelton (Laureate), Benn, London, 1927.

The Less Familiar Nursery Rhymes, Benn, London, 1927.

The Comedies of Terence, Doubleday, New York, 1962; Cassell, London, 1963.

ROBERT GRAVES

Translator

Almost Forgotten Germany, by Georg Schwarz (with Laura Riding), Seizin Press, Deyá, Mallorca, and Constable, London, 1936; Random House, New York, 1936.

The Transformations of Lucius, Otherwise Known as the Golden Ass, by Apuleius, Penguin, London, 1950; Farrar Strauss, New York, 1951.

The Cross and the Sword, by Manuel de Jésus Galvan, Indiana University Press, Bloomington, 1955; Gollancz, London, 1956.

The Infant with the Globe, by Pedro Alarcón, Trianon Press, London, 1955; Yoseloff, New York, 1958.

Winter in Majorca, by George Sand, Cassell, London, 1956.

Pharsalia, by Lucan, Penguin, London, 1956.

The Twelve Caesars, by Suetonius, Penguin, London, 1957.

The Anger of Achilles: Homer's Iliad, Doubleday, New York, 1959; Cassell, London, 1950.

Rubaiyat of Omar Khayyam (with Omar Ali-Shah), Cassell, London, 1967; Doubleday, New York, 1968.

The Song of Songs, Clarkson Potter, New York, 1973; Collins, London, 1973.

The only bibliography, *A Bibliography of the Works of Robert Graves*, is by F. Higginson, Vane, London, 1966.

INDEX

INDEX

Abbott, Charles, purchase of Gravesiana, 506

Adelphi Press, NY, 137

Aesthetic Movement, and deaths in First World War, 74

Agate, James, 224

Agee, James, on *Cry Havoc* film, 454

Aiken, Conrad, 346

Alarcón, Pedro Antonio de, *The Infant with the Globe* (trans. by R.G.), 427

Aldington, Richard, 82, 250 hostile biography of T.E. Lawrence, 496

Aldridge, John, 232, 344, 360
  member of R.G./L.R. 'inner circle', 216, 218, 236, 250, 252, 267
  paintings, 216–17, 246, 248, 249
  'cynical wrapper' for *A Trojan Ending*, 278
  and word 'literal', 307

Allott, Kenneth, 277, 302

Alvarez, Alfred, 534

America, 458, 476
  R. G.'s lectures, 478, 527–8
  television appearance, 480
  poetry reading, 511

American Academy and Institute of Arts, 506, 511

Anderson, Sherwood, 460

Apuleius, Lucius, *The Golden Ass* (trans. by R.G.), 428
  proposed film, 515–16

Ardizzone, Edward,
  illustrates *Ann of Highwood Hall; The Penny Fiddle*, 505

Aristotle, dictum on fiction, 230

Arnold, Malcolm, 488

Arnold, Matthew, 2

Asbaje, Juana de, Mexican poet-prodigy, 467

Asquith, H.H., Earl of Oxford, 121

Atlantic Monthly, 458, 505
  'Mushrooms: Food of Gods', 502

Auden, W. H., 99, 150, 199, 372, 462
  R.G. on, 63, 101, 290, 373
  and Seizin Press, 148
  plagiarisms from L.R., 297, 302, 373
  Symons and, 308
  admirer of Yeats, 405
  and Professorship of Poetry at Oxford, 468, 507, 508, 554
  meeting with R.G., 507

King's Gold Medallist, 552
Spain, 285
Auden, W.H., and Lewis, C. D.,
  Oxford Poetry, 1927, 150
Austin, Alfred, Poet Laureate, 2–3
Australia, sales of *Old Soldiers
  Never Die*, 223
Austria, invasion of, 304

Bachofen, Johann Jacob, 233
  Das Mutterrecht
  (Mother-Right), 387
BBC
  R.G. interview for 'Frankly
    Speaking', 482
  television interview with Huw
    Wheldon, 487
  television serial *I, Claudius*, 566
Bain, A.W., bookseller, 148
Baker, Rev. Shirley, 427
Balcon, Sir Michael, 475
Baldwin, Stanley, first Earl
  Baldwin, 272, 382
Barker, Arthur and R.G./L.R.
  partnership, 224–5
  as R.G.'s publisher, 232, 245–6,
    266, 291
  failure, 358
Barker, George, 373
Barretto, Isabelle de, subject of *The
  Isles of Unwisdom*, 417, 418
Basham, Sergeant Johnny, 33
Bate, Stanley, 499
Bateson, F.W., 75, 82
Beecham, Audrey, 277
Beerbohm, Sir Max, 62, 63, 105
  R.G. on, 433–4;
  Zuleika Dobson, 433
Beggarstaff Brothers, 60
Belcher, George, 62
Bell, Clive, 55
Bennett, Arnold, 121
Bergman, Ingrid, and *Homer's
  Daughter*, 471, 472, 475,
  476, 478

Bible, the, R.G. and, 18, 20, 52,
  119, 285–6, 385, 380
  and Isaiah xxix, 110, 115, 134
  essay on Genesis (*Adam's Rib*),
    426
  changed view of Jesus, 428
  Song of Songs (trans.), 530
Biddle, Francis, US Attorney
  General, 479
Bilignin, 189
Blake, William, 37, 260
Blunden, Edmund, 81, 87, 105
  gassed in First World War, 35,
    80
  relationship with R.G., 80, 107,
    119
  anger at *Goodbye to All That*,
    196–7
  recording of his poems, 552
  Professor of Poetry, 553
  Undertones of War, 191
  'literary' estimation, 192, 193,
    194
Blunt, Wilfred Scawen, 553
Bogan, Louise, 185
  jealousy of L.R., 128, 181
Boland, Bridget, and *Claudius* film
  script, 483, 484, 485
Bold, Alan, 554
Bolt, Robert, 498
Borrow, George, *The Bible in
  Spain*, 268
Bosman, of Dent, 300, 576
Botkins, Rev. Gleb, and Church of
  Aphrodite, 431
Bottomley, Gordon on R.G., 106
  King Lear's Wife, 24
Bowen, J.C.E., trans., of *Rubaiyat*,
  556
Bowra, C. M., 54
Bracken, Brendan, 360
Brando, Marlon, cast to play
  Lawrence, 496, 498
Braziller, George, US publishers,
  461

Bridges, Robert
  Poet Laureate, 3, 289
  R.G. and his poetry, 83, 289
Bridgman, W.C., 58
Briffault, Robert
  R.G.'s debt to, 387
  The Mothers, 387–8
Brill, A.A., translator of Freud, 97
Britten, Benjamin, and *A Song for Sheba*, 488–9
Bronowski, Jacob, 470
  and Eirlys Roberts, 225
  and L.R., 225–6
  disliked by R.G., 226
Brooke, Rupert, 23, 24
  R.G.'s opinion of, 33, 34, 106
  death, 38, 39
  attraction for homosexuals, 74
  Collected Poems (with *Memoir* by Marsh), 106
Brown, John Mason, 480
Brown, Slater, 127
Browne (later Aldridge), Lucie, 216, 250
Browne, Maurice, asks R.G. for a play, 208, 209
Browning, Robert, 2, 260, 516
Buchan, John, Lord Tweedsmuir, 121
Bultmann, Rudolf, 'Form Criticism' of the Gospels, 429
Butler, Patricia, assistant to Watt, 294
Butler, Lord, offers R.G. CLitt, 530–31
Butler, Samuel, R.G. and, 133–4, 242
  Erewhon, 37
  The Way of All Flesh, 23

Cairns, Huntingdon, Director NY National Gallery, 479
Cameron, Norman, xi, 162, 312, 360

character, 150, 303, 304
RC convert, 150
relationship with R.G. and L.R., 150, 181, 216, 218, 220, 222, 316
Education Officer, Nigeria, 186, 216, 222
Ca'n Torrent house, 216, 220, 222, 223, 262
mixture of horror and awe towards L.R., 220–21, 303
resignation as 'Protocol' secretary, 316
disastrous marriage, 316, 435
and R.G./Nancy divorce, 436–7
dies in 1953, 458, 573
collected poems (posth.), 150
rewrite of *Pickwick Papers*, 224
Rimbaud translation (aided by L.R.), 279
'Forgive Me Sire,' 221
'The Wanton's Death', 221
The Winter House, 372

Cameron, Gretl, third wife of above, 150, 435

Campbell, Roy, 266
  Flowering Rifle; The Georgiad, 266

Cambridge University, R.G.'s antipathy towards, 216, 362, 435

Canelluñ, R.G.'s house in Deyá, 203, 206, 214, 217
  building project, 208, 223, 219, 247–8, 249
  L.R.'s 'literal' rule, 233
  atmosphere, 236
  return to in 1946, 412
  'transferred to' R.G. by L.R. (1940), 350, 424

Cape, Jonathan, 39, 224, 266
  published of L.R., 138, 209, 211, 224
  and *Revolt in the Desert*, 141–3
  and *Lawrence and the Arabs*, 141–2

589

and *Goodbye to All That*, 191, 194
Sassoon's anger, 195–6, 210
libel threat over *But It Still Goes On*, 210–11
end of publisher-author relations, 211–12, 224
refuses *The White Goddess*, 395–6
Carthusian, The, R.G., and, 19, 470
Casals, Pablo, R.G. as sponsor, 62
Cassells, publishers to R.G., 294, 301, 383, 396, 429, 449, 459, 481–2, 505
and L.R.'s *Poems*, 301, 305
unable to publish *The White Goddess*, 396
and love poems, 493
Catullus, influence on R.G., 52, 53
Cawston, Richard, television director, 552–3
Caxton, William, *Prologues and Epilogues*, 147
Chamberlain, Neville, 307, 314, 317, 325
Chambers Journal, 64
Chaplin, Charles Spencer, 520
Chase, James Hadley, 531
Château de la Chevrie, Montauban, last shared home of R.G. and L.R., 311, 312, 319, 321
departure from, 328
Chatto and Windus, 309, 322
Chillingworth, John, photographer, 453
Chilver, Elizabeth (Sally), 6, 279, 430
Chilver, Richard, husband of Sally Graves, 279
Chopin, Frédéric, in Mallorca, 203
Christianity, 5, 10, 19, 20
R.G. and, 95, 286, 389–90, 395, 429
failure of, 286
supplants paganism, 389

unsuitable religion for a poet, 392
and orthodoxy, 429
R.G.'s view of Paul, 429–30
Christie, Agatha (Sir Max and Lady Mallowan), 360
Church, Richard, essay on R.G. by, 373
Church of Aphrodite, NY, and *The White Goddess*, 431
Churchill, Sarah, and Vic Oliver, 268
Churchill, Sir Winston, 170, 370, 375
and R.G., 272, 363–4
Churchill, Lady, R.G. and Jenny, 268, 272
and *King Jesus*, 416
Cinema, the, R.G. and, 450–2, 471
Arabian Nights script, 441, 452, 473, 474, 477
Claudius, 473, 474
The Female, 471
Clare, John, part played by R.G. in rescue of reputation of, 87
Clark, Ronald, 56
Clark, Prof. S.D., poetry readings, 87
Classical Review, 461
Clifford, Alex, first husband of Jenny, 362, 410
Cobb, Richard, 534
Cobbold, Richard, *Margaret Catchpole*, Korda and, 292, 296
Cohen, Alexander, invites R.G. to make a musical, 486, 487
Coldstream, Nancy, companion of Louis MacNiece, 373
Coleridge, Samuel T., 98, 371, 545, 554
The Friend, 207
Colne Times, bad review of *Antigua*, 278–9
Conrad, Joseph, *Almayer's Folly*, 2
Constable, publisher, 262, 266, 294

and R.G./L.R. partnership, 246
and *Epilogue*, 247
and *A Trojan Ending*, 269, 278
Constructive Birth Control Society,
79
Cook, William, US expatriate
painter, 190
Cooper (later Graves), Jane, first
wife of A.P., 6, 8
Copthorne, Sussex, R.G. at school,
13
Corelli, Marie, *The Sorrows of
Satan*, 2
Cotterell, Anthony and Geoffrey,
362
Creative Age Press, USA, 343, 358,
383, 411, 416
publish *The White Goddess*,
413, 416–17, 418
and Doubleday's offer for *Isles
of Unwisdom*, 418–19
and *The New Cretans*, 419
see also Garrett, Eileen
Cowan, Louise, 127
Coward, Noël, 531
Cowley, Malcolm, and *Greek
Myths*, 459–60
Crane, Hart
L.R. reviews *White Buildings*,
138
on L.R.'s energy (Laura Riding
Roughshod), 127–8
Crosbie, Charles, Bishop of
Limerick, 5
Crosse, Patrick, second husband of
Jenny, 432–3
Cullen, John xii, 246
Cummings, E.E., 145
R.G. and, 374, 467, 479–80
The Enormous Room, 479
Cunard, Nancy, Hours Press, 211
Curtis Brown, 250
Cyprus, 135

Dahlberg, E., and Read, H., *Truth
is More Sacred*, 515
Daily Express, 468

Daily Herald, 78, 86
Daily Mail, 209, 325
Daily Mirror, 'Shopkeeping on
Parnassus', 88
Daily Telegraph, 274, 307
Dalton, G.C., husband of
Catherine Graves, 362–3
Dalton, Hugh, 382
Davidson, Donald, member of
Fugitives, 124, 126
Davidson, John, 3
Davies, W.H., 24, 86, 105, 205
Day, Douglas, on *Lawrence and the
Arabs*, 142
de la Mare, Walter, 105, 107, 209
de Maria, Bob, 561
Decker, Clarence B., president US
Poetry Society, 500, 501
Defoe, Daniel, *Colonel Jack*, 372
Dehn, Paul, 482
Dent, to publish the *Dictionary*,
307, 321
Devecseri, Gabor, Hungarian poet,
550–51, 561, 562
Deyá, Mallorca, x, 128, 311
foreign residents, 201
physical and natural features,
203–4
choice of by R.G., and L.R., 204
and Casa Salerosa, 206, 214
significance in R.G./L.R.
relationship, 205, 214, 277
position of Gelat, 218, 226, 262
anti-clericalism, 218
Canelluñ project (*see under*)
L.R. as legal owner of
'jointly-owned' properties,
223, 347, 415
sense of happiness, 236
joint purchase of Posada, 243,
248, 249, 262, 438
its memories of L.R., 264
influx of foreign visitors, 441
R.G. and his land ownership,
457
R.G. made an 'adopted' son, 551
hippy era, 560–61

Dickens, Charles
   David Copperfield rewrite, 199, 223-4
   Pickwick Papers rewrite, 224
   Dickensian, The, R.G.'s letter to, 224
Dickinson, Emily, 462
Dobree, Bonamy, R.G. and *The Floating Republic*, 374
Donne, John, 'Sweetest Love, I do not goe', 87, 355
Doubleday Doran, US publishers, 429, 449, 481, 502, 505
   and R.G.'s book on Lawrence, 141, 142
   invite R.G. to join their list, 418
   and *Greek Myths*, 460
   Anchor paperback series, 477
Doughty, C.M., 334
   Arabia Deserta; Adam Cast Forth; Dawn in Britain, 334, 350
Douglas, Keith, 132, 369
Du Gard, Roger Martin, Nobel Prize winner, 297-8
du Maurier, Daphne, 382
   The Scapegoat, 484, 485
Dunn, Capt., 35
Dunn, Dr, saves R.G.'s life, 53
   and *Goodbye to All That*, 197, 198
Dunne, J.W., *Experiment with Time*, 393

Earp, T.W. (Tommy), 54
Egypt, R.G. and, 77, 84, 121, 129-30, 131-3
El Dieff, and annotated copies of R.G.'s works, 196, 199
Eliot, T.S., 3, 99, 124, 372, 374
   R.G. and his poetry, 82, 86, 373
   proto-modernist, 97, 98
   his 'ideal' poet (himself), 98
   and origins of poetry, 98
   and his first wife, 98
   and R.G.'s poetry, 112-13
   his kind of poetry, 113, 114
   attack on anthologists, 145
   and *The White Goddess*, 398-9, 431, 432
   meetings with R.G., 398, 431-2
   and Pound's predicament, 399
   The Sacred Wood, 1920, and detachment in poetry, 98
   and sensibility, 98
   The Waste Land, 86
Ellidge, George, 575
   and *14A*, 246
   marries Honor Wyatt, 246
Ellis, T.P., and Lloyd, J., trans of *The Mabinogion*, 403
Empson, William
   R.G. on, 145
   Seven Types of Ambiguity, 145
Engels, Friedrich, *The Origin of the Family*, 233
Evans, Lt Comd., of HMS *Grenville*, 265
Evans, Joan, *Winged Pharaoh*, 309
Evening Standard, R.G.'s obituary of Lawrence, 259
Every Irishman's Library, 6

Faber and Faber, 223, 232, 266, 355
   and T.E. Lawrence book, 302
   publish *The White Goddess*, 398
Farson, Daniel, 453-4
Fascism, 263-4, 265, 266, 283, 314
   R.G. and, 364
Fawcus, Arnold, and R.G./Beryl's trans. of *Nino de la Bola*, 442
Fernandel, 452, 477
First World War, 564
   outbreak, 31
   initial belief in its brevity, 31, 34
   R.G. in training and arrival in France, 32-4, 36

shatters myth of human progress, 34
nature of its battles, 34–5, 40
trench system, 35
no-man's-land, 39
Somme offensive, 45, 47, 48
behaviour of the Scots, 50
the Armistice, 67
post-war neuroses, 76
Fitzgerald, Edward, his *Rubaiyat* of Omar Khayyam, 530
denigrated by R.G., 556, 557
R.G.'s new translation, 555–8
assisted by Omar Ali-Shah, 555–8
Flecker, James Elroy, 23
Fletcher, Frank, headmaster of Charterhouse, and R.G./monitor encounter, 27, 28
Flint, F.S., 82
Flower, Desmond, publisher to R.G., 301, 302
and L.R.'s *Collected Poems*, 308–9, 320–21
and *King Jesus*, 396
Folk Song Society, 6
Ford, Hugh, and naming of Seizin Press, 146–7
Forster, E.M., 469
Fox, Robin, 'matriarchal' and 'patriarchal' schools of thought (*Kinship and Marriage*), 386–7
Foyle, Christina, 503
£250 Poetry Award to R.G., 503–4
Franco, Francisco, 262–3, 266, 274, 287, 311
Frank, Rose Hirch, 127
Frank, Waldo, *Our America*, 334
Fraser, G.S., on *Undertones of War*, 192
Frazer, Sir James, 98
R.G. and, 119, 383
Folk Law in the Old Testament, 119

The Golden Bough, 387
Freeman, John, 105
French, John, Earl of Ypres, 34–5
Freud, Sigmund, 97, 100
and poetry, 113, 114
Interpretation of Dreams, 97, 119
Studien über Hysterie, 1
Frost, Robert, 42, 119, 501 praised by R.G., 145, 374
R.G.'s meeting with, 500, 501
Fugitive, The, 125
and R.G.'s work, 124
attempt to raise subscriptions, 125–6
Fugitives, the, US poets, 123
role of Hirsch, 123–4
and L.R.'s poetry, 125
and her visits to Nashville, 126–7
Fuller, J.F.C., 382
Fuller, Roy, Professor of Poetry at Oxford, 1968, 554
Fuller, William, solicitor, 261
Furber, Major, portrayed in *Goodbye to All That*, 38–9
Fussell, Paul, *The Great War and Modern Memory*, war/sexuality connection, 73
and R.G., 73, 74
'homoerotic' topic, 73–4
and active homosexuality at the Front, 73–4
homoeroticism among British soldiers, 74
exemplifies Victorians, 74
rates Blunden and Sassoon as war memoirists, 192
and *Goodbye to All That*, 192, 194

Gabarro, Dr, and William, 421
Galmpton, nr Brixham, x,
Farm House, home of R.G. and Beryl, 346, 358–9, 363
visitors, 360, 411
village reaction, 360–61

Galván, Manuel de Jésus, *The
    Cross and the Sword* (trans,
    by R.G.), 427
Gardner, Ava, 446, 484
    in Mallorca, 464–5
    and R.G., 465–6, 471, 541
Garnett, David, 155
    and Phibbs, 159, 165
Garrett, Eileen, publisher
    and R.G., 419–21
    and Matthews, 420
    and L.R.'s 'ethical position' in
        joint undertakings, 425
Gatty, Hester, marriage to Sassoon,
    199
Gay, John, 'The Printer Who
    Pleased Nobody and
    Everybody', R.G.'s use of,
    370–71
Germany
    R.G. and, 29, 31, 283
    and First World War, 35, 48
    and Czechoslovakia, 289, 314
    and Deyá, 311
Gerwing, Howard, purchases
    Gravesiana for University of
    Victoria, 547
Gissing, George, 2
Gittes, Archie and Cicely, 421
Glanville-Hicks, Peggy, *Nausicaa*
    (opera based on *Homer's
    Daughter*), 464, 499
    and Alastair Reid, 499–500, 510
Glenville, Peter, film and theatre
    director, 483, 484
Glover, Gordon, 250
Gnosticism, 148–9
Golding, Louis, 250
Goldschmidt, Karl (Kenneth Gay),
    243, 245
    long friendship with R.G. and
        L.R., 243, 244, 264, 265,
        279, 282, 283, 295
    citizenship difficulties, 307, 319
    and *The Long Weekend*, 346,
        349
    R.G.'s debt to, 415–16, 448

departure of, 543
Gordon (later Tate), Caroline, 127
Gorrell, Lord, 310
Gosse, Sir Edmund, 41
Gottschalk, Louis, divorced first
    husband of L.R., 123, 127,
    131, 137, 138, 140, 141
Gough, Simon, open-air theatre,
    561
Gould, Nat, 283
Grant, Patrick, and R.G.'s alleged
    debt to Bachofen and
    Briffault, 387
Graves (*née* von Ranke), Amalia
    Elizabeth Sophie (Amy)
    mother of R.G., 5, 8–9, 242,
        296
    second wife of A.P., 8
    character, 8, 405–6
    relations with her son, 9–10, 19,
        21, 49, 243, 266, 309
    and First World War, 32, 49
    and R.G.'s 'socialism' and
        religion, 78–9
    disapproval of Nancy, 79
    and her grandchildren, 83, 257
    buys World's End cottage, 91,
        180, 186
    and L.R., 134–5
    and L.R./R.G. ménage, 136–7,
        139, 186
    obsession with 'purity', 405–6
    opinion of Gelat, 415
    last years, 435–6
    and R.G.'s 'moral state', 436,
        437
    dies in 1951, 437
Graves, Alfred Percival (A.P.),
    father of R.G., 5, 6, 7, 10, 13,
        29
    biography, 6, 9
    offspring, 6
    character, 7, 9, 10, 404
    marriage to Amalia, 8
    and his son's enlistment, 32, 33,
        35
    and Rupert Brooke's death, 38

and R.G.'s poems, 42, 43, 79,
241–2
and L.R., 129, 133, 134–5, 136
and L.R./R.G. ménage, 136–7,
139–40, 186
and his wife's 'pure world', 242
dies in 1931, 242
ed. *Every Irishman's Library*, 6
Irish Poems, 6–7
To Return to All That, 35, 49
at Red Branch House, 9
R.G.'s letters from France, 35–9
chapter devoted to R.G., 241

Graves (*née* Pritchard, later
Hodge), Beryl, second wife of
R.G., x, 206, 295, 296, 322,
377
subject of his love poetry, 153,
539
and Canellūn, 248
first meeting with R.G., 292
and Alan Hodge, 292, 296, 297,
299, 301, 302, 313–14, 361
and R.G./L.R. relationship, 293,
314, 341–2, 354
goes to Rennes as secretary,
309–10, 314
R.G.'s love affair and continuing
relationship, 312–17 *passim*,
341, 409, 491, 538, 567
parentage and education,
313–14
character, 322, 539
and her cats, 325, 327, 354
and L.R./Jackson relationship,
335–6
return to England, 340, 345, 346
brings R.G. tranquillity, 353,
354, 358
divorce from Hodge, 361
birth of her children, 383–4, 394
R.G.'s letters to, 394–5
not the Muse or the Goddess,
409
return to Mallorca, 412, 413
marriage to R.G., 436–7
and his Muses (Judith), 441,

443; (Margot), 493, 511,
512, 519, 529
in Israel, 485–6
translations, 427
Graves (later Dalton), Catherine,
daughter of R.G. and Nancy,
91, 267, 296, 362–3, 369,
550, 561
Graves, Charles, Bishop of
Limerick, grandfather of
R.G., 5, 6, 503
Graves, Charles, brother of R.G.,
journalist, 9, 210–11, 267,
278, 325
Graves, Clarissa, sister of R.G., 5,
9, 296
Graves, Clarissa, granddaughter of
R.G., 5
Graves, David, son of R.G., and
Nancy, 18, 83, 296, 362
killed in Second World War, 367
'In Conclusion', 368
Graves, Diana, daughter of Richard
Graves, 294
Graves, Helena Clarissa, later von
Ranke, 5
Graves, John, brother of R.G., xii,
13, 151, 230, 242, 436
at Charterhouse, 51
and Nancy's attitude to L.R.,
129, 139
and R.G.'s resignation from
Cairo University, 133, 135
on R.G./L.R. relationship, 242
satirized in *Antigua, Penny,
Puce*, 253
Graves, John Crosbie, 4, 5
Graves, Juan, son of R.G. and
Beryl, 359, 394, 438, 560
education, 447, 449, 457
Graves, Lucia, daughter of R.G.
and Beryl, 359, 383–4, 394,
438, 486, 511
education, 447, 448–9, 457
later life, 560
Graves, Molly (Mary), R.G.'s
half-sister, 6, 132, 436

Graves (*née* and self-styled
    Nicholson), Nancy, R.G.'s
    first wife, 59
  character, 60, 61, 82, 90, 103–4,
    137
  courtship and marriage, 61–2
  feminism, 61, 71, 77, 78, 90,
    136
  behaviour towards R.G., 69,
    70–71, 75–6, 77, 88, 89, 90,
    103, 107–8, 359
  pregnancies, 69, 71, 75, 83, 91
  quality of R.G.'s feeling for, 74,
    77, 79, 134, 153, 407
  wishes to be 'dismarried', 83–4,
    112, 137
  Boars Hill shop, 88–9
  at Islip, 103–4, 120–21, 136,
    139
  attitude to R.G./L.R. situation,
    129, 132, 136, 137, 139, 154
  and Egypt, 130
  farm worker in Cumberland,
    140
  on barge *Ringrose*, 140, 155
  and L.R./Phibbs entanglement,
    161, 164–5, 166, 179
  lives with Phibbs and her
    children, 166, 170, 172, 173,
    174, 179–80, 182
  final break with R.G., 173, 179
  supported by him, 182, 184, 185
  R.G. resumes communication,
    241, 272–3
  divorce from R.G., 361–2, 436
  and David's death, 368
  R.G.'s poems to, 539
  woodcut to R.G.'s *Treasure
    Box*, 77
Graves, Perceval, 6
Graves, Philip, half-brother of
    R.G., 8, 84, 241
  exposer of 'Protocols of Elders
    of Zion', 6
Graves, Richard, half-brother of
    R.G., and R.G. in Egypt, 132
Graves, Richard (1715–1804),

*Eugenius; The Spiritual
    Quixote*, 4
Graves, Richard (Dick), 6, 29–30,
    485
Graves, Dr Robert, discoverer of
    toxic goitre, 5
Graves, Rev. Robert Perceval,
    curate to the Wordsworths,
    5–6
Graves, Robert (R.G.): Biography,
    1
  parentage and genetic
    influences, 4, 7, 8–10
  education, 12–13; at
    Charterhouse, 13ff., 26
  boxing successes, 18–19, 26, 33
  classical exhibition St John's
    College, Oxford, 26, 27, 83,
    90
  life at Wimbledon, 29
  in Germany, 29
  enlistment in Royal Welch
    Fusiliers, 32
  war experiences, 32–5, 36, 38,
    39–40, 41, 43, 48, 57, 59
  and trench warfare, 36–7, 38,
    43, 48, 52
  Special Reserve Captain, 40
  and Sassoon, 41, 42, 48, 52, 67
  and Somme offensive, 48–9, 53
  wounded at High Wood, 49
  reported dead, 49–50, 51
  in hospital, 50–51, 53
  end of active war service, 53, 54,
    59, 70–72, 76
  Oxford Professor of Poetry
    (1961–66), 54, 468, 507,
    508–9, 512, 514
  falls in love with Nancy, 55, 60
  and Sassoon's anti-militarist
    protest, 56–8
  courtship and marriage to
    Nancy, 66–7, 407, 408
  at University of Cairo, 77, 84,
    121, 129–30, 131–5
  at Boars Hill, Oxford, 81–91,
    105, 108

and Nancy's shop, 88, 89
BLitt, 90, 104
at World's End, Islip, 90, 103–4,
117–21, 129, 132, 134, 136
appearance, 103
and his children, 103, 242,
267–8, 269, 362, 368, 447,
457, 560
socialism, 104
relations with T.E. Lawrence,
108–11 (see also under)
bad state of his marriage,
111–12
begins correspondence with
L.R., 129
resignation from Cairo post,
132, 133, 134–5
and his parents, 133, 134–5,
186, 241–2
collaboration with L.R., 136,
144–6, 345–6
in London, 136, 147, 151, 154,
155 ff., 482
in Vienna with L.R., 139–40
and L.R./Phibbs entanglement,
158, 159, 161, 165–6,
173–7, 179–80
in Ireland, 162
jumps after L.R., 166, 170
parts from Nancy, 167–8, 170,
173, 179
and L.R.'s possible deportation,
170–71
illness after fall, 170, 171, 173
leaves for Mallorca with L.R.,
190, 194
on his lost friendship with
Sassoon, 200
at Casa Salerosa, 204–6
end of sexual relations with
L.R., 205–6
continuing love and devotion for
her, 207–8, 221, 281, 284,
323, 324
move into Canelluñ, 217
ill-health while in Deyá, 249,
261, 269, 271, 273, 276–7,
278, 297, 301
at work on L.R.'s 'Schools'
project, 252, 260, 262, 282,
283, 291
awarded Hawthornden Prize,
254
departure from Mallorca, 264
in London, 266, 267–9, 276,
292, 430, 432
at Denham Studios, 266–7, 273,
292
Swiss visit with L.R., 279–81,
282-92 approaching end of
his relationship with L.R.,
280, 283, 285, 288–9
in Italy, 282, 283, 286
at Ewhurst, 291, 293, 294–8
need for Beryl, 292
operations, 293–4, 495–6, 556,
561–2
forty-second birthday, 295–6
move to Maida Vale, 298,
299–301
'hysterically over-tired', 304
at Rennes, 311
beginnings of his love affair with
Beryl, 312–13, 314, 316,
322, 324, 340
happiness from being loved, 324
to visit America, 325, 328
realization that L.R. love affair
has ended, 329, 332, 340,
426
and Nimrod's Rise, 329, 335
and L.R./Jackson affair, 336,
337, 338, 340–41, 344
return to England, 340, 342, 343
settlement of his joint affairs
with L.R., 339–40, 343
openly admitted new life with
Beryl, 331, 344, 346, 352,
353
delayed divorce from Nancy,
346, 436
throws off L.R.'s spell, 351–2
and return to Mallorca, 369
conversational habits, 374–6

wartime demand for his books, 384–5

on conditions in Mallorca, 412, 413

in Barcelona with William, 421

and possession of his Mallorcan houses, 424

show-business hopes, 427

marriage to Beryl, 436–7

and his mother's death, 437

new state of 'being in love' (Judith), 440–41

lives his private life in the open, 443, 463, 500

period in Palma, 447–9

assumed ownership of Deyá land, 457–8

world fame as poet, 458

and Suez crisis, 469–70

revisits America, 476–9

refuses the CBE, 482–3

in Israel, 485–6

and Nobel Prize, 507–8

refuses CLitt, 530–31

and sale of his letters, 546, 547

poetry readings abroad, 550–51, 561

sets up Graves Prize in Hungary, 551

Olympic Medal for Poetry, 1968, 552–3

sense of enmity against him, 559

in old age, 563

eightieth birthday, 566

Graves, Robert: Character and poetic personality, xi
White Goddess theme, ix (see under Works)

love poet, 2, 68, 74, 153, 524, 544

historical novelist, 2, 225, 229, 301, 358, 377–8, 396–7, 417–18

concepts of poetry and the poetic impulse, 2, 47, 94, 98, 99, 120, 135, 206, 215, 372, 401, 527–8, 536

passion for facts, 5

aspects of his complex character, 8, 27, 28, 43–4, 47, 68–9, 75, 80, 81, 105, 119, 138, 231, 375, 394, 404

childhood fears, 10–11, 12

attitude towards, and delicacy about sex, 10, 12, 14, 19, 21, 22–3, 74, 77, 101, 153, 277

poetry his ruling passion and obsession, 12, 24, 31, 102, 116–17, 149, 153, 377, 378–9, 402

recurring dreams, 13, 14, 15, 149

sense of alienation, 14–19

and his German ancestry, 15, 29, 32

and early 'literary' poetry, 16–17, 23

and orthodox religion, 19–20, 21, 47

'love affair' with 'Dick', 20–22 (see Johnstone, G.H.)

state of terror, 22, 26

romanticism, 22, 23, 81, 116, 375, 422, 491

and disgresion, 23, 24, 25

obsession with ideas of purity and truth, 24–5

vice/sex equation, 26

content of his poems, 26, 68

aversion to 'wetness', 28, 35

and his own poetry, 33

state of depression, 40–41, 105

and David Thomas's death, 45, 47

neurasthenia, 47, 51–2, 59, 67–8, 92, 112, 353

and absolute love between man and woman, 47, 69

death-in-life theme, 51

and existence of lust, 60, 74, 75, 94, 117, 238, 405, 407

on the poet and rules of metre, 65

lyrical gift, 68

external optimism/internal gloom conflict, 70

fear of homosexual feelings, 73, 74, 406

survival of war experiences, 74–5, 76–7

need for a real personal morality, 75, 76, 85, 133

financial affairs, 78, 86, 103, 104, 135, 140, 141, 179, 185, 186–7, 207, 211, 223, 225, 229, 246, 252, 256, 257, 266, 321, 343, 345, 358, 385, 402, 426–7, 449, 467–8, 506

anti-Establishment, 85

choice of poets, 86

sense of guilt, 91, 92, 94, 95

and a psychiatric 'cure', 92, 94

and the poet's Muse, 93, 94, 118, 120, 237, 354, 384, 401–2, 408–9, 438, 439, 491, 518–19, 524–5, 537

longing for a loving wife, 93–4

and the 'unconscious', 98

his ideal poet (himself), 98

necessity of arrogance, 99, 101, 102

origins of poetry in trance, 99–100, 101, 371, 393, 403, 502, 527–8

habit of revision, 100

and humour in poets, 101

'bad' and 'fake' poets, 101, 112

and magic nature of words, 102, 116, 117, 120

disenchantment with Georgian poetry, 105, 107, 113

and modernism, 113

influence of philosophy, 114–15

life as 'goddawful' in anti-poetic sense, 115, 116, 131, 187, 193, 230, 235, 353, 370

increase in poetic power, 116, 153

concept of báraka, 116, 506, 511, 523, 531, 545

and woman as key to truth, 119

and science, 120, 124

disintegration of post-war personality, 131

sense of 'bad luck', 132

alleged socialism, 132

and L.R.'s genius, 137

major part in collaboration, 137–8, 140

'Trinity' of friendship, 139, 140, 154, 155

finds what he needs in L.R., 141, 144, 149, 153

attitude to her enemies, 152, 153

'The Four', 154, 159, 163, 172, 175, 176

and destruction of L.R.'s 'holiness', 175, 176, 177

and Mammonolatry, 186–7

and his 'transformation' by L.R., 187

attitude to the theatre and play-writing, 208

written off by literary world, 212

influence of L.R. on his state of mind and poetry, 215, 234, 236–7

and fictional inventiveness, 230, 231

belief in former matriarchy, 233

proves himself a golden goose, 235

alleged to ignore realities in his poetry, 285

poems about himself, 290

and nature, 291

and meanings of words in poetry, 305

questions L.R.'s authority, 331–2

and L.R.'s intellectual withdrawal, 354

feeling of happiness in being loved (by Beryl), 355

guilty lust gives way to shared love, 355–6

literary reputation as poet and

novelist, x, 107, 112–13, 199, 411, 458–9, 559–60
his vocabulary of criticism, 371
interest in mythology, 383, 386, 400, 402
anthropologically based beliefs, 386, 388, 401
and 'Goats in History', 391–2
undergoes a religious revelation, 401
character of modern poet, 402
knowledge of Oedipus complex, 404
danger of over-systemization, 414–15
lecturing and journalism, 426–7, 428
poetic expression of his love for Judith, 443
poetic output/amorous unrest relationship, 466
poetic presence as a speaker, 466–7
his Protestant conscience, 470, 472–3
central theme of his poetry, 494
attitude to drugs, 501, 502
interpretation of báraka concept, 511, 523, 531, 545
idealism, 517, 523
complaint against women, 521
Black Goddess theme, 518–21
and telepathic communication between lovers, 524, 538
writes to Reeves of his happiness, 526
characteristics of the poet, 527
need to rehabilitate image of the Goddess, 529
years of less powerful poetry (1960s), 530
acquires a new Muse, 533
'true-love' concept of domesticity, 537
monogamy a patriarchal invention, 537–8

songs of obsessional perfectionism, 545
dislike of trained-actors' poetry readings, 552
and 'universal men', 554
disregards most poetry in non-English languages, 559
and 'hippy' end of poetic spectrum, 559, 564
nature of his reactionary modernism, 559–60
final Muse, 563
definition of a poem ('miraculous . . . event . . . in non-history'), 564
poems of final years, 566
remains true to unrest of romantic love, 566
for his Muses (post-L.R.), see Judith; Julie; Laraçuen; Margot

Graves, Robert: Works
'A Restless Ghost', 514
'A Shift of Scene', 538–9
'A Time of Waiting', 516
'A Toast to Ava Gardner', 464
'Act V, Scene 5', 288
Adam's Rib, 426, 442
'Alice', 116
'All I Tell You from my Heart', 524–5
The Anger of Achilles (1954, trans. of Iliad), 504
Ann of Highwood Hall, (1964), 505
Another Future of Poetry (1926), 120, 124
Antigua, Penny, Puce (1936), 230, 233, 243, 253, 260, 261, 262, 267, 273, 274, 278–9, 299
'The Anti-Poet', 371, 515
'Any Honest Housewife', 290
'Apples and Water', 69
'Assumption Day', 314–15
'At the Savoy Chapel', 362

'The Autobiography of Baal',
    unfinished, 210
'The Bards', 199
'Batxóca', 536
'The Beacon', 69–70
'The Beast', 291, 322–3
'The Bedpost', 120
'Between Hyssop and Axe', 537
'Beware, Madam, the Witty
    Serpent', 512–13, 514, 515
'Bins K to T', 27
'The Black Goddess', 526–7
'The Blue-Fly', 443–4, 446, 447
But It Still Goes On (1930), 73,
    193–4, 208–10, 226;
    distinction between 'trench'
    and 'historical' reality, 197–8
'Callow Captain', 206
'Captain Mercies'
!Catacrok! (1956), 481
'Certain Mercies', 234–5, 293
'Children of Darkness', 110, 113
Clark Lectures, 426, 466–7
Claudius the God (1934), 191,
    211, 228–32, 287, 483, 485;
    see also I, Claudius
Collected Poems 1914–1947,
    416
Collected Poems 1938, 7, 16,
    25–6, 133, 206, 237, 291,
    306, 311, 319, 325
Collected Poems (1947), 357
Collected Poems 1955, 73, 460,
    481
Collected Poems 1959, 504
Collected Poems 1965, 494, 530
Collected Poems 1975, final
    volume, 68, 530, 535–6, 545,
    563
Collected Short Stories (1964),
    377, 530
The Common Asphodel (1949),
    96, 97, 120, 247, 413, 414,
    424–6
*Contemporary Techniques of
    Poetry* (1925), 108, 119
'The Cool Web', 22, 296

Count Belisarius (1938), 293–6
    passim, 299–302, 304, 306,
    327, 363–4, 377
'Country House', 284
Country Sentiment (1920), 68,
    77
The Crane Bag (1969), 382, 530
'Crane and Horse', 562
'Creation', 442
The Crowning Privilege (1955),
    459, 467
'The Crusader on his Dead
    Mistress', 109
'Darien', 440–41, 445
'Day of Judgement', 69
'The Dead Boche', 50
'Dead Hand', 534
'The Death Grapple', 494
'The Death Room', 414
'Despite and Still', 354–5, 356
'Dethronement' suppressed, 415
'The Devil's Advice to
    Storytellers', 231, 246,
    370–71
'The Dialecticians', 111
Diary (1935–9), 243, 245,
    248–9, 279, 287, 303, 319,
    327, 330, 357; sale of, 547
Dictionary of Exact Meanings,
    279, 287–8, 300, 305, 307,
    312, 315–19 *passim*, 324,
    327, 340, 345, 347
*Difficult Questions, Easy
    Answers* (1972), 530, 562,
    563
'Down', 91, 94
'Down, Wanton, Down', 199,
    239–40, 355
'Dream of a Climber', 226
The English Ballad (1928), 85
Epilogue I (1935), 225, 244;
    debt to L.R., 247
'Epitaph on an Unfortunate
    Artist', 516
'Escape', 51
Essays on poets, 247
'Está En Su Casa', 415

'The Face in the Mirror', 487–8

Fairies and Fusiliers (1917), 64, 84, 91

The Feather Bed (1923), 108, 124

5 Pens in Hand (1958), 481

'Five Score and Six Years Ago', 382

'The Florist Rose', 293, 302–3

'Flying Crooked', 238–9

Food for Centaurs (1960), 502, 503, 524

'The Foreboding', 445

'From a Private Correspondence on Reality', 331–2

'Full Moon', 117

'Give, ask for nothing', 517

The Golden Fleece (1944), 301, 368, 372, 383–4, 386, 389

Goliath and David (1916), 45–7, 368

Goodbye to All That (1929, 1957), *passim*; 'Dedicatory Epilogue to Laura Riding', 118, 129, 131–2, 161–2, 193

'The Great-grandmother', 305–6

The Greek Myths (1955), 386, 388, 430, 447, 459, 461–2, 504–5

Green-Sailed Vessel (1971), 565

Homer's Daughter (1955), 426, 437, 460, 471–2, 475; operatic version, 464, 511

'The Halls of Bedlam', 274–6

'Have you not read/The words in my head', 355

Hercules, My Shipmate (1945), 358

'Horizon', 518

'Horses', 343, 348, 434

'Hotel Bed', 288

'I, an ambassador of Otherwhere', 458–9

I, Claudius (1934), ix, 299–32, 255–7, 385, 566, 576; TV version, 229–30, 231, 232, plan to film, 243, 249, 253, 257, 260, 273–4, 278, 282, 283, 473

'I Discover Israel', 486

'I sat in my chamber yesternight', 23–4

'I'd die for you, or you for me', 112

'I will write', 527

'In Her Praise', 514

'In Dedication', 431

'In Procession', 85–6

'In the Wilderness', 390–92

'Inkidoo and Queen of Babel', 520

'Intimations of the Black Goddess', 493, 518

The Isles (Islands) of Unwisdom (1950), 417, 418–19

'A Jealous Man', 269–71, 280

'Joan and Derby', 491–2, 510

John Kemp's Wager, 119

'Journal of Curiosities', 209–10

'July the twenty-fourth', 366

'Jungian Mythology', 401

King Jesus (1946), 301, 358, 361, 383, 385, 389, 397, 398, 410, 412, 413, 415, 428; character of Jesus, 390, 392–3; role of Judas, 392–3

'Knowledge of God', 115

La Mejicana', 535

'Largesse to the Poor', 288

'*Lars Porsena, or the Future of Swearing* (1927), 133, 434

'The Laureate', 289

Lawrence and the Arabs (1927), 141–2, 146, 498

'Leaving the Rest Unsaid', 292

'Leda', 293

'Let the weeks end as well they must' (final poem), 566

'Lift-Boy', 488

'Lost Love', 116–17

'Love at First Sight', 75

Love Respelt (1965), 534–5, 538 ('Change'), 544–5

'Love story', 324

Mammon and the Black Goddess (1965), 187, 518, 527

Man Does, Woman Is (1964), 522, 526, 529, 535

'Manifestations', 348

The Marmosite's Miscellany (1925), 119, 138, 159

Meaning of Dreams (1924), 119

'Mid-winter Waking', 357

'Miss Briton's Lady Companion', 406

Mock-Beggar Hall (1924), 115, 117, 121

'The Moon Ends in Nightmare', 330, 332

'Moral Principles in Translation', 380

More Poems 1961, 493, 494, 505, 510, 519

Mount Holyoak (USA) Lectures, 471, 477, 478–9

Mrs Fisher (1928), 115, 116, 193, 434

'Mushrooms: Food of the Gods', 502

My Head! My Head! (1925), 119, 377

Myths of Ancient Greece, see The Greek Myths

'Nature's Lineaments', 291

The Nazarene Gospel Restored (1953), 393, 428–30, 449–50;

Podro's contribution, 430, 449, 450

New Poems 1962, 493, 494, 509, 420

'Nine Hundred Iron Chariots', 527–8

No Decency Left (1932), 212–13, 280

No More Ghosts (1940), 355

'Not to sleep all the night gone', 526

'The Oath', 357

Occupation Writer (1951), 73, 419, 434

'On Dwelling', 199

On English Poetry (1922), 16–19, 101–2, 111, 124

On Poetry (1969; USA only), 530

'On Portents', 237

'One Hard Look', 68, 69

'Or to Perish Before Day', 291

Oratio Creweiana (1962), 520

'Outlaws', 69

'Ouzo Unclouded', 513

Over the Brazier (1916), 42, 79, 84

Oxford Lectures as Professor of Poetry, 494, 516, 518; The Anti-Poet', 371, 515; 'The Dedicated Poet', 371, 514; 'Intimations of the Black Goddess', 493, 518, 520–21; 'The Personal Muse', 515; 'Poetic Craft and Principle', 530; 'Poetic Gold', 501

The Penny Fiddle (1960), 505

The Pier-Glass (1921), 77, 85, 91–3, 107

Poems 1914–1926, 132–3

Poems 1914–27, 92, 132–3, 211

Poems 1926–1930, 211

Poems 1929, 149

Poems 1930–1933, 199, 238

Poems 1938–1945, 355, 357, 402, 410, 411

Poems 1953, 445

Poems 1965–68, 539, 545

Poems About Love (1969), 530

Poems 1970–1972, 25, 563

Poems and Satires 1951, 357, 445

'The Poet in the Nursery', 38

'The Poet's Paradise', 501–2

Poems of Robert Graves (1958), 481

Poems Selected by Himself (1957), 481

Poetic Unreason (1925), 96, 97, 104, 119, 120
Poetry and Politics, 252
'The Portrait', 445, 446, 465
Précis, 155, 171, 184
Proceed Sergeant Lamb (1941), 358, 378, 385
'Prometheus', 445–6
The Real David Copperfield, 224, 225
'Recalling War', 243
'Reproach', 22, 95
'Richard Roe and John Doe', 113, 161, 355
'The Roebuck in the Thicket', *see The White Goddess*
'Ruby and Amethyst', 510–11, 518
'The Sea Horse', 445–6
'The Second-Fated', 231
'Seldom Yet Now', 325–6
Sergeant Lamb of the Ninth (1940), 346, 358, 379
Seven Days in New Crete (1949, one time *The New Cretans*), futurist novel, 301, 313, 418, 419, 421–3, 436, 441
Seventeen Poems Missing from 'Love Respelt', (1967), 538, 545
'The Shout', 209, 117–18, 209; film version, 117, 563
'Sick Love', 149, 153–4, 179
'Some Trench Scenes', 119, 195
Song: 'Come Enjoy Your Sunday', 494
Song: 'Though Once True Lovers', 544
'Song of Contrariety', 110–11
Song for Sheba, 388–9, 486–7
'Spoils', 445
'The Starred Coverlet', 494, 495
Steps (1958), 481, 524, 556
'The Succubus', 238
'The Suicide in the Copse', 318
'Surgical Ward, Men', 495

Survey of Modernist Poetry (1927), 96
'Sweeney Among the Blackbirds', 524
'Symptoms of Love', 511
T. E. Lawrence to His Biographer (1938), 259–60, 302, 306, 319, 498
Ten Poems More (1930), 211
They Hanged My Saintly Billy (1951), R.G.'s last novel, 426, 427, 475, 476, 480
'The Thieves', 324, 354
'Through Nightmare', 355, 539
'To Beguile and Betray', 519
'To Bring the Dead to Life', 246
'To Evoke Posterity', 288
'To Juan at the Winter Solstice', 414
'To R.N.', 83
To Whom Else? (1931), 204, 237
translations, 427–8, 466, 481, 482, 504, 530, 551, 555–8
The Treasure Box (1919), 77
'The Troll's Nosegay', 72, 433
'Troughs of Sea', 492, 493
'Trudge, Body!' 238
'Ulysses', 199, 238
'Under the Olives', 511
'Vain and Careless', 69
Watch the North Wind Rise (1949), 419
Whipperginny (1922), 108, 111, 112, 113, 114
The White Goddess (1948), ix, 10, 12, 93, 117, 187, 205, 215, 237–8, 371, 520; publication, 113, 378, 395–8, 399, 410, 416; climax of R.G.'s poetic development, 354, 389, 395; composition, 358, 383, 388; single grand theme, 392, 393, 402; as a thesis, 399–401; a quest for his Goddess, 402–3, 407, main theme of poetry, 403–4;

about how poets think, 405;
aggressive heterosexuality,
406; relevance to male
experience of women, 408–9;
new material, 410, 413, 414;
final amendment, 413, 414;
US reviewers and, 416–17;
brings repute to R.G., 428;
Reid's film script, 510; his
true Muse, 566
Wife to Mr Milton (1943), 301,
322, 358, 367, 370, 377–80,
441, 524, 538
'Wigs and Beards', 535
'The Window Sill', 445, 455–6
'Witches', 121
'Women and Masks', 551
'Women and Tree', 490–91
'The Young Cordwainers', 524
with Alan Hodge, *The Reader
Over Your Shoulder* (1943),
358, 377, 382, 389, 542; *The
Long Weekend* (1940), 259,
272, 337–8, 346, 349, 353,
364–5, 378
with Raphael Patai, *The Hebrew
Myths* (1964), 505, 516, 530,
550
with Joshua Podro, *Jesus in
Rome* (1957), 426, 481–2;
Nazarene Gospel Restored
(1953), 428
with Alastair Reid, *Quoz* 360,
576n.
with Lauda Riding, *Pamphlet
Against Anthologies* (1928),
137, 145–6; *Survey of
Modernist Poetry* (1927), 96,
137, 138, 140, 143–5; *The
Swiss Ghost*, 280, 291, 295,
296, 319, 321, 339, 348
Graves, Dr Rosaleen, sister of R.G.,
9, 135, 136, 266, 346, 436
Graves, Sally, daughter of Philip,
277, 294, 411, 507
marriage to Richard Chilver,
279

at Oxford, 313
Graves, Sam, son of R.G. and
Nancy, 91, 132, 135, 267–8,
296
at school in Letchworth, 309
Graves, Tomas, last son of R.G.
and Beryl, 457, 486, 560, 561
Graves, William, son of R.G. and
Beryl, xii, 203, 346, 359, 394,
438, 560, 561
bicycle accident, 421
and Eliot, 431
goes to Oundle, 438, 457, 467
Great Bardfield, 216, 217, 267,
346, 464
Greece, R.G.'s television
programme, 508–9, 513
Greene, Graham, 230, 532
Grigson, Geoffrey, xii
on R.G., 517
Guest, Lady Charlotte, and *The
Mabinogion*, 403
Guinness, Alec, 452, 473 and
Claudius, 473, 474, 478, 483,
485
and *World's Delight*, 474, 475
success in *The Prisoner*, 483
cast to play *Ross*, 497, 499

H.D. (Hilda Doolittle), 82
Haas, Robert, US publisher, 232
Hadas, Moses, 479
Hamish Hamilton, and R.G.'s
writings, 424–5
Harcourt Brace, and R.G.'s *David
Copperfield*, 224
Hardwick, Elizabeth, wife of
Robert Lowell, 479
Hardy, Thomas, admired by R.G.,
2, 87–8, 119, 322 and
meliorism, 34
The Dynasts, 87
Jude the Obscure, 2
Harrison, Jane, *Study of Greek
Religion*, 383, 387
Hart, Basil Liddell, 266, 346 and
Ross, 497

T. E. *Lawrence to His Biographer*, 257, 260, 302
Thoughts on War, R.G. and, 384

Harvey, F. W., 64

Hašek, Jaroslav, *Good Soldier Švejk*, 193

Head, Dr Henry, neurologist, 83, 90, 97, 98

Heim, Roger, mushroom, expert, 476

Heinemann, William, 62, 63
  publisher to R.G. 64, 91, 104, 108, 132, 211
  rejects L.R.'s *Collected Poems*, 299

Heller, Joseph, *Catch-22*, 193

Henderson's 'Bomb Shop', 58

Henty, G. A., 301

Herford, C. H., 80–81

Heyward, Leyland, and *A Song for Sheba*, 488

Hilton Farm, 60, 165

Hinde, Thomas (Sir Thomas Chitty), 450

Hirsch, Sidney Mttron, and the Fugitives, 123–4
  quarrels with L.R., 127

History Today, 435

Hodge, Alan, xiii, 267, 272, 277, 360
  in Mallorca, 260–61, 264
  friend and first husband of Beryl, 292, 293, 299, 313
  at Ewhurst, 295, 296
  marriage, 301, 302
  and Symons/R.G. meeting, 308
  at Rennes, 312, 318, 323, 327
  in USA, 335
  and life at Nimrod's Rise, 338
  returns to England with R.G., 340, 342–3
  disgust with L.R., 340
  and imminence of war, 345
  relations with Beryl, 346
  remarriage, 346

collaboration with R.G., 346–7, 349, 351
  and his projected history of poetry, 384
  coeditor *History Today*, 435
  A Year of Damage, 277, 283, 287

Hodge, Jane Aiken, second wife of Alan, 346

Hofmann, Dr Albert, producer of mushroom 'wonder drug', 476

Hogarth Press, 108, 115, 119, 137, 481

Holiday, 'I discover Israel', 486

Homer, *Iliad*, trans. by R.G. (*Anger of Achilles*), 482, 486, 504

Homoeroticism, Victorian, Fussele and, 74

Homosexuality (pseudohomosexuals)
  product of public schools, 14, 20–21
  R.G. on, 22
  at Charterhouse, 27–8
  R.G.'s 'recovery from', 73
  his fear of such emotions, 406

Hope, James, MP, 58

Hopkins, Gerard Manley, 3
  homosexuality, 74, 145

Horne, Lena and *A Song for Sheba*, 488, 489

Houseman, A. E. influence on feelings on death in First World War, 74
  discussed by R.G. and Eliot, 431–2
  homosexuality, 469

Howard, Mrs Michael, and Nancy's shop, 88, 89

Hudson Review, 'Jungian Mythology', 401, 458

Huebsch, B. W., of Viking Press, and *Greek Myths*, 460

Hulton, Edward, of *Picture Post*, 453

Hutchinson, Dorothy, 250, 266

INDEX

Hutchinson, Ward, 246, 250, 266
Huxley, Aldous and Julian, 54, 56
Hypnogogic trance, a now
    established physiological
    state, 99

Illustrated London News, Max
    Beerbohm and, 433
Imagists, 144
Irish Literary Society, 6
Israel, R.G.'s visit, 485–6
Italy, R.G. and Beryl in Portofino,
    432

Jackson, Griselda, daughter of
    Schuyler and Kit, loathing for
    L.R., 335, 339
Jackson, Schuyler, 237
    Matthews praises L.R. to him,
        217–18, 280, 320
    Manifesto, 234
    refuses to endorse 'Covenant of
        Literal Morality', 280, 319
    his fascination for L.R., 280,
        319, 324, 326, 336
    and dictionary project, 288,
        329, 340, 347
    post on *Time*, 319–20, 333, 335
    reviews L.R.'s *Poems*, 326
    relations with Matthews,
        327–8, 333–4, 335, 341
    and Nimrod's Rise, 328
    to leave his wife, 328
    R.G. and, 329, 332, 333, 341
    reciprocal sexual relationship
        with L.R., 330, 332, 335–6
    biography, 332–5
    period in England, 334
    alcohol problem, 341
    and R.G./Beryl relationship,
        341, 349
    financial habits, 345, 346, 348,
        349
    reply to R.G.'s 'literary treatise'
        letter, 349–50

Jackson (*née* Townsend),
    Katherine (Kit), wife of
    Schuyler, 327, 329, 333, 334,
    350
    talks with R.G., 335
    madness, 337, 338, 341, 344,
        347
    RC convert, 337
    accused of being a witch, 337
    divorces Schuyler, 339
Jakobson, Roman, linguist, 479
Jameson, Storm, 287
Jarrell, Randall
    view of *Claudius*, 229
    of *Count Belisarius*, 301
    and *The White Goddess*, 404,
        408
Jeans, James, 53
Jepson, Selwyn, and R.G., 437,
    547, 548
Jews, the, 119, 123, 307
Joad, C. E. M., 382
John Bull, 21, 406
John O'London, 274
Johnson, Lionel, *Essays*, 41
Johnson, Samuel, 378
Johnstone, G. H. (later Baron
    Derwent), R.G.'s platonic
    'love' for, 20, 21, 22, 26–8,
    55
    R.G.'s horror at homosexual
        charge against, 21, 39, 41,
        406, 407
    R.G.'s correspondence with, 39,
        406–7
Jolas, Eugene, *transition 3* (1927),
    138
Jones, David, R.G. on *In
    Parenthesis*, 290
Jonson, Ben, 81, 372
Judd, Forrest
    credentials, 450–51
    film script based on *Arabian
        Nights* story, 451, 452
Judith, post-Riding Muse, 533
    R.G.'s new state of 'being in
        love', 440–47

character, 441, 492
relations with her fiancé, 442–5
    passim, 447, 453, 454
R.G.'s poems to her, 455–7
end of his relationship, 455
R.G. and her mother, 441–3,
    453, 454
Julie, last Muse, 563–4
poems to, 565–6
Jung, Carl Gustav, R.G.'s contempt
    for, 401, 462
Junyer, Joän, 325

Kafka, Franz, *Castle*, 278
'Kain, Saul', pseudonym of
    Sassoon, 41
Keats, John, 37, 111, 371, 403
Kee, Robert, 454
    and a picture-story on R.G., 453
Keith, Warren, Gymnosophy
    movement, 431
Kemp, Alix, 294, 298
    with Riding, Laura *The Left
    Heresy in Literature and Life*
    (1939), 252, 309
Kemp, Harry, 282, 291, 294–5,
    298
Kerellouan, Mme de Comtesse de,
    311
Keyes, Sidney, 369
Keynes, Geoffrey, 30, 467
Kipling, Rudyard, R.G. and, 81,
    517
Knight, G. Wilson, 468
Knopf, Alfred, US publishers, 79,
    91, 124
Korda, Alexander, 266
    plan to film *Claudius*, 243, 257,
        266, 273, 287, 292, 484
    sends R.G. £500, 252
    commissions 'Spanish refugee
        script' from R.G. and L.R.,
        273
    and a *Margaret Catchpole* film,
        292
    financial offer to R.G., 397

option on T. E. Lawrence film
    rights, 498
Korda, Vincent, 266–7, 477
    and a remake of *Claudius*, 473,
        475, 478, 483
Kubler, Otto and *The Isles of
    Unwisdom*, 417–18
Kyllmann, O., of Constable, 271,
    277

Lacey, Mildred, and Lockwood
    Memorial Fund, 506
Lamb, Sergeant, prototype for
    R.G.'s novels, 378
Laraçuen, Aemilia, R.G.'s third
    Muse
    arrival in Deyá, 533 in
        'international jet set', 533,
        535
    relations with R.G., 533–4, 538,
        540, 542–3
    her musician friend, 534, 540,
        541
    status as Muse, 534, 535, 545–5
    R.G.'s poems to, 534–5, 538,
        539
    unpredictable and unpopular,
        541
    R.G.'s disillusionment, 544,
        545, 563, 564
    sales of his letters to her, 546,
        547, 548
    last heard of in Turkey, 549
    trauma of R.G.'s break with her,
        563, 564
Larkin, Philip, Queen's Gold
    Medallist, 552
Latham, Peter, 1
Laughton, Charles, 292
    as Claudius, 243, 287
    as Rembrandt, 266
Lawrence, D. H., 55, 74, 133, 259
    obsession with sex, 145
Lawrence, A. W., brother of T. E.,
    496
    and *Ross*, 496, 497

Lawrence, T. E., 6
  R.G.'s friendship with 30, 75,
    84–5, 108–11, 121, 143,
    186, 254, 258
  Fellow of All Souls, 84, 86, 242,
    374
  compulsion to be punished, 85,
    108–9, 255, 259
  on R.G.'s *The Pier-Glass*, 91, 93
  gifts to R.G., 109–10, 135, 140
  discusses sexual problems with
    R.G., 108–9, 110, 115,
    133–4, 254, 259
  R.G. on his poem (dedicated to
    Dahoum), 109, 110, 111
  vanishes into RAF, 111, 257
  T.E. Shaw, Royal Tank Corps,
    120, 135, 253
  and Egypt, 132
  asked to comment on Isaiah
    xxix, 134
  collaborates in R.G.'s *Lawrence
    and the Arabs*, 141–3
  revives painful memories in
    India, 142–3
  visits L.R. in hospital, 254, 258
  in isolation, 186
  contribution to *No Decency
    Left*, 212–13
  R.G. and his death, 253–4
  letters on man/woman subject,
    254
  R.G. and his break with L.R.,
    254, 257–9
  and Manning, 255
  finds *Claudius* 'sickening', 255
  financial difficulties, 257
  writes his own obituary, 258,
    259
  R.G.'s obituary of him, 259
  Aldington's hostile biography,
    496
  R.G. and the projected film,
    496–7, 497–8
  homosexuality, 496
  The Mint, life in RAF barracks,
    254
  Revolt in the Desert, 135, 140
  Seven Pillars of Wisdom, 89,
    135
  dedicatory poem to 'S.A.'
    (Dahoum), 110, 111
Leach, E.R., anthropologist, 388
Lean, David, and a film on
  Lawrence, 496, 498
Leavis, F. R., 382, 435, 467, 507
Lee, Gipsy Rose, 480
LeGoff, Marcel, *Anatole France at
  Home* (1926), trans. by L. R.,
  137
Lévi-Strauss, Claude, 461, 505
Lewis, Alun
  R.G. and, 368–9
  Ha! ha! Among the Trumpets,
    367, 369
  Raider's Dawn, 369
Lewis, Cecil Day, 554
  and Queen's Medal for Poetry,
    552
  disagreement over Blunden
    reading, 552
  Laureateship, 559
Lewis, Wyndham, 185, 400
Lindsay, Jack, xii
  on R.G. and L.R. in London,
    Fanfrolico and After, 151–2
Lindsay, Vachell, 105
  R.G. on readings of his work, 87
Little, Brown, literary agents, and
  the *Dictionary*, 309, 321, 345
Lloyd, Mrs, mother of John
  Aldridge, 252, 348, 350
Lloyd-George, David, First Earl,
  47, 55
Lodge, Sir Oliver, *Raymond*, 52,
  197
London Mercury, 133, 218, 334
Loraine, Denis, and Cadco Project,
  531, 532
Lorca, Federico Garcia, 559
Lowell, James Russell, 98
Lowell, Robert, 479, 553
Lucan, *Pharsalia* (trans. by R.G.),
  428, 481

Lucas, E. V., 62
Luce, H. R., RC owner of *Time*,
    420
Lucetius, R.G.'s obsession with,
    52–3
Lucy, Mary, Irish poet, 300, 301,
    302
Lye, Jane, 151, 222, 248, 266, 306
    and *Goodbye to All That*, 186
Lye, Len, 151, 246, 266, 306
    films, 279
    No Trouble (letters), 204, 222

MacCarthy, Desmond, 364
McCormacks, the, 269
    take R.G., L.R. and Karl to Italy,
        286
McCormick, Ken, of Doubleday,
    R.G.'s letter to, 499–50
MacDonald, Philip, *The Rasp*, 293
McIntyre, of Little, Brown, 324
    and the 'dictionary', 347–8
Mack, John, and R.G.'s book on
        Lawrence, 142–3
    A Prince of Our Disorder, 573n
Macmillan, USA, refuses *The
        White Goddess*, 399, 410,
        483
Macmillan, Sir Harold, offers R.G.
    a CBE, 482–3
MacNeice, Louis, 199, 373
MacSweeney, Barry, 554
MCA, US agents, 418, 419
Madge, Charles, 372, 373
Magnani, Anna, 477 478, 484
Mahler, Gustav, 1
Malahat Review, 547
    'The Moon Ends in Nightmare',
        330
Mallik, Basanta, Bengali lawyer
        and philosopher, 114–15,
        116, 120
Mallorca (Majorca), ix, x, 301
    natural features, 291–2
    ancient history, 202

Soller port, 203–4, 435, 447,
    454
reign of terror, 262–3, 274, 287
R.G. and L.R. leave, 263–4, 265
return in 1946, 266, 412–14
their joint property, 350, 424
the children at school, 438
see also Canelluñ; Deyá
Mallory, George, 'hero-figure'
    R.G., and, 23, 25, 27, 30, 62
    death on Everest, 120
Malthus, Rev. Thomas, *Theory of
        Population*, 4
Mancroft, Lord, and Foyle Poetry
        Award, 503–4
Manning, Frederick, relations with
        T. E. Lawrence, *Her Privates
        We*, 255
Manwaring, G. E., 374
Margot, R.G.'s Muse, 513, 518,
        529, 533, 535
    arrival in Deyá, 489
    R.G. and his attraction, 491–2,
        493, 494
    reaction of his friends, 492–3,
        512
    elopement with Reid, 510, 521,
        522
    R.G.'s poems to, 510, 517, 522,
        525–7
    R.G. and her role as Goddess,
        518, 520
    on his relationship with her,
        519–20
    as the Black Goddess, 521
    unsent letters to her, 521ff.
    identifies herself as Love
        Goddess, 523
    finish of the affair, 526–7, 529,
        544
Marsh, Sir Edward, 21, 62, 80, 91,
        271
    arbiter of taste, 23, 34
    critic of R.G.'s poetry, 23, 24,
        25, 33, 42–3
    and Sassoon, 50
    letters from R.G., 51, 66

and Brooke, 74, 106
and L.R.'s possible deportation, 170–71
and Lawrence's death, 254
and *Wife to Mr Milton*, 380–81
Georgian Poetry (1912–22), 3, 23, 104, 105, 107, 373–4
Memoir of Rupert Brooke, 106
A Number of People, 373
Marx, Karl, *Das Kapital*, 1
Mas, Anita, at Rennes, 271, 289, 293
Mas, Juan Marroig (Gelat), Mallorcan ally of R.G. and L.R., 218, 219, 236
    position in the village, 218, 262–3
    Canelluñ building project, 219
    power of attorney for L.R.'s Deyá properties, 223, 350, 424
    and purchase of Posada, 243
    financial gains, 248
    and the Left, 261–2, 263
    imprisonment, 287, 289
    release, 293, 311
    R.G.'s post-war reunion, 412, 415
    and R.G.'s attempt to possess his property, 424
Mas, Juan, son of above, 218, 435
Masefield, Catherine
    and R.G. and Nancy, 82, 88–9
    behaviour to husband, 89
Masefield, John, 23, 105
    and R.G. at Oxford, 80, 81, 82
    R.G. and, 81, 82, 119, 289
    The Daffodil Fields, 41
    The Everlasting Mercy, 24, 41, 81
Masson, David, life of Milton, 380
Matthews (*née* Cuyler), Julie, 214, 215, 267, 284, 327
    and R.G./L.R. set up, 329, 335
Matthews, Tom, 230, 246, 267, 375
    on L.R., 122, 217–18, 284
    at Casa Salerosa, 204, 214
    and R.G.'s attitude to L.R., 214–15, 216
    and *Time*, 305, 320, 326, 420
    and L.R.'s *Collected Poems*, 320
    despised by R.G., 324
    and a L.R./Jackson meeting, 327
    relationship with Jackson, 328, 333
    American home, 328
    and R.G. and L.R. in USA, 329
    and L.R./Jackson affair, 336, 337
    and R.G.'s portrait of Milton, 379
    on Auden, 507
    Jacks or Better (UK *Under the Influence*), 214, 363, 572
    The Moon's No Fool (with L.R.'s help), 217, 244
    Name and Address, 332
Mediterranean Institute of Dowling College, USA, in Deyá, 561
Meliorism, myth of human progress, 34
Merrick, Leonard, 287
Merwin, W. S., US poet and translator, 438, 447
    A Mask for Janus, 438
Metcalf, James
    illustrator of *Adam's Rib*, 442
    in Mexico, 552
Methuen, 232
    and *Claudius* books, 358
    and *Sergeant Lamb* books, 358, 378, 385
Mexico, 538, 541, 543, 551–2
Milton, John, R.G. and his poetry, 370, 371, 379
    'trichomania', 380, 389
Mindszenty, Cardinal, basis of *The Prisoner*, 483
Mitchinson, Naomi, 293
Modern Language Quarterly, 96, 97

Monro, Harold, Poetry Bookshop,
    42, 64, 107
    Some Contemporary Poets, 107
Moorhouse, Marion, wife of E. E.
    Cummings, 480
Morgan, Evan, R.G.'s letter to on
    Sassoon, 57–8
Morgan and Morgan, US
    publishers, 462
Morley, Frank, of Faber, 290, 302
Morning Post, 289
Morrell, Lady Ottoline
    Garsington ménage, 54–5
    and Sassoon, 56
Morrell, Philip, pacifist, 54, 55
Morris, William, refuses
    Laureateship, 2
Morris, William, Hollywood agent,
    511
Morton, H. V., *In the Steps of St
    Paul*, 279
Moscow, R.G. and Yevtushenko,
    551
Muse, the *see under* Graves, Robert
Muses, post-Riding, *see* Judith;
    Julie, Laraçuen; Margot

Nagy, Imre, 551
Nation, The, 86, 458
National Poetry Society of
    America, awards R.G. Gold
    Medal, 500
New Criticism, 124–5, 145
New Republic, 'Eminent
    Collaborationist', 515
New Statesman, 411, 467, 517
    and *Epilogue I*, 261
    and *Nazarene Gospel*, 430
New York Times, 417
New Yorker, and R.G.'s poems,
    414, 458
News Chronicle, 278
Nichols, Robert, 65, 97
    one-time friend and
    correspondent of R.G., 74,
    83, 108

neurasthenia, 83
Ardours and Endurances
    (1917), 83
Nicholson, Ben, brother of Nancy,
    60, 78
Nicholson (Graves), Jenny, 231,
    266, 436
    birth, 73
    unbaptized, 79
    career and other problems, 242,
    268, 296
    and R.G.'s brother Charles, 267
    and Sarah Churchill, 268
    WAAF, 362
    marriage to Clifford, 362, 410
    and R.G.'s showbiz hopes, 427,
    471
    Portofino castello, 432–3
    marriage to Crosse, 432–3
    on Bergman, 472
    on Will Price, 484
    in Rome, 484, 486
    and *A Song for Sheba*, 486–7
    sudden death, 532–3
Nicholson, Sir Harold, 468
Nicholson, Nancy (later Graves),
    see Graves, Nancy
Nicholson, Sir William and Lady,
    60, 86, 89, 105, 122, 209
Niebuhr, Reinhold, and *Nazarene
    Gospel*, 429
Nobel Prize for Literature, 297–8,
    507–8
Non-Conscription Movement,
    Russell and, 57
Novello, Ivor, 51

O'Connor, Frank, 161
    and Phibbs, 155, 157, 159
O'Hara, Maureen, one-time wife of
    Will Price, 451, 452
O'Toole, Peter,
    characterization of
    Lawrence, 498
Oaxaca, cult of psilocybin, 479
Oberon, Merle, 243, 286, 287

Observer, 278–9, 504, 505, 509
Old Burseldon, R.G. on, 271
Owen, Harold, 66
Owen, Susan, 63
Owen, Wilfred, war poet, 34, 106
  relations with R.G., 62–3, 64–6, 100
  association with Sassoon, 63, 64, 65, 66
  death in France (1918), 66
  homosexuality, 63, 66, 74
  war neurosis, 113
  'A Terre', 65
  'Disabled', 64, 66
Owl, The (Winter Owl), 105–6
  R.G.'s editorial foreword, 105
Oxford, 54, 508
Oxford Humanist Society, addressed by R.G., 'The Poet's Paradise', 501–2
Oxford Poetry (1927), 150
Oxford University, 31, 80
Oxford University Philological Society, addressed by R.G., 'Poetic Gold', 501
Oxford University Poetry Society, 506
Oxford University Press
  turns down 'dictionary' project, 287
  and *The White Goddess*, 397–8

Palestine, 59, 60, 429
  myth of twin goddess, 523
Palma, x, 190, 201–2, 244, 264, 447–8, 449
  Mare Nostrum hospital, 421
Parkinson, Cyril Northcote, 532
Parry, Adam, and *Anger of Achilles*, 504
Parsons, Ian, 550
  publishes *The World and Ourselves*, 309, 550
Patai, Dr Raphael, 450, 505
Pearson, Lester, Canadian premier, 307

PEN Club, invites R.G. to Budapest, 550, 562
Penguin Books, R.G. and, 426, 428, 430, 459, 460, 467, 481, 504, 567
Pereceval, Helena (later Graves), 4
Perceval, Sir John, first and second Earls of Egmont, 4
Perceval, Spencer, 5
Phibbs, Geoffrey, 187, 188, 241, 353
  biography, 155
  and the 'Trinity', 155
  appearance, 155
  association with L.R., 156–61, 170–72
  disappearance, 160–61, 241
  in Rouen with Norah, 162
  letter to L.R. on his flight, 162–3
  letter to R.G. from Ireland, 163–4
  letter to Nancy, 164–5
  brought back by R.G., 165–6
  wants no more of L.R., 166, 173
  and L.R.'s attempted suicide, 167–8
  association with Nancy, 170–71, 172, 173, 180
  in vengeful mood, 173, 174–5
  interview with R.G., 174–7
  accusations against L.R., 175–7
  demands return of his papers, 177–8, 179, 182
  threatens R.G., 178–9
  slanders R.G., 180–82
  summonses L.R., 183, 184
  subsequent marriage, 184
  Irish Poets of the Nineteenth Century (1951), 155
  The Withering of the Figleaf (1928), 155, 178
Phibbs, Norah, 158, 185
  liaison with Garnett, 159, 165, 166–7
  and her husband's return, 160–61, 164–5
  in Rouen, 162, 163

Phillips, Mary (later Reeves), 250, 261
    see also Reeves, Mary
Picture Post, and R.G., 453
Pinker, Eric, literary agent, 259
Platonism, 297
Pleven, R. J., and Mme, 309
Podro, Joshua, Judaic scholar, 360
    Jewish Jesus thesis, 428–9
Poore, Rear-Admiral Sir Richard, uncle of R.G., 32
Pope, Alexander, criticized by R.G., 81, 370, 371
Porter, Alan, 87
Porter, H. E. L., 30
Porter, Katherine Anne, and The White Goddess, 417
Postgate, Raymond, How to Start a Revolution, 290
Pound, Ezra, 3, 82, 99, 144, 250, 335, 382, 462,
    R.G.'s opinion of, 86, 399, 374, 467
    proto-modernist, 97, 98, 113
    drift into schizo-affective illness, 114
Powell, Anthony, 230
Powell, J. V., moral tutor to R.G., 80
Powell, Marie, wife of Milton, 379, 380, 389
Prescott, Orville, reviewer in New York Times, and The White Goddess, 417
Prewett, Frank, 107, 113
Price, Will, 450–51, 478
    relations with R.G., 451–2, 454, 471, 474–6 and 'Kitten', 451–2
    alcoholism, 452, 474, 484
    and World's Delight film script, 473, 474–5, 477
    and Claudius, 483
Priestley, J. B., 382
Primavera Press, 225
Pritchard, Sir Harold, father of Beryl, 302, 313, 436

for Beryl, see Graves, Beryl
Pryde, James, 60
Psychology, approach to poetry, 97
Publisher's Weekly, 418
Pulman, Jack, and BBC I, Claudius, 566

Quennell, Peter, 76, 103, 107
    on L.R., 122
Quoz, a Reid/R.G. exchange of letters, 462–3

Raine, Kathleen, 554
    and The White Goddess, 430
Raleigh, Sir Walter, and R.G. at Oxford, 80, 87, 104
Random House, US publishers, 244, 278, 308
    mistaken payment to L.R., 348–9
    and R.G.'s novels, 358
Ranke, Heinrich von, grandfather of R.G., 7–8, 29
Ranke, Leopold von
    marriage to Helena Graves, 5
    History of the Popes, 5
Ransom, John Crowe
    and the Fugitives, 123, 124, 127
    R.G. and, 86, 124, 374, 480–81
    and role of poetry, 124
    reviews R.G.'s On English Poetry, 124
    and new criticism, 124–5
    assessment of L.R.'s poetry, 125
    introduces L.R. to R.G., 129, 563
    Grace After Meat, 124, 481
    Poems: Third Edition, 563
    Poems about God, 124
    Selected Poems (1945), 481
Rattigan, Terence, 1
    homosexuality, 496
    Ross, 496, 497

Read, Sir Herbert, 82, 382, 467
  pioneer of depth-psychology
    criticism, 97, 515
  correspondence with Dahlberg,
    Truth is More Sacred, 515
Reeves, David, 268, 314, 326, 328
  book on furniture, 279, 312
Reeves, Ethel, 212
Reeves, James, xi, 216, 218, 266,
    289, 312, 337, 457
  and Bronowski, 226
  and *Epilogue I*, 246
  and R.G. back in England,
    343–4, 360, 411
  and Suez crisis, 470
  hostility towards R.G.'s affair
    with Margot, 492–3,
    514–15, 519, 526, 555
  The Natural Need, 244, 261
Reeves (*née* Phillips), Mary, xi,
    343, 411
  marriage to James, 261, 266,
    360
  and L.R., 344
  in Deyá at the Posada, 492
  and Reid, 512
Reichenthal (*née*), Isobel, sister of
    L.R., 252, 351
  visits Phibbs with Mrs Westgate,
    184
  writes of 'miraculous change' in
    L.R., 352
Reichenthal, Nathaniel, father of
    L.R., 122–3
Reid, Alastair, 479
  relations with R.G., 462–3, 500,
    509, 512
  divorce and remarriage, 464
  and libretto for *Nausicaa*,
    499–500
  claims respect for his privacy,
    509, 512
  love for Margot, 509–10,
    513–14, 519
  elopement, 510, 512
  White Goddess film script, 510
  To Lighten My House, 462

Reid, Jasper, son of above, 464
Reid, Mary, wife of Alastair, 509
Remarque, Erich Maria, *All Quiet
    on the Western Front*, 194,
    195
Rendell, G. H., headmaster of
    Charterhouse, distinction
    between 'erotic' and
    'amorous', 22
Renn, Ludwig, *Kreig*, 193
Rennes
  home of Anita, 271, 289, 293
  R.G. and L.R. at, 309–10,
    311–28
  beginning of R.G./Beryl love
    affair, 312–13, 324
  return to, 1946, 411
Reyles, Carlos, *El Embrujo de
    Seville* (trans. by R.G. and
    Beryl), 466
Rhys, Keidrich
  ed. *Wales*, 397
  'Dog, Lapwing and Roebuck',
    395
Richards, Frank
  Old Soldiers Never Die, 223,
    253
  Old Soldier Sahib, 232, 253
Richards, I. A., 324
Richards, Vyvyan, 267
  and Seizin Press, 147
  Caxton's *Prologues and
    Epilogues*, 147
Riding (*née* Reichenthal), Laura:
    Biography, ix, xi, 114, 559
  'invented' by R.G., 94, 354
  first meeting with R.G., 122,
    123
  appearance, 122, 169
  parentage, 122–3
  education, 123, 573
  marriage to Gottschalk, 123,
    141
  and the Fugitives, 123, 125–6,
    127, 129
  at Nashville, 126–7
  in New York, 127–8

emigration to Europe, 128, 129

departure with R.G. and Nancy, 129, 131

a financial responsibility to R.G., 134, 135, 141, 347–9, 351

relations with Nancy, 136, 137, 141, 163

in Vienna with R.G., 139

attempted suicide, 166, 167, 170, 175, 176, 177, 182, 188

leaves for Mallorca with R.G., 190, 195

end of sexual relationship with R.G., 205, 206, 220, 233–4

effect of sudden access to money, 208, 213, 219–20, 223, 245

university and hotel projects, 219–20, 225, 242, 246, 248, 252, 260, 262, 307

demands money from Cameron, 220, 221, 222

educational project, 252, 260, 262

leaves Mallorca, 264, 265

in London, 266, 267, 292, 299

and R.G./Beryl love affair, 314, 341–2

plans to return to America, 320, 325, 326, 327, 328, 329

reciprocal sexual feelings for Jackson, 330, 332, 336

and Kit's madness, 337, 338

and her joint projects with R.G., 339, 343, 347, 350–51, 425

assigns Mallorcan property to R.G., 350, 424

attacks R.G. in periodicals, 426

R.G. 'still free', 536

Riding, Laura: Character, poetic ideas and personality
debt to R.G., 96, 138, 141, 249

insistence that 'history' has 'finished', 115

persistence in exercising her principles, 122

idealism, 123

non-metrical technique, 125

advancement of her own work, 126, 138

sensitivity to criticism, 126

wrongheaded criticism of others, 128

bizarre personality, 131, 148, 208, 352

influence on and use of others, 131

R.G.'s unchanging early view, 137

R.G.'s subservience to her, 137

relations with Stein, 138

and 'meaning' in 'what has no meaning', 138, 148

prose of post-war years, 138–9

'Trinity' concept, 139, 140, 162

takeover of R.G./Nicholson enterprise, 140

feminism (woman power), 140–41, 271, 273, 274, 277

period of happiness with R.G., 144, 149

concepts of poetry, 148, 206, 208, 305

limited but powerful genius, 148, 288

arouses dislike, 151, 152

denial of intimate relations with R.G., 151, 152

increasing cruel and offensive behaviour towards R.G., 153, 169, 214–15, 314–15, 332, 341

and Phibbs, 156–66 (see also under)

desire for finality, 158, 163

attempted suicide 166, 167, 170, 175, 176, 177, 178, 182, 188

struggle against the flesh, 168, 187

and her own jealousy, 168

unacknowledged vulgarity, 172, 175, 176, 336

as helper to others, 204, 216, 217, 237

'holiness', 205, 221, 285
assumption of leadership and
    rule, 205, 233, 236, 237, 336
behaviour towards visitors, 205,
    214, 219, 236
and 'physicality' postpones
    judgement, 206–7, 220, 235
to form a community dedicated
    to 'truth', 208, 219, 236
alleged 'unreadability', 212
poetic skill compared with R.G.,
    235, 242, 249
as Muse, 237
ill-health, 249, 260, 271, 322,
    325
political ambitions, 262, 280
nearing end of relationship with
    R.G., 264, 269, 273, 280,
    302, 305; official break, 340
to form a group of 'inside'
    people, 280, 284, 285, 303,
    304
'apostasy from poetry', 289,
    333, 341
poems about herself, 290 and
    beauty–sexuality association,
    291
change to 'common plane', 333,
    348
and 'talk' about her in England,
    343
on R.G./.L.R. past relationship,
    347, 351
as presented in R.G.'s poems,
    539
English her only poetic
    language, 559
see also under Graves, Robert:
    Jackson, Schulyer; Phibbs,
    Geoffrey

Riding, Laura: Works Americans,
    225
Anarchism is Not Enough
    (1928), 138, 140
The Close Chaplet (1926), 148;
    first collection, 137, 147
Collected Poems (1938), 301;

aggressive note 'To the
    Reader', 299, 305, 320;
    Desmond Flower's request,
    308–9; publication, 317;
    hostile reviews, 317, 320;
    L.R.'s efforts to publicize
    herself, 320–21
Contemporaries and Snobs
    (1928), 137; 'sense of
    something more real than
    life', 138, 148
Contemporary Poets (1975),
    157; on her emigration to
    Europe, 128
Convalescent Conversations (by
    Madeleine Vara), 244
'The Damned Thing' (sex), 138,
    141
Epilogue I (1935), 225, 244,
    246, 247; 'Preliminaries',
    208, 247; distinction between
    ideas/truth relationship and
    wisdom/truth relationship,
    207
Epilogue II, 244, 247
Epilogue III, 244, 247, 252, 279
Everybody's Letters (ed.), 225;
    and her attempted suicide,
    166
Experts are Puzzled, 209
The First Leaf, (1933), 244
'The First Protocol of the
    Covenant of Literal
    Morality', 280, 309, 342; one
    time 'Letter on International
    Affairs', 282; R.G. and, 282;
    replies to, 283; summarized
    in 'To the Endorsers of the
    Covenant', 283–4; and
    personal values/outer events
    relationship, 284; letters to
    people who get in the way,
    323, 324; 'Second Protocol',
    335, 336, 340
Laura and Francisca (1931),
    128, 204, 240, 244
The Life of the Dead, 225;

illustrated by Aldridge, 216
Lives of Wives, 293, 323; R.G.
and, 306, 311, 317
Love as Love, Death as Death,
147
'March 1937', 286
'The Mask', 169
A Mistake Somewhere (1944),
244
'The Need to Confide', 245
'The New Barbarism and
Gertrude Stein' (1927), 138
No Trouble, 204
Poems: A Joking Word (1930),
209; on her attempted
suicide, 166, 168; on R.G.,
169; on Phibbs, 181
Progress of Stories (1935), 244,
261; R.G.'s aid, 215
'The Quids', 125; R.G. and, 129
'The Second Leaf' (1935), 244
Though Gently (1930), 204
A Trojan Ending, 232, 244–5,
260, 269; R.G. and, 263,
267, 302, 306, 339;
Aldridge's jacket, 278
Twenty Poems Less, 211
*The Vain Life of Voltaire: A
Biographical Fantasy* (1927),
137, 147
The World and Ourselves,
(1938), 301, 303, 304, 316;
and concept of possession,
146–7; R.G. loses money,
207, 332; answers to
questions on 'First Protocol',
282; contents, 284;
withdrawals from project,
306; published by Chatto and
Windus, 309, 550
with George Ellidge, *14A
(roman à clef)*, 161, 166, 171;
judgement on Stein, 191
with Robert Graves, *Pamphlet
Against Anthologies* (1928),
137, 251; argument, 145–6;
A Survey of Modernist Poetry

(1927), 96, 137, 138, 140,
143
with Harry Kemp, *The Left
Heresy in Literature and Life*
(1939), 252, 309
Rieu, E. V., trans of the *Iliad*, 504
Rilke, Rainer, Maria, 559
Duino Elegies, 153
Rimbaud, Arthur, 559
Rivers, W. H. R., neurologist 90, 97
and Sassoon, 83, 97
Freudianism, 83, 113
war neurosis cases, 113
Rizzoli, Italian sponsor, 485
Robbins, Jerome, choreographer,
488, 489, 511
Roberts, Eirlys, xii, 246 companion
of Bronowski, 225
founder of *Which*, 225
Roberts, Michael, 300, 523
Faber Book of Modern Verse,
250
contributions from R.G. and
L.R., 250, 251
Robertson, E. Arnot, *Four
Frightened People*, 293
Rochester, John Wilmot, Earl of,
R.G.'s debt to, 81, 113, 239
Rodakowski, Raymond, R.G.'s
friendship through poetry,
17, 19, 20
Roe, Tom, financier
and 'International Authors', 499
and R.G.'s accounts, 531, 532,
543
Scottish Cadco Pig Project,
531–2
imprisonment, 532
Rose, H. J., *Handbook of Greek
Mythology*, 461
Rosenberg, Isaac, war poet, 106
Rossellini, Roberto, and *Homer's
Daughter*, 471, 472, 475
Rossetti, Dante Gabriel, R.G. and,
398
Rota, Anthony, and sale of
Gravesiana, 546–7

Rothenstein, W., 277
Royal Society of Literature, offers
R.G. CLitt, 530–31
Rusk, Dean, 520
Russell, Bertrand, 55
exploits Sassoon's
anti-militarianism, 56–7, 58,
133
reproved by R.G., 58
Ruth, T. de C., *The Problem of
Claudius*, 228

Sadleir, Michael, of Constable, 246
These Foolish Things, 283
Salisbury, Lord, Unionist ministry,
1
Salvador, Archduke Ludwig, 203
Sand, George, in Mallorca with
Chopin, 203
Winter in Mallorca (trans. by
R.G.), 427
Sanders, George, 537
Sargant, Dr William, *Battle for the
Mind* (R.G.'s contribution),
476
Sartre, Jean Paul, 378
Sassoon, Siegfried ('Mad Jack'), 34,
105, 106, 145
parentage, 41
friendship with R.G., 41–2,
50–51, 52, 67, 75, 80, 104,
119, 186
R.G. and his war poems, 42, 65
on R.G.'s poems, 42, 229
war service, 48, 55, 67
near madness, 55
refusal to serve further in the
war, 55–6
protest at its continuance, 56–7
patient in home for
neurasthenics, 57–9, 63
influence on Owen, 63, 64
'variation between happy
warrior and bitter pacifist'
(R.G.) 67
homosexuality, 74, 192, 209
literary editor *Daily Herald*, 78
pose as 'ordinary man', 113–14
literary estimation of his war
books, 192, 193, 194
angry reaction to *Goodbye to
All That*, 195–6
his and Blunden's annotated
copy, 196–7
exchange of letters with R.G.,
1930, 197–9
marriage to Hester Gatty, 199
Cambridge meeting with R.G.,
1955, 200
Collected Poems, 45
Counter-Attack, 59
The Daffodil Murderer, 41
The Heart's Journey (1928,
USA, 1929), 198
Memoirs of a Fox-Hunting Man,
192
Memoirs of an Infantry Officer
(1930), 192, 198; David
Thomas as 'Dick Tiltwood',
42; R.G. as David Cromlech,
43–4, 50, 194, 231; Russell
as 'Tyrrell', 56
Sherston's Progress, 192
The Tasking (private ed.), 467
Sassoon, Mrs, mother of Siegfried,
spiritualist activities, 52, 195,
197
Schildkraut, Nathan, US lawyer for
L.R., 424
Scholastic, The, 133
Schwarz, George, 279–80, 283
Almost Forgotten Germany
(trans. by R.G. and L.R.),
245, 253
Scott, George, ed. *Truth*, 469
Scottish Cadco Pig Project, 531–2
Searle, Ronald, and R.G.'s *Iliad*,
486
Secker, Martin, publisher to R.G.,
77, 104
Second World War, 39, 222, 324,
345, 365
Seizin Press, R.G./L.R.
collaboration, 151, 274, 350

birth and origin, 143, 146–7
publications, 147, 149, 217, 244
expression of L.R.'s
 'supra-individual', 207
Phibbs and, 159
Karl and, 244
employment of commercial
 printers, 244, 274
financial plight, 293, 297
and Cassells, 294
Epilogue I (the Vulgate), 207,
 225, 244
becomes 'A Critical Summary',
 245, 246
One, 147
The World and Ourselves, 207
Seizin–Constable, 244, 245

Shah, Idries, 114, 505, 520, 522,
 558
and R.G./Laraçuen relationship,
 534
influence on R.G.'s own
 thinking, 555
and *Rubaiyat* of Omar
 Khayyam, 555–8
The Sufis, 505, 557

Shah, Omar Ali-, 505 and *Rubaiyat*
 of Omar Khayyam, 555
 'Jan Fishan' MS, 557–8
 discredited, 558

Shakespeare, William, 129, 145,
 372
Shanks, Edward, 105
Shaw, Charlotte, wife of G.B.,
 confidante of T. E. Lawrence,
 142, 166
Shaw, G. Bernard, 23
 R.G. and, 208–9
Sherriff, R. C., *Journey's End*, 208
Sicre, Ricardo and Betty, 509
 an Ava Gardner in Mallorca,
 464, 465
 and R.G.'s finances, 471
 The Tap on the Left Shoulder,
 464
Simenon, Georges, 230

Simmonds, Dorothy and
 Montague, 312, 319, 324
 and L.R., 327
Simpson/Edward VIII crisis, 272
Simpson, Percy, English tutor to
 R.G., 80–81, 145
Sisson, C. H., *The Avoidance of
 Literature*, 516
Sitwells, the, 82, 108
Sitwell, Edith, 119
 and her poem 'The Sleeping
 Beauty', 135–6
Skelton, John, loved by R.G., 37,
 85, 86, 87, 371
 'Apollo Whirléd Up his Chair',
 133
Smith, Harrison, US publisher,
 232, 253, 278
Smith, Janet (Adam), wife of
 Michael Roberts, 323
Smith, Lees, pacifist MP, 58
Society for the Promotion of
 Christian Knowledge, 241
Solesmes Benedictines, plainsong,
 55
Somerville, Masie, 266, 267, 271,
 300, 306
 and L.R., 291, 302, 304
Sorley, Charles, war poet, 41, 106
Southey, Robert, 371
Spain, 202, 261, 262, 277–8, 283
 R.G./L.R. property, 345, 346
Spanish Civil War, 236, 296, 324,
 364
 Guernica massacre, 289
Spectator, 458
 'Some Trench Scenes', 35
Spiegel, Sam, 531
 projected film about Lawrence,
 496, 498
 and R.G. as adviser, 498–9
Spender, Stephen, 199, 373, 382
 on 'Modern Poetry', 277
 R.G. on, 303
 Collected Poems (1955), 469
Squire, J. C. (Jack), 105
 and Jackson, 334

Stanford, Sir Charles, and 'Father O'Flynn', 6
Starkie, Enid, and Professorship of Poetry, 507, 553, 554
Stead, Christina, 287
Stein, Gertrude, 96, 168, 190, 204
  relations with L.R., 138, 188, 189–90, 191, 205, 574–5
  admired by L.R. and R.G., 149
  homosexuality, 149, 188, 190
  and Seizin Press, 149
  on R.G.'s break with Nancy, 189
  'marriage' to Toklas, 190
  An Acquaintance with Description (1929), 149
  The Autobiography of Alice B. Toklas, 191
  Geography and Plays (1922), 188
Steinbeck, John, Nobel Prizewinner, 508
Stephenson, the Hon. Sir Hugh, key to City of New York, 501
Stewart, John L.
  and L.R.'s *Fugitive* campaign, 126
  on her 'brilliance and energy', 127
Stonier, G. W., reviews R.G.'s *Poems* (1945), 411
Stopes, Dr Marie Carmichael, letter to R.G., 422–3
Stokowski, Leopold, 62
Strachey, Lytton, 55
Strauss Richard, *Till Eulenspiegel*, 1
Strenge, Emmi, companion of Schwarz, 279–80
Stuffed Owl, The, 101
Suetonius, *The Twelve Caesars* (trans. by R.G.), 428, 481
Sufism, mystical branch of Islam, 5, 505–6, 527, 565
  and Black Goddess theme, 520
  influence on R.G.'s thought, 555
  and the *Rubaiyat*, 555, 557–8

Sugrue, Thomas, and *The White Goddess*, 417
Sunday Times, hatchet job on Shah/R.G. *Rubaiyat*, 558
Surrealists, 100
Sutherland, Graham 520
Swinburne, Algernon, C., 3, 517
  'Hertha', 100
Switzerland, R.G., and L.R. in, 279–82
Symonds, John Addington, active pederast, 74
Symons, Julian
  finds L.R. 'oppressive' (*Critical Occasions*), 307, 308
  Twentieth Century Verse, L.R. and 'atomization of his poetry', 307–8

Tambimuttu, ed. *Poetry London*, asks R.G. for a testimonial, 554
Tate, Alan, member of the Fugitives, 123, 124, 126
  on L.R., 127
  marriage to Caroline Gordon, 127, 128
  unhappy love affair with L.R., 132, 374
Taylor, A. J. P., and dictionary project, 306
Taylor, Geoffrey, *see* Phibbs, Geoffrey
Television
  (UK) to interview R.G., 487
  (USA) R.G.'s appearance, 480
Tennant, Stephen, and Sassoon, 198
Tennyson, Alfred, Lord, 2
Terence, *Comedies* (revised by R.G.), 515
Thelin, Frau, 245
Thomas, David, 42
  death at Fricourt, 45
Thomas, Dylan, R.G. on, 372, 373, 462

'The Hand that Signed the Paper', 373

Thomas, Edward (Edward Eastaway), 66
  omitted from *Georgian Poetry*, 373–4

Thomas, Lowell, creator of 'Lawrence legend', 141, 142

Thorneycroft, Hamo, 41

Tiarks (later Ranke), Frau, grandmother of R.G., 8

Time, 214, 216, 305, 331
  Jackson's position, 219–20
  role of book page, 329–30, 420
  and a review of *King Jesus*, 420

Times, The, 317
  R.G.'s letter to (1966), 553 on R.G., 559

Times Literary Supplement, 145, 223, 229, 458
  hostile review of L.R.'s *Collected Poems* (1938), 317
  R.G. *et al.*, spoof sonnet, 297

Toklas, Alice B., relationship with Stein, 188, 189, 190

Tolkein, J. R., 375

Tomorrow, Creative Press quarterly, 416

Trace, Mr, dentist, 295

Trench, Herbert, 119

Trevelyan, George Otto, R. G. and his US War of Independence book, 378

Trianon Press, 442

Turner, W. J., 105

University of Victoria, Canada, purchase of Gravesiana, 547–8

Valldemossa, scene of Chopin/Sand romance, 203

Vellejo, César, Peruvian poet, 305

Vaughan Williams, Ralph, 470

Verney, Edward, 389

vers libre, 97, 100

Vienna, R.G. and L.R. and, 139–40

Viking Press (USA), and *Greek Myths*, 459–60

Villon, François, 559

Voltaire, *Candide*, 394

von Stauffenburg, Count, plot against Hitler, 385

von Sternberg, Josef, director of *The Blue Angel*, 292
  and Claudius, 273–4, 278, 282

Voznozensky, Andrei, 561

Vursell, H. D., vice-president Creative Age
  on reviews of *The White Goddess*, 416–17
  and *The Isles of Unwisdom*, 418
  and L.R.'s character, 425
  behaviour over *The Common Asphodel*, 425

Wabasso, Florida, home of L.R. and Schuyler, 339

Wain, John
  pilgrim to Deyá, 470–71
  battle of letters with R.G., 504, 553

Wain, John (*contd*)
  and Blunden as Professor of Poetry, 553

Wales, 47, 51–2, 67, 296
  R.G. and Harlech, 29, 31, 40, 72, 78, 104, 345

Wales, ed by Keidrich Rhys, 395

Walpole, Sir Hugh, 307
  Vanessa, film version, 261

Walton, Sir William, 488

Warr, Bertram, Canadian airman, 369

Warren, Robert Penn, 123, 374

Watt, A. P. and A.S., literary agents, relations with R.G., 250, 260, 266, 294, 305, 417, 418, 421
  and L.R.'s rights in joint publications, 425

Wasson, R. Gordon
  friendship with R.G., 464, 479, 502–3

interest in psychological effects of hallucinogenic mushrooms, 464, 476, 479
experiments with psilocybin, 501
Wasson, R. G. and V., *Mushrooms, Russia and History*, 464
Wavell, General Lord, Archibald, 367
Wells, H. G., 23
The Time Machine, 2
West, Douglas, 271
West, Rebecca, 267, 467
praise of *Epilogue I*, 261
and L.R., 271, 343
Westgate, Mrs, visits Phibbs with Isobel (L.R.'s sister), 184
Wheldon, Huw, to interview R.G. on television, 487
White, Eric, 552
White, T. H., 532
Whitefield, George, Calvinist Methodist, 4
Wilde, Oscar, 1
homosexuality, 74
Williams, Charles
and *The White Goddess*, 397–8
Poetry at Present, 397
Williams, Emlyn, 243
Williamson, Henry
effects of war experience on, 76
and Lawrence as a guide to Hitler, 253
Wilson, Colin, 561
Wilson, H. W., L.R., on herself in *Authors Today and Yesterday*, 205, 206–7
Windmill, The, 'Conversation at Paphos', 395
Woman's Leader, 'Books at Random', by 'Fuze' (R.G.), 86–7
Woman's Liberation, 405
and Bachofen, 387
and R.G., 388
Woolf, Leonard and Virginia, Hogarth Press, 108

and *Grace After Meat* by Ransom, 124
Woolton, Lord, R.G. and, 496
Wordsworth, William, 6, 371
and his household, 75
search for happiness, 75, 76
criticized by R.G., 467
World's Work, The, 89
Wright, Sir Almroth, anti-feminist, 293
Wyatt, Honor,
marriage to Ellidge, 246
as wife of Glover, 250
The Heathen, 244, 262, 282–3

Yale Review, Jarrell on R.G.'s work, 458
Yeats, W. B., 462, 524
disliked by R.G., 3, 250–51, 324, 469
in Mallorca, 251–2
Schuyler and, 334
poetic presence, 467
dies in 1939, 324
A Vision, 404–5
'Lake Isle of Innisfree', 125, 250
Oxford Book of Modern Verse, 250–51, 252
Poems (1895), 3
Yevtushenko, 504
R.G. and, 551
Young, Brigadier Desmond, reports R.G. called 'cad' and 'traitor', 39
Young, Edward, 98
Young, Geoffrey Winthrop, 30
Youngstein, Mr, fails to back *Claudius* film, 484–5
Yugoslavia, Seventh International Meeting of Writers, Belgrade, 561

Zaubel, Morton, 128
Zuckmayer, Carl
and *Claudius* film, 273, 278
The Devil's General, 273